THE INFORMATION SOCIETY

Critical Concepts in Sociology

Other titles in this series

The State
Edited by John Hall
3 volume set

Power
Edited by John Scott
3 volume set

Citizenship
Edited by Bryan S. Turner
2 volume set

Class
Edited by John Scott
4 volume set

Modernity
Edited by Malcolm Waters
4 volume set

Sexualities
Edited with an introduction by
Ken Plummer
4 volume set

Race and Ethnicity
Edited with an introduction by
Professor Harry Goulbourne
4 volume set

Social Networks
Edited with an introduction by John Scott
4 volume set

Culture
Edited with an introduction by Chris Jenks
4 volume set

Globalization
Edited with an introduction by Roland
Robertson and Kathleen White
6 volume set

Crime
Edited with an introduction by Philip Bean
4 volume set

Islam
Edited with an introduction by
Bryan S. Turner and Akbar Ahmed
4 volume set

Sport
Edited with an introduction by
Eric Dunning and Dominic Malcolm
4 volume set

Family
Edited by David Cheal
4 volume set

The Body
Edited with an introduction by Andrew
Blaikie, Mike Hepworth, Mary Holmes,
Alexandra Howson, Shree
Sartain and David Inglis
5 volume set

Shamanism
Edited by Andrei A. Znamenski
3 volume set

Women and Islam
Edited and with a new introduction by
Haideh Moghissi
3 volume set

Childhood
Edited and with a new introduction
by Chris Jenks
3 volume set

Social Stratification
Edited and with a new introduction
by David Inglis
5 volume set

Social Movements
Edited and with a new introduction by
Jeff Goodwin and James M. Jasper
4 volume set

Sociology of Religion
Edited and with a new introduction
by Malcolm Hamilton
5 volume set

Men and Masculinities
Edited and with a new introduction by
Stephen Whitehead
5 volume set

Transgression
Edited and with a new introduction
by Chris Jenks
4 volume set

Social Exclusion
Edited by David Byrne
4 volume set

Society
Edited and with a new introduction by
Reiner Grundmann and Nico Stehr
4 volume set

Forthcoming

Modern Indian Culture and Society
Edited and with a new introduction by
Knut A. Jacobsen
4 volume set

THE INFORMATION SOCIETY

Critical Concepts in Sociology

Edited by
Robin Mansell

**Volume I
History and Perspectives**

LONDON AND NEW YORK

First published 2009
by Routledge
2 Park Square, Milton Park, Abingdon, Oxon, OX14 4RN, UK

Simultaneously published in the USA and Canada
by Routledge
270 Madison Avenue, New York, NY 10016

Routledge is an imprint of the Taylor & Francis Group, an informa business

Editorial material and selection © 2009, Robin Mansell; individual
owners retain copyright in their own material

Typeset in 10/12pt Times NR MT by Graphicraft Limited, Hong Kong
Printed and bound in Great Britain by
the MPG Books Group

All rights reserved. No part of this book may be reprinted or
reproduced or utilised in any form or by any electronic,
mechanical, or other means, now known or hereafter
invented, including photocopying and recording, or in any
information storage or retrieval system, without permission in
writing from the publishers.

British Library Cataloguing in Publication Data
A catalogue record for this book is available from the British Library

Library of Congress Cataloging in Publication Data
The information society : critical concepts in sociology / edited by Robin Mansell.
p. cm. — (Critical concepts in sociology)
Includes bibliographical references and index.
ISBN 978-0-415-44308-1 (set, hardback) — ISBN 978-0-415-44309-8 (volume 1, hardback)
— ISBN 978-0-415-44310-4 (volume 2, hardback) — ISBN 978-0-415-44311-1 (volume 3,
hardback) — ISBN 978-0-415-44312-8 (volume 4, hardback)   1. Information
society.   I. Mansell, Robin.
HM851.I5324 2009
303.48′33—dc22
2008042128

ISBN 10: 0-415-44308-3 (Set)
ISBN 10: 0-415-44309-1 (Volume I)

ISBN 13: 978-0-415-44308-1 (Set)
ISBN 13: 978-0-415-44309-8 (Volume I)

Publisher's Note

References within each chapter are as they appear in the original
complete work.

CONTENTS

Acknowledgements	XV
Chronological table of reprinted articles and chapters	xvii
Preface	XXV

VOLUME I HISTORY AND PERSPECTIVES

Introduction to Volume I   **1**
ROBIN MANSELL

PART 1
History and early debates   **13**

1   **The structure and function of communication in society**   **15**
HAROLD D. LASSWELL

2   **Effects of the improvements of communication media**   **27**
MARSHALL McLUHAN

3   **The knowledge society**   **37**
PETER F. DRUCKER

4   **The rise of communications policy research**   **45**
ITHIEL DE SOLA POOL

5   **Global implications of the information society**   **58**
MARC URI PORAT

6   **Stocks and flows of knowledge**   **70**
FRITZ MACHLUP

7   **The social framework of the information society**   **80**
DANIEL BELL

CONTENTS

8 Computopia: rebirth of theological synergism   128
YONEJI MASUDA

PART 2
Further reflections and critical perspectives   139

9 Whose new international economic and information order?   141
HERBERT I. SCHILLER

10 Introduction   155
JAMES R. BENIGER

11 From 'post-industrialism' to 'information society': a new social transformation?   183
DAVID LYON

12 The social economics of information technology   197
IAN MILES AND JONATHAN GERSHUNY

13 Deconstructing the information era   215
SOHAIL INAYATULLAH

14 The information society: from Fordism to Gatesism: the 1995 Southam Lecture   235
GAËTAN TREMBLAY

15 Plan and control: towards a cultural history of the Information Society   258
FRANK WEBSTER AND KEVIN ROBINS

16 Porat, Bell, and the information society reconsidered: the growth of information work in the early twentieth century   284
JORGE REINA SCHEMENT

17 Forthcoming features: information and communications technologies and the sociology of the future   309
PETER GOLDING

18 Deciphering information technologies: modern societies as networks   329
NICO STEHR

19 An archaeology of the global era: constructing a belief   341
ARMAND MATTELART

20 Class analysis and the information society as mode of production   363
NICHOLAS GARNHAM

CONTENTS

21 **Making sense of the information age: sociology and cultural studies** 376
FRANK WEBSTER

22 **Putting the critique back into a *Critique of Information*: refusing to follow the order** 395
PAUL A. TAYLOR

23 **Communication, power and counter-power in the network society** 413
MANUEL CASTELLS

VOLUME II   KNOWLEDGE, ECONOMICS AND ORGANIZATION

Acknowledgements ix

Introduction to Volume II 1
ROBIN MANSELL

PART 3
Knowledge and economics 15

24 **Structural change and assimilation of new technologies in the economic and social systems** 17
CARLOTA PEREZ

25 **The dynamo and the computer: an historical perspective on the modern productivity paradox** 38
PAUL A. DAVID

26 **Fast structural change and slow productivity change: some paradoxes in the economics of information technology** 48
CHRISTOPHER FREEMAN AND LUC SOETE

27 **Information: an emerging dimension of institutional analysis** 69
WILLIAM H. MELODY

28 **Beyond interests, ideas, and technology: an institutional approach to communication and information policy** 93
HERNAN GALPERIN

29 **The knowledge-based economy: a Sisyphus model** 111
DON LAMBERTON

vii

CONTENTS

30 **Communications: blindspot of economics**   122
DALLAS W. SMYTHE

31 **The explicit economics of knowledge codification and tacitness**   138
ROBIN COWAN, PAUL A. DAVID AND DOMINIQUE FORAY

32 **Will new information and communication technologies improve the 'codification' of knowledge?**   179
W. EDWARD STEINMUELLER

PART 4
Open networks   195

33 **The power of gifts: organizing social relationships in open source communities**   197
MAGNUS BERGQUIST AND JAN LJUNGBERG

34 **The economics of technology sharing: open source and beyond**   216
JOSH LERNER AND JEAN TIROLE

35 **The transformation of open source software**   239
BRIAN FITZGERALD

PART 5
Inequality and the digital divide   261

36 **Toward a critique of the information economy**   263
PATRICIA ARRIAGA

37 **Inventing the global information future**   284
ERNEST J. WILSON III

38 **An investigation of the impact of information and communication technologies in sub-Saharan Africa**   308
LISHAN ADAM AND FRANCES WOOD

39 **Weaving the western web: explaining differences in Internet connectivity among OECD countries**   328
ESZTER HARGITTAI

40 **From digital divides to digital entitlements in knowledge societies**   351
ROBIN MANSELL

41 **Reconceptualizing the digital divide**   371
MARK WARSCHAUER

CONTENTS

42 Africa as a knowledge society: a reality check   **388**
J. J. BRITZ, P. J. LOR, I. E. M. COETZEE AND B. C. BESTER

43 Digital divide research, achievements and shortcomings   **416**
JAN A. G. M. VAN DIJK

PART 6
Widespread organizational change   437

44 Computerization and social transformations   **439**
ROB KLING

45 New worlds of computer-mediated work   **464**
SHOSHANA ZUBOFF

46 Strategic information systems planning: myths, reality and guidelines for successful implementation   **485**
R. D. GALLIERS

47 Using technology and constituting structures: a practice lens for studying technology in organizations   **505**
WANDA J. ORLIKOWSKI

48 Power, identity and new technology homework: implications for 'new forms' of organizing   **553**
MICHAEL BROCKLEHURST

VOLUME III   DEMOCRACY, GOVERNANCE AND REGULATION

Acknowledgements   vii

Introduction to Volume III   **1**
ROBIN MANSELL

PART 7
Democracy, networks and power   13

49 Information poverty and political inequality: citizenship in the age of privatized communications   **15**
GRAHAM MURDOCK AND PETER GOLDING

CONTENTS

50 **Political science research on teledemocracy**   32
WILLIAM H. DUTTON

51 **Democratic rationalization: technology, power, and freedom**   50
ANDREW FEENBERG

52 **The media and the public sphere**   73
NICHOLAS GARNHAM

53 **New mediation and direct representation: reconceptualizing representation in the digital age**   86
STEPHEN COLEMAN

54 **Real-time politics: the Internet and the political process**   109
PHILIP E. AGRE

55 **Political authority in a mediated age**   149
SUSAN HERBST

56 **The Internet, public spheres, and political communication: dispersion and deliberation**   170
PETER DAHLGREN

57 **Rethinking ICTs: ICTs on a human scale**   190
CEES J. HAMELINK

PART 8
Governing networks   197

58 **Communication policy in the global information economy: whither the public interest?**   199
WILLIAM H. MELODY

59 **Law and borders: the rise of law in cyberspace**   222
DAVID R. JOHNSON AND DAVID POST

60 **The zones of cyberspace**   266
LAWRENCE LESSIG

61 **The Internet and U.S. communication policy-making in historical and critical perspective**   276
ROBERT W. McCHESNEY

62 **The second enclosure movement and the construction of the public domain**   305
JAMES BOYLE

CONTENTS

63 **The telecom crisis and beyond: restructuring of the global telecommunications system**   353
DAL YONG JIN

64 **Internet co-governance: towards a Multilayer Multiplayer Mechanism of Consultation, Coordination and Cooperation (M_3C_3)**   371
WOLFGANG KLEINWÄCHTER

65 **Commons-based peer production and virtue**   391
YOCHAI BENKLER AND HELEN NISSENBAUM

VOLUME IV EVERYDAY LIFE

Acknowledgements   ix

Introduction to Volume IV   1
ROBIN MANSELL

PART 9
Everyday life online and offline   15

66 **Transnational virtual community? Exploring implications for culture, power and language**   17
GUSTAVO LINS RIBEIRO

67 **Multiple subjectivity and virtual community at the end of the Freudian century**   28
SHERRY TURKLE

68 **Social implications of the Internet**   42
PAUL DIMAGGIO, ESZTER HARGITTAI,
W. RUSSELL NEUMAN, AND JOHN P. ROBINSON

69 **Theorizing globalization**   76
DOUGLAS KELLNER

70 **Media literacy and the challenge of new information and communication technologies**   105
SONIA LIVINGSTONE

71 **Complicity and collusion in the mediation of everyday life**   118
ROGER SILVERSTONE

CONTENTS

72 **Identities: traditions and new communities** 137
JESÚS MARTÍN-BARBERO

73 **The three ages of Internet studies: ten, five and zero years ago** 158
BARRY WELLMAN

74 **Where information society and community voice intersect** 165
RAMESH SRINIVASAN

75 **Nation and diaspora: rethinking multiculturalism in a transnational context** 186
KARIM H. KARIM

PART 10
Gender and the cyborg 205

76 **Gender and the information society: a socially structured silence** 207
SUE CURRY JANSEN

77 **A cyborg manifesto: science, technology, and socialist-feminism in the late twentieth century** 228
DONNA J. HARAWAY

78 **What do we know about gender and information technology at work? A discussion of selected feminist research** 272
JULIET WEBSTER

79 **Reflections on gender and technology studies: in what state is the art?** 291
JUDY WAJCMAN

80 **An interrupted postcolonial/feminist cyberethnography: complicity and resistance in the "cyberfield"** 310
RADHIKA GAJJALA

81 **Gendering the Internet: claims, controversies and cultures** 330
LIESBET VAN ZOONEN

PART 11
Privacy and surveillance 347

82 **The surveillance society: information technology and bureaucratic social control** 349
OSCAR H. GANDY, JR.

xii

CONTENTS

83 An electronic panopticon? A sociological critique of surveillance theory 366
DAVID LYON

84 The distribution of privacy risks: who needs protection? 388
CHARLES D. RAAB AND COLIN J. BENNETT

85 Tactical memory: the politics of openness in the construction of memory 412
SANDRA BRAMAN

86 The secret self: the case of identity theft 433
MARK POSTER

Index 456

ACKNOWLEDGEMENTS

The publishers would like to thank the following for permission to reprint their material:

Blackwell Publishing for permission to reprint Ithiel de Sola Pool (1974). The Rise of Communications Policy Research. *Journal of Communication*, 24(2): 31–42.

Blackwell Publishing for permission to reprint Marc Uri Porat (1978). Global Implications of the Information Society. *Journal of Communication*, 28(1): 70–80.

Blackwell Publishing for permission to reprint Fritz Machlup (1979). Stocks and Flows of Knowledge. *Kyklos*, 32(1–2): 400–411.

Blackwell Publishing for permission to reprint Daniel Bell (1980). The Social Framework of the Information Society. In Forrester, T. (ed.), *The Microelectronics Revolution* (pp. 500–549). Oxford: Blackwell.

Harvard University Press for permission to reprint James R. Beniger (1986). 'Introduction'. In *The Control Revolution: Technological and Economic Origins of the Information Society* (pp. 1–27). Cambridge, MA: Harvard University Press, Copyright © 1986 by the President and Fellows of Harvard College.

Sage Publications for permission to reprint David Lyon (1986). From 'Post-Industrialism' to 'Information Society': A New Social Transformation? *Sociology*, 20(4): 577–588.

Sage Publications, Ian Miles and Jonathan Gershuny for permission to reprint Ian Miles and Jonathan Gershuny (1986). The Social Economics of Information Technology. In Marjorie Ferguson (ed.), *New Communication Technologies and the Public Interest* (pp. 18–36). London: Sage.

Elsevier for permission to reprint Sohail Inayatullah (1998). Deconstructing the Information Era. *Futures*, 30(2–3): 235–247.

ACKNOWLEDGEMENTS

Canadian Journal of Communication for permission to reprint Gaëtan: Tremblay (1995). The Information Society: From Fordism to Gatesism: the 1995 Southam Lecture. *Canadian Journal of Communication*, 20(4): 461–482.

Springer Science and Business Media for permission to reprint Frank Webster and Kevin Robins (1989). Plan and Control: Towards a Cultural History of the Information Society. *Theory and Society*, 18(3): 323–351.

Elsevier for permission to reprint Jorge R. Schement (1990). Porat, Bell, and the Information Society Reconsidered: The Growth of Information Work in the Early Twentieth Century. *Information Processing & Management*, 26(4): 449–465.

Sage Publications for permission to reprint Peter Golding (2000). Forthcoming Features: Information and Communications Technologies and the Sociology of the Future. *Sociology*, 34(1): 165–184.

Sage Publications for permission to reprint Nico Stehr (2000). Deciphering Information Technologies: Modern Societies as Networks. *European Journal of Social Theory*, 3(1): 83–94.

Sage Publications for permission to reprint Armand Mattelart (2002). An Archaeology of the Global Era: Constructing a Belief. *Media, Culture & Society*, 24(5): 591–612.

The European Institute for Communication and Culture (EURICOM) for permission to reprint Nicholas Garnham (2004). Class Analysis and the Information Society as Mode of Production. *Javnost–The Public*, 11(3): 93–103.

Manuel Castells for permission to reprint Manuel Castells (2007). Communication, Power and Counter-power in the Network Society. *International Journal of Communication*, 1(1): 238–266.

Disclaimer

The publishers have made every effort to contact authors/copyright holders of works reprinted in *The Information Society (Critical Concepts in Sociology)*. This has not been possible in every case, however, and we would welcome correspondence from those individuals/companies whom we have been unable to trace.

Chronological table of reprinted articles and chapters

Date	Author	Article/Chapter	Source	Vol.	Chap.
1948	Harold D. Lasswell	The structure and function of communication in society	Lyman Bryson (ed.) *The Communication of Ideas*, New York: Harper, pp. 37–51	I	1
1960	Marshall McLuhan	Effects of the improvements of communication media	*Journal of Economic History* 20(4): 566–75	I	2
1969	Peter F. Drucker	The knowledge society	*New Society* 13(343): 629–31	I	3
1974	Ithiel de Sola Pool	The rise of communications policy research	*Journal of Communication* 24(2): 31–42	I	4
1978	Marc Uri Porat	Global implications of the information society	*Journal of Communication* 28(1): 70–80	I	5
1979	Fritz Machlup	Stocks and flows of knowledge	*Kyklos* 32(1–2): 400–11	I	6
1980	Daniel Bell	The social framework of the information society	T. Forrester (ed.) *The Microelectronics Revolution*, Oxford: Blackwell, pp. 500–49	I	7
1980	Yoneji Masuda	Computopia: rebirth of theological synergism	Y. Masuda (ed.) *The Information Society as Post-Industrial Society*, Tokyo: Institute for the Information Society, pp. 146–58	I	8
1980	Herbert I. Schiller	Whose new international economic and information order?	*Communication* 5(4): 299–314	I	9
1981	Dallas W. Smythe	Communications: blindspot of economics	William H. Melody, Liora Salter and Paul Heyer (eds) *Culture, Communication and Dependency: The Tradition of H. A. Innis*, Norwood, NJ: Ablex, pp. 111–25	II	30
1982	Shoshana Zuboff	New worlds of computer-mediated work	*Harvard Business Review* 60(5): 142–52	II	45
1983	Carlota Perez	Structural change and assimilation of new technologies in the economic and social systems	*Futures* 15(5): 357–75	II	24
1985	Patricia Arriaga	Toward a critique of the information economy	*Media, Culture and Society* 7(3): 271–96	II	36

Chronological Table continued

Date	Author	Article/Chapter	Source	Vol.	Chap.
1986	James R. Beniger	Introduction	James R. Beniger *The Control Revolution: Technological and Economic Origins of the Information Society*, Cambridge, MA: Harvard University Press, pp. 1–27	I	10
1986	David Lyon	From 'post-industrialism' to 'information society': a new social transformation?	*Sociology* 20(4): 577–88	I	11
1986	Ian Miles and Jonathan Gershuny	The social economics of information technology	Marjorie Ferguson (ed.) *New Communication Technologies and the Public Interest*, London: Sage, pp. 18–36	I	12
1987	William H. Melody	Information: an emerging dimension of institutional analysis	*Journal of Economic Issues* XXI(3): 1313–39	II	27
1989	Oscar H. Gandy, Jr.	The surveillance society: information technology and bureaucratic social control	*Journal of Communication* 39(3): 61–76	IV	82
1989	Sue Curry Jansen	Gender and the information society: a socially structured silence	*Journal of Communication* 39(3): 196–215	IV	76
1989	William H. Melody	Communication policy in the global information economy: whither the public interest?	Marjorie Ferguson (ed.) *Public Communication – The New Imperatives: Future Directions for Media Research*, London: Sage, pp. 16–39	III	58
1989	Graham Murdock and Peter Golding	Information poverty and political inequality: citizenship in the age of privatized communications	*Journal of Communication* 39(3): 180–95	III	49
1989	Frank Webster and Kevin Robins	Plan and control: towards a cultural history of the Information Society	*Theory and Society* 18(3): 323–51	I	15
1990	Paul A. David	The dynamo and the computer: an historical perspective on the modern productivity paradox	*The American Economic Review* 80(2): 355–61	II	25

Year	Author	Title	Source	Part	No.
1990	Christopher Freeman and Luc Soete	Fast structural change and slow productivity change: some paradoxes in the economics of information technology	*Structural Change and Economic Dynamics* 1(2): 225–42	II	26
1990	Jorge Reina Schement	Porat, Bell, and the information society reconsidered: the growth of information work in the early twentieth century	*Information Processing & Management* 26(4): 449–65	I	16
1991	R. D. Galliers	Strategic information systems planning: myths, reality and guidelines for successful implementation	*European Journal of Information Systems* 1(1): 55–64	II	46
1991	Donna J. Haraway	A cyborg manifesto: science, technology, and socialist-feminism in the late twentieth century	*Simians, Cyborgs, and Women: The Revinvention of Nature*, New York: Routledge, pp. 149–82	IV	77
1991	Rob Kling	Computerization and social transformations	*Science, Technology & Human Values* 16(3): 342–67	II	44
1992	William H. Dutton	Political science research on teledemocracy	*Social Science Computer Review* 10(4): 505–22	III	50
1993	Nicholas Garnham	The media and the public sphere	Craig Calhoun (ed.) *Habermas and the Public Sphere*, Cambridge, MA: MIT Press, pp. 359–76	III	52
1993	David Lyon	An electronic panopticon? A sociological critique of surveillance theory	*Sociological Review* 41(4): 653–78	IV	83
1995	Gaëtan Tremblay	The information society: from Fordism to Gatesism: the 1995 Southam Lecture	*Canadian Journal of Communication* 20(4): 461–82	I	14
1995	Juliet Webster	What do we know about gender and information technology at work? A discussion of selected feminist research	*European Journal of Women's Studies* 2(3): 315–34	IV	78
1996	David R. Johnson and David Post	Law and borders: the rise of law in cyberspace	*Stanford Law Review* 48(5): 1367–402	III	59
1996	Lawrence Lessig	The zones of cyberspace	*Stanford Law Review* 48(5): 1403–11	III	60
1996	Robert W. McChesney	The Internet and U.S. communication policy-making in historical and critical perspective	*Journal of Communication* 46(1): 98–124, and *Journal of Computer-Mediated Communication* 1(4): n.p.	III	61

Chronological Table continued

2000	W. Edward Steinmueller	Will new information and communication technologies improve the 'codification' of knowledge?	*Industrial and Corporate Change* 9(2): 361–76	II	32
2000	Judy Wajcman	Reflections on gender and technology studies: in what state is the art?	*Social Studies of Science* 30(3): 447–64	IV	79
2001	Magnus Bergquist and Jan Ljungberg	The power of gifts: organizing social relationships in open source communities	*Information Systems Journal* 11(3–4): 305–20	II	33
2001	Michael Brocklehurst	Power, identity and new technology homework: implications for 'new forms' of organizing	*Organization Studies* 22(3): 445–66	II	48
2001	Paul DiMaggio, Eszter Hargittai, W. Russell Neuman, and John P. Robinson	Social implications of the Internet	*Annual Review of Sociology* 27: 307–36	IV	68
2002	Philip E. Agre	Real-time politics: the Internet and the political process	*The Information Society* 18(5): 311–31	III	54
2002	Radhika Gajjala	An interrupted postcolonial/feminist cyberethnography: complicity and resistance in the "cyberfield"	*Feminist Media Studies* 2(2): 177–93	IV	80
2002	Douglas Kellner	Theorizing globalization	*Sociological Theory* 20(3): 285–305	IV	69
2002	Robin Mansell	From digital divides to digital entitlements in knowledge societies	*Current Sociology* 50(3): 407–26	II	40
2002	Jesús Martín-Barbero	Identities: traditions and new communities	*Media, Culture & Society* 24(5): 621–41	IV	72
2002	Armand Mattelart	An archaeology of the global era: constructing a belief	*Media, Culture & Society* 24(5): 591–612	I	19
2002	Roger Silverstone	Complicity and collusion in the mediation of everyday life	*New Literary History* 33(4): 761–80	IV	71
2002	Liesbet van Zoonen	Gendering the Internet: claims, controversies and cultures	*European Journal of Communication* 17(1): 5–23	IV	81
2002	Mark Warschauer	Reconceptualizing the digital divide	*First Monday* 7(7): n.p.	II	41

Chronological Table continued

Date	Author	Article/Chapter	Source	Vol.	Chap.
2003	James Boyle	The second enclosure movement and the construction of the public domain	*Law and Contemporary Problems* 66(1–2): 33–74	III	62
2003	Susan Herbst	Political authority in a mediated age	*Theory and Society* 32(4): 481–503	III	55
2004	Andrew Feenberg	Democratic rationalization: technology, power, and freedom	D. M. Kaplan (ed.) *Readings in the Philosophy of Technology*, Lanham, NJ: Rowman & Littlefield, pp. 209–26	III	51
2004	Hernan Galperin	Beyond interests, ideas, and technology: an institutional approach to communication and information policy	*The Information Society* 20(3): 159–68	II	28
2004	Nicholas Garnham	Class analysis and the information society as mode of production	*Javnost–The Public* 11(3): 93–103	I	20
2004	Sonia Livingstone	Media literacy and the challenge of new information and communication technologies	*The Communication Review* 7(1): 3–14	IV	70
2004	Barry Wellman	The three ages of Internet studies: ten, five and zero years ago	*New Media & Society* 6(1): 123–29	IV	73
2005	Stephen Coleman	New mediation and direct representation: reconceptualizing representation in the digital age	*New Media & Society* 7(2): 177–98	III	53
2005	Peter Dahlgren	The Internet, public spheres, and political communication: dispersion and deliberation	*Political Communication* 22(2): 147–62	III	56
2005	Dal Yong Jin	The telecom crisis and beyond: restructuring of the global telecommunications system	*Gazette: The International Journal for Communication Studies* 67(3): 289–304	III	63
2005	Josh Lerner and Jean Tirole	The economics of technology sharing: open source and beyond	*Journal of Economic Perspectives* 19(2): 99–120	II	34
2005	Frank Webster	Making sense of the information age: sociology and cultural studies	*Information, Communication & Society* 8(4): 439–58	I	21

xxiii

2006	Yochai Benkler and Helen Nissenbaum	Commons-based peer production and virtue	*Journal of Political Philosophy* 14(4): 394–419	III	65
2006	Sandra Braman	Tactical memory: the politics of openness in the construction of memory	*First Monday* 11(7): n.p.	IV	85
2006	J. J. Britz, P. J. Lor, I. E. M. Coetzee and B. C. Bester	Africa as a knowledge society: a reality check	*International Information & Library Review* 38(1): 25–40	II	42
2006	Brian Fitzgerald	The transformation of open source software	*MIS Quarterly* 30(3): 587–98	II	35
2006	Cees J. Hamelink	Rethinking ICTs: ICTs on a human scale	*European Journal of Communication* 21(3): 389–96	III	57
2006	Wolfgang Kleinwächter	Internet co-governance: towards a Multilayer Multiplayer Mechanism of Consultation, Coordination and Cooperation (M_3C_3)	*E-Learning* 3(3): 473–87	III	64
2006	Ramesh Srinivasan	Where information society and community voice intersect	*The Information Society* 22(5): 355–65	IV	74
2006	Paul A. Taylor	Putting the critique back into a *Critique of Information*: refusing to follow the order	*Information, Communication & Society* 9(5): 553–71	I	22
2006	Jan A. G. M. van Dijk	Digital divide research, achievements and shortcomings	*Poetics* 34(4–5): 221–35	II	43
2007	Manuel Castells	Communication, power and counter-power in the network society	*International Journal of Communication* 1(1): 238–66	I	23
2007	Karim H. Karim	Nation and diaspora: rethinking multiculturalism in a transnational context	*International Journal of Media and Cultural Politics* 2(3): 267–82	IV	75
2007	Mark Poster	The secret self: the case of identity theft	*Cultural Studies* 21(1): 118–40	IV	86

PREFACE

In this Major Work on the information society, I use the label 'the Information Society' to designate a particular vision of developments arising from the growing use of information and communication technologies (ICT) in the acquisition, storage and processing of information. In the early post-World War II period, scientists, engineers and mathematicians were interested in information and communication control systems and new technologies that might help them to realize their hopes for the contributions of artificial intelligence and robotics. Innovations in ICT provided technologists with new toys. If bigger and better versions could be built, they could be sold to the military-industrial-complex, the richest client for their wares. Economists were searching for a productivity strategy to stimulate growth, and information – although a problematic commodity – was expected to improve productivity in the manufacturing sector and to contribute to the growth of new information-related industries.

Some hoped that the productivity gains reaped by mechanization could be replicated by automation as the dependency of the United States economy on services increased. Policy makers were trying to maintain full employment and growth, and information workers (such as librarians and software engineers) were attempting to increase access to knowledge by crafting better tools for accessing information. Many workers were finding themselves in front of keyboards instead of working with pens and paper. It was widely assumed that enormous benefits would be reaped by those best positioned to enter the information age. Social scientists were trying to understand how all of these changes were transforming societies. They continue to do so and to assess our prospects for the future. In the Information Society, will we become cogs in the machine or system, or empowered savants?

This collection of papers is intended to provide some answers to questions about how social scientists have responded to popular mantras about the Information Society. Should we accept the idea that movement towards the Information Society is creating, or has the potential to create, social exclusion and disadvantage? What have we learned about how this movement influences the way that we live and work?

In the mid-1990s, with the spread of the Internet, research on the Information Society experienced a huge expansion. This collection includes contributions from the late 1940s and extends to the present. Like the

xxv

PREFACE

prevalence of the vision, it reflects a Western bias. Harold A. Innis, a Canadian economic historian, argued that the study of the implications of media and communication 'may enable us to see more clearly the bias of our own civilization' (1951: 90). It was in this spirit of critical inquiry that I made the choices about the papers to include.

Innis warned against the 'ideology of information technology', indicating that the economic, social, cultural and political outcomes associated with a dependence on electronic information should not be straightforwardly associated with enhanced human well-being. I have included papers focusing on the benefits of the Information Society and those offering critiques of the concept and its implications. Frank Webster (2002) suggests that if the Information Society label has any analytical purpose, this must be judged through empirical investigation. For the most part, I have included papers based on empirical studies.

Scientific research in the 1950s focused predominantly on the effects of information and communication to the neglect of the analysis of symbolic meaning. Human beings were conceived of mainly as agents, with little effort made to examine the cultural contexts in which they experienced their lives or acted upon the world. As the scholarly community began to examine the concept of the Information Society from critical perspectives, issues of power and the situated nature of human experience as it is mediated by ICT claimed greater attention. Research relevant to these issues uses many labels, including information economy, post-industrial society, post-modern society, network society, informational capitalism and network capitalism. These terms are used in different ways by the authors of the papers that are included in these volumes, but all are germane to debates about the history and future prospects of this vision.

My selection of papers began with a systematic survey of the literature informed by my knowledge of the field and the boundaries that I had decided upon. This resulted in an initial set of 800 papers, 86 of which figure in these four volumes. Selecting only some 10 per cent of what were often excellent contributions was difficult. I ask for forbearance from those authors who have been excluded. The final selection of papers was reviewed by colleagues and my Routledge editor, but responsibility for the choices made remains with me. I elected to include both papers that have been cited extremely widely and papers by scholars whose work has influenced me but who are not as widely known.

A stage theory of the advance towards a singular Information Society vision in my view is not helpful. A more instructive approach is one that seeks to understand information societies in relation to cultural, social, economic and political life. With the exception of some of the papers chosen to exemplify the early period, most of the papers illustrate the latter perspective, and as seen through the lens of disciplinary approaches in the social sciences. Innovations in ICT during the period from the 1950s to

PREFACE

the present are important, but they should not be seen as determining. They provide the stage and some of the sets for the enactment of the cultural, social, economic and political aspects of information societies.

The arrangement of the papers within each volume is chronological. It does not represent the earliest treatment of an issue by an author, but rather is representative of my effort to include foundational scholarship as well as illustrations of cutting-edge research in reasonably concise papers. Readers may wish to refer to Mansell *et al.* (2007) for a set of original papers which bear on the themes addressed in this Major Work set.

Volume I: History and Perspectives

This volume introduces readers to early contributions, mainly by American authors as it was primarily in the United States that early views of the Information Society originated. Focusing on the period 1980 to the present, the second part of this volume introduces diverse reflections and perspectives, highlighting the need to recognize the plurality of information societies and moving beyond wealth-creating, technology-driven perspectives present in the mainstream of Western scholarship. My plural designation of information societies is intended to signal the importance of differences and distinctions within and between societies.

Volume II: Knowledge, Economics and Organization

This volume emphasizes the role of information and communication in the economy and includes papers concerned with the economics and the political economy of information, the latter of which explicitly acknowledge power as a facet of information societies. These papers address inequality and the digital divide, highlighting concerns about what it means to be excluded from acquiring the capabilities for participating in the predominantly Western conception of the Information Society. Papers illustrating research on organizational changes associated with the introduction of digital ICT are also included, acknowledging that organizational style and power relations are crucial for developments in information societies.

Volume III: Democracy, Governance and Regulation

The actions of state institutions and organizations representing social movements, citizens, consumers and those who are stateless or migratory contribute to shaping information societies. The papers in this volume focus on issues of democratization and the distribution of power at global and local levels. The spread of digital networks is beginning to offer the potential for empowerment to those whose voices have been absent in the past, but, as the papers selected for this volume indicate, empirical evidence on the

PREFACE

consequences of these developments is ambiguous. These papers also provide illustrations of research on the institutions that are emerging at a global level for Internet governance, research on modes of regulation of the infrastructure of information societies, and perspectives on the role of intellectual property in the digital realm.

Volume IV: Everyday Life

This volume includes papers representing research on the way information societies enable new forms of mediated experience, whether as a result of interaction with traditional media or with newer media including the Internet, mobile phones and online social networking applications. The papers selected focus on how everyday life is influenced by perceptions of belonging, ethnicity, identity and gender, and by capacities for achieving literacy, maintaining privacy and managing surveillance in information societies. This research touches upon issues of social (in)justice and inequality and people's abilities to shape their everyday lives, as well as the ways that the forces of globalization mediate identity and allegiances shaped by experience of the local.

Works in the knowledge management tradition and research on intellectual property that are important for understanding information societies are represented only marginally in these volumes as they are the subjects of other Routledge Major Works. Also, for reasons of space, there are only a few references to the debates on the New World Information and Communication Order, many of which resurface in controversies over promotion of the Information Society vision.

Professor Robin Mansell
London School of Economics and Political Science
January 2009

References

Innis, H. A. (1951). *The Bias of Communication*. Toronto: University of Toronto Press.

Mansell, R., Avgerou, C., Quah, D. and Silverstone, R. (eds) (2007). *The Oxford Handbook of Information and Communication Technologies*. Oxford: Oxford University Press.

Webster, F. (2002). *Theories of the Information Society*, second edition. London: Routledge.

INTRODUCTION TO VOLUME I

Robin Mansell

Information is a name for the content of what is exchanged with the outer world as we adjust to it, and make our adjustment felt upon it. The process of receiving and of using information is the process of our adjusting to the contingencies of the outer environment and of our living effectively within that environment.... To live effectively is to live with adequate information. Thus, communication and control belong to the essence of man's inner life, even as they belong to his life in society.

(Wiener 1956: 17–18)

In recorded history there have perhaps been three impulses of change powerful enough to alter Man in basic ways. The introduction of agriculture.... The Industrial Revolution ... [and] the revolution in information processing technology of the computer.

(Masuda 1980b: 3, quoting Herbert A. Simon)

History and early debates

The origins of the emphasis on information and communication control systems, typical of much of literature on 'the Information Society', can be traced to a programme of scientific research, engineering and mathematics in the post-World War II period and the publication in 1948 of Norbert Weiner's *Cybernetics: Or Control and Communication in the Animal and Machine.* As Professor of Mathematics at the Massachusetts Institute of Technology (MIT), he was interested in neurological systems and information processing and feedback systems. A year later, Claude Shannon, an electrical engineer and mathematician, also at MIT, and Warren Weaver, a scientist and Director of Natural Sciences at the Rockefeller Institute, published *A Mathematical Theory of Communication* (Shannon and Weaver 1949). These men were interested in developing new approaches to automation and computerization as a means of providing new control systems for both military and non-military applications. Weiner, especially, was concerned with the philosophical implications of their work. He observed that 'society can only be understood through a study of the messages and the communication facilities that belong to it' (Wiener 1956: 16). Notwithstanding his interest in society, at this time there were few interdisciplinary collaborations with social scientists working on the implications of the insights arising from science and engineering.[1]

Fritz Machlup (1962, 1980–84), an economist, and Marc Porat and Michael Rubin (1977) undertook empirical work aimed at measuring the intensity of information activities and the growth in information-related occupations in the United States economy. This work was to give rise to comparative research aimed at mapping and measuring the Information Society, initially focusing on industrialized countries. Machlup emphasized that over-concentration on information and its delivery systems could deflect attention away from equitable availability and distribution of the benefits of information, and he warned against the temptation to 'measure the unmeasurable' (Machlup and Kronwinkler 1975), counsel that was not particularly well heeded. There has been considerable investment in indicator development, but relatively less effort has been devoted to understanding whether the data collected using these indicators can be used to infer behavioural change or applied to the analysis of the experiential aspects of information societies. In the 1970s research in Japan by Yoneji Masuda was developing a vision of the Information Society. The goal of the plan he devised for the Japanese government, was

> the realization of *a society that brings about a general flourishing state of human intellectual creativity, instead of affluent material consumption.*
>
> (Masuda 1980b: 3, italics in original)

The Information Society was designated a 'computopia', a society that would 'function around the axis of information values rather than material values' and rather idealistically, as one that would be 'chosen, not given' (Masuda 1980a: 146). A different approach to measurement in Japan was Youichi Ito's (1991) work, which involves the many different modes of information and communication, including books, telephone calls, etc.

Daniel Bell's (1973) *The Coming of the Post-Industrial Society: A Venture in Social Forecasting* brought the information age to the attention of social scientists in the United States and Europe, working in many disciplines well beyond those that had always focused on the media or communication systems. For Bell, 'the axial principle of the postindustrial society . . . is the centrality of theoretical knowledge and its new role, when codified, as the director of social change' (1980: 501). He said that the variables it was crucial to study were information and knowledge,[2] and it was now necessary to focus on business and management issues as well as broader societal concerns. Peter Drucker (1969) employed the term 'knowledge society' in arguing that knowledge workers would have to change and adapt to its requirements. For these authors and many others, the task at hand was to forge a strong commitment to technological innovation as the mobilizer of economic and social progress.

Social scientists working in the field of communication in the United States generally emphasized the potentially transformative character of information and communication technology (ICT), although Harold Lasswell (1948, 1972) and Fritz Lazarsfeld and Robert Merton (1948) concentrated on the interactions between mass communication and social action, as did Wilbur Schramm (1955). Lasswell emphasized that the social scientific study of communication meant a focus on 'who says what in which channel to whom with what effect' (1948: 37), setting the stage for a tradition of media effects research with its problematic search for a stable set of effects.

The Canadian, Marshall McLuhan (1962), a Professor of English, popularized the term 'global village'[3] in his *The Gutenberg Galaxy: The Making of Typographic Man*. McLuhan extended the work of fellow Canadian and economic historian Harold Innis (1950, 1951), emphasizing features of communication in the written and oral traditions. McLuhan suggested that 'the advent of a new medium often reveals the lineaments and assumptions, as it were, of an old medium' (1960: 567). This and similar observations sparked vociferous debate – which continues – about whether specific communication technologies are causally related to certain societal configurations. The American scholar Ithiel de Sola Pool (1974) was one of several academics in this period putting ICT at the centre of the case for an Information Society policy. Such policy discussions offered a normative prescription for the optimal way of capitalizing on the benefits of the production and use of ICTs. Information Society as injunction and prescription rather than description, a programme consistent with the dominant values in the wealthy Western countries of the world, was well on its way to being developed. The papers in the second part of this volume have been selected to illustrate some of the arguments of those who criticized this programme.

Reflections and perspectives

Among those who criticized the emerging normative vision of the Information Society was Jacques Ellul (1964), whose outlook was deeply dystopian. Critical reflections in the period from the late 1960s to the present have come from a variety of locations within the social sciences. Some challenge the idea of a progression through stages of social and economic organization to achieve the Information Society. Others criticize the statistical evidence, arguing that the definitions used to collect data are questionable. Still others are concerned about a strong focus on technology and there are those who are emphatic about the significance of information, in either philosophical or symbolic terms.

Mapping and measuring the Information Society

In Britain, Ian Miles and Jonathan Gershuny (1986) examined the empirical evidence suggesting the growing economic significance of information in the economy, concluding that movement toward the Information Society was associated with very diverse tertiary (services) sectors of the economy and, therefore, that analysis must be equally diverse, as the Information Society was a 'moving target' (Miles 2005). Miles and Gershuny advocated debate on the distributional implications of information resources and on the design of new ICTs, commenting that questions 'need to be asked *before* the systems are developed and installed' (1986: 35). This view was echoed by Christopher Freeman and Luc Soete (1990), who called for debate and a resolution of conflicting interests as institutions and ways of living were being reshaped in parallel with technological innovations. Their aim was to humanize the many new and potential applications of ICTs.

Miles (1993) developed research on the interdependencies between manufacturing and services, insisting that arbitrary divisions between services and manufacturing are unhelpful, and emphasizing the need to examine specific services rather than to assume that the take-up of ICT will have the same implications for all kinds of societies. Michel Menou and Richard Taylor (2006) were strongly critical of mapping and measuring efforts, especially those seeking to track advances in information societies in developing countries, arguing that there was little if any coherence in the definitions and indices in use. Other criticisms of research emphasizing ICTs came from those who saw the overemphasis on technology as technological determinism.

Putting society first

In Britain, Peter Golding and Graham Murdock maintained that a priority for social science research should be to develop a theory of society with a focus on the implications of media and communication industry developments for social inequality. As they put it, 'determinism, in its arbitrary allocation of an unwarranted and unsupportable significance to the subject matter at hand, distorts beyond reprieve a balanced view of social structure and process' and leads to a neglect of 'sources of social dissent and political struggle' (Golding and Murdock 1978: 347). In the United States, James Beniger's (1986) book *The Control Revolution: Technological and Economic Origins of the Information Society* underlined the implications of technological convergence, a development that is continuing to spark innovations in information and communication service applications. In contrast to those who contended that the Information Society was being driven by technological advances in tools, Beniger also highlighted the way that organizational systems were contributing to the emergence of 'a single infrastructure of control', an infrastructure that drew upon rather than was determined by the information machinery, and which emerged as the Information Society vision. Also in the United States, Caroline Marvin's (1988) book *When Old Technologies Were New* provided the basis for parallels between current experience and the development of electronic communication in the late nineteenth century.

Understanding power in network relations

During the time since the 1960s, there has been considerable scepticism about the likelihood that fundamental relationships in societies would be altered as a result of innovations in technologies.[4] For example, David Lyon (1986) suggested that it was unlikely that the dynamics of industrial capitalism would be altered substantially by the spread of digital technologies[5] and, instead, that technology should be examined critically rather than taken as a given. A collection of papers edited by Jacques Berleur *et al.* (1990) brought together the work of a number of European and American scholars calling for the need to undertake research on the ethics, ideology, culture, politics and economics of information societies.[6]

In his development of a tradition of research on the political economy of media and communication, Dallas Smythe (1977, 1981), a Canadian, challenged the premise that the Information Society would radically alter relations of political and economic dependency. Similarly, Herbert Schiller (1981, 1984), in the United States, examined concentrations of corporate ownership, which, he argued, were enabling the interests of capitalists to prevail in the Information Society. Together with French scholar Bernard Miège (Schiller and Miège 1990), he argued that there was 'more menace than promise' in information technologies. What mattered, he insisted, was the 'the structural character of the world community and the quality of life and social existence it offers to *all* people' (Schiller 1980: 313).

In Britain, Nicholas Garnham (2000), who contributed substantially to the political economy of the media and communication industries throughout the 1980s and 1990s, by the beginning of the new century had concluded that the concept of the Information Society had failed to achieve much analytical purchase. This, he suggested, was because it is internally incoherent and the use of the terminology simply advances specific interests in the capitalist system. Kevin Robins and Frank Webster had also found fault with the analytical traditions in cultural studies and political economy research, maintaining that 'only when it becomes possible to confront the integral cultural and economic dynamic of contemporary transformations, will it be possible to assess the space for liberatory intervention as against the logic of domination and control in post-modern cultural forms' (1987: 87).

Graham Murdock stressed that, rather than concluding that everything is transformed into a post-modern age as a result of innovations in technologies, the modern era should be seen as 'a complex articulation of formations, operating in different domains and at different levels' (1993: 537). And Brian Winston (1998) found continuity between historical and modern social formations in his research on the period framed by the telegraph and the Internet. In general, in contrast to those who had focused on the disruptive character of innovations in ICTs, many of these scholars acknowledged the opportunities associated with the innovations, but found them to be implemented in ways that replicated the sources of inequality in society. Research undertaken by Armand Mattelart (2002) in France, Jorge Schement (1990) in the United States and Gaëtan Tremblay (1995) in Canada, offered similar criticisms of the dominant discourse of the Information Society vision and its consequences.[7]

The influential work of Manuel Castells (1996, 1997, 1998, 2000) has highlighted the cultural and institutional manifestations of network societies and the importance – or logic – of emergent social formations. Castells work has been criticized by scholars such as Jan van Dijk (1999) and Nico Stehr for its 'modern version of "technological determinism"' (Stehr 2000: 83). Despite this, however, Castells' work is very important for understanding the enabling as well as the disabling characteristics of what he calls 'mass self communication', that is, the possibilities created by the Internet, including an ever-growing number of social networking sites, and greater access to mobile communication.

James Beniger (1990) advocated the development of a general theory of information, communication, decision and control, an approach that was taken up by systems theorists such as Niklas Luhmann (1996). Philosopher Manuel De Landa (1991) was also drawn to systems theory and focused on the chaotic properties in the evolution of systems, re-emphasizing a focus on information processing, to explain developments in intelligent machines, especially those used for military purposes. Suhail Malik (2005) also took a systems perspective in the examination of information societies – in this case making an attempt to integrate insights from developmental systems theory, biology and the social sciences.

Other scholars have begun the quest for a general theory of information paralleled by some political economists' quest for a general theory of society. For example, Tom Stonier envisaged a theory that would encompass 'information, intelligence, meaning, and understanding' (1991: 262). Others, such as Haridimos Tsoukas (1997), while still focusing on information, argued that information overload might diminish understanding in society, while Luciano Floridi (2002) is among those intrigued by the ethical implications of information. Scott Lash maintained that in the information age 'the centrality of the means of production [is] displaced by the means of communication' (2002: 112), that non-linear socio-technical assemblages replace the institutions of earlier societies and, therefore, that a critique of information must emerge from information feedback loops within the communication system itself. Following Luhmann's (1996) systems theory, Lash argues that we can no longer stand outside the system and critique it from a transcendent ideological position.

The proponents of research in the critical traditions of scholarship on the Information Society have struggled to provide a theoretically robust account of how the interpenetration of asymmetrical relationships within today's information societies perpetuates inequalities and injustices. Research in the more critical traditions has had relatively little influence on the priorities of those promoting the Information Society vision. This vision continues to be driven strongly by those in a position to make design and other choices regarding the nature and use of technology, including those individuals using the technology in the search for profit and according to the values of global capitalism.[8] The virtual spaces enabled by the Internet provide opportunities now for more people to represent their views and to participate online in communicative dialogues of many kinds. The uncertainty over these developments is whether these new voices will be heard and responded to by the traditionally powerful actors in society, and whether these voices are heralding a more profound shift of influence and control towards action to address inequality and exclusion.

Conclusion

This volume includes work by information society enthusiasts whose hope for a better world is based on their faith in technological progress and innovations in information processing and organizational control systems. It also includes critiques of the Information Society vision. The scholars in this category call for 'accounts that [are], empirically testable and conceptually sensitive, [and] strive to identify the most consequential characteristics of how we live' (Webster 2005: 454). A substantial amount of research in the social sciences, in both traditions, is being conducted outside North America and Europe. For the reasons noted in the preface, in this volume the North American and European bias is particularly important because it tends to emphasize the claims that the normative vision of the Information Society should be shared globally, notwithstanding criticisms of this vision from some of the papers' authors.

Sohail Inayatullah wrote of the need to 'find ways to enter global conversations, that is, to protect local ways of knowing' (1998: 243) as one means of countering the hegemony of the Information Society vision and its detrimental consequences. Some, including Mark Poster (1990, 2006), have concluded that information societies 'do not reproduce exactly the politics of earlier epochs' (Poster 2006: 83). There is a need for research on whether the new spaces of communication opportunity are engendering outcomes for human beings that are consistent with social justice and greater equality. This possibility is considered further by some of the scholars whose work is included in Volumes II, III and IV of this Master Work on the Information Society.

Notes

1 An exception, in the United States, was the work of Gregory Bateson (1951).
2 Bell (1979) is generally credited with having introduced the term 'Information Society'.
3 The term first coined by Percy W. Lewis (1948) in his *America and Cosmic Man*.
4 For critiques of the Information Society as an analytical concept, see Duff (2000), May (2002) and Webster (2006).
5 Drawing on Kumar (1978).
6 Tom Forester's (1992) 'Megatrends or Megamistakes? What Ever Happened to the Information Society?' also provides a review of a literature that raises similar issues.
7 Douglas Robertson (1990) provides a critical survey of these various arguments.
8 Alternative visions can be found in Mansell and Steinmueller (2000).

References

Bateson, G. (1951). 'Information and Codification: A Philosophical Approach'. In J. Ruesch and G. Bateson (eds), *Communication: The Social Matrix of Psychiatry* (pp. 168–212). New York: Norton & Co.

Bell, D. (1973). *The Coming of Post-Industrial Society: A Venture in Social Forecasting*. New York: Basic Books.

—— (1979). 'The Social Framework of the Information Society'. In M. L. Dertouzos and J. Moses (eds), *The Computer Age: A 20 Year View* (pp. 500–49). Cambridge, MA: MIT Press.

—— (1980). 'The Social Framework of the Information Society'. In T. Forester (ed.), *The Microelectronics Revolution* (pp. 500–49). Oxford: Blackwell.

Beniger, J. R. (1986). *The Control Revolution: Technological and Economic Origins of the Information Society*. Cambridge, MA: Harvard University Press.

—— (1990). 'Conceptualizing Information Technology as Organization, and Vice Versa'. In J. Fulk and C. Steinfield (eds), *Organization and Communication Technology* (pp. 29–45). Newbury Park, CA: Sage Publications.

Berleur, J., Clement, A., Sizer, R. and Whitehouse, D. (eds). (1990). *The Information Society: Evolving Landscapes*. Concord, Ont.: Captus Press.

Castells, M. (1996). *The Information Age: Economy, Society and Culture, Volume I: The Rise of the Network Society*. Oxford: Blackwell.

—— (1997). *The Information Age: Economy, Society and Culture, Volume II: The Power of Identity*. Oxford: Blackwell.

—— (1998). *The Information Age: Economy, Society and Culture, Volume III: End of Millennium*. Oxford: Blackwell.

—— (2000). 'Materials for an Exploratory Theory of the Network Society'. *British Journal of Sociology*, 51(1): 5–24.

De Landa, M. (1991). *War in the Age of Intelligent Machines*. New York: Zone Books.

de Sola Pool, I. (1974). 'The Rise of Communications Policy Research'. *Journal of Communication*, 24(2): 31–42.

Drucker, P. F. (1969). 'Knowledge Society'. *New Society*, 13(343): 629–31.

Duff, A. S. (2000). *Information Society Studies*. London: Routledge.

Ellul, J. (1964). *The Technological Society* (J. Wilkinson, trans.). New York: Vintage Books.

Floridi, L. (2002). 'What Is the Philosophy of Information?' *Metaphilosophy*, 33(1–2): 123–45.

Forester, T. (1992). 'Megatrends or Megamistakes? What Ever Happened to the Information Society?' *The Information Society*, 8(3): 133–46.

Freeman, C. and Soete, L. (1990). 'Information Technology and the Global Economy'. In J. Berleur, A. Clement, R. Sizer and D. Whitehouse (eds), *The Information Society: Evolving Landscapes* (pp. 278–94). Concord, Ont.: Captus Press.

Garnham, N. (2000). *Emancipation, the Media and Modernity: Arguments about the Media and Social Theory*. Oxford: Oxford University Press.

Golding, P. and Murdock, G. (1978). 'Theories of Communication and Theories of Society'. *Communication Research*, 5(3): 339–56.

Inayatullah, S. (1998). 'Deconstructing the Information Era'. *Futures*, 30(2–3): 235–47.

Innis, H. A. (1950). *Empire and Communication*. Toronto: Toronto University Press.

—— (1951). *The Bias of Communication*. Toronto: University of Toronto Press.

Ito, Y. (1991). '"Johoka" as a Driving Force of Social Change'. *Keio Communication Review*, 12: 35–58.

Kumar, K. (1978). *Prophecy and Progress: The Sociology of Industrial and Postindustrial Society*. Harmondsworth: Allen Lane.

Lash, S. M. (2002). *Critique of Information*. London: Sage.

Lasswell, H. D. (1948). 'The Structure and Function of Communications in Society'. In L. Bryson (ed.), *The Communication of Ideas* (pp. 37–51). New York: Harper.

—— (1972). Communications Research and Public Policy. *The Public Opinion Quarterly*, XXXVI(3): 301–10.

Lazarsfeld, P. F. and Merton, R. K. (1948). 'Mass Communication, Popular Taste and Organized Social Action'. In L. Bryson (ed.), *The Communication of Ideas* (pp. 95–118). New York: Harper.

Lewis, P. W. (1948). *America and Cosmic Man*. New York: Doubleday.

Luhmann, N. (1996). *The Reality of Mass Media* (K. Cross, trans.). Stanford, CA: Stanford University Press.

Lyon, D. (1986). 'From Post-Industrialism to Information-Society – A New Social Transformation'. *Sociology*, 20(4): 577–88.

Machlup, F. B. (1962). *The Production and Distribution of Knowledge in the US Economy*. Princeton, NJ: Princeton University Press.

—— (1980–84). *Knowledge: Its Creation, Distribution and Economic Significance*, 4 volumes. Princeton, NJ: Princeton University Press.

—— and Kronwinkler, T. (1975). 'Workers Who Produce Knowledge – Steady Increase, 1900 to 1970'. *Weltwirtschaftliches Archiv-Review of World Economics*, 111(4): 752–59.

McLuhan, H. M. (1960). 'Effects of the Improvements of Communication Media'. *Journal of Economic History*, 20(4): 566–75.

—— (1962). *The Gutenberg Galaxy: The Making of Typographic Man*. Toronto: University of Toronto Press.

Malik, S. (2005). Information and Knowledge. *Theory Culture & Society*, 22(1): 29–49.

Mansell, R. and Steinmueller, W. E. (2000). *Mobilizing the Information Society: Strategies for Growth and Opportunity*. Oxford: Oxford University Press.

Marvin, C. (1988). *When Old Technologies Were New: Thinking about Electric Communication in the Late Nineteenth Century*. Oxford: Oxford University Press.

Masuda, Y. (1980a). 'Computopia: Rebirth of Theological Synergism'. In Y. Masuda (ed.), *The Information Society as Post-Industrial Society* (pp. 146–54). Tokyo: Institute for the Information Society (and 1981 by World Future Society).

—— (1980b). 'Emerging Information Society in Japan'. In *The Information Society as Post-Industrial Society* (pp. 3–22). Tokyo: Institute for the Information Society.

Mattelart, A. (2002). 'An Archaeology of the Global Era: Constructing a Belief'. *Media Culture & Society*, 24(5): 591–612.

May, C. (2002). *The Information Society: A Sceptical View*. Cambridge: Polity Press.

Menou, M. J. and Taylor, R. D. (2006). 'A "Grand Challenge": Measuring Information Societies'. *The Information Society*, 22(5): 261–7.

Miles, I. (1993). 'Services in the New Industrial-Economy'. *Futures*, 25(6): 653–72.

—— (2005). 'Be Here Now'. *Info*, 7(2): 49–71.

—— and Gershuny, J. (1986). 'The Social Economics of Information Technology'. In Ferguson, M. (ed.), *New Communication Technologies and the Public Interest* (pp. 18–36). London: Sage.

Murdock, G. (1993). 'Communications and the Constitution of Modernity'. *Media Culture & Society*, 15(4): 521–39.

Porat, M. U. and Rubin, M. R. (1977). *The Information Economy*, 9 volumes. Washington, DC: Department of Commerce, Government Printing Office.

Poster, M. (1990). *The Mode of Information: Poststructuralism and Social Context*. Chicago, IL: University of Chicago Press.

—— (2006). *Information Please: Culture and Politics in the Digital Age*. Durham, NC: Duke University Press.

Robertson, D. S. (1990). 'The Information Revolution'. *Communication Research*, 17(2): 235–54.

Robins, K. and Webster, F. (1987). 'The Communications Revolution – New Media, Old Problems'. *Communication*, 10(1): 71–89.

Schement, J. R. (1990). 'Porat, Bell, and the Information-Society Reconsidered – the Growth of Information Work in the Early 20th-Century'. *Information Processing & Management*, 26(4): 449–65.

Schiller, H. (1980). 'Whose New International Economic and Information Order?' *Communication*, 5: 299–314.

—— (1981). *Who Knows? Information in the Age of the Fortune 500*. Norwood, NJ: Ablex.

—— (1984). *Information and the Crisis Economy*. Norwood, NJ: Ablex.

—— and Miège, B. (1990). 'Communication of Knowledge in an Information Society'. In J. Berleur, A. Clement, R. Sizer and D. Whitehouse (eds), *The Information Society: Evolving Landscapes* (pp. 161–7). Concord, Ont.: Captus Press.

Schramm, W. (1955). 'Information Theory and Mass Communication'. *Journalism Quarterly*, 32: 131–46.

Shannon, C. E. and Weaver, W. (1949). *Mathematical Theory of Communication*. Urbana, IL: University of Illinois Press.

Smythe, D. W. (1977). 'Communications: Blindspot of Western Marxism'. *Canadian Journal of Political and Social Theory*, 1(3): 1–27.

—— (1981). *Dependency Road: Communications, Capitalism, Consciousness and Canada*. Norwood, NJ: Ablex.

Stehr, N. (2000). 'Deciphering Information Technologies: Modern Societies as Networks'. *European Journal of Social Theory*, 3(1): 83.

Stonier, T. (1991). 'Towards a New Theory of Information'. *Journal of Information Science*, 17(5): 257–63.

Tremblay, G. (1995). 'The Information Society: From Fordism to Gatesism'. *Canadian Journal of Communication*, 20: 461–82.

Tsoukas, H. (1997). 'The Tyranny of Light – the Temptations and the Paradoxes of the Information Society'. *Futures*, 29(9): 827–43.

van Dijk, J. A. G. M. (1999). 'The One-dimensional Network Society of Manuel Castells'. *New Media and Society*, 1(1): 127–39.

Webster, F. (2005). 'Making Sense of the Information Age'. *Information, Communication and Society*, 8(4): 439–58.

—— (2006). *Theories of the Information Society*, third edition. London: Routledge.

Wiener, N. (1948). *Cybernetics: Or Control and Communication in the Animal and Machine*. Cambridge, MA: MIT Press.

—— (1956). *The Human Use of Human Beings: Cybernetics and Society*. New York: Doubleday & Company Inc.

Winston, B. (1998). *Media, Technology and Society: From the Telegraph to the Internet*. London: Routledge.

Part 1

HISTORY AND
EARLY DEBATES

1

THE STRUCTURE AND FUNCTION OF COMMUNICATION IN SOCIETY

Harold D. Lasswell

Source: Lyman Bryson (ed.) (1948) *The Communication of Ideas*, New York: Harper, pp. 37–51.

The act of communication

A convenient way to describe an act of communication is to answer the following questions:

Who
Says What
In Which Channel
To Whom
With What Effect?

The scientific study of the process of communication tends to concentrate upon one or another of these questions. Scholars who study the "who," the communicator, look into the factors that initiate and guide the act of communication. We call this subdivision of the field of research *control analysis*. Specialists who focus upon the "says what" engage in *content analysis*. Those who look primarily at the radio, press, film and other channels of communication are doing *media analysis*. When the principal concern is with the persons reached by the media, we speak of *audience analysis*. If the question is the impact upon audiences, the problem is *effect analysis*.[1]

Whether such distinctions are useful depends entirely upon the degree of refinement which is regarded as appropriate to a given scientific and managerial objective. Often it is simpler to combine audience and effect analysis, for instance, than to keep them apart. On the other hand, we may want to concentrate on the analysis of content, and for this purpose subdivide the field into the study of purport and style, the first referring to the message, and the second to the arrangement of the elements of which the message is composed.

Structure and function

Enticing as it is to work out these categories in more detail, the present discussion has a different scope. We are less interested in dividing up the act of communication than in viewing the act as a whole in relation to the entire social process. Any process can be examined in two frames of reference, namely, structure and function; and our analysis of communication will deal with the specializations that carry on certain functions, of which the following may be clearly distinguished: (1) The surveillance of the environment; (2) the correlation of the parts of society in responding to the environment; (3) the transmission of the social heritage from one generation to the next.

Biological equivalencies

At the risk of calling up false analogies, we can gain perspective on human societies when we note the degree to which communication is a feature of life at every level. A vital entity, whether relatively isolated or in association, has specialized ways of receiving stimuli from the environment. The single-celled organism or the many-membered group tends to maintain an internal equilibrium and to respond to changes in the environment in a way that maintains this equilibrium. The responding process calls for specialized ways of bringing the parts of the whole into harmonious action. Multi-celled animals specialize cells to the function of external contact and internal correlation. Thus, among the primates, specialization is exemplified by organs such as the ear and eye, and the nervous system itself. When the stimuli receiving and disseminating patterns operate smoothly, the several parts of the animal act in concert in reference to the environment ("feeding," "fleeing," "attacking").[2]

In some animal societies certain members perform specialized roles, and survey the environment. Individuals act as "sentinels," standing apart from the herd or flock and creating a disturbance whenever an alarming change occurs in the surroundings. The trumpeting, cackling or shrilling of the sentinel is enough to set the herd in motion. Among the activities engaged in by specialized "leaders" is the internal stimulation of "followers" to adapt in an orderly manner to the circumstances heralded by the sentinels.[3]

Within a single, highly differentiated organism, incoming nervous impulses and outgoing impulses are transmitted along fibers that make synaptic junction with other fibers. The critical points in the process occur at the relay stations, where the arriving impulse may be too weak to reach

STRUCTURE & FUNCTION OF COMMUNICATION IN SOCIETY

the threshold which stirs the next link into action. At the higher centers, separate currents modify one another, producing results that differ in many ways from the outcome when each is allowed to continue a separate path. At any relay station there is no conductance, total conductance or intermediate conductance. The same categories apply to what goes on among members of an animal society. The sly fox may approach the barnyard in a way that supplies too meager stimuli for the sentinel to sound the alarm. Or the attacking animal may eliminate the sentinel before he makes more than a feeble outcry. Obviously there is every gradation possible between total conductance and no conductance.

Attention in world society

When we examine the process of communication of any state in the world community, we note three categories of specialists. One group surveys the political environment of the state as a whole, another correlates the response of the whole state to the environment, and the third transmits certain patterns of response from the old to the young. Diplomats, attachés, and foreign correspondents are representative of those who specialize on the environment. Editors, journalists, and speakers are correlators of the internal response. Educators in family and school transmit the social inheritance.

Communications which originate abroad pass through sequences in which various senders and receivers are linked with one another. Subject to modification at each relay point in the chain, messages originating with a diplomat or foreign correspondent may pass through editorial desks and eventually reach large audiences.

If we think of the world attention process as a series of *attention frames,* it is possible to describe the rate at which comparable content is brought to the notice of individuals and groups. We can inquire into the point at which "conductance" no longer occurs; and we can look into the range between "total conductance" and "minimum conductance." The metropolitan and political centers of the world have much in common with the interdependence, differentiation, and activity of the cortical or subcortical centers of an individual organism. Hence the attention frames found in these spots are the most variable, refined, and interactive of all frames in the world community.

At the other extreme are the attention frames of primitive inhabitants of isolated areas. Not that folk cultures are wholly untouched by industrial civilization. Whether we parachute into the interior of New Guinea, or land on the slopes of the Himalayas, we find no tribe wholly out of contact with the world. The long threads of trade, of missionary zeal, of adventurous exploration and scientific field study, and of global war, reach the far distant places. No one is entirely out of this world.

Among primitives the final shape taken by communication is the ballad or tale. Remote happenings in the great world of affairs, happenings that come to the notice of metropolitan audiences, are reflected, however dimly, in the thematic material of ballad singers and reciters. In these creations far away political leaders may be shown supplying land to the peasants or restoring an abundance of game to the hills.[4]

When we push upstream of the flow of communication, we note that the immediate relay function for nomadic and remote tribesmen is sometimes performed by the inhabitants of settled villages with whom they come in occasional contact. The relayer can be the school teacher, doctor, judge, tax collector, policeman, soldier, peddler, salesman, missionary, student; in any case he is an assembly point of news and comment.

More detailed equivalencies

The communication processes of human society, when examined in detail, reveal many equivalencies to the specializations found in the physical organism, and in the lower animal societies. The diplomats, for instance, of a single state are stationed all over the world and send messages to a few focal points. Obviously, these incoming reports move from the many to the few, where they interact upon one another. Later on, the sequence spreads fanwise according to a few to many pattern, as when a foreign secretary gives a speech in public, an article is put out in the press, or a news film is distributed to the theaters. The lines leading from the outer environment of the state are functionally equivalent to the afferent channels that convey incoming nervous impulses to the central nervous system of a single animal, and to the means by which alarm is spread among a flock. Outgoing, or efferent impulses, display corresponding parallels.

The central nervous system of the body is only partly involved in the entire flow of afferent-efferent impulses. There are automatic systems that can act on one another without involving the "higher" centers at all. The stability of the internal environment is maintained principally through the mediation of the vegetive or autonomic specializations of the nervous system. Similarly, most of the messages within any state do not involve the central channels of communication. They take place within families, neighborhoods, shops, field gangs, and other local contexts. Most of the educational process is carried on the same way.

A further set of significant equivalencies is related to the circuits of communication, which are predominantly one-way or two-way, depending upon the degree of reciprocity between communicators and audience. Or, to express it differently, two-way communication occurs when the sending and receiving functions are performed with equal frequency by two or more persons. A conversation is usually assumed to be a pattern of two-way communication (although monologues are hardly unknown). The modern instruments of mass communication give an enormous advantage to the controllers of printing plants, broadcasting equipment; and other forms of

STRUCTURE & FUNCTION OF COMMUNICATION IN SOCIETY

fixed and specialized capital. But it should be noted that audiences do "talk back," after some delay; and many controllers of mass media use scientific methods of sampling in order to expedite this closing of the circuit.

Circuits of two-way contact are particularly in evidence among the great metropolitan, political and cultural centers in the world. New York, Moscow, London and Paris, for example, are in intense two-way contact, even when the flow is severely curtailed in volume (as between Moscow and New York). Even insignificant sites become world centers when they are transformed into capital cities (Canberra in Australia, Ankara in Turkey, the District of Columbia, U.S.A.). A cultural center like Vatican City is in intense two-way relationship with the dominant centers throughout the world. Even specialized production centers like Hollywood, despite their preponderance of outgoing material, receive an enormous volume of messages.

A further distinction can be made between message controlling and message handling centers and social formations. The message center in the vast Pentagon Building of the War Department in Washington, D.C., transmits with no more than accidental change incoming messages to addressees. This is the role of the printers and distributors of books; of dispatchers, linemen, and messengers connected with telegraphic communication; of radio engineers, and other technicians associated with broadcasting. Such message handlers may be contrasted with those who affect the content of what is said, which is the function of editors, censors, and propagandists. Speaking of the symbol specialists as a whole, therefore, we separate them into the manipulators (controllers) and the handlers; the first group typically modifies content, while the second does not.

Needs and values

Though we have noted a number of functional and structural equivalencies between communication in human societies and other living entities, it is not implied that we can most fruitfully investigate the process of communication in America or the world by the methods most appropriate to research on the lower animals or on single physical organisms. In comparative psychology when we describe some part of the surroundings of a rat, cat, or monkey as a stimulus (that is, as part of the environment reaching the attention of the animal), we cannot ask the rat; we use other means of inferring perception. When human beings are our objects of investigation, we can interview the great "talking animal." (This is not that we take everything at face value. Sometimes we forecast the opposite of what the person says he intends to do. In this case, we depend on other indications, both verbal and non-verbal.)

In the study of living forms, it is rewarding, as we have said, to look at them as modifiers of the environment in the process of gratifying needs, and hence of maintaining a steady state of internal equilibrium. Food, sex, and other activities which involve the environment can be examined on a comparative basis. Since human beings exhibit speech reactions, we can investigate many more relationships than in the non-human species.[5] Allowing for the data furnished by speech (and other communicative acts), we can investigate human society in terms of values; that is, in reference to categories of relationships that are recognized objects of gratification. In America, for example, it requires no elaborate technique of study to discern that power and respect are values. We can demonstrate this by listening to testimony, and by watching what is done when opportunity is afforded.

It is possible to establish a list of values current in any group chosen for investigation. Further than this, we can discover the rank order in which these values are sought. We can rank the members of the group according to their position in relation to the values. So far as industrial civilization is concerned, we have no hesitation in saying that power, wealth, respect, well being, and enlightenment are among the values. If we stop with this list, which is not exhaustive, we can describe on the basis of available knowledge (fragmentary though it may often be), the social structure of most of the world. Since values are not equally distributed, the social structure reveals more or less concentration of relatively abundant shares of power, wealth and other values in a few hands. In some places this concentration is passed on from generation to generation, forming castes rather than a mobile society.

In every society the values are shaped and distributed according to more or less distinctive patterns (*institutions*). The institutions include communications which are invoked in support of the network as a whole. Such communications are the ideology; and in relation to power we can differentiate the political *doctrine,* the political *formula* and the *miranda.*[6] These are illustrated in the United States by the doctrine of individualism, the paragraphs of the Constitution, which are the formula, and the ceremonies and legends of public life, which comprise the miranda. The ideology is communicated to the rising generation through such specialized agencies as the home and school.

Ideology is only part of the myths of any given society. There may be counter ideologies directed against the dominant doctrine, formula, and miranda. Today the power structure of world politics is deeply affected by ideological conflict, and by the role of two giant powers, the United States and Russia.[7] The ruling elites view one another as potential enemies, not only in the sense that interstate differences may be settled by war, but in the more urgent sense that the ideology of the other may appeal to disaffected elements at home and weaken the internal power position of each ruling class.

Social conflict and communication

Under the circumstances, one ruling element is especially alert to the other, and relies upon communication as a means of preserving power. One function of communication, therefore, is to provide intelligence about what the other elite is doing, and about its strength. Fearful that intelligence channels will be controlled by the other, in order to withhold and distort, there is a tendency to resort to secret surveillance. Hence international espionage is intensified above its usual level in peacetime. Moreover, efforts are made to "black out" the self in order to counteract the scrutiny of the potential enemy. In addition, communication is employed affirmatively for the purpose of establishing contact with audiences within the frontiers of the other power.

These varied activities are manifested in the use of open and secret agents to scrutinize the other, in counter intelligence work, in censorship and travel restriction, in broadcasting and other informational activities across frontiers.

Ruling elites are also sensitized to potential threats in the internal environment. Besides using open sources of information, secret measures are also adopted. Precautions are taken to impose "security" upon as many policy matters as possible. At the same time, the ideology of the elite is reaffirmed, and counter ideologies are suppressed.

The processes here sketched run parallel to phenomena to be observed throughout the animal kingdom. Specialized agencies are used to keep aware of threats and opportunities in the external environment. The parallels include the surveillance exercised over the internal environment, since among the lower animals some herd leaders sometimes give evidence of fearing attack on two fronts, internal and external; they keep an uneasy eye on both environments. As a means of preventing surveillance by an enemy, well known devices are at the disposal of certain species, *e.g.,* the squid's use of a liquid fog screen, the protective coloration of the chameleon. However, there appears to be no correlate of the distinction between the "secret" and "open" channels of human society.

Inside a physical organism the closest parallel to social revolution would be the growth of new nervous connections with parts of the body that rival, and can take the place of, the existing structures of central integration. Can this be said to occur as the embryo develops in the mother's body? Or, if we take a destructive, as distinct from a reconstructive, process, can we properly say that internal surveillance occurs in regard to cancer, since cancers compete for the food supplies of the body?

Efficient communication

The analysis up to the present implies certain criteria of efficiency or inefficiency in communication. In human societies the process is efficient to the degree that rational judgments are facilitated. A rational judgment implements value-goals. In animal societies communication is efficient when it aids survival, or some other specified need of the aggregate. The same criteria can be applied to the single organism.

HISTORY AND PERSPECTIVES

One task of a rationally organized society is to discover and control any factors that interfere with efficient communication. Some limiting factors are psychotechnical. Destructive radiation, for instance, may be present in the environment, yet remain undetected owing to the limited range of the unaided organism.

But even technical insufficiencies can be overcome by knowledge. In recent years shortwave broadcasting has been interfered with by disturbances which will either be surmounted, or will eventually lead to the abandonment of this mode of broadcasting. During the past few years advances have been made toward providing satisfactory substitutes for defective hearing and seeing. A less dramatic, though no less important, development has been the discovery of how inadequate reading habits can be corrected.

There are, of course, deliberate obstacles put in the way of communication, like censorship and drastic curtailment of travel. To some extent obstacles can be surmounted by skillful evasion, but in the long run it will doubtless be more efficient to get rid of them by consent or coercion.

Sheer ignorance is a pervasive factor whose consequences have never been adequately assessed. Ignorance here means the absence, at a given point in the process of communication, of knowledge which is available elsewhere in society. Lacking proper training, the personnel engaged in gathering and disseminating intelligence is continually misconstruing or overlooking the facts, if we define the facts as what the objective, trained observer could find.

In accounting for inefficiency we must not overlook the low evaluations put upon skill in relevant communication. Too often irrelevant, or positively distorting, performances command prestige. In the interest of a "scoop," the reporter gives a sensational twist to a mild international conference, and contributes to the popular image of international politics as chronic, intense conflict, and little else. Specialists in communication often fail to keep up with the expansion of knowledge about the process; note the reluctance with which many visual devices have been adopted. And despite research on vocabulary, many mass communicators select words that fail. This happens, for instance, when a foreign correspondent allows himself to become absorbed in the foreign scene and forgets that his home audience has no direct equivalents in experience for "left," "center," and other factional terms.

Besides skill factors, the level of efficiency is sometimes adversely influenced by personality structure. An optimistic, outgoing person may hunt "birds of a feather" and gain an uncorrected and hence exaggeratedly optimistic view of events. On the contrary, when pessimistic, brooding personalities mix, they choose quite different birds, who confirm their gloom. There are also important differences among people which spring from contrasts in intelligence and energy.

Some of the most serious threats to efficient communication for the community as a whole relate to the values of power, wealth and respect.

Perhaps the most striking examples of power distortion occur when the content of communication is deliberately adjusted to fit an ideology or counter ideology. Distortions related to wealth not only arise from attempts to influence the market, for instance, but from rigid conceptions of economic interest. A typical instance of inefficiencies connected with respect (social class) occurs when an upper class person mixes only with persons of his own stratum and forgets to correct his perspective by being exposed to members of other classes.

Research on communication

The foregoing reminders of some factors that interfere with efficient communication point to the kinds of research which can usefully be conducted on representative links in the chain of communication. Each agent is a vortex of interacting environmental and predispositional factors. Whoever performs a relay function can be examined in relation to input and output. What statements are brought to the attention of the relay link? What does he pass on verbatim? What does he drop out? What does he rework? What does he add? How do differences in input and output correlate with culture and personality? By answering such questions it is possible to weigh the various factors in conductance, no conductance and modified conductance.

Besides the relay link, we must consider the primary link in a communication sequence. In studying the focus of attention of the primary observer, we emphasize two sets of influences: Statements to which he is exposed; other features of his environment. An attaché or foreign correspondent exposes himself to mass media and private talk; also, he can count soldiers, measure gun emplacements, note hours of work in a factory, see butter and fat on the table.

Actually it is useful to consider the attention frame of the relay as well as the primary link in terms of media and non-media exposures. The role of non-media factors is very slight in the case of many relay operators, while it is certain to be significant in accounting for the primary observer.

Attention aggregates and publics

It should be pointed out that everyone is not a member of the world public, even though he belongs to some extent to the world attention aggregate. To belong to an attention aggregate it is only necessary to have common symbols of reference. Everyone who has a symbol of reference for New York, North America, the Western Hemisphere or the globe is a member respectively of the attention aggregate of New York, North America, the Western Hemisphere, the globe. To be a member of the New York public, however, it is Essential to make demands for public action in New York, or expressly affecting New York.

HISTORY AND PERSPECTIVES

The public of the United States, for instance, is not confined to residents or citizens, since non-citizens who live beyond the frontier may try to influence American politics. Conversely, everyone who lives in the United States is not a member of the American public, since something more than passive attention is necessary. An individual passes from an attention aggregate to the public when he begins to expect that what he wants can affect public policy.

Sentiment groups and publics

A further limitation must be taken into account before we can correctly classify a specific person or group as part of a public. The demands made regarding public policy must be debatable. The world public is relatively weak and undeveloped, partly because it is typically kept subordinate to sentiment areas in which no debate is permitted on policy matters. During a war or war crisis, for instance, the inhabitants of a region are overwhelmingly committed to impose certain policies on others. Since the outcome of the conflict depends on violence, and not debate, there is no public under such conditions. There is a network of sentiment groups that act as crowds, hence tolerate no dissent.[8]

From the foregoing analysis it is clear that there are attention, public and sentiment areas of many degrees of inclusiveness in world politics. These areas are interrelated with the structural and functional features of world society, and especially of world power. It is evident, for instance, that *the strongest powers tend to be included in the same attention area*, since their ruling elites focus on one another as the source of great potential threat. The strongest powers usually pay proportionately less attention to the weaker powers than the weaker powers pay to them, since stronger powers are typically more important sources of threat, or of protection, for weaker powers than the weaker powers are for the stronger.[9]

The attention structure within a state is a valuable index of the degree of state integration. When the ruling classes fear the masses, the rulers do not share their picture of reality with the rank and rile. When the reality picture of kings, presidents and cabinets is not permitted to circulate through the state as a whole, the degree of discrepancy shows the extent to which the ruling groups assume that their power depends on distortion.

Or, to express the matter another way: If the "truth" is not shared, the ruling elements expect internal conflict, rather than harmonious adjustment to the external environment of the state. Hence the channels of communication are controlled in the hope of organizing the attention of the community at large in such a way that only responses will be forthcoming which are deemed favorable to the power position of the ruling classes.

The principle of equivalent enlightenment

It is often said in democratic theory that rational public opinion depends upon enlightenment. There is, however, much ambiguity about the nature of enlightenment, and the term is often made equivalent to perfect knowledge. A more modest and immediate conception is not perfect but equivalent enlightenment. The attention structure of the full time specialist on a given policy will be more elaborate and refined than that of the layman. That this difference will always exist, we must take for granted. Nevertheless, it is quite possible for the specialist and the layman to agree on the broad outlines of reality. A workable goal of democratic society is equivalent enlightenment as between expert, leader and layman.

Expert, leader and layman can have the same gross estimate of major population trends of the world. They can share the same general view of the likelihood of war. It is by no means fantastic to imagine that the controllers of mass media of communication will take the lead in bringing about a high degree of equivalence throughput society between the layman's picture of significant relationships, and the picture of the expert and the leader.

Summary

The communication process in society performs three functions: (a) *surveillance* of the environment, disclosing threats and opportunities affecting the value position of the community and of the component parts within it; (b) *correlation* of the components of society in making a response to the environment; (c) *transmission* of the social inheritance. In general, biological equivalents can be found in human and animal associations, and within the economy of a single organism.

In society, the communication process reveals special characteristics when the ruling element is afraid of the internal as well as the external environment. In gauging the efficiency of communication in any given context, it is necessary to take into account the values at stake, and the identity of the group whose position is being examined. In democratic societies, rational choices depend on enlightenment, which in turn depends upon communication; and especially upon the equivalence of attention among leaders, experts and rank and file.

Notes

1 For more detail, consult the introductory matter in Bruce L. Smith, Harold D. Lasswell and Ralph D. Casey, *Propaganda, Communication, and Public Opinion: A Comprehensive Reference Guide*, Princeton University Press, Princeton, 1946.
2 To the extent that behavior patterns are transmitted in the structures inherited by the single animal, a function is performed parallel to the transmission of the "social heritage" by means of education.

HISTORY AND PERSPECTIVES

3 On animal sociology see: Warder C. Allee, *Animal Aggregations*, University of Chicago Press, Chicago, 1931; *The Social Life of Animals*, Norton, New York, 1935.

4 Excellent examples are given in Robert Redfield's account of *Tepoztlan, A Mexican Village: A Study of Folk Life*, University of Chicago Press, Chicago, 1930.

5 Properly handled, the speech event can be described with as much reliability and validity as many non-speech events which are more conventionally used as data in scientific investigations.

6 These distinctions are derived and adapted from the writings of Charles E. Merriam, Gaetano Mosca, Karl Mannheim, and others. For a systematic exposition see the forthcoming volume by Harold D. Lasswell and Abraham Kaplan.

7 See William T. R. Fox, *The Super-Powers*, Harcourt, Brace, New York, 1944, and Harold D. Lasswell, *World Politics Faces Economics*, McGraw-Hill, New York, 1945.

8 The distinction between the "crowd" and the "public" was worked out in the Italian, French and German literature of criticism that grew up around Le Bon's over-generalized use of the crowd concept. For a summary of this literature by a scholar who later became one of the most productive social scientists in this field, see Robert E. Park, *Masse und Publikum; Eine methodologische und soziologische Untersuchung*, Lack and Grunau, Bern, 1904. (Heidelberg dissertation.)

9 The propositions in this paragraph are hypotheses capable of being subsumed under the general theory of power, referred to in footnote 6. See also Harold D. Lasswell and Joseph M. Goldsen, "Public Attention, Opinion and Action," *The International Journal of Opinion and Attitude Research*, Mexico City, I, 1947, pp. 3–11.

2

EFFECTS OF THE IMPROVEMENTS OF COMMUNICATION MEDIA

Marshall McLuhan

Source: *Journal of Economic History* 20(4) (1960): 566–75.

The advantage of having a tightly woven thesis to present to you is that it can be used in the introductory paper as a rug to be yanked violently from under my feet. If caution leads Professor Easterbrook "to remain, at least for the time being, in the informational camp," it is obvious that only a total absence of caution would lead me, a professor of English, to venture before the leaders in the field of economic history in the role assigned to me today.

I stand open to the rebuff described in the story of the two goats who were feasting on a junk heap behind a Hollywood studio. One of them, having come upon an old print of the film of *Gone With the Wind* was chomping enthusiastically. He signalled to his companion to come on over and sample his find. The other goat did so, and chewed meditatively for a bit; when the first one said, "How did you like it?" And the second one said, "As a matter of fact, I liked the book better." Just which of these is the media-goat and which the information-goat admits, as Sir Thomas Browne put it, "of a wide solution."

In managerial study of the role of the decision maker today, it is often pointed out that it is difficult under conditions of speeded information flow for anybody to exercise delegated authority. The habits and patterns of delegated authority, with its hierarchy of separate and subordinated functions and jurisdictions, belong quite naturally under the conditions and speeds of written communication.[1] But if within such a structure of written communication there occurs a notable speed-up of information movement, such as takes place with the telephone, the exercise of delegated authority becomes quite unworkable.[2]

HISTORY AND PERSPECTIVES

In an unpublished paper called "New Directions for Organizational Practice,"[3] Professor B. J. Muller-Thym of the Massachusetts Institute of Technology discusses the recent recognition that

> pyramidal organizational structures, with many layers of supervision, and with functional division by specialty, simply did not work. . . . But in these research organizations where work actually got done, when one studied them he found that whatever the organization chart prescribed, groups of researchers with different competences as required by the problem in hand were working together, cutting across organizational lines; that they were establishing most of their own design criteria for the work as well as their intended patterns of association; . . .
>
> The older, many-layered, highly functionalized organizations were characterized by the separation of thinking from doing; thinking was generally allocated to the top rather than the bottom of the pyramid and to "staff" as against "line" components. Whatever the wishes of the company about the decentralized exercise of authority, authority inexorably gravitated toward the top of the structure. There was created a numerous middle management class, spread over an indefinite number of supervisory layers whose actual roles, as many work studies showed, was predominately the passing of information through the system.

Professor Muller-Thym then footnotes:

> It was for this reason that the authors of a now famous article predicted the disappearance of middle managers as an industrial class. The ability to handle the total information for a business system completely, rapidly, and with random access has been made possible by computer technology at the very moment when middle management, because of its size and clumsiness, can no longer perform this task.[4]

The advent of a new medium often reveals the lineaments and assumptions, as it were, of an old medium. The hypertrophy of written messages, which has been dubbed "Parkinson's law" by its author, would appear to be caused not by paper-shuffling and the typewriter, but by the effort of the typewriter to keep pace with the acceleration of information movement created by the telephone and electronic media. Telephone in hand, the decision maker can exercise only the authority of knowledge, not delegated authority. In managerial terms, it would seem that the decision maker who must deal with globally gathered information, moved at electronic speeds, is impelled to acquire a more interrelated and overall type of knowledge

28

EFFECTS OF IMPROVEMENTS OF COMMUNICATION MEDIA

concerning the operations in which he is involved. The new media, in management that is to say, have been directly responsible for the rise of management training centers. The demand increases daily for an ever more liberally educated specialist capable of effective action in ever more decentralized operations.

Much the same pattern of development has occurred, we are told, as a result of the operation of the telephone upon the traditional role of the "call girl." Since the telephone has become a normal feature of our environment, the old red light district has disappeared. Centralism has given way to decentralized operation, as in management, and with the same consequences for the personnel involved. That is to say, the call girl must be, if not cultured, at least at home in a variety of social roles, in contrast to the highly specialized character of her pre-telephonic and localized predecessor. This bizarre instance of social change resulting from great information speed-up, I venture to present in order to illustrate my basic suggestion: that it is the formal characteristics of the medium, recurring in a variety of material situations, and not any particular "message," which constitutes the efficacy of its historical action.

Hjalmar Schacht, in his *Account Settled,*[5] cites the testimony of Albert Speer, German armaments minister in 1942, given at the Nüremberg trials as follows:

> The telephone, the teleprinter and the wireless made it possible for orders from the highest levels to be given direct to the lowest levels, where, on account of the absolute authority behind them, they were carried out uncritically; or brought it about that numerous offices and command centres were directly connected with the supreme leadership from which they received sinister orders without any intermediary. . . . To the outside observer this governmental apparatus may have resembled the apparently chaotic confusion of lines at a telephone exchange, but like the latter it could be controlled and operated from one central source.

Like Parkinson in his indignant moral judgment concerning the operation of technology in office administration, Schacht draws moral conclusions from the operation of the telephone, telegraph, radio and teletype, which are quite irrelevant. What Parkinson and Schacht are both saying is that new technical media for managing information, when used for the older ends established by older media, result in utter confusion and disorganization.

A striking example of this occurs in Oscar Handlin's essay on John Dewey.[6] He points out how John Dewey in the later nineteenth century was baffled by the past-orientation even of vocational training in American high schools. It is the natural bias of print culture to be past-oriented, and above all to be consumer-oriented. Whether with vocational handicrafts or the fine arts,

29

the consumer bias aroused a good deal of comment, not only from John Dewey but from composers and painters and poets, as well as from areas of scientific research. The European, and even the Englishman, when print was new, had a great backlog of oral culture and preprint attitudes which the Gutenberg technology could not entirely obliterate.

We on this continent, on the contrary, had little enough of such preprint backlog, and out of necessity shaped our patterns of association, and our legal, political, and educational establishments on what we did have, namely, the latest European technology: the printing press. Whereas in Europe the printing press had to contend with august and solemn institutions, long established on pre-Gutenberg technology, the range and density of such organizations was in North America almost insignificant. The penetrative powers of the Gutenberg technology, irresistible under any conditions, became the means of forming the very ground plan and the superstructure of social and business institutions.

Concerning the concept of the penetrative powers of the price-system, R. F. Neill, in his "An Exploratory Survey of Industrial Galaxies in Canadian Economic Development," states:[7]

> The term "price-system" can be understood in an "Innisian" sense to mean simply industrialization, economic growth, an economy, or an impersonal force seeking to spread its domination. If we adopt this quasi-poetical use of the term, then the penetrative power of the price-system will depend, not only on the economic efficiency of existing means of communication, but also on the ability of the industrial centre to produce more efficient means of communication. Here there is an interaction in which the extension of markets through the use of more efficient means of communication leads to further division of labor. Further division of labor creates both greater surpluses in production in general and the means of improving the communication system. Greater surplus production, in turn, creates pressures to improve communication in order to further extend the market.

Neill here shows a grasp of Innis which is rare indeed, but Innis in turn had a grasp of causal relationships between media and all levels of social structure from education to industry which would have been invaluable to John Dewey. I would like to enumerate briefly some of the penetrative powers of the Gutenberg technology, even if they are no more than hypotheses or arguments. I have dealt at much greater length with these themes in two essays, "Print and Social Change," and "The Effect of the Printed Book on Language in the Sixteenth Century."[8]

The mechanization of the ancient handicraft of the scribe was effected by segmental arresting of the movements of the scribe in the form of movable

EFFECTS OF IMPROVEMENTS OF COMMUNICATION MEDIA

types. The principle of segmentation has since been applied to almost all handicrafts. Until very recently the assembly line of movable types which formed the basis of print technology had been the unchallenged basis of western industry. Both producer and consumer functions have long depended on the pre-condition of print technology.

Today we are faced on all hands with the obsolescence of the assembly line pattern of industry due to the advent of the non-sequential and instantaneous patterns of electric automation. I do not presume for a moment to explain to this audience matters which it understands far better than I. Purely in media terms, however, the exactly synchronized information flow of an electric circuit can perform many operations at the same instant, which under the conditions of mechanized handicraft or of assembly line were necessarily sequential and one at a time.

The penetrative powers of the new electric technology, as they invade every level of thought and action, have the power to impose their own assumptions, as it were. I have already alluded to the changed patterns of decision making which resulted from the telephone. I will now attempt by a brief enumeration of the patterns of decision making which resulted from Gutenberg technology to convey some idea of the "penetrative powers" of movable types. Most obviously it was the product of the Gutenberg assembly line which appeared to possess in a high degree the qualities of uniformity and repeatability. Since handicraft products do not possess these qualities, it was natural that uniform and repeatable products should make possible new relations between producers and consumers. The message of the uniform commodity is that "this is the same for all men," thus releasing a wave of competitive drive. For among unique products there may be hierarchy but not competition.

In terms of the printed book and the printed page, uniformity and repeatability gave to the political ruler a new instrument of centralism and homogeneity. By means of print the ruler could extend uniform patterns of information and power to the boundaries of his people's vernacular tongue. Uniformity and repeatability gave him the means of mobilizing eventually the entire manpower of his kingdom. Effective mobilization would appear to depend, whether in economic or in military spheres, upon the reduction to homogeneity of an entire population by means of the printed word. What W. W. Rostow calls "the takeoff" occurs in no country that he mentions without this prior homogenization of a people. Whether in the electronic age takeoff can occur in backward or semi-literate areas without long processing by Gutenberg technology remains to be seen.

Another feature of the penetrative powers of print technology, in addition to uniformity and repeatability, is the complimentary of individualism and nationalism. Print makes possible solitary effort and private initiative in a very high degree, everything in fact which David Riesman celebrates in *The Lonely Crowd* as "inner direction." He too seems to treat as a moral failure our tendency to abandon inner direction in the electronic age. But would it not be better to consider where this habit came from in the first place, in the interests of prediction and control? Harold Innis frequently alluded to the close connection between print and nationalism, and Carleton Hayes in *The Historical Evolution of Modern Nationalism*[9] is unable to find any symptoms of it before the Renaissance.

I venture to suggest that all of the reasons for nationalism are included in the penetrative powers of Gutenberg technology. Not only does print vividly discover national boundaries, but the print market was itself defined by such boundaries, at least for early printers and publishers. Perhaps also the ability to *see* one's mother tongue in uniform and repeatable technological dress creates in the individual reader a feeling of unity and power that he shares with all other readers of that tongue. Quite different sentiments are felt by preliterate or semi-literate populations. The type of visualizing fostered by high intensity print technology is quite natural and habitual to highly literate populations, putting them at great disadvantage in a nuclear age, since nuclear structures are *non-visualizable*. That is to say, nuclear structures, whether sub-atomic or in the form of mass-audiences for radio and TV, are, in their instantaneous speed modalities, not capable of comprehension in visual modes, except a la Walt Disney science shorts.

As much as nationalism and individualism, perspective, both psychic and physical, is immediately the child of print technology. Perspective, with arbitrarily fixed point of view and its vanishing point, is natural to the reader of uniform lines of repeatable type. It is not natural at all in our nuclear age when information does not move exclusively in such patterns any more. And Georg von Békésy, in his *Experiments in Hearing,*[10] finds it necessary to criticize the perspective techniques in scientific research, as compared with the mosaic techniques needed in field theory and non-visualizable problems.

This is a possible point at which to introduce a comment on Easterbrook's allusion to the difference between information and media approaches to problems today. The information theory approach, based on statics, is probably self-liquidating by virtue of the electric speeds available to it. It seems to me involuntarily and unnecessarily limited by a "content" concept. Wherever one meets the "content" concept, it is reasonably certain that there has been insufficient structural analysis. Phonetic writing and printing, for example, have content only in the sense that they "contain" another medium, namely, speech. But since the origin of writing, the simultaneous presence of the medium of speech, albeit in low definition, has fostered this habit of dichotomy and content-postulating, which in fact obscures major components in the situations with which we must deal. In the same way, content-postulates seem to have caused game theory to falter to a stop prematurely. I mention this only because I wish to stress how the subliminal legacy of print can have strange effects in the highest scientific quarters of the post-print age. In spite of all this, information theory is able to reveal

EFFECTS OF IMPROVEMENTS OF COMMUNICATION MEDIA

in the person and the paper of Richard Meier that "the degree of substitutability of one resource for another increases when either the stock of knowledge or the flow of communications increases."[11]

Up till now I have attempted merely to indicate in a general way how the penetrative powers of the Gutenberg technology, as of electronic technology, create new patterns of awareness and of human association. Let me tie in my remarks so far with Professor Robinson's paper. It was surely no accident that the Greek revival in design and styling suited so well the needs and tastes of early industrial England. As Robinson puts it:[12]

> Where Wedgwood would have found it utterly impracticable to have assembled or trained in England a staff of highly skilled modellers and free-hand craftsmen capable of working in the sophisticated manner demanded by the Rococo taste, his homespun Staffordshire workmen were as well if not better fitted to the reproduction of simulated antique designs, especially when the workbenches of New Etruria were fortified by the mechanical devices that English ingenuity under the prodding of his practical genius could provide.

Robinson in effect is observing that industrial England, poor in traditional craftsmanship, was rich in the new segmental technology of mechanical lineality. It was precisely this Greek design which Ruskin spent much of his time attacking because of its servility and mechanism. Ruskin became an ardent sponsor of pre-Gutenberg technology, which he called Gothic; only here, he thought, could freedom and spontaneity for the human spirit be found.[18] While the eighteenth century was inspired to make Hellenistic conservatories, Ruskin exhorted his age to discover freedom via the Gothic hencoop.

Let me in manipulating the mosaic of this paper now return to print as staple or natural resource. I have at least pointed out the power of print to penetrate with its patterns all levels of institutional organization and of human awareness. In so changing the modes of human association, print unleashed many new powers in existing situations and resources, but perhaps most important of all, print altered the ratio among the human senses, giving extremely high definition to visual awareness and to visual powers of organizing resources. I would suggest that the penetrative powers of any structure of technology do lie precisely here: namely, that the ratio among sight and sound, and touch and motion, offer precisely that place to stand which Archimedes asked for: "Give me a place to stand, and I will move the world." The media offer exactly such a place to stand, for they are extensions of our senses, if need be into outer space. This is the major fact concealed from us while we concern ourselves with "content." Meier, in the paper already referred to, notes:

We are forced to conclude that natural resources have an informational aspect, in addition to the bulk and utility features mentioned earlier.

But if media as extensions of our senses offer ready access to our inmost lives, putting the lever of Archimedes in the hands of bureaucrat and entrepreneur alike, natural resources can also be seen as media of communication. Richard Dorson, in his *American Folklore,* points out:[14]

> The yeasty oral traditions of the American Negro took form in the plantation culture of the Old South. Northern freedmen who settled in free states before emancipation possess none of this folklore. The Negro song and narrative lore of the West Indies, Brazil, and Surinam, heavy in African elements, shows little correspondence with that of southern colored folk. Southern slave lore developed along its own lines under the particular conditions of the cotton plantation economy. Cotton cultivation from Georgia to Texas, with the growing of rice on the Carolina and Georgia coast, sugar cane in Louisiana, and tobacco in Virginia and Kentucky, molded the southern slaves into homogeneity. After the importation of African slaves ceased in 1808, the Negro community in the United States grew entirely from its own procreation.

The homogeneity achieved in so spectacular a form by the Gutenberg staple, as it were, is nicely paralleled (but in low definition) by the penetrative powers of the cotton plantation economy. Homogeneity of patterns of human association are strikingly apparent consequences of staples, it would seem, whether they be the bulky bale or the resonating radio. Our current alarm about togetherness and conformity may well be the anxiety of a homogeneous literary culture being invaded by an alien homogeneity— a collision of galaxies.

To bring these penetrative powers and patterns back to a directly staple context, let me use the words of K. Buckley in his recent essay:[15] that Innis "used the staple approach to correlate a wide range of political and social developments, and to explain the character of major institutions within Canada."

The penetrative powers of a medium or a staple to impose its patterns and assumptions are in sharp conflict with the concept of social and economic influence and causation which characterize the Gutenberg galaxy. The Gutenberg galaxy, or technology, favors all forms of segmental, fragmental statics rather than dynamic and organic forms. As we move well beyond the first century of the electronic era, we have discovered that our practice can be years ahead of our thought.[16] For more than a century much of our information in the West has moved in the new configurations evoked

EFFECTS OF IMPROVEMENTS OF COMMUNICATION MEDIA

by electronic speeds. We have begun to feel at many levels a consequent change of attitudes towards the temporal and spatial arrangements of our lives and institutions. Professor Cole draws attention to the trend away from static models and toward preoccupation with economic growth to a degree unknown since Adam Smith.[17]

Many people are terrified at the speed of information movement in our electronic time which brainwashes whole populations on the one hand, and eliminates long established roles based on highly specialized knowledge. The interpenetration of Gutenberg and the electronic galaxies is naturally very destructive at many levels. It is hard, for example, to accustom ourselves to the idea that the hot war may have transferred itself from the international scene to the national and domestic one, on the one hand; and that, on the other hand, so far as the international scene is concerned, there has been no *cold* war, but an information hot war all along. Again, it will be hard for educators to face up to a situation of electronic configuration in which civil defense becomes simply protection against media fallout, around the globe and around the clock. To put it in Meier's terms again, with the rise of information levels and speeds, war may cease to be the exchange of bulk or heavy goods, and may become an information exchange before a global public.

If adjustment (economic, social, or personal) to information movement at electronic speeds is quite impossible, we can always change our models and metaphors of organization, and escape into sheer understanding. Sequential analysis and adjustment natural to low speed information movement becomes irrelevant and useless even at telegraph speed. But as speed increases, the understanding of process in all kinds of structures and situations becomes relatively simple. We can literally escape into understanding when the patterns of process become manifest.

Notes

1 Peter F. Drucker, *Landmarks of Tomorrow* (New York, Harpers, 1959), p. 96.
2 H. A. Innis, *The Bias of Communication* (Toronto: University of Toronto Press, 1951), p. 188.
3 Paper prepared for ASME Report: *Ten Year Progress in Management, 1950–1960*.
4 *Cf.*, H. J. Leavitt and T. L. Whisler, "Management in the 1970's," *Harvard Business Review*, XXXVI (Nov.–Dec. 1958), 41–8.
5 Hjalmar Schacht, *Account Settled* (London, 1949), p. 240.
6 Oscar Handlin, "John Dewey's Challenge to Education," *Harpers* (New York, 1959), p. 22.
7 R. F. Neill, *An Exploratory Survey of Industrial Galaxies in Canadian Economic Development* (unpublished M.A. dissertation, University of Toronto, 1960), p. VII.
8 H. M. McLuhan, "Print and Social Change," *Printing Progress* (Cincinnati, 1959), pp. 81–112, and "The Influence of the Printed Book on Language in the Sixteenth Century," from *Explorations in Communication*, edited by Edmund Carpenter and Marshall McLuhan (Boston: Beacon Press, 1960), 125–35.

9 Carelton Hayes, *The Historical Evolution of Modern Nationalism* (London: Macmillan, 1931).
10 Georg Von Békésy, *Experiments in Hearing* (New York: McGraw-Hill, 1960), pp. 3–6.
11 Richard L. Meier, "Information, Resource Use and Economic Growth"; paper read at the Ann Arbor Conference on Natural Resources and Economic Growth, 1959.
12 Dwight E. Robinson, "The Styling and Transmission of Fashions Historically Considered." Economic History Association, 1960.
13 John Ruskin, *The Stones of Venice*; 1851–53. Vol. 1, chap. 6 is on Gothic architecture and man.
14 Richard M. Dorson, *American Folklore* (Chicago: University of Chicago Press, 1959), p. 168.
15 K. Buckley, "The Role of Staple Industries in Canada's Economic Development," THE JOURNAL OF ECONOMIC HISTORY, XVII (Dec. 1958), p. 442.
16 Edward H. Lichfield, "Notes on a General Theory of Administration," *Administrative Science Quarterly*, Vol. 1, No. 1 (June 1956).
17 Arthur H. Cole, *Business Enterprise in its Social Setting* (Cambridge, Mass.: Harvard University Press, 1959), 36–9.

3

THE KNOWLEDGE SOCIETY

Peter F. Drucker

Source: *New Society* 13(343) (1969): 629–31.

> We are living through a major industrial change, where brains
> are resources. The implications include "professionalisation"
> and the need for a two-career life.

The "knowledge industries," which produce and distribute ideas and information rather than goods and services, accounted in 1955 for one quarter of the US gross national product. This was already three times the proportion of the national product that the country had spent on the "knowledge sector" in 1900. Yet by 1965, ten years later, the knowledge sector was taking one third of a much bigger national product. In the late 1970s it will account for one half of the total national product. Every other dollar earned and spent in the American economy will be earned by producing and distributing ideas and information or will be spent on procuring ideas and information.

The figures are impressive enough. In 1900 the largest single group, indeed still the majority of the American people, were rural and made a living on the farm. By 1940, the largest single group, by far, were industrial workers, especially semiskilled (in fact, essentially unskilled) machine operators. By 1960, the largest single group were what the census called "professional, managerial, and technical people," that is, knowledge workers. By 1975, or, at the latest by 1980, this group will embrace the majority of Americans at work in the civilian labour force.

Economists still tend to classify the "knowledge industries" as "services." As such, they contrast them with the "primary" industries—agriculture, mining, forestry, and fishing, which make available to man the products of nature—and with the "secondary" industries—that is, manufacturing. But knowledge has actually become the "primary" industry, the industry that supplies to the economy the essential and central resource of production. The economic history of the last hundred years in the advanced and developed countries could be called "from agriculture to knowledge."

The demand ahead for knowledge workers seems insatiable. In addition to a million computer programmers, the information industry in the United States will need in the next 15 years another half million systems engineers, systems designers and information specialists. It will need, perhaps, two million health care professionals—nurses, dietitians, medical and x-ray technologists, social and psychiatric case workers, physical therapists and so on. These people are both highly trained, well beyond secondary school, and highly skilled. They are fully the equivalent of the skilled machinist or the skilled carpenter with his years of apprenticeship. But their skill is founded on knowledge.

Knowledge work does not lead to a "disappearance of work." The typical "worker" of the advanced economy, the knowledge worker, is working more and more, and there is demand for more and more knowledge workers. The manual worker, the typical worker of yesterday, may have more leisure. He may go home at five in the evening, but the knowledge worker everywhere works increasingly longer hours. The young engineer, the accountant, the medical technologist and the teacher take work home with them when they leave the office. Knowledge work, like all productive work, creates its own demand. And the demand is apparently unlimited.

Knowledge does not eliminate skill. On the contrary, knowledge is fast becoming the foundation for skill. We are using knowledge more and more to enable people to acquire skills of a very advanced kind fast and success-fully. Knowledge substitutes systematic learning for exposure to experience.

"Knowledge," as normally considered by the "intellectual," is something very different from "knowledge" in the context of "knowledge economy" or "knowledge work." For the intellectual, knowledge is what is in a book. But as long as it is in the book, it is only "information" if not mere "data." Only when a man applies the information to doing something does it become knowledge. Knowledge, like electricity or money, is a form of energy that exists only when doing work. The emergence of the knowledge economy is not, in other words, part of "intellectual history" as it is normally con-ceived. It is part of the "history of technology," which recounts how man puts tools to work. When the intellectual says "knowledge" he usually thinks of something new. But what matters in the "knowledge economy" is whether knowledge, old or new, is applicable—for example, Newtonian physics to the space programme.

Knowledge opportunities exist primarily in large organisations. Although the shift to knowledge work has made possible large modern organisations, it is the emergence of these organisations—business enterprise, government agency, large university, research laboratory, hospital—that in turn has created the job opportunities for the knowledge worker. The knowledge

THE KNOWLEDGE SOCIETY

opportunities of yesterday were largely for independent professionals working on their own.

This hidden conflict between the knowledge worker's view of himself as a "professional" and the social reality in which he is the upgraded and well-paid successor to the skilled worker of yesterday, underlies the disenchantment of so many highly educated young people with the jobs available to them. It explains why they protest so loudly against the "stupidity" of business, of government, of the armed services and of the universities. They expect to be "intellectuals." And they find that they are just "staff." Because this holds true for organisations altogether and not just for this or that organisation, there is no place to flee. If they turn their backs on business and go to the university, they soon find out that this, too, is a "machine." If they turn from the university to government service, they find the same situation there.

How did this shift to the knowledge society and knowledge economy come about?

The popular answer is: "Because jobs have been getting more complex and more demanding." But the right answer is: "Because the working lifespan of man has increased so greatly." It is not the demand for labour but the supply that underlies this great transformation of society and economy. And this, in turn, also explains the social and economic problems posed by the emergence of knowledge. The arrival of the knowledge worker changed the nature of jobs. Because modern society has to employ people who expect and demand knowledge work, knowledge jobs have to be created. As a result, the character of work is being transformed. The demands of most jobs have changed but little, at least until recent years.

There is nothing, for instance, in the work of a salesgirl that explains why, 30 years ago, junior high school was considered adequate preparation for the work while today the applicant is expected to have finished high school and preferably a few years of college as well. Nor does today's salesgirl at 18 or 20 produce any more sales than the 15 year old salesgirl of 1935, or the 12 year old salesgirl of 1910.

That the much-vaunted complexity of today's jobs is a myth is also shown by comparing American practice with that of other advanced industrial countries. For, while moving in the same direction, Europe and Japan are still well behind in the educational upgrading of the entire population. Jobs which call for a year or two of college education in the United States are being staffed in Germany, for instance, with men and women who have finished what corresponds roughly to the American junior high school (the German *Ober-Sekunda-Reife*). Yet there is no discernible difference in the demands made on the employee, or in his, or her productivity.

The best example is found in Canada, where there are two educational standards side by side. Toronto and industrial Ontario are on the same educational standard as the American Midwest on which they border. A few hundred miles to the east. Montreal and industrial Quebec are only now starting the "educational explosion." The jobs that, in Ontario, are being filled by high school graduates, preferably with one or two years of college, are staffed by the same employers—supermarket chains, for instance, or commercial banks, or manufacturers—with junior high school graduates in Quebec. They are paid quite differently; yet there is not much difference in the jobs they do or in their productivity.

The direct cause of the upgrading of the jobs is, in other words, the upgrading of the educational level of the entrant into the labour force. The longer he or she stays in school, the more education will be required for entrance into a given job or occupation.

But the extension of the years in school is itself only an effect rather than a cause. It is the result of a long development which drastically changed working-life expectancy in the industrially advanced countries. That life expectancy has gone up sharply in the advanced countries is common knowledge. But few people seem to have noticed that the years of working life have gone up even faster. Around the turn of the century—that is, in the lifetime of people still alive and working today—few members of the labour force could expect to work to full capacity past age 45 or 50.

Before 1850, there was no country where average life expectancy greatly exceeded 33 or 35 years, which limited average working life to 20 years. By 1914 these figures had risen, in the most advanced countries, to around 30 years of working-life expectancy, from starting work at age 15 to disablement or death at age 45 or so. Today working life extends to age 65 for the great majority. If we still expected people to start work around age 14, as we did everywhere up to world war one, we would have a working life of 50 years for the great majority. Even with our later age of entrance into the work force—18 or 20—the working lifespan in the advanced countries today is twice that of a century ago and 50 per cent larger than it was around the time of world war one.

Contrary to popular belief, advances in medicine have had little to do with the lengthening of working lifespan. One main cause was undoubtedly the shift from farming as the occupation of the majority to where it now is the occupation of a very small minority—fewer than 6 per cent of the United States population, for instance. For farm work ages people fast, especially the farm work of 60 years ago, before electricity and modern machinery. Also, in traditional agriculture, disabling accidents occur far more frequently than even in the most dangerous industrial pursuits. The farmer, and especially his wife, tended to be old and disabled by the time their children reached their teens.

The shift from labourer to machine operator was hardly less important. The "navvies" who built the railroads with pick and shovel rarely lasted more than five years or so before they were disabled by accident, liquor, syphilis or plain back-breaking toil. As late as 1900, seamstresses in the garment lofts of New York, London's East End, Paris, or Vienna did not

THE KNOWLEDGE SOCIETY

last much longer. Within ten years most of them had fallen victim to blindness or to TB.

It can be argued that extension of years spent in school reflects a common faith in education as one of the highest human values. It can also be argued that extending the years in school is economic rationality in which people can indulge once they no longer have to worry where the next meal is coming from. By postponing earnings for a few years, they acquire higher earning power for the rest of their lives. There is one more explanation of this sharp increase in years of schooling. People cannot stand a working life of 50 years. It is simply too long for them. School is not seen primarily as desirable in itself nor as a means to a better livelihood. It is seen very largely as a way of keeping the kids off the street while still keeping them out of the labour force for a few years. There is evidence that even a working life of 45 years—that is, a working life that begins at age 20—may be too long, especially for knowledge workers.

Whichever of these three explanations is preferred the results are the same. Extending the years of schooling forces us to create those jobs that apply knowledge to work. The person who has sat on a school bench until he is 18 or 20 may not have learned anything. But he has acquired different expectations. As a result of the change in supply, we now have to create genuine knowledge jobs, whether the work itself demands it or not. For a true knowledge job is the only way to make highly schooled people productive.

Yet no matter how satisfying the individual task, a good many knowledge workers tend to tire of their jobs in early middle age. Long before they reach retirement age, let alone long before they become physically and mentally disabled, the sparkle, the challenge, the excitement, have gone our of their work. For manual workers early retirement seems to offer a solution, as witness the eagerness with which it has been accepted in the American automobile, steel, and rubber industries, in spite of heavy financial penalties. The manual worker does not, it seems, suffer from a "problem of leisure." Time does not hang heavy on his hands, even though he shows little desire for the "cultural pursuits" that are pressed on him by the educated. He can sit in a cottage or trailer in Florida, apparently happy and busy with a small garden, occupied with fishing, hunting and gossiping, without much desire to go back to the mill. The knowledge worker, however, cannot easily retire. If he does, he is likely to disintegrate fast. Knowledge work is apparently habit-forming in a way in which manual work is not. People who have been doing knowledge work for 20-odd years or so cannot stop. But the great majority of them cannot go on either. They do not have the inner resources.

This is not true, it seems, of the few who reach the top, either in terms of power and position or in terms of eminence and leadership in their chosen discipline. They preserve their zest and tend to immerse themselves completely in their work. But the great many members of the educated middle class are only too susceptible to a modern version of the affliction known to the middle ages as *accidie*: the emotional malaise and subacute despair that was the typical disease of the *clerc* who realised, around age 30 or so, that he would be neither saint nor abbot.

Similarly, knowledge workers who, while successful, remain within a specific function or specific discipline until around 45 or so, often become tired, dispirited and bored with themselves and the job. There is, for example, the director of market research in a business or the head of quality control; the comptroller of a navy yard or a training officer in the army with the rank of lieutenant colonel; the senior economist in a government bureau or the senior social worker in a veterans' hospital; even the good "sound" professor on the university faculty.

In business and in government, in the armed services and in the university there is a lot of talk about "retreads," about "recharging a man's batteries," about the need for "sabbaticals," and for "going back to school." But it needs to be recognised that this is not a problem of the individual, but a generic problem. It is a result of the conflict between the knowledge worker's view of himself as a "professional" and the fact that he is within organisation and a successor to yesterday's craftsman rather than to yesterday's "professional." The problem can be converted into an opportunity. We must make it possible for the middle-aged knowledge worker to start a second knowledge career.

The accomplished knowledge journeyman at 45 or 50 is in his physical and mental prime. If he is tired and bored, it is because he has reached the limit of contribution and growth in his first career—and he knows it. He is likely to deteriorate rapidly if left doing what no longer truly challenges him. It is little use to look to "hobbies" or to "cultural interests" to keep him alive. Being an amateur does not satisfy a man who has learned to be a professional. To be a dilettante has to be learned in childhood as all aristocracies have known.

One thing this man usually has is a desire to contribute. The children are grown up by this time, and the house is paid for. He now "wants to give," as so many of these men express it. Today there is little organised opportunity to do so. Yet at the same time, we have—and will continue to have—a growing shortage of personnel in a good many areas of knowledge work. We are having increasing difficulty, for instance, in recruiting young men for the ministry, for teaching, and for medicine. In the past, young men and women had to go into these areas if they wanted to be knowledge workers at all. Now, however, with all the choices open to young people, these occupations are much less attractive, even if they pay well (as, in the United States, both teaching and medicine do). They demand of the young far too early a commitment, far too irrevocable a choice. Twenty years later, however, these are precisely the occupations sought by the man who "wants to give."

THE KNOWLEDGE SOCIETY

Under the present system, the preparation for these careers assumes a youngster who has to learn everything. No allowance is made for the experience and knowledge of a mature man. In fact, at present we do everything to discourage him. I know of a Roman Catholic order of nuns which found, to their surprise, that women they had never considered as possible candidates, such as widows of 50 or so, were greatly interested in entering the order. Many of these women had been schoolteachers in their earlier years—and the order was a teaching order. Yet of a hundred or so applicants only one actually survived the period of probation and took her vows. When the Mother Superior asked her why the other 99 had withdrawn, she was told, "Do you realise that you tell each applicant that she has to start out taking a course in sewing? Most of us have sewn our own clothes and often those of our children or of nieces and nephews for years. If we wanted to sew, we could have stayed right where we were."

Our divinity schools, our schools of social work, of education, of nursing, and of medicine are no different. They also expect the applicant, regardless of his age, to start out "learning to sew." There is no reason, however, why we should not teach experienced, responsible, serious men and women, who have shown their capacity to contribute, how to be effective teachers, ministers, social workers, nurses or doctors and train them in a fraction of the time needed to prepare youngsters without experience. Similarly people of this age need organised opportunities to switch from one institution to another while staying in their technical or functional area—again perhaps with a little training.

I have personally observed in the last decade maybe 50 to 100 military officers, men who reached the rank of commander in the navy or of colonel in the army or air force and who were retired as not promotable any further, around age 48 to 50. When they first left the service they were pitiful— scared of life, weighed down by the belief that theirs had been a narrow and circumscribed environment, and aware also of being tired and drained. There was not one "great man" among them—and not many interesting ones either. They were not always easy to place. But the great majority made a successful transition to a different kind of life: as teacher in a small college or as its business manager, as auditor in an accounting firm or in a local government, as personnel manager in a hospital or as traffic manager in a business, and so on. Without exception each of these men became years younger, and started to grow again and to contribute.

Almost all institutions today have compulsory retirement at age 65. We do, indeed, have to retire people from organisations. The main reason is not that people get old. The main reason is that we have to create opportunities for the young, or they will either not come or not stay. And an organisation that does not have young knowledge workers is an organisation that cannot grow, and can only defend yesterday. But to deny work to a man at any particular age is also needless cruelty and a waste of human resources.

HISTORY AND PERSPECTIVES

Although we need to retire men, we also need organised re-hiring for second careers. We need not do the job as ruthlessly as the military, which retires a man who will go no further whether he likes it or not (though this may be more merciful than to let him stay on, vegetate and destroy himself in frustration and self-pity, as businesses and universities are wont to let him do). But we need to face up to reality the way the military does.

We therefore need to create wholesale opportunities for second careers—and especially for second careers in pursuits where a fixed retirement age is not necessary, that is, where there are no young people bottled up further down the line, like the minister or the physician in private practice. Only with these opportunities will we truly take advantage of that tremendous achievement, the extension of the working lifespan of modern man.

This proposal presupposes the most difficult shift of all: a shift in attitude. Educators are convinced that there is only one curriculum for any area of study. Indeed they see something morally wrong in not insisting on the "required" two years of a course on business economics from the man who, in his working life, has proved himself to be an able economist and who may even, on the side, have taught the very course the rules now require him to take. Executives are still convinced that a man who is no longer challenged by his job has "stopped growing." In his old field he has indeed "stopped growing." But if he was a competent man to begin with—provided, of course, that he is not sick—he may now simply be ready to "grow" in some other field.

The knowledge worker himself will have to change his attitude. He will have to learn that there is no disgrace in starting over again at age 45. He will have to learn that it is relatively easy to do so. And he will have to learn that a second career at this age is a great deal more satisfying—and fun—than the bottle, an affair with a girl, the psychoanalyst's couch, or any of the other customary attempts to mask one's frustration and boredom with work that only a few short years ago had been exciting, challenging and satisfying.

Note

This article is an edited extract from part of the author's book, *The Age of Discontinuity*, published by Heinemann.

4

THE RISE OF COMMUNICATIONS POLICY RESEARCH

Ithiel de Sola Pool

Source: *Journal of Communication* 24(2) (1974): 31–42.

> Technological change transforms entire communications sys-
> tems. Alternative ways of organizing systems confront societies
> with difficult choices. Hard knowledge is needed to make the
> policy decisions of the future.

Ten years ago few communications practitioners thought in terms of any overall communications policy, and few communications researchers would have recognized policy research as an established category. All that has changed. Communications policy has emerged as a field of research.

If we look back 10 or 20 years, we see that universities, research institutes, and research departments of the media themselves were studying audiences, the journalistic profession, and the contents of the media.

Most widespread were the audience studies. After radio came on the scene, audience surveys became the backbone of communications research, particularly where advertisers paid the bills. The surveys covered more than just the ratings. They told us about the tastes, habits, motivations, and responses of the audience, too, but only as a byproduct of the basic necessity of knowing how many were out there listening, reading, and viewing.

Political scientists were interested in themes and ideologies conveyed in the media and in other propaganda, and turned to content and propaganda analysis. Sociologists were also interested in the content of the media as reflections of mass culture and of the society's value system. Academic psychologists, while not much interested in the media as such, contributed a great deal to our understanding of the underlying processes of persuasion and attitude change.

Now an additional research interest is emerging, namely normative research about alternative ways of organizing and structuring society's communications system. Examples are research on such matters as cable television, satellite broadcasting, use of broadcasting in the political process, communications and economic development, or the communications needs of the United Nations.

What accounts for this new trend? One factor is the exponential growth in the rate of technological change. The point becomes apparent if one looks at the dates of the major innovations in communications technology. Table 1 presents the rough length of time since the general introduction of some of these major innovations. The acceleration of change is unmistakable.

Until well within our own lifetimes a student of communications could take the basic parameters of the communication system as given and study how the audience or the professionals behaved within them. In the first decades of this century, historical sociologists such as Simmel or Cooley could examine the role of the press as a century-long force in the transition of society from a traditional community to an impersonal civilization. The process, although revolutionary, was slow enough that a scholar could write about it for his lifetime.

In the 1930's and 1940's, scholars such as Ogburn, Lazarsfeld, Lasswell, Berelson, Katz, Klapper, and others could take note of the major social consequences of the new mass media, particularly radio and the movies. Other scholars such as Schramm, Himmelweit, Steiner, Bogart, and Halloran did similar studies in the 1950's and 1960's on television. While many of the phenomena they studied related to universal human nature, their specific findings turned out to have unqualified relevance for only one or two decades. That was long enough, however, to allow the researcher to present his findings independently of their social parameters. Election studies were thought of as relevant to a general theory of voter behavior, not to a theory

Table 1 Ages of communication media.

Medium	Approximate age in years
Speech	500,000
Writing	4,000
Archives	2,000
Printing	500
Telegraph	140
Typewriter	110
Telephone	100
Radio	50
TV	25
Computer	25
Xerox	20
Satellite	10

of voter behavior in a particular generation. The two-step flow of communication was thought of as a generalization about the relation of the mass media and primary contacts in modern society, not just as a statement about a particular couple of decades. The studies of the impact of television on children were thought to lead to general psychological conclusions. And indeed each conclusion did have some generalizability, even if in specific form it reflected a particular transitory environment. So students of communcations from the 1930's to the 1960's could largely disregard the institutional parameters of their findings, because the parameters still remain valid for a period that was fairly long by the standard of the life of the individual writer. But if the acceleration suggested by our table is valid, that is ceasing to be the case.

We are now at the point, on the exponential acceleration of change, where major innovations in our communications system are coming every decade, and there is no reason to expect that acceleration to stop. We are entering a period in which the whole communications system will be in a process of constant flux. That makes the communications system itself an object of research. The important issues for scholars looking at the next decade are not only how people behave in the existing communications system, but what the communications system itself will be.

In November 1972, the U.S. National Science Foundation issued a notice of intention to make planning grants for new telecommunications policy research programs at nonprofit institutions. Although the funds offered were modest (an average of $75,000 for the establishment of each new program), over 90 applications were submitted. Of those, eight were chosen. Each was required not only to plan the development of an institution but also to undertake one piece of initial research. It may be of interest to note the subjects of the research projects: three (at Lehigh, Michigan State, and Michigan University) deal with cable TV policy and the possibility of delivering new services via a cable system. Another, at the University of Pennsylvania, also deals with the policy and economics of new telecommunications services. The others are investigating television network regulation (Rice University), new ways of providing land mobile radio service (Massachusetts Institute of Technology), telephone regulation (North Carolina State University), and the possibilities of using new technologies as a substitute for travel (University of Southern California).

A number of communications policy research programs already existed in the United States before these new ones were brought into being under NSF sponsorship. Most important, perhaps, is the Rand program directed by Leland Johnson. It has produced extensive economic and technical analysis of the possibilities for cable television. Other significant work on cable prospects is being done at Stanford University, at the MITRE Corporation, and by Peter Goldmark. MITRE is experimenting with means for delivery of highly individualized educational and other social services into the home as an accessory to cable TV, using mainly a device called a frame grabber to deliver different still pictures to subscribers on demand. Peter Goldmark is exploring the possibility of changing the whole ecology of human settlement by providing rural areas by telecommunications with the cultural and social amenities of urban life.

Other communications policy programs are focused on social and political issues rather than on new technologies. Outstanding among them is the Aspen Program on Communications and Society organized by Douglass Cater. It has held a series of conferences and sponsored studies on such matters as the funding of public broadcasting, government and the media, provision of humanistic material for cable TV, and the integration of the national communications system.

At Harvard University, Anthony Oettinger has a general program on communications policy. At the UCLA Law School there is a new program on communications law. Communications economics, which for years was a dead field, has suddenly become lively, with work being done at the Brookings Institution, Yale, Pennsylvania, Stanford, the California Institute of Technology, and the Massachusetts Institute of Technology.

Research within the U.S. government on telecommunications policy is also increasing markedly, particularly thanks to the Office of Telecommunications Policy of the White House, the Office of Telecommunications in the Department of Commerce, and the National Aeronautics and Space Administration (NASA). Most of the planning research regarding possible uses of communications satellites has been initiated by NASA, but interesting studies on such matters as the use of satellites for developing countries, for education, and for international communication have been done at Stanford, M.I.T., and Washington University in St. Louis.

While I am perhaps best informed about the developments in my own country and will therefore probably overrepresent them in this survey, I would not wish to leave the impression that the research trend toward policy research is uniquely American. For example, some of the most interesting research on the uses of new communication technologies to provide remote services and thus to substitute communication for physical travel has been done in England by Alex Reid. Reid's is perhaps the most extensive research to date on teleconferencing. (7) UNITAR and other United Nations groups have been studying the communication needs of the UN and of its affiliated institutions. The UN's chances of becoming a significant force in the world, and a small first counterweight to archaic notions of national sovereignty, depend upon the ability of the UN to talk directly to its staff and to the peoples of the world without going through the censorship of member nations. If the UN is to play an effective role in peacekeeping during crises, it may need means of communication not subject to the control of interested parties. These considerations have led to studies of the UN communications system. (5, 8)

Perhaps the most extensive communications policy studies around the world have been on communication and development. In a developing country one often needs to plan the installing of a new communication system almost from scratch. One must therefore think in policy terms about the structure of that communication system, in a way that one can avoid where one inherits a system that grew incrementally. UNESCO has probably done more than any other single organization to promote study and research of the communication needs of the developing areas. UNESCO studies consider such matters as the needs for radio, press agencies, newsprint, mimeographed newspapers, communication satellites, organized viewing and listening groups, and journalism training in developing countries. It has sponsored institutions and experiments as well as publications and conferences.

Communications media as instruments for development have also been objects of study within research institutes in many of the developing countries themselves. An Indian study, started by Vikram Sarabhai, has explored the use of a satellite to establish TV communication with each of India's 500,000 villages. (3) That study required an integrated attack on technical problems of direct reception and of set maintenance, on operations research problems of relative costs of satellite and terrestrial delivery, on software problems of creating enough material for the broadcast schedule, and on the psychosocial problems of how to reach villagers with advice that would lead them to action. Brazilian satellite planning has involved the same kind of comprehensive policy analysis. A UNESCO-sponsored group is planning for an Andean educational TV satellite. Examples of comprehensive communication policy studies dealing with terrestrial rather than satellite broadcasting are provided by Samoan and Salvadorian (2) educational broadcast experiments and by Iran.

The World Bank has been a major stimulator of policy research on communications and development. In a number of countries, World Bank teams have evaluated the needs for communications investment.

Among the developed countries, Japan has naturally done much communications policy planning. The Research Institute on Telecommunications and Economics in Tokyo has a research program covering the majority of topics referred to in this paper.

Finland is another example of a country from which much interesting and relevant material has recently come. In the late 1960's a long-range planning section was established in Yleisradio, and the broadcasting research organization was made a part of it. Kaarle Nordenstreng has written about the resulting policy research organization and its special outlook. (4)

> *Perhaps the first issue discussed as a matter of communications policy was whether broadcasting should be a government monopoly or a commercial enterprise.*

HISTORY AND PERSPECTIVES

The technical fact that shaped the early discussion of broadcast ownership was that the available channels were natural resources, not made by anyone's labor, and were few in number. Only where ideological commitment to the principle of private enterprise was overwhelmingly strong, as in the United States, did it seem sensible to decision-makers to turn over to more or less arbitrarily chosen individuals such a scarce natural resource as the spectrum, giving the privileged recipients significant wealth and power. Into the technical issues about the spectrum was intermixed the archaic nineteenth-century ideological argument about social *vs.* private ownership. People tried to make the case that state monopoly had some inherent merits over private activity, but it is hard to take that kind of ideologizing seriously in the 1970's, particularly when most of that argument's adherents would be horrified at the suggestion of applying it to print media in the form of a national monopoly press. Clearly the technical fact of the limitation of broadcasting channels was at the heart of the situation in which the issue of public monopoly *vs.* commercial broadcasting could be argued about by people of good will, intelligence, and equal commitment to freedom.

This policy issue comes up for reevaluation in an era of changing technology. The scarcity of channels may no longer be with us. There are new ways of increasing the number of over-the-air channels. On cable an almost indefinite increase in the number of channels is possible. It is tempting to say that we are moving into an era where access to the electronic media can be as open to all as it is, at least in free countries, to the printing press. That, however, would be an oversimplification. Even if cable TV can provide tiny minority groups with their own private channels at a cost of only a few dollars an hour, the whole operation depends on an underlying shared physical plant. Thus a policy issue that promises to be just as central to cable TV as the issue of private *vs.* public ownership was to over-the-air broadcasting is the issue of the desirable relationship between content and conduit. Who should own and build the physical plant, and how should those who have a message they want to send relate to the plant that they use? Hopefully today we can discuss such issues in concrete analytic detail and not become engaged in old-fashioned verbal slogans.

Closely related to these issues of ownership within a medium are the issues of intermedia competition and integration. The patterns of integration found in different countries range from a single ministry of information and communications to prohibitions on cross-ownership.

Whatever the legal requirements on integration or separation may be today, the issue is likely to be reopened by new technologies, the use of which requires that one be able to switch messages between what are now distinct communication modes. An example is the electronic delivery of mail. If bills are to be delivered to the householder on an electronic console, then either the TV cables or the telephone twisted pairs will become functional elements of the postal system. If education is to be delivered to the home by open universities and similar schools, then switched telecommunication along with video displays will become as intertwined with the school system as textbook publishing is today. Such multimodal uses of the basic communications hardware will create a demand for intermodal integration either by regulation of standards for efficient message switching or by cross-ownership.

> *Where does the money come from for communication services?*
> *What rights of control and decision should lie with*
> *those who provide the funds?*

There are other issues of vertical integration besides the conduit-content issue. When is it desirable for users (such as schools or banks) to have their own dedicated communication facilities, and when should they have to purchase services from others? Should delivery organizations follow mercantilist policies of favoring domestically manufactured electronic equipment or buy in a competitive world market?

There are also issues of fiscal control. Where does the money come from for communication services? It may come from taxes, from licenses, from sale of services, or from advertising. Where does investment capital come from? What rights of control and decision should lie with those who provide the funds? What are the proper relations, for example, of publishers and professional editors?

There are also policy questions concerning training. What sort of institutions are needed to produce professionals for the communications media? How should they be recruited and trained? In an era in which the technologies of communication change more than once in a lifetime, practitioners have to be trained and retrained in new ways so that they can cope with their changing environment. Union rules and practices designed originally to protect the practitioners become an incubus on social change and therefore a proper object of policy concern.

Another policy area is the eternal question of how to finance worthwhile material that is not self-supporting. How shall society support the arts? How shall it support new avante-garde experimentation? Wealthy patrons, endowments, foundations, governments, royalities, and the market have all played a role in the past, and in various changing ways will continue to do so.

> *What kinds of discrimination, censorship, and increased costs*
> *will a country tolerate to keep national hegemony*
> *over its communication system?*

Copyright is clearly a communications policy issue. Copyright provided a sensible way to compensate authors of printed books. Since all exemplars of an edition were run off at a central location on a single, easily identified printing press, it became easy to count the number of copies that had been made and pay the author accordingly. The system is of dubious relevance in the era of xerox copiers, loudspeakers, and tape recorders. There is no easy way to measure the frequency of reproduction in some of these newer technologies. International communication also makes the copyright system problematical. In a world in which some countries produce much more program material than they receive and other countries receive much more than they produce, does it make sense for the latter to agree to copyright rules in the interest of the former?

Another set of policy questions concerns rate setting and cost accounting. There are many social costs and hidden subsidies in the economics of communication. If the costs of a postage stamp and a local telephone call are the same everywhere in a country, then rural users are being subsidized by urban ones, for costs of delivery go up where population density is low. Satellite costs per message go up enormously if the space vehicle is not heavily used. There are significant economies of scale. What kinds of international and intermodal sharing make sense as ways of reducing the costs?

There are policy questions about nationalism and international communication. What kinds of discrimination, censorship, and increased costs will a country tolerate to keep national hegemony over its communication system? Relevant issues concern customs duties on products of culture and on electronic equipment, controls of content, cross-border broadcasting, jamming, spectrum allocation, subsidization of translations, cooperative production agreements, and exchange arrangements for programs.

There are also policy issues regarding obscenity, violence, sedition, and libel. People assert with conviction various conclusions about the social effects of the media and how powerful they are in shaping society or in influencing children. What is known as a result of solid research is much less conclusive, though the evidence is gradually improving. Hopefully knowledge will eventually enlighten government action in these emotionally charged areas.

> *What obligations are there on officials to respond to media interrogation, where and when? What documents must be open to public inspection?*

Another social effect of communication is the involvement of people in politics. There are policy choices to be made about the conduct of politics even if we limit our attention to democratic policies designed to secure genuine political involvement. Policy determines such things as fairness of access for different points of view, especially if the available medium is scarce. Policy also may determine the relation of political tendencies to the media—for example, how is TV to be made available to candidates in campaigns? There is a policy question as to what government statements count as partisan declarations deserving a right of reply for the opposition? What obligations are there on officials to respond to media interrogation, where and when? What documents must be open to public inspection?

A major issue in communication policy is centralization *vs.* decentralization of origination. In many developing countries the governments take the view that all broadcasts should originate in the capital so as to discourage parochial tendencies. At the extreme, the government may fear capture of a local broadcasting station by a provincial faction or by insurgents. The national leaders sometimes even fear augmented political popularity for competing local figures. Such a centralist approach is predicated on a theory of nationalism which may well be subjected to the critical eye of research. There is some social science evidence to support the rival view that national loyalty has its roots in loyalty to the local community and that a remote center cannot become an effective object of intense loyalty by itself.

In the United States, broadcast policy is based on a decentralist doctrine. The commitment to local broadcasting is so strong that it is maintained despite resulting inefficiency in the use of the spectrum. If national stations were allowed, most people could receive substantially more TV channels than they now do. A policy choice has been made for localism at a significant and arguable cost.

Language policy is a major issue in many countries. Should broadcasting foster the national language or allow only good diction in it, or should broadcasters speak the languages the people understand, whatever they may be?

Another area affected by communications policy is regional planning. In designing new cities or new districts, investment decisions are made as to what communications facilities to provide. Such decisions can have a profound effect on the human ecology of the next generation. Peter Goldmark, for example, is convinced that we must reverse the trend toward urban concentration by bringing (via telecommunications) the cultural advantages of the city to the residents of the country. (1) Education, music, theater, and better medical care can all be brought by new technologies directly to the rural home. The goal, in Karl Marx's phrase, is to get rid of the idiocy of rural life and to eliminate the distinction between country and city.

> *The role of communications in development is perhaps*
> *the policy issue most urgently in need of study.*

Another policy research issue concerning both communication and human ecology is whether communication can sometimes substitute for transportation. The quantitative relation between these two methods of human contact is obscure. Establishing increased communication with people far away could lead to increased travel so as to carry forward the relationship face

HISTORY AND PERSPECTIVES

to face. Alternatively, better long-distance communication could reduce the need for burning petrol in order to meet in the same room.

The role of communications in development is perhaps the policy issue most urgently in need of study. There is substantial social science evidence for a causal relationship between the growth of mass media and acceleration of modernization. The evidence is carefully reviewed in Frederick Frey's chapter in the new *Handbook of Communication.* (6) The press, movies, and especially radio operate in many ways to foster development. They convey knowledge of new ways of doing things. They raise aspirations. They create identifications on a national and even international scale. They help create a wider market and a less provincial political arena. Few underdeveloped countries have yet taken full advantage of the powerful instrument of development available to them in the communication media. Most fear mass media as a Pandora's box that they do not know how to control. Few have devoted to communication the resources it deserves. Research is gradually providing the evidence for doing more, but there is need of better understanding of the process before the means of communication used will be as they should be for modernization.

Almost all the topics I mentioned have some things in common. In almost every case the impetus to both research and a possible shift in policy is technological change. In almost every case the new technologies open up opportunities for more and better human communication which cannot be fully realized unless we modify in some way the economic and political parameters of the present communications system. In almost every case there are visible consequences of such change, both good and bad. And in almost every case we cannot guess very well what these consequences may be without hard, objective, empirical, and multidisciplinary study. That need for knowledge as a basis for action creates the incentive for the growth and improvement in quality of communications policy research.

> *Every step of progress is bought at some cost. Having described a trend that seems to be taking place, we may ask ourselves to consider both its values and its dangers.*

What can we say about the merits and dangers of this trend toward policy research? Every step of progress is brought at some cost. Having described a trend that seems to be taking place, we may ask ourselves to consider both its value and its dangers.

Its value is obvious. Policy research can help improve decision-making. Communication research in the past may have provided important information for middle-level decisions about such matters as which program to offer the viewing public or how to couch an appeal to them. It seldom entered into the fundamental decisions about what the communication system should be. More enlightenment in the making of such decisions can only help.

The dangers, on the other hand, are the dangers of hubris. There is something very seductive about involvement in the big questions of public policy. It is sometimes fallaciously argued that policy research is by nature less empirical and more theoretical than other research, and that the job of the policy researcher is not so much the cold determination of the facts as it is the philosophical and conceptual-analytic deliberation of goals. If there is anything more than the hubris of intellectual elitism behind that view, it is this: Good policy research has to take account of all factual and normative variables that enter into a decision. No single finding is decisive. A program rating, for example, may be the whole story for an audience research department. It is only one among many urgently needed facts for someone concerned with the entire communication system. More hard facts are needed by the policymaker than by anyone at other levels.

As a result, policy research is inherently multidisciplinary. Fundamental decisions about the nature of the communication system depend upon findings in psychology, sociology, economics, political science, organization theory, engineering, and physical science, as well as upon social value judgments.

Values and social philosophy do play a bigger role in policy research than they did in the conventional audience research of the past, but economics and engineering studies also play a larger role. Economics is the science of the allocation of scarce resources, and any planning effort is an allocation of scarce resources over competing goals. What is or will be technically possible is also an essential input for good communication planning.

The current discussion of direct satellite broadcasting may provide us with an illustration. There is a conflict of values involved. A heated debate is taking place, reflected in the Winter 1974 issue of this *Journal*, between those who would give primacy to the principle of national sovereignty and those who would give primacy to the free flow of information. There are those who believe progress can best be served by allowing all countries, regardless of the character of their regimes, to control the messages that their citizens may receive, and there are those, on the other hand, who think that progress is better served by allowing rival viewpoints to be communicated internationally without regard to the preferences of governments. This is indeed a deep philosophical issue, but there is substantial evidence that the discussion of these rival values is quite academic. It may turn out to be an argument about an economic-technical impossibility.

I am not so characterizing cooperative direct satellite broadcasting where the sending and receiving country work together to solve the thorny problems of spectrum allocation, consistency of standards, and modification of receivers. That will clearly be possible, perhaps in as little as 10 years' time. Nor am I talking of spillover. I am talking about satellite TV broadcasting forced at an acceptable cost by one country onto another country that objects and resists by its own spectrum allocations, terrestrial broadcasts, set design, or refusal of special antennas and adapters to its public. The technical and economic advantages seem so overwhelmingly on the side of the objecting receiver-nation that no sane country will try direct satellite broadcasting of TV to an objecting country at any time that we can now foresee.

Whether those are correct engineering conclusions, however, is not what I wish to argue here. The point I am trying to make is that such hard facts of science and economics must be resolved as prerequisite to any sensible discussion of policy.

If one danger of the growth of policy research arises from the hubris of scholars who would prefer to play philosopher-king rather than be factual researchers, an even greater danger arises from the hubris of policymakers. Too often those in power are convinced that they know best what messages it is good for people to hear. Scientific knowledge, or anything else that enhances the ability of such rulers to implement their preferences about the content of communications, is certainly to be feared. There is much justified anxiety today about the power of science falling into the hands of those who would make others conform to their will. The use of research to increase effectiveness by those in control of media is just one more example of a use of science in a way that can be a force for either good or evil.

The problem of the social use of science is a complex one. People are not going to stop improving their skills because some beneficiaries may misuse such skills. In this area, as in applied science generally, the only realistic goal is to so organize the activities enhanced by technology as to give individuals more choices rather than putting them under more control. Refusal to think about policy will not achieve that goal.

If the notion of communications policy causes some broadcasters and journalists to feel uneasy and to worry about policy becoming a euphemism for the restriction of their freedom, the fears are justified. But the answer is not to bury one's head in the sand. The answer for those concerned with media freedom is to insist that the aim of communication policy be pluralism of expression rather than the dissemination of preferred ideas.

References

1 Goldmark, Peter. New Rural Society, 1972–3. Report to HUD, Contract No. 81695, 1974.
2 Hornik, Robert C. "Television and Educational Reform in El Salvador," Research Report No. 14, Institute for Communication Research. Stanford: Stanford University, August 1973.
3 Maddox, Brenda. *Beyond Babel: New Directions in Communications.* London: André Deutsch, 1972.
4 Nordenstreng, Kaarle. "Broadcasting Research in Scandinavian Countries," in H. Eguchi and H. Ichinoche (Eds.) *International Studies of Broadcasting, 1971.* Tokyo: NHK Radio and TV Culture Research Institute.

THE RISE OF COMMUNICATIONS POLICY RESEARCH

5 Pool, Ithiel de Sola, Philip Stone, and Alexander Szalai. "Communications, Computers and Automation for Development." UNITAR Research Report No. 6, 1971.
6 Pool, I. and W. Schramm (Eds.). *Handbook of Communications*. Chicago: Rand McNally, 1973.
7 Reid, Alex. "New Directions in Telecommunications Research," Communications Studies Group, University College, London, 1971. (Paper for Sloan Commission on Cable Communications.)
8 United Nations Association. "Space Communications: Increasing UN Responsiveness to the Problems of Mankind," Report of a National Policy Panel, UNA of the USA, 1971.

5

GLOBAL IMPLICATIONS OF THE INFORMATION SOCIETY*

Marc Uri Porat

Source: *Journal of Communication* 28(1) (1978): 70–80.

"As with life itself, the prognosis for an information society is mixed, the remedy inconclusive."

The U.S. is now an information-based economy. By 1967, 25 percent of GNP originated in the production, processing, and distribution of information goods and services. In addition, over 21 percent of GNP originated in the production of information services by the private and public bureaucracies for purely internal uses. By 1970, close to half of the U.S. workforce was classified as "information workers," holding a job where the production, processing or distribution of symbols is the main activity. This group of workers earned over 53 percent of all labor incomes.[1]

In this article, I shall discuss some of the many international implications flowing from this transformation of the U.S. economy: How do exports of information goods and services fit into foreign policy? What is "cultural exportation, and how is it viewed internationally? What about human rights issues and the use of information technologies? How important is the export of technological and scientific information?

The group of industries which produce, process, or transmit knowledge, communication and information goods or services are termed the "primary information sector."

On the service side, these industries include the electronic and print media, advertising, education, telecommunications services, components of finance and insurance, libraries, consulting, and research and development firms. On the goods side are included computer, communication, and electronic equipment manufacturers, office and business machines, measuring

GLOBAL IMPLICATIONS OF THE INFORMATION SOCIETY

and control instruments, and printing and printing presses. A detailed measurement effort (covering over 70 industries and over 6,000 products measured at the seven-digit Standard Industrial Classification level) yielded the result that in 1967, 25.1 percent of valued added (GNP) originated in the primary information sector. One quarter of GNP is bound up with the information activity—goods and services for sale.

In addition, we know intuitively that noninformation firms (e.g., auto, steel, and petroleum) and governments produce and consume information of a wholly "internal" type. Every institution consumes some mixture of research and development, design, management, accounting, legal services, clerical and marketing information "services." Firms and governments hire "information labor," (e.g., managers and secretaries) and invest in "information capital," (e.g., computing, communications, and office machines.) These are essentially *information inputs* to noninformation activities. The information services produced in a nonmarket context, i.e., not specifically exchanged in an established market, are labeled the "secondary information sector." A detailed estimate reveals that these activities, often associated with private and public bureaucratic *information overhead*, generated (in 1967) some 21.1 percent of value added (GNP).

Together, the primary and secondary information sectors accounted, in a formal National Income and Product Accounts sense, for 46 percent of GNP in 1967. We assume that the figure is somewhat higher in 1977, although it has not yet been measured.

An economy can also be characterized by the distribution of its workforce across various activities.

The conventional classification of labor is a tripartite sectoring scheme —agriculture, industry, and services. But if we create a fourth sector—information—and include all the workers who hold an informational job,[2] a most interesting picture emerges.

Figure 1 shows the four sector aggregation of the U.S. labor force. In Stage I (1860–1906), the single largest group was agricultural workers. During this stage, the U.S. is characterized as an agricultural society.

In Stage II (1906–1954), we see that the industrial workforce is predominant, reaching a peak of around 40 percent in 1946. During this stage, the U.S. is characterized as an industrial society. In the 1950s, the industrial workforce began to decline, and is presently about 25 percent of U.S. labor.

In Stage III (1954–present), information workers comprise the largest group. From a low of five percent of the workforce in 1860, the information sector of U.S. labor has grown to about 47 percent of the workforce. In 1967, this group earned over 53 percent of all employee compensation, as shown in Table 1.

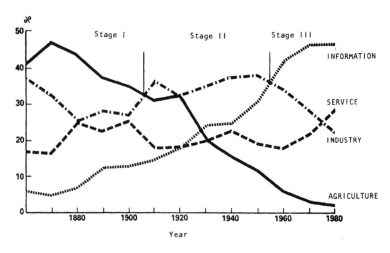

Figure 1 Four sector aggregation of the U.S. work force by percent, 1860–1980. (using median estimates of information workers)

> *On the strength of the GNP and labor data, the U.S. can now be called an "information society."*

There are many phrases for the same phenomenon. Fritz Machlup (4) called it a "knowledge economy."[3] To Brzezinski, it is a "technetronic age," to Dahrendorff, it is "post-capitalist," to Etzioni, it is "post-modern." Daniel Bell first coined the term "post-industrial," and succinctly describes the essence of the transformation as follows:

> In *pre-industrial societies*—still the conditon of most of the world today—the labor force is engaged overwhelmingly in the extractive industries: mining, fishing, forestry, agriculture. Life is primarily a game against nature. . . . *Industrial societies* are goods-producing societies. Life is a game agains fabricated nature. The world has become technical and rationalized. . . . A *post-industrial society* is based on services. Hence, it is a game between persons. What counts is not raw muscle power, or energy, but information.
>
> (1, emphasis added)

The essential difference between an industrial and an information society is that the locus of economic activity and technological change has shifted away from manufacturing "objects" towards handling information and symbols. The plow and farming techniques heralded the agricultural economy; the steam engine and manufacturing techniques transformed first Europe and then the U.S. into an industrial economy; the computer and

GLOBAL IMPLICATIONS OF THE INFORMATION SOCIETY

Table 1 Typology of information workers and 1967 compensation[a].

	Employee compensation ($ millions)
MARKETS FOR INFORMATION	
Knowledge producers	*46,964*
Scientific and technical workers	18,777
Private information services	28,187
Knowledge distributors	*28,265*
Educators	23,680
Public information disseminators	1,264
Communication workers	3,321
INFORMATION IN MARKETS	
Market search and coordination specialists	*93,370*
Information gatherers	6,132
Search and coordination specialists	28,252
Planning and control workers	58,986
Information processors	61,340
Non-electronic based	34,317
Electronic based	27,023
INFORMATION INFRASTRUCTURE	
Information machine workers	*13,167*
Non-electronic machine operators	4,219
Electronic machine operators	3,660
Telecommunication workers	5,288
Total information	243,106
Total employee compensation	454,259[b]
Information as % of total	53.52%

[a] Employee compensation includes wages and salaries and supplements.
[b] Excluding military workers.
Source: Computed using BLS Occupaton by Industry matrix, Census of Population average wages.

telecommunications are now propelling the U.S. into the information economy. This economic realignment, which eventually ripples outside the U.S. borders and onto the shores of our trading partners, has further implications for the nature of the international economy.

> *But is information intrinsically a valuable commodity, or is it a "leech" on the productive sectors of the economy?*

HISTORY AND PERSPECTIVES

No one doubts that information can be a lucrative source of both profits and employment. The primary information sector, which *sells* information goods and services, accounted in 1967 for 25 percent of GNP. The secondary (or overhead) sector employs one out of five workers, and accounted for 21 percent of GNP. But unless the information is *productive*, it is not supportable in the long run.

Consider, for the moment, information as a *resource*, analagous to natural, labor, and capital resources. A firm needs information goods and services (such as computers and managers) to produce its output. A rational firm buys a computer or hires a manager only if it can extract a surplus from the "investment"—the return is greater than the outlay and as large as any alternative investment opportunity.

Information thus enters as a productive input and increases domestic output. In the case of invention, the application of new information mobilizes idle resources, opens new markets, and improves the efficiency of existing processes. Information *creates* wealth in this context.

But the production of information also consumes capital and labor resources, which are "taken" from other sectors of the economy, hence pushing up the price of labor and capital to other sectors of the economy. Assessing the productivity of information workers and bureaucratic process is very hard indeed, leading to a popular (although unproven) assumption that information can be a wasteful activity. In this context, information detracts from domestic input.

Whether information contributes to domestic production through new inventions and increased efficiency—or detracts from it as an unproductive resource "sink"—can only be settled by research which has not yet been done. However, projections of the U.S. labor force reveal that the growth of the information work force has slowed dramatically. According to the Bureau of Labor Statistics, between 1970 and 1980 the information sector will grow at a net rate of 0.04 percent—not much faster than the overall U.S. labor force. It seems that our bureaucracies are glutted and can absorb no more information workers.

The prospects for new growth for the information economy can come from only two sources of demand: domestic and foreign. Domestically, the primary information sector will expand if new entrepreneurial ventures are undertaken: breakthroughs in business and home applications such as "information utilities" and teleconferencing, or new technologies such as microprocessors, fiber optics, and mass storage manufacturing.

Foreign markets are the other obvious sources of demand for U.S. information goods and services. Internal pressures to export information goods and services have already resulted in aggressive marketing by U.S. multinationals —both in the developed countries (including the Soviet Bloc) and the less developed nations. The secondary information sector is now exported as a "hidden cost," as part of the price of a noninformation good, and explicitly in the form of scientific and technological knowledge.

> *An industrial society sheds its chrysalis and becomes an information society when every aspect of its economy becomes dependent on information machines.*

The foreign appetite for U.S. information machines is exceeded only by demand for U.S. guns and butter. The export of computers in 1975 exceeded $2.2 billion. Over $1.1 billion worth of telecommunications systems were bought from U.S. manufacturers. In terms of balance of payments, these information technologies generated a huge $2.4 billion surplus for the U.S. in 1975. The only trade problem on the horizon is the alleged "flooding" of consumer electronics markets by Japanese exporters. (In 1975, the U.S. imported $2,067 million of radios, TVs, high fidelity equipment and calculators, and exported $652 million.) But in the arena of computers, peripherals, microwave, switching equipment, terminal equipment, satellite ground stations, and computer software, U.S. firms are dominant.

The less developed nations, who are grappling with industrial technology, are in the odd position of "leapfrogging" over an entire stage of economic evolution. A country like Brazil is simultaneously developing an industrial *and* information infrastructure. It makes no sense to import modern industrial technology without its concommitants—computer process control, computerized management techniques, and rapid communication between all sectors (business, government, households). Thus as the managerial trappings of modern industry are informational, the demand for U.S. information goods will continue to be strong.

Where computers and communications are used for economic modernization (i.e., in support of industrialization), the U.S. is clearly committed to encouraging such development. The quality of life is at stake, and dovetails with a fixture of U.S. foreign aid policy—raising the developing nation's standard of living.

But modernization or development are not "neutral" words. As they are often equated with Westernization, in a development context, information technology becomes a *political fact* as well as an economic resource. The establishment of U.S. administrative procedures, accounting and financial practices, and managerial control is not an apolitical development. There is nothing inherently political about computers, except that the dearth of native scientific and technical talent often means that U.S. advisors become a part of the technology transfer. And *that* is a political decision.

This point is dramatized by the case of computer exports. The same computer can be used in the service of "modernization" to design a water irrigation project, manage a national innoculation program, or coordinate inter-industry balanced growth. It can also handle logistical support for an army, assist in the design of nuclear weapons, serve as a pinpoint missile guidance control system, or digest foreign intelligence data. A computer is both a tool of economic development and a strategic weapon. It is a plow at one moment, a gun at the next, and this basic duality of purpose cannot easily be severed.

The uses of information systems—both telecommunications and computers —also pose foreign policy problems in the arena of human rights. No one takes issue with a country's basic need to communicate internally and with its neighbors. No modern economy (much less a Western-oriented industrial economy) can survive without efficient domestic telecommunicatons systems. With that presumption, huge exports of advanced systems have recently been approved, mostly to Third and Fourth World nations such as Iran, Saudi Arabia, and Indonesia. But what about the use of telecommunication systems in domestic surveillance—massive eavesdropping and wiretapping— and systematic violation of (what the U.S. defines as) basic human and civil liberties. It is now a fairly simple matter to monitor telephone conversations using highly automated equipment. Telephone pairs of dissidents and political "undesirables" are simply programmed into a computer, and conversations are routinely tapped and recorded.

Computers, a requisite of economic improvement and development, can also be used to maintain extensive personal dossiers on political dissidents. The National Council of Churches recently revealed that an IBM computer system (370/145) might be deployed for just that purpose by DINA, Chile's infamous secret police. DINA has been implicated in numerous violations of human rights, including a regime of sudden "disappearances" of dissidents, extended incarceration without formal charge, and outright torture.[4]

Hence the sale of U.S. information systems can be a highly political decision: Does the U.S. have the right to dictate to its clients how they may or may not use an imported system? How does a nation guarantee in advance that an information system will be used to promote economic development rather than abuse human rights?

*Information services exports are potentially as troublesome
as the export of information goods.*

Information services are divisible into three basic types: (1) financial, insurance, accounting and *data base* information; (2) *cultural exports*, such as film, television, radio, books, newspapers and magazines; and (3) *knowledge exports*, represented by patent royalties, and management and consulting fees. All generate their share of political problems.

U.S. and European firms produce mountains of financial data that flow freely across international borders. This linking of commerce is as natural as the flow of goods in a mercantile or industrial age. The new resource of value is information: invoices, bills of lading, freight movement, personal travel, financial instruments, private bank accounts, personnel records. The European data market alone is projected to exceed $5 billion by 1980.

But some new and troubling policy problems have arisen in connection with the *protection of privacy*. The laws protecting personal information differ considerably between countries, and have not yet been harmonized. Only two nations, Sweden and W. Germany, have passed stringent privacy laws. The EEC and OECD are jointly concerned that a country with weak privacy laws can be used as a "data-haven," wherein an unethical firm subverts its own country's strict privacy laws by setting up a subsidiary in a less stringent foreign host. In fact, the U.S. has been identified as a particularly attractive haven. Foreign firms wishing to fly a U.S. "flag of convenience" can enjoy two advantages: (1) the U.S. does not have comprehensive privacy legislation to cover personal data bases, and (2) the U.S. can offer the necessary technical support—computer hardware and software and advance telecommunications—that may not be available in some other haven such as Turkey.

As a remedy, a convention or a treaty on "transborder data flows" is now under consideration by the OECD. Some U.S. firms maintain that the true purpose of such a treaty is a European attempt to suppress competition from the U.S. firms in the lucrative data markets. This view is rebuffed by European countries, who claim that their true concerns are for the protection of privacy.

> *Another growing source of income from abroad is the sale of U.S. media products like television programming, feature films, books, and magazines.*

Third World nations in particular, often without a developed national media industry, simultaneously seek and resent U.S. cultural products. It is always cheaper to import U.S. entertainment than to produce television and film domestically. A Minister of Culture or Education, facing both a tight budget and the impossible requirement of filling up at least eight hours a day of television programming, has every incentive to import rather than produce domestically.

But the claim is heard that such items are "cultural propaganda," that they are a force of "cultural imperialism," that the portrayal of U.S. lifestyle in television programs transmits ideological fare along with entertainment. The proponents of the "cultural imperialism" argument point to the overwhelmingly dominant position of the U.S. media in the world media market. The defense states that nations can unilaterally restrict such imports by simply refusing to buy. Here the argument takes a new twist: new direct broadcasting technologies by communication statellites may obviate a nation's right to reject U.S. cultural exports. The subject has been repeatedly debated in UNESCO-sponsored conferences. However, it is difficult to assume that many private households could build and conceal illegal rooftop dish antennas to receive satellite transmissions. Thus, the question is wholly political, not technical.

As outputs of the secondary information sector, knowledge exports are embodied in patent royalties, management and consulting fees, and process licensing fees.

Knowledge is being sold—"know-how," "show-how," organizational experience, scientific and technical information, and managerial information. As in the television programming case, a Minister of Science and Industry has little incentive to invest in a domestic "knowledge industry." A research and development lab or a management consulting company is just the tip of a very large iceberg of industrial production experience. Dealing with the global market, in either the role of an importer or exporter, requires sophisticated knowledge. Buying this knowledge is always cheaper than trying to produce it domestically.

In fact, the U.S. has established a foreign aid program specifically in the area of scientific and technical information. Much of the relevant information can be acquired for very little cost; organizations such as the World Bank and the IMF proffer a dose of information along with a low interest loan; many U.S. firms are in the business of "selling" information as a consulting or management contract; and lastly, when a multinational sets up a manufacturing subsidiary as a joint venture with another country, patent royalties and management fees for the use of U.S. technology and U.S. management know-how are often part of the deal.

The concept of "technological colonialism" arises from this last feature. We often see an influx of U.S.-trained technicians, managers, and scientists —a highly visible presence that has often been the target of political criticism. The critics argue that when a country buys technical or scientific knowledge (in the form of patent royalties and management fees), it concurrently imports a form of economic organization that mirrors the West. It is almost unavoidable. Management organizational hierarchy, economic concepts about productive efficiency, the price system, financing tehniques, marketing techniques, demand management—these are the correlates of Western technology.

The export of film and television programs in 1973 amounted to $324 million. By contrast, the knowledge exports (patents, management fees) were $3,034 million—nearly ten times the amount of film rentals and royalties (see 6, Vol. 8, p. 9; 7). A technological system of production, once installed, is a most enduring cultural artifact.

GLOBAL IMPLICATIONS OF THE INFORMATION SOCIETY

> *One of the more assuring propositions about future economic growth is that an information economy is not as constrained by natural resources as an industrial economy.*

The emergence of an information society means that knowledge production and distribution will continue to play critical roles in future economic growth. Firms and individuals that understand the value of information, know how to access and use information, and can discriminate between knowledge and noise, will always be more "successful" than those who cannot.

An information society is geared to the production and distribution of information—its workforce is well-educated, literate, versed in symbol manipulation, comfortable with the use of information machines (such as telephones, computers, photocopiers). An information society can be a vibrant source of new knowledge, invention and progress, whose benefits extend beyond our shores.

An information society is also a technocratic or a bureaucratic society. The creative premium has shifted from physical craftsmanship and pride to specialization and organizational gamesmanship. The manager-scientist-professional is the new knight, absorbing the old powers of the capitalist, the landlord, the general and the priest.

Information is the most curious of all resources. It is infinitely renewable —the act of consumption does not destroy the information, and it can be used repeatedly and simultaneously by many people. Information does not even depreciate with use. On the contrary, the more one uses certain types of information (knowledge, the law), the more valuable they become. Information goods and services do not require huge inputs of natural resources or energy, and generate only modest waste or environmental pollution.

Although this view is appealing on the surface, note that 21 percent of GNP is bound up with bureaucratic information production in non-information firms. In a resource-connected recession, the manufacturing, energy, food, and transportation industries are hard hit. Preliminary evidence indicated that the information bureaucracy is the first economic luxury to hit the street (6, vol. 1, chapter 10). Although the primary information sector is fairly insensitive to resource issues, the secondary information sector is not.

> *The guideposts along the way are domestic and international information policies.*

We can, with guidance, have a bright future as an information society. The capital and human infrastructure is in place, and can be mobilized with great force. But many domestic issues regarding the domestic flows of social and economic issues need to be resolved—contradictions between the Privacy Act and the Freedom of Information Act; First Amendment issues and the bounds of commercial speech; the federal paperwork burden; the Copyright Act—these are all elements of information policy.

Domestic policy will also focus on the structure of the information industries—issues of competition vs. regulation in the telephone industry; the boundary between communicatons and computing; the future of electronic funds transfer systems and electronic mail—these also are elements of information policy. And finally, attention will necessarily focus on the international implications—the exports of information goods and services, cultural exports, and technological and scientific information transfer. We cannot be definitive about the information society because that era is still evolving about us. As with life itself, the prognosis for an information society is mixed, the remedy inconclusive.

Notes

* This article is based on a paper commissioned for the United States Information Agency entitled "The U.S. as an Information Society: International Implications," July 1, 1977.

1 A complete exposition of the definitions, sources, methods, and findings is available in (6).
2 Including teachers, selected managers, selected clerical workers, selected professionals (e.g., accountants, lawyers), and people who work with information machines (e.g., computer and telephone operators). The criterion for including an occupation in the information sector is as follows: The information-handling aspect of the job overshadows the non-information aspects; conversely, the non-information aspects are clearly ancillary to the informational.
3 The quote is attributed to Kenneth E. Boulding, who has also written extensively on the knowledge industries (see 2). The emergence of a large and uncharted service sector was the theme of V. R. Fuchs in *The Service Economy* (3), but he did not, however, carry through Machlup's idea of a "knowledge industry."
4 An overview discussion of the issue, including the viewpoints of the National Council of Churches, Amnesty International, the United Nations, IBM, CDC, and Burroughs, appears in (5). See also the March and May 1977 issues of *Computer Decisions*.

References

1 Bell, Daniel. *The Coming of Post-Industrial Society*. New York: Basic Books, 1973, pp. 126–127.
2 Boulding, K. E. "The Economics of Knowledge and the Knowledge of Economics." In D. M. Lamberton (Ed.) *Economics of Information and Knowledge*. Middlesex, England: Penguin Books, 1971.
3 Fuchs, V. R. *The Service Economy*. New York: National Bureau of Economic Research.
4 Machlup, Fritz. *The Production and Distribution of Knowledge in the United States*. Princeton, N.J.: Princeton University Press, 1962.

5 Nadel, Laurie and Hesh Wiever. "Would You Sell a Computer to Hitler?" *Computer Decisions*, February 1977.
6 Porat, Marc Uri. *The Information Economy: Definition and Measurement* (nine volumes). U.S. Government Printing Office, Washington, D.C., July 1977.
7 Teplin, M. "U.S. International Transactions in Royalties and Fees: Their Relationship to the Transfer of Technology." *Survey of Current Business* 53(12), December 1975.

6

STOCKS AND FLOWS OF KNOWLEDGE

Fritz Machlup

Source: *Kyklos* 32(1–2) (1979): 400–11.

A fundamental distinction is commonly made between stocks and flows, usually with reference to goods, to capital funds, to money. The distinction applies also to knowledge. At any moment of time, there is a stock of knowledge; during any period of time there is a flow of knowledge.

As far as the stock is concerned, we should distinguish between knowledge on record and knowledge in the mind. *Recorded knowledge* may be written, printed, drawn, painted, or engraved on paper or other material, or encoded on disks, tapes, or other implements, for people to read, listen to or decode in order to get it into their heads. Such recorded knowledge is either available to all interested persons or restricted to a selected few. *Knowledge in the mind* is in the memory of an individual person, in the memories of small groups of persons, or in the memories of many members of society.

As to the flows of knowledge, we should distinguish three kinds: transmissions from persons to records, from records to persons, and from person to person without record. Our first task will be to ask whether there are any ways to measure or estimate the magnitudes of the stocks and flows of knowledge.

I. Estimating the stock of recorded knowledge

Various proposals have been made with regard to 'measurements' of society's stock of recorded knowledge, mostly in the form of books and journals stored on the shelves of libraries. The essence of these measures is that they are in terms of physical units, such as volumes or titles. Counts of volumes and counts of titles lead to very different results, not only because one title may involve several volumes (especially in the case of reference works, journals, and other serials), but also because of the holding of duplicates, to

STOCKS AND FLOWS OF KNOWLEDGE

some extent in any one library but mainly in the total of the existing collections (in the country or in the world). None of the title-counts can cope with another problem of duplication: the coverage of the same bits of knowledge in different publications. Some scientometricians – if I may borrow DEREK PRICE's term for measurers of scientific knowledge – have confined themselves to counting journal articles, especially in the natural sciences and technology. They argue that growth of knowledge in society is more meaningfully estimated by the number of articles than by the number of books, particularly on the assumption that scientific journals publish articles refereed for novelty and advancement of knowledge.

Whether estimates of the accumulated journal literature would be more indicative of the stock of recorded knowledge if the number of articles were counted, rather than the number of words, pages, issues, or volumes, is debatable. Is the very short article in which an experimental physicist or biologist reports on his findings an equivalent of a long article (of almost monographic length) in which a historian of science surveys the research achievements of decades or a theorist argues for a major change in a basic 'paradigm' of his scientific discipline? This question may prove to be irrelevant if, over the years, the ratio of short to long articles has not changed very much. A similar question arises with regard to the number of issues per year. Perhaps the simplest kind of estimate would be in terms of volumes, assuming that the issues of a journal for any one year have been bound in one volume. Can we estimate the number of annual volumes of scientific and scholarly journals that would have accumulated on the shelves of a 'universal library' that had not missed or lost a single publication?

A collection of scientific journals

The growth in the number of journals published has been remarkably constant from about 1760 to the present, according to the conjectures of PRICE[1]. If the growth rate is known and has really been constant, and if the number of journals published at present is known, a simple calculation can inform us on the number of annual volumes of journals accumulated in a hypothetical universal library.

PRICE proposed[2] that we use a figure or 50,000 for the number of scientific, technical, and scholarly journals currently published in 1975. The number of journals ever published would be much higher, because the mortality rate of journals has been considerable. But, while many periodicals were discontinued, new ones were started, and the birth rate exceeded the death rate. PRICE estimates that the birth rate is roughly twice the death rate; if this relation was stable over the decades and centuries, the number of journals alive must be about one-half the number of journals ever founded. Taking account only of the surviving scientific journals, PRICE, at one place, estimated that the number of journals published would double every 15 years. This would imply a compound rate of growth of 5 per cent a year. With the volume of journals increasing by 1/20 every year, the total number of volumes published since the beginning (that is, since the publication of the first journal) must be 20 times the number published now in one year. If this number is 50,000, the total accumulation of volumes is 1,000,000.

While the arithmetic of our question is simple, the census of the present population of scientific journals is rather complex. PRICE once had estimated the present population of surviving scientific journals to be 100,000; indeed he had claimed 'an extraordinary regularity' in the growth of journals.[3] This estimate was far too high. The total number of 'serials' listed in the ISSN-Index (International Standard Serial Number) in 1975 was only about 70,000, and this included all sorts of serial publications besides journals. It included, moreover, all sorts of subjects besides science and technology. To be relevant to scholarly (scientific, technological) journals, the overwhelming part of the number of serial publications has to be eliminated.

Such reductions from serials to journals and from all subjects to science and technology have been carried out. Depending on the criteria adopted for recognition as 'primary research journals', the numbers estimated varied between 400 and 4,000[4]. If 4,000 is taken as a plausible number of the present population of scientific and technological journals, and if 5 per cent is still taken as a plausible rate of annual growth of that population, the universal library would have to possess a collection of 80,000 volumes of primary research journals. This would be the stock of recorded knowledge in the natural sciences, mathematics, and technology. The question must be raised, however, whether a growth rate estimated for the kind of periodicals included in a present population of 50,000 periodicals would still be applicable for a more select population of only 4,000 primary-research journals. There is no reason why the ratio of journals in the universe of periodicals should have been constant and, hence, why the rates of growth should have been the same. I conclude that all these speculations about the holdings of our 'universal library' ought not to be taken very seriously.

II. The role of books

We have to recall, moreover, that the foregoing discussion was based on the assumption (or belief) of the scientometricians that all primary research findings in the 'hard sciences' were reported in journals and that books therefore did not matter as a measure of scientific knowledge. Such an assumption, whether valid or not for the natural sciences and mathematics, is surely untenable regarding the accumulation of recorded knowledge in the social sciences and the humanities. In these areas books matter.

An estimate of all books and journals ever published was made by GORE in a paper he presented in 1975 at a conference on academic libraries which was dedicated to the theme: 'Touching Bottom in the Bottomless Pit'. He

STOCKS AND FLOWS OF KNOWLEDGE

estimated that there have been '50 million books published since GUTENBERG; 400,000 new ones each year, plus some 300,000 new serials volumes'[5]. He cited these (perhaps somewhat exaggerated) figures in order to show that the principle or ideal of the great Library of Alexandria – to possess everything that had ever been published – would be both impossible and undesirable. 'Every square foot' of Egypt's surface would be 'occupied by the Alexandrian Library' (p. 170). He held that no university library should aspire to have a collection larger than a reasonable fraction of what its patrons may want to read; and that the libraries should dispose every year of as many old volumes as they acquired new ones. Between three and six national libraries would be the repositories or 'storage libraries' to hold one or two copies of each of the many volumes withdrawn (discarded) by the academic libraries. Gore estimated that initially each of the storage libraries would hold 860,000 volumes, and would add 133,000 volumes per year.

This proposal, bidding farewell to the Alexandrian ideal for academic libraries, implies of course that there would be six quasi-Alexandrian libraries in the United States. That these storage libraries would not hold anything near the 50 million books published since GUTENBERG is due to the fact that none of our libraries has a complete collection, and their discards therefore cannot give the national storage libraries any complete collections. The combined holdings of all academic libraries in the United States are at present (1975) about 440 million volumes, but the largest portion of these consists of multiple copies of the same books. The ratio of titles to copies is estimated to be 1 to 50, which would mean that our combined library collections contain less than 9 million titles.

III. Estimating the stock of knowledge in human minds

One may contend that the stock of knowledge in society is more meaningfully related to what people have in their heads than what there is recorded in their books and journals. It is conceivable that not a single person in the country knows even the smallest fraction of what is printed in the volumes in their library stacks. People may be illiterate and thus incapable of getting to know what *could* be known from the printed records; but even in the most literate society some of the knowledge potentially obtainable from the stored tomes in the libraries is probably unknown to any living person.

To make it quite clear that the size of the accumulated stock of recorded knowledge is not the essential measure for some purposes, one merely has to imagine several different societies of equal population and with exactly the same stock of recorded knowledge on the shelves of their national libraries. In one of these societies, people are completely illiterate; in another, ten per cent of the adult population is literate, and one half of the literates had read and absorbed some tiny fractions of what is stored in the journals and books of the library; and in a third society, 95 per cent of the adult population is literate, between ten and fifteen per cent of the people are so well educated that they have in their heads more than minimal fractions of what the printed pages can transmit, and another five per cent are capable of absorbing much larger quantities of the stored knowlege, and actually do so by various groups specializing in various fields of knowledge. Can anyone doubt that these three societies, despite the equal size of their stocks of recorded knowledge, are totally different in their knowledgeability? From various points of view, 'living knowledge', or what living people know, may be the relevant stock of knowledge in society.

The stock of knowledge accumulated in the head of an individual person is something different from the stock of knowledge shared by two or more persons, let alone by a majority of the members of a community. Phenomenological theory of knowledge[6] significantly began its analysis with the experiences in the daily life of an individual that have gradually built up the private stock of subjective knowledge in his mind, a stock that influences his plans and actions vis-à-vis his fellowmen; the theory proceeded to the problem of inter-subjectivity, communication, and interaction between two individuals with a good deal of shared experiences and, hence, private stocks of subjective knowledge relevant to their common interests and their potential as well as actual dealings with each other; the theory extended the analysis to more anonymous types of actors who share a general social environment, though not necessarily the immediate surrounding, and have learned to orient their individual actions in accordance with their private stocks of subjective, but inter-subjectively valid and partly objectivated knowledge of other minds and other people in the social world in which they live; the theory concluded with the fully objectivated knowledge of a society, a social stock of knowledge which in some sense is the result of a socialization of knowledge and contains at the same time more *and* less than the sum of the private stocks of subjective knowledge: for, if I may quote from the best source, 'the social stock of knowledge contains not only "more" than the subjective, but also "more" than the sum of them', but also ' "less" than any particular subjective stock of knowledge', which 'contains elements which refer back to the biographical "uniqueness" of subjective experiences, and elements which evade an objectivation in language'[7].

This most ingenious phenomenological theory of the stock of knowledge in society is not equipped to deal with the problem that we have raised: the problem of assessing the size of the stock and its growth. As we have decided to focus on the stock of knowledge in the minds of the people, the problems of measuring its size or its growth become forbidding. Of course, there have been attempts to assess the extent of school learning. Several school systems annually rate the cognitive achievements of pupils and students at all levels; and a national assessment of our schools has tried to ascertain how much students at various ages have succeeded in learning in some of the basic subjects taught at school. In the United States, College

STOCKS AND FLOWS OF KNOWLEDGE

Entrance Examinations have been testing the achievements of high-school graduates, and Graduate Record Examinations have tested the verbal and numerical aptitudes of college graduates and their mastery of particular subjects. In all these cases, not the complete stock of knowledge in the heads of the examined students is measured, but only the degree to which they have mastered particular batches of knowledge in well-circumscribed areas.

If we are interested not only in how well certain things are known to a certain group of persons in school, but also in the scope of their knowledge, we are confronted with again another problem. There arises the question how the social stock of knowledge is related to the private stock of knowledge in the mind of each individual in society. Should we claim 'additivity' of the individuals' stocks of knowledge? Should we for each bit or bite of knowledge find out the number, or the percentage, of the people who know it?

In any case, the conception of 'growth' becomes highly complex if we want to apply it to the stock of knowledge in society. This stock is increased if more people come to know – to absorb and retain – a given quantum of knowable things, but also if a given number of persons come to know more. The same thing may be known to more people or more things to the same people. But what weights should be assigned to different accretions of knowledge? If knowledge of the multiplication table is successfully transmitted to an additional five million people, does this represent more or less growth in the stock of knowledge in society than if knowledge of gene-splicing and recombinant *DNA* is transferred to an additional five hundred people? We may want both, but choices are often necessary, and indeed are being made, between more new knowledge in the heads of a few and old knowledge in more heads.

Such choices are made even if the stock of knowledge in society cannot be measured and its growth cannot be quantified. The weights that are assigned to various kinds of growth, or rather the priorities that are assigned to alternative directions and advancements of knowledge in society, are probably not very consistent. The decisions are either compromises between different preferences of different political factions, or majority votes of the legislatures or other collective bodies in charge of such decisions. We have seen that the appropriation of public funds for space explorations – generating knowledge accessible to very few – have successfully competed with appropriations for remedial education of retarded, neglected or unwilling learners, but the latter, in turn, have outranked the funding of enriched or accelerated education of especially gifted youth. Political decision-making does not and cannot wait for solutions of unsolved problems of measuring the probable consequences of these decisions. Thus we must content ourselves with raising questions and pondering the difficulties of finding good answers.

IV. Estimating the flow of knowledge

One should think that the problems of quantifying the flow of knowledge are just as difficult as those connected with the stock of knowledge in society. Indeed, in some economic applications – to wit, in the case of some nonperishable good – flows are measured by changes in stocks. This is not so in the case of flows of knowledge. Flows of knowledge are different, in a very special and important sense, from flows of material goods. A flow of goods from one person to another reduces the stocks of the former and increases the stocks of the latter. By contrast, a flow of knowledge may increase the recipient's stock of knowledge without reducing the stock of the transmitter. This implies that every flow of knowledge may bring about an increase in the combined stock of knowledge.

I have said 'may', because it is not necessarily so. While the flow never reduces the stocks of knowledge possessed by the transmitters, it does not always increase the recipients' stocks. First, a recipient may not fully comprehend. Secondly, he may be unable to retain what was supposedly disseminated[8]. Thirdly, knowledge may be perishable, ephemeral: that is, it may quickly lose relevance for the recipient. The third reason will not often apply to scientific and scholarly knowledge, but it often applies to information of a mundane type, especially pastime knowledge, but also practical knowledge needed for actions today, not tomorrow or any time later. Many information services, highly valued and paid for, are not designed to increase the stock of knowledge for any length of time, or, if they do increase it, the increment may be subject to rapid obsolescence.

While the preceding statements were made with reference to flows from person to person, they could be reformulated for transfers of knowledge from persons to records and from records to persons. The only difficulty would be that some of the formulation might imply additivity of knowledge in man-made records and knowledge in human minds, which would compound the problems of quantification and estimation. This can be avoided by assuming that all newly recorded knowledge is actually read (listened to, decoded) and absorbed by at least one mind. Those scientometricians who are resolved to measure the flow of knowledge in terms of physical units have chosen the alternative of concentrating on recorded knowledge.

Not in all areas of knowledge transmission will it be possible to count physical units, but such counts are feasible in publishing, library operation, broadcasting, motion pictures, performing arts, telephone service, to mention some examples. The physical units are not comparable, however, either among the different branches of knowledge production or even within any one branch. We need only note the difference in volumes, titles and copies of books; in the numbers of journals, issues, subscriptions, articles, pages, and words printed; in library materials acquired and circulated; in hours of broadcasting, the number of receiving sets, and the size of the audience;

STOCKS AND FLOWS OF KNOWLEDGE

in the numbers of motion-picture films produced or presented, the footage of film shown, the cinemas, the audience; at various levels of education the numbers of teachers employed, students enrolled, degrees granted, hours spent in classrooms; and so on. Every single one of these units, and especially their rates of growth, may be meaningful for *some* purposes, but none lends itself for a measurement or estimate of the magnitude of the annual flow of knowledge.

There is, however, one common denominator: dollars spent, or dollars collected, for any of the activities during the period; and the dollar figures can be compared with such large aggregates as the national income or the gross national product. Costs or revenues expressed in dollars permit the one measure or estimate that applies to all types of knowledge disseminated within a period[9]. It can even be broken down, though only on the basis of imaginative and arbitrary judgments, by different types of knowledge and, within intellectual knowledge, by field or subject matter. The production and distribution of knowledge in the United States is, in essence, the annual flow of knowledge disseminated at a cost (defrayed or borne by some members of our society).

V. Accumulation, replacement, current input, consumption, and waste

A set of concepts deserves a brief side-glance in connection with the dichotomy of stocks and flows of knowledge. A flow of knowledge – from person to person, by word of mouth or via some sort of record – may be regarded as accumulation, replacement, current input, consumption, or waste – but sometimes as a combination of two or more of these alternatives.

A flow of knowledge will give rise to *accumulation* if it results in a net addition to the stock of knowledge in society. It will be *replacement* to the extent that it, though a gross addition to the stock, offsets (compensates for) parts of the stock that have been forgotten, become obsolete, or were wiped out by the death of the persons in whose minds it had been stored. It will be *current input* if it serves the current production of other goods and services but is not expected to aid such production in the future. (I have elsewhere commented on knowledge as an intermediate product used in current production.) The flow will be *consumption* if it serves the current enjoyment of the recipients. It will be *waste* if it does none of the four things.

It is easy to see that combinations of the five possibilities are quite normal. If a given flow of knowledge is designed as entertainment or some other form of immediate satisfaction, but succeeds only partially – for example, because it is mixed with excessive amounts of unwanted knowledge, non-comprehended knowledge, or unpleasant noise, so that it is boring instead of amusing, or if it is produced at excessive cost, the outcome will be judged to be a combination of waste and consumption. If a given flow of

HISTORY AND PERSPECTIVES

knowledge constitutes a gross addition to the stock of knowledge in society, usually some share of that addition will be considered a replacement of knowledge lost by the various kinds of attrition (death, loss of memory, obsolescence[10]). The same flow of knowledge may be partly current input and partly accumulation for future use in production. To give an example of a triple combination, a given flow of knowledge may be regarded as yielding current consumption (immediate enjoyment by the recipients), accumulation of a stock of knowledge expected to yield future benefits, and some waste, too.

Virtually every flow of knowledge may have an admixture of waste, some of the efforts of producing knowledge proving either abortive or superfluous. Incidentally, if efforts at disseminating knowledge are abortive, the failure may be the fault of the transmitters, lacking understanding, discernment or skill, or the fault of would-be recipients, being ill-prepared, uninterested or otherwise nonreceptive. On the other hand, the admixture of waste may often be so small compared with the benefits derived from the contributions which the flow of knowledge makes to consumption and production that the effort devoted to the dissemination may still be fully worth while. Where the benefits exceed the costs by a sufficiently wide margin, one may be inclined to overlook the waste involved in the fact that the benefits *could* be higher or the cost *could* be lower.

In some particular areas of knowledge dissemination it is possible to undertake estimates of waste by some analyses of the cost-effectiveness of resources employed or by comparisons of the benefits and costs of alternative techniques. However, where questions of the actual or potential stocks of knowledge enter the argument, we had better acknowledge that attempts at quantification are not promising; the essential concepts are not statistically operational and, hence, neither accumulation nor replacement are subject to estimation, let alone measurement. To say this, however, is not to question the significance of the conceptual framework for the analysis of fundamental relationships which remain important as long as we are satisfied with understanding the social world without insisting on measuring the nonmeasurable.

Notes

1 PRICE [1975, pp. 164–165].
2 PRICE, in a letter to me, May 19, 1977.
3 PRICE [1975, p. 165].
4 For a survey of estimates see MACHLUP/LEESON *et al.* [1978, Chapter 3.1].
5 GORE [1976, p. 171].
6 SCHUTZ/LUCKMANN [1973, especially Chapter 3 on 'Knowledge of the Life-World' and Chapter 4 on 'Knowledge and Society'].
7 SCHUTZ/LUCKMANN [1973, p. 364].
8 There is the problem of subconscious retention: a message received but not consciously retained may on later occasions, as a result of an appropriate stimulus,

STOCKS AND FLOWS OF KNOWLEDGE

be retrieved or reconstructed. Should such potential recovery of knowledge lost for the time being be included in the accumulated stock?

9 BOULDING reminds us of 'the measuring rod of money' employed in the *Economics of Welfare* by Pigou. See BOULDING [1966, p. 2].

10 It was BOULDING who, in a review of the first edition of my book, raised the question of replacement of knowledge lost by death, loss of memory, and obsolescence. BOULDING [1963, p. 37]. Perhaps we should add retirement of trained people from active service as an additional factor of attrition calling for replacement.

References

BOULDING KENNETH E.: 'The Knowledge Industry', *Challenge* (1963), May.

BOULDING KENNETH E.: 'The Economics of Knowledge and the Knowledge of Economies', *American Economic Review*, Papers and Proceedings, Vol. 56 (1966), May.

GORE DANIEL: 'Farewell to Alexandria: The Theory of the No-Growth, High-Performance Library', in: D. GORE (Ed.), *Farewell to Alexandria: Solutions to Space, Growth, and Performance Problems of Libraries*, Greenwood Press, Westport, Connecticut, 1976.

MACHLUP FRITZ: *The Production and Distribution of Knowledge in the United States*, Princeton, Princeton University Press, 1962.

MACHLUP FRITZ and LEESON K. *et al.*: *Information through the Printed Word: The Dissemination of Scholary, Scientific and Intellectual Knowledge*, New York, Praeger 1978.

PRICE DEREK DE SOLLA: *Science since Babylon*, New Haven, Vale University Press, 1961. Second Enlarged Edition 1975.

SCHUTZ ALFRED and LUCKMANN THOMAS: *The Structures of the Life-World*, translated by RICHARD M. ZANER and A. TRISTRAM ENGELHARDT, Jr. Evanston, Ill., Northwestern University Press, 1973.

7

THE SOCIAL FRAMEWORK OF THE INFORMATION SOCIETY

Daniel Bell

Source: T. Forrester (ed.) (1980) *The Microelectronics Revolution*, Oxford: Blackwell, pp. 500–49.

> The endless cycle of idea and action,
> Endless invention, endless experiment,
> Brings knowledge of motion, but not of stillness. . . .
> Where is the Life we have lost in living?
> Where is the wisdom we have lost in knowledge?
> Where is the knowledge we have lost in information?
> *T. S. Eliot: Choruses from "The Rock"*

Information and telecommunications in the postindustrial society

In the coming century, the emergence of a new social framework based on telecommunications may be decisive for the way in which economic and social exchanges are conducted, the way knowledge is created and retrieved, and the character of the occupations and work in which men engage. This revolution in the organization and processing of information and knowledge, in which the computer plays a central role, has as its context the development of what I have called the postindustrial society.[1] Three dimensions of the postindustrial society are relevant to the discussion of telecommunications:

(1) The change from a goods-producing to a service society.
(2) The centrality of the codification of theoretical knowledge for innovation in technology.
(3) The creation of a new "intellectual technology" as a key tool of systems analysis and decision theory.

THE SOCIAL FRAMEWORK OF THE INFORMATION SOCIETY

The change from a goods-producing to a service society can be indicated briefly. In the United States in 1970, sixty-five out of every hundred persons in the labour force were engaged in services, about thirty per cent in the production of goods and construction, and under five per cent in agriculture. The word *services* of course covers a large multitude of activities. In preindustrial societies a sizeable proportion of the labour force is engaged in household or domestic service. (In England until the 1870s the single largest occupational class was servants.) In an industrial society services are auxiliary to the production of goods, such as transportation (rail and truck), utilities (power and light), banking, and factoring. Postindustrial services are of a different kind. They are human services and professional services. The human services are teaching, health, and the large array of social services; professional services are those of systems analysis and design and the programming and processing of information. In the last two decades, the net new growth in employment has been entirely in the area of postindustrial services, and while the rate of growth has slowed (particularly because of the financial costs of education and the cutbacks in social services in urban communities), the general trend continues.

The axial principle of the postindustrial society, however, is the centrality of theoretical knowledge and its new role, when codified, as the director of social change. Every society has functioned on the basis of knowledge but only in the last half of the century have we seen a fusion of science and engineering that has begun to transform the character of technology itself. As Cyril Stanley Smith, the distinguished metallurgist, has observed: "In only a small part of history has industry been helped by science. The development of a suitable science began when chemists put into rational order facts that had been discovered long before by people who enjoyed empirical diverse experiment."[2]

The industries that still dominate society – steel, motor, electricity, telephone, aviation – are all "nineteenth-century" industries (though steel began in the eighteenth century with the coking process of Abraham Darby, and aviation in the twentieth with the Wright Brothers) in that they were created by "talented tinkerers" who worked independently of or were ignorant of contemporary science. Alexander Graham Bell, who invented the telephone about one hundred years ago (though the actual fact is in some dispute), was an elocution teacher who was looking for some means to amplify sound in order to help the deaf. Bessemer, who created the open-hearth process (to win a prize offered by Napoleon III for a better means of casting cannon), did not know the scientific work of Henry Clifton Sorby on metallurgical processes. And Thomas Alva Edison, who was probably the most prolific and talented of these tinkerers (he invented, among other things, the electric light bulb, the phonograph, and the motion picture), was a mathematical illiterate who knew little and cared less about the theoretical equations of Clerk-Maxwell on electromagnetic properties.

Nineteenth-century inventing was trial-and-error empiricism, often guided by brilliant intuitions. But the nature of advanced technology is its intimate relations with science, where the primary interest is not in the product itself but in the diverse properties of materials together with the underlying principles of order that allow for combination, substitution or transmutation. According to Cyril Smith:

> All materials came to be seen in competition, with the emphasis only on the properties that were needed. Thereafter every new development in advanced technology – radar, nuclear reactors, jet aircraft, computers and satellite communications to name a few – has served to break the earlier close association of materials research with a single type of manufacture, and the modern materials engineer has emerged.

The nature of this change, in technology and in science, has been to enlarge the "field of relation" and the range of theory so as to permit a systematic synergism in the discovery and extension of new products and theories. A science, at bottom, is a set of axioms linked topologically to form a unified scheme. But as Bronowski has observed: "A new theory changes the system of axioms and sets up new connections at the joints which changes the topology. And when two sciences are linked to form one (electricity and magnetism, for instance, or evolution with genetics), the new network is richer in its articulation than the sum of its two parts."[3]

While modern science, like almost all human activities, has moved towards a greater degree of specialization in its pursuit of more detailed knowledge, the more important and crucial outcome of its association with technology is the integration of diverse fields or observations into single conceptual and theoretical frameworks offering much greater explanatory power. Norbert Wiener, in his autobiographical *I Am a Mathematician*, points out that his first mathematical papers were on Brownian motion and that at the same time electrical engineering work was being done on the so-called shot effects, or the movement of electric current through a wire. The two topics were unrelated; yet twenty years later the situation had changed dramatically.

> In 1920 very little electrical apparatus was loaded to the point at which the shot effect became critical. However the later development – first of broadcasting and then of radar and television – brought shot effect to the point where it became the immediate concern of every communications engineer. The shot effect was not only similar in origin to the Brownian movement, for it was a result of the discreteness of the universe, but had essentially the same mathematical theory. Thus, my work on the Brownian motion became some twenty years later a vital tool for the electrical engineer.[4]

THE SOCIAL FRAMEWORK OF THE INFORMATION SOCIETY

Wiener's theory of cybernetics joins a variety of fields in the common framework of statistical information theory. "The development of ideas on the structure of synthetic polymers," Cyril Smith writes, "eventually came to bridge the gap between the nineteenth-century chemist's molecule and the early twentieth-century crystal, so paving the way for the unified structural view of all materials which we see taking shape today."[5] The development of solid-state physics, which is the foundation of the electronic revolution, arose out of the work of metallurgists and physicists on the structure of conductor devices.

The methodological promise of the second half of the twentieth century is the management of organized complexity: the complexity of theories with a large number of variables and the complexity of large organizations and systems which involve the coordination of hundreds of thousands and even millions of persons. Since 1940 there has been a remarkable efflorescence of new fields and methods whose concern is with the problems of organized complexity: information theory, cybernetics, decision theory, game theory, utility theory, stochastic processes. From these have come specific techniques such as linear programming, statistical decision theory, Markov chain applications, Monte Carlo randomizing, and minimax strategies, which allow for sampling from large numbers, alternative optimal outcomes of different choices, or definitions of rational action under conditions of uncertainty.

Since technology is the instrumental mode of rational action, I have called this new development "intellectual technology", for these methods seek to substitute an algorithm (i.e., decisions rules) for intuitive judgements. These algorithms may be embodied in an automatic machine or a computer program, or a set of instructions based on some statistical or mathematical formula, and represent a "formalization" of judgements and their routine application to many varied situations. To the extent that intellectual technology is becoming predominant in the management of organizations and enterprises, one can say that it is as central a feature of postindustrial society as machine technology is in industrial society.

A knowledge theory of value

If one compares the formal properties of postindustrial society with those of industrial and preindustrial society (see Table 1), the crucial variables of the postindustrial society are information and knowledge.

By information I mean data processing in the broadest sense; the storage, retrieval, and processing of data become the essential resource for all economic and social exchanges. These include:

(1) Data processing of records: payrolls, government benefits (e.g. social security), bank clearances, credit clearances, and the like. Data processing

Table 1 The postindustrial society: a comparative schema.

Mode of production	Preindustrial extractive	Industrial – Fabrication	Postindustrial – Processing; Recycling	
Economic sector	*Primary*	*Secondary*	Services	
	Agriculture	Goods-producing	*Tertiary*	*Quaternary*
	Mining	Manufacturing	Transportation	Trade
	Fishing	Durables	Utilities	Finance
	Timber	Nondurables		Insurance
	Oil and gas	Heavy construction	*Quinary*	Real estate
			Health, Education	
			Research, Government,	
			Recreation	
Transforming resource	*Natural power*	*Created energy*	*Information*	
	Wind, water, draft animal, human muscle	Electricity – oil, gas, coal, nuclear power	Computer and data-transmission systems	
Strategic resource	Raw materials	Financial capital	Knowledge	
Technology	Craft	Machine technology	Intellectual technology	
Skill base	Artisan, manual worker, farmer	Engineer, semiskilled worker	Scientist, technical and professional occupations	
Methodology	Common sense, trial and error; experience	Empiricism, experimentation	Abstract theory, models, simulations, decision theory, systems analysis	
Time perspective	Orientation to the past	Ad hoc adaptiveness, experimentation	Future orientation: forecasting and planning	
Design	Game against nature	Game against fabricated future	Game between persons	
Axial principle	Traditionalism	Economic growth	Codification of theoretical knowledge	

for scheduling: airline reservations, production scheduling, inventory analysis, product-mix information, and the like.

(3) Data-bases: characteristics of populations as shown by census data, market research, opinion surveys, election data, and the like.

By knowledge, I mean an organized set of statements of fact or ideas, presenting a reasoned judgement or an experimental result, which is transmitted to others through some communication medium in some systematic form. Thus, I distinguished knowledge from news or entertainment. Knowledge consists of new judgements (research and scholarship) or presentations of older judgements (textbooks, teaching, and library and archive materials).

In the "production of knowledge", what is produced is an intellectual property, attached to a name or a group of names and certified by copyright or some other form of social recognition (like publication). This knowledge is paid for – in the time spent in writing and research, in the monetary compensation by the communications and educational media. The response of the market, along with administrative and political decisions of superiors or peers, judge the worth of the result and any further claim on social resources that might be made in its behalf. In this sense, knowledge is part of social overhead. More than that, when knowledge becomes involved in some systematic form in the applied transformation of resources (through invention or social design), then one can say that knowledge, not labour, is the source of value.

Economists in their formal schemes to explain production and exchange, use as key variables "land, labour and capital", though institutionally-minded economists such as Werner Sombart and Joseph Schumpeter added the notion of an acquisitive spirit or entrepreneurial initiative. The analytical mode used by economists, the "production function", sets forth the economic mix only as capital and labour – a system that lends itself easily to a labour theory of value, with surplus labour value as congealed capital, but neglects almost entirely the role of knowledge or of organizational innovation and management. Yet with the shortening of labour time and the diminution of the production worker (who in Marxist theory is the source of value, since most services are classified as nonproductive labour), it becomes clear that knowledge and its applications replace labour as the source of "added value" in the national product. In that sense, just as capital and labour have been the central variables of industrial society, so information and knowledge are the crucial variables of postindustrial society.

Intellectual foundations of the revolution in communications

For Goethe, the basis of the human community was communication. Decades before other persons spoke of such projects, he envisaged a Panama Canal, a Suez Canal, and a canal between the Rhine and the Danube as the means by which the human community might become more closely intertwined. But it was the Canadian economic historian Harold Innis, more than any other person, who saw changes in the modes of communication, rather than production and property relations, as the key to transitions from one stage of society to another.

> Western civilization has been profoundly influenced by communication ... [and can be] divided into the following periods in relation to media of communication: clay, the stylus and cuneiform script from the beginnings of civilization in Mesopotamia; papyrus, the brush and hieroglyphics and hieratic to the Graeco-Roman period, and the reed pen and the alphabet to the retreat of the Empire from the west; parchment and pen to the tenth century of the dark ages; and overlapping with paper, the latter becoming more important with the invention of printing; paper and the brush in China, and paper and the pen in Europe before the invention of printing or the Renaissance; paper and the printing press under handicraft methods to the beginning of the nineteenth century, or from the Reformation to the French Revolution; paper produced by machinery and the application of power to the printing press since the beginning of the nineteenth century to paper manufactured from wood in the second half of the century; celluloid in the growth of the cinema; and finally the radio in the second quarter of the present century. In each period I have attempted to trace the implications of the media of communication for the character of knowledge and to suggest that a monopoly or an oligopoly of knowledge is built up to the point that equilibrium is disturbed.[6]

Innis was a technological determinist. He thought that the technology of communication was basic to all other technology, for if tool technology was an extension of man's physical powers, communication technology, as the extension of perception and knowledge, was the enlargement of consciousness. He argued not only that each stage of Western civilization was dominated by a particular medium of communication but that the rise of a new mode was invariably followed by cultural disturbances.[7]

One can say that the new media of communication today are television or the computer, or the variant modes of storage, retrieval and transmission that will arise through the "fusing" of technologies. But the core of the present communications revolution is not a specific technology but the set of concepts represented by the term *information theory*.

The statistics of language

Information theory arose from the work of Claude Shannon on switching circuits to increase "channel capacity", the design for which he derived from

THE SOCIAL FRAMEWORK OF THE INFORMATION SOCIETY

the algebra of logic. The algebra of logic is an algebra of choice and deals with the range of choices in a determinate sequence of alternative possibilities in the routing of a message. The parlour game of "Twenty Questions" is often taken as a conventional illustration of how one narrows a range of possibilities by asking a series of yes or no questions. As Shannon points out in the article on information theory that he wrote for the *Encyclopaedia Britannica*: "The writing of English sentences can be thought of as a process of choice: choosing a first word from possible first words with various probabilities; then a second with probabilities depending on the first; etc. This kind of statistical process is called a stochastic process, and information sources are thought of, in information theory, as stochastic processes."

The information rate of written English can be translated into bits (*binary digits* 1 and 0), so that if each letter occurred with equal frequency, there would be 4.76 bits per letter. But since the frequencies are unequal (*E* is common, *Z*, *Q*, and *X* are not), the actual rate is one bit per letter. Technically, English is said to be eighty per cent "redundant", a fact that one can immediately ascertain by "deciphering" a sentence from which various vowels or consonants have been deleted. By knowing the statistical structure of a language, one can derive a general formula that determines the rate at which information can be produced statistically and create huge savings in transmission time. But though transmission was the impetus to the formulation of information theory, the heart of the concept is the idea of coding. Messages have to go through "channels"; inevitably, they are distorted by "noise" and other forms of "resistance" that arise from the physical properties of the channel. What Shannon found was that it is possible to encode a message that can be accurately transmitted even if the channel of communication is faulty, so long as there is enough capacity in that channel.

Shannon's mathematical theory had immediate application to industry. The theoretical and statistical underpinnings seemed to confirm the more general theory of Wiener's *Cybernetics*, a work that had been commissioned by an obscure publisher in France after the war and became an immediate bestseller on its publication by Wiley in 1948. What Shannon's and Wiener's work seemed to promise was the move toward some general unified theory of physics and human behaviour (at least in physiology, psychology and linguistics) through the concept of information. As Shannon himself wrote in his *Britannica* essay:

> A basic idea in communication theory is that information can be treated very much like a physical quantity such as mass or energy. . . . The formula for the amount of information is identical in form with equations representing entropy in statistical mechanics, and suggests that there may be deep-lying connections between thermodynamics and information theory. Some scientists believe that a proper statement of the second law of thermodynamics requires

a term relating to information. These connections with physics, however, do not have to be considered in the engineering and other applications of information theory.[8]

But this is a confusion of realms – compounded by the facile use of the word *entropy* to equate the degree of disorder or noise (i.e., the loss of accuracy) in communication with the loss of heat or energy in transformational activities in physics. As Wiener put it in his *Cybernetics*, resisting the easy comparisons of living with mechanical organisms: "Information is information, not matter or energy. No materialism which does not admit this can survive at the present day."[9]

However true it may be as a statistical concept that information is a quantity, in its broadest sense – to distinguish between information and fabrication – information is a pattern or design that rearranges data for instrumental purposes, while knowledge is the set of reasoned judgements that evaluates the adequacy of the pattern for the purposes for which the information is designed. Information is thus pattern recognition, subject to reorganization by the knower, in accordance with specified purposes. What is common to this and to all intellectual enterprises is the concept of relevant structure. This concept is what underlies the shift, in the works of Cyril Stanley Smith, from "matter to materials", from the classificatory and even combinational arrangements of elementary properties of matter that began with the pre-Socratics to our present-day understanding of the structural relations of the properties of materials.

These structural relations – in science, as in the economy – fall into two separate domains. The first is the transformation of matter and energy, from one material form into another. The second is the transformation of information from one pattern into another. As Anthony Oettinger puts it in an aphorism: "Without matter there is nothing; without energy matter is inert; and without information, matter and energy are disorganized, hence useless."

The use of models

Technological revolutions, even if intellectual in their foundations, become symbolized if not embodied in some tangible "thing", and in the postindustrial society that "thing" is the computer. If, as Paul Valéry said, electricity was the agent that transformed the second half of the nineteenth century, in a similar vein the computer has been the "analytical engine" that has transformed the second half of the twentieth century. What electricity did – as the source of light, power and communication – was to create "mass society"; that is, to extend the range of social ties and the interaction between persons and so magnify what Durkheim called the social density of society. In that respect, the computer is a tool for managing the mass society, since it is the mechanism that orders and processes the transactions whose huge number has been mounting almost exponentially because of the increase in social interactions.

The major sociopolitical question facing the mass society is whether we can manage the economy effectively enough to achieve our social goals. The development of computers has allowed us to construct detailed models of the economy. Wassily Leontieff recently described the extraordinary expansion of the input-output system:

> The first input-output tables describing the flow of goods and services between the different sectors of the American economy in census years 1919 through 1929 were published in 1936. They were based on a rather gross segregation of all economic activities in 44 sectors. Because of the lack of computing facilities, these had to be further grouped into only 10 sectors, for the purposes of actual analytic calculations.
>
> The data base, the computing facilities, and the analytical techniques have advanced much further than could have been anticipated forty years ago. National input-output tables containing up to 700 distinct sectors are being compiled on a current basis, as are tables for individual, regional, state and metropolitan areas. Private enterprise has now entered the input-output business. For a fee one can now purchase a single row of a table showing the deliveries of a particular product, say, coated laminated fabrics or farming machine tools, not only to different industries but to individual plants within each industry segregated by zip code areas.[10]

Though it is clear that economists are able to model the economy and do computer simulations of alternative policies to test their consequences, it is much less clear whether such models allow us to manage the economy. The critical point is that the crucial decisions for any society are the political ones, and these are not derivative from economic factors.

Can one model a society? One immediate problem is that we do not have any persuasive theories of how a society hangs together, though paradoxically, because of our understanding of technology, we have a better idea of how societies change. One can only model a closed or finite system; the econometric models operate within a closed system. Yet society is increasingly open and indeterminate, and as men become more conscious of goals there is greater debate about decisions. Decisions on social policy become more and more a matter within the purview of the political system rather than of aggregate market decisions, and this, too, weakens our ability to model a society.

Beyond this there may be reasons intrinsic to the structure of "large numbers" that could prevent the computer from becoming the instrument

HISTORY AND PERSPECTIVES

for the modelling and prediction of any complex system. John von Neumann, one of the pioneers in the development of the theory of electronic computing, thought that the prediction of weather would be possible once computers became sophisticated enough to handle all the numerous interacting variables in the atmosphere. Yet as Tjalling Koopmans and others have pointed out, beyond a certain threshold introducing added complexity results in answers that are less and less reliable. Thus, the effort to optimize an objective by seeking for complete information may be self-defeating. The social world is not a Laplacean universe where one can plot, from the initial values, the determinate rates of change of other phenomena. If so many parts of the physical world now require us to deal with a calculus of possibility rather than determined regularities, this is even more true in a social world where men are less and less willing passively to accept existing arrangements but instead work actively to remake them. By letting us know the risks and probabilities, the computer has become a powerful tool for exploring the permutations and combinations of different choices for calculating their consequences, the odds of success or failure. The computer does this by using a binary code that with the speed of light can answer a question with a yes or a no. What it cannot do, obviously, is to decide like a roulette wheel whether to stop on the yes or on the no.

The economics of information

Information is central to all economic transactions – indeed, perfect information is the indispensable condition for perfect competition in general equilibrium theory. Yet we have no economic theory of information, and the character of information, as distinct from the character of goods, poses some novel problems for economic theorists.

In a price and market economy, the condition for efficiency, or optimal use of resources, is complete information among buyers and sellers, so that one can obtain the "best" price for one's goods or services. But with the widening of markets and the reduction of distances by transportation and communication – which also enlarges the sphere of competition – efficiency increasingly demands not only a knowledge of contemporary alternatives but of the likely future ones as well, since political decisions or new technologies may radically alter prices. A political embargo may cut off the supplies of a resource. A tax cut or a tax rise will affect the level of spending. New technologies may sharply cut the price of a product (witness the extraordinary changes in two years in the price of small electronic calculators), leaving firms with large inventories or committed to older production techniques at a great disadvantage.

Information, as Kenneth Arrow puts it, reduces uncertainty.[11] The random-walk theory that one cannot "beat the stock market" is based on the assumption that stock prices reflect new information about companies

THE SOCIAL FRAMEWORK OF THE INFORMATION SOCIETY

so quickly that investors have little chance to earn better-than-average returns on their money. Therefore the wiser strategy is to place one's money in an index fund that reflects the average prices of the market as a whole. The job search in the labour market is enhanced by access to a wider pool of information. Accurate crop reporting controls the vagaries of the futures market in commodities. One can multiply the illustrations indefinitely.

But information is not a commodity, at least not in the way the term is used in neoclassical economics or understood in industrial society. Industrial commodities are produced in discrete, identifiable units, exchanged and sold, consumed and used up, like a loaf of bread or an automobile. One buys the product from a seller and takes physical possession of it; the exchange is governed by legal rules of contract. In the manufacture of industrial goods, one can set up a "production function" (i.e., the relative proportions of capital and labour to be employed) and determine the appropriate mix relative to the costs of each factor.

Information, or knowledge, even when it is sold, remains with the producer. It is a "collective good" in that once it has been created, it is by its nature available to all.[12] In fact, the character of science itself, as a cooperative venture of knowledge, depends on the open and complete transmission of all new experiments and discoveries to others in the field. Multiple discoveries of the same theory or experimental result or technique, which Robert Merton argues is a more dominant pattern in science than the image of the lonely genius or scholar, are one result of this openness and the rapid spread of knowledge.[13]

If knowledge is a collective good there is little incentive for any individual enterprise to pay for the search for such knowledge, unless it can obtain a proprietary advantage, such as a patent or a copyright. But increasingly, patents no longer guarantee exclusiveness, and many firms lose out in spending money on research only to find that a competitor (particularly one overseas) can quickly modify the product and circumvent the patent; similarly, the question of copyright becomes increasingly difficult to police when individuals or libraries can Xerox whatever pages they need from technical journals or books or when individuals and schools can tape music off the air or record a television performance on video discs. But more generally, the results of investing in information (i.e., doing research), are themselves uncertain. Because firms are averse to risk, they tend to undervalue such investments from the social point of view, and this leads to underinvestment in private research and development.

If there is less and less incentive for individual persons or private enterprises to produce knowledge without particular gain, then the need and effort fall increasingly on some social unit, be it university or government, to underwrite the costs. And since there is no ready market test (how does one estimate the value of basic research?), it is a challenge for economic theory to design a socially optimal policy of investment in knowledge (including how much money should be spent for basic research; what allocations should be made for education, and for what fields; in what areas of health do we obtain the "better returns"; and so on) and to determine how to "price" information and knowledge to users.[14]

The merging of technologies

Through the nineteenth and up to the mid-twentieth century, communication could be divided roughly into two distinct realms. One was mail, newspapers, magazines and books, printed on paper and delivered by physical transport or stored in libraries. The other was telegraph, telephone, radio and television, coded message image or voice sent by radio signals or through cables from person to person. Technology, which once made for separate industries, is now erasing these distinctions, so that a variety of new alternatives are now available to information users, posing, for that very reason, a major set of policy decisions for the lawmakers of the country.

Inevitably, large vested interests are involved. Just as the substitution of oil for coal and energy and the competition of truck, pipeline, and railroad in transportation created vast dislocations in corporate power, occupational structures, trade unions, geographical concentrations and the like, so the huge changes taking place in communications technology will affect the major industries that are involved in the communications arena.

Broadly, there are five major problem areas:

(1) The meshing of the telephone and computer systems, of telecommunications and teleprocessing, into a single mode. A corollary problem is whether transmission will be primarily over telephone-controlled wires or whether there will be independent data-transmission systems. Equally, there is the question of the relative use of microwave relay, satellite transmission and coaxial cables as transmission systems.
(2) The substitution of electronic media for paper processing. This includes electronic banking to eliminate the use of cheques; the electronic delivery of mail; the delivery of newspapers or magazines by facsimile rather than by physical transport; and the long-distance copying of documents.
(3) The expansion of television through cable systems, to allow for multiple channels and specialized services, and the linkage to home terminals for direct response to the consumer or home from local or central stations. A corollary is the substitution of telecommunication for transportation through videophone, closed-circuit television and the like.
(4) The reorganization of information storage and retrieval systems based on the computer to allow for interactive network communication in team research and direct retrieval from data banks to library or home terminals.

(5) The expansion of the education system through computer-aided instruction, the use of satellite communications systems in rural areas, especially in the underdeveloped countries, and the use of video discs both for entertainment and instruction in the home.[15]

Technologically, telecommunications and teleprocessing are merging in a mode that Anthony Oettinger has called "compunications" (see Fig. 1). As computers come increasingly to be used as switching devices in communications networks and electronic communications facilities become intrinsic elements in computer data processing services, the distinction between processing and communication becomes indistinguishable. The major questions are legal and economic. Should the industry be regulated or competitive? Should it be dominated, in effect, by AT&T or by IBM?[16]

The entry of specialized carriers into the business field, undercutting AT&T prices, threatens its consumer rate structure as well, and would create large political unheavals. Yet the "computer" proponents have argued that technological innovation in the telephone field has been stodgy, whereas the energetic and bustling computer field has demonstrated its ability to

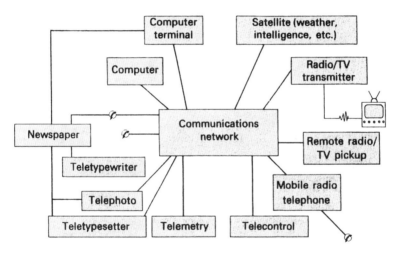

Figure 1 The changing telecommunications network. As of 1974, the 144 million plain old telephones still predominated, but many other devices are now attached to a network that has become an infrastructure basic to most social functions, including many that reach directly into the home. As computers and computer terminals have become increasingly pervasive over the last two decades, the network has developed towards an integrated computer communications or "compunications" network. From Paul J. Berman and Anthony G. Oettinger, *The Medium and the Telephone: The Politics of Information Resources*, Working Paper 75-8, 15 December 1975, Harvard Program on Information Technologies and Public Policy, Cambridge, Mass.

innovate rapidly and reduce costs and prices, so that competition in transmission, in the end, would serve the country as a whole.

The questions I have been raising about the fusion of communications technologies – the rise of compunications – are not only technological and economic but, most important, political. Information is power. Control over communications services is a source of power. Access to communication is a condition of freedom. There are legal questions that derive directly from this. The electronic media, such as television, are regulated, with explicit rules about "fairness" in the presentation of views, access to reply to editorials, and the like. But ultimately the power is governmental. Decisions about the station's future lie with the Federal Communications Commission. The telephone industry is regulated on its rates and conditions of service. The computer industry is unregulated and operates in an open market. The print media are unregulated, and their rights on free speech are zealously guarded by the First Amendment and the courts. Libraries have largely been private or locally controlled; now great data banks are being assembled by government agencies and by private corporations. Are they to be under government supervision or unregulated? All of these are major questions for the future of the free society and bear on the problem of a national information policy.

The quantitative dimensions of the information society

In 1940, Colin Clark, the Australian economist, wrote his path-breaking *Conditions of Economic Progress*, in which he divided economic activity into three sectors, primary (principally extractive), secondary (primarily manufacturing), and tertiary (services). Any economy is a mixture of all three sectors, but their relative weights are a function of the degree of productivity (output per capita) in each sector. Economic progress is defined as the rate of transfer of labour from one sector to another, as a function of differential productivity. As national incomes rise, the expansion of the manufacturing sector is followed by a greater demand for services and a further corresponding shift in the slope of employment. In this fashion, Clark was able to chart the rate of change from a preindustrial into an industrial society and then into a service society.

The difficulty remains the definition of services. In classical economics, beginning with Adam Smith, services were thought of as unproductive labour. Marx, accepting that distinction, had based one of his theories on the crisis of capitalism, that of the falling rate of profit, on the proposition that as a higher proportion of output shifted from "variable capital" (productive labour) to "constant capital" (machinery, for example), the rate of profit would fall since the base on which surplus value was produced would be shrinking (unless overcome by more intensive exploitation, such as lengthening the working day or speeding up the pace of work). As the notion that services were unproductive became increasingly dubious, economists were faced with a double problem of redefinition: first, determining which services were unproductive (e.g., domestic servants) and which were productive (e.g., education, by increasing the skill of labour, or medicine, by making persons healthier or prolonging working life); second, developing a more adequate set of distinctions within the services category. Some writers sought to restrict the tertiary sector to auxiliary blue-collar work, such as transportation, utilities, repair (e.g., motor mechanics), and personal services (laundry, barbers, and so on), and to define a *quaternary* sector made up essentially of the white-collar industries, such as banking, insurance and real estate, and a *quinary* sector, made up of knowledge activities like scientific and technical research, education and medicine. While such distinctions are useful for indicating the complexity of occupational distributions, with them one loses the thrust implicit in the original Colin Clark scheme, with its emphasis on differential productivity as the mechanism for the transition from one type of society to another.

Without pretending to be exhaustive, I have adopted a scheme for the postindustrial society of classifying economic sectors as extractive, fabrication and information activities. The underlying sociological rationale is that it seeks to look at the character of work as a shaper of the character of individuals. The scheme is based on the distinction that some societies are primarily engaged in games against nature, others in games against fabricated nature (things), and others in games between persons. It also derives from the propositions I have put forward regarding the centrality of knowledge in the postindustrial society, the primacy of a knowledge theory of value as against a labour theory of value, and the growth of information processing within the traditional sectors, such as agriculture, manufacture and services, which is beginning to transform the character of those sectors as well.

The measurement of knowledge

In 1958, Fritz Machlup, then at Princeton University, made the first efforts to measure the production and distribution of knowledge. The definition of knowledge was somewhat unsatisfactory, for Machlup rejected "an objective interpretation according to *what* is known", as against a subjective interpretation derived from what a knower designates as being known.[17] And Machlup worked from the standard national accounts, although in important details he varied from standard usages.[18]

Still, Machlup's painstaking work was crucial. In his accounting scheme, he grouped thirty industries into five major classes of knowledge production, processing, and distribution: (1) education, (2) research and development, (3) media of communication, (4) information machines, and (5) information services. The categories were broad. Education, for example, included education in the home, job and church as well as in school. Communications media included all commercial printing, stationery and office supplies. Information machines included musical instruments, signalling devices, and typewriters. Information services included money spent for securities brokers, real-estate agents and the like.

Machlup estimated that $136,436m was spent for knowledge, or twenty-nine per cent of gross national product (GNP),[19] and that thirty-one per cent of the labour force was engaged in that sector. Of equal importance, he estimated that between 1947 and 1958, the knowledge industries expanded at a compound growth rate of 10.6 per cent a year, which was double that of the GNP itself during the same period. In 1963, Gilbert Burck, an editor of *Fortune*, replicated Machlup's estimates and calculated that in that year knowledge produced a value added of $159 billion, or thirty-three per cent of the GNP.[20] Five years later, Professor Jacob Marschak, one of the most eminent economists in the United States, in computations made in 1968, said that the knowledge industries would approach forty per cent of the GNP in the 1970s.[21]

The last decade has in fact seen enormous growth in the "information economy", which includes various fields. In education, while the rate of growth of college education has slowed down, there has been a continuing increase in adult education, which in fact has maintained its rise. In health, the expansion of health services continues, particularly with the multiplication of federal legislation. Information and data processing continue to rise, particularly as the volume of transactions and record keeping increases. Telecommunications finds its major area of growth in international communications, particularly with the launching of new satellites. Television is on the threshold of a number of major changes with the growth of both cable television and video discs.

Still, if one wanted to measure the actual economic magnitudes of the information economy, the difficulty is that there is no comprehensive conceptual scheme that can divide the sector logically into neatly distinct units, making it possible to measure the trends in each unit over time. A logical set of categories might consist of the following: knowledge (which would include situses – locations or social positions – such as education, research and development, libraries and occupations that apply knowledge, such as lawyers, doctors and accountants); entertainment (which would include motion pictures, television, the music industry); economic transactions and records (banking, insurance, brokerage); and infrastructure services (telecommunications, computers and programs, and so on).

Two somewhat different approaches have been adopted. Anthony Oettinger and his colleagues have taken the "information industries" from the Standard Industrial Classification used by the US Census and listed their gross revenues in order to provide some crude baselines to measure changes. The difficulty here is that merging technologies and double counting defeat such efforts. The second approach, a more difficult and pioneering effort, is that of Marc Porat, which is to use the National Income Accounts to define a primary sector, the direct sale of information services (like education, banking, advertising) to consumers, and then to define a secondary sector – the planning, programming and information activities of private and public bureaucracies in enterprises and government – and impute the value added by such activities to the national product and national income.

The information economy

Marc Porat has broken down the National Income Accounts for 1967 in order to see what portions may be attributable, directly and indirectly, to information activities. In doing this, he has used three measures to compute gross national product. One is "final demand" (which eliminates the intermediate transactions that would add up to double counting), the second is "value added", which is the actual value added by a specific industry or component of an industry to the product, and the third is the income or compensation received by those who create these goods and services. Theoretically, the totals of all three figures should be equal; in fact, for statistical reasons, in part owing to different methods of collection, the figures do not always dovetail exactly. But the virtue of using all three is that one can make different analytical distinctions. For my purposes, the most important measure is that of value added, for with it one can seek to determine the actual services provided by information activities and then check these figures against the income or compensations received by those engaged in providing the services.

Porat's work is the first empirical demonstration of the scope of information activities since Machlup, but it goes far beyond Machlup's work, not only because it uses finer categories and makes three different kinds of estimations, but also because it seeks to establish an input-output matrix that would permit, once the accounts were complete, an estimation of the impact on other parts of the economy of a change, say, from a "paper economy" to an "electronic transmission" economy or from books to video discs as modes of instruction, along with hundreds of similar questions. Here, however, I am interested primarily in Porat's findings on the value of information activities in the economy.[22]

Porat sets up a six-sector economy. There is a primary information sector which includes all industries that produce information machines or market information services as a commodity. (This includes the private sector, which contributes about ninety per cent of the primary information products and services, and the government, which accounts for the remaining ten per cent.) There is a secondary information sector with two segments, the public bureaucracy and those private bureaucracies whose activities are not directly counted in the national accounts as information services – such as the planning, programming, scheduling and marketing of goods or services – yet who are actually engaged in information and knowledge work. The value of these activities has to be imputed (for example, by factoring out the income or compensation of those persons within a manufacturing firm who are engaged in such work). The three remaining sectors consist of the private productive sector, producing goods; the public productive sectors (building roads, dams, and so on); and the household sector.

The primary information sector is the one that is most easily measurable, since it sells its products in a market. It includes industries and activities as diverse as computer manufacturing and services, telecommunications, printing, media, advertising, accounting and education; it is the productive locus of an information-based economy.[23] In 1967, sales of information goods and services in the primary information sector to the four major sectors of final demand amounted to $174.6 billion, or 21.9 per cent of GNP. In other words, seventeen cents of every consumer dollar represented direct purchase of information goods and services. If one looks at the income side, in 1967 nearly twenty-seven per cent of all income originated with information goods and services. The civilian government was the most information-intensive – almost forty-three per cent of all federal, state and local wages were paid to federal primary information-creating personnel such as Postal Service workers or education workers.

Strikingly, as Porat points out, over forty-three per cent of all corporate profits originated with the primary information industries. All corporations in the United States earned some $79.3 billion in profits in 1967; the primary information industries earned $33.7 billion. After removing the government's share of the primary information sector's national income ($37.2 billion), the information industries alone accounted for twenty-one per cent of national income but forty-two per cent of corporate profits. Each dollar of employee compensation generated thirty-four cents in profits, as against a ratio in the overall economy of twenty-one cents – a difference that Porat attributes to the large profits earned by the telephone and banking industries with their high profit-to-labour ratios. Calculating value added, about twenty-five per cent of total GNP originated in the primary information industries. In all, over $200 billion of the total GNP of $795.4 billion originated in information goods and services.

The most interesting and novel aspect of Porat's work is the definition and measurement of the secondary information sector, a sector that Porat derives from Galbraith's notion of the "technostructure". This is the section of an industry that is directly engaged in information work but whose activities are not measured as such, for while the goods produced may be sold in the market (and thus are reflected in the GNP as manufactured goods like automobiles or transportation activities like airline flights), the information components in those enterprises – the planning, scheduling, and marketing

THE SOCIAL FRAMEWORK OF THE INFORMATION SOCIETY

activities in automobiles; the computerized reservation processes in airline flights – are not counted directly in the GNP.

The secondary information sector expands for several reasons. One is the inherent tendency for bureaucracies to grow, which while true is a quite simple-minded explanation since there are always constraints of costs. A second, more serious reason is the multiplication of technical activities that comes with size, complexity and advanced technology – such as research, planning, quality control, marketing, and the like. And third is the fact that firms integrate or coordinate to economize on information costs. Thus a group of independent, high-quality hotels in different cities recently banded together to create a common reservation service as a means of competing with the large hotel chains by saving on communications costs. In fact, as Porat points out, there are quasi-industries hidden within the secondary sector that under some circumstances could become independent, primary (i.e., directly measurable) industries. One is the hypothetical "reservations industry". This "industry" sells its services to airlines, trains, hotels, theatre box offices and automobile rental companies through computerized data networks. In actual fact, each of the industries or firms maintains its own reservations systems, so the information costs are counted within the product cost. Yet if a single company created an efficient reservations network that it could sell to all these industries to replace the in-house services they maintain themselves, then these information activities would be measured in the "final demand" of GNP.

Other than these quasi-information industries, the bulk of the secondary information sector consists of planning and financial control, the administrative superstructure that organizes and manages the activities of firms or government agencies – in short, the private and public bureaucracies. In 1967, according to Porat, twenty-one per cent of GNP originated in the secondary information sector – 18.8 per cent in the private bureaucracies and 2.4 per cent in the public bureaucracies. Of the $168.1 billion in value added, some eighty-three per cent ($139.4 billion) originated in compensation to information workers, some 3.5 per cent ($5.8 billion) represented depreciation charges on information machines, and the balance was earned by proprietors performing information tasks. In sum, nearly fifty per cent of GNP, and more than fifty per cent of wages and salaries, derive from the production, processing and distribution of information goods and services. It is in that sense that we have become an information economy.

The growth of the secondary sector is, of course, the growth of the bureaucratic society. In 1929, some thirteen per cent of the national income originated in the secondary sector, but by 1933 it had fallen to nine per cent. During the depression, the secondary sector shrank from seventy-two per cent of the size of the primary information sector to forty per cent. But it is in the war and postwar years, with the expansion of government and the growth of corporate size, that the secondary information sector begins to swell, so that by 1974, about twenty-five per cent of the national income could be attributed to the secondary information sector and about twenty-nine per cent of the national income to the primary sector.

The final necessary component is the change in the composition of the workforce itself over time. From 1860 to about 1906, the largest single group in the workforce was in agriculture. In the next period, until about 1954, the predominant group was industrial. Currently, the predominant group consists of information workers. By 1975, the information workers had surpassed the noninformation group as a whole. On the basis of income received, the crossover came earlier, since those in information occupations, on the average, earn a higher income. By 1967, some fifty-three per cent of the total compensation was paid to information workers.

The accompanying graph (Fig. 2) and Tables 2 and 3 illustrate the change. In 1930, there were twelve million workers in the information sector, almost 10.5 million in agriculture, eighteen million in industry, and ten million in services. By 1970, there were thirty-seven million in the information sector, less than 2.5 million in agriculture, 22.9 million in industry, and 17.5 million in services. In percentage terms, the labour force in the information sector today is over forty-six per cent; in agriculture, three per cent, in industry 28.6 per cent, and in services 21.9 per cent.

What of the future? Extrapolations can be deceptive. The information sector has grown hugely in the last decade and a half, but that has been a result of both the rapid introduction of new technology in computers and telecommunications and the economic growth rate that financed it. In many sectors, such as education, public policy is the decisive variable. Although

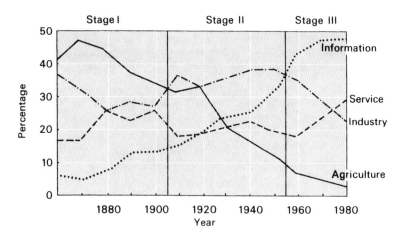

Figure 2 Four-sector aggregation of the US workforce, 1860–1980 (using median estimates of information workers).

Table 2 Four-sector aggregation of the US labour force (median definition).

	Experienced civilian workforce				
Year	Information sector	Agriculture sector	Industry sector	Service sector	Total
1860	480,604	3,364,230	3,065,024	1,375,525	8,286,283
1870	601,018	5,884,971	4,006,789	2,028,438	12,521,216
1880	1,131,415	7,606,590	4,386,409	4,281,970	17,406,384
1890	2,821,500	8,464,500	6,393,883	5,074,149	22,754,032
1900	3,732,371	10,293,179	7,814,652	7,318,947	29,159,149
1910	5,930,193	12,377,785	14,447,382	7,044,592	39,799,952
1920	8,016,054	14,718,742	14,492,300	8,061,342	45,288,438
1930	12,508,959	10,415,623	18,023,113	10,109,284	51,056,979
1940	13,337,958	8,233,624	19,928,422	12,082,376	53,582,380
1950	17,815,978	6,883,446	22,154,285	10,990,378	57,844,087
1960	28,478,317	4,068,511	23,597,364	11,661,326	67,805,518
1970	37,167,513	2,466,883	22,925,095	17,511,639	80,071,130
1980[a]	44,650,721	2,012,157	21,558,824	27,595,297	95,816,999

Percentages

1860	5.8	40.6	37.0	16.6	100
1870	4.8	47.0	32.0	16.2	100
1880	6.5	43.7	25.2	24.6	100
1890	12.4	37.2	28.1	22.3	100
1900	12.8	35.3	26.8	25.1	100
1910	14.9	31.1	36.3	17.7	100
1920	17.7	32.5	32.0	17.8	100
1930	24.5	20.4	35.3	19.8	100
1940	24.9	15.4	37.2	22.5	100
1950	30.8	11.9	38.3	19.0	100
1960	42.0	6.0	34.8	17.2	100
1970	46.4	3.1	28.6	21.9	100
1980[a]	46.6	2.1	22.5	28.8	100

[a] Bureau of Labour Statistics projection.

the cohort of younger people will begin to shrink – in absolute numbers it is still growing, but the rate is slowing rapidly – there is an evident desire on the part of many in the adult population to undertake continuing education. Thus many community colleges are finding themselves transformed into adult schools. Whether or not society can afford these costs or wants to pay them is a different question. But aside from issues of public policy the expansion of the information economy will largely depend on two developments. One is automation – in industry and in the white-collar occupations. The second is the growth of information and its retrieval – data-bases, scientific information networks, and the explosion of international communications.

HISTORY AND PERSPECTIVES

Table 3 Two-sector aggregation of the US labour force.

| | Experienced civilian workforce | | | | |
| | Inclusive definition | | Restrictive definition | | |
Year	Information workers	Noninformation workers	Information workers	Noninformation workers	Total
1860	580,040	7,706,243	372,883	7,913,400	8,286,283
1870	788,837	11,732,379	500,849	12,020,367	12,521,216
1880	1,340,292	16,066,092	887,726	16,518,658	17,406,384
1890	2,980,778	19,773,254	2,480,189	20,273,843	22,754,032
1900	4,286,395	24,872,754	3,120,029	26,039,120	29,159,149
1910	7,283,391	32,516,561	4,537,196	35,262,756	39,799,952
1920	9,963,456	35,324,982	6,023,362	39,265,076	45,288,438
1930	16,031,889	35,025,090	8,883,914	42,173,065	51,056,979
1940	16,470,313	37,112,067	9,883,428	43,698,952	53,582,380
1950	21,691,532	36,152,555	13,940,424	43,903,663	57,844,087
1960	30,851,510	36,954,008	19,256,767	48,548,751	67,805,518
1970	40,529,588	39,541,542	29,464,497	50,606,633	80,071,130
1980[a]	49,154,120	46,662,879	39,955,688	55,861,311	95,816,999

Percentages

1860	7.0	93.0	4.5	95.5	100
1870	6.3	93.7	4.0	96.0	100
1880	7.7	92.3	5.1	94.9	100
1890	13.1	86.9	10.9	89.1	100
1900	14.7	85.3	10.7	89.3	100
1910	18.3	81.7	11.4	88.6	100
1920	22.0	78.0	13.3	86.7	100
1930	31.4	68.6	17.4	82.6	100
1940	30.7	69.3	18.4	81.6	100
1950	37.5	62.5	24.1	75.9	100
1960	45.5	54.5	28.4	71.6	100
1970	50.6	49.4	36.8	63.2	100
1980[a]	51.3	48.7	41.7	58.3	100

[a] Bureau of Labour Statistics projection.

Future problems: the retrieval of information

In his *Sartor Resartus*, Thomas Carlyle wrote ironically: "He who first shortened the labour of the Copyists by the device of movable type was disbanding hired Armies . . ." He was, of course, referring to Johann Gutenberg (and praising him as well for "cashiering most Kings and Senates and creating a whole new Democratic world: he had invented the art of printing"). Yet such "technological" displacement, characteristically, had contradictory results. While old-fashioned calligraphers no longer could

THE SOCIAL FRAMEWORK OF THE INFORMATION SOCIETY

practise their skill and thus were relegated to the artisan scrap heap, more jobs were created by the increased demand for printed materials, and newer, less artistic but differently skilled men found employment.

And yet initially the pace of change was not so abrupt and rapid as to create wholesale turnovers in the print trade of the time. The printing press of the eighteenth century was little different from that used by Gutenberg three hundred years before. It was a wooden handpress on which a flat plate was laid upon a flat piece of paper with pressure created by the tightening of screws. Wood was eventually replaced by metal and the screw by a double lever, which allowed the speed of printing to be increased by half. By 1800 a radically new method of printing using a rotating cylinder – the basis of the modern press until the development of photographic technologies – was invented and with its greater speed began gradually to displace the flat press. The double rotary cylinder, developed for newspapers in the 1850s, made it possible to print two sides of a piece of paper at once. By 1893, the *New York World*'s octuple rotary press was printing 96,000 copies of eight pages in a single hour, whereas seventy years before the average was 2500 pages an hour.[24]

Such developments, understandably, went hand in hand with complementary technologies. The Linotype, developed by Mergenthaler in 1868, replaced monotype by selecting and casting type by keyboard, reducing composition costs by half while quintupling the speed of typesetting. The paper industry, which until the early nineteenth century was a time-consuming hand process using rags, was transformed in the middle of the century by the Fourdrinier process which mechanized the production of paper with the use of wire webs and cylinders. At the same time the development of wood pulp and a practical pulping process displaced rags, so that paper which had cost almost $350 a ton at the mid-century had come down to $36 a ton by the end of the century. Each of these developments was sped by new sources of energy. Printing presses, originally turned by hand and briefly even by horse (in America at least), became powered by steam and then by electricity. Papermaking, dependent initially on waterpower, came to use hydraulic power accelerated by electric turbines.

But what is so striking is how long it took, from the time of Gutenberg, for all this to develop. It is only in the twentieth century that one finds the mass production of newspapers (with millions of copies of a single issue printed overnight), magazines (set and printed in widely dispersed places using common tapes), and books. And now, with the revolution in communications, all this will change. The information explosion is a set of reciprocal relations between the expansion of science, the hitching of that science to a new technology, and the growing demand for news, entertainment and instrumental knowledge, all in the context of a rapidly increasing population, more literate and more educated, living in a vastly enlarged world that is now tied together, almost in real time, by cable, telephone and international

HISTORY AND PERSPECTIVES

satellite, whose inhabitants are made aware of each other by the vivid pictorial imagery of television, and that has at its disposal large data banks of computerized information.

Given this huge explosion in news, statistical data and information, it is almost impossible to provide any set of measurements to chart its growth. Yet there is one area – the growth of scientific information – where some reconstruction of historical trends has been carried out, and I will use that as a baseline for understanding the problems of the next twenty years.

The historical picture of the knowledge explosion was first formulated statistically by Derek de Solla Price in 1963, in his work *Little Science, Big Science*. The first two scientific journals appeared in the mid-seventeenth century, the *Journal des savants* in Paris and the *Philosophical Transactions of the Royal Society* in London. By the middle of the eighteenth century, there were only ten scientific journals, by 1800 about 100, by 1850 perhaps 1000. Today? There are no exact statistics on the number of scientific journals being published in the world. Estimates range between 30,000 and 100,000, which itself is an indication of both the difficulty of definition and the difficulty of keeping track of new and disappearing journals. In 1963, Price estimated that 50,000 journals had been founded, of which 30,000 were still surviving. A UNESCO report in 1971 put the figure at between 50,000 and 70,000. *Ulrich's International Periodicals Directory* (a standard library source) in 1971–72 listed 56,000 titles in 220 subjects, of which more than half were in the sciences, medicine and technology; but these were only of periodicals in the Latin script and excluded most Slavic, Arabic, Oriental and African languages.

Perhaps the most directly measurable indicators are university library holdings. The Johns Hopkins University in 1900 had 100,000 books and ranked tenth among American university libraries. By 1970, it had over $1^1/_2$ million volumes, a growth of 3.9 per cent per year, although it had dropped to twentieth place. In the same period, the eighty-five major American universities were doubling the number of books in their libraries every seventeen years, for an annual growth rate of 4.1 per cent. (The difference between 3.9 and 4.1 per cent may seem slight, yet it relegated the Johns Hopkins Library to the bottom of the second decile.)

A 1973 OECD survey of all the extant studies of the growth in scientific knowledge came to the following conclusions.

(1) In all the case studies, growth follows a geometric progression, the curve being exponential.
(2) However, the growth rates varied considerably, the lowest one being 3.5 per cent yearly, the highest 14.4 per cent.
(3) The lowest growth rates are shown by the number of scientific periodicals published, covering a 300-year period, and the number of specialized bibliographical periodicals involved in indexing and abstracting over a

THE SOCIAL FRAMEWORK OF THE INFORMATION SOCIETY

140-year period. In the case of scientific journals, the annual growth rate has been 3.5, 3.7 or 3.9 per cent, depending whether the number published in 1972 is taken as 30,000, 50,000, or 100,000. The growth rate for indexing and abstracting organizations has been 5.5 percent a year. In 1972 there were 1800 such services in science.

(4) A recent series reporting the number of articles by engineers in civil engineering journals (from 3000 pages of technical articles in three specialized periodicals in 1946 to 30,000 pages in forty-two specialized periodicals in 1966) shows growth rates of 12.3 per cent a year.

(5) The growth rate in the number of international scientific and technical congresses increased almost fourfold in twenty years, rising from 1000 in 1950 to over 3500 in 1968.[25]

The multiplication in the number of scientific reports and documents has naturally led to the conclusion that such progression cannot continue indefinitely, that at some point a slowdown would take place, probably in the form of a logistic curve that would symmetrically match the exponential rise of the ascent. The crucial question has been to identify the point of inflection where the reverse trend would begin. Derek de Solla Price argued in 1963 that "at some time, undetermined as yet but probably during the 1940s or 1950s, we passed through the mid-period in general logistic curve of science's body politic." In fact, he concluded, saturation may have already arrived.[26]

Yet as Anderla noted in his study for the OECD: "Today it is absolutely certain that these forecasts, repeated without number and echoed almost universally, have failed to materialize, at any rate so far." As evidence, he assembled the number of abstracts published between 1957 and 1971 for nineteen scientific disciplines and demonstrated that between 1957 and 1967 the output increased by nearly two and a half times, for an annual growth rate of 9.5 per cent. Over the fourteen years from 1957 to 1971, the volume increased more than fourfold, for a growth rate of 10.6 per cent, so that there was an escalation in growth rather than the predicted reverse.[27]

The major reason for this continued escalation is the tendency for science to generate more and more subspecialities, each of which creates its own journals and research reports system. At the same time, cross-disciplinary movements arise to bridge some of the subspecialities, extending the proliferation process even further.

What then of the future? The production of scientific literature is determined in the first instance, by the projected rate of increase in the scientific population. It is calculated that in 1970 the scientific population represented about two per cent of the total labour force. The rate of increase has been estimated variously at between 4.7 and 7.2 per cent a year (a fifteen-year and a ten-year doubling time, respectively), although certain categories, such as computer scientists, have been increasing by more than ten per cent annually. Taking 1970 as a base, one can estimate the likely size of the scientific population in 1985 by making three assumptions: an unyielding exponential increase to the horizon year of 1985; a break occurring in 1980, with the logistic curve beginning to slow down at that time; or the point of inflection coming as early as 1975. Given these assumptions, the number of scientists, engineers and other technicians in 1985 could account for a low of 3.8 per cent to a high of 7.2 per cent of the total labour force. If one takes the midpoints, between four per cent and 5.7 per cent of the total working population would be scientists and engineers in 1985.

In order to project the volume of information that is likely to be produced, we can take as a base a survey of the US National Academy of Science which revealed that in the early 1970s about 2,000,000 scientific writings of all kinds were issued each year, or between 6000 and 7000 articles and reports each working day. For an internally consistent time series, the most reliable indicators are the statistics of abstracts of articles in the leading specialized reviews, which from 1957 to 1971 increased exponentially at a rate of more than ten per cent a year. As with the growth rates in the number of scientists, one can assume breaks in the logistic curves at 1975, 1980 or 1985 and then take a median figure. According to these computations, there is every indication that projections to within a year or two of the 1985 horizon might well lie within the index range of some 300 to 400. In other words, the number of scientific and technical abstracts would be three or four times the present number.

The end of the Alexandrian Library

Clearly, if the explosion in information continues, it cannot be handled by present means. If by 1985 the volume of information is four (low estimate) or seven times (high estimate) that of 1970, then some other ways must be found to organize this onslaught of babel. In one of these pleasant exercises that statisticians like to undertake, it is estimated that under present projections, the Yale University Library would need a permanent staff of 6000 persons in the year 2040 to cope with the books and research reports that would be coming annually into the library. (Such projections recall earlier ones that if the US telephone system had to handle the current volume of calls solely through operator-assisted methods, then every female in the labour force – a sexist remark obviously made before women's lib – would now be working for AT&T.)

Obviously, the information explosion can only be handled through the expansion of computerized and subsequently automated information systems. The major advance to date has been the computerization of abstracting and indexing services. Most of the printed abstract index bulletins in research libraries are prepared from computer tape. The Chemical Abstract Service (CAS), the largest in the field, is a case in point. Before computerization, it

THE SOCIAL FRAMEWORK OF THE INFORMATION SOCIETY

took the CAS about twenty months to produce an annual index; these are now available twice a year, while the unit costs for indexing have decreased from $18.50 to $10.54. Moreover, as the new substances are recorded in the Chemical Registry System – there are now 3,000,000 items in the files – it is possible to store, recreate and display structure diagrams on video terminals from the computer-readable structure records stored in the system. A further development is the rise of computer-based searching services, drawn from the tape initially used to expedite the printing of indexes. Two American firms, the Systems Development Corporation and Lockheed Information Systems, provide on-line searching to over thirty bibliographic data-bases. Together they provide immediate access to over fifteen million citations, with an annual increase of approximately 3.5 million citations.[28]

The logic of all this is that the range of the Alexandrian Library – the single building like the Bibliothèque Nationale, the British Museum or the Library of Congress – where all the world's recorded knowledge is housed in one building may become a sad monument of the printed past. Data-based stores of information, especially in the scientific and technical field, will come from specialized information centres, transmitted through computer printouts, facsimile, or video display to the user, who will have consulted an index through on-line searching to locate items of interest and then order them on demand.

All this supposes two things. One, the creation of large-scale networks in which a national system is built through the linkage of specialized centres. And two, the automation of data banks so that basic scientific and technical data, from industrial patents to detailed medical information, can be retrieved directly from computers and transmitted to the user. But both suppositions raise two very different problems. One is the intellectual question of the distinction between programming a data-base, and constructing a program for use as a knowledge base. Retrieving some census items from a data-base is a simple matter; but finding kindred and analogous conceptual terms – the handling of ideas – raises all the problems that were first encountered, and never successfully solved, in the effort to achieve sophisticated machine translation of languages.

As early as the pre-Socratics, when philosophy was first becoming self-conscious, there was an awareness of the ambiguities of language and the hope, as with the Pythagoreans, that certainty could be expressed through mathematical relations. Descartes, in creating his analytical geometry, thought he could substitute the "universal language of logic" for the messy imprecisions of ordinary language, as Spinoza felt he could create a "moral geometry" to deal with ethical questions. In each generation that hope has arisen anew. In 1661 a Scotsman, George Dalgarno, published his *Ars Signorum* in which he proposed to group all human knowledge into seventeen sections (such as "politics" and "natural objects") and to label each with a Latin consonant. Vowels would be used to label the subsections into which each section was

107

HISTORY AND PERSPECTIVES

to be divided, and the process of subdivision was to be continued with consonants and vowels alternating. In this way, any item of knowledge would have a specific reference and identification.[29]

In the twentieth century we have had the effort of Whitehead and Russell to formalize all logic using a mathematical notation, the effort of the logical positivists such as Carnap to construct (in theory) a language that would avoid the ambiguities of ordinary discourse and to propose (in practice) a verifiability principle that would specify which propositions were testable and could be held to "make sense", as against those that were (pejoratively) metaphysical, emotive or theological and could not, given the nature of language, be "proved". And most recently, in the *Britannica* 1, Mortimer Adler has proposed a new scholastic ordering of knowledge, the *Propaedia*, that would guide encyclopedia users to interrelated sets of relevant terms, as his earlier *Synopticon* sought to be an intellectual index to the 101 major "ideas" of human thought.

The attempts to discipline human knowledge and create a vast and unified edifice, as Dalgarno and even Leibniz sought to do, were bound to fail. The effort to formalize knowledge or construct artificial languages has proved inadequate. The scholastic orderings of Mortimer Adler may help an individual to trace the bibliographic cross-relationships of ideas, but if the purpose of a library, or a knowledge-based computer program, is to help a historian to assemble evidence or a scholar to "re-order" ideas, then the ambiguity of language itself must be confronted. Terms necessarily vary in different contexts and lend themselves to different interpretations, and historical usages shift over time (consider the problem of defining an intellectual, or the nature of ideology), making the problem of designing a "knowledge" program quite different from designing an "information" program.

The process of creating new knowledge (reasoned judgements) proceeds by what Léon Walras, the great mathematical economist, called *tâtonnement*, trial-and-error tapping, by taking fragments of intellectual mosaics whose larger shapes cannot be predicted in advance and fitting them together in different ways or by regarding large conceptual structures from a new angle, which opens up wholly new prisms of selection and focus. A sophisticated reader, studying a philosophical text, may make use of the existing index at the back of the book, but if he is to absorb and use the ideas in a fruitful way, he has necessarily to create his own index by regrouping and recategorizing the terms that are employed. As John Dewey pointed out in *Art as Experience*, the nature of creativity is to rearrange perceptions, experiences and ideas into new shapes and modes of consciousness. In this process, no mechanical ordering, no exhaustive set of permutations and combinations, can do the task. Descartes once thought that the geometer with a compass could draw a circle more exactly than an artist could freehand. But a perfect circle, or even a set of interlocking circles, is not art without some larger conceptual context that "redesigns" an older or

THE SOCIAL FRAMEWORK OF THE INFORMATION SOCIETY

different way of arranging shapes. Art, and thought, as modes of exploration, remain primarily heuristic.

A more mundane yet sociologically important problem is the lack of a national information policy on science and technical information, let alone on library resources generally. Should there be a national scientific and technical computer network? Should there be a government corporation or utility with direct responsibility to scientific and technical users or simply a major, governmentally organized data-base (like the census) made available to commercial services that meet specific consumer needs? Such questions have been raised since the creation of the Office of Science Information within the National Science Foundation in 1958, and they have been asked over and over again in a number of governmental and National Academy of Science studies in subsequent years. No answers have been forthcoming; no policy exists. Yet if science information is the end product of the $35 billion annual investment that the nation makes in research and development, and information, broadly defined, accounts for almost fifty per cent of the gross national product, then some coherent national policy is in order.

The policy questions of the information society

My basic premise has been that knowledge and information are becoming the strategic resource and transforming agent of the postindustrial society. Inevitably, the onset of far-reaching social changes, especially when they proceed, as these do, through the medium of specific technologies, confronts a society with major policy questions. Here I can only schematically indicate some of the questions society will face in the next two decades.

The new infrastructure

Every society is connected by diverse channels that permit trade and discourse between its members. These modes, or infrastructures, have usually been the responsibility of government – as builder, financier, maintainer or regulator. The first infrastructure was transportation – roads, canals, railroads, airways – which breaks down the segmentation of society and allows for the movement of people and goods. Caravans and trade routes formed the social framework of older human societies. The second infrastructure has been the energy utilities – waterpower, steam pipes, gas, electricity, oil pipelines – for the transmission of power. By mobilizing technological rather than natural sources of energy and linking them into power grids, not only have we transformed the lives of cities through lighting, but we have provided power for the fabrication of goods and the use of consumer appliances. The third infrastructure has been communications – first the mails and newspapers, then telegraph and telephone, now radio and television – as media for the mounting explosion of messages, the bombardment of

HISTORY AND PERSPECTIVES

sensory experiences, and the increased degree of social and psychic inter-action between persons that is now accelerating exponentially.

In the next two decades, there is little likelihood of any major develop-ments in the first infrastructure, that of transportation. The adoption of the Concorde or other supersonic airplanes, if it comes, may halve the time for crossing the ocean, but the effect will be minor compared to the reduction in the time needed to cross the Atlantic in the last hundred years, from several weeks by steamship to six days by fast boat, to sixteen hours by propeller plane, to seven hours by jet. Mass transit in the cities, if it returns, is unlikely to replace the automobile or other modes of personal movement unless fuel prices rise so high as to overthrow the hedonistic way of life that has become entrenched in advanced industrial societies. The rising demand for personal transportation in the newer developing countries and increases in congestion may lead to new combinations of taxis, leasing and motor utilities (in which one shares in a common pool). But much of the vaunted experimental innovations, such as monorails or automated elevated speedways or even hovercraft, have proved to be either uneconomic or technologically too complicated.

In the second infrastructure, energy, there are clearly major new develop-ments requiring large capital expenditures, involving conservation (insulating housing), better extractive techniques for coal and its gasification, potential uses of nuclear energy, research in tapping solar sources of energy, and more efficient modes of electricity transmission, such as superconductivity. These efforts, if made, will stimulate a huge expansion in the areas of research and development (and of engineers and technically trained personnel), and, if successful, will establish new energy grids that will supply a steady source of renewable power and once again bring down the price of energy relative to other goods. But such changes, large as they may be, are primarily sub-stitutes for existing energy sources and modes of transmission. They do not presage huge upheavals in the role energy plays in the society.

The really major social change of the next two decades will come in the third major infrastructure, as the merging technologies of telephone, com-puter, facsimile, cable television and video discs lead to a vast reorganization in the modes of communication between persons; the transmission of data; the reduction if not the elimination of paper in transactions and exchanges; new modes of transmitting news, entertainment and knowledge; and the reorganization of learning that may follow the expansion of computer-assisted instruction and the spread of video discs.

One may be sceptical, as I am, about extravagant claims regarding the quantum leaps in level of education that computer-assisted instruction and video discs will bring. Learning, as I think we have learned, is a function of both the ability to learn and the cultural milieu; any technology is only instrumental, and its impact depends on other social and cultural factors. But in the realm of data transmission (especially in the world of business)

THE SOCIAL FRAMEWORK OF THE INFORMATION SOCIETY

and in the development of knowledge networks (particularly in science and research), what Anthony Oettinger has called compunications certainly will stimulate vast social changes.

This upheaval in telecommunications and knowledge poses two economic-political policy problems, one structural, the other intellectual. The structural question is what kind of technical-economic organization is best designed to be efficient, meet consumer (i.e., industrial, commercial, financial, scientific, library) use, and remain flexible enough to allow for continuing technological development. One proposal is for a single computer utility that would centralize and provide a single source for information and transmission of data for consumer use, either government-owned (as are the telephone and broadcasting systems in many European countries) or privately owned but government-regulated, like AT&T and the major broadcast networks in the United States. Among different versions of the computer utility idea, there is a proposal for diverse sources of information (i.e., different data banks operated publicly or privately) based on a single transmitting system (such as the present telephone quasi-monopoly) or, conversely, a centralized set of data-bases with diverse means of transmission. Against these are the proposals for a completely unregulated, competitive market system, in which different "producers" would be free to set up diverse informational services and transmission would be through cable, microwave, or satellite communication operated by different combines, each competing for the business. These are the issues whose economic aspects Noll has addressed.[30]

It has been argued that a single national computing service, interconnecting all user terminals from geographically dispersed data banks, would achieve vast economies of scale, and if run as a government utility (like TVA) would avoid the concentration of vast power in the hands of a single private enterprise. Against this, as Noll points out, computer systems sell not merely computational power or data processing but "information", and the large and varied needs of thousands of different kinds of users for different kinds of information – medical, technical, economic, marketing – would best be served by specific firms that would be responsive, in the way efficient markets can be, to the diverse needs of consumers. Others have argued that government control could be as dangerous, if not more so, than private concentration since it could be more easily misused for political purposes. And there is the further question of whether a competitive decentralized system would not be more flexible technologically, and more innovative, than a large monopoly system, either public or private. The record so far, in the instance of the computer versus the telephone, would indicate that technological innovation has come more rapidly and more responsively in an unregulated and competitive atmosphere than in the government-regulated sphere.

On the traditional grounds of economic efficiency and technological responsiveness, it seems to me that Noll makes a convincing case for the primacy of the market and for a market system. Yet he also points out that

HISTORY AND PERSPECTIVES

regulators tend to see prices as taxes to be levied according to some calculus of social worth, favouring one group over another, rather than seeing prices as signal-covering information about costs that induce buyers to make economically efficient decisions. He is, I believe, right in his observation. Yet is the policy itself so wrong? Where markets are open and competitive, the allocation of resources does respond most efficiently to the preferences and demands of consumers, and this is the justifiable defence, theoretically, of the market as the arbiter of economic activity. Yet if in the institutional world income distribution is grossly distorted, or various social groups are discriminated against, then redress through subsidy may be one means of achieving equity, even if sometimes at the expense of efficiency. Also, there is the growing realization that markets do not often reflect the larger range of social costs that are generated in the process, and these may be unfairly distributed. As Arthur Okun has pointed out, the trade-off between efficiency and equity presents a real problem. The point is not to disguise the issue but to make it as explicit as possible, so that one knows the relative gains and losses in equity and efficiency that result from market and regulatory decisions.

The second problem posed by the upheaval in telecommunications is intellectual rather than structural and concerns the question of a national information policy, particularly the dissemination of science and technical information. The government is obviously committed to the furtherance of research and development. Increases in productivity depend increasingly on the more efficient distribution of necessary knowledge, but so far there is no unified government policy or an organized system to bring scientific and technical information to diverse users, to speed the process of innovation, and shorten the time of development and diffusion.

After Sputnik, there was a flurry of sides reviewing the problem. A report by William C. Baker of Bell Laboratories stated the unexceptionable principle that the flow of scientific information was necessary. A second report in 1962 by J. H. Crawford for the president's Office of Science and Technology recommended that each agency of government set up a specific office to produce scientific information, and these were created in the Department of Defence, the Atomic Energy Commission, and the National Aeronautic and Space Agency. In 1963, a report by Alvin Weinberg of the Oak Ridge National Laboratory argued that the government had the further responsiblity to organize the dissemination of research information in order to avoid costly duplication of effort. The government did create a coordinating body called COASTI (Committee on Scientific and Technical Information) to implement this effort.

Yet the odd if not surprising fact is that little has been done. During the Nixon administration, COASTI, the Office of Science and Technology, and the Science Information Council were dismantled. Inevitably the number of hortatory studies multiplied. In 1969, the National Academy of Sciences and the National Academy of Engineering brought forth the SATCOM (Committee

THE SOCIAL FRAMEWORK OF THE INFORMATION SOCIETY

on Scientific and Technical Communication) report, which involved more than 200 scientists, calling for a national policy-making body to deal with information policy. In 1972, the Federal Council on Science and Technology and the National Science Foundation commissioned yet another report, by Dr Martin Greenberger of Johns Hopkins University, which concluded, unsurprisingly, that the government was not well organized to deal with the problems of scientific and technical information facing the country.

It still is not. Meanwhile, the number of scientific papers and the volume of scientific information continue to rise. There is a growing trend towards cross-disciplinary information which the single-disciplinary systems (such as abstracting and indexing) are not equipped to handle. The proliferation of diverse types of material, stored in different ways from books, films, computer tapes, video tapes and so on, makes it difficult to keep track of everything. And finally, the number of users continues to increase.

All trends pose a large variety of policy issues. Should there be, as Fernbach suggests,[31] a national Library of Data, like the Library of Congress, to store all basic data and programs in giant memories? Should this library – if such a Library of Babel as Jorge Luis Borges envisaged ever comes about – also concern itself with the dissemination of data, as the government's Medlars system does for medical information, or should it be available for private companies, such as Lockheed or Systems Development Corporation or the *New York Times*, to provide specialized services for subscribers through proprietary communications and terminal systems?

The growth of shared communications systems and on-line terminals makes a national scientific and technical information network a tangible possibility. Denicoff describes the development of the interactive computer network invented in 1968 by Dr L. G. Roberts for the Advanced Research Projects Agency (ARPA), which was first employed by the Defence Communications Agency in 1976.[32] Its most valued result, according to Denicoff, was the emergence of a "user community". The operational reality of such a community, he writes, is the proof of the gains we have made in scientific cooperation. In the same vein, Joseph Becker has argued that:

> a national scientific and technical information network implies the interconnection of discipline-oriented and mission-oriented information systems for remote use through standard communications. Unless cohesive development takes place, the separate systems will remain insulated from one another and from their users. But, if maximum communication can be established among them, the array can be converted into a national resource of immense value to America's scientific enterprise.[33]

H. G. Wells, in one of his megalomaniacal visions of the future, proposed a "world brain" that like a vast computer would bring together in one place all organized scientific knowledge and make it available through communication networks to the "new samurai", the coming scientific elite of the world. Is such a technological phantasmagoria feasible (as some computer scientists claim it is) or desirable (as others do), or is it simply one of those marvellously simple visions (like that of Sidney Webb) of tidily and neatly organized bundles of knowledge that can be separated and reassembled by pressing the right button? If the last, it is a deceptive vision, which misunderstands the way the mind actually works, and which makes the sociological error of assuming that some central knowledge system can function better than the decentralized, self-organizing system in which demand specifies the organizational and market response to the needs of the users. This is an issue that should remain open to extended debate, for it is too serious and too costly to be settled on purely ideological grounds.

And finally, on a more mundane level, there is the legal and economic question of what is an "intellectual property" – at least where the intellectual product is clearly defined (such as a book or a journal article), let alone where the boundaries are blurred, as in the instance of a computer program. How does one balance the rights of fair use as demanded by libraries against the economic rights of authors and publishers? As books become stored in computer memories and can be retrieved on tapes and printed by attached photocopying devices, who is to pay for what? Should Xerox and IBM receive financial returns while the intellectual producers gain only the psychic satisfaction of the widespread reproduction of their words?

The courts and the Congress have been struggling with these questions for years. Clearly no solution will completely satisfy those who press for the widest possible dissemination of intellectual material under some fair-use and information-need concept, or those who demand payment for any use of copyright material. But we need a clarification of the legal and philosophical issues at stake.

Social and economic transformations

The major determinant of policy issues, as I have indicated, is the question of what kind of infrastructure will be created out of the merging technologies of computers and communications. Inevitably this will give rise to more diffuse policy issues deriving from the economic and social transformations that may come in their wake. I will conclude by examining five central issues of this kind.

(1) The location of cities

Historically, all cities were formed at the crossroads of overland caravan routes, at the strategic confluence of rivers, or at large, protected ports on seaways and oceans as entrepôts and trading centres. Almost all the major

THE SOCIAL FRAMEWORK OF THE INFORMATION SOCIETY

cities in the world have been located on rivers, lakes, and oceans since transportation – and particularly waterways for heavy barge loads – tied areas together in the first infrastructure.

In the industrial age, cities were located near major resource bases, such as coal and iron, as one sees in the English Midlands or the German Ruhr and most strikingly in the great industrial heartland of the United States, where the great iron-ore resources of the Mesabi Range in upper Minnesota were connected to the great coal regions in southern Illinois and western Pennsylvania through a network of lakes and rivers. In this way the great industrial cities of Chicago, Detroit, Cleveland, Buffalo and Pittsburgh were intricately linked in one huge complex.

In the transition to a service economy, the metropolitan cities became the major financial centres and headquarters for the great enterprises. The histories of New York and London form striking parallels. Both began as port cities through which goods could be sent overseas or transported inland. New York was a large, ice-free port, protected by two great bays, yet connected through the Hudson River and the Erie Canal system to the midwestern Great Lakes complex. As trade increased, banking, factoring and insurance arose as auxiliary services to commerce; later, with the rise of industry, they became nerve centres for financial and stock transactions. In its third phase, New York became a large headquarters city, where the major corporations located their head offices to take advantage of the external economies offered by the concentration of banking, legal, publishing, and communications services.

In economic geography, the resource base was the decisive locational factor up to the last forty years, when all this began to change. In the United States in the postwar years, the economic map of the country was reworked largely through politics, since the new large aircraft, space and missile companies were created entirely by government contracts, and the decisions to locate them in areas like the Pacific Northwest, southern California and southwest Texas were made on political grounds. With the rise of air cargo, we have witnessed a phenomenon in which new "airplane cities", such as Dallas–Fort Worth, Houston, Denver and Atlanta, rather than water and rail cities, serve as regional hubs for industrial and commercial spokes. And now, as the increasing spread (and cheapness) of telecommunications reduces the former external economies of physical proximity, we see the dispersal of corporate headquarters and major white-collar concentrations like the insurance industry from the decaying central cities to the suburbs. The location of research laboratories, new universities, and large hospital complexes is less dependent on the traditional factors of economic geography and more influenced by the nearness of educational facilities, easier lifestyles, and political factors. Phenomena like the development of "Silicon Valley" in California – the electronics and computer firms around San Jose – and Route 128 around Boston were a response to the availability of university research facilities, plus more pleasant space for the smaller-sized physical plants and offices than the industrial areas could provide.

C. A. Doxiades has envisaged the growth of linear cities without the older focal piazzas and market centres of the classical European towns. B. F. Skinner has suggested that in an age of advanced communication, networks of towns will replace the large, increasingly ungovernable cities. The question of whether these apocalyptic visions will be realized is moot; the life and death of cities is a long historical process. But what is changing is the concept of "urbanism" itself. Thirty years ago Louis Wirth wrote a famous essay entitled "Urbanism as a Way of Life", in which he summed up the characteristics of urbanism as a highly interactive, heavily mobile, culturally and politically attentive mode, as against the older small-town and rural patterns centred on the church and the family. What is happening today is that the entire nation (if not large parts of the world) is becoming urbanized in the psychological sense, though increasingly more dispersed geographically.

The changes in the character and pattern of telecommunications pose problems of national land use, of the social costs of dispersions and concentrations, the management of the decay of old cities, and the control of the sprawl of new ones. Inevitably, the decisions will reflect the interplay of market and political forces, since neither one can be decisive in itself. But it is the exact mix of the two that remains as the interesting sociological question for the next decades.

(2) The possibilities of national planning

Leon Trotsky once said that a capitalist society is one where each man thinks for himself and no one thinks for all. That a single "one" can think for "all" is probably impossible and, if so, would be monstrous, since the "one" would be some giant bureaucracy and the "all" a putative single interest equally applicable to all citizens in the society. As Alan Altshuler of MIT has remarked:

> Those who contend that comprehensive planning should play a large role in the future evolution of societies must argue that the common interests of society's members are their most important interests and constitute a large proportion of all their interests. They must assert that conflicts of interests in society are illusory, that they are about minor matters, or that they can be foreseen and resolved in advance by just arbiters [planners] who understand the total interest of all the parties.

In this respect, Altshuler is probably correct, yet such a view unduly restricts the meaning of planning in all its possible varieties. The different kinds of planning can be arrayed in a simple logical ladder:

THE SOCIAL FRAMEWORK OF THE INFORMATION SOCIETY

(a) Coordinated information

Almost all major enterprises make five- and even ten-year plans (for product development, capital needs, manpower requirements, new plants) as a necessary component of their own planning. And various services, such as the McGraw-Hill survey of capital spending budgets or the federally financed University of Michigan surveys of consumer intentions, seek to provide more comprehensive information for firms about these trends to aid them in their planning. A national computerized information service, through the Bureau of the Census or some similar government body, could bring together all such relevant information – just as the various econometric models now in use make forecasts of the annual GNP and its major components, which become the basis of both governmental and private policies. To this extent, the idea of a coordinated information system is simply an extension of the planning process that is now so extensive in the corporate and governmental sectors.[34]

(b) Modelling and simulation

Using an input-output matrix, such as that developed by Wassily Leontieff, one could test alternative economic policies in order to weigh the effects of different government policies on different sectors of the economy. In a more radical version, the Russian economist Leonid Kantorovich has argued that a national computerized economic system, registering the different prices and allocations of items, could spot items that deviate from planned or targeted goals or the disproportionate use of resources in various sectors.

(c) Indicative planning

In this model, which is used by the French Commissariat du Plan, several thousand industry committees coordinate their plans regarding economic activities, and these plans become the basis of governmental decisions to stimulate or inhibit certain sectors, largely by easier credit facilities or credit restrictions.

(d) National goals

In this scheme, the government would stipulate certain major goals – the expansion of housing or levels of economic growth – and monitor the economy to see whether such goals were being achieved as a guide to which further measures (tax cuts, investment credits, credit allocations, preferred sections such as housing) might be necessary to achieve them.

HISTORY AND PERSPECTIVES

(e) Mobilized targets

This is, in effect, a "war economy", such as that exemplified by the War Production Board in the United States during World War Two or the British Ministry of Supply; in practice, it is the actual nature of Soviet "planning". In this system, certain key targets are specified (level of steel output, kind of machine tools, number of tanks and aircraft, and so on), and the government physically allocates, by a priority system, the key materials and manpower to designated factories. In this respect, the entire economy is not planned, but key sectors are controlled.

These different modes of planning range from direct controls and policing at one end to "simple" information coordination at the other. Which kind of planning society will adopt is a political question. Given the degree of interdependence and the spillover effects of various individual decisions, some larger degree of planning – analogous to the rise of environmental monitoring and regulation planning – than we now have is probably inevitable. The computer and the large-scale information systems that are being developed will make it feasible; but how one reconciles planning with various kinds of individual freedom is a very different and more difficult question.

(3) Centralization and privacy

Police and political surveillance of individuals is much more possible and pervasive because of sophisticated advances in the information process. In a survey of federal agencies' use of computerized data banks, former Senator Sam Ervin wrote in the preface to a report by the Senate Judiciary Committee's Subcommittee on Constitutional Rights:

> The subcommittee has discovered numerous instances of agencies starting out with a worthy purpose but going so far beyond what was needed in the way of information that the individual's privacy and right to due process of law are threatened by the very existence of files. . . . The most significant finding is that there are immense numbers of government data banks, cluttered with diverse information on just about every citizen in the country. The 54 agencies surveyed were willing to report 858 [data banks] containing more than $1\frac{1}{4}$ billion records on individuals.

Government demand for information can be highly costly to enterprises and institutions. Derek Bok, the president of Harvard, reported that the demand of the governmental agency enforcing the affirmative action programme for detailed information on every aspect of employment practices and the need to keep records of all job searches for applicants to teaching and other positions cost the university over a million dollars a year. What

THE SOCIAL FRAMEWORK OF THE INFORMATION SOCIETY

information is necessary and what is not is a difficult question to decide, particularly in the abstract. Yet the tendency of almost every bureaucracy, reflecting an aspect of Parkinson's Law, is to enlarge its demands on the principle that (a) "all" information might conceivably be necessary; and (b) it is easier to ask for everything than to make discriminations.

The simple point, for it is one of the oldest and most important truisms of politics, is that there is an inherent potential for abuse when any agency with power sets up bureaucratic rules and proceeds without restraint to enforce them. The other, equally simple, point is that control over information lends itself more readily to abuse – from withholding information at one end to unlawful disclosure at the other, both processes exemplified by Watergate – and that institutional restraints are necessary, particularly in the area of information, to check such abuses.

(4) Elite and mass

Every society we have known has been divided, on one axis or another, into elite and mass. On a different axis, a society may be designated as open or closed. In the past, most societies have been elite and closed in that aristocracies have been hereditary. Even when there has been an examination system for choosing mandarins, as in Imperial China, the selection process has been limited to a small class of persons.

In the West the major elites have traditionally been landed and propertied elites. Even in an occupation like the military, which requires some technical skill, until about a hundred years ago (in Britain, for example) commissions could be purchased. The older ladders of social mobility were "the red and the black", the army and the church. Modern capitalist and industrial society began to break open those moulds. In business, there was the rise of the entrepreneur, the engineer and the manager. With the succeeding breakdown of "family capitalism", the managerial elites were no longer children of previous owners but men who earned their way up by technical competence. In government, there was the expansion of the administrative bureaucracy, in which top positions were achieved, as in France, through a rigorous selection system by rites of passage through the *grandes écoles*, or by patronage, as was usual in the United States.

Modern societies, in contrast with the past, have become more open societies, but at the same time, as knowledge and technical competence have become the requirement for elite positions, the selection process has fallen more and more on to the educational system as the sluicegates that determine who shall get ahead. The result has been increasing pressure on the educational system to provide "credentials" for those who want to move up the escalator of social mobility. In the postindustrial society, the technical elite is a knowledge elite. Such an elite has power within intellectual institutions – research organizations, hospital complexes, universities and

119

HISTORY AND PERSPECTIVES

the like – but only influence in the larger world in which policy is made. Inasmuch as political questions become more and more intricately meshed with technical issues (from military technology to economic policy), the knowledge elites can define the problems, initiate new questions, and provide the technical bases for answers; but they do not have the power to say yes or no. That is a political power that belongs, inevitably, to the politician rather than to the scientist or economist. In this sense, the idea that the knowledge elite will become a new power elite seems to me to be exaggerated.

But what is equally true is that in contemporary society there is a growing egalitarianism fostered in large measure by sectors of the knowledge elite, especially the younger ones, and given the most vocal support by those in marginal positions and marginal occupations in the knowledge sector. Within institutions, this has taken the form of attacks on "authority" and "professionalism" as elitist and demands that all groups have some share in the decision-making power. In certain European universities, for example, even the nonprofessional staffs are given a voice and representation in university affairs, while on academic issues, from curriculum to tenure decisions, the three "estates" of students, junior faculty and senior faculty have equal corporate rights. How far this egalitarianism will go remains to be seen.

The fear that a knowledge elite could become the technocratic rulers of the society is quite far-fetched and expresses more an ideological thrust by radical groups against the growing influence of technical personnel in decision making. Nor is it likely, at least in the foreseeable future, that the knowledge elites will become a cohesive "class" with common class interests, on the model of the bourgeoisie rising out of the ruins of feudalism to become the dominant class in industrial society. The knowledge class is too large and diffuse, and there seems little likelihood, either in economic or status terms, that a set of corporate interests could develop so as to fuse this stratum into a new class. What is more likely to happen, as I have argued previously, is that the different situses in which the knowledge elites are located will become the units of corporate action. One can identify functional situses, such as scientific, technological (applied skills like engineering, medicine and economics), administrative, and cultural, as well as institutional situses, such as economic enterprises, government bureaux, universities, research organizations, social service complexes (like hospitals), and the military. The competition for money and influence will be between these various situses, just as in the communist world the major political units are not classes but situses such as the party, the government machine, the central planners, factory managers, collective farms, research institutes, cultural organizations and the like.

What one sees in contemporary society is the multiplication of constituencies and consequently the multiplication of elites; and the problem of coordinating these elites and their coalitions becomes increasingly complex.

THE SOCIAL FRAMEWORK OF THE INFORMATION SOCIETY

(5) International organization

The problems of creating a new infrastructure for telecommunications (or compunications) on a national scale are magnified when the questions are projected on the international scene. Just as within the last thirty years the United States has become a "national society", so in the next thirty years we will have an international society – not as a political order, but at least within the space-time framework of communications. Here not only is the scale enormously larger, but more importantly there is no common political framework for legislating and organizing the creation of a world-wide infrastructure.

International telephone traffic, for example, has been growing by about twenty per cent a year, and international communications are handled by Intelstat, an international commercial satellite organization with ninety-odd member countries. Yet Intelstat has been largely dependent on one American aerospace company (Hughes Aircraft) to build the satellites and on the American space agency to launch its satellites into orbit. The day-to-day financial and technical management of Intelstat has been in the hands of an American corporation, Comsat, whose ownership is distributed half among ordinary shareholders and half by the large communications companies, among which AT&T has a prominent voice. The question of such dominance is bound to become more and more of an international political issue in the next decades.

On a different level, the creation of worldwide knowledge data banks and services becomes an important issue as more and more countries and their scientific, technical and medical organizations seek to share in the enlarged computerized systems and on-line networks that are being developed in the advanced industrial societies.

And finally – although this is only a sampling of the international issues that will play a role in the transformation of contemporary society – there is the question of the spread of computers, specifically the sharing of advanced computer knowledge and the creation of international computer data-transmission systems. In the period before World War One, steel production was the chief index of the strength of nations, and when Germany began to overtake Great Britain and France as a steel producer, it was a tangible sign of the growth of her economic and military power. A few years ago, the Soviet Union overtook the United States in steel output, a fact that received only passing mention in the back pages of the *New York Times*. Yet the Soviet Union is far behind the United States in the production of computers and their degree of sophistication. The export of computers – to the Soviet Union and to China – is still a political, not commercial, question, for one of the chief uses of computers has been for military planning, the design of military hardware, and most importantly the creation of guided missiles and "smart" bombs.

HISTORY AND PERSPECTIVES

Turning points and promises

I have been arguing that information and theoretical knowledge are the strategic resources of the postindustrial society, just as the combination of energy, resources and machine technology were the transforming agencies of industrial society. In addition – is the claim extravagant? – they represent turning points in modern history.

D. S. L. Cardwell has identified four major turning points in the rise of scientific technology.[35] One was the era of invention at the close of the late Middle Ages, signalled by the development of the clock and the printing press. The second, the scientific revolution, was symbolized by Galileo, with his emphasis on quantitative measurement and his technical analyses of the strength of materials and the structure of machines (for example, the square-cube law on the nature of size and growth). The third, the industrial revolution of Newcomen and Watt, was the effort to realize a Baconian programme for the social benefits of science. The fourth is represented in the work of Carnot and Faraday, not only because it produced new conceptions of thermodynamics and field theory but also because it provided the bridge to a more integral relationship between science and technology.

The new turning points are of two kinds. One lies in the changing character of science. The transmutation of materials made possible by knowledge of the underlying structure of the properties of matter and the reorganization of information into different patterns through the use of the new communication technologies, particularly the computer, are transforming the social organization of science. On the one hand they create Big Science and on the other enhanced communication through on-line networks, cooperative ventures in the discovery of new knowledge and the experimental testing of results. Science as a "collective good" has become the major productive force in society.

The second turning point is the freeing of technology from its "imperative" character to become almost entirely instrumental. It was – and remains – a fear of humanists that technology would more and more "determine" social organization because the standardization of production or the interdependence of skills or the nature of engineering design forces the acceptance of one, and only one, "best" way of doing things – a theme that itself was fostered by prophets of the industrial age like Frederick W. Taylor. But the nature of modern technology frees location from resource site and opens the way to alternative modes of achieving individuality and variety within a vastly increased output of goods. This is the promise – the fateful question is whether that promise will be realized.

THE SOCIAL FRAMEWORK OF THE INFORMATION SOCIETY

Notes

1 For an elaboration of this concept, see my book, *The Coming of Post-Industrial Society* (Basic Books, New York, 1973). A paperback edition with a new introduction appeared in 1976 (Harper & Row, Colophon Books, New York).

2 Cyril Stanley Smith, "Metallurgy as a Human Experience", *Metallurgical Transactions A*, 64, No. 4 (April 1975), p. 604. Professor Smith adds: "As an undergraduate (a half century ago) I had to decide whether to enrol as a ferrous or a non-ferrous metallurgist; I heard little about ceramics and nothing whatever about polymers. The curriculum, though refined in detail, had pretty much the same aim as the eighteenth century courses in the mining academy in Frieberg and the Ecole de Mines in Paris." (ibid., p. 604.)

3 Jacob Bronowski, "Humanism and the Growth of Knowledge", in Paul A. Schlipp (ed.), *The Philosophy of Karl Popper* (Open Court Publishing Company, LaSalle, III, 1974), p. 628.

4 Norbert Wiener, *I Am a Mathematician* (MIT Press, Cambridge, Mass., 1970), p. 40. (The book was first published in 1956 by Doubleday, New York.)

5 Smith, loc. cit., pp. 620–1.

6 Harold A. Innis, "Minerva's Owl", in *The Bias of Communication* (University of Toronto Press, Toronto, 1951), p. 3, given as the presidential address to the Royal Society of Canada in 1947.

7 For example:

> The use of clay favored a dominant role for the temples with an emphasis on priesthood and religion. Libraries were built up in Babylon and Nineveh to strengthen the power of monarchy. Papyrus and a simplified form of writing in the alphabet supported the growth of democratic organization, literature, and philosophy in Greece. Following Alexander, empires returned with centres at Alexandria and elsewhere and libraries continued as sources of strength to monarchies. Rome extended the political organization of Greece in its emphasis on law and eventually on empire. Establishment of a new capital at Constantinople was followed by imperial organization on the oriental model particularly after official recognition of Christianity. Improvement of scripts and wider dissemination of knowledge enabled the Jews to survive by emphasis on the scriptures and the book. In turn Christianity exploited the advantages of parchment and the codex in the Bible. With access to paper the Mohammedans at Baghdad and later in Spain and Sicily provided a medium for the transmission of Greek science to the Western world. Greek science and paper with the encouragement of writing in the vernacular provided the wedge between the temporal and the spiritual power and destroyed the Holy Roman Empire. The decline of Constantinople meant a stimulus to Greek literature and philosophy as the decline of Mohammedanism had meant a stimulus to science. Printing brought renewed emphasis on the book and the rise of the Reformation. In turn new methods of communication weakened the worship of the book and opened the way for new ideologies. Monopolies or oligopolies of knowledge have been built up in relation to the demands of force chiefly on the defensive, but improved technology has strengthened the position of force on the offensive and compelled realignments favoring the vernacular.
>
> (ibid., pp. 31–2.)

HISTORY AND PERSPECTIVES

Marshall McLuhan, as is evident, was a disciple of Harold Innis (he wrote the introduction to the paperback edition of *The Bias of Communication*) and derived most of his major ideas from him. But McLuhan not only "hyped up" and vulgarized Innis's ideas, he also reversed the thrust of his argument, for Innis feared that the tendency of new media was to extend centralization and concentrate power, while McLuhan, though propagating the notion of a "global village", argued that the newer media would encourage decentralization and participation.

8 *Encyclopedia Britannica* (1970 ed.), s.v. "information theory".

9 Norbert Wiener, *Cybernetics* (Wiley, New York, 1948), p. 155.

10 Wassily Leontieff, "National Economic Planning: Methods and Problems", *Challenge*, July–August 1976, pp. 7–8.

> Referring to the further consequences of this new capacity, Leontieff writes: Such systematic information proves to be most useful in assessing structural – in this particular instance technological – relationships between the input requirements on the one hand, and the levels of output of various industries on the other. In the case of households these relationships would be between total consumers' outlay and spending on each particular type of goods. Stocks of equipment, buildings and inventories, their accumulation, their maintenance and their occasional reduction are described and analyzed in their mutual dependence with the flows of all kinds of goods and services throughout the entire system. Detailed, as contrasted with aggregative, description and analysis of economic structures and relationships can indeed provide a suitable framework for a concrete, instead of a purely symbolic description of alternative methods of production, and the realistic delineation of alternative paths of technological change.
>
> (ibid., p. 8.)

11 Indeed information is merely the negative measure of uncertainty, so to speak. Let me say immediately that I am not going to propose a quantitative measure. In particular, the well-known Shannon measure which has been so useful in communications engineering is not in general appropriate for economic analysis, for it gives no weight to the value of the information. If beforehand a large manufacturer regards it as equally likely whether the price of his product will go up or down, then learning which is true conveys no more information, in the Shannon sense, than observing of the toss of a fair coin.
Kenneth J. Arrow, *Information and Economic Behavior*, Office of Naval Research Technical Report No. 14 (Washington, DC), pp. 4–5.

12 As Arrow remarks:

> The presumption that free markets will lead to an efficient allocation of resources is not valid in this case. If nothing else, there are at least two salient characteristics of information which prevent it from being fully identified as one of the commodities represented in our abstract models of general equilibrium: (1) it is by definition indivisible in its use, and (2) it is very difficult to appropriate.
>
> (ibid., p. 11.)

13 Robert K. Merton, "Singletons and Multiples in Science", in Norman W. Storer (ed.), *The Sociology of Science*, the papers of Merton (University of Chicago Press, Chicago, 1900), p. 356.

THE SOCIAL FRAMEWORK OF THE INFORMATION SOCIETY

14 The problem is that economists have no direct measures of such "inputs" and treat them as "residuals", not accounted for by direct increases in the productivity of capital or labour. As Michael Spence writes:

> The difficulty in measuring information has hampered research concerned with the effects of information on [economic] growth. It is common practice to estimate the effect of education and knowledge on growth in GNP by first estimating the impact of real factors like the increase in capital stock, the labour force, and so on. One then attributes the growth that is not explained in these real factors to increases in knowledge.

15 There is a huge and growing literature on all these questions. I have drawn largely on the reports of the Harvard Programme on Information Technology and Policy for the material in this section.

16 In 1976, AT&T introduced a bill in Congress to allow it to buy out its microwave competitors, and it wants Congress to require anyone plugging specialized services into its lines to buy a connecting device from the phone company. IBM has entered into a direct challenge to AT&T by setting up the Satellite Business Systems Company jointly with Aetna Insurance and Comsat General to operate a satellite communications service that would transmit the full range of "compunications" by 1979.

17 See Fritz Machlup, *The Production and Distribution of Knowledge in the United States* (Princeton University Press, Princeton, 1962). For a detailed discussion of Machlup's types of knowledge in comparison with those of Max Scheler and my own, see Bell, *The Coming of Post-Industrial Society*, pp. 174–7. Since, for me, the heart of the postindustrial society is the new ways in which knowledge becomes instrumental for science and social policy, I have attempted an "objective definition" that would allow a researcher to plot the growth and use of knowledge.

18 Marc Porat has reformulated the 1967 National Income Accounts to make them consistent with accepted practices, and despite some admitted deficiencies, he has hewed to the standard usages. As Porat points out,

> Machlup's accounting scheme innovated rather liberally on the National Income Accounts and practices whereas this study does not. . . . His work includes an admixture of "primary" and "secondary" type activities, whereas this study keeps them distinct. Third, a variant of *final demand* is used by Machlup as a measure of knowledge industry size, whereas this study uses primarily the value added approach but reports both sets of figures. . . .

"The Information Economy" (Ph.D. diss., Stanford University, 1976), vol. 1, pp. 81–2.

HISTORY AND PERSPECTIVES

19 Machlup's key data can be presented in tabular form:

Distribution of proportion of Gross National Product spent on knowledge, 1958.

Type of knowledge and source of expenditures	Amount in millions of dollars	Percentage of total
Education	60,194	44.1
Research and development	10,090	8.1
Communication media	38,369	28.1
Information machines	8,922	6.5
Information services (incomplete)	17,961	13.2
Totals	136,436	100.0
Expenditures made by:		
Government	37,968	27.8
Business	42,198	30.9
Consumers	56,270	41.3
Totals	136,436	100.0

(*Source*: Machlup, *Production and Distribution of Knowledge*, pp. 360–1. Arranged in tabular form by permission.)

20 Gilbert Burck, "Knowledge, the Biggest Growth Industry of Them All", *Fortune*, November 1964.
21 Jacob Marschak, "Economics of Inquiring, Communicating, Deciding", *American Economic Review*, 58, No. 2 (1968), pp. 1–8.
22 The statistics and tables here, except where noted, are taken from Porat, "The Information Economy", vol. 1. The page citations refer to that volume. The figures on trends in the workforce are from a briefing packet that Mr Porat had prepared for presentation at an OECD conference. I am grateful to him for making these materials available to me, and for his correspondence in clarifying some of my questions. His revised work is scheduled to be published by Basic Books.
23 Porat divides the sector into eight major classes of industries: (1) the knowledge production and inventive industries; (2) information distribution and communication industries; (3) risk-management industries, including components of finance and insurance; (4) search and coordination industries, including all market information and advertising vendors; (5) information processing and transmission services, both electronic and nonelectronic; (6) informations goods industries, including information machines; (7) selected government activities that have direct market analogs in the primary information sector, including Postal Service and education; and (8) support facilities such as office and education buildings.

These eight major groups are further subdivided into 116 industries, which can be located in the Standard Industrial Classification; the monetary figures can be located in the National Income Accounts.
24 I am indebted for this technological information to a research paper by Paul DiMaggio, a graduate student of sociology at Harvard.
25 Georges Anderla, *Information in 1985. A Forecasting Study of Information Needs and Resources* (OECD, Paris, 1973), pp. 15–16.
26 D. de Solla Price, *Little Science, Big Science* (Columbia University Press, New York, 1963), p. 31. For a critical discussion of the use of logistic curves and some questions about Price's various starting points, see my *The Coming of*

THE SOCIAL FRAMEWORK OF THE INFORMATION SOCIETY

Post-Industrial Society, chap. 2. "The Measurement of Knowledge and Technology", pp. 177–85.

27 Anderla, *Information in 1985*, p. 21. The major specialist journals were: *Chemical Abstracts* and *Biological Abstracts* (which between them accounted for more than 550,000 items, more than half of the one million produced in 1971), *Engineering Index Monthly, Metals Abstracts, Physics Abstracts, Psychological Abstracts*, and a Geology Index Service.

28 The figures are taken from a paper by Lee Burchinal of the National Science Foundation, "National Scientific and Technical Information Systems", presented to an international conference in Tunis, 26 April 1976. I am grateful to Dr Burchinal for the reprint.

29 Cited by Colin Cherry, "The Spreading Word of Science", *Times Literary Supplement*, 22 March 1974, p. 301.

30 Roger G. Noll, "Regulation and Computer Services" in Dertouzos and Moses, op. cit.

31 Sidney Fernbach, "Scientific Use of Computers", in Dertouzos and Moses, op. cit.

32 Marvin Denicoff, "Sophisticated Software: The Road to Science and Utopia", in Dertouzos and Moses, op. cit.

33 Remarks made at the Science Information Policy Workshop, National Science Foundation, Washington, DC, 17 December 1974.

34 One major difficulty is the inadequacy of our statistics. As Peter H. Schuck remarks:

> What is perhaps more disturbing, given the imminence of national economic planning, is the abject poverty of our economic statistical base, upon which a good theory must be grounded. In recent years the inadequacy and inaccuracy of a broad spectrum of economic indices – including the wholesale price index, the consumer price index, the unemployment rate, and business inventory levels – have become quite evident. The wholesale price index, for example, reflects only list prices rather than actual transaction prices (which are often lower) and uses anachronistic seasonal adjustment factors; yet it is considered a bellwether statistic in economic forecasting.

("National Economic Planning: A Slogan without Substance", *The Public Interest*, Fall 1976, p. 72.)

35 D. S. L. Cardwell, *Turning Points in Western Technology* (Science History Publications, New York, 1972).

8

COMPUTOPIA

Rebirth of theological synergism

Yoneji Masuda

Source: Y. Masuda (ed.) (1980) *The Information Society as Post-Industrial Society*, Tokyo: Institute for the Information Society, pp. 146–58.

A vision of computopia

As I come to the final chapters of this book about the information society, I want to round off my discussion with *A Vision of Computopia* (abbreviation of Computer Utopia) [15]. Looking back over the history of human society, we see that as the traditional society of the Middle Ages was drawing to a close, the curtain was rising on the new industrial society. Thomas More, Robert Owen, Saint Simon, Adam Smith and other prophets arose with a variety of visions portraying the emerging society. The one that is of special interest to me is Adam Smith's vision of *a universal opulent society*, [26] which he sets out in 'The Wealth of Nations.' Smith's universal affluent society conceives the condition of plenty for the people, economic conditions that should free the people from dependence and subordination, and enable them to exercise true independence of spirit in autonomous actions.

Smith presented The Wealth of Nations to the world in 1776. Strangely, James Watt's first steam engine was completed in the same year, but although the Industrial Revolution was under way, Smith's grand vision of a universal society of plenty was still far off when he died in 1790. His vision seems to be half-realized two centuries later, as society reaches Rostow's High Mass Consumption stage. [27] The High Mass Consumption stage means that the material side of Smith's vision of people having material wealth in plenty is partially accomplished, at least in the advanced countries. The wider vision he had of individual independence and autonomy that would follow has clearly not been realized, because the axis around which the mass production and consumption of industrial goods turns in industrial society comprises machines and power. Capital investments are necessarily immense, with the result that the concentration of capital and corresponding centralized power are the dominating factors. This is the fundamental structure of all industrial societies, something that transcends the question of a society being capitalistic or socialistic.

Industrial societies are characterized by centralized government supported by a massive military and administrative bureaucracy, and in capitalist states supra-national enterprises have been added that make the modern state dependent on the trinity of industry, the military, and the government bureaucracy. In industrial societies the individual has freedom to take social action in three ways. A person is able to participate indirectly in government policy by voting in elections once every few years. One has the freedom of using income (received as compensation for subsistence labor) to purchase food and other articles necessary to sustain life, which implies freedom to use free time on weekends and holidays as one likes. This freedom of selection, however, is freedom only in a limited sense, quite removed from the voluntary action selection that Adam Smith envisioned.

As the 21st century approaches, however, the possibilities of a universally opulent society being realized have appeared in the sense that Smith envisioned it, and the information society (futurization society) that will emerge from the computer communications revolution will be a society that actually moves toward a universal society of plenty.

The most important point I would make is that the information society will *function around the axis of information values rather than material values,* cognitive and action-selective information. In addition, the information utility, the core organization for the production of information, will have the fundamental character of an infrastructure, and knowledge capital will predominate over material capital in the structure of the economy.

Thus, if industrial society is *a society in which people have affluent material consumption,* the information society will be *a society in which the cognitive creativity of individuals flourishes throughout society.* And if the highest stage of industrial society is the high mass consumption society, then the highest stage of the information society will be *the global futurization society,* a vision that greatly expands and develops Smith's vision of a universal opulent society; this is what I mean by 'Computopia'. This global futurization society will be a society in which everyone pursues the possibilities of one's own future, actualizing one's own self-futurization needs by acting in a goal-oriented way. It will be *global, in which multi-centered voluntary communities of citizens participating voluntarily in shared goals and ideas flourish simultaneously throughout the world.*

Computopia is a wholly new long-term vision for the 21st century, bearing within it the following seven-fold concepts:

HISTORY AND PERSPECTIVES

Pursuit and realization of time-value

My first vision of Computopia is that it will be *a society in which each individual pursues and realizes time-value*. In Japan, the advanced welfare society is often talked about, and people are now calling for a shift of emphasis from rapid economic growth to stable growth, stressing social welfare and human worth, sometimes expressed as a shift from a GNP society to a GNW society, i.e. gross national welfare. The current idea of an advanced welfare society, however, tends to place the emphasis on the importance of living in a green environment where the sun shines. Obviously, in seeking to escape from the pollution and congestion of cities, and from the threat of a controlled society, this concept is significant, as indicative of our times. Yet it does not embrace a dynamic vision of the future, which I feel is its greatest weakness. The disappearance of pollution and congestion or even escape from the cities will not alone bring satisfaction. Human needs are of a very high dimension that must be actively satisfied, the need for self-realization. The futurization society, as I see it, will be a society in which each individual is able to pursue and satisfy the need for self-fulfillment.

The self-realization I refer to is nothing less than the need to realize time value, and time value, of course, involves painting one's own design on the invisible canvas of one's future, and then setting out to create it. Such self-fulfillment will not be limited merely to individuals all pursuing their own self-realization aims, but will expand to include mini-groups, local societies, and functional communities.

Freedom of decision and equality of opportunity

My *second* vision is *freedom of decision and equality of opportunity*. The concepts of freedom and equality grew out of the Puritan Revolution (1649–1660) which occurred in England around the end of the Middle Ages. Initially the ideas of *freedom from absolute authority* and *legal equality* underlay these concepts, backed by the theories of social contract and individual consent as the basis of political authority, theories that maintain that freedom and equality are natural rights for all people. These two ideas provided the theoretical base for the formation of modern civil society.

As the capitalist economic system came into being, freedom and equality developed conceptually to include 'freedom to work at something of one's own choice', 'equality of ownership', and 'freedom to select an occupation,' and 'industrial equality,' more commonly referred to as free competition.

The information society will offer new concepts of freedom and equality, embodying *freedom of decision* and *equality of opportunity*.

As I have said, the information society will be a society in which each individual pursues and realizes time value. In this type of society the freedom that an individual will want most will be *freedom to determine voluntarily*

COMPUTOPIA: REBIRTH OF THEOLOGICAL SYNERGISM

the direction of time value realization in the use of available future time. Call it 'freedom of decision.' Freedom of decision is the freedom of decision-making for selection of goal-oriented action, and refers to the right of each individual to voluntarily determine how to use future time in achieving a goal. This will be the most fundamental human right in the future information society.

'Equality of opportunity' is *the right that all individuals must have, meaning that the conditions and opportunities for achieving the goals they have set for themselves must be available to them.* This will guarantee that all individuals have complete equality in all opportunities for education, and the opportunity to utilize such opportunities for action selection. Guaranteed equality of opportunity will, for the first time, assure that the people will share equally the maximum opportunities for realizing time value.

Flourishing diverse voluntary communities

My *third* vision is that there will be a *flourishing of diverse voluntary communities.* A society composed of highly educated people with a strong sense of community has long been a dream of mankind, and several attempts have been made to bring it into being. Recently communes have been formed by young groups, and a number of cooperative communities have been formed in Japan. One was the *Yamagishi-kai,* formed after the war. The rapid growth of information productive power built around the computer will see some big advances and developments beyond the ideas and attempts of the past. There will be enhanced independence of the individual, made possible for the first time by the high level of the information productive power of the information society. The development of information productive power will liberate man by reducing dependence on subsistence labor, with rapidly increasing material productive power as the result of automation, thus increasing the amount of free time one can use. There will also be an expanded ability to solve problems and pursue new possibilities, and then to bring such possibilities into reality; that is to say, it will expand one's ability for futurization.

The development of this information productive power will offer the individual more independence than can be enjoyed now.

Another point to be noted is the autonomous expansion of creativity that will follow. The keynote of utopian societies in the past has been the establishment of communal life through the common ownership of the means of production, based more or less on the prototype of primitive communism. This type of society has inevitably operated with a relatively low level of productive power; but the future information society will ensure more active voluntary communities, because humans will be liberated from dependence on subsistence labor, and because of the expanded possibilities for future time-value realization.

As a consequence, utopian societies will move on from being merely cooperative societies, where most time must still be given to sustaining existence, to become dynamic and creative voluntary communities. It is people with common goals who will form the new voluntary communities, communities that will always be carried on by voluntary activity and the creative participation of individuals; individual futurization and group futurization will be harmoniously co-ordinated with societal futurization. In the mature information society of the future, nature communities, non-smoking communities, energy conservation communities, and many other new types of voluntary communities will prosper side by side.

Interdependent synergistic societies

My *fourth* vision is *the realization of interdependent synergistic societies.* A synergistic society is one that develops as individuals and groups cooperate in complementary efforts to achieve the common goals set by the society as a whole. The functioning societal principle is *synergism,* a new principle to replace the free competition of the current capitalistic society.

In the future information society, information utilities, whose structure of production is characterized by self-multiplication and synergy, will take the place of the present large factories, and become the societal symbol of the information society. These information utilities will be the centers of productive power, yielding time value that will be the common goal of voluntary communities, because of *the self-multiplication* that characterized production in the information utility. Unlike material goods, information does not disappear by being consumed, and even more important, the value of information can be amplified indefinitely by constant additions of new information to the existing information. People will thus continue to utilize information which they and others have created even after it has been used, and, at macro level, the most effective way to increase the production and utilization of information will be for *people to work together to make and share societal information.* This economic rationality means that the information utility itself will become part of the infrastructure. It will be the force behind the productive power which gives birth to socio-economic values, and corresponding new socio-economic laws and systems will come into being as a matter of course. *Synergistic feedforward* will function as the new societal principle to establish and develop social order, with the resulting societies becoming voluntary communities.

Functional societies free of overruling power

My *fifth* vision is of *the realization of functional societies free of overruling power.* The history of the rule of man over man is long, continuing right into the present, simply changing form from absolute domination by an

COMPUTOPIA: REBIRTH OF THEOLOGICAL SYNERGISM

aristocracy linked with religion in feudal society to economic domination of enterprises in capitalist society, and to political domination by the bureaucracy in both socialist and capitalist society. The future information society, however, will become a *classless society,* free of overruling power, the core of society being voluntary communities. This will begin as informational and local communities comprising a limited number of people steadily develop and expand. A voluntary community is a society in which the independence of the individual harmonizes with the order of the group, and the social structure is a multi-centered structure characterized by mutual cohesion. By 'multi-centered' I mean that *every individual and group in a voluntary community is independent, and becomes a center.*' Mutual cohesion' means that *both individuals and groups that constitute the centers share a mutual attraction to form a social group.* Behind this mutual attraction lies the common goal, the spirit of synergy, with the ethics of self-imposed restraints. In other words, as individuals pursue their own time value, they work synergetically as a group to achieve a shared goal, and all exercise self-restraint so that there will be no interference with the social activities of others. This social structure is the overall control system of a voluntary community. In the political system, democracy based on participation of the citizens will be the general mode of policy making, rather than the indirect democracy of the parliamentary system. The technological base to support this participatory democracy will consist of (1) information networks made possible by the development of computer-communications technology, (2) simulation of policy models, and (3) feedback loops of individual opinions; with the result that policy making will change from policy making based on majority versus minority rule to policy making based on the balance of gain and loss to individuals in the spectrum of their areas of concern, both in the present and in future time. In policy making by this means, the feedback and accumulation of opinions will be repeated many times until agreement is reached, to insure the impartial balance of merits and demerits of the policy decision as it affects individuals and groups with conflicting interests.

The present bureaucratic administrative organization will be converted into *a voluntary management system of the citizens.* Only a small staff of specialists will be needed to carry out administrative duties, officers who are really professionals responsible for the administrative functions. The bureaucratic organization of a privileged class will disappear. In this voluntary civil society, ruling, coercion, and control over others will cease. Society will be *synergistically functional,* the ideal form that the information society should take.

Computopia: can it become a reality?

Can these visions of Computopia be turned into reality? We cannot escape the need to choose, before it is established, either 'Computopia' or an

HISTORY AND PERSPECTIVES

'Automated State'. These inescapable alternatives present two sharply contrasting bright and dark pictures of the future information society. If we choose the former, the door to a society filled with boundless possibilities will open; but if the latter, our future society will become a horrible and forbidding age.

As far as present indications go, we can say that there is *a considerable danger that we may move toward a controlled society.*

This is seen in the following tendencies:

During the first fifteen to twenty years of their availability, computers were used mainly by the military and other government organizations and large private institutions. Medium and small enterprises and individuals were generally barred from using computer-communications technology, since large scale computers at the early stages of automation were extremely costly. This situation caused a significant delay in democratic applications of computers. Initially, computers were used mainly for automatic control and labor-saving purposes, rather than 'problem-solving' applications. The development of automatic control of separate systems to integrated real-time control systems covering broad areas is increasing the danger of a controlled society.

The utilization of computers for major scientific and technological applications, such as space development, has led us to neglect the need for coexistence with nature, while our impact on nature has grown immeasurably. The development of 'big' science and technology has operated in such a way as to further increase the imbalance between human and nature systems.

If computerization continues in this direction, the possibility of a controlled society increases alarmingly.

However, I believe and predict that *the catastrophic course to an 'Automated State' will be avoided,* and that our choice will be to follow the path to 'Computopia.' I give you two logical reasons for my confidence.

The first theoretical basis is that *the computer as innovational technology is an ultimate science.* By 'ultimate science' I mean *a science that will bring immeasurable benefits to humanity if wisely used, but which would lead to destruction if used wrongly.* Nuclear energy, for example, can be an extremely useful source of energy, but it could kill the greater part of the human race in an instant. The computer may, in one sense, be more important, as an ultimate science, than atomic energy.

If computers were to be used exclusively for automation, a controlled society, the alienation of mankind and social decadence would become a reality. But if used fully for the creation of knowledge, a high mass knowledge creation society will emerge in which all people will feel their lives to be worth living. Further, an on-line, real-time system of computers connected to terminals with communication lines would turn society into a thoroughly managed society if utilized in a centralized way, but if their

COMPUTOPIA: REBIRTH OF THEOLOGICAL SYNERGISM

utilization is decentralized and open to all persons, it will lead to creation of a high mass knowledge creation society. Similarly, if data banks were to be utilized by a small group of people in power to serve their political purposes, it would become a police state, but if used for health control and career development, every person can be saved from the sufferings of disease, and be enabled to develop full potentialities, opening up new future opportunities and possibilities.

The computer thus confronts us with these alternatives: An "Automated State" or a "Computopia." So it is *not the forecasting* of the state of a future information society, *but our own choice* that is decisive. There is only one choice for us—the road to computopia. We cannot allow the computer, an ultimate science, to be used for the destruction of the spiritual life of mankind.

The second theoretical basis of my confidence is that *the information society will come about through a systematic, orderly transformation.* The information society will be such that information productive power will develop rapidly to replace material productive power, a development that will bring about a qualitative conceptual change in production, from production of material goods to the production of systems. What I mean is the production of far-reaching systems that include everything from production systems for material goods (such as automated factories), to social systems (wired cities, self-education systems), to political systems (direct citizen participation systems), and even to ecological systems.

Obviously, information productive power centering on the computer communications network will be the powerful thrust to bring about societal systems innovations. New social and economic systems will be created continuously, and society as a whole will undergo dynamic changes, not the drastic social changes of the past, typified by the power struggles of ruling classes, wars between nation states, and the political revolutions of mass revolt. It will be achieved through *systematic, orderly transformation.* As old socio-economic systems gradually become ineffectual and unable to meet the needs of the times, they will atrophy, and new, responsive socio-economic systems will take their place, in the way that a metamorphosis takes place with an organism, the useless parts of the body atrophying and other parts developing in response to the new demands.

Moreover, this systematic transformation of the societal structure will be brought about by citizen action, *changing means-and-goal oriented modes of action into cause-and-effect modes of action.* I have pointed out that human modes of action will become goal-oriented in the information society. These modes of goal-oriented action will evolve to the point where they function as a goal principle, to become the principle of social action. When this happens, social action will be logical, means-oriented action for the pursuit of common goals. So we can replace the term, 'goal-means oriented action,' with the term, 'cause-effect relationship,' following the idea

HISTORY AND PERSPECTIVES

of Max Weber, who changed this concept of goal-means relationship into a concept of cause-effect relationship. In the information society, the social actions of citizens in general will become goal-means relationships that operate as cause-effect relationships.

The rebirth of theological synergism of man and the supreme being

The final goal of Computopia is *the rebirth of theological* synergism of man and the supreme being, or if one prefers it, the ultimate life force, expressions that have meaning both to those of religious faith and the irreligious. This can be called the ultimate goal of Computopia. The relation existing between man and nature was the beginning of civilization. For many thousands of years man was completely encompassed by the systems of nature, which he had to obey or be destroyed by them. Five or six thousand years ago, man succeeded in harnessing these systems of nature in a limited way to increase agricultural production, and the first civilizations were built. This marked the beginning of man's conquest of nature. But with the Industrial Revolution the conquest of nature meant the destruction of nature, and now nature's retaliation has begun, the sequel to man's relation with nature that turned into destruction.

Now, a new relationship is beginning. At last, man and nature have begun to act together in a new ecological sense, on a global scale, in synergistic society. At the base of this conversion of human society into an ecological system is the awareness of the limitations of scientific technology. It means awareness that scientific technology is simply the application of scientific principles, and that these can not be changed by man, nor can he create new principles to work and live by. It is also a new awareness of the commonality of man's destiny, in that there is no place where man can live except on this earth, which first gave him life; from this very awareness is emerging the idea of a synergistic society where man and nature must exist in true symbiosis.

This is the assertive, dynamic idea that *man can live and work together with nature, not by a spirit of resignation that says man can only live within the framework of natural systems;* but, not living in hostility to nature, man and nature will work together as one. Put another way, man approaches the universal supra life, with man and god acting as one.

God does not refer to a god in the remote heavens; it refers to nature with which we live our daily lives. The scientific laws that we have already identified and are aware of are simply manifestations of the activity of this supreme power. The ultimate ideal of the global futurization society will be for man's actions to be in harmony with nature in building a synergistic world.

This synergism is a modern rebirth of the theological synergism which teaches that *'spiritual rebirth depends upon the cooperation of the will of man*

136

and the grace of God,' however it may be expressed. It aims to build an earthly, not a heavenly, synergistic society of god and man.

When we open the book of history, we see that when man brought about the accumulation of wealth and an increase in productive power, various choices had to be made. The Greeks built magnificent temples to Apollo and carved beautiful statues of Venus. The Egyptians built gigantic pyramids for their Pharaohs, and the Romans turned the brutalities of the Colosseum into a religious rite. The Chinese built the Great Wall to keep out the barbarians. Now man has made the fires of heaven his own, and left footprints on the craters of the moon.

We are moving toward the 21st century with the very great goal of building a Computopia on earth, the historical monument of which will be only several chips one inch square in a small box. But that box will store many historical records, including the record of how four billion world citizens overcame the energy crisis and the population explosion; achieved the abolition of nuclear weapons and complete disarmament; conquered illiteracy; and created a rich symbiosis of god and man without the compulsion of power or law, but by the voluntary cooperation of the citizens to put into practice their common global aims.

Accordingly, the civilization to be built as we approach the 21st century will not be a material civilization symbolized by huge constructions, but will be virtually *an invisible civilization.* Precisely, it should be called an 'information civilization.' *Homo sapiens,* who stood at the dawn of the first material civilization at the end of the last glacial age, is now standing at the threshold of the second, the information civilization after ten thousand years.

References

1. H. A. Simon, *'The Impact of the Computer on Management'*, Presented at the 15th CIOS World Conference, Tokyo, Japan, 1969.
2. Y. Masuda, *'A New Development Stage of the Information Revolution'*, Applications of Computer/Communications Systems, DECD Informatics Studies 8. Paris: DECD, 1975.
   The Plan for Information Society: A National Goal toward the 2000 Year. Tokyo: Japan Computer Usage Development Institute, 1971.
3. *Toward the Information Society.* Report of the Industrial Structure Council, Ministry of International Trade and Industry. Tokyo: Computer Age, 1969.
4. *The International Opinion Poll on 'The Plan for Information Society.* JCUDI Report, Tokyo: Japan Computer Usage Development Institute, 1973.
5. *Report on Tama CCIS Experiment Project in Japan.* Tokyo: Living-Visual Information System Development Association, 1978.
6. *Report on Hi-OVIS Experiment Project.* Tokyo: Living-Visual Information System Development Association, 1979.
7. J. C. Madden, *Videotex in Canada.* Ottawa: Department of Communications, Government of Canada, 1979.

HISTORY AND PERSPECTIVES

8. *Telecommunications and Regional Development in Sweden*. Stockholm: A Progress Report of Swedish Board for Technical Development, 1977.

9. Y. Masuda, '*Social Impact of Computerization. An Application of the Pattern Model for Industrial Society*, Challenges from the Future. Tokyo: Kodansha, 1970.

10. Y. Masuda, '*The Conceptual Framework of Information Economics*, IEEE Transaction on Communications, October 1975. New York: IEEE Communications Society.

11. S. Kuznets, *Modern Economic Growth: Rate, Structure and Spread*. New Hayen and London: Yale University Press, 1966.

12. J. Ota, *Amoeba*, NHK Books. Tokyo: Nihon Hoso Shuppan Kyokai, 1960.

13. Y. Masuda, '*Computopia vs. Automated States: Unavoidable Alternatives for the Information Era*' The Next 25 Years, Crisis and Opportunity. Washington D.C.: World Future Society, 1975.

14. K. E. Boulding, *The Economy of Love and Fear: A Preface to Grants Economics*. California: Wadsworth, 1973.

15. Y. Masuda, '*Triple Concept of Information Economics*', Proceedings of the 2nd International Conference on Computer Communication, Stockholm, 1974.

16. Y. Masuda, '*Future Perspectives for Information Utility*', Proceedings of the International Conference on Computer Communication, Kyoto, Japan, 1978.

17. Y. Masuda, '*A New Era of Global Information Utility*', Proceedings of Eurocomp 78, London, 1978.

18. Y. Masuda, *Information Economics*. Tokyo: Sangyo Noritsu University Press, 1976.

19. Y. Masuda, '*Privacy in the Future Information Society*', Computer Networks, Special Issue, 1979. Amsterdam: North-Holland.

20. Y. Masuda, '*Management of Information Technology for Developing Countries: Adaptation of Japanese Experience to Developing Countries*', Data Exchange, April 1974. London: Diebold Europe.

21. Y. Masuda, '*A Plan for the Information Society in Developing Countries*', Presentation at the 5th Brazil Telecommunication Congress, Sao Paulo, 1979.

22. H. Otsuka, *Method of Social Science*. Tokyo: Iwanami Publishing Co., 1966.

23. W. M. Kitzmiller, R. Ottinger, *Citizen Action: Vital Force for Change*. Washington D.C.: Center for a Voluntary Society, 1971.

24. *Aktuellt*, Bulletin of VISIR. Stockholm: VISIR. The Smoking Digest: Progress Report on a Nation Kicking the Habit. Washington D.C.: US Department of Health, Education, and Welfare, 1977.

25. Y. Masuda, *Computopia*. Tokyo: Diamond, 1966.

26. A. Smith, '*An Early Drft of the Wealth of Nations*' in W. R. Scott, Adam Smith as Student and Professor. Glasgow: 1937.

27. W. W. Rostow, *The Stage of Economic Growth*. London: The Syndics of the Cambridge University Press, 1960.

Part 2

FURTHER REFLECTIONS AND CRITICAL PERSPECTIVES

9

WHOSE NEW INTERNATIONAL ECONOMIC AND INFORMATION ORDER?

Herbert I. Schiller

Source: *Communication* 5(4) (1980): 299–314.

"We conclude our work, therefore, not with another recommendation but with an exhortation: with all the force at our command, we urge the government of Canada to take immediate action to alert the people of Canada to the perilous position of their collective sovereignty that has resulted from the new technologies of telecommunications and informatics; and we urge the Government of Canada and the governments of the provinces to take immediate action to establish a rational structure for telecommunications in Canada as a defence against the further loss of sovereignty in all its economic, social, cultural, and political aspects."*

Production sites in the world economy are shifting. They are being relocated globally by transnational corporations seeking maximum profits by taking advantage of international differentials in wages, taxes, raw material availabilities, and political complaisance. Simultaneously, a spectacular growth of new communication technologies facilitates the operation of those companies that carry on business in dozens of countries.

While this is the reality, a different set of expectations has prevailed in much of the world for at least the last twenty years, expressed in the demands for a new world economic and—later—information order. These demands were predicated on the determination of people in the former colonial, and other dominated areas, to shake off their shackles of poverty, forged by economic and cultural dependency.

Yet deep structural changes in the social and productive spheres, *inside both* the dominating and dominated states, have always been a precondition for the realization of equal relationships between poor and rich nations. The full dimensions of a new world economic order, from this perspective, have never been fully articulated. Still it is clear that most of the prevailing economic assumptions and relations governing production and distribution and, indeed, what constitutes "development" itself, are open to review and revision.

The demand for a new world information order—a demand which emerged more slowly—reflected similar impulses. The definition and presentation of everyday reality, nationally and internationally, have been the prerogatives of a score of media conglomerates. The concentrated control of information by Western monopolies has created enormous difficulties for those seeking economic self-determination and political autonomy. By its myth-making and information control, the Western media system has also provided transnational corporate business with confused and pacified domestic publics in their home territories. Finally, information management for years permitted the dominating centers to ignore or misrepresent Third World demands for new arrangements.

Now new tendencies can be seen. The far reaching industrial and technological shifts occurring under the initiatives and guidance of transnational business provide an opportunity for the centers of domination to adopt the *language*, if not the substance, of socially desirable change. The new electronic industries, the changing sites of industrial production, and the sophisticated instrumentation that permits high volume, instantaneous international communication are imposing a new form of dependency on much of the world. At the same time, these developments are being described as facilitating a new global economic and informational order. But this is an "order" quite unlike the one perceived originally by Third World and Non-Aligned Nations. It arises not out of dependency and the desire to overcome it—the inspiration of the poor world. The current vision springs from the beneficiaries of domination and their intention of perpetuating it.

The economic and social transformations now taking place around the world, and the effort to present these changes as the answer to longstanding Third World demands for a substantively new economic and informational order, are the subjects of this paper.

Transformation in the Western industrialized economies

What is happening, it is important to state at the outset, is not a linear, preconceived, and predetermined transformation of the international political economy. The energizing stimuli heavily influencing what now is occurring are the relatively recent substantive changes in the American and a few other industrially advanced economies. Briefly put, change on a global scale is being activated by a complex set of pressures, initiatives, and requirements arising out of domestic developments in a few core industrial areas, foremost of which is the United States. A review of some of the significant changes in the American economy since the end of the Second World War is indicative and suggestive (though it should be noted that the following account accepts unquestioningly descriptions of the American economy as "pluralistic" and controlled by "middle management administration"):

> Consider the shrinking percentage of blue-collar workers in the labor force, with the near-doubling (inflation discounted) of the gross national product since W. W. II; the expansion of research and development in governmental and business budgets and the flowering of major new industries built on the technologies of solid-state electronics and information processing: the transformation of family-owned big businesses into multinational conglomerates under multilayered middle-management administration; the substantial growth of the not-for-profit private governmental sectors of the pluralistic U.S. economy; the proliferation of the control functions of the Federal Government into many aspects of the economy. . . .[1]

Within the overall pattern, the most striking development is the phenomenal growth of the so-called information sector, a not-too-clearly defined category that includes the production of information technology and goods and the information services utilized by the rest of American industry (and society). New industries have appeared in the last thirty years, producing a spectacular range of electronic instrumentation which, in turn, has been installed rapidly, though unevenly, in manufacturing and services across the country. The productivity of the domestic economy is more and more reliant on information processes and electronic systems. According to one estimate, thirty percent of the labor force is "currently in contact with computers on a daily basis." In the early 1980s, it is claimed that the figure will increase to 50 percent and reach 70 percent by 1985.[2] Rarely encountered twenty years ago, computers and microprocessors today are literally household items.

While the domestic importance of computerization grows almost daily, the well-being of the information industries which provide the hardware and services is itself increasingly dependent on the *world* market for growth and sales. In a magazine forum reviewing the status of the semiconductor industry, organized by *Datamation*, two key figures in the field emphasized the importance of the international market for U.S. producing companies. H. Gunther Rudenberg, senior staff member of Arthur D. Little, Inc. observed: ". . . It's an international production scene and an international marketing scene. . . ." Roger Bender, president of NEC Microcomputers, added; ". . . Fortunately—or unfortunately, depending on your point of view—the U.S. semiconductor industry is world-oriented; it invests heavily in R & D, and it is not going to roll over and be absorbed by foreign manufacturers."[3] Information machinery, information services, information products and information "know how" have become increasingly significant items and components in American foreign trade, as well as supplying dynamism to the domestic economy. An Arthur D. Little study estimated that the world market for telecommunications equipment would more than double between 1977 and 1987, going from $30 to $65 billion, with the greatest market potential in the developing nations.[4]

In contrast with other sectors of American manufacturing, where exports have been stagnating, trade figures for 1978 showed that "The U.S. favorable balance of trade in computers and related equipment increased by almost half a billion dollars. . . . The favorable balance was $3.439 billion, compared with $3.011 billion the previous year." Altogether, "The U.S. exported almost $4.2 billion in computers and related equipment during 1978, up from $3.26 billion the year before. . . ."[5] In services too, the processing and transmission of data, U.S. firms are increasingly active internationally. "U.S. computer firms" one observer notes, "are major world suppliers, deriving about half of their revenues from overseas sales; overseas revenues of U.S. computer firms from sales of services was one billion dollars in 1976 for both on-line and software services and may increase to more than two billion dollars by 1981."[6]

Another dimension adds significance to the information sector. It has been recognized for some time that familiar cultural products and services —film, TV programs, books, news, records, etc.—besides offering entertainment, are ideological items embodying social values and messages and consequently influencing the organization of the entire social enterprise. Such vital matters as the locus of decision-making—the issue of centralization or local control—are affected, if not determined, by the structure and operation of the (imported) electronic telecommunications facilities. So, too, questions of the organization of the workplace and labor's role in production are bound up with the information systems now being introduced. Dominique Wolton of the University of Paris spent several months in the United States, interviewing journalists and publishers about the new communication technologies. He was startled to find that there was practically no attention given to the question of the impact of the new systems and instrumentation on the character of the work and the work process itself. He wrote:

> The fact that the transition from paper to computers is bound to modify the process of intellectual creation was never mentioned. Yet the new technology necessarily makes this creative process more abstract, involving an essentially visual, rather than a material or tactile, relationship to writing, which now occurs within the fixed space of the display screen. Who can deny that here we have the seeds of a change in the journalist's relation to his work? . . .
>
> Again, little was said about changes in the organization of this work; journalists instead made the point that electronic editing allows them greater control over their copy. Yet this advance raises the question of what will happen to the line dividing the activities

of the journalist from those of typesetters and other production workers. The question gains urgency as the technical capabilities of the former encroach on those of the latter. . . .[7]

Wolton also expressed surprise that no consideration seems to have been given to what may be the consequences of the substitution of selective computerized information on demand for the more general information customarily supplied by newspaper and other large circulation organs of information.

For both economic and ideological reasons, therefore, the information industries and their ancillary activities have become vital determinants of existing and future power relations *within* and *between* nations. An official British paper, for example, notes that "It is the view of the United Kingdom that information processing and handling in all its aspects is now *the* critical technology for advanced industrial countries."[8] A recent French study, likewise, states that ". . . data processing has become a strategic sector in most countries."[9] Similar appraisals are found in the United States. Some have begun to sketch in the larger meaning of informational supremacy in the time ahead. Relating information to global economic developments of recent years, one senior analyst made this connection:

A small but increasingly powerful group of decision-makers—in government as well as in industry—are now coming to believe that an ideal way to relate to the world economy is as an idea and knowledge exporter, based on sophisticated information tools. For example, publications, software, and data can be sold abroad for export revenue, and the knowledge and our natural resources still remain at home—you can sell information over and over again and still have it. . . .[10]

Another voice, speaking perhaps for the "powerful group of decision-makers," is that of John Eger, formerly director of the now defunct (Nixon Administration's) White House Office of Telecommunications Policy. Eger urges an acceleration in the transformation of the domestic economy, eliminating as quickly as possible older, less profitable manufacturing industries. In truth, his vision comprehends a massively reorganized division of labor, worldwide. In this reorganization, the United States would provide the vital information function. To be sure, such an approach necessitates difficult decisions—which Eger is prepared fully to recommend: "If we do proceed to bargain on information flow," he states, "we will have to be prepared to make trade concessions in other areas, where our technological advantage is smaller and our labor costs greater. The results could well be a loss of jobs in older domestic industries in exchange for guarantees that our growing information industry will continue to expand."[11]

HISTORY AND PERSPECTIVES

The design for a worldwide redistribution of industrial production is, of course, not unilaterally American. It takes into account historical factors that have been pushing things in this direction for some time. Manufacturing capacity, especially in basic industrial fields, has developed in many countries outside the North American and West European centers. Two world wars and innumerable regional conflicts have contributed heavily to this movement. More important still, the rapid expansion of transnational corporate activity in the last three decades has created a substantial number of manufacturing facilities in the less industrially developed nations. These innumerable manufacturing enclaves are now striving to enter the world market with their outputs, and the outcry of some U.S. industries for "protection" against these goods is indicative of the heavy weather ahead. Efforts to encourage the re-deployment of the manufacturing base have to be understood in this overall context.

The rationale of comparative advantage

The public rationale for proposed redistribution of industrial manufacturing worldwide rests heavily on a doctrine developed in the 19th century known as comparative advantage. It argues that optimum benefits occur when each nation exchanges what it produces most advantageously, i.e., at lowest cost. The doctrine contains less than the whole truth. Most disturbingly, it accepts conditions of differential capacity or advantage as fixed, ignoring the historical factors that may have contributed to present relationship. In this way the doctrine presents itself as timeless truth, permitting no change in the underlying conditions and relationships of those caught up in its operation.

Applying comparative advantage to international data communications, two enthusiasts describe how benefits are supposed to derive from the doctrine's application:

> In societies in which information activities generate up to half of the GNP, substantial gains in productivity will arise from efficiency gains in that sector. Thus there is good economic reason to use the cheapest, fastest, most accurate, and most complete information facilities available, wherever they may be located. Just as international trade in physical commodities has raised living standards in the world community by allowing use of commodities produced in the most advantageous places, so societies half of whose economic activities consist of information operations will gain mutual advantage from shared use of information resources, with each nation working especially at activities in which it has a comparative advantage. Energy and other scarce resources can be saved by linking distributed activities electronically, rather than duplicating expensive facilities in many physical locations.[12]

WHOSE INTERNATIONAL ECONOMIC & INFORMATION ORDER?

Actually, this near eulogistic tribute to comparative advantage is addressed to the developed market economies in Western Europe—the OECD countries. It is these industrializad economies which at this time are challenging the "advantage" of United States-based information industries and threatening to curtail their operation in Europe.

The modern proponents of comparative advantage are silent about the appalling inequities and dependencies that historically have accompanied the doctrine's implementation. The early post-World War Two efforts by Third World countries to overcome economic backwardness and dependency were directed largely at the effects of comparative advantage, as they had accumulated in Asia, Africa, and Latin America. So it is a bitter irony that the exploited countries, some of which are now embarked on at least limited industrialization, are again being pushed into unequal economic and informational relationships under the guise of comparative advantage.

It should be understood that the shifts, proposed and actual, in the world division of labor, based on an ever-increasing utilization of information in the productive process as well as in continuously expanding service industries, do not imply a fully-developed plan with each participant neatly and consciously assigned a particular slot in the global economy of the future. What is occurring, rather, is a projection of some developments that have taken place already and others that are becoming apparent. It is not predestined but it may be predictable. Daniel Bell writes:

> ... because of a combination of market and political forces, a new international division of labor is taking place in the world economy ... It is likely that in the next decades traditional, routinized manufacturing, such as textile, shipbuilding, steel, shoe, and small consumer appliances industries, will be centered in this new tier (e.g., Brazil, Mexico, South Korea, Taiwan, Singapore, Algeria, Nigeria) that is beginning to industrialize rapidly.

Bell believes that this global realignment in production will not be achieved easily or smoothly:

> The response of the advanced industrial countries will be either protectionism and the disruption of the world economy or the development of a 'comparative advantage' in, essentially, the electronic and advanced technological and science-based industries that are the feature of post-industrial society. How this development takes place will be a major issue of economic and social policy for the nations of the world in the next decade.[13]

Bell does not discuss why this large scale shift in productive activity worldwide may be expected to be troublesome, but that is the nub of the problem.

The changing division of labor internationally is being initiated, guided, and implemented largely by the transnational corporate system, and that system is the chief beneficiary of the changes occurring.

The worldwide media system, for the most part also under transnational corporate control, ignores or misrepresents what is transpiring. When the shift is presented at all, it is described as historically progressive, a step toward "modernization," and in the interest of people everywhere. The costs and burdens—most of which are still to be experienced—are over-looked and unmentioned. An elementary lesson in capitalistic enterprise is being played out on a world stage: benefits are going to the holders of capital while burdens are being borne by the vast majority without property stakes.

More than a hundred industrially weak and exploited nations since the second world war have sought to create a new international environment in which the economic, political, and cultural fetters that prevented their autonomous development would be broken. Now both the economic and informational movements have been incorporated as vehicles to facilitate the global relocation and control of economic activity. Under transnational corporate direction, production in conventional industrial goods and services is being transferred worldwide to sites with impoverished workers, tax exemptions, and complaisant governments. Information industries are, at the same time, taking over as the central foci of economic activity in the earlier industrialized core areas. As this relocational process unfolds, the New International Economic Order is itself recast but hardly into a progressive arrangement.

The new industrial producer nations are being brought into the existing world structure, carrying on their newly-developed industrial activities under market rules and with market criteria that date back at least a century and a half. A United Nations resolution, adopted in 1975, explains and validates the overall process:

> Developed countries should facilitate the development of new policies and strengthen existing policies, including labor market polic-ies, which would encourage the redeployment of their industries which are less competitive internationally to developing countries, thus leading to structural adjustments in the former and a higher degree of utilization of natural resources in the latter.[14]

One writer sees the international division of labor, resulting from what he terms this "integrative approach," as leading to a familiar condition:

> The main directionality of the linkages in this division of labor— and the international system of which it is a part—is thus such that the developed countries provide the consumption patterns,

technology, skills, capital, etc. to the developing countries which then establish production facilities to service the markets of the North.[15]

All of this leads to the bleak conclusion that such an international economic order "with its reliance on transnational enterprises is not likely to be a framework for a new and more equitable world economic order but rather designed to stabilize the present order and thus contain a further deterioration of the position of the developing countries."

The new international *information* order falls neatly into this general context. As information is crucial for the operation of the transnational corporate system, there is every reason to expand international communications. Increased linkages, broadened flows of information and data, and above all, installation of new communication technology are expected to serve the world business system.

Operationalizing the new communications technology in the new order

Technology plays a vital role in the emerging new scheme of things, first to integrate the transnational corporate system and second to deepen the dependence of the peripheral world on hardware, software, training, and administration supplied by that system. Less developed nations are not to be denied the new technology. Rather, technology is being pressed on the poorer countries in an atmosphere of urgency. "We must offer to expand communication systems abroad," urges one promoter of U.S. information policy. "Imaginative use of our satellites and earth stations, shared time on our broadcasting channels, crash projects to produce cheap newsprint—all and more are readily possible. . . ."[16] It is reasonable to believe that this is intended to assure the implantation of Western developmental models— of production, administration, consumption, and education.

The effect will be dependency. Writing about the possible transfer of information technology, one observer notes:

> Even if the U.S. Government did subsidize access to U.S. data banks and "information resources" [the U.S. proposal at the UNESCO 1978 Paris meeting and elsewhere], it is questionable how useful this information would be . . . In order for information to have real utility it has to be tailored to the needs and circumstances of the user, and this simply is not achieved through the installation of an international data network. However, once the technical, financial, and management skills and infrastructures have been developed, as in the case of Taiwan, Hong Kong, Malaysia, and others, then the export of information is related to the export of capability and "comparative advantage."[17]

HISTORY AND PERSPECTIVES

Suggestive of the efforts undertaken to create an international atmosphere of encouragement, if not urgency, for the rapid adoption of new communications technology, the International Telecommunications Union (ITU) organized a forum in Geneva in September, 1979, the introductory section of which was called Telecommunication Perspectives and Economic Implications. The subjects under discussion were: "strategies for dealing with evolving international telecommunications; industrial products and transfer of technology for effective operation; telecommunication services and networks; [and] financing of telecommunications."

Offering views on these important questions was a panel of speakers recruited almost exclusively from the most powerful companies producing equipment in the transnational corporate system. Among them, were: The President of RCA, the Vice-President and Chief Scientist of IBM, the President of Siemens AG, the Vice-President of the Executive Board at Philips; the Executive Vice-President of A.T.&T; the Vice-President and Group Executive of Hughes Aircraft; and similar ranking officers from Thomson-CSF, *NASA*, Comsat, and Ericsson (Sweden). Supplying the new instrumentation and processes would mean consolidating longterm Western control in international markets, over equipment, replacement parts, servicing, and finance, and so even mild attempts to establish international specifications and protective standards are rebuffed and labelled "premature."[18]

1. Information inequality in the center of the system

Though this is small consolation to the rest of the world, in the global shift of economic and informational activity now proceeding, *the center of the system, no less than the periphery, experiences deepening inequalities.*

To the developing nations, the new communications technology is promoted as a means of lessening social gaps in education and literacy and as a means of leapfrogging into the modern age, with classrooms and businesses informed from satellite broadcasts. For the already industrialized countries, the promise is of electronic democracy, including plebiscites and polls carried out at home by the touch of a button on the living room TV console. These are claims the transnational corporate system circulates through its transnational media circuits, but actual developments in the United States and elsewhere present another reality.

Evidence is beginning to come in. According to one report on the computer-telecommunications industry, ". . . policy trends now in motion will favor the development of business, government or specialized network service for large users . . . Most of the *Fortune 500* companies and about one-third of the medium-sized companies in the nation will account for almost 80% of network usage." As a result of these trends, the study hypothesizes that by the 1990s in the United States, "the issue will be one of inequality of access to information, with the specialized networks doing

150

quite well financially because of the valuable and efficient services they will be providing." At the same time, "evidence of societal and economic split will become apparent through the growing incidence of small business failures no longer able to purchase the information they need to remain competitive as information becomes increasingly available only in electronic form."[19] Thus, in the very heart of the most advanced information society, it is predicted that, contrary to widely-publicized claims, the introduction of electronic information systems will deepen information inequality in the social order.

2. The free flow of information

In the period from 1940–1970, "the free flow of information" was a major element in United States information and foreign policy.[20] It generally was limited to the market needs of the American media industries, though it was also directed against the socialist nations.

But now it transcends the question of expanded markets for American media interests. Information gathering, processing, and transmission have become essential elements in corporate America's quest for hegemony in a new international economic order. The free flow of information concept, one analyst writes, "... is the pillar not only of U.S. civil liberties and individual freedoms, but the market economy as well ... And many U.S. commentators and officials have avowed that the concept of free flow is a wholly non-negotiable item."[21] Similarly, the Director of Security Programs for *IBM* writes:

> I believe the paramount objective should be the preservation of the free flow of information across and within national borders balanced by considerations for privacy and national security. This must be the single most important objective simply because of the immense economic and political impact of free information flow in today's society. So much of this information flow takes place beneath the surface of our conscious activities that we literally take it for granted. Perhaps we would only realize its true value and impact if it were restricted.[22]

But historically and currently, the free flow of information is a myth. Where the flow *does* move freely is in privately organized circuits between corporate affiliates in the international sphere. Selectors and controllers continue, as they always have, to sift and shape the messages that circulate in society. It is always a matter of who the selectors are and whom they represent.

The information industries support and facilitate the operation of the hefty American-owned slice of the transnational corporate system. Public

HISTORY AND PERSPECTIVES

scrutiny is avoided and strong efforts are made to keep matters as they are. As new technology makes all communications processes increasingly interchangeable—i.e., messages, whatever the form (record, voice, visual) are reducible to electric impulses—transnational businesses have the opportunity to reach large audiences and publics on their own terms, possibly through their own informational circuits. A recent study notes: "The ability to communicate with masses of people is spreading beyond the 'institutional media.'" And a United States Supreme Court decision in 1978 approved the principle that "a telephone company, or any other corporation, has First Amendment rights."[23] Moreover, in recent years, United States policy-makers have defended American broadcasters' rights to use direct satellite broadcasting—when it became available—without submitting to national oversight from any country.

Will the new international economic and information order be achieved?

Industrial competition, technological developments, social movements, and national policies are changing the contours of the international economy and the global information system, and the main activators and controllers of this change have been the transnational corporations—TNCs. In Canada, a recent study commissioned with some urgency by the Government recommended a "national awareness campaign" to explain the social, economic, and cultural implications of the new electronic information society, and to alert Canadians to the increasing threat (from American TNCs) to their "collective sovereignty."[24] National campaigns to inform people of the dangers facing them can be an important element in the effort to create resistance to developments underway. But specific measures, nationally formulated and implemented, are indispensable if some success in countering the TNCs is to be expected. Their penetration and domination is bound up inextricably with the property structure and institutions of the host country.

The impact of the changing international division of labor will be felt deeply both in the industrialized and the industrializing societies. The experiences of the industrializing process in the 19th century suggest that those in command might attempt to push the entire burden of the dislocations onto the working population, and how that would affect political stability and the social order remains to be seen. Still, there are not the same opportunities for industrialization to proceed as it did in Western society a century ago. Resources are not available to allow the profligacy that accompanied early capitalist expansion in the West. And the turbulence of anti-imperialist movements in the twentieth century is too great to allow passive acceptance of socio-economic institutions that are deeply exploitative and structurally inequitous.

WHOSE INTERNATIONAL ECONOMIC & INFORMATION ORDER?

Critical to the outcome everywhere will be the understanding that what is at issue is not technical change or resource availabilities, though of course they are related matters. At issue is the structural character of the world community and the quality of life and social existence it offers to *all* people.

Notes and references

* *Telecommunications and Canada*, report of the Consultative Committee on the Implications of Telecommunications for Canadian Sovereignty (The Clyne Report) Ottawa, March, 1979, page 76.

1 Eli Ginzberg, "The Professionalization of the U.S. Labor Force," *Scientific American*, Vol. 240, No. 3, March 1979, p. 48.
2 E. Drake Lundell, "Greater Penetration Viewed as Critical DP Issue," *Computerworld*, February 19, 1979.
3 "The Chip Revolution . . . A Candid Conversation," *Datamation*, June, 1979, Vol. 25, No. 7, pp. 98–107.
4 *Computerworld*, April 17, 1979, p. 80.
5 *Ibid.*, June 4, 1979.
6 W. Fishman, "International Data Flow: Personal Privacy and Other Matters," paper presented to the Fourth International Conference on Computer Communication, Kyoto, Japan, February 3, 1978.
7 Dominique Wolton, "Do You Love Your VDT?" *Columbia Journalism Review*, July/August, 1979, Vol. XVIII, No. 2, pp. 36–39.
8 "Taking A Stand On A Critical Technology," editorial in *Computing*, September 7, 1978, London, emphasis in original.
9 Simon Nora and Alain Mine, "L'Informatisation de la Societe," La Documentation Francaise, Paris, 1978.
10 Vincent E. Guiliano, "Electronic Office Information Systems and the Information Manager," *Bulletin of the American Society for Information Science*, Vol. 4, No. 3 (February) 1978, p. 13.
11 John M. Eger, "Protest of Global 'Information War' Poses Biggest Threat to U.S.," *The Washington Post*, January 15, 1978.
12 Ithiel de Sola Pool and Richard J. Solomon, "Transborder Data Flows: Requirements for International Co-Operation," Organization for Economic Cooperation and Development (OECD), Working Party on Information, Computer and Communications Policy, DSTI/ICCP/78.21, Paris, 26th July, 1978, pp. 17–18.
13 Daniel Bell, "Communications Technology—for better or for worse," *Harvard Business Review*, Vol. 57, No. 3, May–June, 1979, p. 26.
14 "Development and International Economic Cooperation," Resolution 3362 (S-VIII), UN General Assembly, Seventh Special Session, 16 September 1975.
15 Karl P. Sauvant, "The Role of Transnational Enterprise in the Establishment of the New International Economic Order: A Critical Review," Ervin Laszlo and Jorge Alberto Lozoya, eds., *Strategies for the NIEO* (Oxford: Pergamon, 1979), p. 24.
16 Leonard R. Sussman, "A New World Information Order?" *Freedom at Issue*, November/December, 1978, No. 48, p. 9.
17 John H. Clippenger, "The Hidden Agenda," *Journal of Communication*, Winter, 1979, Vol. 29, No. l, pp. 197–203.
18 The U.S. Delegate to the Strategies and Policies for Informatics (SPIN) meeting in Torremolinos, Spain, in August, 1978, stated this explicitly.

19 Herbert S. Dordick, Helen G. Bradley, Burt Nanus, and Thomas H. Martin, "The Emerging Network Marketplace," F35, December, 1978. Center for Futures Research, Graduate School of Business Administration, University of Southern California, Los Angeles, CA.

20 Herbert I. Schiller, *Communication and Cultural Domination*, (New York: M. E. Sharpe, 1976), ch. 2.

21 Clippenger, *op. cit.*, p. 199.

22 Harry B. DeMaio, "Transnational Information Flow: A Perspective," *Data Regulation: European and Third World Realities*, p. 170.

23 William H. Read, "The First Amendment Meets the Second Revolution," Working Paper W-79-3. Harvard University Program on Information Resources Policy, Cambridge, Massachusetts, March, 1979, pp. 25–26.

24 *Telecommunications and Canada*, report of the Consultative Committee on the Implications of Telecommunications for Canadian Sovereignty (The Clyne Report), Ottawa, March, 1979. "These are some of the dangers foreseen if protective measures are not urgently devised and implemented. Greater use of foreign, mainly U.S., computing services and growing dependence on them will ... facilitate the attempts of the government of the United States to make laws applicable outside U.S. territory ..." (page 64).

10

INTRODUCTION

James R. Beniger

Source: James R. Beniger (1986) *The Control Revolution: Technological and Economic Origins of the Information Society*, Cambridge, MA: Harvard University Press, pp. 1–27.

> Here have we war for war and blood for blood, controlment for controlment.
> —King of England to the French ambassador
> (Shakespeare, *King John*)

One tragedy of the human condition is that each of us lives and dies with little hint of even the most profound transformations of our society and our species that play themselves out in some small part through our own existence. When the earliest *Homo sapiens* encountered *Homo erectus*, or whatever species was our immediate forebear, it is unlikely that the two saw in their differences a major turning point in the development of our race. If they did, this knowledge did not survive to be recorded, at least not in the ancient writings now extant. Indeed, some fifty thousand years passed before Darwin and Wallace rediscovered the secret—proof of the difficulty of grasping even the most essential dynamics of our lives and our society.

Much the same conclusion could be drawn from any of a succession of revolutionary societal transformations: the cultivation of plants and the domestication of animals, the growth of permanent settlements, the development of metal tools and writing, urbanization, the invention of wheeled vehicles and the plow, the rise of market economies, social classes, a world commerce. The origins and early histories of these and many other developments of comparable significance went unnoticed or at least unrecorded by contemporary observers. Today we are hard pressed to associate specific dates, places, or names with many major societal transformations, even though similar details abound for much lesser events and trends that occurred at the same times.

This condition holds for even that most significant of modern societal transformations, the so-called Industrial Revolution. Although it is generally conceded to have begun by mid-eighteenth century, at least in England,

155

the idea of its revolutionary impact does not appear until the 1830s in pioneering histories like those of Wade (1833) and Blanqui (1837). Widespread acceptance by historians that the Industrial Revolution constituted a major transformation of society did not come until Arnold Toynbee, Sr., popularized the term in a series of public lectures in 1881 (Toynbee 1884). This was well over a century after the changes he described had first begun to gain momentum in his native England and at least a generation after the more important ones are now generally considered to have run their course. Although several earlier observers had described one or another of the same changes, few before Toynbee had begun to reflect upon the more profound transformation that signaled the end—after some ten thousand years—of predominantly agricultural society.

Two explanations of this chronic inability to grasp even the most essential dynamics of an age come readily to mind. First, important transformations of society rarely result from single discrete events, despite the best efforts of later historians to associate the changes with such events. Human society seems rather to evolve largely through changes so gradual as to be all but imperceptible, at least compared to the generational cycles of the individuals through whose lives they unfold. Second, contemporaries of major societal transformations are frequently distracted by events and trends more dramatic in immediate impact but less lasting in significance. Few who lived through the early 1940s were unaware that the world was at war, for example, but the much less noticed scientific and technological by-products of the conflict are more likely to lend their names to the era, whether it comes to be remembered as the Nuclear Age, the Computer Age, or the Space Age.

Regardless of how we explain the recurrent failure of past generations to appreciate the major societal transformations of their own eras, we might expect that their record would at least chasten students of contemporary social change. In fact, just the opposite appears to be the case. Much as if historical myopia could somehow be overcome by confronting the problem head-on, a steadily mounting number of social scientists, popular writers, and critics have discovered that one or another revolutionary societal transformation is now in progress. The succession of such transformations identified since the late 1950s includes the rise of a new social class (Djilas 1957; Gouldner 1979), a meritocracy (Young 1958), postcapitalist society (Dahrendorf 1959), a global village (McLuhan 1964), the new industrial state (Galbraith 1967), a scientific-technological revolution (Richta 1967; Daglish 1972; Prague Academy 1973), a technetronic era (Brzezinski 1970), postindustrial society (Touraine 1971; Bell 1973), an information economy (Porat 1977), and the micro millennium (Evans 1979), to name only a few. A more complete catalog of these and similar transformations, listed by year of first exposition in a major work, is given in Table 1.

The writer who first identified each of the transformations listed in Table 1 usually found the brunt of the change to be—coincidentally enough

INTRODUCTION

Table 1 Modern societal transformations identified since 1950.

Year	Transformation	Sources
1950	Lonely crowd	Riesman 1950
	Posthistoric man	Seidenberg 1950
1953	Organizational revolution	Boulding 1953
1956	Organization man	Whyte 1956
1957	New social class	Djilas 1957; Gouldner 1979
1958	Meritocracy	Young 1958
1959	Educational revolution	Drucker 1959
	Postcapitalist society	Dahrendorf 1959
1960	End of ideology	Bell 1960
	Postmaturity economy	Rostow 1960
1961	Industrial society	Aron 1961; 1966
1962	Computer revolution	Berkeley 1962; Tomeski 1970; Hawkes 1971
	Knowledge economy	Machlup 1962; 1980; Drucker 1969
1963	New working class	Mallet 1963; Gintis 1970; Gallie 1978
	Postbourgeois society	Lichtheim 1963
1964	Global village	McLuhan 1964
	Managerial capitalism	Marris 1964
	One-dimensional man	Marcuse 1964
	Postcivilized era	Boulding 1964
	Service class society	Dahrendorf 1964
	Technological society	Ellul 1964
1967	New industrial state	Galbraith 1967
	Scientific-technological revolution	Richta 1967; Daglish 1972; Prague Academy 1973
1968	Dual economy	Averitt 1968
	Neocapitalism	Gorz 1968
	Postmodern society	Etzioni 1968; Breed 1971
	Technocracy	Meynaud 1968
	Unprepared society	Michael 1968
1969	Age of discontinuity	Drucker 1969
	Postcollectivist society	Beer 1969
	Postideological society	Feuer 1969
1970	Computerized society	Martin and Norman 1970
	Personal society	Halmos 1970
	Posteconomic society	Kahn 1970
	Postliberal age	Vickers 1970
	Prefigurative culture	Mead 1970
	Technetronic era	Brzezinski 1970
1971	Age of information	Helvey 1971
	Compunications	Oettinger 1971
	Postindustrial society	Touraine 1971; Bell 1973
	Self-guiding society	Breed 1971
	Superindustrial society	Toffler 1971
1972	Limits to growth	Meadows 1972; Cole 1973
	Posttraditional society	Eisenstadt 1972
	World without borders	Brown 1972
1973	New service society	Lewis 1973
	Stalled society	Crozier 1973

157

HISTORY AND PERSPECTIVES

Table 1 (cont'd)

Year	Transformation	Sources
1974	Consumer vanguard	Gartner and Riessman 1974
	Information revolution	Lamberton 1974
1975	Communications age	Phillips 1975
	Mediacracy	Phillips 1975
	Third industrial revolution	Stine 1975; Stonier 1979
1976	Industrial-technological society	Ionescu 1976
	Megacorp	Eichner 1976
1977	Electronics revolution	Evans 1977
	Information economy	Porat 1977
1978	Anticipatory democracy	Bezold 1978
	Network nation	Hiltz and Turoff 1978
	Republic of technology	Boorstin 1978
	Telematic society	Nora and Minc 1978; Martin 1981
	Wired society	Martin 1978
1979	Collapse of work	Jenkins and Sherman 1979
	Computer age	Dertouzos and Moses 1979
	Credential society	Collins 1979
	Micro millennium	Evans 1979
1980	Micro revolution	Large 1980, 1984; Laurie 1981
	Microelectronics revolution	Forester 1980
	Third wave	Toffler 1980
1981	Information society	Martin and Butler 1981
	Network marketplace	Dordick 1981
1982	Communications revolution	Williams 1982
	Information age	Dizard 1982
1983	Computer state	Burnham 1983
	Gene age	Sylvester and Klotz 1983
1984	Second industrial divide	Piore and Sabel 1984

—either in progress or imminent. A recent best-seller, for example, surveys the sweep of human history, notes the central importance of the agricultural and industrial revolutions, and then finds in contemporary society the seeds of a third revolution—the impending "Third Wave":

> Humanity faces a quantum leap forward. It faces the deepest social upheaval and creative restructuring of all time. Without clearly recognizing it, we are engaged in building a remarkable new civilization from the ground up. This is the meaning of the Third Wave . . . It is likely that the Third Wave will sweep across history and complete itself in a few decades. We, who happen to share the planet at this explosive moment, will therefore feel the full impact of the Third Wave in our own lifetimes. Tearing our families apart,

INTRODUCTION

rocking our economy, paralyzing our political systems, shattering our values, the Third Wave affects everyone.

(Toffler 1980, p. 26)

Even less breathless assessments of contemporary change have been no less optimistic about the prospect of placing developing events and trends in the broadest historical context. Daniel Bell, for example, after acknowledging the counterevidence of Toynbee and the Industrial Revolution, nevertheless concludes, "Today, with our greater sensitivity to social consequences and to the future . . . we are more alert to the possible imports of technological and organizational change, and this is all to the good" (1980, pp. x–xi).

The number of major societal transformations listed in Table 1 indicates that Bell appears to be correct; we do seem more alert than previous generations to the possible importance of change. The wide variety of transformations identified, however, suggests that, like the generations before us, we may be preoccupied with specific and possibly ephemeral events and trends, at the risk of overlooking what only many years from now will be seen as the fundamental dynamic of our age.

Because the failures of past generations bespeak the difficulties of overcoming this problem, the temptation is great not to try. This reluctance might be overcome if we recognize that understanding ourselves in our own particular moment in history will enable us to shape and guide that history. As Bell goes on to say, "to the extent that we are sensitive [to the possible importance of technological and social change], we can try to estimate the consequences and decide which policies we should choose, consonant with the values we have, in order to shape, accept, or even reject the alternative futures that are available to us" (1980, p. xi).

Much the same purpose motivates—and I hope justifies—the pages that follow. In them I argue, like many of the writers whose names appear in Table 1, that society is currently experiencing a revolutionary transformation on a global scale. Unlike most of the other writers, however, I do not conclude that the crest of change is either recent, current, or imminent. Instead, I trace the causes of change back to the middle and late nineteenth century, to a set of problems—in effect a crisis of control—generated by the industrial revolution in manufacturing and transportation. The response to this crisis, at least in technological innovation and restructuring of the economy, occurred most rapidly around the turn of the century and amounted to nothing less, I argue, than a revolution in societal control.

The Control Revolution

Few turn-of-the-century observers understood even isolated aspects of the societal transformation—what I shall call the "Control Revolution"—then

159

HISTORY AND PERSPECTIVES

gathering momentum in the United States, England, France, and Germany. Notable among those who did was Max Weber (1864–1920), the German sociologist and political economist who directed social analysis to the most important control technology of his age: bureaucracy. Although bureaucracy had developed several times independently in ancient civilizations, Weber was the first to see it as the critical new machinery—new, at least, in its generality and pervasiveness—for control of the societal forces unleashed by the Industrial Revolution.

For a half-century after Weber's initial analysis bureaucracy continued to reign as the single most important technology of the Control Revolution. After World War II, however, generalized control began to shift slowly to computer technology. If social change has seemed to accelerate in recent years (as argued, for example, by Toffler 1971), this has been due in large part to a spate of new information-processing, communication, and control technologies like the computer, most notably the microprocessors that have proliferated since the early 1970s. Such technologies are more properly seen, however, not as causes but as consequences of societal change, as natural extensions of the Control Revolution already in progress for more than a century.

Revolution, a term borrowed from astronomy, first appeared in political discourse in seventeenth-century England, where it described the restoration of a previous form of government. Not until the French Revolution did the word acquire its currently popular and opposite meaning, that of abrupt and often violent change. As used here in Control Revolution, the term is intended to have both of these opposite connotations.

Beginning most noticeably in the United States in the late nineteenth century, the Control Revolution was certainly a dramatic if not abrupt discontinuity in technological advance. Indeed, even the word *revolution* seems barely adequate to describe the development, within the span of a single lifetime, of virtually all of the basic communication technologies still in use a century later: photography and telegraphy (1830s), rotary power printing (1840s), the typewriter (1860s), transatlantic cable (1866), telephone (1876), motion pictures (1894), wireless telegraphy (1895), magnetic tape recording (1899), radio (1906), and television (1923).

Along with these rapid changes in mass media and telecommunications technologies, the Control Revolution also represented the beginning of a restoration—although with increasing centralization—of the economic and political control that was lost at more local levels of society during the Industrial Revolution. Before this time, control of government and markets had depended on personal relationships and face-to-face interactions; now control came to be reestablished by means of bureaucratic organization, the new infrastructures of transportation and telecommunications, and system-wide communication via the new mass media. By both of the opposite definitions of *revolution*, therefore, the new societal transformations—rapid innovation in information and control technology, to regain control

INTRODUCTION

of functions once contained at much lower and more diffuse levels of society —constituted a true revolution in societal control.

Here the word *control* represents its most general definition, purposive influence toward a predetermined goal. Most dictionary definitions imply these same two essential elements: *influence* of one agent over another, meaning that the former causes changes in the behavior of the latter; and *purpose*, in the sense that influence is directed toward some prior goal of the controlling agent. If the definition used here differs at all from colloquial ones, it is only because many people reserve the word *control* for its more determinate manifestations, what I shall call "strong control." Dictionaries, for example, often include in their definitions of control concepts like direction, guidance, regulation, command, and domination, approximate synonyms of *influence* that vary mainly in increasing determination. As a more general concept, however, *control* encompasses the entire range from absolute control to the weakest and most probabilistic form, that is, any purposive influence on behavior, *however slight*. Economists say that television advertising serves to control specific demand, for example, and political scientists say that direct mail campaigns can help to control issue-voting, even though only a small fraction of the intended audience may be influenced in either case.

Inseparable from the concept of control are the twin activities of information processing and reciprocal communication, complementary factors in any form of control. Information processing is essential to all purposive activity, which is by definition goal directed and must therefore involve the continual comparison of current states to future goals, a basic problem of information processing. So integral to control is this comparison of inputs to stored programs that the word *control* itself derives from the medieval Latin verb *contrarotulare*, to compare something "against the rolls," the cylinders of paper that served as official records in ancient times.

Simultaneously with the comparison of inputs to goals, two-way interaction between controller and controlled must also occur, not only to communicate influence from the former to the latter, but also to communicate back the results of this action (hence the term *feedback* for this reciprocal flow of information back to a controller). So central is communication to the process of control that the two have become the joint subject of the modern science of cybernetics, defined by one of its founders as "the entire field of control and communication theory, whether in the machine or in the animal" (Wiener 1948, p. 11). Similarly, the pioneers of mathematical communication theory have defined the object of their study as purposive control in the broadest sense: communication, according to Shannon and Weaver (1949, pp. 3–5), includes "all of the procedures by which one mind may affect another"; they note that "communication either affects conduct or is without any discernible and probable effect at all."

Because both the activities of information processing and communication are inseparable components of the control function, a society's ability to maintain control—at all levels from interpersonal to international relations —will be directly proportional to the development of its information technologies. Here the term *technology* is intended not in the narrow sense of practical or applied science but in the more general sense of any intentional extension of a natural process, that is, of the processing of matter, energy, and information that characterizes all living systems. Respiration is a wholly natural life function, for example, and is therefore not a technology; the human ability to breathe under water, by contrast, implies some technological extension. Similarly, voting is one general technology for achieving collective decisions in the control of social aggregates; the Australian ballot is a particular innovation in this technology.

Technology may therefore be considered as roughly equivalent to that which can be done, excluding only those capabilities that occur naturally in living systems. This distinction is usually although not always clear. One ambiguous case is language, which may have developed at least in part through purposive innovation but which now appears to be a mostly innate capability of the human brain. The brain itself represents another ambiguous case: it probably developed in interaction with purposive tool use and may therefore be included among human technologies.

Because technology defines the limits on what a society *can* do, technological innovation might be expected to be a major impetus to social change in the Control Revolution no less than in the earlier societal transformations accorded the status of revolutions. The Neolithic Revolution, for example, which brought the first permanent settlements, owed its origin to the refinement of stone tools and the domestication of plants and animals. The Commercial Revolution, following exploration of Africa, Asia, and the New World, resulted directly from technical improvements in seafaring and navigational equipment. The Industrial Revolution, which eventually brought the nineteenth-century crisis of control, began a century earlier with greatly increased use of coal and steam power and a spate of new machinery for the manufacture of cotton textiles. Like these earlier revolutions in matter and energy processing, the Control Revolution resulted from innovation at a most fundamental level of technology—that of information processing.

Information processing may be more difficult to appreciate than matter or energy processing because information is epiphenomenal: it derives from the *organization* of the material world on which it is wholly dependent for its existence. Despite being in this way higher order or derivative of matter and energy, information is no less critical to society. All living systems must process matter and energy to maintain themselves counter to entropy, the universal tendency of organization toward breakdown and randomization. Because control is necessary for such processing, and information, as we have seen, is essential to control, both information processing and communication, insofar as they distinguish living systems from the inorganic universe, might be said to define life itself—except for a few recent artifacts of our own species.

Each new technological innovation extends the processes that sustain life, thereby increasing the need for control and hence for improved control technology. This explains why technology appears autonomously to beget technology in general (Winner 1977), and why, as argued here, innovations in matter and energy processing create the need for further innovation in information-processing and communication technologies. Because technological innovation is increasingly a collective, cumulative effort, one whose results must be taught and diffused, it also generates an increased need for technologies of information storage and retrieval—as well as for their elaboration in systems of technical education and communication—quite independently of the particular need for control.

As in the earlier revolutions in matter and energy technologies, the nineteenth-century revolution in information technology was predicated on, if not directly caused by, social changes associated with earlier innovations. Just as the Commercial Revolution depended on capital and labor freed by advanced agriculture, for example, and the Industrial Revolution presupposed a commercial system for capital allocations and the distribution of goods, the most recent technological revolution developed in response to problems arising out of advanced industrialization—an ever-mounting crisis of control.

Crisis of control

The later Industrial Revolution constituted, in effect, a consolidation of earlier technological revolutions and the resulting transformations of society. Especially during the late nineteenth and early twentieth centuries industrialization extended to progressively earlier technological revolutions: manufacturing, energy production, transportation, agriculture—the last a transformation of what had once been seen as the extreme opposite of industrial production. In each area industrialization meant heavy infusions of capital for the exploitation of fossil fuels, wage labor, and machine technology and resulted in larger and more complex systems—systems characterized by increasing differentiation and interdependence at all levels.

One of the earliest and most astute observers of this phenomenon was Emile Durkheim (1858–1917), the great French sociologist who examined many of its social ramifications in his *Division of Labor in Society* (1893). As Durkheim noted, industrialization tends to break down the barriers to transportation and communication that isolate local markets (what he called the "segmental" type), thereby extending distribution of goods and services to national and even global markets (the "organized" type). This, in turn, disrupts the market equilibrium under which production is regulated by means of direct communication between producer and consumer:

HISTORY AND PERSPECTIVES

Insofar as the segmental type is strongly marked, there are nearly as many economic markets as there are different segments. Consequently, each of them is very limited. Producers, being near consumers, can easily reckon the extent of the needs to be satisfied. Equilibrium is established without any trouble and production regulates itself. On the contrary, as the organized type develops, the fusion of different segments draws the markets together into one which embraces almost all society ... The result is that each industry produces for consumers spread over the whole surface of the country or even of the entire world. Contact is then no longer sufficient. The producer can no longer embrace the market in a glance, nor even in thought. He can no longer see limits, since it is, so to speak, limitless. Accordingly, production becomes unbridled and unregulated. It can only trust to chance ... From this come the crises which periodically disturb economic functions.

(1893, pp. 369–370)

What Durkheim describes here is nothing less than a crisis of control at the most aggregate level of a national system—a level that had had little practical relevance before the mass production and distribution of factory goods. Resolution of the crisis demanded new means of communication, as Durkheim perceived, to control an economy shifting from local segmented markets to higher levels of organization—what might be seen as the growing "systemness" of society. This capacity to communicate and process information is one component of what structural-functionalists following Durkheim have called the problem of *integration*, the growing need for coordination of functions that accompanies differentiation and specialization in any system.

Increasingly confounding the need for integration of the structural division of labor were corresponding increases in commodity flows through the system—flows driven by steam-powered factory production and mass distribution via national rail networks. Never before had the processing of material flows threatened to exceed, in both volume and speed, the capacity of technology to contain them. For centuries most goods had moved with the speed of draft animals down roadway and canal, weather permitting. This infrastructure, controlled by small organizations of only a few hierarchial levels, supported even national economies. Suddenly—owing to the harnessing of steam power—goods could be moved at the full speed of industrial production, night and day and under virtually any conditions, not only from town to town but across entire continents and around the world.

To do this, however, required an increasingly complex system of manufacturers and distributers, central and branch offices, transportation lines and terminals, containers and cars. Even the logistics of nineteenth-century armies, then the most difficult problem in processing and control, came to

INTRODUCTION

be dwarfed in complexity by the material economy just emerging as Durkheim worked on his famous study.

What Durkheim described as a crisis of control on the societal level he also managed to relate to the level of individual psychology. Here he found a more personal but directly related problem, what he called *anomie*, the breakdown of norms governing individual and group behavior. Anomie is an "abnormal" and even "pathological" result, according to Durkheim (1893, p. 353), an exception to his more general finding that increasing division of labor directly increases normative integration and, with it, social solidarity. As Durkheim argued, anomie results not from the structural division of labor into what he called distinct societal "organs" but rather from the breakdown in communication among these increasingly isolated sectors, so that individuals employed in them lose sight of the larger purpose of their separate efforts:

> The state of anomie is impossible wherever solidary organs are sufficiently in contact or sufficiently prolonged. In effect, being contiguous, they are quickly warned, in each circumstance, of the need which they have of one another, and, consequently, they have a lively and continuous sentiment of their mutual dependence ... But, on the contrary, if some opaque environment is interposed, then only stimuli of a certain intensity can be communicated from one organ to another. Relations, being rare, are not repeated enough to be determined; each time there ensues new groping. The lines of passage taken by the streams of movement cannot deepen because the streams themselves are too intermittent. If some rules do come to constitute them, they are, however, general and vague.
>
> (1893, pp. 368–369)

Like the problem of economic integration, anomie also resulted—in Durkheim's view—from inadequate means of communication. Both problems were thus manifestations, at opposite extremes of aggregation, of the nineteenth-century control crisis.

Unlike Durkheim's analysis, which was largely confined to the extremes of individual and society, this book will concentrate on intervening levels, especially on technology and its role in the processing of matter, energy, and information—what might be called the *material economy* (as opposed to the abstract ones that seem to captivate most modern economists). Chapter 6 includes separate sections on the production, distribution, and consumption of goods and services in the industrializing economy of the United States in the nineteenth century and on the new information-processing and communication technologies—just emerging during Durkheim's lifetime—that served to control the increasing volume and speed of these activities. We will find that, just as the problem of control threatened to reach crisis proportions late in the century, a series of new technological and social solutions began to contain the problem. This was the opening stage of the Control Revolution.

Rationalization and bureaucracy

Foremost among all the technological solutions to the crisis of control—in that it served to control most other technologies—was the rapid growth of formal bureaucracy first analyzed by Max Weber at the turn of the century. Bureaucratic organization was not new to Weber's time, as we have noted; bureaucracies had arisen in the first nation-states with centralized administrations, most significantly in Mesopotamia and ancient Egypt, and had reached a high level of sophistication in the preindustrial empires of Rome, China, and Byzantium. Indeed, bureaucratic organization tends to appear wherever a collective activity needs to be coordinated by several people toward explicit and impersonal goals, that is, to be *controlled*. Bureaucracy has served as the generalized means to control any large social system in most institutional areas and in most cultures since the emergence of such systems by about 3000 B.C.

Because of the venerable history and pervasiveness of bureaucracy, historians have tended to overlook its role in the late nineteenth century as a major new control technology. Nevertheless, bureaucratic administration did not begin to achieve anything approximating its modern form until the late Industrial Revolution. As late as the 1830s, for example, the Bank of the United States, then the nation's largest and most complex institution with twenty-two branch offices and profits fifty times those of the largest mercantile house, was managed by just three people: Nicholas Biddle and two assistants (Redlich 1951, pp. 113–124). In 1831 President Andrew Jackson and 665 other civilians ran all three branches of the federal government in Washington, an increase of sixty-three employees over the previous ten years. The Post Office Department, for example, had been administered for thirty years as the personal domain of two brothers, Albert and Phineas Bradley (Pred 1973, chap. 3). Fifty years later, in the aftermath of rapid industrialization, Washington's bureaucracy included some thirteen thousand civilian employees, more than double the total—already swelled by the American Civil War—only ten years earlier (U.S. Bureau of the Census 1975, p. 1103).

Further evidence that bureaucracy developed in response to the Industrial Revolution is the timing of concern about bureaucratization as a pressing social problem. The word *bureaucracy* did not even appear in English until the early nineteenth century, yet within a generation it became a major topic of political and philosophical discussion. As early as 1837, for example, John Stuart Mill wrote of a "vast network of administrative tyranny . . . that system of *bureaucracy*, which leaves no free agent in all France, except the man at Paris who pulls the wires" (Burchfield 1972, p. 391); a decade

INTRODUCTION

later Mill warned more generally of the "inexpediency of concentrating in a dominant bureaucracy... all power of organized action... in the community" (1848, p. 529). Thomas Carlyle, in his *Latter-Day Pamphlets* published two years later, complained of "the Continental nuisance called 'Bureaucracy'" (1850, p. 121). The word *bureaucratic* had also appeared by the 1830s, followed by *bureaucrat* in the 1840s and *bureaucratize* by the 1890s.

That bureaucracy is in essence a control technology was first established by Weber, most notably in his *Economy and Society* (1922). Weber included among the defining characteristics of bureaucracy several important aspects of any control system: impersonal orientation of structure to the information that it processes, usually identified as "cases," with a predetermined formal set of rules governing all decisions and responses. Any tendency to humanize this bureaucratic machinery, Weber argued, would be minimized through clear-cut division of labor and definition of responsibilities, hierarchical authority, and specialized decision and communication functions. The stability and permanence of bureaucracy, he noted, are assured through regular promotion of career employees based on objective criteria like seniority.

Weber identified another related control technology, what he called *rationalization*. Although the term has a variety of meanings, both in Weber's writings and in the elaborations of his work by others, most definitions are subsumed by one essential idea: control can be increased not only by increasing the capability to process information but also by decreasing the amount of information to be processed. The former approach to control was realized in Weber's day through bureaucratization and today increasingly through computerization; the latter approach was then realized through rationalization, what computer scientists now call *preprocessing*. Rationalization must therefore be seen, following Weber, as a complement to bureaucratization, one that served control in his day much as the preprocessing of information prior to its processing by computer serves control today.

Perhaps most pervasive of all rationalization is the increasing tendency of modern society to regulate interpersonal relationships in terms of a formal set of impersonal and objective criteria. The early technocrat Claude Henri Comte de Saint-Simon (1760–1825), who lived through only the first stages of industrialization, saw such rationalization as a move "from the government of men to the administration of things" (Taylor 1975, pt. 3). The reason why people can be governed more readily *qua* things is that the amount of information about them that needs to be processed is thereby greatly reduced and hence the degree of control—for any constant capacity to process information—is greatly enhanced. By means of rationalization, therefore, it is possible to maintain large-scale, complex social systems that would be overwhelmed by a rising tide of information they could not process were it necessary to govern by the particularistic considerations of family and kin that characterize preindustrial societies.

In short, rationalization might be defined as the destruction or ignoring of information in order to facilitate its processing. This, too, has a direct analog in living systems, as we shall see in the next chapter. One example from within bureaucracy is the development of standardized paper forms. This might at first seem a contradiction, in that the proliferation of paperwork is usually associated with a growth in information to be processed, not with its reduction. Imagine how much more processing would be required, however, if each new case were recorded in an unstructured way, including every nuance and in full detail, rather than by checking boxes, filling blanks, or in some other way reducing the burdens of the bureaucratic system to only the limited range of formal, objective, and impersonal information required by standardized forms.

Equally important to the rationalization of industrial society, at the most macro level, were the division of North America into five standardized time zones in 1883 and the establishment the following year of the Greenwich meridian and International Date Line, which organized world time into twenty-four zones. What was formerly a problem of information overload and hence control for railroads and other organizations that sustained the social system at its most macro level was solved by simply ignoring much of the information, namely that solar time is different at each node of a transportation or communication system. A more convincing demonstration of the power of rationalization or preprocessing as a control technology would be difficult to imagine.

So commonplace has such preprocessing become that today we dismiss the alternative—that each node in a system might keep a slightly different time—as hopelessly cumbersome and primitive. With the continued proliferation of distributed computing, ironically enough, it might soon become feasible to return to a system based on local solar time, thereby shifting control from preprocessing back to processing—where it resided for centuries of human history until steam power pushed transportation beyond the pace of the sun across the sky.

New control technology

The rapid development of rationalization and bureaucracy in the middle and late nineteenth century led to a succession of dramatic new information-processing and communication technologies. These innovations served to contain the control crisis of industrial society in what can be treated as three distinct areas of economic activity: production, distribution, and consumption of goods and services.

Control of production was facilitated by the continuing organization and preprocessing of industrial operations. Machinery itself came increasingly to

INTRODUCTION

be controlled by two new information-processing technologies: closed-loop feedback devices like James Watt's steam governor (1788) and preprogrammed open-loop controllers like those of the Jacquard loom (1801). By 1890 Herman Hollerith had extended Jacquard's punch cards to tabulation of U.S. census data. This information-processing technology survives to this day—if just barely—owing largely to the corporation to which Hollerith's innovation gave life, International Business Machines (IBM). Further rationalization and control of production advanced through an accumulation of other industrial innovations: interchangeable parts (after 1800), integration of production within factories (1820s and 1830s), the development of modern accounting techniques (1850s and 1860s), professional managers (1860s and 1870s), continuous-process production (late 1870s and early 1880s), the "scientific management" of Frederick Winslow Taylor (1911), Henry Ford's modern assembly line (after 1913), and statistical quality control (1920s), among many others.

The resulting flood of mass-produced goods demanded comparable innovation in control of a second area of the economy: distribution. Growing infrastructures of transportation, including rail networks, steamship lines, and urban traction systems, depended for control on a corresponding infrastructure of information processing and telecommunications. Within fifteen years after the opening of the pioneering Baltimore and Ohio Railroad in 1830, for example, Samuel F. B. Morse—with a congressional appropriation of $30,000—had linked Baltimore to Washington, D.C., by means of a telegraph. Eight years later, in 1852, thirteen thousand miles of railroad and twenty-three thousand miles of telegraph line were in operation (Thompson 1947; U.S. Bureau of the Census 1975, p. 731), and the two infrastructures continued to coevolve in a web of distribution and control that progressively bound the entire continent. In the words of business historian Alfred Chandler, "the railroad permitted a rapid increase in the speed and decrease in the cost of long-distance, written communication, while the invention of the telegraph created an even greater transformation by making possible almost instantaneous communication at great distances. The railroad and the telegraph marched across the continent in unison . . . The telegraph companies used the railroad for their rights-of-way, and the railroad used the services of the telegraph to coordinate the flow of trains and traffic" (1977, p. 195).

This coevolution of the railroad and telegraph systems fostered the development of another communication infrastructure for control of mass distribution and consumption: the postal system. Aided by the introduction in 1847 of the first federal postage stamp, itself an important innovation in control of the national system of distribution, the total distance mail moved more than doubled in the dozen years between Morse's first telegraph and 1857, when it reached 75 million miles—almost a third covered by rail (Chandler 1977, p. 195). Commercialization of the telephone in the 1880s,

169

and especially the development of long-distance lines in the 1890s, added a third component to the national infrastructure of telecommunications.

Controlled by means of this infrastructure, an organizational system rapidly emerged for the distribution of mass production to national and world markets. Important innovations in the rationalization and control of this system included the commodity dealer and standardized grading of commodities (1850s), the department store, chain store, and wholesale jobber (1860s), monitoring of movements of inventory or "stock turn" (by 1870), the mail-order house (1870s), machine packaging (1890s), franchising (by 1911 the standard means of distributing automobiles), and the supermarket and mail-order chain (1920s). After World War I the instability in national and world markets that Durkheim had noted a quarter-century earlier came to be gradually controlled, largely because of the new telecommunications infrastructure and the reorganization of distribution on a societal scale.

Mass production and distribution cannot be completely controlled, however, without control of a third area of the economy: demand and consumption. Such control requires a means to communicate information about goods and services to national audiences in order to stimulate or reinforce demand for these products; at the same time, it requires a means to gather information on the preferences and behavior of this audience —reciprocal feedback to the controller from the controlled (although the consumer might justifiably see these relationships as reversed).

The mechanism for communicating information to a national audience of consumers developed with the first truly mass medium: power-driven, multiple-rotary printing and mass mailing by rail. At the outset of the Industrial Revolution, most printing was still done on wooden handpresses —using flat plates tightened by means of screws—that differed little from the one Gutenberg had used three centuries earlier. Steam power was first successfully applied to printing in Germany in 1810; by 1827 it was possible to print up to 2,500 pages in an hour. In 1893 the New York *World* printed 96,000 eight-page copies every hour—a 300-fold increase in speed in just seventy years.

The postal system, in addition to effecting and controlling distribution, also served, through bulk mailings of mass-produced publications, as a new medium of mass communication. By 1887 Montgomery Ward mailed throughout the continent a 540-page catalog listing more than 24,000 items. Circulation of the Sears and Roebuck catalog increased from 318,000 in 1897 (the first year for which figures are available) to more than 1 million in 1904, 2 million in 1905, 3 million in 1907, and 7 million by the late 1920s. In 1927 alone, Sears mailed 10 million circular letters, 15 million general catalogs (spring and fall editions), 23 million sales catalogs, plus other special catalogs—a total mailing of 75 million (Boorstin 1973, p. 128) or approximately one piece for every adult in the United States.

INTRODUCTION

Throughout the late nineteenth and early twentieth centuries uncounted entrepreneurs and inventors struggled to extend the technologies of communication to mass audiences. Alexander Graham Bell, who patented the telephone in 1876, originally thought that his invention might be used as a broadcast medium to pipe public speeches, music, and news into private homes. Such systems were indeed begun in several countries—the one in Budapest had six thousand subscribers by the turn of the century and continued to operate through World War I (Briggs 1977). More extensive application of telephony to mass communication was undoubtedly stifled by the rapid development of broadcast media beginning with Guglielmo Marconi's demonstration of long-wave telegraphy in 1895. Transatlantic wireless communication followed in 1901, public radio broadcasting in 1906, and commercial radio by 1920; even television broadcasting, a medium not popular until after World War II, had begun by 1923.

Many other communication technologies that we do not today associate with advertising were tried out early in the Control Revolution as means to influence the consumption of mass audiences. Popular books like the novels of Charles Dickens contained special advertising sections. Mass telephone systems in Britain and Hungary carried advertisements interspersed among music and news. The phonograph, patented by Thomas Edison in 1877 and greatly improved by the 1890s in Hans Berliner's "gramophone," became another means by which a sponsor's message could be distributed to households: "Nobody would refuse," the United States Gramaphone Company claimed, "to listen to a fine song or concert piece or an oration—even if it is interrupted by a modest remark, 'Tartar's Baking Powder is Best'" (Abbot and Rider 1957, p. 387). With the development by Edison of the "motion picture" after 1891, advertising had a new medium, first in the kinetoscope (1893) and cinematograph (1895), which sponsors located in busy public places, and then in the 1900s in films projected in "movie houses." Although advertisers were initially wary of broadcasting because audiences could not be easily identified, by 1930 sponsors were spending $60 million annually on radio in the United States alone (Boorstin 1973, p. 392).

These mass media were not sufficient to effect true control, however, without a means of feedback from potential consumers to advertisers, thereby restoring to the emerging national and world markets what Durkheim had seen as an essential relationship of the earlier segmental markets: communication from consumer to producer to assure that the latter "can easily reckon the extent of the needs to be satisfied" (1893, p. 369). Simultaneously with the development of mass communication by the turn of the century came what might be called *mass feedback* technologies: market research (the idea first appeared as "commercial research" in 1911), including questionnaire surveys of magazine readership, the Audit Bureau of Circulation (1914), house-to-house interviewing (1916), attitudinal and opinion surveys (a U.S. bibliography lists nearly three thousand by 1928), a Census of Distribution

171

HISTORY AND PERSPECTIVES

(1929), large-scale statistical sampling theory (1930), indices of retail sales (1933), A. C. Nielsen's audimeter monitoring of broadcast audiences (1935), and statistical-sample surveys like the Gallup Poll (1936), to mention just a few of the many new technologies for monitoring consumer behavior.

Although most of the new information technologies originated in the private sector, where they were used to control production, distribution, and consumption of goods and services, their potential for controlling systems at the national and world level was not overlooked by government. Since at least the Roman Empire, where an extensive road system proved equally suited for moving either commerce or troops, communications infrastructures have served to control both economy and polity. As corporate bureaucracy came to control increasingly wider markets by the turn of this century, its power was increasingly checked by a parallel growth in state bureaucracy. Both bureaucracies found useful what Bell has called "intellectual technology":

> The major intellectual and sociological problems of the post-industrial society are ... those of "organized complexity"—the management of large-scale systems, with large numbers of inter-acting variables, which have to be coordinated to achieve specific goals ... An *intellectual technology* is the substitution of algorithms (problem-solving rules) for intuitive judgments. These algorithms may be embodied in an automatic machine or a computer program or a set of instructions based on some statistical or mathematical formula; the statistical and logical techniques that are used in dealing with "organized complexity" are efforts to formalize a set of decision rules.
>
> (1973, pp. 29–30)

Seen in this way, intellectual technology is another manifestation of bureaucratic rationality, an extension of what Saint-Simon described as a shift from the government of men to the administration of things, that is, a further move to administration based not on intuitive judgments but on logical and statistical rules and algorithms. Although Bell sees intellectual technology as arising after 1940, state bureaucracies had begun earlier in this century to appropriate many key elements: central economic planning (Soviet Union after 1920), the state fiscal policies of Lord Keynes (late 1920s), national income accounting (after 1933), econometrics (mid-1930s), input-output analysis (after 1936), linear programming and statistical decision theory (late 1930s), and operations research and systems analysis (early in World War II).

In the modern state the latest technologies of mass communication, persuasion, and market research are also used to stimulate and control demand for governmental services. The U.S. government, for example, currently

INTRODUCTION

spends about $150 million a year on advertising, which places it among the top thirty advertisers in the country; were the approximately 70 percent of its ads that are presented free as a public service also included, it would rank second—just behind Proctor and Gamble (Porat 1977, p. 137). Increasing business and governmental use of control technologies and their recent proliferation in forms like data services and home computers for use by consumers have become dominant features of the Control Revolution.

The Information Society

One major result of the Control Revolution had been the emergence of the so-called Information Society. The concept dates from the late 1950s and the pioneering work of an economist, Fritz Machlup, who first measured that sector of the U.S. economy associated with what he called "the production and distribution of knowledge" (Machlup 1962). Under this classification Machlup grouped thirty industries into five major categories: education, research and development, communications media, information machines (like computers), and information services (finance, insurance, real estate). He then estimated from national accounts data for 1958 (the most recent year available) that the information sector accounted for 29 percent of gross national product (GNP) and 31 percent of the labor force. He also estimated that between 1947 and 1958 the information sector had expanded at a compound growth rate double that of GNP. In sum, it appeared that the United States was rapidly becoming an Information Society.

Over the intervening twenty years several other analyses have substantiated and updated the original estimates of Machlup (1980, pp. xxvi–xxviii): Burck (1964) calculated that the information sector had reached 33 percent of GNP by 1963; Marschak (1968) predicted that the sector would approach 40 percent of GNP in the 1970s. By far the most ambitious effort to date has been the innovative work of Marc Uri Porat for the Office of Telecommunications in the U.S. Department of Commerce (1977). In 1967, according to Porat, information activities (defined differently from those of Machlup) accounted for 46.2 percent of GNP—25.1 percent in a "primary information" sector (which produces information goods and services as final output) and 21.1 percent in a "secondary information" sector (the bureaucracies of noninformation enterprises).

The impact of the Information Society is perhaps best captured by trends in labor force composition. As can be seen in Figure 1 and the corresponding data in Table 2, at the end of the eighteenth century the U.S. labor force was concentrated overwhelmingly in agriculture, the location of nearly 90 percent of its workers. The majority of U.S. labor continued to work in this sector until about 1850, and agriculture remained the largest single sector until the first decade of the twentieth century. Rapidly emerging, meanwhile, was a new industrial sector, one that continuously employed at

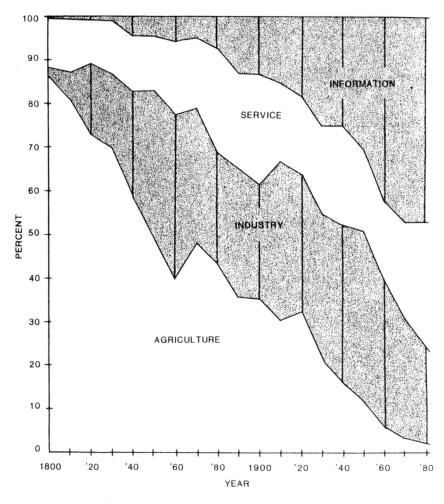

Figure 1 U.S. civilian labor force by four sectors, 1800–1980.

least a quarter of U.S. workers between the 1840s and 1970s, reaching a peak of about 40 percent during World War II. Today, just forty years later, the industrial sector is close to half that percentage and declining steadily; it might well fall below 15 percent in the next decade. Meanwhile, the information sector, by 1960 already larger (at more than 40 percent) than industry had ever been, today approaches half of the U.S. labor force.

At least in the timing of this new sector's rise and development, the data in Figure 1 and Table 2 are compatible with the hypothesis that the Information Society emerged in response to the nineteenth-century crisis of control. When the first railroads were built in the early 1830s, the information sector employed considerably less than 1 percent of the U.S. labor force; by the

INTRODUCTION

Table 2 U.S. experienced civilian labor force by four sectors, 1800–1980.

| Year | Sector's percent of total | | | | Total labor force (in millions) |
	Agricultural	Industrial	Service	Information	
1800	87.2	1.4	11.3	0.2	1.5
1810	81.0	6.5	12.2	0.3	2.2
1820	73.0	16.0	10.7	0.4	3.0
1830	69.7	17.6	12.2	0.4	3.7
1840	58.8	24.4	12.7	4.1	5.2
1850	49.5	33.8	12.5	4.2	7.4
1860	40.6	37.0	16.6	5.8	8.3
1870	47.0	32.0	16.2	4.8	12.5
1880	43.7	25.2	24.6	6.5	17.4
1890	37.2	28.1	22.3	12.4	22.8
1900	35.3	26.8	25.1	12.8	29.2
1910	31.1	36.3	17.7	14.9	39.8
1920	32.5	32.0	17.8	17.7	45.3
1930	20.4	35.3	19.8	24.5	51.1
1940	15.4	37.2	22.5	24.9	53.6
1950	11.9	38.3	19.0	30.8	57.8
1960	6.0	34.8	17.2	42.0	67.8
1970	3.1	28.6	21.9	46.4	80.1
1980	2.1	22.5	28.8	46.6	95.8

Sources: Data for 1800–1850 are estimated from Lebergott (1964) with missing data interpolated from Fabricant (1949); data for 1860–1970 are taken directly from Porat (1977); data for 1980 are based on U.S. Bureau of Labor Statistics projections (Bell 1979, p. 185).

end of the decade it employed more than 4 percent. Not until the rapid bureaucratization of the 1870s and 1880s, the period that—as I argue on independent grounds in Chapter 6—marked the consolidation of control, did the percentage employed in the information sector more than double to about one-eighth of the civilian work force. With the exception of these two great discontinuities, one occurring with the advent of railroads and the crisis of control in the 1830s, the other accompanying the consolidation of control in the 1870s and especially the 1880s, the information sector has grown steadily but only modestly over the past two centuries.

Temporal correlation alone, of course, does not prove causation. With the exception of the two discontinuities, however, growth in the information sector has tended to be most rapid in periods of economic upturn, most notably in the postwar booms of the 1920s and 1950s, as can be seen in Table 2. Significantly, the two periods of discontinuity were punctuated by economic depressions, the first by the Panic of 1837, the second by financial crisis in Europe and the Panic of 1873. In other words, the technological origins of both the control crisis and the consolidation of control occurred in periods when the information sector would not have been expected on other economic grounds to have expanded rapidly if at all. There is therefore no reason to reject the hypothesis that the Information Society developed as a result of the crisis of control created by railroads and other steam-powered transportation in the 1840s.

A wholly new stage in the development of the Information Society has arisen, since the early 1970s, from the continuing proliferation of micro-processing technology. Most important in social implications has been the progressive convergence of all information technologies—mass media, telecommunications, and computing—in a single infrastructure of control at the most macro level. A 1978 report commissioned by the President of France—an instant best-seller in that country and abroad—likened the growing interconnection of information-processing, communication, and control technologies throughout the world to an alteration in "the entire nervous system of social organization" (Nora and Minc 1978, p. 3). The same report introduced the neologism *telematics* for this most recent stage of the Information Society, although similar words had been suggested earlier—for example, *compunications* (for "computing + communications") by Anthony Oettinger and his colleagues at Harvard's Program on Information Resources Policy (Oettinger 1971; Berman and Oettinger 1975; Oettinger, Berman, and Read 1977).

Crucial to telematics, compunications, or whatever word comes to be used for this convergence of information-processing and communications technologies is increasing digitalization: coding into discontinuous values —usually two-valued or binary—of what even a few years ago would have been an analog signal varying continuously in time, whether a telephone conversation, a radio broadcast, or a television picture. Because most modern computers process digital information, the progressive digitalization of mass media and telecommunications content begins to blur earlier distinctions between the communication of information and its processing (as implied by the term *compunications*), as well as between people and machines. Digitalization makes communication from persons to machines, between machines, and even from machines to persons as easy as it is between persons. Also blurred are the distinctions among information types: numbers, words, pictures, and sounds, and eventually tastes, odors, and possibly even sensations, all might one day be stored, processed, and communicated in the same digital form.

In this way digitalization promises to transform currently diverse forms of information into a generalized medium for processing and exchange by the social system, much as, centuries ago, the institution of common currencies and exchange rates began to transform local markets into a single world economy. We might therefore expect the implications of digitalization to be as profound for macrosociology as the institution of money was for macroeconomics. Indeed, digitalized electronic systems have already begun

INTRODUCTION

to replace money itself in many informational functions, only the most recent stage in a growing systemness of world society dating back at least to the Commercial Revolution of the fifteenth century.

Societal dynamics reconsidered

Despite the chronic historical myopia that characterizes the human condition as documented in the opening pages of this chapter, it is unlikely that the more astute observers of our era would fail to glimpse—however dimly —even a single aspect of its essential social dynamic. For this reason the ability of a conceptual framework to subsume social changes noted by previous observers might be taken as one criterion for judging its claim to portray a more fundamental societal transformation. We shall see that the various transformations identified by contemporary observers as listed in Table 1 can be readily subsumed by the major implications of the Control Revolution: the growing importance of information technology, as in Richta's scientific-technological revolution (1967) or Brzezinski's technetronic era (1970); the parallel growth of an information economy (Machlup 1962, 1980; Porat 1977) and its growing control by business and the state (Galbraith 1967); the organizational basis of this control (Boulding 1953; Whyte 1956) and its implications for social structure, whether a meritocracy (Young 1958) or a new social class (Djilas 1957; Gouldner 1979); the centrality of information processing and communication, as in McLuhan's global village (1964), Phillips's communications age (1975), or Evans's micro millennium (1979); the information basis of postindustrial society (Touraine 1971; Bell 1973); and the growing importance of information and knowledge in modern culture (Mead 1970).

In short, the argument that motivates our investigation of the nineteenth-century crisis of control and the resulting Control Revolution is that particular attention to the material aspects of information processing, communication, and control makes possible the synthesis of a large proportion of the literature on contemporary social change. It will be useful, however, to consider first the broader theoretical and historical context of industrialization and technological change. A more detailed review of the literature on contemporary social change will therefore be postponed until the nineteenth-century developments, our own Information Society, and the emerging world system have been examined in greater detail. We now turn to the analytic groundwork for this larger task, consideration of information processing and control at the more general level of living systems.

References

Abbot, Waldo, and Richard L. Rider. 1957. *Handbook of Broadcasting: The Fundamentals of Radio and Television*, 4th ed. New York: McGraw-Hill.

177

HISTORY AND PERSPECTIVES

Aron, Raymond. 1961. *18 Lectures on Industrial Society*, trans. M. K. Bottomore. London: Weidenfeld and Nicolson, 1967.

—— 1966. *The Industrial Society: Three Essays on Ideology and Development*. New York: Simon and Schuster, Clarion, 1967.

Averitt, Robert T. 1968. *The Dual Economy: The Economics of American Industry Structure*. New York: Norton.

Beer, Samuel H. 1969. *British Politics in the Collectivist Age*, rev. ed. New York: Random House, Vintage.

Bell, Daniel. 1960. *The End of Ideology: On the Exhaustion of Political Ideas in the Fifties*. New York: Free Press, rev. ed. 1965.

—— 1973. *The Coming of Post-Industrial Society: A Venture in Social Forecasting*. New York: Basic Books.

—— 1979. "The social Framework of the Information Society." Pp. 163–211 in *The Computer Age: A Twenty-Year View*, ed. Michael L. Dertonzos and Joel Moses. Cambridge, Mass.: MIT Press.

—— 1980. "Introduction." Pp. vii–xvi in Simon Nora and Alain Minc, *The Computerization of Society: A Report to the President of France*. Cambridge, Mass.: MIT Press.

Berkeley, Edmund Callis. 1962. *The Computer Revolution*. Garden City, N.Y.: Doubleday.

Berman, Paul J., and Anthony G. Oettinger. 1975. *The Medium and the Telephone: The Politics of Information Resources*, Working Paper 75–8 (December 15). Cambridge, Mass.: Harvard University Program on Information Technologies and Public Policy.

Bezold, Clement, ed. 1978. *Anticipatory Democracy: People in the Politics of the Future*. New York: Random House, Vintage.

Blanqui, Jérôme Adolphe. 1837. *History of Political Economy in Europe*, trans. Emily J. Leonard. New York: G. P. Putnam's Sons, 1880.

Boorstin, Daniel J. 1973. *The Americans: The Democratic Experience*. New York: Random House, Vintage.

—— 1978. *The Republic of Technology: Reflections on Our Future Community*. New York: Harper and Row.

Boulding, Kenneth E. 1953. *The Organizational Revolution: A Study in the Ethics of Economic Organization*. New York: Harper.

—— 1964. *The Meaning of the Twentieth Century: The Great Transition*. New York: Harper and Row.

Breed, Warren. 1971. *The Self-Guiding Society*. New York: Free Press.

Briggs, Asa. 1977. "The Pleasure Telephone: A Chapter in the Prehistory of the Media." Pp. 40–65 in *The Social Impact of the Telephone*, ed. Ithiel de Sola Pool. Cambridge, Mass.: MIT Press.

Brown, Lester R. 1972. *World Without Borders*. New York: Random House.

Brzezinski, Zbigniew. 1970. *Between Two Ages: America's Role in the Technetronic Era*. New York: Viking Press.

Burchfield, R. W., ed. 1972. *A Supplement to the Oxford English Dictionary*, vol. 1. Oxford: Oxford University Press, Clarendon.

Burck, Gilbert. 1964. "Knowledge: The Biggest Growth Industry of Them All." *Fortune* (November): 128–131 ff.

Burnham, David. 1983. *The Rise of the Computer State*. New York: Random House.

INTRODUCTION

Carlyle, Thomas. 1850. *Latter-Day Pamphlets*. New York: Charles Scribner's Sons, 1898.

Chandler, Alfred D., Jr. 1977. *The Visible Hand: The Managerial Revolution in American Business*. Cambridge, Mass.: Belknap Press of Harvard University Press.

Cole, H. S. D., Christopher Freeman, Marie Jahoda, and K. L. R. Pavitt, eds. 1973. *Models of Doom: A Critique of the Limits to Growth*. New York: Universe Books.

Collins, Randall. 1979. *The Credential Society: An Historical Sociology of Education and Stratification*. New York: Academic.

Crozier, Michel. 1973. *The Stalled Society*. New York: Viking Press.

Daglish, Robert, ed. 1972. *The Scientific and Technological Revolution: Social Effects and Prospects*. Moscow: Progress Publishers.

Dahrendorf, Ralf. 1959. *Class and Class Conflict in an Industrial Society*. Stanford, Calif: Stanford University Press.

—— 1964. "Recent Changes in the Class Structure of European Societies." Pp. 291–336 in *A New Europe?* ed. Stephen R. Graubard. Boston: Houghton Mifflin.

Dertouzos, Michael L., and Joel Moses, eds. 1979. *The Computer Age: A Twenty-Year View*. Cambridge, Mass.: MIT Press.

Dizard, Wilson P., Jr. 1982. *The Coming Information Age: An Overview of Technology, Economics, and Politics*. New York: Longman.

Djilas, Milovan. 1957. *The New Class: An Analysis of the Communist System*. New York: Praeger.

Dordick, Herbert S., Helen G. Bradley, and Burt Nanus. 1981. *The Emerging Network Marketplace*. Norwood, N.J.: Ablex.

Drucker, Peter F. 1959. *Landmarks of Tomorrow*. New York: Harper and Row.

—— 1969. *The Age of Discontinuity*. New York: Harper and Row.

Durkheim, Emile. 1893. *The Division of Labor in Society*, trans. George Simpson. New York: Free Press, 1933.

Eichner, Alfred S. 1976. *The Megacorp and Oligopoly: The Micro Foundations of Macro Dynamics*. Cambridge: Cambridge University Press.

Eisenstadt, Shmuel N., ed. 1972. *Post-Traditional Societies*. New York: Norton.

Ellul, Jacques. 1964. *The Technological Society*, trans. John Wilkinson. New York: Knopf.

Etzioni, Amitai. 1968. *The Active Society: A Theory of Societal and Political Processes*. New York: Free Press.

Evans, Christopher. 1979. *The Micro Millennium*. New York: Washington Square/Pocket Books.

Evans, Lawrence B. 1977. "Impact of the Electronics Revolution on Industrial Process Control." *Science* 195 (March 18): 1146–1151.

Fabricant, Solomon. 1949. "The Changing Industrial Distribution of Gainful Workers: some comments on the American Decennial Statistics for 1820–1940." *Studies in Income and Wealth*, vol. 11. New York: National Bureau of Economic Research.

Feuer, Lewis S. 1969. *Marx and the Intellectuals: A Set of Post-Ideological Essays*. Garden City, N.Y.: Anchor Books.

Forester, Tom, ed. 1980. *The Microelectronics Revolution*. Cambridge, Mass.: MIT Press.

HISTORY AND PERSPECTIVES

Galbraith, John Kenneth. 1967. *The New Industrial State*. Boston: Houghton Mifflin, 3rd rev. ed., 1978.

Gallie, Duncan. 1978. *In Search of the New Working Class*. Cambridge: Cambridge University Press.

Gartner, Alan, and Frank Riessman. 1974. *The Service Society and the Consumer Vanguard*. New York: Harper and Row.

Gintis, Herbert. 1970. "The New Working Class and Revolutionary Youth." *Continuum* 8(1, 2): 151–152.

Gorz, André. 1968. *Strategy for Labor*. Boston: Beacon Press.

Gouldner, Alvin W. 1979. *The Future of Intellectuals and the Rise of the New Class*. New York: Seabury Press, Continuum.

Halmos, Paul. 1970. *The Personal Society*. London: Constable.

Hawkes, Nigel. 1971. *The Computer Revolution*. New York: Dutton.

Helvey, T. C. 1971. *The Age of Information: An Interdisciplinary Survey of Cybernetics*. Englewood Cliffs, N.J.: Educational Technology Publications.

Hiltz, Starr Roxanne, and Murray Turoff. 1978. *The Network Nation: Human Communication via Computer*. Reading, Mass.: Addison-Wesley.

Ionescu, Ghita, ed. 1976. *The Political Thought of Saint-Simon*. Oxford: Oxford University Press.

Jenkins, Clive, and Barrie Sherman. 1979. *The Collapse of Work*. London: Eyre Methuen.

Kahn, Herman. 1970. *Forces for Change in the Final Third of the Twentieth Century*. Croton-on-Hudson, N.Y.: Hudson Institute.

Kant, Immanuel. 1788. *Critique of Practical Reason*, trans. Lewis W. Beck. Indianapolis, Ind.: Bobbs-Merrill, 1956.

Lamberton, Donald M., ed. 1974. *The Information Revolution*. Annals of the American Academy of Political and Social Science, vol. 412. Philadelphia: American Academy of Political and Social Science.

Large, Peter. 1980. *The Micro Revolution*. London: Fontana.

—— 1984. *The Micro Revolution Revisited*. Totowa, N.J.: Rowman and Allanheld.

Laurie, Peter. 1981. *The Micro Revolution: Living with Computers*. New York: Universe Books.

Lebergott, Stanley. 1964. *Manpower in Economic Growth: The American Record since 1800*. New York: McGraw-Hill.

Lewis, Russell. 1973. *The New Service Society*. London: Longman.

Lichtheim, George. 1963. *The New Europe: Today and Tomorrow*. New York: Praeger.

Machlup, Fritz. 1962. *The Production and Distribution of Knowledge in the United States*. Princeton, N.J.: Princeton University Press.

—— 1980. *Knowledge: Its Creation, Distribution, and Economic Significance*, vol. 1. Princeton, N.J.: Princeton University Press.

McLuhan, Marshall. 1964. *Understanding Media: The Extensions of Man*. New York: McGraw-Hill.

Mallet, Serge. 1963. *La Nouvelle Classe Ouvrière*. Paris: Editions du Seuil.

Marcuse, Herbert. 1964. *One-Dimensional Man: Studies in the Ideology of Advanced Industrial Society*. Boston: Beacon Press.

Marris, Robin. 1964. *The Economic Theory of Managerial Capitalism*. New York: Free Press.

Marschak, Jacob. 1968. "Economics of Inquiring, Communicating, and Deciding." *American Economic Review* 58(2): 1–8.

INTRODUCTION

Martin, James. 1978. *The Wired Society*. Englewood Cliffs, N.J.: Prentice-Hall.

—— 1981. *The Telematic Society: A Challenge for Tomorrow*. Englewood Cliffs, N.J.: Prentice-Hall.

Martin, James, and David Butler. 1981. *Viewdata and the Information Society*. Englewood Cliffs, N.J.: Prentice-Hall.

Martin, James, and Adrian R. D. Norman. 1970. *The Computerized Society*. Englewood Cliffs, N.J.: Prentice-Hall.

Mead, Margaret. 1970. *Culture and Commitment: A Study of the Generation Gap*. New York: Doubleday, Natural History Press.

Meadows, Donella H., Dennis L. Meadows, Jorgen Randers, and William W. Behrens III. 1972. *Limits to Growth: A Report for the Club of Rome's Project on the Predicament of Mankind*. New York: Universe Books.

Meynaud, Jean. 1968. *Technocracy*, trans. Paul Barnes. London: Faber and Faber.

Michael, Donald N. 1968. *The Unprepared Society: Planning for a Precarious Future*. New York: Harper and Row, Colophon.

Mill, John Stuart. 1848. *Principles of Political Economy, with Some of their Applications to Social Philosophy*, 2 vols. Boston: Little, Brown.

Nora, Simon, and Alain Minc. 1978. *The Computerization of Society: A Report to the President of France*. Cambridge, Mass.: MIT Press, 1980.

Oettinger, Anthony G. 1971. "Compunications in the National Decision-Making Process." Pp. 73–114 in *Computers, Communications, and the Public Interest*, ed. Martin Greenberger. Baltimore: Johns Hopkins University Press.

Oettinger, Anthony G., Paul J. Berman, and William H. Read. 1977. *High and Low Politics: Information Resources for the 80's*. Cambridge, Mass.: Ballinger.

Phillips, Kevin P. 1975. *Mediacracy: American Parties and Politics in the Communications Age*. Garden City, N.Y.: Doubleday.

Piore, Michael J., and Charles F. Sabel. 1984. *The Second Industrial Divide: Possibilities for Prosperity*. New York: Basic.

Porat, Marc Uri. 1977. *The Information Economy: Definition and Measurement*. Washington: Office of Telecommunications, U.S. Department of Commerce.

Prague Academy. 1973. *Man, Science, and Technology: A Marxist Analysis of the Scientific Technological Revolution*. Prague: Academia Prague.

Pred, Allan R. 1973. *Urban Growth and the Circulation of Information: The United States System of Cities, 1790–1840*. Cambridge, Mass.: Harvard University Press.

Redlich, Fritz. 1951. *The Molding of American Banking, Men and Ideas*. New York: Johnson Reprint Corporation, 1968.

Richta, Radovan, ed. 1967. *Civilization at the Crossroads: Social and Human Implications of the Scientific and Technological Revolution*. White Plains, N.Y.: International Arts and Sciences Press.

Riesman, David. 1950. *The Lonely Crowd: A Study of the Changing American Character*, with Reuel Denney and Nathan Glazer. New Haven, Conn.: Yale University Press.

Rostow, Walt W. 1960. *The Stages of Economic Growth*. Cambridge: Cambridge University Press.

Seidenberg, Roderick. 1950. *Posthistoric Man: An Inquiry*. Chapel Hill: University of North Carolina Press.

Shannon, Claude E., and Warren Weaver. 1949. *The Mathematical Theory of Communication*. Urbana: University of Illinois Press.

HISTORY AND PERSPECTIVES

Stine, G. Harry. 1975. *The Third Industrial Revolution.* New York: G. P. Putnam's Sons.

Stonier, Tom. 1979. "The Third Industrial Revolution—Microprocessors and Robots." In *Microprocessors and Robots: Effects of Modern Technology on Workers.* Vienna: International Metalworkers' Federation.

Sylvester, Edward J., and Lynn C. Klotz. 1983. *The Gene Age: Genetic Engineering and the Next Industrial Revolution.* New York: Scribner's.

Taylor, Keith, ed. 1975. *Henri Saint-Simon (1760–1825): Selected Writings on Science, Industry and Social Organisation.* New York: Holmes and Meier.

Thompson, Robert Luther. 1947. *Wiring a Continent: The History of the Telegraph Industry in the United States, 1832–1866.* Princeton, N.J.: Princeton University Press.

Toffler, Alvin. 1971. *Future Shock.* New York: Bantam Books.

—— 1980. *The Third Wave.* New York: William Morrow.

Tomeski, Edward Alexander. 1970. *The Computer Revolution: The Executive and the New Information Technology.* New York: Macmillan.

Touraine, Alain. 1971. *The Post-Industrial Society.* New York: Random House.

Toynbee, Arnold. 1884. *Lectures on the Industrial Revolution of the Eighteenth Century in England.* London: Longmans, Green, 1920.

U.S. Bureau of the Census. 1975. *Historical Statistics of the United States, Colonial Times to 1970,* 2 vols. Washington: U.S. Government Printing Office.

Vickers, Geoffrey. 1970. *Freedom in a Rocking Boat: Changing Values in an Unstable Society.* London: Allen Lane, Penguin.

Wade, John. 1833. *History of the Middle and Working Classes.* London: E. Wilson, 3rd ed., 1835.

Weber, Max. 1922. *Economy and Society: An Outline of Interpretive Sociology,* 3 vols., ed. Guenther Roth and Claus Wittich. New York: Bedminster Press, 1968.

Whyte, William H., Jr. 1956. *The Organization Man.* New York: Simon and Schuster.

Wiener, Norbert. 1948. *Cybernetics: or Control and Communication in the Animal and the Machine.* Cambridge, Mass.: MIT Press, 2nd ed., 1961.

Williams, Frederick. 1982. *The Communications Revolution.* Beverly Hills, Calif.: Sage.

Winner, Langdon. 1977. *Autonomous Technology: Technics-out-of-Control as a Theme in Political Thought.* Cambridge, Mass.: MIT Press.

Young, Michael. 1958. *The Rise of the Meritocracy 1870–2033: An Essay on Education and Equality.* Harmondsworth, England: Penguin, 1961.

11

FROM 'POST-INDUSTRIALISM' TO 'INFORMATION SOCIETY': A NEW SOCIAL TRANSFORMATION?

David Lyon

Source: *Sociology* 20(4) (1986): 577–88.

The rapid introduction and widespread diffusion of information technology (IT) within the advanced societies raises numerous questions of great interest for sociology. Among them is the broad question of whether we are at the threshold of a new kind of society. Naturally enough, this issue features prominently in futurist television shows, popular paperbacks, and the press. But the kinds of claims made – such as that we are constructing a 'wired society' (Martin 1978) or experiencing a 'third wave' (Toffler 1980), dependent on the 'wealth of information' (Stonier 1983) – warrant more systematic social analysis.

Among the concepts put forward to encapsulate what is going on, the 'information society' is clearly a leading candidate. Given the newness of the technologies, and the relatively recent realization of their potential to affect all areas of life, it would be surprising if sociological debate were already crystallizing around a single concept. But the growing number of references to the 'information society' (or to related categories, such as 'information workers') makes it a suitable focus for discussion of research on the social dimensions of the new technology, and the specific question of whether we should revise one of our basic means of characterising 'society' today.

The emergence of this concept within serious social analysis is explicable. Firstly, the social (not to mention economic and political) significance of information technology is rapidly being established as a phenomenon worthy of social investigation (sometimes on dubious grounds, as we shall see). Secondly, whereas 'post-industrialism', the only previous potential usurper of 'industrial society' concepts, was *negatively* and thus rather vaguely defined, 'information society' promises concrete clues as to the dominant features of the burgeoning social formation. Thirdly, just as Daniel Bell more than any other single contributor placed 'post-industrialism' on the sociological agenda, so he has also put his weight behind the 'information society' concept.

Some discussions of 'information society' evoke a sense of *déjà vu*, not to mention impatience, in the light of extensive critiques which have already been made of 'post-industrialism' (Kleinberg 1973, Kumar 1978). On the other hand, the 'social forecast' of 'post-industrial society' was issued by Bell and others well before the technological breakthroughs associated with the silicon chip. While it may appear premature to hail the consequences of this as a 'Micro Revolution' (Large 1984), the increases in speed, flexibility and efficiency in information handling, along with the decreases in component costs, do have far-reaching actual and potential social ramifications. Trying to gauge the extent and meaning of such ramifications, whether or not they amount to 'information society', is a valid sociological enterprise.

In what follows, I examine the current debate over the 'information society' concept. Firstly, I uncover the roots of this concept in the literatures of post-industrialism, of futurism, and of what might be called the 'social consequences of new technology'. Secondly, I survey attempts to clarify or criticise the idea of 'information society', with particular reference to the social role of 'information' and of 'information activities'. I also comment on the failure to include analysis of power relations (local and global) in some versions of the 'information society' thesis. Thirdly, I suggest where the most fruitful lines of inquiry seem to lie. While this need not necessarily entail abandonment of the 'information society' concept, I propose a number of crucial qualifications. In particular, the spectres of economic and technological determinism must be laid, and renewed emphasis given to the social *shaping* as well as the social *consequences* of new technology.[1]

The roots of the information society idea

The roots of the information society idea are intertwined in a fairly complex manner. It is hard to disentangle the diverse strands of attempted social prediction, government policy, futuristic speculation and empirical social analysis. For instance, a Canadian government report, *Planning now for the information society* (Science Council of Canada 1982), is clearly geared towards identifying a national technological strategy in microelectronics. But it depends on social scientific concepts such as the 'information economy', indulges briefly in quoted 'predictions' (for instance that by the year 2000 'smart' highways for semiautomated driving will enter early development), and refers to empirical studies of the impact of microelectronics on, among other things, women's work.

FROM 'POST-INDUSTRIALISM' TO 'INFORMATION SOCIETY'

One strand that is readily identifiable, however, is the idea of post-industrialism, especially the version associated with Daniel Bell. Several writers refer hopefully to the 'information society' future (for instance, Nora and Mine 1981), but frequently fall back on the language of post-industrialism. In essence, this is the view that, as 'agrarian' was replaced by 'industrial' society as the dominant economic emphasis shifted from the land to manufacture, so 'post-industrial' society emerges as a result of the economic tilt towards the provision of services. The increased part played by science in the productive process, the rise to prominence of professional, scientific and technical groups, plus the introduction of what we now call 'information technology', all bear witness to a new 'axial principle' at the core of the socioeconomic system. This 'axial principle', the 'energising principle that is the logic for all the others', is the centrality of 'theoretical knowledge' (Bell 1974:14).

Bell argues that the information society is developing in the context of postindustrial society. He forecasts the emergence of a new social framework based on telecommunications which 'may be decisive for the way economic and social exchanges are conducted, the way knowledge is created and retrieved, and the character of work and occupations in which men (sic) are engaged'. The computer plays a central role in this 'revolution' (1980:500).

Bell also sketches other significant features of information society. Information and telecommunications, as they shorten labour time and diminish the production worker, actually replace labour as the source of 'added value' in the national product. Knowledge and information supplant labour and capital as the 'central variables' of society. He comments on the 'pricing' of information, and the way in which the 'possession' of information increasingly confers power on its owner. Bell acknowledges but sidesteps the ambiguities involved in identifying a 'service sector' by proposing that economic sectors be divided into 'extractive, fabrication, and information activities'. This way, he claims, one may monitor the penetration of information activities into more traditional areas of agriculture, manufacturing and services.

Bell underlines what he sees as the expansion of these areas in the wake of information technology. He foresees major social changes resulting from the establishment of new telecommunications infrastructures. These in turn will intensify concern about population distribution, national planning, centralization, privacy, and so on. The 'fateful question', when all is said and done, is whether the promise will be realised that 'instrumental technology' will open 'the way to alternative modes of achieving individuality and variety within a vastly increased output of goods' (1980:545).

Of course, Bell's is not the only version of the postindustrialism thesis. Alain Touraine's European alternative, for instance, takes account of the same socioeconomic trends as those isolated by Bell, but views the post-industrial society as a somewhat less harmonious product of them. Arguing that our image of class has been too deeply bound up with the 'era of capitalist industrialization', Touraine challenges the bland postindustrial assumption that class struggle is a thing of the past, and invites us to consider the 'fundamental importance of class situations, conflicts and movements in the programmed society' (1974:28). He identifies the major new cleavage between on the one hand the technocrats, and on the other a more disparate grouping whose livelihood and lifestyle is governed by their practice. The principal opposition between the two great classes or groups of classes hinges not so much on property-ownership but 'comes about because the dominant classes dispose of knowledge and control *information*' (1974:61).

During the 1970s a number of theories appeared, purporting both to document the emergence of 'new classes' – 'the knowledge class' (Gouldner 1979) or the 'professional-managerial class' (Ehrenreich 1979) – and to bid 'farewell to the working class' (Gorz 1980). Novel class alignments, it appeared, were bound up with changing technologies and shifts in educational qualification and skill. As we shall see, however, the effort to identify new lines of class cleavage has sometimes deflected attention from those which still operate within societies adopting IT, namely, property relations.

Social forecasters and social planners

The roots of the 'information society' idea are not only found in sociology. Futurists (such as Toffler 1980, Naisbitt 1984) and 'social impact of technology' commentators also contribute. They tend to share the belief that technology 'shapes' social relationships.

One of the many cheerful 'social forecasts' comes from Tom Stonier. 'Living in a post-industrial world' he avers, 'means that not only are we more affluent, more resourceful and less likely to go to war, but also more likely to democratise' (1983:202). Increasing prosperity is a common 'information society' theme.

By 'more resourceful' Stonier means that IT will enable us to conquer the environmental and ecological problems associated with industrialism. Again he touches on a common theme. James Martin also stresses the 'non-polluting, nondestructive' quality of IT itself as a major point in its favour (Martin 1978:4). New communications technologies hold out the next promise – the demise of war ('as slavery disappeared in the industrial era' Stonier 1983:202). And lastly, IT ushers in the world of 'computer democracy'. More information availability, plus pushbutton referenda, open the door for the first time to genuinely responsive participatory government. This, along with the burden of administration being thoroughly automated, is the contented futurist's world of 'information society'.

A short step away from the futurist's vision is the forecaster's proposal. Japan was first to produce such a proposal, in the shape of *The plan for information society: A national goal toward the year 2000* (1972). Lacking natural energy resources, the Japanese were acutely aware of the fragility of their economy in the face of recession. Yoneji Masuda's work (translated into English as *The information society as post-industrial society*, 1981) has been central to the process of establishing the 'national plan'. The idea of 'computopia' is given concrete shape by Masuda, who links together the futurist dream ('the goal. . . . is a society that brings about a general flourishing state of human intellectual creativity, instead of affluent material consumption', 1981:3) with actual 'new towns' in Japan and 'information society infrastructures' elsewhere.

Japan's Tama New Town, with its built-in network of coaxial cables, Canada's *Telidon* (videotex) programme, and Sweden's *Terese* project, which monitors regional development using new telecommunications, are cited as relevant examples of such 'infrastructures'. They are significant because Masuda sees information society as 'a new type of human society'. For him, *production of information values and not material values will be the driving force'*. At the same time, past experience within industrial society may be used as a *historical analogical model for future society'* (1981:29).

Masuda's assumption that the history of industrial society may be used as an analogy for what will happen in information society brings us back to the core of the sociological question. Is it legitimate to claim that the steam engine was to industrial society what the computer is to information society, so that, one, the new technology shapes the resulting social and political formation, and two, a qualitatively different kind of society emerges?

Within the same sociological question lies the problem of exactly what the social consequences – and the social determinants – of the diffusion of information technology are? Even if one remains sceptical about the capacity of the computer to transform the world in quite the way envisaged by a Stonier or a Masuda, it is clear that IT is a major phenomenon with a broad potential social impact.

Some predictions about IT's effects exude confidence, especially those whose plausibility rests on identifying a big proportion of the work-force as 'information processors'. Barron and Curnow, for example, put the proportion at around 40% (1979). Against this, Trevor Jones is more cautious (1980). He insists that a sector-by-sector analysis is required before any overall survey can be attempted. Productivity varies between sectors, as does the pace of change and new technology take-up rates. Close analysis also reveals job-loss, deskilling, and increased workplace surveillance associated with new technology, which suggests continuities rather than discontinuities with 'industrial society'.

Clearly, other factors than 'technology' enter the picture. Government policy for example has an impact on the way IT is developed. In Britain, the Alvey programme for developing IT is heavily weighted in favour of commercial rather than university research, which affects both the traditional role of the latter, and the kinds of 'product' of research.

HISTORY AND PERSPECTIVES

This brings us to the sociological critique of the 'information society' concept. The further one moves from grand national IT plans and from futuristic forecasts of the conditions prevailing within the computerised society, and the nearer one gets to actual social analysis in which technology is not perceived as a quasi-autonomous force acting upon society, the more questionable the information society concept appears.

The critique of 'information society'

The 'information society' concept has inherited several symptoms of the troubles which beset 'postindustrialism'. The postindustrialists failed to justify the significance given to trends such as the growth of theoretical knowledge and 'services'. Their idea of a leisure society, based on automated manufacture, and a vast array of services, with a cultural system embodying self-expression, political participation, and an emphasis on the quality of life, does not seem to have materialised, at least not for the majority of the populations of the advanced societies.

Much of the exaggeration and sociological sleight of hand involved in postindustrialism has been adequately exposed (most economically in Kumar 1978). For instance, the *quantity* of research and development (R&D) in a given economy tells us nothing about the social *role* of scientific and technical knowledge, the price put on it, or the power of those who manipulate it. The fact that R&D is often financed for political rather than social reasons, and developed for military rather than economic purposes, gives the lie to any idea that universities may have become crucibles of power in the new world. (Add to this the current squeeze on university funding, plus the politicization of science and technology policy, and the notion of 'powerful' universities becomes even more of a chimera.) The so-called 'new class' is probably less strong than some postindustrialists imagined, either as an enlightened elite or as an exploitative class (see further, Badham 1984).

Kumar, whose work draws together diverse strands of the critique of postindustrialism, concludes that a qualitatively different social world has not appeared. When one has distinguished between 'white collar' and 'service' work, shown that some 'professionalization' in fact involves 'relabelling' (the plumber becomes a 'heating engineer'), and deflated the idea that more PhDs means a bigger stock of social knowledge, the claims about a 'new social transformation' begin to wear somewhat thin. The agenda of questions for postindustrial society, says Kumar, is remarkably reminiscent of the agenda for *industrial* society. In his words,

> Beneath the postindustrial gloss, old scarred problems rear their heads: alienation and control in the workplaces of the service economy; scrutiny and supervision of the operations of private and

FROM 'POST-INDUSTRIALISM' TO 'INFORMATION SOCIETY'

public bureaucracies, especially as they come to be meshed in with technical and scientific expertise. Framing all these is the problem of the dominant constraining and shaping force of contemporary industrial societies: competitive struggles for profit and power between private corporations and nation states, in an environment in which such rivalries have a tendency to become expansionist and global.

(1978:231)

Kumar points out that the early sociologists foresaw in *industrialism* exactly those trends which are now touted as signs of postindustrialism, such as Weber's observation of the increasing application of calculative rationality to the productive order. Something not dissimilar applies to 'information society' as well.

Having said that, today's 'information society' theorists lay great store by the notion that 'information work' is becoming increasingly significant within the economy, especially as IT is more widely diffused. It is not just that theoretical knowledge is more important for production, but that so-called 'information operatives' are increasingly visible within all kinds of occupations. The big question, of course, is who these information operatives are, and what contribution their work makes to patterns of social relationship.

Studies of the occupational structure made by Marc Porat (1977) are frequently taken as the basis for bold predictions. Taking the US national accounts as his basis, Porat calculated (in 1967) that almost 50% of the workforce was engaged in the 'information sector', and received just over 50% of total employee remuneration. But Porat fails to explain what is meant by 'information', so that while rent collectors and judges *are* in the 'information' sector, doctors are an 'ambiguous occupation', straddling the 'service' and 'information' sectors. He simply defines 'information' as 'data that have been organized and communicated', and decides who is and is not an 'information worker' on the basis of whether the worker derives an income from handling such information. No reference is made to the purpose, function, or context of 'information work', and thus any clues about informative *power* are missing.

'Information work' is a category deserving careful analysis, without which we cannot know who makes decisions, and on what basis, or with what effect. Newman and Newman (1985) argue that a theory of information is a vital prerequisite to that. They propose the (economist's) formula that information is 'that which destroys uncertainty'. Information's importance to the economy lies in its contribution to economic adaptation through decisions made by firms, unions, governments, regulatory bodies, and consumers. And it must be seen in relation to organizational processes which shape labour markets and work situations. On this showing, 'information work' has to do with specific decision-taking (as in top management), while 'knowledge work' (as with the R&D scientist) has to do with the broader framework within which 'information' questions are asked.

Beyond this, the 'information society' thesis stands or falls on the question of which sectors of the economy are actually expanding, and which contracting. Politically, this is a crucially sensitive area. Government puts all its eggs into the IT basket on the assumption that IT will contribute to the creation of wealth and employment in the long run. It is to this question we now turn.

Information: a new socio-economic factor?

In *The new service economy*, (1983) Jonathan Gershuny and Ian Miles attempt to break out of the sectoral paradigm which has guided popular economic thinking since the 1960s. They doubt whether much sense may be made of today's social-economic realities by appealing to the traditional 'march through the sectors' of development, from primary through secondary and into tertiary production. Both postindustrial and information society theories are dubious because they are built on this 'march' idea. They obscure, for instance, the extent to which the tertiary services sector grew *because of* growth in manufacturing, and thus the extent to which services would not simply soak up surplus labour displaced from manufacturing.

Gershuny and Miles offer both an alternative reading of sectoral shifts, which details many nuances *within* the too-frequently homogenised services sector, and indicate the growing significance of information technology within the service sub-sectors. Thus they acknowledge that 'information' (-processing, -storing, and -transmitting) is a factor which must increasingly be taken into account in contemporary social-economic analysis. But they rightly stress that 'information' cannot validly be viewed as a 'separate' sector. *All* sectors are becoming more 'information intensive'.

The 'march through the sectors' appears more and more 'simplistic and naive' as one follows Miles and Gershuny's (1986) arguments further. By distinguishing on the one hand between marketed and non-marketed services, and on the other between intermediate producer and intermediate consumer services (the latter often refer to services finally controlled by the consumer, involving entertainment or DIY) they illustrate that far more than mere 'consumer demand' is operating. Political and management decisions are also crucially important.

The work of Gershuny and Miles helps collapse the 'information society' idea into a question of *alternative* possibilities rather than the 'evolution' of the next 'stage of development'. But I do have a caveat which I think is more than a cavil. It centres on the use of the term *'wave'*. They say that 'informatics are clearly central' to 'a future growth wave' (1986:26).

FROM 'POST-INDUSTRIALISM' TO 'INFORMATION SOCIETY'

A recent revival of interest in the 'Kondratiev wave' has stimulated analytical debate, especially among those searching for a way out of economic recession (see, for example, Freeman 1984, but also Marxist versions such as Wallerstein 1980). The difficulty, as Tom Kitwood (1984) points out, is that a metaphor may be raised to the status of theory, at the expense of careful analysis both of actions of the *dramatis personae*, and of major social processes such as militarism and government policy. Given Miles and Gershuny's critique of technological determinism, and their awareness of the problems surrounding the new 'informatics' infrastructure, their use of the 'wave' metaphor seems a little surprising.

Nevertheless, the main message derived from Gershuny and Miles about the 'information society' stands: the 'march through the sectors' idea is of little help in determining what role 'information' has today. Information activities take place throughout the economy, for varying reasons, and with differing impacts on processes such as employment.

At the same time, informatics has risen very rapidly over the past decade as a source of 'added value' and a means of wealth creation. Is this another reason for revising our concepts? Are we moving 'beyond' industrial capitalism?

Information society: beyond industrial capitalism?

It is hard to justify the claim that 'information society' takes us beyond industrial capitalism. On the one hand, information is being treated as though it were a commodity, to be priced within the marketplace. Vast transnational corporations such as IBM are involved in the commercial exploitation of information-related hardware, software, and services. On the other hand, the kinds of issues which have absorbed social analysts of industrial capitalism are reappearing in the information-intensive context – alienation and exploitation of the labour force, management and state monitoring and surveillance, and ethnic, gender and class cleavages.

In the USA, Herbert Schiller's critique of the 'information society's' transcendence of capitalism is probably best known (1981). In his words,

> The new communications technologies that have been discovered, the mode of their invention, the processes by which they have been installed, the factors which determine their utilization, the products that have been forthcoming, and the beneficiaries of the new systems and means of information transfer, are phenomena understandable best in terms of long-established and familiar market-based criteria.
>
> (1981:xii)

As in Britain, big corporations are given public assistance at the R&D stage, then the enterprises have to 'pay their own way' in the market. Needless to say, those who *cannot* pay (either for new cable television 'entertainment' or for new educational, commercial, personal or medical services) will rapidly become aware of what is termed 'information inequality'. It would indeed seem that property relations retain their importance *within* the 'information economy'.

But it is not only within nations that information inequality seems to be growing. The so-called 'information explosion' is a global phenomenon, in which the less developed countries are at a distinct disadvantage. The transfer of technology and skills happens slowly, if at all, so that indigenous growth is unlikely. But the transnational corporations not only continue to locate their plant in the most economically viable settings within the so-called Third World, they also maintain a commanding position because of their superior technological capabilities (See Rada 1982, Littler and Salaman 1984).

Britain also has its 'information society' critics. Frank Webster and Kevin Robins, for instance, see the activities of the transnationals which monopolise IT and shape innovation as expressions of the 'needs of capital'. They argue that the British Conservative government's 'free market/strong state' policy shows extensive collusion between it and big business. IT will actually 'facilitate the institution of the rule of capital across ever wider spheres of social existence'. This is felt, they say, both in the workplace (through the discipline of the labour process), the public sphere (as a tool of administrative and political processes), and the private sphere (through the further privatisation of leisure) (1981:266–7, and forthcoming).

The rapid growth of IT raises the question of what exactly is happening to capitalism, which is of particular interest to Marxists (see Mandel 1978). Harry Braverman's controversial work on 'deskilling' is also about the restructuring of capital, hence 'labour *and monopoly capital*' (1974). The quest for profit within capitalism, and its impact on relations between labour and capital, is crucial here. In its 'monopoly' phase, capitalism has developed at least two kinds of response to the crisis which has been with us since the 1960s. One has to do with labour intensification, technological innovation, and the rationalization of work, the other with the international movement of capital via multinational corporations.

Debate over Braverman's work (for instance, Wood 1982) has served to highlight the question of whether or not capitalism is being 'transcended' in 'information society'. The extent to which Braverman is correct to claim that deskilling and labour control are part of a capitalist ploy to extract surplus value (an alternative view is sketched in Rosenbrock 1984) cannot be determined here. But it is clear that resistance to deskilling and to management control and pacing of tasks is at the core of a number of socialist and union strategies to cope with new technology, as well as more academic attempts to explain its social impact (Gill 1985[2]).

One other area of concern is IT and women's employment. The two main aspects of this are, firstly, the lack of opportunities for technical education

FROM 'POST-INDUSTRIALISM' TO 'INFORMATION SOCIETY'

and training for women, and secondly, that women continue to bear the brunt of deskilling, low pay and unemployment as word processors, automation and IT-enabled homeworking are extended (see, e.g. Cockburn 1983). Are these concerns qualitatively different from those which have exercised the minds of students of industrial capitalism, especially since the last war? It would seem that only one thing has changed: the debate is now focused around the diffusion of information technology.

Information society as a problematic

Given the massive alterations in the way of life and in patterns of social, economic and political relationship which actually and potentially accompany the diffusion of information technology, focusing sociological attention on these is clearly a priority. The danger (in view of who pays for research) is that the scope of such studies will be restricted to the social *consequences* of new technology, and on 'adaptation to change'. It is a danger because the technology is then taken as given, rather than as the outcome of economic, political, and technical choices (although the socially-constraining effects of those choices should also be analysed)[3].

So what concepts should we use in attempting to analyse these changes? My own suggestion is that, rather than discarding the 'information society' concept, we should grant it the status of a 'problematic'. A 'problematic' is a 'rudimentary organization of a field of phenomena which yields problems for investigation' (Abrams 1982:xv). What would its features be?

Firstly, it must be very clear what 'information society' does *not* involve. The technological determinism lying not far beneath the surface of some accounts is rejected. Likewise the idea that a new 'technocracy', in which power resides with a knowledgeable or 'information-rich' class, is vulnerable to critique from both within and outside of marxism. Also, any view which ignores the palpable fact that no social-economic development takes place today in isolation from the *world* economic system must be subjected to severe criticism.

Secondly, alternative explanations must be offered. Technological determinism may be countered with analyses of the *social shaping* of new technology, the diverse contributions of governments, labour unions, corporations, universities, and consumers (see MacKenzie and Wajcman 1985). Predictions about the growing power of intellectuals or, rather, the technically knowledgeable are thrown in doubt by the continuing salience of property relations to the analysis of IT. The same economic activities are also inherently *international* in scope.

Negatively and positively, then, such criteria alert us to significant features of the 'information society' problematic. Two final comments are in place. Firstly, social analysis must grapple with the social implications of the *fusion* of technologies represented by the phrase 'information technology'

HISTORY AND PERSPECTIVES

(as begun, for instance in Bannon 1982, Bjorn-Andersen 1982, and Forester 1985). This involves eroding the conventional division of labour between 'communication studies' on the one hand, and 'computing/automation studies' on the other. For instance, issues raised by the decline of public service broadcasting are no longer relevant only to 'communications and media studies'. The burgeoning of communication between computers, and the emergence of the commercial database brings 'public service' questions to the heartland of computing (journals such as *Media, Culture and Society* are relevant here).[4]

Secondly, as social analysis exposes *alternative* options in the adoption of new technology which are in fact available to governments, industry, and the public, discussion of strategies for *shaping* new technology will become more relevant. Such analysis can serve to indicate the conditions under which ethical considerations and social hopes might be released. The yawning credibility gap between futurist dreams and the hard realities of government, transnational, and military involvement in IT demands a sense of urgency about research within the 'information society' problematic. It also indicates a vital role for serious social analysis within the policymaking process.

Notes

1 Comments from Jay Blumler, Howard Davis, Anthony Giddens, and anonymous referees helped my revision of this article.
2 See also the new journal, *New Technology, Work and Employment*, issued to supplement *The Journal of Industrial Relations*.
3 Relevant literature is monitored in *New Technology: social and economic impacts*, a periodical edited by Lesley Grayson, and published by Technical Communications, 100, High Avenue, Letchworth, SG6 3RR, UK.
4 For instance, the journal *Media Culture and Society* has now committed itself to debating the 'information society' concept. See the editorial by Nicholas Garnham and Richard Collins in volume 7, number 1, January 1985.

References

BADHAM, R. 1984 'The sociology of industrial and postindustrial society', *Current Sociology*, 32:1

BANNON, L. (*et al*, eds.) 1982 *Information Technology: impact on the way of life.* Dublin: Tycooly.

BARRON, I. and CURNOW, R. 1979 *The Future with Microelectronics.* Milton Keynes: Open University Press.

BELL, D. 1974 *The coming of postindustrial society: a venture in social forecasting.* Harmondsworth: Peregrine.

BELL, D. 1980 'The social framework of the information society,' in Forester 1985, q.v.

BJORN-ANDERSEN, N. (*et al*, eds.) 1982 *Information Society: for richer, for poorer.* Oxford: North-Holland.

BRAVERMAN, H. 1974 *Labour and Monopoly Capital*. New York: Monthly Review Press.

COCKBURN, C. 1983 *Brothers: Male dominance and technological change*. London: Pluto.

FERGUSON, M. (ed.) 1986 *New Communications Technologies and the Public Interest*. London: Sage.

FORESTER, T. (ed.) 1985 *The Information Technology Revolution*. Oxford: Basil Blackwell.

FORESTER, T. (ed.) 1980 *The Microelectronics Revolution*. Oxford: Basil Blackwell.

FREEMAN, C. 1984 'Keynes or Kondratiev: How can we get back to full employment?' in Pauline Marstrand (ed.) 1984, q.v.

GERSHUNY, J. and MILES, I. 1983 *The New Service Economy*. London: Frances Pinter.

GILL, C. 1985 *New Technology, Unemployment and Work*. Cambridge: Polity Press.

GORZ, A. 1980 *Farewell to the Working Class*. London: Pluto.

GOULDNER, A. 1979 *The Rise of the Intellectuals and the Future of the New Class*. London: Macmillan.

JONES, T. (ed.) 1980 *Microelectronics and Society*. Milton Keynes: Open University Press.

KITWOOD, T. 1984 'A farewell wave to the theory of long waves,' *Education, Culture and Society (Universities Quarterly)* 38:2, 158–78.

KLEINBERG, B. 1973 *American Society in the Post-Industrial Age*, Columbus: Merril.

KUMAR, K. 1978 *Prophecy and Progress: the sociology of industrial and postindustrial society*, Harmondsworth: Allen Lane.

LARGE, P. 1984 *The Micro Revolution*. London: Fontana.

LITTLER, C. and SALAMAN, G. (eds.) *Class of Work*. London: Batsford.

MACKENZIE, D., and WAJCMAN, J. (eds.) 1985 *The Social Shaping of Technology*. Milton Keynes: Open University Press.

MANDEL, E. 1978 *Late Capitalism*. London: Verso.

MANDEL, E. 1980 *Long Waves in Capitalist Development*. Cambridge: Cambridge University Press.

MARSTRAND, P. (ed.) 1984 *New Technology and the Future of Work and Skills*. London: Frances Pinter.

MASUDA, Y. 1981 *The Information Society as Postindustrial Society*. Bethesda MD: World Futures Society.

MARTIN, J. 1978 *The Wired Society*, Harmondsworth: Penguin.

MILES, I., and GERSHUNY, J. 1986 'The social economics of information technology', in Ferguson 1986, q.v.

NAISBITT, J. 1984 *Megatrends*. New York: Warner Books.

NEWMAN, J. and NEWMAN, R. 1985 'Information work: the new divorce?', *British Journal of Sociology* 24: 497–515.

NORA, S., and MINC, A. 1980 *The Computerisation of Society*. Cambridge MA: MIT Press (ET of *L'informatisation de la société*, Paris: La Documentation Française)

RADA, J. 1982 'A third world perspective,' in Gunter Friedrichs and Adam Schaff, *Microelectronics and Society: for better or worse*. London: Pergamon.

REINECKE, I. 1984 *Electronic Illusions*. Harmondsworth: Penguin.

ROSENBROCK, H. H. 1984 'Designing automated systems: need skill be lost?' in Pauline Marstrand (ed.) 1984.

HISTORY AND PERSPECTIVES

SHILLER, H. 1981 *Who Knows: information in the age of the Fortune 500*. Norwood NJ: Ablex.

SCIENCE COUNCIL OF CANADA 1982 *Planning Now for an Information Society: tomorrow is too late*. Ottawa: Science Council of Canada.

STONIER, T. 1983 *The Wealth of Information*. London: Thames Hudson.

TOFFLER, A. 1980 *The Third Wave*. London: Pan.

TOURAINE, A. 1974 *The Postindustrial Society*. London: Wildwood House.

WALLERSTEIN, E. 1980 *The Capitalist World Economy*. Cambridge: Cambridge University Press.

WEBSTER, F. and ROBINS, K. 1981 'Information technology: futurism, corporations and the state,' *Socialist Register*, 247–269.

WEBSTER, F. and ROBINS, K. (forthcoming) *Information Technology: a Luddite analysis*. Norwood, NJ,: Ablex.

WOOD, S. (ed.) 1982 *The Degradation of Work? Skill, deskilling, and the labour process*. London: Hutchinson.

12

THE SOCIAL ECONOMICS OF INFORMATION TECHNOLOGY

Ian Miles and Jonathan Gershuny[1]

Source: Marjorie Ferguson (ed.) (1986) *New Communication Technologies and the Public Interest*, London: Sage, pp. 18–36.

'Information society': a second coming of post-industrial society?

From post-industrial society to the information economy

According to a widely accepted view of economic development, the economy can best be seen as consisting of three main sectors: agriculture and other primary production, industries such as construction and (especially) manufacturing, and a tertiary or 'residual' sector producing services. Economic development is then viewed as a progressive shift in the focus of activity, first from the primary to the secondary sector, and then from the secondary to the tertiary.

Post-war developments seem at first sight to demonstrate the usefulness of this view. Agricultural employment declined rapidly with the introduction of mechanized, fertilizer-intensive and factory-farming methods. And service employment grew more rapidly than manufacturing, so that by the 1960s economists were talking of the 'service economy': more than 50 percent of all workers were employed in the service sector in the 1970s for the European Economic Community (EEC) as a whole. If we include workers from white-collar and other service-type jobs in the primary and secondary sectors, the dominance of such 'non-production' work is overwhelming.

The idea of a march of workers from primary through secondary to tertiary employment was taken to mean that there was little reason to be alarmed by the prospect of automation in manufacturing industry. The service industries would soak up surplus employment, it seemed – although close inspection of the data would have revealed that rather little of the growth in tertiary employment represented a migration of employees from the secondary sector into these industries of the future.

The implications of this process for social development more generally were elaborated in terms of certain assumptions about changes in social values. The progression through the economic sectors was attributed to shifts in consumer demand resulting from affluence and social equality. As people's basic needs were satisfied, the role of foodstuffs in their expenditure declined relative to that of manufactures (Engels' Law). And as they became satiated with material abundance, their desires for intangibles such as health and education grew in prominence. This hierarchy of values explains the march through the three economic sectors, and in turn has other social consequences that justified an intellectual shift from service *economy* to post-industrial *society*. 'Post-industrialism' became a dominant diagnosis of the present, and prognosis for the future, of the Western world.[2]

Social and economic developments were seen to be mutually reinforcing. As people's attitudes shifted away from a concern with the bare necessities of life, there would be a growth in demand for political participation, for care of the environment and for weaker members of society. These concerns, rather than the traditional issues of management of the economy, entered the political agenda in the late 1960s and early 1970s – what Inglehart called the 'silent revolution'. Furthermore, with the growth of white-collar and knowledge-intensive work, increasing power would be vested in scientific and technical workers, in people whose work depends upon their intellectual or interpersonal abilities, rather than in the owners of capital or other traditional bearers of power. Emerging as a dominant force in post-industrial society is a *new service class* of 'knowledge workers', with the values, skills and resources appropriate for the new agenda of political and economic development.

Thus there would be a shift toward greater social planning, and a subordination of business interests to values of meritocracy and welfare. The existence of some stresses and strains was conceded – such as the conflict between libertarian and personal-growth values and those of preserving high culture and maintaining media standards – but the general expectation was that of an end of ideology. Disagreement over social goals would be reduced to a minimum (especially as East–West conflict subsided with the convergence of both blocs towards post-industrial societies); that over the means to achieve the goals would be transformed into a technical debate in which tools such as technology assessment, social indicators and computer simulation would allow for the fine-tuning of social progress. . . .

Despite the traumas of the last decade, the term 'post-industrial society' remains remarkably respectable. Admittedly it tends to be used as a hand-waving description – but, as we shall argue, many of the underlying assumptions of post-industrialism are still commonly reproduced, and enter into the currently fashionable concept: the 'information society'.

The information society literature has moved on in some respects from the post-industrialists. Concern over job loss and de-skilling has become prominent with the industrial application of microelectronics, so the literature is more marked by disagreement over positive and negative consequences of technological and organizational changes than was the case for the post-industrialists. One recent study lists debates over whether informatics leads to: decentralization or increased centralized decision-making, upgrading or de-skilling of work, increased computer literacy or alienation from everyday technology, economic dualism or a more participatory economy, and intensified or debilitated interpersonal relationships. Most authors see one pole to be the logical consequence of current tendencies, rather as post-industrialists saw their future to be a logical consequence of social evolution: but in the economic climate of the 1980s the information society commentators add the imperative for countries to compete to make use of new processes and to produce new products to gain comparative advantages in international trade. Information society (perhaps with concomitant future shock and unemployment) or economic failure (with even more stress and unemployment): this is the implicit choice. But there remain a number of fundamental points where agreement between the 'post-industrial' and the 'information' society schools is strong.

The march through the sectors underpins much information society literature. However, some influential writers have proposed updating the three-sector model. Recognizing that the model loses much of its usefulness when an extremely diverse set of tertiary industries rise to the prominence which they now occupy, these authors suggest adding a fourth sector – the information sector. They similarly describe information occupations – all formal employment that is largely concerned with the production, processing or distribution of information, or with the installation, operation and maintenance of associated physical, electronic and mechanical infrastructure – which have formed an increasing proportion of the labour force (more than a third of all employment in the UK and North America by the 1980s).

Information society, then, rests upon the expansion of economic activities concerned with information flows. This expansion is attributed the centrality that was earlier accorded to the services. New technologies may check the growth of employment in information occupations by enabling increases in labour productivity; but they will also dramatically reduce the costs of information, leading to a considerable growth in demand for existing information services and informatics products, and the development of a host of new ones. Information services are seen as particularly important emerging areas of public demand (manipulated by media moguls according to some critical accounts). Industries too are seen as being forced to become more information-intensive owing to the changing nature of products and markets, and because of the drive for increased productivity. (For example,

HISTORY AND PERSPECTIVES

it is argued that rapid shifts in product design – corresponding to innovation or fashion – require production technologies that can be readily geared to different volumes of production and designs, as in computer-aided design–computer-aided manufacture (CADCAM).)

The debate over the relative rates of job replacement and job generation in information activities, relating closely to public and media concerns about unemployment, has helped raise the concept of information society to greater prominence than that achieved by post-industrial society. But other concerns have also surfaced: fears about the erosion of public service broadcasting (and the standards it has promoted) by cable and satellite services, and fears of surveillance and other forms of insidious social control, in particular. While this means that there is more critical thought about the prospects afforded by informatics, the shared core of assumptions here is suspiciously like that used by the post-industrialists. Is there any essential difference between the information workers, and the older new class of knowledge workers? What is it about information that makes it sufficiently desirable to form a base for a future general expansion? What will consumers be doing with all the information produced by the expanding army of information workers? The literature is rather short on answers to these workers.

Beneath the trends

Let us look a little more closely at the factors that underpin the growth of the service economy. The tertiary sector includes very diverse types of economic activity, which, as they have grown to be major areas of employment, appear increasingly incongruous when lumped together. More detailed classifications give a rather different picture of the rise of the service economy.[3]

For one thing, not all tertiary activities have been growing. In the UK, employment in personal services has declined since the last war. Employment in transport and distribution has been declining since the 1960s. In contrast, employment has increased in social services and also in producer services – that is, services sold to firms. Thus the growth in service sector employment in part reflects political choices and changes in industrial structure rather than changes in private demand for services. But has not private demand for services increased – and does this not reflect a shift away from materialist values?

Demand for services has increased with increasing affluence – but so has demand for goods. There is little evidence for services *per se* having a greater income elasticity than goods. There has been a shift in household expenditure along Engels' Law-like lines, away from basic purchases such as food and shelter and towards education, entertainment, etc. But within these latter categories, there has been a shift in private expenditure *away from services and towards goods*. Thus more money is spent on cars, televisions and washing machines, less on rail, theatre and laundry services. This

THE SOCIAL ECONOMICS OF INFORMATION TECHNOLOGY

would mean, other things being equal (which they are not), that service employment would decline relative to that in manufacturing – with the creation of some new service employment, for example in garages, TV studios and domestic equipment repairs. These service the use of manufactured goods by consumers producing their own final services (the shift to domestic production that Toffler suggests in his neologism of 'prosumers'), rather than supplying final services. Just as the producer services are supplying intermediate services to industries, we have here intermediate consumer services. Thus a portion of service sector growth derives from these two types of intermediate service, which appear to be contributing largely to the manufacture and operation of goods.

But service sector employment has grown mainly under the impetus of two other factors. First, increases in labour productivity have been lower in most services than in most other economic sectors. (This is why we suggested above that not all other things were equal.) Similar rates of demand increase across sectors will mean shifts in relative employment to those with lower rates of productivity growth. Second, collectively-provided services have been responsible for a very large share of the growth in tertiary employment. Again, as far as can be established given the problematic accounting methods available here, low productivity growth is involved in the rapid expansion of employment in these sectors.

The view of the service economy provided by this analysis is radically different to that of the post-industrialists. Rather than there being an inherent bias in favour of the purchasing of services with increasing affluence, the growth of services reflects rather complex political and economic trade-offs made by the state, firms and households. In several countries the growth of many skilled occupational categories in the first few post-war decades had much to do with the aerospace industry and the Cold War; and the expansion of social services can be related to the strength of socialist and social-democratic movements in different Western countries. Firms have participated in an increasing division of labour and found it expedient to purchase many of the services that might otherwise have been provided in-house: this choice, shaped by technological change, fiscal policy and employment protection legislation and unionization, has led to the development of new intermediate producer service industries. And while consumers have been more concerned with sophisticated luxury expenditure, the choice about how to make that expenditure has increasingly been weighted toward goods rather than services. This reflects a variety of factors shaping the relative cost and convenience of different modes of provision of final services, and hardly bears out the idea of a growth of post-material attitudes; indeed, the groups most prepared to endorse Inglehart's 'post-bourgeois' values have the highest aspirations for material affluence.

The future of the service economy, then, cannot be as rosy as post-industrialists imagined. The march through the sectors is less a disciplined advance than a scattering of the tribes. There are at least four distinct elements in the service sector (the intermediate producer and consumer service, and the marketed and non-marketed final service, subsectors). Low productivity growth in tertiary sectors may lead to increased limits on public expenditure and increased shifting of consumers to goods rather than services. Or, if the use of new technologies does permit more innovation in tertiary industries, service employment may be restricted through job displacement: unless, that is, new service products can find mass markets.

What does this imply about accounts of information society, which follow the post-industrialists in projecting a march through the sectors, but provide little substantial analysis of the growth of what are quite heterogeneous varieties of activity? Lumping together a variety of 'new' activities under a common heading is a gesture of recognition to the problem, not a step toward solving it. If the tertiary sector is internally diverse, the 'information sector' is equally so. The range of occupations covered under the heading of information workers includes research scientists, typists, broadcasters, telephone operators and television repairers. It can be useful to group together all these jobs as belonging to one industry: the ones we have chosen could all be associated with television, and one could relate their patterns of development together as part of a systems analysis of the industry. But when we consider that there are a host of industries in which these categories of occupation are found, the notion of information occupations begins to look more like a handy slogan ('vanguard of the information age') than a concept of any real explanatory relevance. The Organization for Economic Cooperation and Development (OECD) does list such a range of 'information occupations', and distinguishes between primary information industries (whose purpose is the production of information as a final commodity or benefit), and secondary information industries (which provide information as an input to the production of material commodities); but it fails to reveal the diverse prospects for growth within these categories.

A better understanding of the rise of information-related activities, and the potential transformations that may be associated with the introduction of informatics, really requires an analysis of large-scale processes of social change. But in the first instance, we can take the distinction between information work concerned with production, processing, distribution and infrastructure as a helpful guide to the sorts of activity that might take place in any location. In addition to this we would distinguish between activities that are intermediate inputs to producers, intermediate inputs to consumers, and final inputs to consumers, and between those that are marketed and non-marketed. Within these different types of activities there are information flows, and different applications for informatics. 'Information work' has different meanings within these different sectors. The development of these activities is closely interrelated: by considering the costs and benefits to the different actors involved we may gain some idea of the likely course of social change in the future, the possibilities for use of new technology, and the conflicts and broader consequences that might result.

Long-run processes of social change

The end of the post-war boom

Can our account of the growth of the tertiary sector account for the drastic way in which the predictions of post-industrial theory were undermined by the changes of the 1970s and 1980s?

To a large extent, the end of the post-war boom reflects the erosion of the various structures that formed the post-war political settlement – and the basis for the pattern of growth described above, and the view of the post-industrial future it fostered. The growth of welfare states and the application of Keynesian counter-cyclical measures was part of the post-war political settlement within the West. These arrangements helped regulate demand and provide markets for a wide range of other products, including those central to the boom, and facilitated a large growth in service sector activities. The breakdown of the post-war settlement was related to internal problems of these arrangements as well as to international travails. A view of long-run social change is required to grasp this process.

With the world economic crisis has come renewed interest in the 'long waves of economic life', and researchers have focused on the technical paradigms in manufacturing industry that characterize each of these waves. They argue that long downswings are associated with industries maturing and their technological systems becoming subject to cost-cutting, rationalizing innovation. The upswings are in contrast associated with new products and processes, with new industries and technological systems. Innovations in 'heartland technologies' permit the development of diverse new products and processes, and the development of infrastructure makes possible the diffusion and widespread application of these new technologies. But these researchers have paid little attention to social innovations: changes that people make in their ways of life so as to take advantage of the opportunities offered by new technologies – and to cope with the changed social relationships that are thus created. Whether or not they are 'cycles' with a definite periodicity, long waves should be interpreted in terms of the growth, maturity and stagnation of socio-technical systems, of which technical paradigms form just one, albeit important, part.[4]

The post-war boom involved considerable change in technologies – and in ways of life. The key industrial sectors – consumer durables and automobiles – relied on new methods of mass production and industrial organization (which meant, among other things, the 'tertiarization' of secondary industries), and sold their products to newly affluent populations. Infrastructures

HISTORY AND PERSPECTIVES

– mains electricity, telecommunications and modern road systems – made possible the widespread application of these products, changing their cost and convenience relative to other modes of service provision. New ways of life were developed in which the automobile and telephone, washing machine and television played an important role, and often involving shifts away from the purchase of final services to self-service provision of transport, domestic services, entertainment, etc. And collective provision of social services expanded, reflecting changes in the family, the workforce, and in social aspirations.

Women's employment (and part-time working) grew, with the expansion of the services and the greater division of labour, and domestic technology was used to reduce 'their' housework load. While some de-skilling of work was the norm for many traditional occupations and within whole industrial sectors, there was also considerable growth of white-collar posts of various kinds, and the expansion of the services – especially, as noted, non-marketed and producer services – meant the creation of large numbers of professional and semi-professional posts. Employees belonging to these groups became bearers of 'post-bourgeois values', and a major social basis for many of the new social movements of the 1970s and 1980s.

But the growth of state expenditure of the post-war boom fuelled inflationary tendencies. The expansion of employment in the services meant an increasing proportion of national income going to the relatively lagging sectors of the economy – and the new public sector unionism placed obstacles in the way of attempts to keep wages at low levels here. The market was showing signs of maturity and stagnation by the end of the 1960s. No radically new products were emerging, worldwide overproduction was becoming apparent in several sectors – if not actually saturating, markets were no longer as elastic as they had been. Government policies in the UK and many other countries were directed towards shoring up mature and traditional industries rather than stimulating innovation; and these industries were rationalizing rather than developing substantially new products. The post-war boom petered out, with constraints being placed upon public expenditure, with the downturns of business cycles creating increasing unemployment – a general exhaustion of a pattern of growth involving a particular set of products, processes, infrastructure and ways of life. The destabilization of the international economy, and the appearance of a baby boom generation (born in the upswing) on the labour market, set the scene for a long period of economic trauma.

The transformation that we are undergoing, then, involves more than just technical change – although new technologies would form part of any return to long-term growth, if a future growth wave is to resemble past experience. Informatics are clearly central, if for no other reason than that they offer to reduce the bottlenecks in information flow created during the post-war boom. But changes in institutions, infrastructures and ways of life

204

are also required for the opportunities they present to be seized. The design of products and infrastructures has considerable relevance to the ways of life that may evolve, the values and practices that are integral to a new sociotechnical system. But the question is not really about the *impact* of informatics on ways of life, values and culture, but the way in which societies reproduce and adapt themselves, using and reshaping technologies in the process.

An informatics upswing?

Informatics provides heartland technologies for process innovations: CADCAM, rapid information transfer and retrieval, new paradigms of industrial organization. It provides new products: home computers, control devices for household equipment, new telecommunications facilities. It involves new infrastructures: cable and satellite systems. But innovations in people's ways of life would be both precondition and consequence of the widespread adoption of informatics.

The potential uses of new technology extend well beyond the proliferation of video games and television channels, which do not exactly sound like the recipe for renewed economic growth. A new telecommunications infrastructure could permit the development of new services, and the transformation of many existing ones. Changes in entertainment are obvious enough. Distribution and transport could be transformed through teleshopping, improved travel booking and scheduling, telebanking, telework. Education could move more to Open University-type formats, with public information utilities for informal and community education and training. In medicine, in addition to remote diagnosis and monitoring services for chronic disorders, preventative advice and improvement of community care could involve informatics. Even domestic services might be the focus of innovation: pensioners' safety, household security and energy use can be monitored, payments and purchasing could be substantially automated, and so on.

Cable TV and home computers may be dominant at present, but this does not mean that the other innovations are unlikely. Indeed, the advent of improved telecommunications infrastructure is a prerequisite for most of the services outlined above to be effective. The development of an infrastructure for entertainment purposes may precede its use for a much broader range of interactive services – although this may well depend crucially upon appropriate design of the systems.[5]

There are many different ways in which informatics could be developed within our society, with correspondingly varied implications for economic expansion and the details of ways of life. To reduce the rate of diffusion of new technologies in industry would be likely to lead to continued stagnation. To concentrate on improving industrial efficiency by process innovation could lead to considerable improvements in delivery of many existing products – although in practice this seems likely simply to mean labour-saving and cost-cutting change in non-marketed services, and an overall reduction in employment. A combination of product and process innovation, of infrastructural and way-of-life changes is also possible: while this may not be able to restore full employment as understood in the post-war boom, we can outline areas where formal employment might begin to expand.

On the one hand, we can expect to see some jobs created in the manufacture of informatics equipment and the installation of the infrastructure, although neither may be as demanding of labour as some optimists hope. We might see some loss of work in final services, although this *could* be offset by improvements in service quality: for example, increased efficiency of travel services, and the associated tasks of booking and scheduling, might go some way toward reversing the trend away from public transport. Political choices are very important here: again, it is not the potential of the technology, but the application of that potential that is the key issue.

As for intermediate services, contradictory trends would operate in the case of producer services (increased labour productivity through the use of informatics, but also increased need for information services of various kinds), but there may be considerable growth of intermediate consumer services. Consumer uses of informatics like those discussed above often require extensive backup services including, as well as maintenance and related functions, various sorts of information brokerage. And the intermediate consumer services would involve people in the production of software, which we understand to mean more than the material that is purchased (or pirated) to run on computers, to cover information encoded on media for use in informatics hardware more generally. Software production involves the embodiment of applied human skills in information-storage devices for use in the production of services, then; it spans recorded entertainment and expert systems, the writing of video games and that of Teletext pages. This means seeing actors in a television studio as producing software (the TV broadcast or video) as an intermediate consumer service, to be used by consumers in their application of their manufactures (TV sets); in contrast the actor on the public stage is providing a final entertainment service (with the aid of a built infrastructure rather than a telecommunications one). (The self-same actor may provide both sorts of service at once, just as one production process in industry may yield two different products simultaneously, or yield one product which can be used both as a capital good and as a consumer item.)

This pattern of introduction and reshaping of informatics might be compatible with social and economic innovation in general, with the establishment of a new sociotechnical system rather than the recuperation of the existing one. The diffusion of domestic equipment and infrastructure might be led by demands for entertainment and further education. But existing services

THE SOCIAL ECONOMICS OF INFORMATION TECHNOLOGY

might be transformed: and there could be the emergence of new information and advice services, and the growth of interactive informal use of telematics (to establish like-minded or like-needful groups for car-sharing, pressure groups, romantic liaisons, consumer advice, bartering of child-care or do-it-yourself (DIY) work, personal advice, the sponsorship of performances and cultural events . . .). Some shift away from formal provision of final services to self-service provision might be expected to continue, even to accelerate. The key questions of political choice here relate to the future of collective services: will informatics be used to substitute for existing provisions, or to expand and augment them?

Social choice and information societies

We have suggested that distinctive periods of growth and stagnation in the world economy are related to the 'life cycle' of vigour and exhaustion of particular sociotechnical systems, of specific constellations of process and product technology, infrastructure, social organization and ways of life. These constitute different ways of representing and satisfying consumer demands through the political economy. The choice between the different available *modes of provision* of final service functions – i.e. between, on the one hand, purchases of final services, or, on the other, communal- or self-servicing (cars versus public transport, laundry versus washing machine, traditional performance versus information-technology-mediated entertainment etc.) – has become as important as the shifting of priorities from one of these functions to another.

Informatics may well help underpin a wave of innovation, but it has not arrived like the fifth cavalry at the whim of a benevolent scriptwriter. Its emergence is built upon the achievements of the last long upswing, and is a response of technicians and engineers to their perception of the developing problems in that growth paradigm. (This is one of the reasons why our view of informatics is liable to be blinkered, to be framed too much in terms of incremental solutions to pressing problems, such as the costs of clerical work.) A leap in the dark is inevitable in any major process of technological change. Can we avoid stumbling into some of the obstacles which are more likely to be encountered by less innovative strategies? What implications for social organization and political choice are raised by our analysis?

Employment and industrial organization

It is evident that employment in primary and secondary production is likely to continue its decline. In addition, employment in many of the 'information occupations' of the traditional services is likely to be reduced by the application of informatics, even though some compensation for this labour-saving might be brought about by increased demand due to reduced prices

HISTORY AND PERSPECTIVES

related to innovation in the services. More significantly, informatics could also be used to bring about quality improvements in services – reduced waiting time and delay, more personalized services, resources freed from routine business to deal with priority cases. This might stem or reverse the trend from services to goods in some areas, and also defuse opposition to expenditure on social services (where anger about cuts is attenuated by the perception that costs have risen much more than output). Some producer services may continue to expand, and new consumer services, especially information services and other intermediate consumer services, may undergo rapid growth.

These developments are unlikely to restore the total amount of formal work to a level sufficient to restore full employment as it has been known. Two extreme consequences would be the development of a highly dualistic economy, with regional and class differences sharpened between those with employment, those in insecure work, and the permanently unemployed; and the redistribution of work through reduced lifetime working hours and the expansion of lifelong education, community activities, etc. Informatics could be used to support either kind of development – arguments that it inevitably fosters either one, or can magically restore the previous sociotechnical system to its full vigour, should be discounted. The new technology might increase the strains of a dualistic economy: for example, accentuating awareness of the extremes of poverty and wealth that coexist. On the other hand, new security systems, new types of pass and credit card, surveillance and psy-ops methods could be used to bolster up an increasingly repressive social order. Or 'bread and circuses' could be the order of the day: wall-to-wall video games and computer nasties.

Despite ominous portents, there are prospects for more positive changes – not least in the public discussion over information society. One of the problems, however, is the relative paucity of analysis of the interrelations of social and technical innovation. Trade unionists have been pressing for substantial reductions in the working week, and have begun to pay attention to the design of technologies as well as to their introduction into the workplace. But the sorts of innovation required for a new sociotechnical system are more wide-ranging. The point of our analysis is not that anything can happen, but that it is necessary to establish linkages between different sorts of change around which shared interests could be mobilized.

For example, reduced working lifetimes have social implications that could bring together diverse social interests. Women might see this as an element in a strategy to reconstruct the sexual division of labour, since men typically blame their evasion of child-care, etc. upon the requirements of full-time breadwinning. Recurrent training may be necessitated by a rapid pace of technological change, so sectors of management could support changes in this direction, which educationalists would doubtless welcome. Many leisure industries would benefit from a more equitable distribution of leisure time.

Education and entertainment – and various forms of meaningful leisure – also offer possibilities for innovative applications of informatics to the delivery of final and intermediate services.

What of the quality, rather than the quantity, of employment? The post-war boom involved the de-skilling of many traditional production activities, with a growth of middle-skill jobs in secondary and tertiary sectors alike. Informatics offers the prospect of subjecting service occupations to a similar 'capital-deepening' and division of labour. The tertiarization of the secondary sector is likely to be complemented by a secondarization of the tertiary sector. Despite some increase in scientific and technical skills, many existing semiprofessional jobs could be substantially de-skilled, leading to polarization of the labour force within industries. (This has obvious implications for the prospects for reduced lifetime working hours and retraining discussed above.) Again, this is not an inevitable consequence of the potential of the technology, nor is it necessarily the preferred management strategy. In manufacturing industry, lessons are being learned from Japanese methods of production, where the Taylor/Ford types of assembly-line division of labour are modified so as to give workers more responsibility for a coherent set of tasks (with the eminently non-altruistic goal of reducing costs incurred in bottlenecks and stockpiles). The automation of tasks only means a de-skilling of jobs if the range of tasks covered by a job remains fixed: in this instance conventional demarcation systems may run counter to improving the quality of working life.

There is considerable opportunity for different actors to intervene in the resolution of these contradictory tendencies. Outcomes are liable to be quite different in firms of different sizes and based in different sectors. Legislation over working conditions and training processes may make a difference, as will the organizational culture of firms from different national bases. But on balance, we would expect that the relative autonomy enjoyed by many service workers will be somewhat decreased, with informatics used to introduce more monitoring of operations into areas of activity where control and accountancy has to date remained more formal than substantial.

Another issue of industrial organization concerns the spatial and managerial dimensions of economic restructuring. Informatics can support a wide variety of different combinations of centralized and decentralized information processing and decision-making. The strategy of larger corporations, at least, seems to involve increased centralized monitoring and control of the overall performance of more specialized subunits or branches, with these given more responsibility for their own data processing and specialized decision-making. There may be considerable reduction of the middle ranges of the managerial pyramid, with the functions that are now typically performed by these levels in the head office being partly shifted upward and partly distributed among branches. This would reinforce the occupational trends discussed above.[6]

Households and lifestyles

Post-industrialists' theories that mass communications would bring about a massification of society, with increased commonality of opinions and practices across different social groups, have proved inaccurate to date. The social developments of the post-war boom supported heterogeneity, although this can be a mutually rewarding 'cultural pluralism' or a destructive 'social fragmentation': recent trends have displayed elements of both processes. Narrowcasting and interactive services might permit these processes to continue apace. The privatization of individual households might be accompanied by a greater segregation of social groups distinguished in lifestyle terms. But the choice of lifestyle, and the access to diverse views and practices, could also be widened.

Lifestyles remain overwhelmingly structured by class and stage in the family/employment life cycle. Thus the evolution of the employment situation – in terms of greater dualism or a decreased emphasis on formal employment in everyday life – would be an important determinant of the evolution and diversity of household consumption patterns. A dualistic labour market may mean a dualistic market more generally: for example, shops, products and discount rates that cater for owners of 'intelligent' credit cards, increased differentiation between luxury and basic goods. Working life is also extremely relevant to the development of lifestyles: and a culturally active society would be more likely to develop were informatics used to upgrade working conditions and skills and reduce weekly hours of employment.

Informatics could be used by an active citizenry to engage in more varied leisure and cultural activities, and to take part in and create new forms of social participation. Indeed, using the technology in this way – by making interactive services available to individuals and communities – might render increased leisure more attractive for many working people. We would see household consumption shifting from services to goods, with people applying informal labour to help produce many of their own final services. In some cases this 'production' would imply little more creativity than that involved in selecting a videotape; but the potential would be there for access to more educational opportunities, more networking of people with common interests, more use of recreational facilities and development of specialist services.

Social welfare

The shift toward self-servicing may be expected to continue within areas that are largely catered for by social services. Many services are likely to remain a matter of collective organization, and the main issues may

THE SOCIAL ECONOMICS OF INFORMATION TECHNOLOGY

surround 'community care' versus central provision. Informatics could be used to improve community facilities – monitoring the circumstances of pensioners, relating the need for services to provisions at a local level, supplying access to expert systems for paraprofessionals in health and welfare (along the lines of the computerized benefit claim systems used by some Citizens' Advice Bureaux).

The trend toward community care is deeply ambiguous. It combines genuine recognition of the problems of impersonal, bureaucratized service organizations – oriented toward cure rather than prevention, labelling and institutionalizing their clients, allowing them little autonomy and creating dependency – with cynical efforts to reduce costs and to shift the burden of care onto charities and families. And in the background in Britain is the pressure towards the privatization of (profitable) areas of social service. This tendency toward a two-tier structure of welfare services is found sufficiently threatening by most employees in public services to reduce their interest in innovation: it is difficult constructively to criticize what one is desperately struggling to defend. By and large, privatization means allowing the relatively privileged to jump queues and segregate themselves from other social strata. But valuable experiments in care for the elderly, education, and self-help are taking place outside of the public services (though often with their financial support). Furthermore, alongside institutional moves in the direction of community care are attempts to develop alternative services along the lines of free schools and self-help health groups. (Social innovators could learn a great deal from the experience of different countries in these respects: for example, the extremely original educational experiments of the Folk High Schools in Denmark.) It would be possible to direct informatics toward advancing and promoting their methods.

These strategies will interact with the ongoing shift toward self-service provision. Self-servicing in areas of health and education (and social and political organization) is bound to grow with the cheapening of informatics. Public and voluntary services, then, need to capitalize on these developments. This might mean pressing for community access to informatics facilties (so that these do not remain the preserve of the more affluent or better educated), and designing appropriate intermediate services. It might involve improving the scope and quality of both routine and non-routine service delivery, as part of a wider strategy of rebuilding social services to cater for the needs of late industrial society. Just as new technologies, by offering possibilities for product and process change, simultaneously threaten employment in private services and offer possibilities for demand expansion through reduced costs or new facilities, so may public services face a choice of whether merely to rationalize existing practices, and thus save costs, or to develop new services, and perhaps gain wider public support for their efforts.

HISTORY AND PERSPECTIVES

Critical issues for information society

We have contrasted a strategy of social innovation with other possible information societies: societies based on protectionism and greater social dualism. But the leap in the dark that we have tried to illuminate is by no means assured of a comfortable landing. Any process of technical change unevenly benefits people at different locations in a structure of social inequality. People may differ in their financial or cognitive abilities to make use of the technology, or to assess how its use by others will impinge upon them. Some inequalities could be amplified. Therefore the reduction of major inequalities should be explicitly incorporated as a goal in the design of information society. Otherwise, poorer communities are liable to receive poorer services, women are likely to be accorded greater burdens of caring, etc. the key issues include:

- the *distribution* of informatics resources. Infrastructural provision is of considerable importance in *regional* development and in the rise and decline of *urban* areas. Given the potential of informatics for making training and information services available, the provision of facilities for *social groups* disadvantaged by restructuring is of considerable importance. This may involve policies of positive discrimination, and adaptation of different media (or their 'programmes') to different social groups.
- the *design* of informatics. How far do the technologies permit interactivity rather than just expand the transmission of information in hierarchical structures? This raises questions for the design of infrastructure: whether the nodes of the cable systems can communicate with each other, rather than act as mere passive receivers of broadcast information as in a root-and-branch system; whether the systems have sufficient channel capacity to carry two-way video signals, and so on. The state and the market are unlikely to promote – or even formulate – the whole range of social innovations here. It will be necessary for a wide range of interest groups to evaluate technical alternatives and affect the process of technical change. Given that choices with long-term consequences are already under way, it is important that debate and analysis of these alternatives be promoted more widely.

Given the eventual importance of these issues for the future quality of life, the *public debate* on these issues is muted to the point of inaudibility. The questions posed above, together with those about the implications for privacy and the possibilities of public surveillance and control, all need to be asked *before* the systems are developed and installed. Firms and telecommunications authorities, in this country and elsewhere, are busily designing and building: where is the debate?

Notes

1 The authors are currently funded by the Joseph Rowntree Memorial Trust, to which we express our gratitude. Rather than provide numerous notes, we cite below only the main texts relevant to our arguments.

2 The main theoretical contribution on post-industrial society is Bell (1974); see also Kahn *et al.* (1976). Probably the best critique of the political assumptions of post-industrialism is Kleinberg (1973). The 'silent revolution' in values is the theme of Inglehart (1977). An early statement of our views concerning the social and psychological approaches of this school is Miles (1975); see also Miles (1980). The information society dichotomies we outline are drawn from Colombo and Lanzavecchia (1982); for similar perspectives see a related collection, Barry *et al.* (1982). The most influential proponent of an information sector is Porat (1977).

3 Our discussion follows Gershuny and Miles (1983). See also Gershuny (1983) and Gershuny and Miles (1985). The term 'prosumer' is introduced in Toffler (1981), one of the better popular books attempting to explicate information society. The OECD text is an output of its series 'Information Computer Communications Policy' (1981).

4 The most interesting study of long waves is Freeman, Clark and Soete (1982). For the relation between automation and the economic crisis, see Kaplinsky (1984). See also various papers (especially those by Freeman and Coombes) in Martstrand (1984).

5 For a wide-ranging account of potential uses of cable systems, see the CNET/INA volume (1983); also relevant are the collections on information society referred to in note 2, and the popular discussions of Grossbrenner (1983) and Nilles (1982).

6 Our thinking here has been enriched by the work of Carlota Perez Perez: in particular by discussions around her papers in *Futures* (1983) and *World Development* (1985).

References

Barry, U., L. Bannon and O. Holst (eds) (1982) *Information Technology: Impact on the Way of Life.* Dublin: Tycooly.

Bell, D. (1974) *The Coming of Post-Industrial Society.* New York: Basic Books.

CNET/INA (1983) *Images pour le Cable.* Paris: La Documentation Française. (Centre National d'Etude des Télécommunications/Institut National de la Communication Audiovisuelle).

Colombo, J. and G. Lanzavecchia (1982) 'The Transition to an Information Society', in N. Bjorn-Andersen, M. Earl, O. Holst and E. Mumford (eds), *Information Society: For Richer, For Poorer.* Amsterdam: North Holland.

Freeman, C., J. Clark and L. Soete (1982) *Unemployment and Technical Innovation.* London: Frances Pinter.

Gershuny, J. (1983) *Social Innovation and the Division of Labour.* London: Oxford University Press.

Gershuny, J. and I. Miles (1983a) *The New Service Economy.* London: Frances Pinter.

Gershuny, J. and I. Miles (1983b) 'Towards a New Social Economies', in B. Roberts, R. Finnegan and D. Gallie (eds), *New Approaches to Economic Life.* Manchester: Manchester University Press. (Published in 1985.)

Grossbrenner, A. (1983) *Personal Computer Communications*. New York: St Martin's Press.

Inglehart, R. (1977) *The Silent Revolution*. Princeton: N.J., Princeton University Press.

Kahn, H., W. Brown and L. Martell (1976) *The Next 200 Years*. New York: Morrow.

Kaplinsky, R. (1984) *Automation*. London: Longman.

Kleinberg, B. (1973) *American Society in the Post-Industrial Age*. Columbus, Ohio: Charles E. Merril.

Martstrand, P. (ed.) (1984) *New Technology and the Future of Work and Skills*. London: Frances Pinter.

Miles, I. (1975) *The Poverty of Predication*. Farnborough, Hants: Saxon House.

Miles, I. (1980) 'Effacing the Political Future', *Futures*, (12) 6: 436–52.

Nilles, J. M. (1982) *Exploring the World of the Personal Computer*. Englewood Cliffs, N.J.: Prentice-Hall.

OECD (1981) *Information Activities, Electronics and Telecommunications Technologies*. Vol. 1. Paris: Organization for Economic Cooperation and Development.

Perez Perez, C. (1983) 'Structural Change and Assimilation of New Technologies in the Economic and Social Systems', *Futures*, October: 357–74.

Perez Perez, C. (1985 forthcoming) 'Microelectronics, Long Waves and World Structural Change', *World Development*.

Porat, M. (1977) *The Information Economy*. Office of Technology Special Publication, US Department of Commerce; Washington, D.C.: Government Printing Office.

Toffler, A. (1981) *The Third Wave*. London: Pan.

13

DECONSTRUCTING THE INFORMATION ERA

Sohail Inayatullah

Source: *Futures* 30(2–3) (1998): 235–47.

> Information theory, while claiming universality, ignores civilisation and spiritual perspectives of knowledge. Moreover, the information society heralded by many as the victory of humanity over darkness is merely capitalism disguised but now commodifying selves as well. This essay argues for a more communicative approach wherein futures can be created through authentic global conversations—a gaia of civilisations. Current trends, however, do not lie in that direction. Instead, we are moving towards temporal and cultural impoverishment. Is the Web then the iron cage or can a global *ohana* (family, civil society) be created through cybertechnologies? Answering these and other questions are possible only when we move to layers of analysis outside conventional understandings of information and the information era and to a paradigm where communication and culture are central.

The time for the liberation of heart and mind has not come yet . . . This is not your final destination.[1]

Has the future arrived?[2] Ended? Cyberspace and cloning; postmodernity and globalism are creating worlds where the future as a place of possibility and as a site of critique of the present, no longer exists. With virtual reality, cyberworld and genetics having arrived, the future and, indeed, history has ended. Our imaginations have become real—the fantastic has become the real.

However, perhaps the 'cyber/information era' view of the future is overly linear, exponentially so, and forgetful that two-thirds of the world does not have a phone and much of the world lives over 2 hours from a phone connection. While postmodernity has speeded up time for the elite West and the elite in the non-West, for the majority of the world there is no information era. Moreover, in the hyperjump to starspace, we have forgotten that while ideas and the spirit can soar, there are cyclical processes, such as the life and death of individuals, nations and civilisations that cannot be so easily transformed. While certainly there are more people making their living by processing ideas,[3] perhaps we are engaged in a non-productive financial/information pyramid scheme where we are getting further and further away from food production and manufacturing, building virtualities on virtualities until there is nothing there, as in *advaita vedanta*[4] wherein the world is *maya*, an illusion. And perhaps it is important to remember from the history of previous empires that decline is in order when the capitalist class grows only from financing and knowledge creation, giving up manufacturing and losing vital resource to insecure peripheries.[5]

The coming of the information era, ostensibly providing untold riches in bits of freedom for all, in fact limits the futures of others because it robs them of their future alternatives—it certainly does not create a communication gaia of civilizations,[6] a new planetary future. Reality has become constructed as the worldwideweb, but perhaps this web is Max Weber's iron cage—the future with no exit, wherein there is an inverse relationship between data and wisdom, between quick bytes and long term commitment, between engagement to technology and engagement with humans, plants and animals. We know now from email culture that the twin dangers of immediacy and speed do not lead to greater community and friendship, rather they can lead to bitter misunderstandings.[7] Email then becomes not the great connector leading to higher levels of information but the great disconnecter that gives the mirage of connection and community.[8] Email without occasional face to face communication can transform friendships into antagonistic relationships. Just as words lose the informational depth of silence, email loses information embedded in silence and face to face gestures. The assimilation and reflection as well as the intuition and the insight needed to make sense of intellectual and emotional data are lost as the urgent need to respond to others quickens. Slow time, lunar time, women's time, spiritual timeless time, cyclical rise and fall time and circular seasonal time are among the victims, leading to temporal impoverishment, a loss of temporal diversity where '21C' is for all instead of peculiar to Western civilisation.[9]

Cybertechnologies thus create not just rich and poor in terms of information, but a world of quick inattentive time and slow attentive time. One is committed to quick money and quick time, a world where data and information are far more important than knowledge and wisdom. It is a world where history is exponential versus a world that is cyclical: that believes the only true information worth remembering is humility; that civilisations that

DECONSTRUCTING THE INFORMATION ERA

attempt to touch the sky burn quickly down; that economies that become so far removed from the real economy of goods and services, of agriculture, of the informal women's economy and that become utterly dependent on cybertransactions can easily melt down.

It is thus a mistake to argue that there will only be an information rich and poor, rather there will be information quick and slow. Time on the screen is different from time spent gazing at sand in the desert or wandering in the Himalayas. Screentime does not slow the heart beat down relaxing one into the superconsciouos, rather we become lost in many bits, creating perhaps an era of accelerating information but certainly not a knowledge future or a future where the subtle mysteries of the world, the spiritual ever present is felt.

Dark side of the Earth

There are two clear positions. In the first, the information era provides humans with the missing technologies to connect all selves. In the other, 'Cyberspace is the darkside of the West' to use Zia Sardar's provocative language.[10] He argues that cyberspace is the West caving in on itself, leaving no light to see outside of its own vision.[11] It is a Spenglarian collapse. While cyberspace claims community, there is in fact none, it is anonymous. There is no responsibility towards others since there is no longer term relationship —there are no authentic selves, all exist for immediate short term pleasure and not for the larger task of working together towards a shared goal. People are because they struggle through projects/missions together, not just because they exist in shared virtual worlds.

This quickening of the self was anticipated by McLuhan in 1980. 'Excessive speed of change isolates already fragmented individuals. At the speed (speech) of light man has neither goals, objectives or private identity. He is an item in the data bank—software only, easily forgotten—and deeply resentful'.[12]

Selves lose reflective space, jumping from one object to another, one Website to another, one email to another. It is not a communicative world that will transpire but a world of selves downloading their emotional confusion onto each other. Writes Sardar, 'Far from creating a community based on consensus, the information technologies could easily create state of alienated and atomised individuals, glued to their computer terminal, terrorising and being terrorised by all those whose values conflict with their own'.[13] It is as if we have all become psychic with all thoughts interpenetrating creating a global schizophrenia.[14]

Virtual realities have and will prosper not for the glimpse they give to us of other worlds but because they detach us from this world. Among the main virtual projects is the continued silencing of women from the technological discourse. Virtual technologies are growing because of their ability

HISTORY AND PERSPECTIVES

to simulate sexual pleasure. Once these technologies are fully developed, men will no longer need to connect emotionally or with commitment to women (and some women to men as well), rather they will simulate their relationships with virtual dolls, creating worlds where women exist only as male representation. What Playboy has not yet accomplished because of the flat dimension of centrefold spreads, virtual full dimension will realise it. Men will then continue to locate women as pleasure objects, and create them as standardised beauty forms. The first step is the reduction of women to the hormone maddened images of adolescent males. The next stage is the elimination of women through virtual simulcras. Through genetics (the first phase as cloning but more important is the artificial womb), they will not be needed for procreation as well. While this perhaps might be too bold a statement, certainly the new genetics cannot in anyway be seen as nature or women-oriented technologies. While Finland, for example, extends the metaphor of the home into a caring State, genetics will lead to the opposite: the total penetration of the State into the home and then the body of women.[15]

The great leap forward

Virtual reality thus fulfils the homoerotic male fantasy of a world of just men. However, some argue that virtual reality is a new technology whose future development is up for grabs, that computing does not have to be male based, that women can enjoy user groups dominated by men. While the technology is certainly male-dominated,[16] Sherman and Judkins give the banal advice that women[17] should educate themselves on the positive and negative dimensions of this new technology and then make it into their own (of course, forgetting the reasons why it is male dominated).[18] Fatma Aloo, however, of the Tanzanian Media Women's Association argues that the internet is a necessarily evil.[19] Even though it is male-dominated and the technology in itself is male—cultures, women endanger themselves more by not using these new technologies. Her association and the numerous other NGO's hope to empower women through the net. Through the net, they are able to tell their stories of suffering, of marginalisation as well as their victories to others—at the same level then, isolation can disappear.

But for cyber enthusiasts, these new technologies are not necessarily evils but grand positives that do more than merely provide information, they give more choice. They reduce the power of Big business and Big State, creating a vast frontier for creative individuals to explore. 'Cyberspace has the potential to be egalitarian, to bring everyone into a network arrangement. It has the capacity to create community; to provide untold opportunities for communication, exchange and keeping in touch.'[20] Cybertechnologies will allow more interaction creating a global ecumene—authentic global communication. They create wealth, indeed, a jump in wealth. The new technologies promise a transformational society where the future is always

DECONSTRUCTING THE INFORMATION ERA

beckoning, a new discovery is yearly[21]—and as our memory of the past becomes increasingly distant, humans become important not for themselves but for the new genetic/cyber species they create. The evils of the past slowly disappear as we know each other more intimately. The oppressive dimensions of bounded identity—to nation, village, gender, culture—all disappear as we move in and out of identities and communities. History is then exponential with visions of collapse, of the perpetual cycle, of the weight of history, merely fictions of the past. Our children will live in a world without gravity, believes Nicholas Negroponte. In *Being Digital* he argues that, 'Digital technology can be a natural force drawing people into great world harmony',[22] where historical social divisions will disappear. Predictably Bill Gates writes that 'we are watching something historical happen and it will affect the world seismically, rocking us in the same way the discovery of the scientific method, the invention of the printing, and the arrival of the industrial age did'.[23] Mark Pesce goes even further than Negroponte and Gates, believing the web to be 'an innovation as important as the printing press—it may be as important as the birth of language itself . . . in its ability to completely refigure the structure of civilization'.[24] This is the moment of *kairos*, the appropriate moment, for a planetary jump to a new level of consciousness and society. It is the end of scarcity as an operating myth and the beginning of abundance, of information that wants to be free. The late 20th century is the demarcation from the industrial to the information/knowledge era. Progress is occurring now. Forget the cycle. That was misinformation.

But while the growth data looks impressive and the stock of Microsoft continues upward, there are some hidden costs. For example, what of negative dimensions of the new technologies such as surveillance? Police in Brisbane, Australia use up to 100 hidden cameras in malls to watch for criminal activities.[25] Hundreds more are anticipated creating an electronic grid in central Brisbane. While this might be possibly benign in Brisbane (Aborgines might have different views though), imagining a large grid over Milosevic's Yugoslavia or Taliban's Afghanistan (or under Ziaul Haq's Pakistan where every 'immoral' gaze would have led to arrest) it is enough to frighten the most fanatical techno-optimist. Or is it? Many believe that privacy issues will be forgotten dimensions of the debate on cyberfutures once we each have our own self-encryptors so that no one can read or enter us (the 21st century chastity belt). Technology will tame technology. Over time, the benefits of the new technologies will become global with poverty, homelessness and anomie all wiped out. All will eventually have access—even the poorest—as the billions of brains that we are, once connected, will solve the many problems of oppression.[26] While we have always imagined such a future, it is only now that technology allows it so.

The new cybertechnologies will also change how we war with each other. 'The world is in the early stages of a new military revolution. The

HISTORY AND PERSPECTIVES

technologies include digital communications, which allow data to be compressed; a 'global positioning system' (GPS) of satellites, which makes more exact guidance and navigation possible, radar-evading 'stealth'; and, of course, computer processing.'[27]

But they will also create a world in perpetual war with itself.

> The new warfare will be 'multi-dimensional', meaning not only that air, sea and land operations will be increasingly integrated, but also that information and outerspace will be part of modern war. 'Information warfare' could mean disabling an enemy by wrecking his computing, financial, telecoms or air-traffic control systems. The relevant weapons might be computer viruses, electro-magnetic pulses, microwave beams, well-placed bombs or anything that can smash a satellite.[28]

Competitive advantage will go to those who are the most information dependent, thus creating information gaps between themselves and others. This dependence, however, is a weakness, both sapping innovation by leading to a closed surveillance society and allowing others not dependent on instant information to attack from non-information paradigms. It is enantiodromia in action—one's excellence is one's fatal flaw.

Access to global conversations

At the metalevel, at issue is not just the access of individuals to technologies but more how the new technologies have taken over the discourse of global conversations, how they have infected our deep social grammar. While certainly it is important to have a global language—a way of communicating —the internet not only privileges English, it anglicises the world such that other languages lose their ability to participate in global futures. It continues global standardisation. Who needs, cloning, writes Kiirana@unm.edu when you already have global standardisation in the form of global coca-colaisation.[29]

The web creates a voice, a rhetoric, a certain kind of rationality which is assumed to be communicative. But while certainly web pages that provide information on airline flight arrivals and departures or on hard to find books are instrumentally useful, information retrieval is not communication. Communication proceeds over time through trauma and transcendence. In trauma, communication occurs when human suffering is shared with others. In transcendence, communication occurs when differences are understood and mutuality discovered, when beneath real differences in what it means to be human, similarities in how we suffer and love are realised. Merely having a web page does not mean one is communicating with others except at the banal level of an electronic business card.

DECONSTRUCTING THE INFORMATION ERA

A web page, like a Coca-Cola ad on the moon or on Mars for visiting aliens, provides some information but certainly not at a level most civilisations in the world would find satisfactory. It amplifies a certain dimension of self, however, as with all such amplifications, far more interesting is to note what is not sent, what is not said, then what is officially represented in email or on a website.

While Marshall McLuhan was certainly correct in writing that we create technologies and thereafter they create us, he did not emphasise enough that technologies emerge within civilisational contexts (where politics are naturalised, considered absent). Technology creates the possibility of a global village but in the context of the Los-Angelisation of the plant. It is the global city of massive pollution, poverty and alienation that is the context. In addition, the more vicious dimension of the village—the history of landlords raping farmers, of exclusive ideologies and of feudal relations is often forgotten in the metaphor of the global village, indeed, a global colony would be a far more apt metaphor. But new technologies do create differences in world wealth, access to power and access to the creation of alternative futures.

Cyber-enthusiasts rightfully point to the opportunities of the one world created by new technologies. But they need to remember that the one world of globalisation remains fundamentally capitalistic with the local (local economy and power over one's future) increasingly being attacked. The tiny Pacific Island of Niue recently discovered that 10% of its national revenue was being sucked out through international sex-line services.[30] The information era as P R Sarkar points out is late capitalism, a system in which all other *varnas*—psychosocial classes and ways of knowing (the intellectual, the worker and the warrior)—become the 'boot lickers of the merchants'.[31] And: 'In order to accumulate more and more in their houses, they torture others to starvation . . . they suck the very living plasma of others to enrich the capabilities'.[32] While intellectuals invent metaphors of postmodernity and post-industrialism, capital continues to accumulate unevenly, the poor become poorer and less powerful (however, they can now have a Website). The information era still exists in the context of the world capitalist system—it is not an external development of it, and it will not create the contradictions that end it. The knowledge society or non-material society that many futurists imagine conveniently forget human's very real suffering. But for virtual realities, we have virtual theories. The words 'I make friends' from the genetic engineer character in the movie *Blade Runner* take on a different meaning. Making friends becomes not an 'exchange' of meanings but the manufacturing of like-minded life forms—friendly robots in this movie. One can easily imagine scenarios with corporations making happiness, love and life (not to mention providing passports/passwords). The advertising genius of the 20th century will pale in comparison to what is to come in the next.

The politics of conversations

Current global conversations are not communicative spaces of equal partners but conversations wherein one party has privileged epistemological, economic and military space. Certainly the emerging Palestinian world can not have a meaningful conversation with the power of Israel—they do not enter the conversation as equals. Moreover the language of such conversations uses the categories and assumptions of those that have designed the metaconversation. We do not enter conversations unencumbered, as Foucalt, Heidegger and many others have pointed out. Trails of discourses precede our words. We do not own words, indeed, it is not even so much that we speak but that discourse creates the categories of 'we'. That is to say, it is not that we speak English, but that we language the world in particular ways.

Remembering the Unesco MacBride Commission report, Majid Tehranian argues that the major problem in global communication is the lack of a meaningful dialogue between West and non-West. Each cannot hear the other—their paradigms are too different, for one. Second, the West does not believe that as the losers in history, Asia, Africa, the Pacific have the right to speak. Only Confucianist societies (who present an economic challenge) and Islamic societies (who do not accept their fate and challenge the positioning of the West) are problematic for the future of the West.

The West desires the non-West to procreate less; the non-West points out that the West argues for population limits only after it has robbed the future of the world's resources and without contesting the structural relations of imperialism. After all, Los Angeles uses the same amount of energy as India. As Gayatri Spivak writes: 'A large part of this deplorable state of affairs is lodged between the legs of the poor women of the South. They're having too many children. At Halloween, one day in the United States, more than 300 million dollars was spent on cards, 72 million dollars on costumes and more than 700 million on candy. More than a billion dollars. One of those children is 300 times (in terms of consumption) one of the children in the South. So what kind of body count is that'.[33] Spivak thus locates the problem in consumption-oriented capitalism and not in Indian women who do not need information on world population trends.

The West desires a free-flow of information, the non-West (and France) wants to protect its culture, arguing that the real flow is downward from Disneyland to Islamabad and rarely the other way around. This is not because Western culture is superior, because truth really did begin in Greece, but because the West has technological and financial advantages and because over the past 500 years they have defined what is beauty, truth and humour. Free flow can exist when lines of videos, television and music are, in fact, authentically based on market relations. Currently the West has structural advantages. However, the West believes that it is bringing faster,

DECONSTRUCTING THE INFORMATION ERA

quicker and more exciting global culture, and that the non-West is using these excuses as a way to deny their citizens global culture, to protect their culture industries and to oppress dissent in their home countries. For example, East Asian nations have used Confucianism as an argument against liberal democracy. New technologies then will merely continue a dialogue that others cannot hear but they do so at many levels now—the space of nationalism becomes wider and thus sovereignty harder to maintain. But while it might be argued that this is so for the US and European nations, that the Net limits their sovereignty, this forgets that the creators, the designers and the value adders are mainly from the US.

Thus, before we enter global conversations we need to undo the basis of such conversations asking who gets to speak; what discourses are silenced; and, what institutional power points are privileged? We need to ask how the language of conversation enables particular peoples and not others (peoples as well as animals[34] and nature). We need to see particular linguistic movements as fragile spaces—as the victory of one way of knowing over other ways of knowing. Our utterances are political in that they hide culture, gender and civilisation. Conversations come to us as neutral spaces for created shared agreement but they are trojan horses carrying worldviews with them. For example, centre nations often want to enter into political reconciliation conversations with indigenous peoples but the style and structure of such conversations almost always reinscribe European notions of self and governance instead of indigenous notions of community and spirituality. By entering, for example, a parliament house or a constitutional convention, the indigenous person immediately enters a terrain outside of his and her value considerations—in fact, outside his or her non-negotiable basis of civilisation. As traditional Hawaiians say, the *aina* (land) is not negotiable, cannot be sold—it is rooted to history, to the ancestors and cannot enter exchange relations.[35] Hawaiians have been prodded by the US Federal government to engage in a constitutional convention to articulate their ideal state, governance system. As with traditional American conventions, delegates are to run and lobby for election, each one to act as a delegate and thereby somehow representing their nation. During the convention, they are to follow discussions and enter in conversations as bounded by Robert's Rules of Order. However, for many Hawaiians entering a constitutional convention already limits the political choice they have. Ho'pono'pono, for example, as a method of negotiation—wherein ancestors are called, where all others are forgiven, where a shared spiritual and social space is created—is far more meaningful than the power worlds of suits and ties.

As a Maori elder has argued: Westerners want us to have a governance system based on parliamentary democracy wherein electoral legitimacy is based on full representation and attendance of delegates. In this system, the Maori are often chided for not showing up to meetings.

HISTORY AND PERSPECTIVES

What Westerners do not recognise, is that 'they' is not only constituted by 'physical beings'. More important than particular individuals showing up is if the *mana* shows up. If the mana is not there then it does not matter if all voted in unanimity. Having or not having mana determines civilisational success. Merely voting, while perhaps a necessary condition, is not a sufficient condition. One's relationship with the mana is. Representation by the Maori and the Hawaiians is made problematic—one person, one vote is part of the story but it misses the expanded communicative community of other cultures, including the special voices of elders (those who dream the past) and of angels (and other non-human beings who affect day to day life) as well as of the community as whole. Finally it misses the mana, that there is more to a person or to a community than its human population.

Conversation then is more than being able to access different web pages of Others. A global village is not created by more information transfer. Conversation is also more about equals meeting around a table but also asking what type of table should we meet around. What type of food is served? Who is fasting. Should food be eaten on the ground? Who should serve? Is there prayer before eating? When should there be speech? When silence?[36] What constitutes information transfer? When is there communication? The meanings we give to common events must be civilisationally contextualised. Libraries, for example, create knowledge categories that are political that is, they reflect the history of Western knowledge. These divisions of knowledge—the floors of a library—bear little relationship to the orderings of other civilisations where reality does not consist of divisions between art, science, social science, government documents and other. The Web, however, does to some extent create a new global library, which allows for democracy in terms of what is put on the Web and in terms of how it is accessed. Categories are more fluid, allowing for many orderings of information. At the same time, the Web flattens realities to such an extent where all information is seen as equal, the vertical gaze of hierarchical knowledge—of knowing what is most important, what is deeper, what is lasting—is lost. Immediacy of the present, all categories being equal, results with the richness of epistemological space lost.

A real information society

A real information society, an *ilm* (knowledge in the Islamic worldview) world system would thus be one that was diverse in how it viewed knowledge, appreciating the different ways civilisations ordered the real. It would not just be technical but emotional and spiritual as well and ultimately one that used knowledge to create better human conditions, to reduce *dhukka* (suffering) and realise *moksa* (spiritual liberation from the bonds of action and reaction). The challenge then is not just to increase our ability to produce and understand information but to enhance the capacity of the deeper layers of mind, particularly in developing the *vijinanamaya kosa* (where knowledge of what is eternal and temporal is realised). Certainly, even though the Web is less rigid than a library, it is not the total information technology some assume—spiritual energies and shamanistic dissenting spaces cannot enter. Of course, underlying an alternative view of information society is a commitment to *prama* or a dynamic equilibrium wherein internal/external and spiritual/material are balanced.

The issue is more than equality but the illumination of difference—difference at the level of political-economy, at the level of epistemology, of worldview. Information is not information and knowledge is not knowledge.

But for the moderns, these concepts are understood by characterising the other as existing in religious worldviews. Following Comte and Spencer, as the intellect develops, philosophy and then later science flourishes—real knowledge, objective science, that can lead to commercial success arises. Other ways of knowing become characterised as backward, or in more generous terms as not having access to enough information. With full information, ignorance is reduced and the objective revealed. In contrast, for non-Western civilisations, it is the subjectivisation of information that is far more important (with Islam trying to balance the subjective and objective).[37] Moreover, the division between secular and religious is less strict.

But the techno-optimists of the information postmodern society believe that these differences between worldviews can be accommodated. By decentralising power, the new technologies allow the spirit of the individual to thrive. Through the internet, we will all be wired one day happily communicating all day long—that difference will lead to a space of communicating equals all sharing a confidence in world connectivity. The noosphere imagined by Teilhard de Chardin is just years away. But what type of connectivity will it be? While certainly email helped the Belgrade student and opposition movement of 1997 gain world—Western—support, the Algerian Muslims equally deprived of electoral victory have received few hits on their Websites. What happened to our image of an objective information rich society where more information leads to wiser and fairer decisions?

Postmodern nets

Time writer Julian Dibble believes that the Belgrade revolt was an internet revolution since it was the one media the fascist Milosevic regime did not manage to control. Certainly access to the rest of the world through email provided important emotional support and it provided an antidote to the pro-Milosovic government reporting, as evidenced in Australian TV newscoverage through the SBS channel. However, the revolution 'succeeded' because of other factors: the US's clear warning to Milosevic that violence to protestors would have severe repercussions (at the very least the reinstatement of sanctions), the creative non-violent tactics of students (the revolt tactician was a theatre director) and loss of right-wing nationalistic (fascist) support to Milosevic since he was now seen not as the father of a Serbian homeland but the one who sold out the Serbs in Krajina. The internet was neither a necessary nor a sufficient factor. Mass protest, a neutral Army, support from the powerful military nations, threat of UN sanctions and courage of individual women and men in the face of policy brutality were. But the process of the mythification of the internet continues.

Information optimists remain convinced that more information about others leads automatically to a better world. For example, in an article by Anthony Spaeth at the recent Davos World Economic Forum, he writes that South African Thambo Mbeiki, the Executive Deputy President, said that if South Africa had been connected, there would not have been apartheid.[38] Somehow despots are undermined by the Web, racism disappears once we have more information about events. However, in the very same issue of *Time* we are told that the best predictor of one's view of American footballer O J Simpson's guilt or innocence was race.[39] Irrespective of any evidence or objective information, black Americans were far more likely to believe in his innocence, white Americans in his guilt. Clearly being wired is only one factor in determining how one sees the world. The US is internet connected and yet two groups separated only by a bit of skin colour can see the world so differently. Information is obviously not so flat. For Blacks the trial was about history, about inequity in the US as well as about how they see themselves constructed by white Americans (as an inch removed from barbarism). For Whites it was more evidence that blacks are dangerous irrespective of their 'white' credentials. To assume that more information leads to insight into others, misses the point. We make decisions based on many factors—conceptual information is just one of them. Our own personal history, the trauma each one of us has faced. Our moments of transcendence when we have gone beyond the trauma and not others (ie as less or evil or as a reified social category). Civilisational factors and of course institutional barriers are other variables that mediate both the introduction and dissemination of technology but as well as how technology is constituted.

But others believe the Net can be about transcendence. Sherry Turkle argues that the internet allows us to delink from our physical identity and gain some distance from our personal traumas.[40] We can play at being female or male, human or animal, diseased or healthy. She describes stories of healing where women and men understand their own pathologies better through play with other identities. However, she was not so thrilled when others created a character called Dr Sherry, that is the foundational basis for her identity was suddenly questioned. Of course, it is easier to play (assuming other identities in fun) when one has a sovereign coherent identity and when one is still making one's historical identity. Identity play as postmodern irony is a far more painful episode when one had identity systematically removed. Among others, Asians and Africans are currently undergoing such a trauma, between imposed selves, a range of historical selves and desired futures selves. What Turkle forgets is that it is not just Web-surfers who have many identities. Colonised people have always had an ability to be multi-selved, not for play, though, but for survival. For example, survival for Indians during British rule meant creating a British self, holding on to a historic self and a synthetic self. While multi-tasking might be the craze today and for Douglas Rushkoff[41] the most important ingredient for success tomorrow, it is not just playing on computers that create multi-tasking, as any mother will tell, having children is the true teacher of multi-tasking.

Internet enthusiasts forget that the wiring of the globe means the wiring of the worst of ourselves and best of ourselves. Evil and goodness can travel through broadband. Technology is political, constitutive of values and not merely a carrier. The information era remains described in apolitical terms forgetting the culture of technology creating it, forgetting the class (Marx) and *varna* (Sarkar) basis of these technologies, that is, they exist in the end days of capitalism, and it forgets that the Net privileges certain values over others. We need to remember that if there were 100 people with all existing ratios the same, 70 would be unable to read, 50 would suffer from malnutrition, 80 would live in substandard housing, and only one would have a college education.[42]

Also forgotten is that merely entering a cyberworld makes no promise of justice or global fairness. And as South African Mikebe will find out, his nation will enter the world information system on their terms, their categories, their view of history, on the views of those with the most definitional power. Currently, the world guilt ratio favours South Africa. That will certainly change as it is currently with US anger at South Africa's selling of arms to Syria (ethical arms trading, it is now called).

At the same time, even with the limits of Webspace, as the Zapatista have managed to do, a revolution of land and labor can, while not be won in cyberworld, certainly be kept alive there.[43] Through numerous Web sites and quick access to international human rights organisations and other NGO's, the power of the Mexican state to obliterate the Zapatistas is dramatically reduced. When local power is not enough, movements can enter the global ecumene and find moral power from international society, speeding up the creation of a global *ohana*. Clearly the Web has changed the relationships between oppressor and oppressed, between national totalitarianism and movements of dissent. Indeed, Sardar writes that CD-ROM has the potential to change power relations between individuals and religious scholars (who served as human memory banks controlling the interpretations of what one should or should not do as a Muslim). By making vast

HISTORY AND PERSPECTIVES

amounts of information easy to access and thus allowing Muslims to interpret themselves truth claims made by a particular class of people 'Islamic culture could be remade, refreshed and re-established by the imaginative use of a new communication technology'.[44] But perhaps this is too hopeful, expert information systems can be designed that reinforce the views of the mullah class, interpretations can be framed so that their power base and their view of Islam continues.

The ubiquitous power of the Web is such that one cannot escape it—there is no luddite[45] space available, one has to enter the technology and do one's best to make it reflect one's own values and culture. But technology more than a site of progress must be located as a site of contending politics.

We thus need to ask if the Web and the promised information world change the hegemony of the West (here now extending West outside of its geographical borders to cosmology, a way of knowing)—ie definitional power, deciding what is truth, reality and beauty; temporal power, deciding what historical landmarks calender the world, eg that 21C is arriving; spatial power, imagining space as urban, secular (without *feng shui* or local knowledge) and to be owned; and economic power (upward movement of wealth from the periphery to the centre). Clearly it does not. It does give more pockets of dissent and it has now once again packaged dissent as a Website—with the right graphics, name, format and sexy catch words (and payment to search engines to ensure one's Website comes up first).

The challenge for cultures facing cyberworld ahead is to find ways to enter global conversations, that is, to protect local ways of knowing and at the same time enter the end of history with new ways of knowing—worlds beyond the information era. This is a far more daunting task than cross-cultural communication. It is a vision of a gaia of civilisations. It is a deep global conversation that admits metaconversations.[46] To do so, one cannot be a luddite. Historical change happens because of environmental clash and cohesion and because of the clash of ideas. But it also occurs because of a desire for something other—an attraction to the Great, in sanskrit, for *ananda.* Science and technology thus must be seen in cultural terms (what ways of knowing they privilege) but also in terms of their political economy (who owns them and how the benefits are distributed) but even as we evoke nonlinear images of time, space and spirit, there is a crucial linear progressive dimension to history, of increasing rights for all, of some possibility of decreasing levels of exploitation (through social innovation). The enlightenment project, however, must be seen in the context of others—civilisations and worldview. Moreover, it is not perfection of society that must be sought as in the Western project, since this means the elimination of all that is other, nor is it the perfection of the self as in the Hindu tradition, since this avoids structural inequity. It is the creation of eutopias—good societies. Technology balanced with the finer dimensions of human culture can provide that upward movement in history and Antonio Gramsci warned, we must not be excited by rubbish—a gaia of civilisations cannot occur in the context of the deep inequity of the world capitalist system.

A gaia of civilisations

We thus need to imagine and help create social spaces so the new technologies participate in and allow for the coming of a real planetary culture, a gaia of civilisations; one where there is deep multi-culturalism and where the epistemologies of varied cultures—how they see self and other are respected—flourish. To realise this, open communication and travel are necessary factors but they are not sufficient. Interaction amongst equals and not merely information transfer, that is to say a right to communication is needed as well.

Finally, instead of seeing culture as rigid and fixed, we need to remember that cultures have more resilience than governments give them credit for. For example, while India might be made problematic by Disneyland, India civilisation will not be since it has seen the rise and fall of claims to world empire repeated many times. Pax Americana will go the way of the British Empire, which went the way of the Moguls. Indeed, the strength of Indian culture and other historical civilisations (especially the West and particularly the United States) is its ability to localise the foreign, to localise english, to localise western MTV, to create its own culture industries. Culture and identity then is fluid. When the powerless meet the powerful, confrontation need not be direct. It could be at different levels, wherein the powerful are seduced then changed—where, at least in the Indian tradition, all enter as foreigners but leave culturally transformed, as eclectic Hindus.

What we also learn from other cultures is that the new electronic technologies are just one of the possible technologies creating world space. Indeed they just act at the most superficial levels. As important as cyberspace is microvita space or the noosphere being created through our world imaginations. Indian mystic P R Sarkar reminds us that behind our wilful actions is the agency of microvita—the basic substance of existence, which is both mental and physical, mind and body. Microvita can be used by minds (the image of monks on the Himalayas sending our positive thoughts is the organising metaphor here, as is the Muslim prayer in unison throughout the world with direction and focus) to change the vibrational levels of humans, making them more sensitive to others, to nature and to the divine. And as Sheldrake reminds us, as images and beliefs of one diverse world become more common it will be easier to imagine one world and live as one world, as a blissful universal family. The Web then can participate in the historical decolonisation process giving power to communities and individuals in the overall context of global human, economic, environmental and cultural rights.

Or can it?

HISTORY AND PERSPECTIVES

Acknowledgements

With thanks to Leanne Holman and Linda Crowl.

Notes and references

1 The words of Pakistani socialist poet Faiz Ahmed Faiz.
2 Nearly every brochure on the benefits on the new communication technologies begins with that phrase. The future is seen solely in technological terms.
3 See, for example, Halal, W. E., The rise of the knowledge entrepreneur. *The Futurist*, 1996, **20**(7), 13–16. Halal writes that in the US 'Blue-collar workers should dwindle from 20% of the US work force in 1995 to 10% or less within a decade or two . . . non-professional white-collar workers [will be reduced] from 40% to 20%–30%. The remaining 60%–70% or so of the work force may then be composed of knowledge workers . . . meanwhile, productivity, living standards and the quality of life will soar to unprecedented levels', p. 13. Also see, The Think Tank Directory in which it is reported that the number of think tanks have exploded from 62 in 1945 to 1200 in 1996. For more information on this email: grs@cjnetworks.com, or write to 214 S.W. 6th Avenue, Suite 301, Topeka, KS 66603, USA.
4 One of the six schools of classical Indian philosophy. Only Brahman, the supreme consciousness, is postulated as real. Everything else is but an illusion—*maya*.
5 Tehranian, M., Totems and Technologies. *Intermedia*, 1986, **14**(3), 24.
6 I am indebted to Ashis Nandy for this term, although he calls it, 'A gaia of cultures'. See Masini, E. and Atal, Y. (eds.), *The Futures of Asian Cultures*. UNESCO, Bangkok, 1993, for more on this theme.
7 See, Gwynne, S. C. and Dickerson, J. F., Lost in the E-Mail. *Time*, 21 April 1997, pp. 64–66. They report on the dangers in businesses when bosses use email to berate employees, creating considerable ill-will and inefficiencies. Email exports the anger of the sender to the receiver. Diane Mores Houghten writes that 'E-mail leaves a lot of blank spaces in what we say, which the recipient tends to fill with the most negative interpretation' (p. 65). To avoid sending the wrong message, four rules are suggested: '(1) Never discuss bad news, never criticize and never discuss personal issues over email. And if there's a chance that what you say could be taken the wrong way, walk down the hall to discuss it in person or pick up the phone' (p. 66).
8 Lyn Simpson, former head of the School of Communications, Queensland University of Technology reports on a disastrous result of an email sent to school students. Asked if they were interested in greater liaison/representation of students in faculty committees, she was treated to a barrage of obscenities. When reminded that email was a privilege and not a right of registered students, the obscenities did not subside. Whether this was because of pent up frustration of students towards the university or a response to the formal tone of Professor Simpson's message is not clear. Certainly, none of them would have expressed vulgarities in face to face communication. Moreover, they were not bothered by the fact that their messages had their return email addresses on them, that is to say, they could be easily identified.
9 For more on the temporal hegemony, particularly in the construction of the 21st century as neutral universal timing instead of as particular to the West, see Inayatullah, S., Listening to non-Western perspectives. In *1998 Education Yearbook*, ed. D. Hicks and R. Slaughter, Kogan Page, 1998.

DECONSTRUCTING THE INFORMATION ERA

10 Sardar, Z., alt.civilisations.fax Cyberspace as the darker side of the west. *Futures*, 1995, **27**(7), 777–995.

11 On one public newsgroup the following message on 6 May 1996 was posted to the question: what would you do with an unconscious woman's body? According to Walter Sharpless, he would: Well if it were an 8 year old boy's body, I would . . . the rest is too pornographic (even from extreme libertarian positions) to report especially since it concludes with . . . Thank you for all your time, it has been very satisfying knowing you will read this. In response, was an equally stunning reply from Max Normal: 'Now here's a guy that needs therapy . . . the twelve gauge kind! a 44 mag would be more in line . . . with the brain that is'. What is not contested is the pornographic nature of the initial question ie 'what would you do with an . . . '. Internet as necessarily a progressive form of knowledge? Perhaps not.

12 Marshall McLuhan quoted in New Internationalist special issue entitled, Seduced by technology: the human costs of computers. *New Internationalist*, 1996, **286**, 26.

13 Sardar, Z., The future of democracy and human rights. *Futures*, 1996, **28**(9), 847.

14 Inayatullah, S., Frames of reference, the breakdown of the self and the search for reintegration. In *The Futures of Cultures*, ed. E. Masini and Y. Atal. Unesco, Bangkok, 1993.

15 See Jarva, V., *Feminist Research, Feminist Futures, Futures* (forthcoming). Also see, Jarva, V., Towards female futures studies. In *The Knowledge Base of Futures Studies: Directions and Outlooks*, ed. R. Slaughter, Vol. 3. DDM Media Group, Melbourne, 1996, pp. 3–20. Women's inner circle of reproduction and the home will thus be transformed but without entry into the male sphere of production and the public—they will lose their traditional source of power and history, and as they are not participating in the creating of the new technologies, they will enter a new unfamiliar world with few sites to locate their selves. Indeed, the new technologies are attempts, argues Jarva, to dismantle the women's sphere dimensions of the welfare state.

16 See Spender, D., *Nattering on the Net: Women, Power and Cyberspace.* Spinifex Press, North Melbourne, 1996; Cherny, L. and Reba Weise, E. (eds.), *Wired Women: Gender and New Realities in Cyberspace.* Seal Press, Seattle, 1996. For an excellent review, see Shute, C., Women with byte. *Australian Women's Book Review*, 1996, **8**(3), 8–10.

17 Some, of course, are already doing this in sophisticated ways. Margarat Grace, June Lennie, Leonie Daws, Lyn Simpson and Roy Lundin argue in Enhancing rural women's access to interactive communication technologies (Interim report, The Communication Centre, Queensland University of Technology, April 1997) that email is a soft technology, it can be led in appropriate directions given the appropriate context. In their research, they have found that by guided moderation, by creating conditions in which community and connectedness can develop, email can be beneficial for all concerned. Thus, it is not just the technology but the cultural framework. In their case, they found that a community was created among rural women in Queensland, Australia. While contentious issues were not swept away, they were raised in gentle ways, wherein women would 'test the waters' to see if a certain behavior was ok with others. It was done in a way not to make others wrong but to learn from each other. This is in contrast to many user groups, private email communication, wherein since the emotional, face-to-face dimensions are not visible, small issues lead to troublesome relationships, undoing rather than enhancing communication. The conclusion by Grace and others is that email, given appropriate moderation and an appropriate cultural

HISTORY AND PERSPECTIVES

contest (in this case a womanist framework) can be a medium that helps create a more communicative society, a least among rural women.

18 Sherman, B. and Judkins, P., *Glimpses of Heaven, Visions of Hell: Virtual Reality and its Implications*. Hodder and Stoughton, London, 1992; see Ch. 14, 'A new world for women'.

19 Comments given after the presentation of my paper on: Communication, information and the Net. Paper presented at the 'Women and the Net', UNESCO/ SID meeting held in Santiago de Compostelo, Spain, 20 May 1997. Wendy Harcourt is the principle organizer of this group. Lourdes Arzipe has provided the UNESCO leadership behind the women and the net project.

20 Dale Spender quoted in Shute, C., *Women With Byte*, p. 9.

21 Serageldin, I., Islam, science and values. *International Journal of Science and Technology*, 1996, **9**(2), 100–114. An impressive array of statistics are compiled. 'Items in the Library of Congress are doubling every 14 years and, at the rate things are going, will soon be developing every 7 years . . . In the US, there are 55,000 trade books published annually. . . . The gap of scientists and engineers in North and South is vast with 3800 per million in the US and 200 per million in the South . . . [Finally], currently a billion email messages pass between 35 million users, and the volume of traffic on the Internet is doubling every 10 months', pp. 100–101. Of course, why anyone would want to count email messages is the key issue—as ridiculous would be to count the number of words said daily through talking, or perhaps even count the silence inbetween words.

22 Negroponte, N., *Being Digital*. Hodder and Stoughton, London, 1995, p. 230. For a critical view of such claims, see the brilliant essay by Robins, K., The new communications geography and the politics of optimism. In *Cultural Ecology: The Changing Dynamics of Communications*, ed. D. Cliche. International Institute of Communications, London, 1997, pp. 199–210.

23 Gates, B., *The Road Ahead*. Viking, London, 1995, p. 273, quoted in Robins, K., *op cit*, ref. 22.

24 Pesche, M., Proximal and distal unity. Paper available at: http:www.hyperreal.com/ mpesce/pdu/html. Quoted in Elgin, D. and Drew, D., *Global Consciousness Change: Indicators of an Emerging Paradigm*. The Millennium Project, San Anselmo, CA, 1997. See, in particular, pp. 6–9 on the global consciousness and the communications revolution. They are hopeful that the emerging global brain—signified by the ever increasing web of communication conducted through the internet —will achieve a critical mass and turn on (p. 8). Writes Peter Russell, 'Billions of messages continually shuttle back and forth, in an ever-growing web of communication, linking billions of minds of humanity into a single system'. See Russell, P., *The Global Brain Awakens*. Global Brain, Palo Alto, CA, 1995, p. 8.

25 Stated on the television show 'Sixty Minutes', Channel 9, Brisbane, Australia, 16 March, 1997.

26 While these are optimistic forecasts, Roar Bjonnes reports that according to *The Nation Magazine* '368 of the world's richest people own as much wealth as 40% of the world's poor'. In other words, 368 billionaires own as much as 2.5 billion poor people. Moreover, the trend is towards greater inequity with the share of global income between the world's rich and the world's poor doubling from 30 to 1 in 1960 to 59 to 1, in 1989. The information revolution will have to be quite dramatic to reverse these figures. Email: Rbjonnes@igc.apc.org, 13 August 1995. Bjonnes is former editor of *Commonfuture and Prout Journal*.

27 Staff, The future of warfare. *The Economist*, 8 March 1997, p. 21.

28 *Ibid*.

DECONSTRUCTING THE INFORMATION ERA

29 For more on this, Inayatullah, S., United we drink: inquiries into the future of the world economy and society. *Papers De Prospectiva*, April 1995, pp. 4–31.

30 Niue takes moral stand on sex lines. *The Courier-Mail*, 20 February 1997, p. 19.

31 Sarkar, P. R., *The Human Society*. AM Publications, Calcutta, 1984, p. 97.

32 Sarkar, P. R., *Problem of the Day*. AM Publications, Ananda Nagar, India, 1959, p. 3. The corporatist framework of the information superhighway removes them from state control and from people's democratic control. 'This technology legitimates the hegemony of corporate interests', writes Kosta Gouliamos. See Kosta Gouliamos, 'The information highway and the diminution of the nation-state', p. 182 in Cliche, D., *Cultural Ecology, op cit.*

33 Stephens, J., Running interference: an interview with Gayatri Chakravorty Spivak. *Australian Women's Books Review*, 1995, **7**(3/4), 27.

34 For more on the silence of animals, that is how discourse silences them, see *New Renaissance*, 1995, **5**(2). The focus of that issue is on the silence of the lambs.

35 Of course, few Islanders have managed to maintain this level of purity. Rather, land has been sold to others for short term profits. However, by selling land (and not using it to develop through agro-industries and manufacturing), Pacific Islands remain locked at the bottom of the world capitalist system.

36 For more on the communicative role of silence, see *The Unesco Courier*, May 1996. The issue focuses on the ontology of silence.

37 Email transmission from Acarya Abhidevanada Avadhuta, March 1997. On Ananda-net.

38 Spaeth, A., @ the web of power. *Time*, 17 February 1997, p. 67.

39 Darden, C., Justice is in the colour of the beholder. *Time*, 17 February 1997, 30–31.

40 Turkle, S., *Life on the Screen: Identity in the Age of the Internet*. Weidenfeld and Nicolson, London, 1996.

41 Rushkoff, D., *Children of Chaos*. Harper Collins, New York, 1997.

42 What's happening in the global village. *Asian Mass Communication Bulletin*, 1996, **26**(5), 17. Also important is to note that 'electricity is still not available for two billion people and many others have only intermittent access'. See, *The Global Futures Bulletin*, 1 July 1997, No. 38/39. Available on-line from the Institute of Global Futures Research, P.O. Box 683, NSW 2022, Australia, igfr@peg.apc.org.

43 Grassel, K., Mexico's Zapatistas: revolution on the Internet. *New Renaissance*, 1997, **7**(2), 22–23. They are just one example, hundreds of non-governmental organisation use the internet as a way to pressure governments and corporations by making their policies more public. Email campaigns for world peace, to stop torture of prisoners throughout the world or to save vegetarian orphanages as, for example, in Romania (on Ananda-net) where, for example, vegetarians successfully campaigned against a preliminary decision by a Romanian agency (Protection of Minors Agency) to close an award winning Ananda Marga school since it did not feed students dead/cooked animals, ie meat. Inundated with faxes and letters from all around the world, including the entire gamut of vegetarian/health organisations, the Romanian agency relented. Whether this was because of the international nature of the pressure—because they did not want to be seen as parochial—or because of a change of heart towards dietary practices is not clear.

44 Sardar, Z., Paper, printing and compact disks: the making and unmaking of Islamic culture. *Media, Culture and Society*, 1993, **15**, 56.

45 Although Kirkpatrick Sale's recent article makes this word now problematic. He argues that Ned Ludd's efforts were not simplistic attacks on technology but

an understanding that the new technologies were increasing the power of the masters. 'The Luddite idea has . . . flourished wherever technology has destroyed jobs, ruined lives and torn up communities'. Sale, K., Ned Ludd live! *New Internationalist*, 1996, **286**, 29. The entire issue is a must read. Ashis Nandy has taken a similar position in his essays sympathetic to the Gandhian critique of technology.

46 For the problems and possibilities of this approach see, Hamelink, C. J., Learning cultural pluralism: can the 'Information Society' help? In *Cultural Ecology*, ed. D. Cliche. International Institute of Communications, London, 1997, pp. 24–43.

14

THE INFORMATION SOCIETY

From Fordism to Gatesism: the 1995 Southam Lecture

Gaëtan Tremblay

Source: *Canadian Journal of Communication* 20(4) (1995): 461–82.

Abstract

The information society model claims that the new information hegemony is transforming industrial society. But is it not the case that the major change has to do with the increasingly greater integration of information and communication into the functioning of the economy and society, in the submission of information and communication to the operative rules of industrial society, in sum, in the commodification of information, culture, and communication? Rather than a "post-industrial society," the period of transition which we are experiencing consists more modestly in the shift from one industrial mode of organization to another mode of industrial organization, that is, from Fordism to Gatesism.

Introduction

Current events, technological developments, and the evolution of our societies continually provide us with subjects, themes, and problems which greatly influence our work. Communication researchers are particularly sensitive to these influences, as is borne out by the analysis of publications in our field.[1] Such permeability to contemporary preoccupations is surely positive in many respects. It roots us in our society and incites us to participate in major public debates. It also helps us continually to adapt our teaching to the evolution of the world of communications. But it also carries certain dangers and often presents us with difficulties. Things evolve so rapidly that our research findings are often out of date even before they are published. And, above all, drawn into the heat of the action, we often lack the distance necessary for rigorous and impartial analysis of the phenomena we are studying. It is often difficult to distinguish our own discourse from the normative and prophetic discourses of other social actors. Indeed, at times we even contribute to nourishing and renewing them. In sum, it is too often the case that our discourse does not demarcate itself from that of the political and economic promoters of these new communication technologies. If this is the case, are we fulfilling our roles as researchers, academics, intellectuals, and critical, impartial analysts?

For some years, decades even, certain recurring themes have imposed themselves with force. Extremely fast-paced developments in technology have led us to focus attention on its immense possibilities and predict the arrival of what has been variously termed "the global village," "the cabled city," "the information economy," "the knowledge economy," and "the information society." Within the same time frame and movement of thought, transformations in the economic system have led us to emphasize globalization and its social and cultural consequences. The most recent development, propelled by the highest political authorities, has focused these preoccupations into the "electronic highways" or "information highways" metaphor. Countless newspaper and magazine articles, television programs, conferences, and public addresses have been devoted to this subject over the past two years. The culminating moment was attained when the G7 members decided to make it the theme of their February 1995 meeting in Brussels.

The subject of my talk is not that of information highways. Rather, I wish to focus on its subtending project, one that has continually been taken up and reactualized over the past few decades, namely, the emergence of a new society characterized as an "information society" (see Lacroix, Miège, & Tremblay, 1994). I would like to explore, in the form of a paper, the following questions: Where does communication theory stand on these issues? How can it help us to conceptualize these phenomena? And how is the evolution of communication theory influenced by these phenomena?

Reactions to technological developments in the field of communication are typically classified into two broad categories: optimist and pessimist. The former views innovations as elements of ineluctable progress, while the latter sees increasing alienation. This dichotomous categorization has been imposed to such an extent and functions so well that whosoever expresses the least criticism is quickly classified as a pessimist, and anyone who mentions the positive outcomes is labelled an optimist. I wish to avoid such a Manichean approach and warn you at the same time that my initial perspective takes nothing from visions of a concentration camp universe or of better things to come, from Orwell and Huxley, or Martin and Chagnon. I merely wish to question, in a critical manner to be sure, the basis of the postulates and concepts we use in the analysis of the above-mentioned phenomena, something which the convenient classification into optimist and pessimist too often occludes and eludes. I begin by discussing some epistemological obstacles facing our conceptualization of the changes affecting our societies. This is followed by a discussion of the meanings we have given to the notion of an information society. Lastly, I propose a change in perspective and offer an hypothesis for explaining current transformations.

Epistemological obstacles

There are many different types of obstacles lying in the path of a more objective—or, if you like, the most desubjectivized possible—understanding of the transformations currently taking place in the most industrialized societies, to speak only of them. I will identify three from among many others.

Let us be honest: we are spontaneously sympathetic to the idea that we are moving towards an information society, even before taking the facts into consideration. This notion is pleasing to us, not only because its usual descriptions evoke the idea of a society in which knowledge and information will be readily accessible and greatly shared (i.e., a more just, more prosperous, and more democratic society), but because it comforts us in our own personal choices: we really are engaged in important matters, we who have chosen to devote our professional lives to the study of communication. We were right. Our work is at the heart of the changes traversing contemporary societies.

This quite natural sympathy constitutes the first obstacle we need to surmount in our efforts to theorize the phenomenon. And we should take note that it will not be easy, particularly since this sympathy finds an easy justification in the Innisian postulate—that nearly all of us accept—to the effect that communications are central to the constitution and life of empires (Innis, 1950/1972, 1951/1968). What could be more normal than for communicologists to adopt this perspective? Are sociologists not convinced of the importance of social facts, psychologists of mental and affective processes, economists of markets, and so forth?

The information society thus flows logically from the historical importance that communication has always occupied in the lives of societies. But if communication media have always played a central role, then why is this characteristic reserved only for the society unfolding before our eyes? Should we not be more precise in how it is qualified, more specific in terms of its characteristics?

The second obstacle is also intimately related to our choice of the field of communication as the object of our professional activities. Despite our explicit denials, we find it difficult to distance ourselves from technological determinism. We are spontaneously given to according considerable and at times inordinate importance to communication media. We tend to begin with the technological, to analyze its characteristics, and to study or deduce its social, economic, cultural, and political consequences. Too often, our work implicitly assumes that technology has an autonomous, independent status relative to socioeconomic structures and actions of social actors. This obstacle is just as difficult to overcome as the previous one because it, too, appears natural, just as it also strikes us as normal that we should conduct ourselves like other social science professionals who give priority to their object of study and their own perspective. In addition, perhaps we are fascinated by ever more powerful technology, the functioning of which we understand poorly!

The centrality of technology has been a characteristic of communication scholarship since its beginning. With few exceptions—such as semiotics and rhetoric—communication theories, from Shannon & Weaver's information theory to mass communication theory and Innis and McLuhan, have been developed as a function of, or reaction to, the development of modern communication technology. However understandable it may be, this tendency to situate technology at the centre of our work needs to be questioned, particularly since we go so far as to draw general conclusions about the type of society in which we live or which we foretell.

The third epistemological obstacle I wish to mention concerns our latent progressivism. The dominant discourse on communication technologies, particularly on what is with some confusion called "the new information and communication technologies" (NICTs), is characterized by an optimism which, though not always overflowing or without nuance, is nevertheless fundamentally convinced that we are progressing. The least one can say is that Jacques Ellul has been left aside! One hardly ever hears, with respect to communication technologies, the same criticisms and doubts abundantly expressed in every other field by the ecology movement. Indeed, communication technology is considered to be essentially positive: it does not pollute, can replace transportation, even allow the movement to organize itself, etc. This optimism is tempered only by the threat posed to individual privacy by the establishment of all manner of electronic files.

Let me be clear: it is not my claim that the pessimists are right after all. At the outset, I stated that I wanted to avoid this dichotomy. I would simply like to point to a recurring theme in the dominant discourse on NICTs, which, even when it tries to have a balanced view of things, tends to present the positive consequences as inevitable, as self-evident, as the natural outcome of the introduction and use of technology, while the negative consequences are viewed as simple possibilities that can be avoided or minimized, given adequate policies and strategies. Without wishing to advocate a catastrophic vision, it seems to me that this prejudice constitutes a significant epistemological obstacle to the apprehension of current changes. It is hardly compatible with the systematic doubt characteristic of any scientific undertaking.

There are thus three obstacles lying on the road to our understanding of changes related to the introduction and spread of NICTs in our societies:

The discourse of the information society

There have been many attempts to name the changes to post-Second World War society and to identify the resulting new society. These have included "mass society," "leisure society," "programmed society," "post-industrial society," "consumer society," "information society," and so on. If certain authors are to be believed, society types change as often as governments! Historians will no doubt sort matters out in a few decades. But one already suspects that despite the fantastic acceleration of the rate of change over the last half century, profound transformations of society are less rapid and certain developments, hailed as fundamental, will not have as dramatic an effect on the system's base as had been anticipated. In this light, to what does the notion of "information society" refer? What are its characteristics? And do they represent a radical transformation justifying claims of a new type of society, of a change as important as that of the industrial revolution, the invention of the printing press, or even the invention of writing?

The argument presenting the advent of the information society as a radical change essentially rests on two kinds of consideration: (1) extremely rapid developments in information processing and transmission, and (2) the growing strategic importance of information and knowledge in the entire arena of human activities. Let me briefly summarize what has been said on this matter over the last few decades by discussing four themes: (1) an interconnected society, (2) an information economy, (3) an interactive society, and (4) informatics as a new form of writing. I will conclude this point with an assessment of the utility of the notion of the information society.

An interconnected society

The first speculations about the information society arose in the 1970s, contemporaneously with the first sense of the immense development possibilities of cable, satellite communications, fibre optics, and micro-informatics. In his 1978 book, *The Wired Society*, James Martin, for example, traces an often-echoed but rarely surpassed portrait. From the new technical possibilities of information transmission and processing, he inferred a number of consequences for the organization of work, social relations, education, political life, the environment, and so on, which led him to sketch a portrait of an idyllic society. In the book's second chapter, entitled "New Highways"—as if the metaphor were not so recent—he writes:

HISTORY AND PERSPECTIVES

Imagine a city ten or twenty years in the future, with parks and flowers and lakes, where the air is crystal clear and most cars are kept in large parking lots on the outskirts. The high rise buildings are not too close, so they all have good views, and everyone living in the city can walk through the gardens or rain-free pedestrian mall to shops, restaurants, or pubs. The city has cabling under the streets and new forms of radio that provide all manner of communication facilities. The television sets, which can pick up many more channels than today's television, can also be used in conjunction with small keyboards to provide a multitude of communication services. The more affluent citizens have 7-foot television screens, or even larger.

There is less need for physical travel than in an earlier era. Banking can be done from the home, and so can as much shopping as is desired. . . .

Some homes have machines that receive transmitted documents. With these new machines one can obtain business paperwork, new items selected to match one's interests, financial or stock market reports, mail, bank statements, airline schedules, and so on. . . .

There is almost no street robbery, because most persons carry little cash. . . . Citizens can wear radio devices for automatically calling police or ambulances if they wish. Homes have burglar and fire alarms connected to the police and fire stations. . . .

Industry is to a major extent run by machines. . . . There is almost no machine tool that does not contain a miniature computer. Paperwork is largely avoided by having computers send orders and invoices directly to other computers and by making most payments, including salary payments, by automatic transmission of funds into the appropriate bank accounts. To avoid unemployment, long weekends have become normal and are demanded by the labor unions.

Inventing and producing ways to fill the increased leisure time is a major growth industry. . . .

Above all, there is superlative education. History can be learned with programs as gripping and informative as Alistair Cooke's *America*. University courses modeled on England's *Open University* use television and remote computers; degrees can be obtained via television. . . . To prepare such programs, there has grown up an industry as large as Hollywood and just as professional. Program production is expensive, but one program is often used by hundreds of thousands of students. . . .

The communication channels provide excellent medical facilities, some computerized and some via the videophones and large television screens. Remote diagnostic studios are used, employing powerful television lenses and many medical instruments. . . .

THE INFORMATION SOCIETY: FROM FORDISM TO GATESISM

> Technical innovation has changed the news media. Citizens can watch their political representatives in action and can register approval or protest. . . .
>
> If new telecommunications has changed the city, it has changed the rural districts even more. . . .
>
> Many country villages have a satellite antenna. People can have their own garden or farmstead and can walk in the fields and woods; they eat fresh vegetables and bread from the local bakery; but they are no longer cut off from the world. . . . There is a growing trend to small communities which are self-dependent except for their use of the new telecommunications highways.
>
> (Martin, 1978/1981, pp. 8–12)

It is curious that Martin did not entertain the possibility that these networks might be used for other ends. There is nothing in his book predicting the use of the Internet by movements on the extreme right or the extreme left. There is nothing that might allow for anticipating the events in Oklahoma City. Nor is there anything about the infatuation of television viewers with events like the O. J. Simpson trial rather than with city council debates. What lovely optimism! What lovely naïveté! What utopianism!

What is striking about this type of discourse is not so much the prediction of technological developments—which are not all that wrong-headed—as the manifest absence of any appreciation of the complexity of social, cultural, political, and economic processes. After all, the telecommunications infrastructures have been largely developed and household equipment has been improved. Not as much can be said, however, for the ecological, erudite, policed, and idyllic society depicted by Martin.

But the tone had been set. Many government documents and articles were to be produced with the same visionary accents, the same type of reasoning which consists in extrapolating a host of improvements in every walk of social life solely on the basis of the spread of new information and communication technologies. Such is the background to the dominant discourse of the information society.[2]

An information economy

The work of Daniel Bell (1973) and Marc Porat (1977) represents another type of vision centred on technological potential. More specifically, their vision is predicated on the importance of knowledge and information in contemporary economies. In Bell's view, knowledge has become the most important production factor in modern economies. It is the basis of the exercise of power, it produces gains in productivity, and it ensures business competitiveness. And in Porat's view, America's post-war economy can be characterized by the rise in importance of activities related to information production, processing, and transmission. Since an economy can be defined by the type of activities occupying the majority of its workers, we can talk in terms of an information economy, just as one spoke of an industrial economy when manufacturing and transformation were the dominant activities, or an agrarian economy when the majority of workers were in the primary sector.

It is undeniable that knowledge is now one of the most important factors in production. While this has always been true to a lesser extent, it must be admitted that technical and scientific knowledge plays a much more important role in contemporary economies than in the economy of, for example, the first industrial revolution. Porat's argument in this respect, however, is subject to certain problems, as William Leiss points out in his systematic critique (Leiss, 1982). Let me only mention that Porat's conclusions rely on disputable statistical aggregates. In order to show the supreme importance of information-related activities in contemporary economies, Porat lumps together very different trades and professions, which all touch upon information production and processing, but in degrees that vary considerably. In certain respects, insurance agents, computer programmers, secretaries, telephone operators, scholars, writers, accountants, journalists, and so forth are all communicators. However, their relationships to producing, processing, and diffusing information are extremely different. In this light, the meaning of the expressions "information economy" or "information society" is problematic.

There is another characteristic generally attributed to the information society, its place of honour due to progress in digitalization, the modernization and expansion of telecommunications networks (via satellite, cable, and airwaves), and the advent of multimedia products: interactivity. With the most advanced technologies now capable of interactivity, the information society will become much more interactive, which is, of course, presented as constituting considerable progress.

Lastly, the information society, predicated on the generalization of informatics, would involve a major cultural revolution, comparable to those which followed the invention of the printing press and writing itself. These two points merit closer attention.

An interactive society

In the campaign promoting the new communication technologies, as well as the so-called information highways, much is made of interactivity, claimed as their essential and revolutionary characteristic. But are we not both victims and accomplices of this propaganda?

The potentialities of interactive multimedia are indeed fabulous, if still poorly defined. But is this enough to infer the coming of a profound social and cultural change? Upon what is this prediction based? On three a priori: (1) that these technological potentialities will necessarily become concrete

THE INFORMATION SOCIETY: FROM FORDISM TO GATESISM

features of social reality, (2) that the media have until now kept audiences in a passive state, and (3) that interactivity is necessarily a good thing, and, as a corollary, that all that is not interactive is uninteresting.

Though I discussed the first a priori above, it is important to come back to it here: our field of study has difficulty in freeing itself from technological determinism. This can be seen once again in thought about interactivity. Since the technology is interactive, it will necessarily foster interactive uses. The history of media, however, is rife with examples demonstrating that "technological potential" does not necessarily fulfill itself and that uses do not flow naturally from the characteristics of a given technique (Flichy, 1991). Allow me a single example. Writing is a medium that allows for interactivity and creativity. But are these its most everyday and widespread uses?

The second a priori concerning the passive nature of traditional media reception flies in the face of a few decades of research. It has been known for some time that the receiver is not merely a photographic plate, that even watching a television program involves selective perception, decoding, and recoding of messages. Interlocution already exists. Its extension to inter-action with machines and the profusion of remote interactive possibilities does not in itself constitute a revolution. Before jumping to this conclusion, however, there is a need for rigorous analysis of how interactive uses of NICTs, about which we still know little, will transform the conditions of interactivity in our societies.

The third a priori rests on an undisputed claim regarding the positive value of interactivity. Passivity is automatically assigned a negative sign and interactivity a positive one. Interactivity is good in itself, passivity is bad. Passivity entails a hierarchic relationship between a sender and receivers. In contrast, interactivity fosters equality and symmetry in the relationship. Traditional television exploited the passivity of its viewers, the new media encourage interactivity. The advent of these new media, therefore, indisput-ably constitutes progress. Users will spontaneously recognize this fact and the passive use of media, television among others, will disappear. Interactive television will soon replace mass television. We have finally entered the *EMEREC* era, that is, according to the neologism coined by Jean Cloutier from *ÉMEtteur* (sender) and *RÉCepteur* (receiver), an age in which receivers can at the same time be senders (Cloutier, 1973).

You might well find that the above borders on caricature. I do not believe it is. This a priori is rarely explicitly stated, but it subtends most of the work on interactivity. This unconditional valuing of interactivity generally omits to take a certain number of relatively elementary things into consideration:

(a) that there are several types of interactivity, and that there is a funda-mental difference between, for example, accessing a data bank, playing a video game, and a telephone conversation. A typology of the different forms of interactivity is a prerequisite to any rigorous research into the question.

(b) that listening (which is not a purely passive phenomenon) is not necessarily inferior to speaking; my apologies for the following analogy of questionable taste: one might enjoy cooking, but it is not obvious that one always eats better at home, or in a cafeteria, than in the fief of a master chef!

(c) that the pleasure of being told a story or of watching a show considerably predates the invention of modern media, and that it will probably survive the advent of interactive multimedia technology.

(d) that interactivity does not always translate into egalitarian relationships and does not produce only happy results. As is the case in interpersonal relationships, conflict and mutual misunderstanding are equally possible results of electronic exchanges.

(e) that the real uses of this technology will be the result of a long and complex process of creation, and that, though it is difficult to predict the result, it is unlikely that it will establish itself as a function of a rectilinear logic which will lead to the replacement of all passive uses by active uses.

What can we take from all this? Two things: (1) it is true that recent technology displays interesting interactive possibilities, and (2) it is not obvious that this will lead to qualitative social change. In any event, it remains to be seen. The information society will not necessarily be more interactive than the preceding ones.

Informatics: a new form of writing?

Are the consequences of the invention of informatics as significant as those of the invention of the printing press and of writing, as is claimed by authors whose theories have made the bestseller list?[3] Historians of the next few decades, if not centuries, will no doubt be in a better position to judge the validity of this assertion.

It is undeniable that informatics products have spread to every sector of human activity. In the factory, at the office, and in the home, a vast array of objects now incorporate computer chips. While not yet universal, the use of the computer is widespread and the expansion of telematics networks ensures an ever-widening electronic diffusion of information. Neither the computer nor telecommunications has caused paper to disappear, as has been predicted several times over, but it is not unreasonable to suggest that the volume of electronic exchanges will soon be equal in importance to that of printed material. The construction of information highways is likely to reinforce this trend. The comparison with the printing press would appear to be justified.

THE INFORMATION SOCIETY: FROM FORDISM TO GATESISM

The comparison with writing, however, is more complex and less obvious. To be sure, very complex "informatics languages" that rely on formal logic do exist. But these particular "languages" remain the preserve of a small number of specialists. While the use of computers is now widespread, the same is not the case with learning computer programming. The use of a spreadsheet, a word processor, or desktop publishing, or graphics software requires a certain learning period, but it has nothing to do with computer programming.

Far from relying on the spread of a new informatics culture, manufacturers do their utmost to produce user-friendly software that resembles natural languages as much as possible. Less and less energy is devoted to teaching humans how to speak "machine language" and more and more time to teaching machines how to speak "human language." All specialists are unanimous in thinking that the information highways will never truly have mass appeal unless their use modes and navigational instruments become more user-friendly. The same requirement of simplicity of use applies to the generalization of multimedia products.

Under these conditions, it is very difficult to speak of the generalization of an "informatics writing," the impact of which is comparable to that of the invention of alphabetic writing.

It remains to raise the eventuality of a mode of multimedia thought, which will be the result of the simultaneous use of writing, sounds, and images, and a non-linear approach to the production and use of these products. Given the embryonic state of multimedia, all claims in this regard are much more in the nature of prophecies than of analysis.

The information society: an overly vague notion

The notion of an "information society" was coined to describe the type of society that would result from the expansion of communication technology, the generalization of digitalization technology, and the strategic importance of information and knowledge in modern economies. Its description often assumes lyric proportions. This society is the stuff of dreams, especially in the context of current difficulties. But, as we saw above, this notion lacks rigour due to a deterministic vision amplified by a naïve progressivism.

This notion is too vague to be of any use. The notion of information encompasses an overly vast range of objects, extending from current affairs to scientific inventions and entertainment products. To speak of an information society strikes me as being no more enlightening than to speak of an economic society, a political society, or a sociological society. It describes all societies. It is necessary to be more specific in the characterization of the phenomena. All societies are information societies. One must not confuse the "computerization of society" with "information society." We need to develop more rigorous typologies, such as sociologists have done in distinguishing primitive societies, traditional societies, and industrial societies, and as economists have done in distinguishing barter economies, market economies, planned economies, and so forth.

Moreover, it is necessary to be able to articulate the changes being produced in the world of communication in conjunction with other major trends in our societies in order to be able to claim to characterize them: population aging, the crisis of the welfare state, modifications of the family unit, demographic changes, ecological consciousness, globalization of the economy, and so forth. In a world that is globalizing and complexifying, there is, alas, little global thinking in the field of communication; one only finds globalizing discourses which proceed—as was taught in the methodology courses I took as a student—by way of unwarranted and hasty generalizations.

I doubt that you expect me to meet all these requirements and present you with a fully elaborated model. For the moment, I will settle for sketching the avenues of research we are developing at GRICIS.

For a change in perspectives

The eulogists of the information society argue that we must begin to conceive society and the economy essentially in terms of the production and circulation of information. In their view, information has become the most important production factor and product of economic life. The model places information and communication at the very heart of the functioning of societies. It is this new centrality of information that is the main characteristic of the changes affecting advanced industrial societies. Such a perspective leads to thinking of the information society as surpassing industrial society, as the advent of something completely different, obeying a new set of rules and opening horizons which have been unknown until the present. We have thus gone from a traditional rural society to an industrial urban society (which underwent a first, then a second, revolution), and we are now entering an information society. The importance of energy will give way to that of information, manufacturing will take second place to conception, and the secondary sector will drop behind the tertiary sector. Dynamic economies of the future will be based essentially on businesses producing and processing information. Traditional manufacturing activities will become the lot of second-order, if not underdeveloped economies.

It is true that in recent decades companies in search of cheap labour have tended to move their production activities to less-developed countries. It is also true that Western countries have been obliged to undertake painful restructuring of several underperforming sectors of their economies (iron and steel, textiles, pulp and paper, etc.). And it is true that the information and communication sector—production of informatics and telecommunications material, production of cultural contents, software, and so forth—has experienced remarkable growth and now accounts for a growing share of the gross domestic product. But between this and the conclusion that the future essentially resides in the reinforcement of this sector, there is a gap. It too quickly overlooks the fact that the most powerful economies—the United States, Japan, and Germany—are still the planet's greatest industrial powers, and that the new dynamic economies of Southeast Asia owe the greater part of their growth to industrial activity.

Before jumping to the conclusion that a radical change in the economy and society is taking place, it strikes me as necessary to consider other possible interpretations of present changes. The information society model claims that the new information hegemony is transforming industrial society. But, to the contrary, should we not ask ourselves whether it is not rather the expansion of capitalist logic, more triumphant than ever, that is transforming the world of information and communication? Is it not the case that the major change has to do with the increasingly greater integration of information and communication into the functioning of the economy and society, in the submission of information and communication to the operative rules of industrial society—in sum, in the commodification of information, culture, and communication. From this point of view, present transformations should be seen as a new phase of capitalism, as an extension of commercial and industrial logic to sectors which had previously eluded it. Rather than a "post-industrial society," the period of transition which we are experiencing consists more modestly in the shift from one mode of industrial organization to another mode of industrial organization, that is, from Fordism to Gatesism. This proposition is no doubt less exciting than the dream of a new society promised us by the prophets of the information society, but it raises no fewer significant changes in economic, social, and political organization.

This perspective recentres the problem. Information and communication technologies are neither pushed aside nor classified as secondary factors, but they are no longer the only factors that need to be taken into consideration. This re-orientation of the problematic requires an understanding of communication phenomena, including technological development, in terms of interests, power, and the conflicts resulting from their affirmation.

A working hypothesis: from Fordism to Gatesism

Without ever having expressed the desire, Henry Ford gave his name to a form of production and a form of consumption which came to characterize a form of capitalism. Bill Gates readily admits his ambition to become the Henry Ford of informatics and new communication technologies. Will his name become synonymous with a new norm of production and consumption, characteristic of a new development in capitalism? No doubt, Gates would not object.

Fordism refers, of course, to a mode of production and organization of work: mass production, the assembly line, a Taylorian conception of work. But this model also entails a mode of social regulation and a norm of consumption. Collective bargaining, a certain type of unionism, and the development of the welfare state have become its main mechanisms for resolving conflicts and antagonisms, managing growth and recessions, and framing needs and social demands. It also fostered the development of purchasing power and the creation of a consumer market for mass-produced goods. Franklin Roosevelt's New Deal institutionalized this mode of organization, not only in economic terms, but in social and political terms as well.

The diagnosis proffered by numerous economists is confirmed daily by current events: Fordism is in a state of crisis. The modes of production and consumption and the organization of work are being transformed. And the development of information technologies and products is a non-negligible factor in this reorganization. But this simple observation, with which we are all too often satisfied, does not constitute an explanation. It is not enough to identify a product or a technique. One must show how work is being reorganized, how new modes of social regulation are being established, how new uses develop and create a new consumer market. In this transition period, it is difficult to visualize the end result with any degree of precision. At most, we can identify a few trends and formulate several questions.

The reorganization of work

This aspect of the crisis is well known. Faced with deficits and accumulated debts, the State is deregulating and privatizing. Faced with competition, business is rationalizing. The result: a high rate of unemployment that is giving no indication of reducing itself. Computerization and improvements in telecommunications are part of this process. They permit savings and foster rationalization. Our leaders assure us that they will be sources of new jobs. They are indeed responsible for new job creation, but not at the same rate as layoffs. Is this the normal lag experienced in transition periods? Perhaps, but there is no guarantee. In past industrial revolutions, the agricultural and the manufacturing, the freed-up labour force was always eventually re-absorbed. Laid-off workers in the primary sector shifted to the secondary sector, and those in the secondary sector moved on to the tertiary sector, after often long and painful transition periods. But there are no more sectors. Where will laid-off tertiary sector workers turn to? The construction of new communication networks will provide employment for a certain period of time. But what will these workers do once these networks have been put in place? The demand for new products will also create opportunities, but will they suffice to absorb the available labour force? What exactly does the quaternary sector mentioned by some authors consist of?

THE INFORMATION SOCIETY: FROM FORDISM TO GATESISM

This leaves us with work sharing. It looks good on paper, but runs into many problems and resistances, as much from management as unions. For the moment, rationalization entails precarious job security, an increase in the rate of unemployment, and greater workloads for those who keep their jobs.

It is curious that eulogists of the information society either do not take these problems into consideration or give them short shrift by reminding us that past technological revolutions always led to improved working conditions. One would like to believe them, especially since, for once, they are telling us that nothing has changed under the sun and that things will go along as they did before.

In reaction to these new conditions, the number of independent workers is on the rise. It now appears as if one must create one's own job without, however, either permanence or job security, privileges acquired in industrial society. This is no doubt the prosaic version of working at home, free from transportation and disciplinary constraints.[4] If this is what the future holds, it effectively represents a dramatic change from industrial society which took workers out of the home and put them into factories. If, however, it works, with good salaries and improved working conditions, then there is cause to rejoice. But the reality depicted by current studies is something else entirely.

At present, the transition induced by the crisis of Fordism, created and nourished by developments in communication technology, has not resulted in significant gains for workers. Rather, it has led to a deep crisis marked by a decrease in job security and a high rate of unemployment. The leisure society, such as it is characterized by Dumazedier (1967), is one of forced leisure for those without access to the labour market, and heavy workloads for those who manage to remain.

With developments in informatics, production cannot only be automated, but mass production can be replaced by production on demand. Distribution can be made "just-in-time," and inventories can be managed much more efficiently. No doubt there will be profound changes to production norms. But the organization of work will also be turned upside down, and little is known about how to deal with the consequences. For some time now, Taylorism has ceased to set the standard for the organization of work. Judging by the profusion of management models put forward in recent decades—from "small is beautiful" to the re-engineering of business processes and total quality—one is justified in asking what its replacement will be. Either we are still in a transition period that continues to make it difficult to identify it or the future will see a plurality of production norms.

There have been several empirical studies of the introduction of new information technologies into the workplace.[5] And many more will be needed to come to a satisfactory understanding of the reorganization process still in progress. But one thing stands out from these studies: one must take care

249

Modes of social regulation

The welfare state is also undergoing a crisis. Confronted with important budget deficits and an accumulated debt that in many cases has reached alarming proportions, states, too, have begun to rationalize: privatization, reductions in services and programs, and reductions in personnel. Not all governments share the same ideology, but they are all adopting measures aimed at limiting government spending and action and are increasingly relying on the market and civil society to ensure social regulation.

Internationalization and the resulting increase in interdependence reveal the limits of nation-states. Policies and regulations are increasingly obliged to adjust to one another. Governments which stray too far from general trends are quick to suffer the consequences and are obliged sooner or later to realign themselves.

Once again, the notion of the information society is of little use in understanding what is taking place. Visions of a global village, the possibilities of the rapid interconnection of all points on the planet, and the virtues of electronic democracy shed little light on the real processes of social regulation currently being redefined. To mention only one problem, will the information society ensure the integration of individuals, ethnic groups, and diverse cultures? At a time when the traditional mechanisms of integration have broken down in most countries throughout the world, and when all manner of conflicts can erupt into violence, a global vision of society cannot ignore these issues.

Over the past few years, in the wake of the privatization and deregulation movement in the field of communication, a number of strategic international alliances between the most important players in the various theatres have begun to take shape: telephony, cable, producers and publishers of contents, satellite operators, software manufacturers, generalist and specialized programmers, and so forth.[6] The advantage of such alliances is that they permit the coverage of all potential development sectors and ensure a diversified expertise while sharing risks.

It is these few large groups or consortiums that will take the lion's share of deregulated national markets which have been opened up to competition. Concerned about protecting their interests, they exercise considerable influence over the public agencies responsible for redefining the rules ordering the lifting of barriers—public service ones in particular—that hinder their access to markets and the development of their activities. They can regularly be seen confronting one another at CRTC public hearings, for example. It is

THE INFORMATION SOCIETY: FROM FORDISM TO GATESISM

through these confrontations and subsequent decisions that new modes of social regulation in the fields of culture and communication are being progressively defined.

It is for this reason that it is important to conduct a detailed and rigorous analysis of the evolution of the industrial structure as well as the strategies adopted by the main actors with a stake in the introduction of NICTs: the various public agencies, as well as the major private groups. We would be wrong to assume that they all have the same interests and pursue identical objectives. In fact, in this transition period, the horizon is still quite hazy and the dust is far from settled. Public service is regressing and the welfare state is being questioned, but, for the moment, we are hardly in a position to identify its replacement model.

Uses and consumption

"Those who claim to know where we are headed with all this business about information highways are peddling fantasies!"[7] This quotation is not from a Marxist sociologist but a senior executive of a major informatics and communication company owned by General Motors. It neatly summarizes the reality of things. Notwithstanding all the megaprojects and all the hopes invested in the construction of information highways, it is impossible at present to predict consumer reaction. History teaches us that uses for new communication technologies are constructed slowly and involve a series of factors, of which the characteristics of the technology is only one element. Uses are the result of a long process of social construction, and they often contain surprises for the initiators of the technological supply.

Whatever the case, big capital, desperate for new niches in order to accrue its surplus value, has decided to invest in the fields of culture and communication. In this regard, technological progress offers significant possibilities. I am convinced that the electronic highways megaproject must be interpreted in light of these major interests. The industrialization of culture and communication began a long time ago. Despite its catastrophic visions, the Frankfurt School should be given its due for having foreseen subsequent developments. The major stakes involved in the information highways pertain to the creation of both a professional and a mass market that will foster the redeployment of our economies. What has until now been offered free of charge, that is, inscribed in a public service logic, will henceforth be offered in a paying mode, that is, inscribed in a commercial logic.

Scientific and technical information has always had a certain economic and strategic value. One only need think of patents and military secrets to validate this claim. At the same time, however, it obeyed a logic of diffusion and sharing that rendered it accessible and kept it largely sheltered from market logic. Scientists who were not bound by military or industrial contracts hoped for the widest possible diffusion of their works. The goal of

251

those promoting information highways is to extract payment for this access, if only for the telecommunications link.

The same is true for literary and artistic work. Reproductions and copies are now accessible by telecommunications. The extent to which creators will benefit from this will depend on copyright legislation and agreements. One of the major issues that will be a source of tension in international conflicts and negotiations in the coming decades will no doubt be the copyright issue. We saw it emerge recently in trade discussions between China and the United States. Other indicators can be found in the race by large corporations—Microsoft, among others—to acquire ownership of or access to the world's large image and data banks. Moreover, while Canada managed to exclude culture from its free trade agreements with Mexico and the United States, it should not be forgotten that copyright fees are an integral part of these agreements, as is the case with the GATT agreements.

With respect to this major issue of intellectual property, the development of communication networks exacerbates the always latent conflict between distributors and producers of content.[8] The interests of the latter reside in the highest possible copyright payments. The former, to the contrary, seek a reduction of these payments to a minimum as a means of reducing their costs and offering consumers maximum use of their networks at the lowest possible price. In this context, two legal traditions are opposed to one another: the French tradition, which accords greater rights to creators, and the American tradition, which concedes these same rights to producers.

The same tendency is having an effect on mass market cultural productions. The service logic model of supplying television products is being demolished. What was once free, that is, financed by government funding, licence fees, or advertising, will increasingly be offered in discrete units, on a pay-per-view basis. It is unlikely that generalist broadcasters will disappear, if only because of the needs of the advertising market, but the pay-per-view and remote commercial transaction markets will no doubt experience sustained growth over the coming years—at least that is what corporations willing to invest billions of dollars in the development of information highways are gambling on (Tremblay, in press; Lacroix, Tremblay, Wilson, & Ménard, 1994).

If we are still uncertain about the shape of the future reorganization of work and social regulation, we are even more so about future uses of NICTs. We are beginning to get a glimpse of the implications of privatization, deregulation, and rationalization. But we are still completely in the dark with respect to consumer responses to networks which have yet to be installed or to multimedia products not yet available on the market. One hardly need add that in the area of predictions, the prophets of the information society are even less credible. The general public will not be fooled as easily as the experts by the sirens of technology. The real utility, available time and income, ease of use, the pleasure felt, and needs satisfaction will ultimately count for more in the success of a given technology than its theoretical potential.

In this respect, allow me a brief return to the notion of interactivity. We are told that the new technologies are revolutionary in that they allow for, facilitate, and promote interactivity. Users replace receivers. This is actively entailed by NICT use. Over and above the theoretical rediscovery of the effective participation of interlocutors in all communication situations, should we not interpret the recurrence of this discourse, which is almost presented in the form of an injunction, as a fundamental requirement of the new form of consumption being established? Does interactivity not require the development by consumers of new skills and competencies? I suspect that the notion of servuction, which refers to the effective participation of consumers in the reception of services, might be useful in conceptualizing this phenomenon (Eiglier & Langeard, 1987). Consumers must not only choose from among the various services offered to them, but they must also actively mobilize a knowledge and perform a number of operations in order for them to receive a desired service. Is this not the underside of the computerization of production processes? From this perspective, interactivity and the user's mandatory participation that it implies represent much more than technological possibilities or theoretical rediscoveries. They would constitute the conditions for the elaboration of the new norm of consumption under Gatesism: While computerization would require less activity on the part of human service providers, it would inversely require a greater participation on the part of beneficiaries of these services.

Gatesism: a useful notion?

Why speak of Gatesism instead of the information society? Am I not committing the same sin that I criticized at length earlier? Is Gatesism just another label in the long series of propositions employed in characterizing change? Perhaps. I admit to succumbing to the temptation of wanting to be provocative in using the term "Gatesism." But my other reason for doing so stems from the parallels with Fordism. And this is much more fundamental. Fordism identifies a form of capitalism, along with a norm of production, a norm of consumption, and a specific system of regulation. Bill Gates is another symbol in our contemporary society. He is not only the wealthiest man in the United States and the most recent model of the self-made man. He also incarnates success in the cutting-edge domain of informatics and telecommunications. In addition, he heads up one of the sector's most powerful and ambitious corporations. As was the case with Henry Ford, his name could be used to synthesize the changes currently underway. Ultimately, however, the term chosen makes no difference. I am not particularly interested in promoting the image of Bill Gates. It is the implied perspective that counts, meaning:

(a) that the changes accompanying NICT development should not necessarily be interpreted as auguring a radical rupture with industrial society, but, to the contrary, they should be understood within the framework of a dynamic specific to capitalist industrial societies.
(b) that these changes nevertheless translate into a shift from one mode of organization to another, from one production and consumption norm to other production and consumption norms.
(c) that the search for new modes of social regulation is part of this process of change.
(d) that the computerization of society, a transformation process currently underway, is not necessarily tantamount to the information society, a utopian model of society, the realization of which is more than unlikely.
(e) that it is necessary to conduct meticulous studies of the organization of work, modes of regulation, and social uses before making globalizing claims about the "information revolution."
(f) that we must rid ourselves of technological determinism and restore the importance of social, economic, legal, cultural, and political factors if we want to be able to provide a global explanation of current phenomena.

If a Gatesism phenomenon—or whatever we choose to call it—does exist, it has yet to be described and explained. In any event, this strikes me as a hypothesis worth exploring, one that is as rich as, if not richer than, that of the "information society."

Conclusion

I can already hear certain individuals asking me: "But the perspective you are proposing contains nothing specific to communications. Where is the theory of communication in all this?" The question is not without relevance. However, I would reply: "Neither do the theories of the 'information society' that I discussed. Rather, it is the thinking that generalizes about the future of our societies on the basis of a reductive technologism." Communication studies has a globalizing ambition. I have nothing against this ambition. It represents a challenge that we are as well suited to meet as our colleagues in the human sciences. But if this is our goal, then let us rise to the requirements, difficulties, and complexities of the task.

With regard to important transformations in the organization of work, modes of social regulation, and consumer practices, as well as the concrete problems they engender, one is constrained to admit that communication theory has contributed little. Too often, we remain at the level of McLuhanesque determinism. We make too many prophesies and analyze too little. We are either too enthusiastic or too depressing, but we do not theorize enough.

I cannot tell you what the world of tomorrow will be like, but I can assure you that it will be nothing like the one predicted by the eulogists of the information society. They provide us with a globalizing but ultimately simplistic model. If communication theorists wish to participate in the effort to understand society as a whole and the transformations traversing it, they will truly have to come to grips with its complexity and propose something other than a determinist vision centred only on technology and its effects.

To be sure, immense progress has been made in informatics and telecommunications in recent decades. But the spread of these technologies and models of implementation and use are the result of complex social, economic, and political processes, themselves not determined only by the features of technologies. Attentive observation of the definition and evolution of electronic highway projects shows this to be the case. Huge economic interests are at stake, interests that are calling for a redefinition of the rules regulating broadcasting and telecommunications in the countries concerned. The objective is to create and exploit a new cultural and communication market, both professional and domestic. The barriers to the attainment of this objective must be brought down. This is what the industrialists interested in these new markets are demanding, as they clearly made known when they met at the Brussels G7 conference last February.

In order to take the pulse of current changes, communication research must undertake a systematic analysis of the transformations taking place in production and distribution modes, the organization of work, social uses, and modes of social regulation. It is after these meticulous studies have been completed that we can theorize the importance of current changes. Perhaps we will conclude that a radical rupture with a past situation has taken place. But we will also be obliged to ask ourselves whether recent technological achievement is not rather the apogee—for the moment—of developments begun with the invention of the electric telegraph in the middle of the last century,[9] of which electronic highways are merely the most recent metaphorical formulation.

Acknowledgments

An earlier version of this article was presented as the Southam Lecture keynote address to the Canadian Communication Association Annual Meeting, Montreal, Quebec, 1995. I would like to thank Juan Carlos Miguel de Bustos, Marc Ménard, and Jean-Guy Lacroix for their interesting comments on the first draft of this paper, and Richard Ashby for the translation of this paper.

Notes

1 In this regard, see Lacroix & Lévesque (1985a, 1985b), Lacroix (1988), Salter (1988), McFadyen, Hoskins, Finn, & Lorimer (1994).

HISTORY AND PERSPECTIVES

2 An analysis of the social function of this dominant discourse is provided in Lacroix, Miège, & Tremblay (1994).
3 See, for example, Lévy (1987, 1990).
4 Will the rise in independent workers supplant wages as the main mode of work remuneration?
5 In particular, see several issues of *Technologies de l'information et société* (Paris: Dumont).
6 In this connection, see Carlos de Miguel (1993).
7 Liberal translation of remarks made by John R. Harris, head of EDS's communications division, quoted in *El Pais*, May 25, 1994.
8 A more nuanced analysis of the situation requires that one distinguish between the interests of creators and those of production companies.
9 In this connection, see the excellent analysis provided in Carey (1989).

References

Bell, Daniel. (1973). *The coming of post-industrial society: A venture in social forecasting.* New York: Basic Books.

Carey, James W. (1989). Technology and ideology: The case of the telegraph. In James W. Carey (Ed.), *Communication as culture: Essays on media and society.* Boston: Unwin Hyman.

Carlos de Miguel, Juan. (1993). *Los grupos multimédia, estructuras y estrategias en los medios europeos.* Barcelona: Bosch Communicación.

Cloutier, Jean. (1973). *L'ère d'émérec.* Montreal: Presses de l'Université de Montréal.

Dumazedier, Joffre. (1967). *Vers une civilization du loisir.* Paris: Éditions du Seuil.

Eiglier, P., & Langeard, E. (1987). *Servuction. Le marketing des services.* Montreal: McGraw Hill.

Flichy, Patrice. (1991). *Une histoire de la communication moderne, espace publique et privée.* Paris: La Découverte.

Innis, H. A. (1972). *Empire and communications.* Toronto: University of Toronto Press. (Original work published 1950)

Innis, H. A. (1968). *The bias of communication.* Toronto: University of Toronto Press. (Original work published 1951)

Lacroix, J.-G. (1988). Les études sur les médias au Québec: État de la question. *Communication, 9*(2), 59–84.

Lacroix, J.-G., & Lévesque, B. (1985a). L'émergence et l'institutionnalisation de la recherche en communication au Québec. *Communication, 7*(2), 7–32.

Lacroix, J.-G., & Lévesque, B. (1985b). Principaux thèmes et courants théoriques dans la litérature scientifique en communication au Québec. *Communication, 7*(3), 153–211.

Lacroix, J.-G., Miège, B., & Tremblay, G. (Eds.). (1994). *De la télématique aux autoroutes électroniques: le grand projet reconduit.* Montreal: Presses de l'Université du Québec et Grenoble: Presses de l'Université de Grenoble.

Lacroix, J.-G., Tremblay, G., Wilson, K., & Ménard, M. (1994). L'autoroute électronique, plus qu'une métaphore? *Interface, 15*(5), 12–25.

Leiss, William. (1982). *The information society: A new name for some old tricks.* 1982 Annual Departmental Colloquium, Department of Sociology, University of Calgary, March 24–26.

THE INFORMATION SOCIETY: FROM FORDISM TO GATESISM

Lévy, Pierre. (1987). *La machine univers: création, cognition et culture informatique.* Paris: La Découverte.

Lévy, Pierre. (1990). *Les technologies de l'intelligence.* Paris: La Découverte.

Martin, James. (1981). *The wired society.* Englewood Cliffs, NJ: Prentice-Hall. (Original work published 1978)

McFadyen, Stuart, Hoskins, Colin, Finn, Adam, & Lorimer, Rowland (Eds.). (1994). Cultural development in an open economy [Special issue]. *Canadian Journal of Communication, 19*(3–4).

Porat, Marc U. (1977). *The information economy.* Washington, DC: U.S. Department of Commerce.

Salter, L. (1988). Les études en communication au Canada: un état présent. *Communication, 9*(2), 31–58.

Tremblay, G. (in press). Hacia la sociedad de la información o el mercado electrónico? Una perspectiva critica. *Comunicación,* Valencia.

15

PLAN AND CONTROL

Towards a cultural history of the Information Society

Frank Webster and Kevin Robins

Source: *Theory and Society* 18(3) (1989): 323–51.

Every gain in knowledge and efficiency and every outworn symbol or causal explanation displaced by more realistic analysis, is potentially a gain in ease and richness of living. But when this new knowledge is not put to work in the service of all the people, when it is only partially applied to those able to "pay for it" or bright enough to learn it unaided, or when it is used by those with power in order to exploit others, this knowledge may be either largely barren or, worse, it tends to become a disruptive factor.

Robert S. Lynd, Knowledge For What? (1939)

What is the Information Revolution? The answer to this question may seem to be self-evident. A united host of industrialists, politicians, and academics is now engaged in making sure that we know that recent developments in the miniaturization of electronics components (the "microelectronics revolution") are laying the foundations, particularly through their impact on computing and telecommunications, for a new era of information wealth and abundance. An array of reports and publications make clear to us that the eighties mark a unique watershed in human history as we now experience a second Industrial Revolution. According to one observer, "the first Industrial Revolution enormously enhanced the puny muscular power of men and animals in production; this new development will similarly extend human mental capacity to a degree which we can now only dimly envisage."[1] It is the exploitation (and industrialization) of information and knowledge that marks an epochal shift from industrial to post-industrial society. The promise is that through new technologies (advanced computers, robotics, communications satellites, etc.) the puny powers of human intelligence and reason may be enhanced beyond our wildest dreams. As such,

PLAN AND CONTROL: TOWARDS A CULTURAL HISTORY

the "Information Revolution" reflects the symbiotic relationship between human evolution and scientific and technological progress.

In this discursive cocktail of scientific aspiration and commercial hype, there are a number of implicit but significant assumptions. First, it is assumed that the decisive shift has been brought about by recent technological innovations: the association of information revolution and information technologies seems tautologically self-evident. Thus, discussion of the Information Revolution is located within the history of technological development and the discourse of technological "progress." Secondly, the assumption is made that this technological revolution, like the earlier Industrial Revolution, marks the opening of a new historical era. The flaccid terms "industrial" and "post-industrial" society – which, through a process of ideological elision, often translate into "capitalist" and "post-capitalist" – mark this transition from a period of constraint and limits to one of freedom, democracy, and abundance. A third assumption is that of the novelty of the Information Revolution. For the first time, in the late twentieth century, as a consequence of the development and convergence of telecommunications and data-processing, it has become possible to harness human intelligence and reason in a systematic and scientific way. Associated with this, of course, is the unquestioned assumption that organized knowledge and information are socially beneficial. Information is the major asset and resource of a post-industrial society: "it is . . . the raw material of truth, beauty, creativity, innovation, productivity, competitiveness, and freedom."[2] Information in all places and at all times – that is the Utopian recipe. Finally, the issue is seen substantially as an economic matter, and information as pre-eminently an economic category. The revolution is about "making a business of information."[3] According to Tom Stonier, "the accumulation of information is as important as the accumulation of capital," because "as our knowledge expands the world gets wealthier."[4] Information is the key to economic growth and productivity, and to the bigger pie from which we shall all have bigger slices. Reflecting this economic annexation of information and knowledge is the fast expanding field of information economics.[5]

In the following discussion, which radically questions the unsubstantiated optimism of the information society scenario, we aim to confront and challenge these assumptions and their complacent promise of technological progress, economic growth, and human betterment. Thus, our own attempt to explore the significance of the new communications and information technologies in terms of their genealogy, leads us to be skeptical of the idea that they constitute a technological revolution. Whilst we would, of course, accept the scale of innovation in this area, and the degree of its exploitation (in the context of long-term national and international recession), we believe that these new technologies are "revolutionary" only in a rather trivial sense.

Of course, we do not want to imply that there are not important transformations in the form and nature of capitalist societies in the 1980s, and the new information and communications technologies are surely implicated in these transformative processes.[6] Some commentators have described a historical shift from organized capitalism to disorganized capitalism while others have conceptualized the present period in terms of a change in the dominant regime of accumulation, from the system of Fordism to one characterized, still rather inadequately, as neo-Fordist or post-Fordist. Within this latter perspective, there has been, in our view, a strong tendency to over-emphasize elements of rupture: to focus on the shift from centralization to decentralization, massification to demassification, concentration to dispersal, rigidity to flexibility. However, there are others working within this framework who have stressed the elements of continuity between Fordism and its successor regime of accumulation. The work of Joachim Hirsch stands out as a particularly trenchant analysis of continuities in the mode of domination and control. In his account post-Fordism is emerging as a new system of "hyperindustrialization," characterized by the "microelectronic reorganization of Taylorism" and by the regulatory form of "authoritarian statism," which combines "decentralized and segmented corporatism" with new (and perhaps more flexible) technologies and strategies of repression and surveillance.[7]

The issue is clearly one of change and continuity, and this is a matter of disentangling different historical temporalities. Thus, although many have rightly focused on significant transformations in the structure and organization of the labor process, it is the case that forms of control, through the mobilization of information and communications resources, operate in terms of a longer periodicity.

Against those accounts that see the information society in terms of a technological revolution it is also important to emphasize that the appropriation of information and information resources has always been a constitutive aspect of capitalist societies quite outside of any technological context. The appropriation of knowledge (skill) in the factory, for example, may operate solely through hierarchical control. Similarly, at the level of the social totality there have been plenty of examples of totalitarianism to make us realize that states can oppress without benefit of computer technologies. Both here, and in wider contexts, organizational structures – culminating in bureaucratic institutions – may establish effective mechanisms for the control and management of information resources. The gathering, recording, aggregation, and exploitation of information can be – and has, of course, been – achieved on the basis of minimal technological support.

Our point is that the "Information Revolution" is inadequately conceived, as it is conventionally, as a question of technology and technological innovation. Rather it is better understood as a matter of differential (and unequal) access to, and control over, information resources. That is, far from being a technological issue, what should concern us is the management and control of information within and between groups. Raising this widens unavoidably the scope of discussions of social change, taking it far from "technology effects" considerations, at the same time as it, necessarily, politicizes the process of technological development itself by framing it as a matter of shifts in the availability of information. Conversely, attempts to divert analysis and debate into technical and technocratic channels serve to repress these substantial political questions.

In a similar way, the prevailing tendency to consider information and information technology chiefly in terms of economic growth, productivity, and planning again puts it in a strongly technical, calculative, and instrumental context (with the major issue being that of the allocation of wages and profits). Against this orthodoxy, our own approach focuses upon information and information technologies in terms of their political and cultural dimensions. In both these aspects what are raised are the complex relations among technology, information, and power. In the case of the former, what is on the agenda, in the workplace and in society as a whole, is the relationship between management and control. And in the case of the cultural dimension, what is of concern is the micro-politics of power, what Foucault calls the capillary forms of power's existence. What this raises is the shaping influence of information and communication technologies on the texture, pattern, organization, and routines of everyday life.[8] What is apparent, at both levels we believe, is the indissociable relation between information/knowledge and power.

In tracing the cultural and political contexts in which information and communications technologies have taken shape, we suggest that they have performed two distinct but related functions, both of which are absolutely central to the cohesion and reproduction of capitalist societies. On the one hand, they have been the mechanism for social management, planning, and administration; and, on the other, they have been at the heart of surveillance and control strategies. Our argument is that these two functions are closely interrelated and mutually reinforcing. To echo Foucault's words, it is not possible for social planning and administration to be exercised without surveillance, it is impossible for surveillance not to reinforce administrative cohesion, efficiency, and power.[9] There is no point in dreaming of a time when planning and management will be simply a technical and instrumental matter – the administration of things – and will cease to be embroiled in the business of power, surveillance, and control.

Planning and control

The recent work of Anthony Giddens throws light on this relationship between planning and control. He argues that the state must maintain an effective hold on both "allocative resources" (planning, administration) and "authoritative resources" (power, control). Central to this project, argues Giddens, is information gathering and storage, which "is central to the role of "authoritative resources" in the structuring of social systems spanning larger ranges of space and time than tribal cultures. Surveillance – control of information and superintendence of the activities of some groups by others – is in turn the key to the expansion of such resources."[10] If information-gathering, documentation, and surveillance are vital to this end, it is also the case, Giddens argues, that the regularized gathering, storage, and control of information is crucial for administrative "efficiency" and power.

In the modern nation state administrative/allocative control and authoritative control converge insofar as each comes to depend on the continuous, normalized, and increasingly centralized surveillance and monitoring of subject populations. Tendentially, moreover, allocative control comes to prevail through its ability to combine (and legitimate) both administrative and authoritative functions: "surveillance as the mobilizing of administrative power – through the storage and control of information – is the primary means of the concentration of authoritative resources involved in the information of the nation-state."[11] In advanced capitalist societies it is this administrative-technocratic machinery of surveillance that expresses the prevailing relations of power and designates the inherently totalitarian nature of the modern state. "The possibilities of totalitarian rule," Giddens writes, "depend upon the existence of societies in which the state can successfully penetrate the day-to-day activities of most of its subject population. This, in turn, presumes a high level of surveillance . . . the coding of information about and the supervision of the conduct of significant segments of the population."[12] It is, we shall go on to argue, precisely these possibilities that are opened up by the new information technologies.

Further evidence of the tendency toward control through surveillance and monitoring that Giddens identifies can be seen in the field of economic analysis. For instance, one way of conceptualizing transactions in the economic market place has been in terms of information theory. Thus, Hayek writes of the "price system as . . . a mechanism for communicating information"[13] and argues that "the problem of what is the best way of utilizing knowledge initially dispersed among all the people is at least one of the main problems of economic policy."[14] Hayek's own solution to this problem was, famously, to eschew central planning – "direction of the whole economic system according to one unified plan" – in favor of competition, which he refers to as "decentralised planning by many separate persons."[15] Other economists, however, have lived less comfortably with this "problem of the utilization of knowledge not given to anyone in its totality."[16] The tendency in the late twentieth century has been for the economy to assume ever greater complexity. The relation between the national economy and international markets; the relation between finance and industrial sectors; the management of technological innovation; the coordination of production and consumption; the internal articulation of dispersed multinational

PLAN AND CONTROL: TOWARDS A CULTURAL HISTORY

conglomerates – these all become pressing issues of economic management. Alfred Chandler has argued that this reflects a point in history "when the volume of economic activities reached a level that made administrative co-ordination more efficient and more profitable than market co-ordination"; a point at which "the visible hand of management replaced the invisible hand of market forces."[17] What becomes crucial is precisely the gathering in of dispersed knowledge, the concentration and centralization of information, and the elaboration of a unified plan. Economic management in the age of multinational capital necessarily tends toward that process of administrative control by a "directing mind" of the kind that Hayek[18] so despises. The necessity for effective and centralized information management becomes the preoccupation of an increasing number of economists. Thus, Charles Jonscher, referring to the "increase in the complexity of economic systems," refers to the enormous "organizational or informational task of co-ordinating the diverse steps in the production chain . . . [and] the number of trans-actions within and among productive units." "The largest untapped oppor-tunities for improving economic performance," he concludes, "lay in the area of information handling. Consequently large research and development resources began to be directed to the creation of technologies which process, store, transport and manipulate information."[19]

We are especially suspicious of the "information society" scenarios sketched by the likes of Daniel Bell,[20] where information/knowledge is represented as a beneficial and progressive social force. Information, we suggest, has long been a key component of regulation in the modern nation state and in capitalist economies. And the history of information management suggests that technocratic and economic exploitation should be understood within the wider context of its disciplinary and political deployment.[21] Particularly significant in this context has been the process whereby authoritative con-trol has become subsumed within the machinery of allocative control: power expresses itself through the discipline of calculative and rational social man-agement and administration. Historically, this process has occurred without significant technological mediation. Increasingly, however, new technologies are drawn upon: because as Lewis Mumford has argued, "mechanization, automation, cybernetic direction" overcome the system's weakness, "its original dependence upon resistant, sometimes actively disobedient servo-mechanisms, still human enough to harbour purposes that do not always coincide with those of the system."[22] Whether bureaucratic or technological, however, the thrust of administrative control is toward extensive and intensive documentation and surveillance of internal populations. "With the mechanisms of information processing (the bureaucracy using people; the computer using machines), the ability to monitor behaviour is extended considerably," Mark Poster argues: "The mode of information enormously extends the reach of normalizing surveillance, constituting new modes of domination that have yet to be studied."[23] This disciplinary and calculative

263

management of existence in advanced capitalist societies transforms itself into their culture, their way of life, their prevailing social relations.

The dark side of the Information Revolution

We would stress that the logic of planning and control has always been contested. In an environment of increasing complexity and uncertainty, the urge to control may become more intensive and more neurotic, but it does not, for that, become more cohesive.[24] The logic of control invokes that of resistance. Populations are never simply and absolutely fixed and compartmentalized; they remain obdurately fluid and mobile. The power of resistance is an integral and dynamic aspect of the control system, and it would be quite wrong to regard it as only a residual force. Nonetheless, if we do not underestimate the significance of this counter-force,[25] then any balanced consideration should encourage us also not to underestimate the tenacity and resourcefulness of diverse control agencies. Thus, in the present context of a potential historical transition beyond Fordism, it seems to us that there are also important transformations in the modalities of surveillance and control. While control is often understood as an external and directly repressive force, its real dynamics are more complex and insidious, and, in fact, ideally exploit the compliance and even the creativity of its subjects. There are clear signs that, after a period of "desubordination" and destabilization, the present period is very much about the reassertion, and the streamlining, of control strategies. This is apparent in the image of the new model worker, the flexible, compliant, self-motivated, and self-controlling worker; and also in the new model student, again self-directed, flexible, enthusiastic, and docile.[26] As cognitive intrusion and surveillance become increasingly normalized, pervasive, and insidious, so does the logic of control – of power through visibility of "knowability" – become internalized.

The following sections aim to explore this dark underside of the information revolution, and to do this on the basis that serious, rather than just well-meaning, political responses are only possible if we confront, not just the repressive potential of information/knowledge, but more significantly the integral and necessary relation between repressive and possible emancipatory dimensions. In the following discussion we draw attention to the administrative and disciplinary exploitation of information resources and technologies, first in a discussion of the role of information in the economic contexts of production, markets, and consumption, and then through an account of the relations among information technologies, communications, and the political system. Such discussion remains selective and incomplete. Our ambition here is to provide an overview, a cartography of the information society, to trace the cohesion in what might seem to be quite disparate developments. Whilst the exploitation of information/

PLAN AND CONTROL: TOWARDS A CULTURAL HISTORY

knowledge has a considerable history, our argument here is that the really significant moment occurs early in the twentieth century. It is at this time, and particularly in the complex matrix of forces surrounding the Scientific Management of Frederick Winslow Taylor, that the information society may be said to have been truly inaugurated.[27]

The new machine: Scientific Management and consumer capitalism

Though the image of the Industrial Revolution is one of vast, impersonal mills in which multitudinous "hands" were ruthlessly exploited by distant capitalists, the reality was that most work – arduous though it undeniably was – took place in small units of perhaps a dozen or so employees overseen by a master. It was in the later years of the century that size became an issue when the logic of competition and cartels brought into being the kind of corporate Leviathans that have dominated the industrial landscape ever since. With direct supervision of labor now increasingly impossible, what became necessary was a mechanism for coordinating and integrating the complex, fragmented processes and divisions of production. It was here that the philosophy and practice of F. W. Taylor was so crucial, with its application of Scientific Management to production: expert direction by engineers, factory planning, time and motion study, standardization, the intensive division of labor. The keyword in the application of engineering principles to the industrial system of production was efficiency. Taylor "proposed a neat, understandable world in the factory, an organization of men whose acts would be planned, co-ordinated, and controlled under continuous expert direction. His system had some of the inevitableness and objectivity of science and technology."[28] Factory production was to become a matter of efficient and scientific management: the planning and administration of workers and machines alike as components of one big machine.

Now, two observations here relate to our broader argument. First, within the Taylor system, efficient production and administration (planning) is indissociably related to control over the workforce. Although these two aspects are often treated as distinct (and emphasis is often placed on the disciplinary function), we would argue that planning and control are each an integral part of the other: efficiency translates into domination and the engineering of people becomes subsumed within the engineering of things. The second point is that administration and control are a function of managerial appropriation of skills, knowledge, and information within the workplace. According to Taylor, workers should be relieved of the work of planning, and all "brain work" should be centered in the factory's planning department. In Anthony Giddens's terms, the collation and integration of information manifests itself in terms of both administration and surveillance. It is this dual articulation of information/knowledge for "efficient" planning and for control that is at the heart of Scientific Management, and which, in our view, characterizes it as the original Information Revolution.

Importantly, Taylorism as a system of factory control does not depend on technological support: information gathering and surveillance do not depend to any large extent upon information technologies. Its capacity to "reduce the labour of the ordinary employee to an automatic perfection of routine"[29] is a consequence of organizational forms and of direct managerial intervention, of technique rather than technology. As such it may be inscribed within Mumford's history of the non-technological megamachine – the military is a paramount example – which is "an invisible structure composed of living, but rigid, human parts, each assigned to his special office, role, and task, to make possible the immense work-output and grand design of this great collective organization."[30] If, however, this form of megatechnics, which replaces interpersonal modes of control with more rational and calculative procedures, establishes a certain degree of automaticity, it is the case that machinery can implement this principle more effectively. Insofar as it subordinates unreliable human components to the precise routines of machinery, technology enhances both efficiency and control.[31] It is this realization that constitutes Henry Ford's major contribution to the scientific management of production. Not only did Ford appropriate information/knowledge within the production process, but he also incorporated it into the technology of his production lines to achieve technical control over the labor process.[32]

Although we can touch on it only fleetingly here, the subsequent history of capitalist industry, we would argue, has been a matter of the deepening and extension of information gathering and surveillance to the combined end of planning and controlling the production process, and it is into this context that the new communications and information technologies of the 1980s are inserting themselves. Thus, computer numerical control, advanced automation, robotics and so on, intensify this principle of technical control. And the new technologies now spreading through office and service work threaten to "Taylorize" intellectual labor itself. Managements have carefully analyzed their information routines and requirements and are aiming to introduce information technologies that will make information flows more effective, efficient, and cost-effective.[33] The new technologies are also crucial in managing and coordinating ever more complex organizational and productive structures. The establishment of a system of transnational corporations depends upon effective computer communications systems to handle financial transactions, corporate directives, and organizational coordination.

Yet Taylorism is more than just a doctrine of factory management. It became, in our view, a new social philosophy, a new principle of social revolution, and a new imaginary institution in society. Outside the factory gates, Scientific Management became a new form of social control, not just in the dominative sense of this term, but also in the more neutral sense of the "capacity of a social organization to regulate itself."[34] Taylor and his various epigones believed that the idea of rational, scientific, and efficient management and regulation could be extended beyond the workplace to other social activities. They spoke of "social efficiency," by which they meant "social harmony" under the leadership of "competent" experts.[35]

In 1916, Henry L. Gantt took a "dramatic step from the planning room of the factory to the world at large," with the formation of the "New Machine," an organization of engineers and sympathetic reformers under Gantt's leadership, which announced its intention to acquire political as well as economic power.[36] The association is made between society and the machine; society is to be regulated and maintained by social engineers. Experts and technocrats are to be the orchestrators of a programmed society.[37] As in the factory, this calculative and instrumental regime entails a combined process of administration/planning and surveillance, and depends upon the centralized appropriation and disposal of information resources. It implies "the intelligence of the whole," and this in the form of instrumental, theoretical, quantified data. The legitimacy of technocratic rule is justified by the command of knowledge/information: it assumes "an objective and universal rationality based on superior knowledge."[38]

A further legitimating aspect of Scientific Management was its undoubted capacity to increase productivity, economic growth, and, consequently, social wealth. As Charles Maier argues, it promised "an escape from zero-sum conflict" between labor and capital: what Taylorism "offered – certainly within the plant, and ultimately, according to its author, in all spheres of government and social life – was the elimination of scarcity and constraint."[39] Inherent in mass production was the system of mass consumption and the promise of the consumer Utopia. In Scientific Management was a broad social philosophy, a promise of reform through growth and expansion, which had great appeal to social theorists and politicians of the Progressive era (and coincided, in Britain, with Fabian principles and beliefs).

This complex and expanding system of mass production and mass consumption could only be coordinated and regulated if the criteria of efficiency and optimality were extended from the factory to the system as a whole (the social factory). The system of consumption, particularly, must be brought under the practices of Scientific Management. It became increasingly apparent that both economic and social stability depended upon continuous and regular consumption, and upon the matching of demand to cycles and patterns of production. Ultimately what was required was the Scientific Management of need, desire, and fantasy, and their reconstruction in terms of the commodity form.[40] Thus, Taylorist principles of calculation must extend into the marketing sphere.[41] The steady movement of such commodities as clothing, cigarettes, household furnishings and appliances, toiletries or processed foods required the creation of ways of reaching customers, taking heed of their needs, wants, and dispositions, and responding by persuasion and even redesign of products to make them more or newly attractive.[42]

In this project of systematizing the management of consumption, it was Henry Ford's counterpart at General Motors, Alfred P. Sloan who played an important and formative role. It was Sloan who, in the twenties, introduced installment selling, used-car trade-ins, annual model changes, styling and brand image, to the automobile industry.[43] The objective was both to integrate production and demand, and also to intensify and "speed up" consumption. As such, "Sloanism" exemplified the principle of modern marketing, with its ambitions toward the Scientific Management of commodity markets and consumer behavior.

The system of mass consumption (and the consumer society) is dependent upon the collection, aggregation, and dissemination of information. One consequence of this imperative to accumulate data on patterns of consumption was the rise of market-research organizations, specializing in the aggregation of demographic and socioeconomic information, and in the detailed recording of trends and patterns in sales. The embryonic company, International Business Machines, quickly developed technologies to service record-conscious and surveillance-conscious corporations. Henry C. Link, a polemical advocate of scientific marketing, described the relation between early forms of information technology and the informational needs of business:

> The most highly developed technique for measuring buying behaviour is that made possible by the electric sorting and tabulating machines. These ingenious devices have made it feasible to record and classify the behaviour of the buying public as well as the behaviour of those who serve that public, on a scale heretofore impracticable. Whereas by ordinary methods hundreds of transactions may be recorded, by this method thousands may be recorded with greater ease. Not only have comprehensive records been made possible but, what is more important, the deduction from these records of important summaries and significant facts have been made relatively easy. The technique developed by various merchants, with the use of these devices . . . is the quantitative study and analysis of human behaviour in the nth degree.[44]

It is also vital, of course, to convey information to the consumer, and this informational task gave rise most obviously and pre-eminently to advertising (though it was also evident in packaging and branding commodities and in their display). In a paean to American productivism, David Potter suggests that "advertising [is] an instrument of social control"; it is, he continues, "the only institution which we have for instilling new needs, for training

PLAN AND CONTROL: TOWARDS A CULTURAL HISTORY

people to act as consumers, for altering men's values, and thus for hastening their adjustment to potential abundance."[45] Through their exploitation of information resources and channels, the early advertising corporations were searching "for a means of translating Frederick W. Taylor's ideal of scientific management into the selling and distribution processes."[46] What became apparent was that information resources (and information and communications technologies in their early incarnations) were the life-blood of modern corporations and of the national and international business system.

During the second and third decades of the century, these developments were coming together to constitute a more systematic, calculative, and rationalized management of economic life. There was a concern with information management, with an emphasis on quantification and on professional and "scientific" procedures. Thus, in advertising, concepts from psychological research were introduced and campaigns more thoroughly prepared by pre-testing and careful analysis of advertising copy and presentation; broadcast ratings were promoted and refined to differentiate types of audience, patterns of behavior, and preferences;[47] public relations developed as "the attempt, by information, persuasion, and adjustment, to engineer public support," and quite self-consciously proclaimed that "engineering methods can be applied in tackling our problems."[48] Informing these trends toward more effective control and planning was the faith that innovations were motivated, not by vulgar self-interest, but by the search for efficiency, expertise, and rationality in the administration of both things and people.

It is in the context of this historical outline that we can begin to understand some aspects of the current "Information Revolution." Our argument is that what is commonly taken as innovation and "revolution" is, in fact no more – and no less – than the extension and intensification of processes set under way some seventy or so years ago. It was the exponents of Scientific Management, in its broadest sense, who unleased an Information Revolution. And particularly important here were the strategies of the "consumption engineers"[49] to regulate economic transactions and consumer behavior. It was these advocates of big business who first turned to the "rational" and "scientific" exploitation of information in the wider society, and it is their descendents – the multinational advertisers, market researchers, opinion pollers, data brokers, and so on – who are at the heart of information politics in the eighties. It is they who are promoting and annexing cable systems, communications satellites, telecommunications links, computer resources, and so on. Their objective is the elaboration of what has been termed a global "network market place"[50] in which ever more social functions and activities come "on-line" (education, shopping, entertainment, etc.). What is new in their enterprise is its scale, and also its greater reliance on advanced information and communications technologies to render the scientific management of consumer life more efficient and automatic. The objective of a cybernetic market place, and the fantasy of society as a

HISTORY AND PERSPECTIVES

producing and consuming machine, goes back, however, to Taylor, Gantt, and the rest.

World marketing in the era of multinational capital demands global market research and advertising, the ability to undertake surveillance and monitoring of markets and to launch persuasive propaganda on behalf of a particular product or corporation. The information and intelligence agencies that undertake these tasks of "mind management" are themselves transnational enterprises and increasingly integrated across the whole information business. Thus, Saatchi and Saatchi, the world's number one advertising agency following its takeover of the Ted Bates group, has, during its meteoric rise, established skills and expertise in public relations, market research, management consultancy and sales promotion as well as in its central advertising concerns. The strategy of Saatchi and Saatchi is explicit to direct its informational expertise toward the "multinational advertisers [who are moving] towards greater co-ordination in their international marketing activities"[51] and who account for 80% of America's top spenders on advertising. World marketing necessitates a major strategy of surveillance and intelligence: the "analysis of all demographic, cultural and media trends" so that marketers "can survey the world battlefield for their brands, observe the deployment of their forces, and plan their international advertising and marketing in a coherent and logical way."[52] The important point, made by a Saatchi employee, is that "a coordinated approach to multinational brand marketing is only as good as the information which supports it, information about consumer habits, consumer perceptions and attitudes."[53]

The spread of global marketing is manifest, not only in new information politics, but also in its impact on communications media. The press, radio, and television have long been shaped, often in decisive ways, by the pressures of advertising, and it seems likely that the new information and communications technologies will be harnassed to the same consumerist ends.[54] The possibilities exist now both for global advertising and also for more targeted advertising reaching particular segments of the audience ("narrowcasting"). Cable television is particularly important here in that its two-way communication facility allows (and, indeed, requires) the recording and surveillance of precise viewing habits. This routine logging of consumer preferences can also be enhanced by the use of such devices as "people meters," through which each member of a monitored family is assigned a personal code which they "tap in" when viewing and "tap out" when leaving the set.[55] Yet a further extension of this surveillance and information gathering is the recording of data from supermarket check-out scanners in order to establish a basis for designing specifically "addressed" commercials to particular consumer groups. Similarly, the growth in credit cards permits the monitoring of purchasers and gives access to information about what people buy, at what price, how regularly, where, and how readily they foot the bill. Already there are gargantuan data banks holding information on credit worthiness: Infolink, for example, has records on the entire electoral register of 42 million persons, which it processes at the rate of 48,000 transactions an hour.[56]

What the new technologies enhance, we would suggest, is the Scientific Management of marketing. "Teleshopping," global and targeted advertising, and electronic market research surveillance, all combine to establish a more rationalized and "efficient" network market place.[57] Information, surveillance, efficiency: the very principles of Taylorism become intensified, extended, and automated through the application of new communications and information technologies. One fundamental aspect of the "communications revolution" has been to refine that planning and control of consumer behavior that were already inherent in the early philosophy of Scientific Management.

From public sphere to cybernetic state

The growth of a "programmed" market, of a regulated and coded consumer society, is a fundamentally cultural phenomenon. The stimulation of needs, the recording of tastes, the surveillance of consumption, all reflect a more rationalized and regulated way of life. (This does not, of course, imply the necessary success of such strategies, nor does it deny the ability of individuals to derive pleasure and creativity from consumer goods.) We want now to turn to a second set of forces that have been central to the historical development of the "information society." We are referring to the role of information and communications resources in the political process. Here too we can trace the tendency towards combined planning and control, and here too this has been of profound significance for the cultural life of modernity.[58]

We have already referred to Anthony Giddens's argument that the state, and particularly the nation-state, has always been propelled into the business of surveillance and information gathering. Giddens suggests that "storage of authoritative resources is the basis of the surveillance activities of the state," and such surveillance, he argues, entails "the collation of information relevant to state control of the conduct of its subject population, and the direct supervision of that conduct." The storage of authoritative resources and control depends upon "the retention and control of information or knowledge."[59] Information and communications capabilities have been fundamental to the state and the political sphere in a number of respects. First, they have been indispensable prerequisites for administrating and coordinating – maintaining the cohesion and integrity – of complex social structures. Secondly, they have played an important part in policing and controlling "deviant" members of the internal population, and in the surveillance of external (potential enemy) populations. And, thirdly, they have been central to the democratic process of political debate in the public sphere. In the following discussion we want to outline the specific shape and force that these various information functions have assumed in political life during this century.

Our historical account of the relation between information/knowledge and the political system gives rise to a number of observations that can usefully be detailed at the outset. First, we should emphasize that neither planning nor surveillance depends upon technological support. Thus, Theodore Roszak notes that the English Utilitarians recognized, early in the nineteenth century, "the persuasive force of facts and figures in the modern world": "All the essential elements of the cult of information are there – the façade of ethical neutrality, the air of scientific rigor, the passion for technocratic control. Only one thing is missing: the computer."[60] And the principles of disciplinary surveillance, too, have non-technological and Benthamite origins in the architecture of the Panopticon. The issue we are addressing is fundamentally about relations of power, though, having said that, we must emphasize that technologies have increasingly been deployed in the twentieth century to render the exercise of power more efficient and automatic. Our second point is that the functions of administration and control have increasingly coalesced and regulatory and disciplinary tendencies have increasingly expressed themselves through the calculative and "rational" machinery of administration. Thirdly, we argue that the idea of a democratic "conversation" in the public sphere has given way to that of the instrumental and "efficient" Scientific Management of political life. Along with this, surveillance has become associated with a transformation of the political identity and rights of the internal population, and comes to be directed against the "enemy within." Finally, we argue that, although there has always been an information politics, a particularly important moment in these processes occurred early in the twentieth century and was associated with the project of Taylorism.

To clarify these arguments, let us begin with the ideal role of information and communications in democratic political theory. In his classic account of the emergence of the bourgeois public sphere, Habermas describes the historical convergence of democratic principles, the new channels of communication and publicity, and the Enlightenment faith in Reason.[61] The public sphere is the forum, open equally to all citizens, in which matters of general and political interest are debated and ideas exchanged. It remains distinct and separate from the state, and, indeed, insofar as it is the locus of critical reasoning, it operates as a curb on state power. The fundamental principles are that "opinions on matters of concern to the nation and publicly expressed by men [sic] outside the government . . . should influence or determine the actions, personnel, or structure of their government," and that "the government will reveal and explain its decisions in order to enable people outside the government to think and talk about those decisions."[62] Such democratic discussion within the frontiers of the extended nation state

PLAN AND CONTROL: TOWARDS A CULTURAL HISTORY

depends necessarily upon an infra-structure of communication and publicity. Indeed, it is only on this basis that the idea of a public can have any meaning. It is through these media that channels of communication and discourse, and access to information resources, are assured. On this basis the public use of reasoning could be assured. Gouldner describes the bourgeois public sphere as "one of the great historical advances in rationality."[63]

That was the aspiration, though many critics of Habermas have doubted whether the bourgeois public sphere – and the "ideal speech situation" that it presupposes – were ever significant historical realities. For the present argument, however, these objections are not important. What concerns us now are the subsequent transformations of the public sphere, which do have manifest historical palpability. One process that occurs is the intrusion of market and commodity relations into the public sphere, and this results in the transformation of reasoning into consumption.[64] But perhaps even more important has been that process through which political debate has come to be regulated by large corporate bodies and by the state ("refeudalisation" is Habermas's term for it). The "public" is then "superseded, managed and manipulated by large organizations which arrange things among themselves on the basis of technical information and their relative power positions," and what results is "the dominance of corporative forms within which discussion is not public but is increasingly limited to technicians and bureaucrats," with the public now becoming "a condition of organizational action, to be instrumentally managed – i.e. manipulated."[65] What Habermas and Gouldner both discern is the technocratic and administrative rationalization of political life, the Scientific Management of the public sphere and of public information and communication. Gouldner goes further, however, in recognizing that this rationalizing tendency is, ironically, already present in the very foundations of the public sphere. He demonstrates that "the means to bring about the communicative competence that Habermas requires for rational discourse presuppose precisely the centralization and strengthening of that state apparatus which increasingly tends to stifle rather than facilitate the universalization of the rational, uninhibited discourse necessary for any democratic society."[66]

The most important cultural change with regard to the public sphere is the historical shift from a principle of political and public rationality, to one of "scientific" and administrative rationalization. As Anthony Giddens argues, there are problems in the very scale and complexity of the modern nation state. Social integration depends upon a strengthening and centralization of the state, and one aspect of this is the development and regulation of communication and information resources. The rationale and justification of such tendencies become a "technical" matter of "efficient" management and administration over the extended territory of the nation state. On this basis, political debate, exchange, and disagreement in the public sphere can come to seem "inefficient," an inhibiting and frictive obstacle to the rational management of society. Rational and informed discourse in the public sphere gives way to rational, scientific management of society by technicians and bureaucrats. In this process, the very nature and criteria of rationality have been transformed. In the first case, appeal is made to the reason and judgment of the individual citizen. In the second, it is made to the scientific rationality of the expert, and to the rationality of the social system. The more "objective" rationality of scientific management seems to promise a more "efficient" democratic order than the often inarticulate and irrational citizen. Reason thus becomes instrumental, the mechanism for administrating, and thereby effectively controlling, the complex social totality. The Enlightenment ideal of Reason gives birth to what Castoriadis calls the "rationalist ideology": the illusion of omnipotence, the supremacy of economic "calculus," the belief in the "rational" organization of society, the new religion of "science" and technology.[67]

This technocratic tendency is, of course, reflected in the positivist philosophy of Saint-Simon and Comte, which, as Gouldner persuasively argues, was inimical to the ideal of a politics open to all and conducted in public, and which maintained that public affairs were in fact scientific and technological problems, to be resolved by professionals and experts.[68] But it is with a later form of practical sociology, that associated with the extension of the principles of Scientific Management to the wider society, that such social engineering assumed its most sustained form and the systematic exploitation of information and communications resources was taken up in earnest. And an emblematic figure here was Walter Lippmann. Scientific Management, especially when placed within the conditions of industrial democracy, embodied in the factory regime what these progressive thinkers such as Walter Lippmann envisioned within society at large.[69]

Lippmann points to two dilemmas of the modern, mass society.[70] The first refers to the political competence of citizens in democratic society: "The ideal of the omnicompetent, sovereign citizen is, in my opinion, such a false ideal. It is unattainable. The pursuit of it is misleading. The failure to produce it has produced the current disenchantment."[71] The second dilemma is that society has attained "a complexity now so great as to be humanly unmanageable."[72] The implication is that central government has been compelled to assume responsibility for the control and coordination of this increasingly diffuse social structure. And this entails "the need for interposing some form of expertness between the private citizen and the vast environment in which he is entangled."[73] As in the Taylorist factory, this depends on "systematic intelligence and information control"; the gathering of social knowledge, Lippmann argues, must necessarily become "the normal accompaniment of action."[74] If social control is to be effective, the control of information and communication channels is imperative. With the scientific management of social and political life through the centralization of communications and intelligence activities, "persuasion . . . become[s] a

PLAN AND CONTROL: TOWARDS A CULTURAL HISTORY

self-conscious art and a regular organ of popular government" and the "manufacture of consent improve[s] enormously in technique, because it is now based on analysis rather than rule of thumb."[75]

What is especially important here, we believe, is the association of public opinion theory with the study of propaganda in contemporary political discourse. Propaganda has commonly, and common-sensibly, been seen as inimical to rational political debate, as a force that obstructs public reasoning. In the context, however, of the social complexity and citizen "incompetence" observed by Lippmann, propaganda assumed the guise of a more positive social force in the eyes of many social and political thinkers in the early decades of the century. An increasingly pragmatic and "realistic" appraisal of the political process suggested that "in a world of competing political doctrines, the partisans of democratic government cannot depend solely upon appeal to reason or abstract liberalism."[76] It became clear that "propaganda, as the advocacy of ideas and doctrines, has a legitimate and desirable part to play in our democratic system."[77] The very complexity of the modern nation state is such that a "free market" of ideas and debate must be superseded by the management and orchestration of public opinion. Harold Lasswell makes the point succinctly: "The modern conception of social management is profoundly affected by the propagandist outlook. Concerted action for public ends depends upon a certain concentration of motives . . . Propaganda is surely here to stay; the modern world is peculiarly dependent upon it for the co-ordination of atomized components in times of crisis and for the conduct of large scale 'normal' operations."[78]

Propaganda is understood here in terms of the regulation and control of channels of communication and information in democratic societies. At one level, this is a matter of disseminating and broadcasting certain categories of information.[79] At another level, it is a matter of restricting access to specific categories of information. As Walter Lippmann makes clear, "without some form of censorship, propaganda in the strict sense of the word is impossible. In order to conduct a propaganda there must be some barrier between the public and the event."[80] For Lippman, propaganda and censorship are complementary as forms of persuasion and public opinion management. There has been a shift from the idea of an informed and reasoning public, to an acceptance of the massage and manipulation of public opinion by the technicians of public relations. The state function has increasingly come to subsume and regulate the democratic principle; and this to the point that it now seems indissociable from that principle.[81]

We have spent some time in outlining the development of rationalized political management and information control because we feel, again, that this is an important historical context for the development of new information and communications technologies. Through the impetus of Scientific Management, and the development of propaganda and public opinion research, it became clear that social planning and control depended upon the exploitation of information resources and technologies. This was the historical moment of the Information Revolution. The most recent technological developments – space and satellite technologies, data processing, telecommunications – only extend what was in reality a fundamentally political "revolution" in information (and communication) management. It was this historical conjuncture that spawned the "modern" industries and bureaucracies of public relations, propaganda, public (and private) opinion polling, news management, image production and advocacy, political advertising, censorship and "official" secrecy, think tanks, and so on. Innovations in the eighties came only with the increase in scale and the exploitation of technological resources.

An important rationale for the deployment of new information technologies is, then, the regulation of political life and the engineering of public opinion. Jeremy Tunstall describes the technological streamlining of political management in the United States: election campaigns "are now managed via computers"; electronic mailing permits "separate mailing shots... targetted at particular occupational groups or types of housing area"; electronic databases provide political and demographic information.[82] In Britain, too, electioneering is increasingly a matter of electronic techniques, with the development of software programs to analyze voter groups and behavior, the growth of targetted mail, and computerized planning of campaigns.[83] The centrality of information control became apparent also in the defeat of the mineworkers during 1984–85, which owed much to the National Coal Board's use of private opinion polls and of modern communications and public relations strategies to bypass the unions.[84]

Conclusion

"Is closer and closer social control the inevitable price of 'progress,' a necessary concomitant of the continued development of modern social forms?"[85] We believe that this is indeed the case. Against those who see the new communications technologies as the basis for a coming "communications era,"[86] and the new information technologies as the panacea for our present "Age of Ignorance,"[87] our own argument is that their development has, in fact, been closely associated with processes of social management and control. The scale and complexity of the modern nation state has made communications and information resources (and technologies) central to the maintenance of political and administrative cohesion.

The "Information Revolution" is, then, not simply and straightforwardly a matter of technological "progress," of a new technological or industrial revolution. It is significant, rather, for the new matrix of political and cultural forces that it supports. And a crucial dimension here is that of organizational form and structure. Communication and information resources (and technologies) set the conditions and limits to the scale and nature of

PLAN AND CONTROL: TOWARDS A CULTURAL HISTORY

organizational possibilities. What they permit is the development of complex and large-scale bureaucratic organizations, and also of extended corporate structures that transcend the apparent limits of space and time (transnational corporations). They also constitute the nervous system of the modern state and guarantee its cohesion as an expansive organizational form. Insofar as they guarantee and consolidate these essential power structures in modern society, information and communication are fundamental to political-administrative regulation, and consequently to the social and cultural experience of modernity.

The exploitation of information resources and technologies has expressed itself, politically and culturally, through the dual tendency towards social planning and management, on the one hand, and surveillance and control, on the other. In historical terms, this can be seen as the apotheosis of Lewis Mumford's megamachine: technology now increasingly fulfils what previously depended upon bureaucratic organization and structure. But the central historical reference point is the emergence, early in the twentieth century, of Scientific Management (as a philosophy both of industrial production and of social reproduction). It was at this moment that "scientific" planning and management moved beyond the factory to regulate the whole way of life. At this time, the "gathering of social knowledge" became "the normal accompaniment of action," and the manufacture of consent, through propaganda and opinion management, was increasingly "based on analysis rather than on rule of thumb."[88] If, through Scientific Management, the planning and administration of everyday life became pervasive, it also became the preeminent form and expression of social control. Planning and management were, necessarily and indissociably, a process of surveillance and of manipulation and persuasion. To the extent that these administrative and dominative information strategies were first developed on a systematic basis, it was at this historical moment, we believe, that the Information Revolution' was unleashed. New information and communications technologies have most certainly advanced, and automated, these combined information and intelligence activities, but they remain essentially refinements of what was fundamentally a political-administrative "revolution."

Recent innovations in information and communications technologies have generally been discussed from a narrow technological or economic perspective. It has been a matter of technology assessment or of the exploitation of new technologies to promote industrial competitiveness and economic growth. This, in the light of our discussion, seems a partial and blinkered vision. The absolutely central question to be raised in the context of the "Information Revolution" of the eighties, is, we believe, the relation between knowledge/information and the system of political and corporate power. For some, knowledge is inherently and self-evidently a benevolent force, and improvements in the utilization of knowledge are demonstrably the way to ensure social progress.[89] Information is treated as an instrumental and technical resource that will ensure the rational and efficient management of society. It is a matter of social engineering by knowledge professionals and information specialists and technocrats. For us, the problems of the "information society" are more substantial, complex, and oblique.

This, of course, raises difficult political and philosophical issues. These are the issues that Walter Lippmann comes up against when he recognizes in the Great Society "that centralization of power which deprives [citizens] of control over the use of that power," and when he confronts the disturbing awareness that "the problems that vex democracy seem to be unmanageable by democratic methods."[90] They are the issues that Lewis Mumford addresses when he argues that "the tension between small-scale association and large-scale organization, between personal autonomy and institutional regulation, between remote control and diffused local intervention, has now created a critical situation."[91] And they are the monumental issues that concern Castoriadis in his analysis of instrumental reason and the "rationalist ideology," those "myths which, more than money or weapons, constitute the most formidable obstacles in the way of the reconstruction of human society."[92]

Among the significant issues to be raised by the new information technologies are their relation to social forms of organization, their centrality to structures of political power, and their role in the cultural logic of consumer capitalism. Sociological analysis is naive, we believe, when it treats the new telecommunications, space, video, and computing technologies as innocent technical conceptions and looks hopefully to a coming, post-industrial Utopia. Better to look back to the past, to the entwined histories of reason, knowledge, and technology, and to their relation to the economic development of capitalism and the political and administrative system of the modern nation state.

Acknowledgments

We would like to thank Maureen McNeil and the anomymous referees of *Theory and Society* for their helpful and constructive comments.

Notes

1 Alexander King, "For Better or For Worse: The Benefits and Risks of Information Technology," in N. Bjorrn-Anderson *et al.*, *Information Society: For Richer, For Poorer* (Amsterdam: North-Holland, 1982).
2 Jacques Maisonrouge, "Putting Information to Work for People," *Intermedia*, 12(2) March, 1984.
3 Information Technology Advisory Panel, *Making a Business of Information* (London: HMSO, September 1983).

PLAN AND CONTROL: TOWARDS A CULTURAL HISTORY

4 Tom Stonier, *The Wealth of Information* (London: Thames Methuen, 1983).

5 Fritz Machlup, *Knowledge: Its Creation, Distribution, and Economic Significance, vol. 3: The Economics of Information and Human Capital* (Princeton: Princeton University Press, 1984).

6 In referring throughout this essay to capitalist societies, we leave open the question of how much these ideas relate, or do not relate, to other social forms. Nonetheless, it would be hard to deny that the impulse to "command and control" is very highly developed in state socialist societies where totalitarianism is most evident. Some commentators might seize on this convergence of East and West to suggest that the increase in surveillance and computer communications technologies is indicative of a neutral technological progress or the necessity of control in advanced societies. We would refute such reasoning, pointing to the absence of consideration of relations of power in these perspectives.

7 Joachim Hirsch, "Fordismus and Postfordismus: die gegenwärtige gesellschaftliche Krise und ihre Folgen," *Politische Vierteljahresschrift*, 26(2), 1985; Joachim Hirsch, "Auf den Wege zum Postfordismus? Die aktuelle Neuformierung des Kapitalismus und ihre politischen Folgen," *Das Argument*, (151), 1985.

8 Kevin Robins and Frank Webster, "Cybernetic Capitalism: Information, Technology, Everyday Life," in V. Mosco and J. Wasko, editors, *The Political Economy of Information* (Madison: University of Wisconsin Press, 1988), 44–75.

9 Cf. "Knowledge and power are each an integral part of the other, and there is no point in dreaming of a time when knowledge will cease to be dependent on power. . . . It is not possible for power to be exercised without knowledge, it is impossible for knowledge not to engender power." Michael Foucault, "Prison Talk: An Interview," *Radical Philosophy*, no. 16, Spring 1977, 15.

10 Anthony Giddens, *The Nation State and Violence* (Cambridge: Polity Press, 1985), 2.

11 Ibid., 181.

12 Ibid., 302.

13 F. A. Hayek, "The Use of Knowledge in Society," *American Economic Review*, 35(4), 1945, 526.

14 Ibid., 520.

15 Ibid., 521.

16 Ibid., 520.

17 Alfred D. Chandler, *The Visible Hand: The Managerial Revolution in American Business* (Cambridge, Mass.: The Belknap Press, 1977), 8, 12.

18 F. A. Hayek, "Economics and Knowledge," *Economica*, 4, February, 52.

19 Charles Jonscher, "Information Resources and Economic Productivity," *Information Economics and Policy*, 1(1), 1983, 21, 15.

20 Kevin Robins and Frank Webster, "Information as Capital: A Critique of Daniel Bell," in J. D. Slack and F. Fejes, editors, *The Ideology of the Information Age* (Norwood, New Jersey: Alblex, 1987), 95–117.

21 This is not, of course, to imply the necessary effectiveness of technocratic rule. Technocracy probably always approximates more to what S. M. Miller calls "pseudo-technocratic Society." See S. M. Miller, "The Coming of Pseudo-Technocratic Society," *Sociological Inquiry*, 46(3–4), 1976. And the "human components" always remain recalcitrant and resistant in the face of attempted social engineering.

22 Lewis Mumford, "Authoritarian and Democratic Technics," *Technology and Culture*, 5, 1964, 5.

23 Mark Poster, *Foucault, Marxism and History* (Cambridge: Polity Press, 1984), 103, 115.

HISTORY AND PERSPECTIVES

24 Scott Lash and John Urry, *The End of Organized Capitalism* (Cambridge: Polity Press, 1987).

25 David F. Noble, *Forces of Production* (New York: Alfred A. Knopf, 1984); Kevin Robins and Frank Webster, "Luddism: New Technology and the Critique of Political Economy," in L. Levidow and B. Young, editors, *Science, Technology and the Labour Process*, vol. 2 (London: Free Association Books, 1985), 9–48.

26 John Holloway, "The Red Rose of Nissan," *Capital and Class*, (32), Summer 1987; Kevin Robins and Frank Webster, *The Technical Fix: Education, Computers and Industry* (London: Macmillan, 1989), ch. 7.

27 See Frank Webster and Kevin Robins, *Information Technology: A Luddite Analysis* (Norwood, N.S.: Ablex, 1986), Part Three. James R. Beniger, *The Control Revolution: Technological Origins of the Information Society* (Cambridge: Harvard University Press, 1986) offers a parallel argument to ours, that the Information Revolution was essentially completed by the thirties. However, his perspective is one of sociological functionalism, arguing that the "control revolution" that creates the Information Society stems from the "needs" of "industrialization." We reject such technological determinism, which is devoid of any account of the dynamics of interests, values, and contestations in the genesis of the Information Society.

28 Samuel Haber, *Efficiency and Uplift: Scientific Management in the Progressive Era, 1890–1920* (Chicago: University of Chicago Press, 1964), xi.

29 J. A. Hobson, "Scientific Management," *Sociological Review*, 6(3), July, 1913, 198.

30 Lewis Mumford, *The Myth of the Machine: Technics and Human Development* (London: Seeker and Warburg, 1967), 189.

31 Michael Burawoy, "Toward a Marxist Theory of the Labor Process," *Politics and Society*, 8(3–4), 1978, 294.

32 Richard Edwards, *Contested Terrain: The Transformations of the Workplace in the Twentieth Century* (London: Heinemann, 1979).

33 Mike Cooley, "The Taylorization of Intellectual Work," in L. Levidow and B. Young, editors *Science, Technology and the Labour Process*, vol. 1 (London: CSE Books, 1981).

34 Morris Janowitz, "Sociological Theory and Social Control," *American Journal of Sociology*, 81(1), July, 1975, 84; cf. David A. Hounshell, *From the American System to Mass Production 1800–1932: The Development of Manufacturing Technology in the United States* (Baltimore: The John Hopkins University Press, 1987), ch. 8.

35 Samuel Haber, *Efficiency and Uplift*, x.

36 Ibid., 44.

37 Edwin Layton, "Veblen and the Engineers," *American Quarterly*, Spring, 1962.

38 Magali Sarfatti-Larson, "Notes on Technocracy: Some Problems of Theory, Ideology and Power." *Berkeley Journal of Sociology*, 17, 1972, 19.

39 Charles S. Maier, "Between Taylorism and Technocracy: European Ideologies and the Vision of Industrial Productivity in the 1920," *Journal of Contemporary History*, 5(2), 1970, 31–32.

40 See, for example, Stuart and Elizabeth Ewen, *Channels of Desire*, (New York: McGraw-Hill, 1982), and Jean Baudrillard, *La Société de Consommation* (Paris: Gallimard, 1970).

41 Herbert Casson realized early on that "what has worked so well in the acquisition of knowledge and in the production of commodities may work just as well in the distribution of those commodities." Herbert N. Casson, *Ads and Sales: A Study of Advertising and Selling from the Standpoint of the New Principles of Scientific Management* (Chicago: A. C. McClurg & Co., 1911), 71.

PLAN AND CONTROL: TOWARDS A CULTURAL HISTORY

42 Daniel Pope, *The Making of Modern Advertising* (New York: Basic Books, 1983); Raymond Williams, "Advertising: the Magic System," in Raymond Williams, *Problems in Materialism and Culture* (London: Verso, 1980), 170–195.

43 Alfred P. Sloan, *My Years with General Motors* (London: Sidgwick and Jackson, 1965), ch. 9.

44 Henry C. Link, *The New Psychology of Selling and Advertising* (New York: Macmillan, 1932), 248.

45 David M. Potter, *People of Plenty: Economic Abundance and the American Character* (Chicago: University of Chicago Press, 1954), 168, 175.

46 Quentin J. Schultze, *Advertising, Science, and Professionalism* (University of Illinois at Urbana-Champaign, unpublished Ph.D. thesis, 1978), 116.

47 Donald L. Hurwitz, *Broadcast Ratings: The Rise and Development of Commercial Audience Research and Measurement in American Broadcasting* (University of Illinois at Urbana-Champaign, unpublished Ph.D. thesis, 1983).

48 Edward L. Bernays, *The Engineering of Consent* (Norman: University of Oklahoma Press, 1955), 3–4, 9; cf. Abram Lipsky, *Man the Puppet: The Art of Controlling Minds* (New York: Frank-Maurice Inc.), 1925.

49 Roland Marchand, *Advertising the American Dream: Making Way for Modernity, 1920–1940* (Berkeley: University of California Press, 1985), 25.

50 Herbert S. Dordick, *et al.*, *The Emerging Network Marketplace* (Norwood, New Jersey: Ablex), 1981.

51 Kenneth Gill, "Chairman's Review," in Saatchi and Saatchi Company plc, *Annual Report 1983.*

52 Saatchi and Saatchi Company plc, *Review of Advertising Operations 1984* (London: Saatchi and Saatchi, 1985).

53 Steve Winram, "The Opportunity for World Brands," *International Journal of Advertising*, 3(1), 1984, 25; Ivan Fallon, *The Brothers: The Rise and Rise of Saatchi & Saatchi* (London: Hutchinson, 1988), 197–217.

54 Kevin Robins and Frank Webster, "The Revolution of the Fixed Wheel: Television and Social Taylorism," in P. Drummond and R. Paterson, editors, *Television in Transition* (London: British Film Institute, 1985); Kevin Robins and Frank Webster, "Broadcasting Politics: Communications and Consumption," *Screen*, 27(3–4), May–August, 1986.

55 Oscar H. Gandy, "Media Technology and Targeting: Patching the Cracks in Hegemony." Paper for the Political Economy and Communications Technology Sections, International Association for Mass Communication Research, XIV Congress, Prague, August, 1984; compare the paper by Chief Executive of AGB Television International John Clemens, "Electronic TV Measurement Techniques: Today, Tomorrow and Tomorrow." Economic and Social Research Council Conference, Madingley Hall, Cambridge, April, 1988.

56 *Financial Times*, 25 March, 1986.

57 Dominic Cadbury, "The Impact of Technology on Marketing." *International Journal of Advertising*, 2(1), 1983, 72, 70.

58 Philip Corrigan and Derek Sayer, *The Great Arch: English State Formation as Cultural Revolution* (Oxford: Basil Blackwell, 1985).

59 Anthony Giddens, *A Contemporary Critique of Historical Materialism, vol. 1, Power, Property and the State* (London: Macmillan, 1981), 94.

60 Theodore Roszak, *The Cult of Information* (Cambridge: Lutterworth Press, 1986), 156.

61 Jürgen Habermas, *Strukturwandel der Öffentlichkeit* (Darmstadt: Luchterhand, 1962).

HISTORY AND PERSPECTIVES

62 Hans Speier, "Historical Development of Public Opinion." *American Journal of Sociology*, 55, January, 1950, 376.
63 Alvin Gouldner, *The Dialectic of Ideology and Technology* (London: Macmillan, 1976); cf. Nicholas Garnham, "The Media and the Public Sphere," in Peter Golding, Graham Murdock, and Philip Schlesinger, editors, *Communicating Politics: Mass Communications and the Political Process* (Leicester University Press, 1986), 37–53.
64 Jürgen Habermas, *Strukturwandel*, 194.
65 Alvin Gouldner, *Dialectic of Ideology*, 139–140.
66 Paul Piccone, "Paradoxes of Reflexive Sociology," *New German Critique*, (8), Spring, 1976, 173.
67 Cornelius Castoriadis, "Reflections on 'Rationality,' and 'Development,'" *Thesis Eleven*, (10/11), 1984/85.
68 Alvin Gouldner, *Dialectic of Ideology*, 36–37.
69 Samuel Haber, *Efficiency and Uplift*, 90, 93, 97–98.
70 Kevin Robins, Frank Webster, and Michael Pickering, "Propaganda, Information and Social Control," in J. Hawthorn, editor, *Propaganda, Persuasion and Polemic* (London: Edward Arnold, 1987), 1–17.
71 Walter Lippmann, *The Phantom Public* (New York: Harcourt, Brace & Co., 1925), 39.
72 Walter Lippmann, *Public Opinion* (London: Allen and Unwin, 1922), 394.
73 Ibid., 378.
74 Ibid., 408.
75 Ibid., 248.
76 William Albig, *Public Opinion* (New York: McGraw-Hill, 1939), 301.
77 Harwood L. Childs, *Public Opinion: Nature, Formation and Role* (Princeton: Van Nostrand, 1965), 282.
78 Harold D. Lasswell, "The Vocation of Propagandists" [1934], in *On Political Sociology* (Chicago: University of Chicago Press, 1977), 235, 234.
79 Edward Bernays refers to this as "special pleading" and Harold Lasswell writes of "the function of advocacy," suggesting that "as an advocate the propagandist can think of himself as having much in common with the lawyer." Indeed, according to Lasswell, society "cannot act intelligently" without its "specialists on truth": "unless these specialists are properly trained and articulated with one another and the public, we cannot reasonably hope for public interests." Edward L. Bernays, *Crystallizing Public Opinion* (New York: Boni and Liveright, 1923); Harold D. Lasswell, *Democracy Through Public Opinion* (Menasha, Wis.: George Banta Publishing Company (The Eleusis of Chi Omega, vol. 43, no. 1, part 2), 1941), 75–76, 63.
80 Walter Lippmann, 1922, *Public Opinion*, 43.
81 As Francis Rourke observes "public opinion (has) become the servant rather than the master of government, reversing the relationship which democratic theory assumes and narrowing the gap between democratic and totalitarian societies," Francis E. Rourke, *Secrecy and Publicity: Dilemmas of Democracy* (Baltimore: Johns Hopkins Press, 1961), xi.
82 Jeremy Tunstall, "Deregulation is Politicization," *Telecommunications Policy*, 9(3), September, 1985, 210.
83 Paul Sullivan, "Voters go on Disk Drives," *Observer*, 7 July, 1985.
84 See Bill Schwarz and Alan Fountain, "The Role of the Media: Redefining the National Interest *and* The Miners and Television," in Huw Beynon, editor, *Digging Deeper: Issues in the Miners' Strike* (London: Verso, 1985), 123–135.

85 James B. Rule, *Private Lives and Public Surveillance* (London: Allen Lane, 1973), 43.
86 Tom Stonier, "Intelligence Networks, Overview, Purpose and Policies in the Context of Global Social Change," *Aslib Proceedings*, 38(9), September, 1986.
87 Michael Marien, "Some Questions for the Information Society," *The Information Society*, 3(2), 1984.
88 Walter Lippmann, 1922, *Public Opinion*, 408, 248.
89 Kenneth E. Boulding and Lawrence Senesh, *The Optimum Utilization of Knowledge: Making Knowledge Serve Human Betterment* (Boulder, Colorado: Westview Press), 1983.
90 Walter Lippmann, *The Phantom Public*, 189–190.
91 Lewis Mumford, "Authoritarian and Democratic Technics," 2.
92 Cornelius Castoriadis, 1984/85, "Reflections," 35.

16

PORAT, BELL, AND THE INFORMATION SOCIETY RECONSIDERED

The growth of information work in the early twentieth century

Jorge Reina Schement

Source: *Information Processing & Management* 26(4) (1990): 449–65.

Abstract

In this article the author analyzes the growth of U.S. information work in order to test Bell and Porat's view of the information society as post-industrial. The findings presented here indicate that the information work sector grew significantly in the 1920s, rather than in the 1950s, due to the expansion of American corporate bureaucracies. Contrary to post-industrial explanations, it is concluded that any theory of the information society must construct a single explanation for the rise of early 20th century information work, as well as for growth after World War II.

1. Introduction

World satellite systems now make distance and time irrelevant. We witness and react to crises simultaneously with their happening. Networks of telephones, telex, radio, and television have exponentially increased the density of human contact. More people can be in touch with one another during any single day in the new communications environment than many did in a lifetime in the fourteenth century. The convergence of telecommunications and computing technologies distribute information automation to the limits of the world's communication networks. We are well past the point of having the capability to transform most of human knowledge into electronic form for access at any point on the earth's surface.

FREDERICK WILLIAMS, 1982, p. 201

As fewer workers in the rich nations have engaged in physical production, more have been needed to produce ideas, patents, scientific formulae, bills, invoices, reorganization plans, files, dossiers, market research, sales presentations, letters, graphics, legal briefs, engineering specifications, computer programs, and a thousand other forms of data or symbolic output. This rise in white-collar, technical, and administrative activity has been so widely documented in so many countries that we need no statistic here to make the point. Indeed, some sociologists have seized on the increasing abstraction of production as evidence that society has moved into a 'post-industrial' stage.

ALVIN TOFFLER, 1980, p. 186

Williams and Toffler evoke an image that today is largely taken as fact. The basis for the image rests upon the idea that we are entering a new age characterized by the recent evolution of the information society, which may be observed by following the course of three recent events: the information economy, information technology and information work.

According to this widely held view, interaction among these three events led to a profound socio-economic shift in the history of the United States. Information-oriented activities grew into the primary sector of the economy and information became a major commodity of exchange. Computers and other information technologies, produced by big science, arrived to shape the production and distribution of information, as well as reframing the context of everyday life. Information work spread as the primary form of employment necessary to produce the new devices and transmit the primary commodity. From this convergence of social forces, an information society began to emerge in the United States during the 1950s, '60s and '70s.

Porat's (1977) pioneering work, *The Information Economy*, is the original source of data for this interpretation of the rise of the information society. His description of the changes in the U.S. work force underlies the majority view on the growth of information work (Bell, 1979; Dizard, 1982; Katz, 1988; Nora and Minc, 1978; Ochai, 1984; Toffler, 1980; Williams, 1982) and is often linked with Bell's (1976) theory of post-industrial society.

Most scholars of the information society accept Porat's premise that information work became the dominant kind of work in the U.S. at about the same time that the information sector of the economy became the largest economic sector. Moreover, they tend to relate these events to the development and diffusion of the computer. Thus, the dominant image in the literature pictures the late twentieth century as an era when the economy and the labor force underwent a profound transformation, probably driven by a revolution in computing technology.

Information work forms a key component in this explanation, because it impacts most directly on daily life and reflects the actual activities of the members of society. Work, the source of sustenance for modern men and women, began to change in the late 1950s from manipulation of materials to manipulation of information, so that the arrival of the information age was personally felt by individuals confronting changes in the work place – or so the argument goes according to Porat.

The purpose of this paper is to examine the portion of this explanation that proposes that information work emerged as a dominant sector within the labor force in the 1950s and 1960s. In section 2, this paper reviews approaches to the measurement of information work. In section 3, Machlup's interpretation of the existence of a knowledge work force is reviewed, along with Bell's subsequent proposal of a theory of post-industrial society. Section 4 examines and critiques sources of bias in Porat's construction of information occupations for his four sector analysis of the work force. In section 5, a new four sector analysis is presented based on the critique of Porat and data for recent years. The findings of the two studies are compared and contrasted in section 6. Based on the new findings presented here, section 7 suggests that the information work sector grew to prominence in the 1920s, rather than in the 1950s. It is further suggested that the early growth of the information work sector was due to the expansion of American corporate bureaucracies during the heyday of American industrialization.

Only data presented for the twentieth century are incorporated in this paper, although Porat's analysis goes back to 1860. This is because data for the twentieth century are the most relevant to the question asked here. Moreover, data for the nineteenth century are not of sufficient reliability to be of use to the analysis presented in this paper.

2. Approaches to the conceptualization and measurement of information work

Determining precisely who is an information worker and what is information work presents a severe test to the social scientist. Obviously all human activities require some measure of information processing or manipulation. Every human task, no matter how routine, depends on an intellectual capacity. Indeed, humans continuously process and manipulate information in order to adapt to their social and physical environments. In the case of manual work, the goal of these information activities is to facilitate the performance of a physical task. Thus, the assembly line worker must interpret what he or she sees and depend on an understanding of management's directives in order to carry out the appropriate task, even if it is no more complicated than fitting a washer onto a bolt.

Machlup (1962), the first to enter this field, sought to define knowledge as an operational concept, in order to establish a systematic basis for constructing his concept of knowledge industries. He required a model of the knowledge work force to answer questions derived from his attempt to redefine the GNP. But he left his model to the last chapter of the study. Not surprisingly, his analysis of the knowledge labor force lacks the thoroughness of his analysis of the knowledge sector of the economy. Nevertheless, his was the first comprehensive attempt. But while his studies of the nature of knowledge and information shed light on these difficult phenomena (Machlup and Mansfield, 1983), his, and subsequent operationalizations of knowledge production continue to be awkward.

For example, the production of "new knowledge," is difficult to operationalize. Machlup identified one kind of new knowledge producer as an "original creator" who,

> although drawing on a rich store of information received in messages of all sorts, adds so much of his own inventive genius and creative imagination, that only relatively weak and indirect connections can be found between what he has received from others and what he communicates
>
> (Machlup, 1962, p. 33)

In principle, he resisted any interpretation of original creators as limited solely to those in the "upper strata" (his phrase). But, he limited his group of original creators to scientists and engineers, though he acknowledged that the bulk of time spent doing scientific and engineering work involves little original creation in the above sense. Furthermore, he conceded that original creativity could also be present in the work of a newspaper columnist but he could not say exactly how (Machlup, 1962, p. 349). Machlup (1962, p. 386) found that knowledge producers constituted 31.6% of the labor force in 1959, and that if one included students ninth grade and up as members of the labor force, the figure increased to 42.8% (Fig. 1).

Bell (1976) noted the rise of the service work force and its importance to the shape of a postindustrial society (see Fig. 2). He sought to describe a new knowledge class, primarily composed of professional and technical workers with a scientific elite at its core (Bell, 1976, pp. 228–232). According to his theory, they constituted the class of technocrats that would lead postindustrial society. Even more than Machlup, Bell focused on "new knowledge" as the basis for his division of the work force. Bell ignored the possibility that workers outside the elite class might originate, synthesize, and apply information in order to produce "new knowledge." His 1972 prediction that American society would evolve into a technocracy led by an

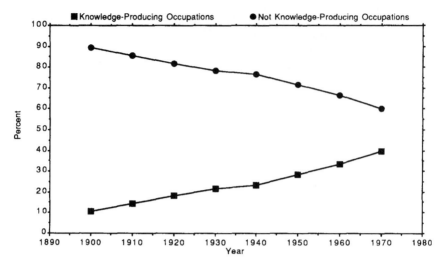

Figure 1 Growth of knowledge-producing activities in the labor force: 1900–1970 (Machlup).
Compiled from: Machlup, F. and Kronwinkler, T. (1975). Workers who produce knowledge: a steady increase, 1900 to 1970. *Weltwirtschaftliches Archiv. 37*. pp. 752–759. Their source: *1900–1950: Historical Statistics of the United States*, pp. 75–78.

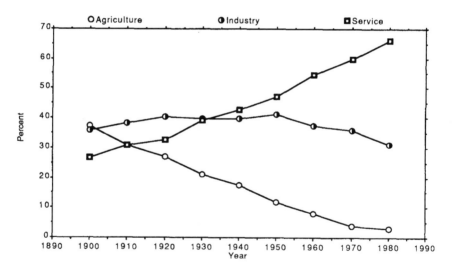

Figure 2 3 sector aggregation of the U.S. work force: 1900–1908 (Bell).
Compiled from: Bell, D. (1976) *The Coming of Post-Industrial Society.* New York: Basic Books, pp. 134, 137.

elite class of knowledge creators continues to hold interesting implications. But his exclusive focus on technocrats limited understanding of the extent and content of information work.

Porat was first to break away from the conceptual constraints of operationalizing new knowledge. He did so by introducing the more inclusive term "information" and sought to determine the extent to which the production, processing, and distribution of information goods and services contributed to the U.S. GNP. He specifically steered away from the problem posed by the recognition that information processing is present in all work.

> We are trying to get at a different question: Which occupations are *primarily* engaged in the production, processing, or distribution of information as the output, and which occupations perform information processing tasks as activities ancillary to the primary function?
>
> (Porat, 1977, p. 105)

Having identified the "information economy," he aggregated the number of "information workers" active in these new sector of the economy. For this reason, Porat's study was brilliant yet limiting. His reanalysis of the economy uncovered the strength of the contribution of information activities. He altered thinking on the character of the U.S. economy, so that the phrase, "information economy," soon entered the literature and popular speech and the idea of an information sector within the economy has taken firm hold. His focus on "information" rather than "knowledge" avoided Machlup's conceptual pitfall, and imposed a broader, more realistic framework for measuring the extent of this kind of work. Nevertheless, he continued in the tradition of Machlup. Porat admitted that information work might occur outside of the information sector, in some agricultural occupations for example. But since these were located outside of the information sector, he could not analyze them within his framework. Even given these limitations, he found that information workers earned 53% of all labor income in 1967 (Porat, 1977, pp. 8, 117).

Machlup's and Porat's economic analysis shed first light on the phenomenon of information work. Yet their economic approach also directed inquiry away from the study of information work as a social phenomenon within the information society.

The Expert Group at OECD attempted to fill in the blanks by constructing a typology of information occupations, utilizing the 1968 International Standard Classification of Occupations (ISCO) as their point of departure. They divided information work into four groups of occupations:

1 information producers;
2 information processors;

HISTORY AND PERSPECTIVES

3   information distributors; and
4   information infrastructure occupations.

Their success led to other studies analyzing information work as occupational behavior wherever it occurs, rather than as an activity present within the information sector of the economy. Because OECD identified information occupations, rather than directly aggregating information workers as did Machlup and Porat, they opened the door for the direct study of information occupations and workers. Moreover, the use of the ISCO classifications provided the opportunity to compare empirical data from numerous countries. Especially valuable are those studies focusing on less developed countries where information sectors are small, but where information workers are widely distributed throughout the work force. As a result of the Expert Group's breakthrough, researchers have begun to accumulate data on information occupations and work forces in many countries (Katz, 1988; Singlemann, 1978).[1]

Schement and Lievrouw (1984) focused on the informational content of work. They assumed Porat's given, that "intellectual content is present in every task, no matter how mundane" (Porat, 1977, p. 105). But beyond the recognition that human workers process information, they observed patterned information activities increasingly integrated into many occupations, even traditional ones. For example, Sears mechanics routinely fill out numerous forms prior to performing any assignment on an automobile brought in for service. Taxi drivers spend significant amounts of time communicating with dispatchers, processing directions, and maintaining logs of their transactions. All occupations, even traditional ones, contain patterned information activities as part of the work task, and some traditional occupations contain surprisingly high levels of information processing. But in information occupations, manipulation of information defines product, task, and worker. Schement and Lievrouw (1984, p. 235) identified five categories of workers:

1   information producers;
2   information recyclers;
3   information maintainers;
4   information technology producers; and,
5   information technology maintainers.

Their study of the Dictionary of Occupational Titles (DOT), the basic document for describing occupations, reinforced the hypothesis that information work occurs across all sectors of the work force. As one would expect, they found that 96.9% of the DOT's information sector (divisions 00–29) met their definitions of information occupations. Similarly, they determined that 49.6% of those occupations in the service sector (30–38) could be considered informational. But Schement and Lievrouw also found that information occupations comprised 25.1% of the industrial sector (50–99) and 26.1% of the agricultural sector (40–46). Moreover, while the Department of Labor correctly identified an information sector within the labor force, its definitions were excessively narrow since other sectors also contained significant numbers of information occupations. Of the total number of occupations recognized in the U.S. labor force, 40% were informational.[2] Thus, information occupations were found across all divisions of the 1977 DOT indicating that information work takes place in all areas of the economy.

Social scientists have grappled with the concept of information work since Machlup's first attempt at an economic analysis of the production of knowledge. In the intervening years, a general picture has emerged with some variation depending on the assumptions of the interpreter. As attempts to define information work have evolved, they encompass a basic set of behaviors consistent across all definitions. The following definition summarizes these points.

Information work occurs when the worker's main task involves information processing or manipulation in any form, such as information production, recycling, or maintenance. Moreover, the consequence of information work is more information, whether in the form of new knowledge or repackaged existing forms. Unlike the assembly line worker, an information worker, such as a telephone operator, processes and manipulates information as an end in itself. Information defines the task, the product, and the worker.

3. Earlier findings and updates

Machlup focused solely on those workers who produce knowledge as opposed to those who do not. His data indicated a steady growth of knowledge workers throughout the twentieth century. Assuming his trend, identified in Fig. 1, knowledge workers would have been expected to pass the 50% mark around 1980 or soon thereafter. Rubin and Huber, with Taylor, (1986) updated Machlup's 1962 findings, carefully adhering to his classification scheme of occupations. By carrying forth a project begun by Machlup and unfinished at the time of his death in 1983, they found all knowledge-producing workers to comprise 41.23% of the total economically active population in 1980 (p. 196). This falls considerably below Machlup's earlier estimate. Because Machlup's scheme was not as inclusive as Porat's and others, he and his followers consistently give lower figures for the share of information work. Neither Machlup, nor Ruben *et al.*, attempts a breakdown into four work force sectors.

Bell proposed that the growth of the service sector of the work force (see Fig. 2) had transformed the reality of life for Americans. In postindustrial society individuals engage in work whose product is quality of life; whereas,

HISTORY AND PERSPECTIVES

before they engaged in work whose product was a material good. At the core of the service work force, Bell hypothesized the existence of a scientific elite creating new knowledge and forming the intellectual impetus for post-industrial society. In turn, this elite drew support from an infrastructure of technical workers. His findings indicated that these professional and technical workers comprised 12.2% of the total work force in 1963 (Bell, 1976, p. 217). Bell's subsequent writings (1979) on the growth of a technocratic elite within post-industrial society, and within the information society, rely on Porat's data.

4. Operationalizations and sources of bias in Porat's information occupations

Porat identified five groups of information occupations found in three markets for information services. Workers producing or distributing information commodities for sale in the marketplace fell into the first and largest group of information occupations. In the second group, he placed those occupations concerned with the processing, movement, or manipulation of information for purposes of planning, or coordinating activities that result in the sale of goods and services. The last group comprised occupations involved in the operation of information machines, or technologies, for the purpose of supporting the first two groups (see Fig. 3).

4.1 Splitting occupational categories

Porat made operational decisions regarding the inclusion of a number of occupations which affected the relative sizes of his categories. He addressed the problem of defining those occupations in which some workers primarily manipulate information, but others do not. In particular, he saw that some

---

Markets for Information
1. Knowledge producers (scientific and technical, producers of private information services).
2. Knowledge distributors (educators, public information disseminators, communication workers).

Information in Markets
3. Market search and coordination specialists (information gatherers, search and coordination specialists, planning and control workers).
4. Information processors (nonelectronic based, electronic based).

Information Infrastructure
5. Information machine workers (nonelectronic machine operators, electronic machine operators, telecommunication workers).

Figure 3 Porat's (1977) typology of information workers.

PORAT, BELL & INFORMATION SOCIETY RECONSIDERED

Physicians	Sales Clerks, Retail Trades
Registered Nurses	Misc. Clerical Workers
Dietitians	Mangers, Retail Trade, Salaried
Health Record Technologies	Managers, Personal Services, Salaried
Radiological Technologies	Managers, Personal Services, Self-
Counter Clerks, exc. food	Employed
Officers, Pilots, Pursers on Ships	Managers, Business Services, Salaried
Officials of Lodges, Societies, Unions	Managers, Business and Repair
Demonstrators	Services, Self-Employed
Hucksters	Receptionists

Figure 4 Occupations allocated 50% to service and 50% to information (Porat, 1977, p. 119).

service occupations (e.g., physicians, registered nurses) underwent rapid changes in the 1960s and '70s, so that they might reasonably be considered informational in the near future. But at the time of Porat's research, he recognized them as occupations in transition, so he attempted to sift out the informations work portion and split eighteen occupations, allocating one half to the service sector (see Fig. 4) (Porat, 1977, p. 119).

By splitting the occupational categories identified by the available census data, Porat questioned the utility of traditional definitions and opened for consideration, the possibility that information work might occur in occupations that did not conform to intuitive definitions. He argued that lumping together foremen who were information workers, with foremen who were industrial workers, confused occupational labels, thus implicitly challenging Bell's (1976) identification of the knowledge work force. Other researchers, such as Schement and Lievrouw (1984), pursued this line of questioning by studying the extent to which information work behavior had penetrated the entire work force.

Porat's decision partially solved the problem of recognizing occupations in transition, but created a systematic bias inflating the size of the information work sector for the early decades of the century. Medical doctors provide an example of why the operational decision to split occupations between information work and noninformation work is misleading. For the 1970s and '80s, an excellent claim can be made for classifying general practitioner (GP) physicians as information workers. Typically, a GP meets the patient and elicits information about the suspected illness in a clinical setting. Then the GP diagnoses the illness and prescribes treatment. The patient takes the prescription to a pharmacist who interprets the physician's instructions and physically dispenses the medication. The patient then performs self treatment by ingesting the medication. The pharmacist and the patient perform the physical aspects of the treatment. The physician performs the informational components of data collection and diagnosis. Indeed, diagnosis stands

HISTORY AND PERSPECTIVES

Foreman, NEC
Inspectors, Scalers, Graders, Lumber
Chainmen, Rodmen (Surveying)
Checkers, Examiners, Inspectors (Manufacturing)
Graders and Sorters (Manufacturing)

Figure 5 Occupations allocated 50% to industry and 50% to information (Porat, 1977).

at the core of the medical profession's definition of itself. Thus, Porat's claim considering GPs as information workers is valid for recent decades. However, in the first half of the century, GPs performed surgery, dispensed medication, gave injections, and took blood samples, in addition to performing diagnoses. Thus, it is unlikely that even 50% of all GPs were information workers prior to the 1960s, the decade when doctors quit making house calls and providing individual treatment.

Porat faced the same problem with some industrial occupations. Foremen, for example, have increasingly assumed tasks of coordinating activities and disseminating information. Moreover, throughout the twentieth century, automation and unionization resulted in converting foremen from industrial workers into information workers. However, this transformation did not occur at a uniform rate for all foremen. Some, especially those in small construction businesses, continue to play the role of lead worker. Porat also split workers in these occupations between the industrial and information sectors (see Fig. 5).

In the above cases, Porat recognized these occupations as containing a significant amount of information work. But his decision to allocate half of their numbers as information workers gave the false impression that, in the first half of the century, these occupations contained large numbers of information workers. It would have been more accurate to judge the presence of information work on a decade-by-decade basis. That way, he would have allowed for the uneven rate of change. To be fair, such detailed analysis would have been virtually impossible for reasons outlined in section 5.1.

4.2 Assigning occupations from the service sector to the industrial sector

Of more profound effect on Porat's four sector analysis was his decision to shift some occupations from the service sector to the industrial sector (see Fig. 6). He chose to redefine these occupations as industrial occupations reasoning that, since some of these workers (plumbers and glazers) manipulated physical objects, their occupations should be considered industrial. Furthermore, he also reallocated some transportation occupations on the

PORAT, BELL & INFORMATION SOCIETY RECONSIDERED

Railroad brakemen   Truck drivers
Barge captains   Glazers
Plumbers
All skilled crafts whether based in factories or not.
All occupations involved in the transport of bulk commodities.

Figure 6 Service occupations allocated to industry (Porat, 1977, p. 117).

premise that, "transportation of bulk commodities is an essential feature of an industrial economy" (Porat, 1977, p. 117). With these seemingly innocuous changes, Porat effectively redefined the meaning of "industry" and "service," and by doing so, increased the number of occupations in the industrial sector at the expense of the service sector.

This operational decision left a source of confusion greater than splitting occupations between two sectors. Changing the grouping of the occupations but leaving the traditional labels in effect led to the assumption that the industrial sector contained only those occupations conventionally thought of as industrial. Certainly, this was not Porat's intention. Porat wrote *The Information Economy* as his dissertation and probably performed the reassignment of occupations in response to suggestions from committee members seeking a more rational basis for differentiating occupations in the industrial sector from those in the service and information sectors.[3] But since the main purpose of the report was to measure the extent of information activity in the U.S. economy, the discussion of the work force is supplementary and limited to chapter seven. The brief explanation on operationalizing occupations within the industrial sector is buried in the text, not likely to be noticed (Porat, 1977, p. 117).

Therefore, one reason for the high percentage of industrial workers in Porat's data is that he included a variety of service jobs as industrial occupations. Moreover, since many of these groups have been less susceptible to mechanization, they represent large numbers in the work force. By locating plumbers, glazers, railroad brakemen, truck drivers, and all skilled crafts (whether factory-based or not) in the category of industrial work, he inflated the industrial work force while deflating the service work force, thus contributing to the illusion that industrial workers dominated well into the 1950s.

5. Porat's findings and the interpretations based on these findings

Porat (1977) took Machlup (1962) as his point of departure, and expanded the division of the labor force from two sectors to four sectors (see Figs. 1, 7, & 8). Like Machlup, he found information workers approaching 50% of the

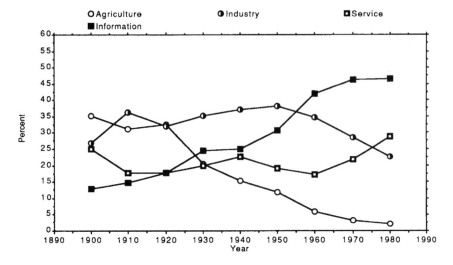

Figure 7 4 sector aggregation of the U.S. work force: 1900–1980 (Porat).
Source: Porat, M.U. (1977) *The Information Economy: Definition and Measurement*. (OT Special Publication 77-12 (1)). Washington, DC: Office of Telecommunications, U.S. Department of Commerce, p. 121.

Year	Agriculture	Industry	Service	Information
1900	35.3	26.8	25.1	12.8
1910	31.1	36.3	17.7	14.9
1920	32.5	32	17.8	17.7
1930	20.4	35.3	19.8	24.5
1940	15.4	37.2	22.5	24.9
1950	11.9	38.3	19	30.8
1960	6	34.8	17.2	42
1970	3.1	28.6	21.9	46.4
1980	2.1	22.5	28.8	46.6

Figure 8 Percentages of the United States work force by sector: 1900–1980 (Porat, Bell).
Compiled from: Bell, D. (1979). "The Social Framework of the Information Society," in M. L. Dertouzos and J. Moss (Eds). *The Computer Age: A Twenty-Year View*. Cambridge, MA: MIT Press, pp. 163–211.

work force in 1980. In his analysis, information workers overtook service workers in 1920, and surpassed agricultural workers at the end of the same decade. But they did not reach parity with industrial workers until 1955. Thus, according to Porat, information workers did not come into their own as the primary work force group until the late fifties. The timing of the trend line for information workers coincides with the period when computers were growing in visibility, the late fifties and early sixties. Porat interpreted the coincidence of these two trends as reflecting the coming of an information society. Similarly, Bell's (1976) theory of post-industrial society was premised on the seemingly recent growth of the service sector. In a later review of Porat's research, Bell (1979, pp. 180–186) supported Porat's interpretation equating post-industrial society with the information society. Their main point is that the information society is a post-industrial society precisely because the explosion in information technology and the rise of the information sector of the work force are recent. The recency of these two developments demonstrates the passing of the old industrial society of the late nineteenth and early twentieth centuries. However, one basis for this interpretation, the rise of the information sector of the work force, may not be so recent.

6. An analysis of the four sectors of the work force with corrections for biases identified in section 4

An analysis of the U.S. work force in the twentieth century was conducted in order to determine the relative sizes of the four sectors and to test Porat's data. In order to reduce the systemic bias in Porat's earlier approach, two changes were introduced departing from his organization of the four sectors of the work force. First, the census data were reevaluated in an attempt to accurately measure the representation of information workers in those composite occupation groups that include information and noninformation workers, and that evolved a greater information orientation between 1900 and 1980 (see Figs. 4 and 5). Second, Porat's reassignment of service occupations to the industrial sector was reversed (see Fig. 6), so that conventional groupings of occupations were maintained.

6.1 Measurement of numbers of workers in composite occupations

The gross nature of occupational statistics gathered by the census presents a major difficulty for this type of analysis. For one thing, the census combined or divided occupational categories in 1910, 1920, 1950, 1960, and 1970 making it difficult to calculate the numbers of information workers within the affected categories. For example, *Express messengers and railway mail clerks*, suddenly appear in 1910 in large numbers, as do *Foremen, construction*; and, *Motion picture projectionists*. These insertions give the impression that groups of information occupations came into existence suddenly, where none existed before. On the other hand, *Musicians and music teachers* disappear as a separate group beginning with the 1970 census, their numbers being subsumed within the total for *Professional, technical, and kindred workers*.

As mentioned above, foremen pose daunting problems when trying to separate information from noninformation workers. For the 1940 census, foremen in nonrailway transportation industries were divided into *Foremen, transportation, except railroad*; and, *Foremen, telecommunications, utilities,*

& sanitary services. Then in the 1970 census, they were recombined into one group to also include *Foremen, railroads and railway express service.* Knowing the numbers of foremen in separate industries will contribute to our understanding of how the information work sector grew. But the answer cannot be teased from the census data.

Some groups of information workers were combined in occupations so that the information workers could not be separated from the noninformation workers. For example, *Jewelers, watchmakers, goldsmiths and silversmiths; Fruit, nut, and vegetable graders and packers, excluding factory;* and, *Airplane pilots and navigators,* include both information and noninformation workers. The case of jewelers and watchmakers is difficult because watchmakers produce information devices. Similarly, vegetable graders generate information but packers do not. In both cases, cycles of automation and foreign trade have affected information and noninformation workers differentially, making it difficult to determine the proper ratio for one census period, much less nine. In the case of the commercial airline industry, these cycles have produced a stable ratio of around two pilots to one navigator since 1920, but even this cannot be determined without resorting to numerous outside sources. Therefore, while one suspects that the ratio of information workers to noninformation workers is significant in these occupation groups (especially for recent decades), no simple ratio can be applied.

Lastly, the 1950, 1960, and 1970 censuses show discrepancies between the numbers of workers in the occupations listed and the subtotals for occupation groupings. For example, when one adds the number of workers listed in the 1970 census for all occupations comprising *Professional, technical, and kindred workers,* the sum is 7,897,000. But the total given by the census is 11,561,000. Three million six hundred and sixty-four thousand workers were "lost" because the census total included persons for whom occupations were not reported. In the case of the subtotals for these years, some also included occupations not shown separately. Undoubtedly, information occupations fell within these unspecified catch-all categories. I encountered insurmountable difficulties in deciding how to classify these hidden groups of workers and occupations, as did Machlup and Porat. The task was akin to attempting a portrait with a house painter's brush.

Upon review of the operational possibilities for resolving the problems inherent in the census data, no solution promised greater accuracy in determining the number of information workers. Ultimately, all attempts to accurately measure the numbers of information workers hidden in suspected occupations were equally defeated. Given its implicit bias, Porat's operational decision to split occupational groups on a 50/50 basis offers no advantage in terms of accuracy. Since one goal of this study is to test Porat's 4 sector construction of the work force, a conservative approach was chosen. In selecting occupations to be included in the information sector, I only included occupations which easily fell within the dimensions of information work outlined in section 2. Of those composite occupations listed in Figs. 4 and 5, only *Managers; Checkers, examiners, inspectors (manufacturing)*; and *Graders and sorters (manufacturing)*, were included as information workers.

6.2 Allocation of occupations to the industrial and service sectors

In keeping with a conservative approach to this test of Porat's study, all occupations identified in Fig. 6, were placed within the service sector. In so doing, conventional assumptions were maintained regarding the "industrial nature" or "service nature" of an occupation. Accordingly, the revised industrial and service sectors avoided the systematic bias which exaggerated the size of Porat's industrial sector.

7. Comparison of findings from all of the studies

7.1 Similarities

The data from all of the studies (including Machlup's) show an increase in the percentage of information workers in the work force. Porat (1977) and the data collected for this paper show information workers overtaking agricultural workers during the 1920s. All three studies indicate that information occupations experienced little growth during the depression years. Porat found a diminished rate of growth for information workers, from 1960 to 1970, and the findings in the reanalysis support him. All of the studies show information workers approaching 50% of the work force in the 1980s.

7.2 Differences

Porat's data (Fig. 7 & 8) indicate that the percent of information workers reached a level higher than the percent of industrial workers in the 1950s, while the service sector increased beyond the industrial sector in the mid 1970s. However, the data gathered for this paper show that the information work sector overtook the industrial work sector by 1930, and that the service work sector intersected the industrial work sector during the 1940s.

By correcting for the systematic biases in Porat's work categories, the data in Figs. 9 and 10 show important work force shifts occurring during the 1920s and 1930s. They show the information work sector rising to primacy by 1930, stalled during the depression, and continuing to grow after 1940. The crucial decades for the emergence of the information work force seem to be 1920–1940. In this period, the United States passed the threshold into a work force where information workers formed the single largest group. At the same time, service workers reached near parity with industrial workers, and farm workers finally fell below the other major groups. Throughout the post World War II era, the industrial work sector

HISTORY AND PERSPECTIVES

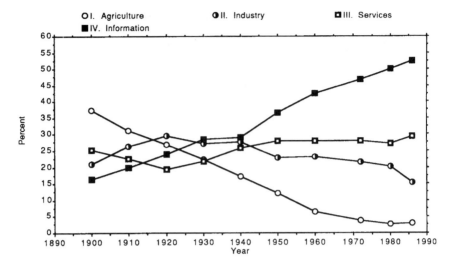

Figure 9 4 sector re-aggregation of the U.S. work force: 1900–1986.
Compiled from: Table 627. *Employed Persons, by Sex, Race, and Occupation: 1986.* U.S. Bureau of the Census. *Statistical Abstract of the United States: 1988.* (108th Ed.). Washington, DC, 1987. Table 675. *Employed Persons by Sex, Race, and Occupation: 1972 and 1980.* U.S. Bureau of the Census. *Statistical Abstract of the United States: 1981.* (102nd Ed.). Washington, DC, 1981. Series D 233–682. *Detailed Occupation of the Economically Active Population: 1900 to 1970.* U.S. Bureau of the Census. *Historical Statistics of the United States, Colonial Times to 1970* (Bicentennial Ed.). Part 1. Washington, DC, 1975.

Year	Agriculture	Industry	Service	Information
1900	37.5	20.9	25.3	16.4
1910	31.1	26.4	22.5	20
1920	26.9	29.6	19.5	24
1930	22.4	27.1	21.9	28.6
1940	17.3	27.6	25.9	29.1
1950	12.2	23	28.1	36.7
1960	6.6	23.1	27.9	42.4
1972	3.7	21.5	28	46.8
1980	2.8	20.2	27.1	50
1986	2.9	15.2	29.3	52.6

Figure 10 Percentages of the United States work force by sector: 1900–1980 (Schement).
Compiled from: Table 627. *Employed Persons, by Sex, Race, and Occupation: 1986.* U.S. Bureau of the Census. *Statistical Abstract of the United States: 1988.* (108th Ed.). Washington, DC, 1987. Table 675. *Employed Persons by Sex, Race, and Occupation: 1972 and 1980.* U.S. Bureau of the Census. *Statistical Abstract of the United States: 1981.* (102nd Ed.). Washington, DC, 1981. Series D 233–682. *Detailed Occupation of the Economically Active Population: 1900 to 1970.* U.S. Bureau of the Census. *Historical Statistics of the United States, Colonial Times to 1970* (Bicentennial Ed.). Part 1. Washington, DC, 1975.

placed third and diminished steadily. Information workers surpassed 50% after 1980, becoming the majority of the work force.

Based on the growth trend between his 1960 and 1970 data, Porat forecast a leveling off of the information work force after 1970. He implied that information work might reach a point of saturation as it approached 50% of the work force. Collected twelve years later, the data in Figs. 9 and 10 show no actual leveling. During the seventies, the growth rate of the information sector approximated that of the booming fifties. From 1980 to 1986, growth slowed to a rate similar to that of the sixties. As of 1986, the information portion of the labor force continued to gain against other sectors and stood at 52.6% of the total work force. While no leveling off has been observed, there can be no doubt that the information work sector will eventually peak at a point somewhere beyond 50%.[4]

The differences are significant because Porat's data show the information work sector reaching primacy in the years after World War II and the industrial work sector succumbing to the service work sector more recently. Taken at face value, his body of data provide evidence for a recent shift into a work force dominated by information workers, thereby reinforcing a view of the information society as taking the place of industrial society. After Porat's study was published, Bell endorsed Porat's position in an important review article. Bell retranslated Porat's data within the context of his own theory of post-industrial society (Bell, 1979). When reinforced by Porat's data, Bell's theory projects a seemingly potent interpretation tying the growth of the information work force to post World War II developments in science and technology.

In contrast, the data presented in this paper pose a paradox, since they suggest that the information work sector surpassed the other work sectors by the end of the third decade of the century. Thus, the post-industrial interpretation is flawed. Furthermore, although the rise of post war science and the computer certainly affected the development of the information work force and influenced the direction of the information society, they cannot be considered a primary cause, since the pattern of information work was set decades before the emergence of the first or the diffusion of the second. The rise of the information work force needs to be understood within the context of the history which shaped industrial society in the United States, rather than as part of a post-industrial transformation. Indeed, the pattern of information work can best be seen as a manifestation of the forces that created industrial society.

8. Modern management and the growth of information work in the early twentieth century as an alternative explanation

The powerful forces that propelled information work to the forefront of the American economy converged in the earliest decades of the century, during the height of the "industrial" period. They did so in response to the problems which industrialization itself posed for managers.

By the middle decades of the nineteenth century, entrepreneurs began to realize the tremendous profit potential of industrial production. Their key insight recognized that the advantage of the industrial system lay in its capacity for sustained growth. When entrepreneurs increased the numbers of units produced in their factories, they drove down the cost per unit of production. Nineteenth century industrial entrepreneurs discovered economies of scale and built empires on this principle (Chandler, 1977, pp. 240–244; Heilbroner and Singer, 1984, pp. 175–176).

However, the very size of the empires presented immense problems of control for their directors. Styles of management, typical of the entrepreneurs who rose to become captains of industry, collapsed when companies reached sizes that prevented personal attention to each factory, warehouse, and railroad yard owned by the firm. As each new industry – the railroads, steel, oil, meat packing, chemicals, automobiles – grew, it encountered the same problems of size and control. The solution, first discovered by managers of railroads, required the creation of an entirely new system of supervision (Beniger, 1986, pp. 219–287; Chandler, 1977, pp. 81–187; Heilbroner and Singer, 1984, pp. 143–167; Schement, 1989, pp. 41–44).

The new system of administrative management demanded that managers, first, believe in the superiority of systematic decisions arrived at rationally, and, second, that they invent ways and means for supplying managers with information. The rational management systems necessary for bringing order from the chaos of sprawling industrial empires relied on information as the foundation resource.

So when Alfred P. Sloan Jr. conducted an organization study of General Motors, in 1920, and recommended that each GM division develop statistics for determining the relation between net return and invested capital in order to assist senior management in deciding the allocation of resources to each division, he set in motion the building of a vast information infrastructure within the corporation (Sloan, 1963, pp. 53–54). In 1921, before the implementation of Sloan's organization study, GM contained 40 separate corporate staffs and 14 manufacturing divisions each with its own staffs (Sloan, 1963, p. 56). By 1925, with the reorganization of GM well under way, there were 41 corporate staffs and 32 manufacturing divisions with staffs organic to their operations (Sloan, 1963, p. 115). Furthermore, the invention of organizations based on the flow of information occurred in every corporate sphere. As of 1902, the directors of the United States Rubber Company received information from 36 corporate level staffs and 51 divisions (Chandler, 1977, pp. 436–437). The directors of Armour & Company, in 1907, reported 23 corporate staffs, and 9 divisions containing 71 separate staffs (Chandler, 1977, pp. 394–395). American managers like Sloan had discovered that the profitability of large corporations depended

PORAT, BELL & INFORMATION SOCIETY RECONSIDERED

Yr.	1 Clerical*	2 Professional**	3 Total [1 + 2]	4 Government†	5 Gvt. % [4 ÷ 3]
1900:	877	1,234	2,111	239	11.3%
1930:	4,336	3,311	7,647	601	7.8%
1960:	9,617	7,336	16,953	2,398	14.1%

*Clerical = Clerical and kindred workers.
**Professional = Professional, technical and kindred workers.
†Government = Total federal government employees [including non information workers].

Figure 11 Comparison of selected information workers to selected government
information workers (in thousands): 1900, 1930, 1960.
Compiled from: Machlup, F., & Kronwinkler, T. (1975). Workers who produce knowledge: a
steady increase, 1900 to 1970. *Weltwirtschaftliches Archiv.*, *111*(4), 752–759. Series Y 308–317.
Paid Civilian Employment of the Federal Government 1816 to 1970. U.S. Bureau of the Census.
Historical Statistics of the United States, Colonial Times to 1970 (Bicentennial Ed.). Part 1.
Washington, DC, 1975.

on efficient management, and that efficient management depended on
information.

As a result, the number of information workers employed by large corporations grew rapidly in the first decades of the twentieth century (see
Fig. 11). For example, clerical and kindred workers increased by nearly
500% between 1900 and 1930, whereas their numbers increased by 220%
between 1930 and 1960. The numbers of professional, technical and kindred
workers increased by nearly 270% from 1900 to 1930; between 1930 and
1960, their numbers increased by 220% (Machlup and Kronwinkler, 1975,
pp. 754–755).[5]

However, one might reasonably argue that in order to judge the relative
importance of corporate bureaucracies in creating the information work
force, it is necessary to know something of the extent to which the rise of
information work was influenced by the growth of government civil service.
Total federal government employees (including non information workers)
increased by 360% between 1900 and 1930, whereas their numbers increased
by 400% between 1930 and 1960. Nevertheless, during the first decades of
the century, the percentage of federal government employees shrank in comparison to all clerical, professional, technical and kindred workers as the
growth of corporate bureaucracies outdistanced the growth of the federal
government (see Fig. 11).[6] In 1900, federal civil servants made up 11.3% of
all clerical, professional, technical and kindred workers. In 1930, the first
census year to record the primacy of the information work sector, their
share dropped to 7.8%. In 1960, in the wake of government growth due
to World War II and the Cold War, federal civil servants rose to 14.1%.
The inclusion of government noninformation workers means that the actual
numbers of government information workers is somewhat less than these

figures. Moreover, the total for all information workers is larger than the number of clerical, professional, technical and kindred workers. Therefore, one can see that government information workers were not the major source of growth for the information work force in the first decades of the century.

The creation of an information work force in the early twentieth century resulted from efforts to more efficiently exploit the productivity of industrial workers. That the growing ranks of information workers were interdependent with the industrial work force can be seen in Figs. 9 and 10. During the Great Depression, the effect of shutting down factories was felt by both industrial and information workers. Industrial workers lost jobs directly from the factory floor. But, less obviously, information workers lost jobs since they also figured into the calculus of corporate profitability. Thus, both the industrial and information work forces stagnated between 1930 and 1940. The point is that the information work force of 1930 was the direct result of industrial production. Moreover, continued demand for information workers of increasing specialization fulfilled the needs of the new corporate bureaucracies coming into existence and formed the technostructure of the new industrial state (Galbraith, 1967).

On the other hand, the information work force of 1980 contained a source of production in its own right – the producers of information commodities. Therefore, the recession of 1981–1983 did not duplicate the trend lines of 1930. In 1981–83, the information work force continued to grow, while the industrial work force declined.

What is counterintuitive in this alternative explanation is that the image of the information worker is a recent one associated with the 1980s, not the 1930s. The stereotype of the information worker sitting at a desk with a personal computer resonates because it entered the public imagination along with the idea of the information society. No comparable image from the pencil-and-paper era of the '20s and '30s seems fitting. Yet the evidence seems to indicate otherwise.

The theory of post-industrial society/information society proposed by Bell, based on Porat, and generally followed in the literature, is grounded in an interpretation of the growth of the information work force as part of social and technological changes that occurred in the U. S. after World War II. Moreover, the concept of the recent rise of information work is integral to the idea of the information society as a post-industrial society. Thus, once information work is shown to have arisen prior to World War II, one of the three conceptual legs of the theory is removed.

If new studies reinforce the interpretation that information work rose to primacy in the 1920s, then new hypotheses must be sought to explain the timing of its emergence and, consequently, the relationship between industrial society and the information society. That is not to say that important economic and technological changes did not occur over the last 30 years. It is simply to say that any theory of the information society must accept a more complex view and explain the growth of the information work force in the '20s and '30s, along with changes that occurred in the '60s, '70s, and '80s. From this perspective, post-industrial explanations appear invalid.

9. Conclusion

In contrast to the visibility of material technologies like the railroad, the automobile, or the computer, the diffusion of the technology of modern management took place with less public notice. The gradualness of pace meant that today we see it in the background rather than in the foreground of history. But what is not seen clearly may have profound effects.

We know little of the underlying dynamics that stimulated the proliferation of new information occupations in the first half of the century. Although, as expressed by Adam Smith, the reasons for this proliferation are clear enough.

> The greatest improvement in the productive powers of labor, and the greater part of the skill, dexterity, and judgement with which it is anywhere directed, or applied, seems to have been the effects of the division of labor.
>
> (Smith, 1776/1902, p. 43)

Smith is equally clear on the significance of work to the modern state,

> The annual labor of every nation is the fund which originally supplies it with all the necessaries and conveniences of life which it annually consumes, and which consist always either in the immediate produce of that labor, or in what is purchased with that produce from other nations.
>
> According, therefore, as this produce, or what is purchased with it, bears a greater or smaller proportion to the number of those who are to consume it, the nation will be better or worse supplied with all the necessities and conveniences for which it has occasion.
>
> (Smith, 1776/1902, p. 39)

As to gaining a fuller picture of the dynamics of information work, there are limits to what we can know along the line of inquiry pursued in this paper. It is one thing to statistically analyze the presence of information work as a historic pattern in the distribution of the work force. It is another thing to understand what it means to labor as an information worker at an information job in an information age.

HISTORY AND PERSPECTIVES

In the case of the United States today, "the immediate produce of this labor" is information. Moreover, it is through information work that the majority of the members of society have and will experience the information age in a form of direct significance to their lives. The image of a computer programmer of the eighties working at Fairchild Electronics is indelibly etched on the public memory of the age. But the image of a 1920s distribution clerk routing crates of apricots picked on land that now houses Fairchild Electronics does not come to mind as easily. Explanations of the information society should encompass both.

Acknowledgement

The author wishes to acknowledge Professors Hartmut Mokros, Getinet Belay, and Richard Budd of Rutgers University, Loy Singleton of the University of Alabama, and Terry Curtis of California State University at Chico, for providing valuable criticism to the draft of this paper.

Notes

1 At about this time, Debons, King, Mansfield, and Shirey (1981) were conducting their survey of information professionals. They also followed an occupational approach, but limited their analysis to "professionals" only, that is those whose occupations required them to hold a bachelor's degree or higher. Thus, their analysis shed useful light on the characteristics of information professionals within the labor force, but did not attempt to gain insight into the pattern of distribution of information work.
2 Schement, J. R. and Lievrouw, L. (1984), pp. 330–333. In the DOT for 1977, 55% of all occupations are found in the industrial sector. The preponderance of industrial occupations, in contrast to the actual number of industrial workers, can be attributed to the longer period of time available for industrial occupations to subdivide and specialize, as well as to the pro-industrial bias built into the DOT at its inception during the Depression years. The information work sector was already the largest sector during the Depression. Yet the idea of information work would not arrive for forty years.
3 Personal communication recorded in 1977.
4 A further note on the transformation of the work force since 1980: The 1981 recession represents a good confidence test of the analysis presented in this article. This period saw massive layoffs of industrial workers and the growth of low paying jobs in the service sector. Some of these new jobs went to unemployed industrial workers. Figure 9 shows a decline in the percent of industrial workers and an increase in the percent of service workers from 1980 to 1986, indicating that the data reflect actual labor displacement which occurred in the economy.
5 For an excellent treatment of the social and political dynamics affecting the 19th and 20th century growth of the professional work force, see Abbott (1988).
6 State and local government employment figures were either incomplete or unreliable for 1900–1930; most state, and territorial governments (Oklahoma, Arizona, and New Mexico), were small in numbers of employees. The inclusion of federal government employees who were not information workers appears to be a reasonable compensation for the absence of figures on state and local government employees.

References

(1975). Series D 233–682. Detailed occupation of the economically active population: 1900 to 1970. Historical statistics of the United States, colonial times to 1970. Washington DC: GPO.

(1975). Series Y 308–317. Paid civilian employment of the federal government 1816 to 1970. U.S. Bureau of the Census. Historical Statistics of the United States, colonial times to 1970. Washington DC: GPO.

(1981). Table 675. Employed persons by sex, race, and occupation: 1972 and 1980. Statistical abstract of the united states: 1981. Washington DC: U.S. Bureau of the Census.

(1987). Table 627. Employed persons, by sex, race, and occupation: 1986. Statistical abstract of the united states: 1988. Washington DC: Bureau of the Census.

Abbott, A. D. (1988). *The system of professions: An essay on the division of expert labor.* Chicago, IL: University of Chicago.

Bell, D. (1976). *The coming of post-industrial society.* New York: Basic Books.

Bell, D. (1979). The social framework of the information society. In M. L. Dertouzos & J. Moss (Ed.), *The computer age: A twenty-year view* (pp. 163–211). Cambridge, MA: MIT Press.

Beniger, J. R. (1986). *The control revolution.* Cambridge, MA: Harvard University Press.

Chandler, A. D. Jr. (1977). *The visible hand: The managerial revolution in American business.* Cambridge, MA: Harvard University Press.

Debons, A., King, D. W., Mansfield, U., & Shirey, D. L. (1981). *The information professional: Survey of an emerging field.* New York: Marcel Dekker, Inc.

Dizard, W. P. J. (1982). *The coming information age: An overview of technology, economics, and politics.* New York: Longman.

Galbraith, J. K. (1967). *The new industrial state.* New York: The New American Library.

Heilbroner, R. L., & Singer, A. (1984). *The economic transformation of America: 1600 to the Present.* (2nd ed.). New York: Harcourt Brace Jovanovich.

Katz, R. L. (1988). *The information society.* New York: Praeger.

Machlup, F. (1962). *The production and distribution of knowledge in the United States.* Princeton, NJ: Princeton University Press.

Machlup, F., & Kronwinkler, T. (1975). Workers who produce knowledge: a steady increase, 1900 to 1970. *Weltwirtschaftliches Archiv., 111*(4), 752–759.

Machlup, F., & Mansfield, U. (1983). *The study of information: Interdisciplinary messages.* New York: John Wiley & Sons.

Nora, S., & Minc, A. (1978). *L'Informatisation de la societe.* La Documentation Française.

Ochai, A. (1984). The emerging information society. *International Library Review, 16*(4), 367–372.

Porat, M. U. (1977). *Information economy: Definition and measurement* (OT Special Publication 77–12 (1)). Washington DC: Department of Commerce/Office of Telecommunications.

Rubin, M. R. and Huber, M. T., with Taylor, E. L. (1986). *The knowledge industry in the United States 1960–1980.* Princeton, NJ: Princeton University Press.

Schement, J. R. (1989). The Origins of the Information Society in the United States: Competing Visions. In J. Salvaggio (Ed.), *The information society* (pp. 29–50). New York: Lawrence Erlhbaum.

Schement, J. R., & Lievrouw, L. A. (1984). A behavioural measure of information work. *Telecommunications Policy, 8*(4), 321–334.

Singlemann, J. (1978). *From agriculture to services.* Beverly Hills, CA: Sage.

Sloan, A. P. J. (1963). *My years with General Motors.* New York: Doubleday.

Smith, A. (1776/1902). *An inquiry into the nature and causes of the wealth of nations.* New York: American Home Library.

Toffler, A. (1980). *The third wave.* New York: William Morrow.

Williams, F. (1982). *The communications revolution.* Beverly Hills, CA: Sage.

17

FORTHCOMING FEATURES

Information and communications technologies and the sociology of the future

Peter Golding

Source: *Sociology* 34(1) (2000): 165–84.

Abstract

This article explores the social impact of new information and communication technologies (ICTs). It argues that they are best understood, not as heralding a substantially new 'information society', but as significant technologies emerging in but inherently part of late modernity. This argument is developed by examining themes from post-materialism, globalisation and information society theories. It is suggested there are two types of technology, those changing and extending existing processes and those facilitating wholly new activities, and that recent innovations in information and communication technology are rather better construed as the former. By examining empirically questions of identity, inequality, power and change the recent and future impact of ICTs is explored, and it is argued that current trends suggest increasing convergence (economic and organisational as much as technological), differentiation and deregulation.

Sociology is always writing the history of the future, yet routinely declares itself unready for the task. Somehow, whenever we sense the emanation of epochal change, sociology is deemed to be wanting. In the intense debate of the 1960s, Alvin Gouldner, predicting then the 'coming crisis of western sociology', argued that the sheer success of the discipline in entering the mainstream of popular culture had stunted its aspirations and achievements.

HISTORY AND PERSPECTIVES

Yet paradoxically, as social theory was being put to one side, those few that persisted in such work ignored the very real transformations of the society around them. Such theorists 'work within a crumbling social matrix of paralysed urban centres and battered campuses. Some may have cotton in their ears, but their bodies still feel the shock waves' (Gouldner 1971:vii).

Curiously, a generation later, recurrent attempts to prevent sociology succumbing to a 'flight from a reason' have been provoked by another succession of perceived disciplinary crises (Alexander 1995; Mouzelis 1995). Professional modesty feeds a prevailing sense of inadequacy in the face of apparently colossal, indeed millennial social change. This is, though, the eternal condition of sociology, and indeed its very genesis. As Smith notes, in recent years the imminent end of an era has frequently been signalled by analyses reporting on the end of history, of organised capitalism, of modernity, or of Western civilisation (Smith 1990:1). The grand narratives of classic sociology both responded to the urgent need to understand the emergence of industrial and modern urban society, and constructed clear dichotomies to characterise the difference between new and old. We are, it seems, always on the cusp of a new sociality.

At the end of the twentieth century this urge to inhabit the dawn is fostered above all by the spread of new information and communication technologies (ICTs). This article briefly assesses the extent and character of the changes consequent to their arrival, and the adequacy of sociology to understand them. Its simple theme is that continuity exceeds discontinuity. While recognising the very real and substantial changes provoked and enabled by such technologies, we need to see these, in Webster's phrase, as 'an informatisation of life which stems from the continuity of established forces' (Webster 1995:218). In part this is an insistence on the endurance of modernity and the intellectual and political baggage that comes with it. In part it is a plea for a stay of execution of the core tools and methods of the sociological imagination, and a reminder that the basis of prediction lies in examining social dynamics rather than technological innovation.

The imagery of the future looms over the landscapes of the present; tomorrow is ever-present in the cultural icons of everyday experience. For the *parti-pris*, like the world's richest man, Bill Gates, the information highway along which Microsoft is transporting us 'is going to give us all access to seemingly unlimited information, anytime and any place we care to use it' (Gates 1995:184). Technophiliac rebellion against decades of bleak paranoia about the portent of an Orwellian future has spawned belief in 'a new digital Jerusalem . . . Advertisements for cars, mobile phones, digital and satellite consumer goods all ask us to reflect on how new technologies will transform not just our social and cultural environments but the very idea of what it is to be human' (Sardar 1999:25). Consequently, we run towards the sound of funfair, as the increasing digitisation of everyday technologies apparently opens vistas of freedom from the constraints of material scarcity, and from the mundane barriers of power, privilege and place. This is not, however, the stuff of serious sociology.

New for old: interpreting the information society

Understanding the sociology of the shifts engendered by the rapid expansion of ICT has drawn on a number of key concepts, of which three will be briefly examined here.

The first is the notion *of post-materialism* arising especially from extensive empirical work by Inglehart and his collaborators. Rooted in Maslow's psychological concept of a needs hierarchy, and something akin to a principle of marginal utility, the thesis has two key hypotheses (Inglehart 1990). These seek to explain why cultural change is 'leading to the de-emphasis of economic growth as the dominant goal of society' (p. 3). The first, the 'scarcity hypothesis', suggests people place first and highest priority on those things least available to them. The second, the 'socialisation hypothesis', suggests a person's values will continue to reflect those prevailing in their maturing, pre-adult years (pp. 56, 68). Added together these produce an account of cultural history in Western countries since 1945 which argues that unprecedented prosperity, peace, prevailing affluence and social stability have nurtured a shift from materialist values, rooted in concern for material and physical security, to post-materialist values, concerned with quality of life, expressiveness, the environment and so on. From a cohort of somewhat dull and aspiring workaholics has been bred a generation of underachieving aesthetes.

The thesis has been the basis for a substantial industry of empirical, largely survey research, and an extensive literature addressing the conceptual as well as methodological assumptions and reservations which this now massive, influential (especially in political science) and sophisticated body of work has attracted (see *inter alia*, Scarbrough 1995; Warwick 1998), not least the vexed issue of whether what is being tapped are generational or cohort effects. The essential narrative is straightforward and nicely nurtures a growing esteem for the sociology of lunching and shopping. Indeed, a burgeoning fascination with garden centres, DIY and designer clothing would seem to complement Inglehart's work. The relevant issue here is not the wider assessment of post-materialism, but its inextricable linkage with the notion of an information society, to which we turn shortly. For Inglehart, post-materialism arises from a societal shift in which scarcity disappears, and post-materialist values nurture the emergence of a 'new class' within the knowledge and information occupations. However, an alternative reading of these trends is that post-materialism becomes the acceptable ideology of occupational and educational elites: 'these variables are the bearers, at the individual level, of the effects of macrolevel changes in the economic and social environment' (Scarbrough 1995:149). Not surprisingly large proportions of

HISTORY AND PERSPECTIVES

the populations of Western industrial societies turn out to be firmly, and sensibly, rooted in materialist concerns for an income, the next meal and a roof over their heads.

The inevitably ideological character of concepts fuelled by ICT developments is equally reflected in the notion of *globalisation.* Again, it is impossible here to give adequate attention to the important debates provoked by this notion. Suffice to note the emphasis in the literature on globalisation on the ability of new ICTs to emancipate human experience from the familiar ties of social and economic formation. Waters (1995:124), for example, suggests that globalisation means 'material and power exchanges in the economic and political arenas . . . progressively becoming displaced by symbolic ones, that is by relationships based on values, preferences and tastes rather than by material inequality and constraint'. The parallel with post-materialism is obvious, and hard to reconcile with the continuing evidence of inequalities on a planet in which 70 per cent of resources are consumed by 15 per cent of the population. As I have argued elsewhere (Golding and Harris 1997:8),

> We are a long way, surely, from believing that parallel style wars among the urban youth of Tokyo, Dar-Es- Salaam, Lima, and New York are a greater reality than the desperate efforts to eke out some form of subsistence among the billion or so of the world's inhabitants living on less than a dollar a day.

The concept of globalisation also underestimates the persistence of the nation-state as political form and economic entity, albeit in dynamic and changing structure (cf. Weiss 1998). While the new international division of labour has certainly relocated production and the circuits of goods, people and capital, the varied extent of success between national economies suggests something other than globalisation. Despite the undoubted increase in global flows of capital and labour, most remain within national boundaries. The United States, in particular, remains immune to such dissolution of nation-state frontiers. As for capital so too for consciousness. As Billig (1995) has recently reminded us, what he terms the daily 'flagging' of nation and nationality forms an inescapable and formative backdrop to everyday experience and rhetoric. The boundaries between 'us' and 'foreigners' are not just the lines around which the racism of ethnic antagonisms is drawn, though they serve that purpose only too well. 'These habits of thinking persist, not as vestiges of a past age, having outlived their function; they are rooted to forms of life, in an era in which the state may be changing, but has not yet withered away' (Billig 1995:139). The ability of ICTs to enhance as well as banish the frontiers of modernity is too often ignored. While some can buy their books, drugs, cars and pornography on-line trans-nationally, others remain locked into the constraints of local economy. That their protection from low-wage regimes imposed by Nike and Nintendo in Asian factories depends on national legislation, not the will of the north-American or European consumers of their work, underlines the persistent if variable role of the nation-state boundary in human experience in the medium term future.

The third notion briefly assessed here is the most fundamental – a broad encapsulation of the argument that the growth of ICTs has fostered a whole-sale shift in the social order. The idea of an *information society* lurks behind several other such general characterisations, including those considered above, and its various manifestations nurture much futurology. Its ideological aspects have never been obscure, and have attracted frequent commentary (cf. Slack 1984). Originating in Japanese observation, in the notion of *johoka-shakai*, usually translated as 'the information society', its influence has been profound (Duff *et al.* 1996). In its Western lineage the focus has been on employment and the economy, not least in measures of sectoral employ-ment and shifting profiles of occupational activity (cf. Machlup 1962). The most enduring development has been in the scholarly and influential work of Daniel Bell (1976, 1979). The post-industrial tag, for Bell, was the context for the emergence of a new economic order characterised by the central importance of information and theoretical knowledge, and by a shift from a goods-producing to a service society.

It is this latter observation that is central here. As Webster (1995:34–46) and others have crucially observed, the movement to a service economy has, in fact, been a long-term trend, thoroughly pre-dating recent rapid innova-tions in ICTs. But the notion of an information society rests fundamentally on this presumed shift. In Britain, for one, the proportion of the labour force in manufacturing has been relatively stable for much of the last cen-tury, the more significant shift being the decline of agriculture and the growth in services. But this also disguises some tacit assumptions about the nature and function of work. The wage-slave welded to a desk, word-processing invoices for Ford Motors, is information processing in one sense, but pro-ducing cars in another and more meaningful sense. Those computers and faxes easing the path of the 'weightless economy' emerge from plastic, metal ore, steel and assembly line industries somewhere around the world. In fact, much of the shift in recent years has been within sectors. Analysis by Gershuny showed that of the increase in 'knowledge workers' during the sample period in the 1970s he examined, 'less than a quarter appears to be due to the growth in the service industries, while, more than three-quarters comes from the increase in the proportion of employees in service occupa-tions within industries' (Gershuny 1983:107). Changes in work practice, work relations, but not the industrial order emerge as the 'information society' becomes more evident (cf. OECD 1981).

The notion of an information society has been equally profound in the politics of prophecy. If the birth of the information society is inevitable, it will none the less not lack for powerful and rhetorically insistent midwives.

In preparing for office the rapidly modernising British Labour party confidently declared:

> We stand on the threshold of a revolution as profound as that brought about by the invention of the printing press. New technologies, which enable rapid communication to take place in a myriad of different ways across the globe, and permit information to be provided, sought, and received on a scale hitherto unimaginable, will bring fundamental change to all our lives.

It went on to note that 'In the new information society, we can either allow the technology to drive these changes forward in a haphazard and incoherent fashion, or we can choose to shape them for the benefit of our community as a whole' (Labour Party 1997:1). The new government's initial attempts to nudge the process along included a plethora of select committees and reports, the DTI Multi-Media Industry Advisory Group and the same department's Information Society Initiative (Phillips 1997).

At European level the same anxiety to hasten the inevitable has been fuelled by an obsession to see off competition from Japan and the United States, but with a wholly contradictory double focus on, on the one hand, the need to protect and foster a presumed European culture and, on the other, the need to enhance European industrial and economic progress in the ICT sector. Both in the United Kingdom and at European level it is plainly the latter which prevails, as the emergence of the information society is embodied in the imposition of commercial need and corporate strategy onto the remnants of cultural and social policy in the communications field (Murdock and Golding 1999). The EU fifth Framework Programme seeks to embrace and deliver a 'user-friendly information society'. From the premise, uncompromisingly proclaimed, that 'We are undergoing a fundamental transformation: from an industrial society to the information society', it slips awkwardly between concern that 'Europe's industrial competitiveness . . . depends on it being at the leading edge of the development' and that the same developments will 'contribute to cohesion in the European Union' by overcoming isolation in remote communities (European Commission 1997a:1). Strangely, by the time we get to the final report of the European Union's expert group on the information society this ambiguity is beginning to resolve. We now learn that 'New commercial opportunities . . . will focus in the first instance on those activities with the most commercial potential . . . Seen from this angle a generalised European directive on an extended USO [universal service obligation in telephony] is unlikely to contribute in any real sense to regional cohesion' (European Commission 1997b:37). Information society policy both anticipates and celebrates the privatisation of information, and the incorporation of ICT developments into the expansion of the free market. The launch of a *Magna Carta* for the information age sets this firmly in the libertarian rhetoric of US political economy; 'the key principle of ownership by the people – private ownership – should govern every deliberation. Government does not own cyberspace, the people do' (Calabrese 1997:16).

One member of the EU expert group was Manuel Castells, and his powerful and encyclopaedic survey of the 'information age' represents the most important recent examination of the information society thesis. Castells distinguishes carefully between the information society (which could apply to almost all past societies) and the 'informational society', 'in which information generation, processing, and transmission become the fundamental sources of productivity and power' (Castells 1996:21). In such societies ICT promotes networking as a 'dynamic, self-expanding form of human activity' which 'transforms all domains of social and economic life' (Castells 1998:336–7). Castells's exhaustive and massively researched elaboration of this argument is a major contribution to social analysis, and cannot be adequately addressed here. None the less, with its echoes of the 'modernisation' thesis – a hint that all societies will move inexorably over the next twenty years to the condition of late twentieth-century southern California (though Castells eschews both futurology and historicism) – his analysis has inevitably prompted dissent.

Garnham (1998), for example, in a forceful and compelling critique, notes that the presumption that ICTs engender vast expansion in the productive capacity of those societies in which they are pervasive, is not borne out by the evidence – rapid growth of productivity in Japan and Germany was in periods in which they were relatively low in ICT development. Castells makes much of the 'spirit of informationalism' – as he puts it himself, 'Schumpeter meets Weber in the cyberspace of the network enterprise' (Castells 1996:199). As Garnham notes, there is an almost mystical dependence on this concept, which is not only tautologous, but also parallels many of the less certain features of post-modernism, not least in that it is ideological 'in the sense of distracting from underlying, more deeply rooted, structures of interest' (Garnham 1998:114). Garnham argues that these developments are not new, or at least not epochal, but reflect the continuing need to create value with information commodities.

The spirit of technological determinism is hard to exorcise from many renderings of information society theory. In place of what Raymond Williams (1974:15) succinctly describes as a 'continuing complex of need and invention and application', is a heightened regard for the fundamental social shifts presumed inevitable and inherent in new media of communication. The danger is that the fascination of the new distracts sociology from its proper focus on what Winston, in his book-length assault on technological determinism, describes as 'the law of the suppression of radical potential' (Winston 1998: *passim*), in other words the solidity and endurance of social and economic formations in the face of technical novelty. But how new is new?

HISTORY AND PERSPECTIVES

Means and ends: two types of technology

Technology may be construed as the mechanisms by which human agency manipulates the material world. We can conceive of two forms of technological innovation. Technology One allows existing social action and process to occur more speedily, more efficiently, or conveniently (though equally possibly, with negative consequences, such as pollution or risk). Technology Two enables wholly new forms of activity previously impracticable or even inconceivable. In essence many new ICTs are more obviously Technology One than Technology Two.

Compared with the 'miracle' of telephony – speaking over vast distances, in real time, to unseen interlocutors contacted accurately from among millions of potential alternatives – the hype surrounding the impact of e-mail seems extravagant. The capacity of the internet to facilitate on-line communities through Usenet and newsgroups is indisputable, but overstatement of their social importance might be compared with an equally implausible claim that enthusiasm for pen-pals created a new social order among the literate. Equally, and even earlier, the profound social impact of the telegraph vastly exceeded, at least so far, that of more recent ICTs. As Carey notes, a full account of the telegraph would describe how it 'altered the spatial and temporal boundaries of human interaction, brought into existence new forms of language as well as new conceptual systems', and not least enabled the networking of a national commercial middle class in the United States. Not surprisingly, he claims, 'the innovation of the telegraph can stand metaphorically for all the innovations that ushered in the modern phase of history' (Carey 1989:202–4).

Interestingly, at its birth the telegraph attracted the same form of almost spiritual accreditation as Castells accords new ICTs; what Leo Marx terms 'the rhetoric of the technological sublime' (cited in Carey 1989:206). As the telegraph was unleashing and enabling North American commercial expansion, so too it provided the nervous system of empire. Submarine telegraphy made contact with the outposts of the British empire independent of intermediate countries, and further enabled central control from London. By 1870 permanent lines installed at the Foreign and Colonial Offices completed the circuit (Standage 1999:96–7, 148). The unmistakable link between the telegraph and the contours of imperialism – possibly among the most profound global legacies of later modernity – is still readily discernible, not just in the geometry of international telecommunications but in the topography of post-colonialism.

By contrast with the Technology One character of most recent ICTs, developments in biotechnology presage real change in what human action and activity might obtain and pursue. They represent examples of Technology Two. Advances in genetics, or the as yet uncertain ripples from the human genome project, posit the possibility of manipulation of human biology at the molecular or even chromosomal level, such that, as Rose has suggested (1999) in the age-old debate about the primacy of nature or nurture, sociology finds itself disconcerted by the novelty that it may be easier to change human genetics than social or cultural context. If the nineteenth century was the age of the telegraph and telephony, and the twenty-first becomes that of biotechnology, it is not necessarily the case that the intervening era of late modernity is best conceived as the 'information age'.

Towards a sociology of the information age: fallacies and futures

The theme of this article is the robust relevance of the key terms of sociological enquiry, as they emerge from an engagement with capitalism and modernity, to the social changes inherent in and consequential to new ICTs. Four such terms can very briefly be listed here to illustrate, though not adequately to demonstrate, this point. In so doing at least four potential fallacies of the information age thesis come into view.

The first is *identity: the fallacy of the postmodern subject.* For Tony Hall, chief executive of BBC News, one unique value and virtue of the BBC is its capacity to show it 'can be good to be British'. However dynamic and difficult to define, 'Britishness is still based on a profound sense of fair play, personal liberty and voluntary commitment. We still queue at the slightest provocation, while ball-tampering is practically a hanging offence' (Hall 1999). But the ubiquity of ICTs is seen by many as precisely the means by which identity is playfully disposable and malleable, a matter of choice and demonstration rather than imposition, of achievement rather than ascription. Not just 'Where do you want to go today?' but 'Who do you want to be today?'

The fallacy of the postmodern subject finds its keenest expression in much writing on computer-mediated communication (cf. Jones 1998; Ito 1996; Bromberg 1996). Much analysis of the sociology of cyberspace apes, but does not match, the visionary fiction of William Gibson. Turkle, of whom this is not true, however, argues that the internet is 'changing the way we think, the nature of our sexuality, the form of our communities, our very identities' (Turkle 1996:10). Her case studies of participants in multi-user computer games (MUDs, and the like) signify a wider context in which we find 'eroding boundaries between the real and the virtual, the animate and the inanimate, the unitary and the multiple self' in the patterns of everyday life (1996:10). There are here, essentially, two problems.

First, identity continues to reflect the resilience of national and state boundaries, albeit in increasingly complex and protean formation. Billig's insistence (1995) on the perpetuity of 'banal nationalism' reminds us that it is one of the obstinate contours of identity formation. As Keohane and Nye (1998:82, 85) argue, 'Prophets of a new cyberworld, like modernists before

HISTORY AND PERSPECTIVES

them, often overlook how much the new world overlaps and rests on the traditional world in which power depends on geographically based institutions . . . the information revolution exists in the context of an existing political structure'. Secondly, presuming a shift from a politics of distribution to a politics of identity elides the supply side of symbolic circulation. The media, and more generally the communication and cultural industries, provide the symbolic resources that people use to make sense of their lives and their relationships with social institutions. These resources are increasingly controlled and rationed by surprisingly few, largely corporate, interests. Stuart Hall notes that the erosion of national identities by the global postmodern is countered by resistance locally to globalisation. More crucially, as he points out, cultural (not just national) identity comes from representation. The very decentring of the subject at the core of the postmodern analysis means we are 'confronted by a bewildering, fleeting multiplicity of possible identities', including those of the narrative of nation (Hall 1992:277, 292). But this multiplicity is not infinite, and depends significantly on powerful flows of representation. As Morley and Robins (1995:19, 38–9) point out, for example, the retreat of public service broadcasting across Europe dismantles a political culture in which questions of identity and citizenship were bound together. The space within which the symbolic resources for addressing such questions can be found 'is shaped and maintained by transnational capital: it is the space of IBM and AT&T, of Murdoch and Berlusconi.' Information society theses, like some kinds of post-modernist theory, remain preoccupied with image, simulation, and spectacle (Morley and Robins 1995:39). The manufacturers and distributors of the raw resources of identity construction are to be found elsewhere, in familiar and very material locations.

The second term is *inequality:* in the future, it is claimed, ICTs will unlock the door to a society of unlimited resources. The plenitude of the information economy will end deprivation and need. Here we run into the fallacy of universal abundance. The diffusion of new consumer goods in the past has inevitably moved from more affluent groups rapidly through to the less affluent, until widely, even ubiquitously, available. However, recent communications goods and resources do not replicate this pattern for two reasons (Golding 1990; Golding and Murdock 1989). First, earlier innovations were introduced in a period of rapid economic growth, rising popular affluence, and diminishing inequality, none of which obtain now or in the medium-term future. Secondly, ICT goods require recurrent investment. The PC needs updating or regular replacement, feeding with software, garlanding with add-ons – a modem, a printer, a scanner, on-line costs. The consequence for the distribution of such goods is inevitable. As Fortner (1995:142) notes, in the United States 'the only information technology that has consistently high penetration regardless of income is television'. The pattern for the United Kingdom is presented in Table 1.

FORTHCOMING FEATURES

Table 1 Household Ownership of Selected Communications Facilities, United Kingdom 1997–98.

	Proportion (%) of households owning item in each income group					
Consumer goods	*Lowest 20%*	*Second quintile*	*Third quintile*	*Fourth quintile*	*Highest 20%*	*All*
Telephone*	79	92	96	98	100	93
Mobile phone*	3	6	12	21	38	16
Satellite dish *	7	16	20	26	28	19
Home computer*	8	12	22	34	57	27
VCR†	65	76	91	94	97	84

Sources: *Office of National Statistics (1997:154).
†Office of National Statistics (1998:135).

The cliché that ICT development leads to information poor and information rich is nowhere more evident and substantiated than in the growth of the internet. Director of the MIT Media Lab and digital visionary Nicholas Negroponte argues that: 'Some people worry about the social divide between the information-rich and the information-poor, the haves and the have-nots, the first and Third Worlds. But the real cultural divide is going to be generational' (Negroponte 1996:6). But he has the wrong demographic variable. Table 2 sets out recent figures for internet access in the United Kingdom. Increasing evidence of consistency in such figures suggests a settling pattern of high users and excluded non-users which will provide a digital underpinning to structures of material inequality that are more likely to become self-replicating than abating.

The third fallacy concerns *power.* The distribution of new ICTs can provide the vehicle for the conquest of *dirigiste* and centralised government; the push-button democracy or electronic forum is but a few cables away. That presumption, the fallacy of interactivity, is found most prevalently in preliminary analyses of politics and the internet, and its analysis would extend beyond the space available here (cf. Golding 1998). As the net has become

Table 2 Demographic Correlates of Internet Access: United Kingdom, 1998.

Socio-Economic Group	*% with a PC at home*	*% with internet access*
AB	64	27
C_1	50	17
C_2	41	9
DE	26	6
All (15+)	44	14

Source: BMRB (1999:5, 7).

more and more a commercial medium, from the point in 1995 when .com domains exceeded in number all others, the politics has itself become part of the commercial embrace. As Huber put it, 'By providing efficient integrated global data connections, telecommunications companies now offer voters the ultimate shopping experience: shopping for better government' (Huber 1996:142).

Among the frequently observed dangers inherent in 'direct' democracy is its evacuation of secondary association, what Coleman (1999:18) describes as 'techno-populism', serving as 'a chilling warning of the kind of plebiscitary authoritarianism which lies not far beneath the surface rhetoric and imagery of the Global Village Meeting House'. The promise of interactivity is that voters will have direct access to their political rulers. The electronic referendum would provide a recurrent check for accountability and democratic politics, and political information for citizenship would be boundless and instantly accessible.

The digital Athenian democracy this conjures up also, among sceptical observers, prompts the reminder that in Athens neither women nor slaves got much of a political look in. Not only that but the character of the politics envisaged in these scenarios changes the essential nature of democracy. As Stoll points out, 'This electronic town hall removes valid reasons for representative government. What's the purpose of a representative when each of us can vote immediately on every issue?' (1995:33). There is here the potential for a fundamental individualisation of politics. In cyberdemocracy the role of representative and intermediary organisations – trade unions, community groups, political parties, pressure groups – atrophies. As a result, as Dutch analysts Van de Donk and Tops suggest, 'representative organisations may disappear . . . A direct plebiscitarian democracy becomes feasible when the "demos" . . . can come together "virtually"' (Van de Donk and Tops 1995:16). But the presupposition of universal access, itself illusory, is also based on a fiction about the nature of interactivity. Home shopping on the web has not yet taken off because people want to touch, see and interact with what they are buying and those from whom they purchase it. But that may change as systems become more reliable and secure; by 1999 selling goods to the public over the internet was already a $500 million business, and website advertising, the more likely growth area ('on-screen real estate') was attracting an estimated $325 million. Interactivity on the web, far from a mechanism for democratic debate and influence, will distil, as Besser (1995:63) sardonically notes, into 'responding to multiple-choice questions and entering credit card numbers on a key pad'. Thus individualisation, unequal access, and disenfranchisement maybe the outcome of net politics.

The fourth potential fallacy relates to *change*: crucial to the fundamental shift assumed to be endemic in the social order of the information society is the compression of time and space, and indeed the 'death of distance', 'probably the single most important force shaping society in the first half of the next century' (Cairncross 1998:1). The flow of people, images, goods, information and materials is so fast, and often instantaneous, it is suggested, that physical space diminishes as a dimension in human experience, finally and fully colonised by human sovereignty over communication and movement. How far this fallacy accords with the evidence of urban gridlock, air travel whose average speed from destination to destination has changed little in decades, or the frustrations of 'computer rage', driving e-mail addicts to reach for a postage stamp or the phone, bears further investigation. Theoretically the shift is forward from the consequence of modernity described by Giddens, in which 'time–space distanciation' means that the present and propinquity are not the only, or even primary contexts and determinants of action and understanding. 'The advent of modernity increasingly tears space away from place by fostering relations between 'absent' others, locationally distant from any given situation of face-to-face interaction' (Giddens 1991:18). From here we come to Castells's argument that the decline in the power (though not the influence) of the state allows individual subjects, with sovereignty over self-defined and plural identities, autonomy from the state-bounded definitions of time and space (Castells 1997:243). This process extends so far in the network society that reflexively organised life-planning, for Giddens a characteristic feature of modernity, becomes impossible for most, inhibited by 'the systemic disjunction between the local and the global' (Castells 1997:11). Civil societies disintegrate, and what Castells terms 'project identity', or 'collective action', emerges only from communal resistance (cf. Melucci 1996).

As Bauman has noted, even if this account were to reflect the experiential realities of some, it is certainly not the fate of all or even many. Time (and also distance) is, as they say, money. Commenting on the notion of the 'end of geography', Bauman notes that "distance" is a social product'. But, as Bauman (1998:12, 18) goes on, this polarises rather than homogenises experience.

> For some people it augurs an unprecedented freedom from physical obstacles and unheard-of ability to move and act from a distance. For others it portends the impossibility of appropriating and domesticating the locality from which they have little chance of cutting themselves free in order to move elsewhere.

Time and space are mediated by material resources, and both are social to the extent that they impinge on and derive from other dimensions of collective experience. Extensive travel may be desirable if voluntary and in attractive locations, avoided or resented if provoked by long-distance commuting or the mobile office. Time is only a resource if positively and enjoyably occupied. Increases in work hours, for example, suggest a compression of leisure time driven socially and economically, not technologically, creating among other things, the phenomenon of the 'resource rich and time poor'.

The evidence of untrammelled and instant movement is less than compelling. A sharp transference from public to private travel in recent years, from bus and train to car, is manifest. But in 1998 in the United Kingdom about 13 million people did not have access to a car. Average speed of travel in those cars in the Greater London area declined from 18 m.p.h. in 1970 to 16 m.p.h. in 1996 (*Social Trends* 29:196). Not everyone was airborne. While only 1 per cent of miles travelled was by air, the car reigned supreme (*Social Trends* 29:Table 12.2). Most travel is wholly functional (commuting and shopping), and while commuting trips are increasing in volume (and discomfort) they remain relatively short (Office for National Statistics 1999: Table 1.8; Banister and Gallent 1998). Many travel seldom and parochially. In the United Kingdom 41 per cent of the population in 1998 took no holiday away from home at all during the year, a figure which has scarcely fluctuated in the last twenty years. Jones notes the paradoxical effect of some new ICTs to abolish not distance but proximity; 'we may eschew some forms of proximal communication . . . for ones that distance us', e-mailing our nearest and dearest, or at least local colleagues rather than encountering them in person over the photocopier (Jones 1998:xiii).

Twenty years ago the coming of ICTs was threatening the end of work (cf. Jones 1982; Jenkins and Sherman 1981). The 'death of work' is certainly not reflected in data on the labour force. The growth of new technologies has in many areas compressed time through the expansion of work, and changed the nature of space, rather than eliminating it, by diffusing the spatiality of work into other zones. The unleashing of an embarrassing excess of leisure opportunities forecast in the 1970s and 1980s is now confronted by evidence of both longer working hours and the increase, particularly among women, of participation rates. Between 1984 and 1997 the UK labour force increased from 24 million to 26.7 million, especially enlarged by the growth of the female labour force from 9.9 million to 12 million in the same period. Work hours have not reduced to compensate. Average hours worked were 44.3 per week in 1984 for men, and 44.1 in 1997. For women, more concentrated in part-time work, the average has none the less remained static (actually rising from 30 to 30.8 hours per week over the period). The total volume of paid employment time, as an aggregate for the population, is thus substantially higher now than a generation ago (Office of National Statistics 1999). This trend defies the more usual presumption that 'the growth of employment in the expanding industries (especially the IT sector) is not enough to counterbalance the declining industries and to accommodate the growing population' (Van Den Besselaar 1997:389). As the efficiencies of new ICTs displace traditional occupations, instead of the triumph of leisure we obtain both increases in unemployment but also the expansion of insecure, low-paid and largely female paid employment in a labour market expanded to embrace work previously located in the informal or service sectors.

This is especially true of the kind of paid work facilitated by new ICTs, notably home working. Analyses of homeworking highlight great uncertainty about their numbers, though it is quite certainly a largely female labour force, and one that has possibly trebled since 1981 (Felstead 1996). The impact on differential opportunity for time–space compression (emancipation for some, confinement for others), is nowhere more intense than in the homeworking of the information age, 'telework'. As Stanworth shows, the anticipated liberation arising from 'virtual organisations' has rarely arrived, while flexible 'outsourcing' creates a dependent and insecure online labour force. Although for some the mobile phone and laptop service a mobile office, releasing the hot-desking sales manager onto the motorway and rail network, for others it is simply the transfer of the costs of production from employer to employee. Telework is only growing very slowly, and much new work is in routine tasks such as data entry. However, 'there is clear evidence of the perpetuation of labour market segmentation and the continued importance of gender and class divisions in the teleworkforce' (Stanworth 1998:59). As in so much else in this debate, one is compelled to mutter, *plus ça change* . . .

Trends and continuities: the sociology of impatience

The recent and rapid emergence of new ICTs among the vistas of everyday experience, not least for the intelligentsia and literati, has fuelled a powerful sense of having crossed a fissure into tomorrow. Impatient for a wholly different social order we prematurely discover its embryo in contemporary innovation. But the techno-centric core to this sensibility is occasion for sociological caution. In assessing the impact, both recent and immanent, of these technologies, we find, above all, the abiding fault lines of modernity. Three broad trends emerge – convergence, deregulation and differentiation.

The digitisation of various communications media enables the common distribution and storage of information, knowledge and entertainment across what were previously quite distinct platforms or media. This is not yet the death of the book, but it does underpin what is widely seen as the accelerating *convergence* of ICTs, abolishing any meaningful distinction between film, video, television, publishing or the internet. The consolidation of computing, telecommunications and broadcasting especially, rewrites the previously distinct character of analogue media. More importantly, however, convergence should be read as an organisational and economic phenomenon, recognisable most obviously at the level of corporate strategy and structure.

In Europe this activity has been mainly in telecommunications, in the United States in the audio-visual sector, and in Japan in electronics. The wider trend of mega-mergers in the audio-visual sectors has included the take-over by Canadian wine and drinks giant Seagram of MCA, which controls Universal Studios; Time Warner's buy out of Turner Broadcasting; Disney's purchase of Capital Cities (including the ABC network); and the take-over by Westinghouse of the CBS network. Time–Warner, the largest purely media corporation on the planet, embraces *Time* magazine, Warner music and Warner Bros. studios, the Home Box Office TV channel, and major holdings in cable systems and channels, as well as the mammoth operation in book-selling operated by Time Life Books, and Time–Warner Telecom.

The growth of vertical integration strategies which this trend represents places the audio-visual sector in a key position, as distribution becomes the next priority for internet commercialisation. This is well represented by the 1994 purchase by media giant Viacom, which controls the MTV channels, of the Paramount movie studios. Viacom also owns publisher Simon and Schuster, the Nickelodeon chain, and Blockbuster video. The merger in 1999 of Viacom with CBS in a \$36 billion deal created a content and distribution combine of unprecedented proportions and market reach. Behind the new giant, Disney, previously second only to Time–Warner as a media corporation, controls search engine Infoseek. America Online, now the dominant player in internet services since its take-over of CompuServe, finds itself under growing competition from software colossus Microsoft, which fends off antitrust assaults while expanding into cable television and news networks. British Telecom has formed an alliance with AT&T for data, voice and video services. The 1999 merger of Excite, provider of internet services to 28 million registered users, with the Home Service TV footprint of more than 65 million homes world-wide, illustrates what the new company's chief executive described as 'the dawn of a new Internet era that will revolutionise the way consumers view and interact with communication, information, and entertainment services' (company press release). Somehow the dream of Jeffersonian democracy through optic fibres had been transposed into the opportunity to save a twenty-minute round trip to the video rental store.

The atrophy of public service broadcasting is emblematic of decreased certainty about the role of the state in relation to communications institutions (Golding and van Snippenberg 1995). Eternal conflict over the twin, but contradictory role of communications as both the raw resource for citizenship, governed by criteria of need, rights and communality, but also as commodities for consumers, governed only by market power, has continued to challenge policy debate. New ICTs provide a wider range of distribution channels but do not in principle address that contradiction. European policy has continued along twin tracks, unclear which is the priority, while G7 direction is insistently neo-liberal.

Regulation of information and communication has traditionally sought to inhibit presumed harmful or 'anti-social' material, while promoting the productive, socially desirable and educational. The terms of this debate become ever less certain as the boundaries of public and private, culture and difference, disintegrate. The trend of recent years has normally been seen as *deregulation*, the retreat from direct statutory intervention by the state into communications institutions. But, while most evident in the expansion of private sector broadcasting and the waning of public corporations, more widely the issue becomes the re-regulation of the relationship between the state and the production and distribution of information and communication goods and services.

The third broad trend that may be discerned is that of *differentiation.* The tables presented above simply provide a snap-shot of the rapid translation of income inequalities into ICT stratification. For the reasons advanced earlier, this is more likely to be a stable pattern than a transient state. What was once the 'syndication of experience' becomes niche culture. Increasingly, differentiated cultural consumption across social sectors constricts access to common experience, and thus thwarts the shared interrogation of cultural symbols which is at the core of a social and political order. Evidence from many industrial societies would seem to point to an intensified segmentation of cultural consumption and, with the transfer from public to private of much of the communication order, a further move away from a public sphere of any recognisable vitality.

How these changes will shape the cultural landscape of Britain in 2025 is plainly difficult to predict. The theme of this article is the persistence of familiar patterns of social structure and experience. The growing prevalence and prominence of new ICTs, however, may have two beneficial consequences for the discipline's capacity to assess and analyse those patterns. First, the pervasive impact of new technologies on the worlds of work, leisure, consumption and education will, or should, ensure that any theory construction addressed to their understanding will necessarily engage with crucial questions of social and public policy across a range of institutional spheres. The accidental organisational and disciplinary rift between sociology and social policy which emerged in post-war British social science may be bridged as a consequence. Secondly, the welcome re-emphasis in sociology on the cultural in recent years, has also, and in parallel, seen the growing autonomy of studies of the cultural zones of human life – the media and popular culture especially – into quasi disciplines. But culture has its structural and institutional dynamics too, and the renewed permeability of these areas of interest and study by the core concerns of sociology would be to the benefit of both.

It is easy to construct a visionary epic from the impact of new ICTs, peopled by cyborgs and digitised into a Utopian landscape of limitless expressive leisure, or alternatively a bleak wasteland of panoptic centralisation and anomic screen-bound cultural dupes. Prediction is the snare of the social scientist, and a folly to be resisted. But the key lesson of our experience to date of the startling and rapid innovations in communications technologies is the enduring centrality of the key analytical elements of modernity, explored here as identity, inequality, power and change. The sociology of the future is ineluctably the sociology of the present.

References

Alexander, J. C. 1995. *fin de Stècle Social Theory: Relativism, Reduction, and the Problem of Reason.* London: Verso.

Banister, C. and Gallent, N. 1998. 'Trends in Commuting in England and Wales – Becoming Less Sustainable'. *Area* 30:331–41.

Bauman, Z. 1998. *Globalization: The Human Consequences.* Cambridge: Polity Press.

Bell, D. 1976. *The Coming of Post-Industrial Society: A Venture in Social Forecasting.* Harmondsworth: Penguin Books.

Bell, D. 1979. 'The Social Framework of the Information Society'. In M. L. Dertouzos and J. Moses (eds.), *The Computer Age: A Twenty Year View.* Cambridge, Mass.: MIT Press.

Besser, H. 1995. 'From Internet to Information Superhighway'. In J. Brook and I. Boal (eds.), *Resisting the Virtual Life: The Culture and Politics of Information.* San Francisco: City Lights.

Billig, M. 1995. *Banal Nationalism.* London: Sage.

British Market Research Bureau (BMRB) 1999. *Is IT For All?* London: BMRB.

Bromberg, H. 1996. 'Are MUDs Communities? Identity, Belonging and Consciousness in Virtual Worlds'. In R. Shields (ed.), *Cultures of Internet: Virtual Spaces, Real Histories, Living Bodies.* London: Sage.

Cairncross, F. 1998. *The Death of Distance: How the Communications Revolution Will Change our Lives* London: Orion Books.

Calabrese, A. 1997. 'Creative Destruction? From the Welfare State to the Global Information Society'. *Javnost – The Public* 4(4):7–23.

Carey, J. 1989. 'Technology and Ideology: The Case of the Telegraph'. In J. Carey, *Communication as Culture: Essays in Media and Society.* London: Unwin Hyman.

Castells, M. 1996. *The Rise of the Network Society.* London: Blackwell.

Castells, M. 1997. *The Power of Identity.* London: Blackwell.

Castells, M. 1998. *End of Millennium.* London: Blackwell.

Coleman, S. 1999. 'Can the New Media Invigorate Democracy?' *Political Quarterly* 70:16–22.

Duff, A. S., Craig, D. and McNeill, D. A. 1996. 'A Note on the Origins of the "Information Society"'. *Journal of Information Science* 22:117–22.

European Commission 1997a. *Creating a User-Friendly Information Society.* Working document on the Information Society Technologies (IST) Programme, COM (97) 553. Brussels: Commission of the European Union.

European Commission 1997b. *Building the European Information Society for Us All.* final Policy Report of the High-level Expert Group. Directorate-General V for Employment, Industrial Relations, and Social Affairs. Unit V/B/4. Brussels: Commission of the European Union.

Felstead, A. 1996. 'Homeworking in Britain: The National Picture in the mid-1990s'. *Industrial Relations Journal* 27:225–38.

Fortner, R. S. 1995. 'Excommunication in the Information Society'. *Critical Studies in Mass Communication* 12:133–54.

Garnham, N. 1998. 'Information Society Theory as Ideology: A Critique'. *Loisir et Société* 21:97–120.

Gates, B. 1995. *The Road Ahead.* New York: Viking Books.

Gershuny, J. 1983. *Social Innovation and the Division of Labour.* Oxford: Oxford University Press.

Giddens, A. 1991. *The Consequences of Modernity.* Cambridge: Polity Press.

Golding, P. 1990. 'Political Communication and Citizenship: The Media and Democracy in an Inegalitarian Social Order'. In M. Ferguson (ed.), *Public Communications: The New Imperatives.* London: Sage.

Golding, P. 1998. 'World Wide Wedge: Division and Contradiction in the Global Information Infrastructure'. In D. K. Thussu (ed.), *Electronic Empires: Global Media and Local Resistance.* London: Arnold.

Golding, P. and Harris, P. 1997. 'Introduction'. In Golding and Harris, *Beyond Cultural Imperialism: Globalisation, Communication, and the New International Order.* London: Sage.

Golding, P. and Murdock, G. 1989. 'Information Poverty and Political Inequality: Citizenship in the Age of Privatised Communications'. *Journal of Communication* 39:180–95.

Golding, P. and van Snippenberg, L. 1995. 'Government, Communications and the Media'. In O. Borre and E. Scarbrough (eds), *The Scope of Government.* Oxford: Oxford University Press.

Gouldner, A. W. 1971. *The Coming Crisis of Western Sociology.* London: Heinemann.

Hall, S. 1992. 'The Question of Cultural Identity'. In S. Hall *et al.* (eds.), *Modernity and Its Futures.* Cambridge: Polity Press.

Hall, T. 1999. 'Best of British'. *The Guardian*, 9 April.

Huber, P. 1996. 'Cyberpower'. *Forbes Magazine*, December:142–7.

Inglehart, R. 1990. *Culture Shift in Advanced Industrial Society.* Princeton, NJ: Princeton University Press.

Ito, M. 1996. 'Virtually Embodied: The Reality of Fantasy in a Multi-User Dungeon'. In D. Porter (ed.), *Internet Culture.* London and New York: Routledge.

Jenkins, C. and Sherman, B. 1981. *The Leisure Shock.* London: Eyre Methuen.

Jones, B. 1982. *Sleepers, Wake! Technology and the Future of Work.* Brighton: Wheatsheaf.

Jones, S. G. 1998. 'Introduction'. In S. G. Jones (ed.), *Cybersociety 2.0: Revisiting Computer-Mediated Communication and Community.* London: Sage.

Keohane, R. O. and Nye J. S. 1998. 'Power and Independence in the Information Age'. *Foreign Affairs* 77(5): 81–92.

Labour Party 1997. *Communicating Britain's Future: A Labour Party Report.* London: The Labour Party.

Machlup, F. 1962. *The Production and Distribution of Knowledge in the United States.* Princeton, NJ: Princeton University Press.

Melucci, A. 1996. *Challenging Codes: Collective Action in the Information Age.* Cambridge: Cambridge University Press.

Morley, D. and Robins, K. 1995. *Spaces of Identity: Global Media, Electronic Landscapes and Cultural Boundaries.* London: Routledge.

Mouzelis, N. P. 1995. *Sociological Theory: What Went Wrong? Diagnosis and Remedies.* London: Routledge.

Murdock, G. and Golding, P. 1999. 'Common Markets: Corporate Ambitions and Communication Trends in the UK and Europe'. *Journal of Media Economics* 12: 117–32.

Negroponte, N. 1996. *Being Digital.* London: Coronet.

OECD 1981. *Information Activities, Electronics and Telecommunications Technologies: Impact on Employment, Growth and Trade.* Paris: Organisation for Economic Co-operation and Development.

Office of National Statistics 1997. *Family Spending.* London: HMSO.

Office of National Statistics 1998. *Family Spending.* London: HMSO.

Office of National Statistics 1999. *Labour Force Survey.* London: HMSO.

Phillips, Lord 1997. 'Information Society: Agenda for Action in the UK'. *Journal of Information Science* 23:1–8.

Rose, N. 1999. Comments as panel member 'Sociology and Biology'. British Sociological Association, Glasgow, April.

Sardar, Z. 1999. 'The Future Is Ours to Change'. *New Statesman*, 19 March:25–7.

Scarbrough, E. 1995. 'Materialist–Postmaterialist Value Orientations'. In J. W. van Deth and E. Scarbrough (eds.), *The Impact of Values.* Oxford: Oxford University Press.

Slack, J. 1984. 'The Information Revolution as Ideology'. *Media, Culture and Society* 6:247–56.

Smith, D. 1990. *Capitalist Democracy on Trial: The Transatlantic Debate from Tocqueville to the Present.* London: Routledge.

Standage, T. 1999. *The Victorian Internet: The Remarkable Story of the Telegraph and the Nineteenth Century's Online Pioneers.* London: Phoenix.

Stanworth, C. 1998. 'Telework and the Information Age'. *New Technology, Work and Employment* 13:51–62.

Stoll, C. 1995. *Silicon Snake Oil: Second Thoughts on the Information Highway.* London: Macmillan.

Turkle, S. 1996. *Life on the Screen: Identity in the Age of the Internet.* London: Weidenfeld and Nicolson.

van de Donk, W. B. H. J. and Tops, P. W. 1995. 'Orwell or Athens? Informatization and the Future of Democracy'. In de Donk and Tops (eds.), *Orwell in Athens: A Perspective.* Amsterdam: IOS Press.

Van Den Besselaar 1997. 'The Future of Employment in the Information Society: A Comparative, Longitudinal and Multi-Level Study'. *Journal of Information Science* 23:373–92.

Warwick, P. V. 1998. 'Disputed Cause, Disputed Effect: The Postmaterialist Thesis Re-examined'. *Public Opinion Quarterly* 62:583–609.

Waters, M. 1995. *Globalisation.* London: Routledge.

Webster, F. 1995. *Theories of the Information Society.* London: Routledge.

Weiss, L. 1998. *The Myth of the Powerless State.* Cambridge: Polity Press.

Williams, R. 1974. *Television: Technology and Cultural Form.* London: Fontana.

Winston, B. 1998. *Media Technology and Society: A History from the Telegraph to the Internet.* London: Routledge.

18

DECIPHERING INFORMATION TECHNOLOGIES

Modern societies as networks

Nico Stehr

Source: *European Journal of Social Theory* 3(1) (2000): 83–94.

Abstract

This essay advances two sets of critical observations about Manuel Castells's suggestion and detailed elaboration of the idea that modern society from the 1980s onwards constitutes a network society and that the unity in the diversity of global restructuring has to be seen in the massive deployment of information and communication technologies in all spheres of modern social life. The criticism attends to the possibility that the emphasis on the social role of information technologies in advanced society amounts to a modern version of 'technological determinism'. A discussion of the so-called productivity paradox shows that cultural and social processes rather than technological regimes continue to be more important for the evolution of society.

In a series of imaginative and empirically grounded, studies, Manuel Castells (1996) suggests that modern society from the 1980s onwards constitutes a *network society* and that the unity in the diversity of global restructuring has to be seen in the massive deployment of information and communication technologies in all spheres of modern social life. Innovations in the field of communication and information technologies therefore represent, not unlike the eighteenth-century industrial revolution, a major historical event and a fundamental change in the material as well as the social structure and culture of society. Echoing what has been generally stated in its most uncompromising form by Marx, the transformation of the 'material culture' of modern society on the basis of the information revolution since the 1980s amounts to a historically new formation of capitalism (Castells and Henderson, 1987).[1] But Castells also emphasizes that the reshaping of advanced capitalism cannot be reduced to a manifestation of mere capitalist interests.

In this brief essay, I should like to take up what I consider to be two clearly related basic questions posed by Castells's general theory of modern society as network societies or *informational capitalism*:

1 First, there is what can only be described as the puzzling issue of 'technological determinism' as well as the associated question of how the notion of a network society differs from designating modern society an *information society*; after all, both terms rely to a crucial extent on references to efforts to decipher the social and economic impact of more efficient 'information processing' on social conduct.

2 Second, there is what economists have called the puzzle of the productivity paradox. Castells (1996: 17) makes it the very premise of his observations that the source of productivity in the new form of capitalism 'lies in the *technology* of knowledge generation, information processing, and symbol communication' (emphasis added).

In social science discourse, the first issue I have identified is, depending on one's perspective, hardly a novel theoretical dilemma or promise; however, the second question represents a unique challenge because, as the *New York Times* (17 April 1999) expresses it, quoting the economist Robert Solow: 'You can see the Computer Age everywhere but in the productivity statistics.' The challenge is the inability of economists, marshalling conventional indicators of economic success, to trace any significant financial payoff from the massive corporate and state investments in information and communication technologies.

Although Castells in his own study continually stresses the enormous efficacy and impact of the new technological means as the major productivity-inducing factors in modern nations, as far as I can tell he fails to refer to the productivity paradox and the extensive literature that has grown around this topic.[2] The reference to the productivity paradox does not mean that investments in information technologies have been ineffectual. Increased productivity is indeed of major importance, not only for the competitive advantages of firms and countries, but also for wages and salaries paid, the ability of the state to maintain entitlement regimes, and standards of living.

Technological determinism?

According to Castells, the new society or network society in which the state continues to occupy a decisive function[3] originates as the result of a new technological paradigm and therefore a dynamic process that is propelled by information processing or informationism. Given Castells's description of the network society with its essential dependence on the operation of communication technologies, the question that arises is in what way, if at all, does his term 'the network society' differ from the more frequently used concept of modern society as an information society?

The difference to which Castells himself points, and which in his self-assessment constitutes a progressive conceptual step in our analytical understanding of modern society as well as the theoretical model of the information society, can be explicated in analogy to the distinction between 'industry' and 'industrial'. At first glance, such a differentiation would not appear to yield much in the way of differences. Information (society) and informational (society) results, Castells (1996: 21) suggests, are distinct ways of viewing and knowing. The concept of information or, as he also calls it, the 'communication of knowledge', implies nothing more or less than the assertion that information is of importance in all possible social formations and represents an anthropological constant found in all human societies. In contrast to information, 'the term informational indicates the attribute of a specific form of social organization in which information generation, processing, and transmission become the fundamental sources of productivity and power, because of new technological conditions emerging in this historical period'. Information becomes an immediately productive force (Stehr, 1994: 99–104).

The term 'information', which Castells therefore locates on the same logical plane as knowledge, remains but skin deep, while the concept 'informational' refers to the probability that social conduct is affected in its inner constitution by information and that the social organization of social action is transformed because of the utilization of information.

The close alliance of Castells's theory of society with the development of information and communication technologies, as well as his conscious conflation of knowledge and information,[4] make it rather difficult to detect any decisive and robust differences between the notions of an information and a network society. After all, for most observers, the information revolution is understood in the first instance as a technical one. The gadgets change but not the socio-cognitive frames, immediately productive knowledge, the language of entitlements and scientific regimes.

Although Castells is not a strict proponent of technological determinism, a number of theses in his study tend to resonate unavoidably with the paradigm of technological determinism that stresses context-insensitive consequences of technical products rather than the social processes of innovation and deployment. Technology, along with knowledge (information), is often treated as a black box: that is, as stable and robust entities or processes whose embeddedness into the circumstances of their production and use are hidden. It is self-evident that technology plays a crucial role in the modern life-world and in the course of economic 'progress' (Mokyr, 1990).[5] However, technology needs to be examined not from a 'disembodied' perspective but from one that is cognizant of the social conditions within which it emerges and is employed.[6]

Alain Touraine ([1984] 1988: 104) has argued, convincingly I believe, that the specificity of a particular society should not hinge on a given technology: 'It is just as superficial to speak of a computer society or of a plutonium society as it is of steam-engine society or an electric motor society. Nothing justifies the granting of such a privilege to a particular technology, whatever its economic importance.'[7]

The productivity paradox

Castells (1996: 80) throughout his study reiterates that 'productivity is the source of the wealth of nations'. Global competition represents the linkage path that connects information technology, organizational change and productivity growth. However, in the last two decades economists have been puzzled about the apparent lack of measurable productivity gains in industry and services in OECD countries in response to or conjunction with the immense investments in recent years in information and communication technologies. The choice of the label of a productivity paradox results from the disjuncture between the immense economic expectations and promises that have been engendered by the 'computer age', on the one hand, and the apparent lack of economic payoffs resulting from the enormous investments by corporation and the state in information and communication technologies, on the other hand.

Indeed, for a number of decades now information technology investments in the United States have consumed a growing proportion of all investments. Overall investments have remained fairly constant over this period of time. In 1990 alone, US businesses invested $61 billion in hardware, $18 billion in software and $75 billion in data processing and computer services (US Department of Commerce, 1991). As a share of all investments in equipment (hardware) by US corporations, investment in information technology has surpassed 50 percent.

Attewell (1994: 24) sums up previous research on the productivity paradox, affirming its existence and commenting 'no study documents substantial IT effects on productivity'. Although conceptual, methodological and data difficulties that extend to the very definition of productivity obviously also exist with respect to the statistics utilized in generating observations about the productivity paradox, these quandaries do not appear to invalidate the results completely.

None the less, the variety of research and accounts of the productivity paradox exemplify the growing and deepening division of labor in social science and its essentially contested nature. For some observers, the productivity paradox does not exist in reality. The productivity puzzle is a measurement construct, or indicative of a mismeasurement of outputs that conceals real gains that are made (cf. Quinn, 1996; Diewert and Fox, 1997). But even if the puzzle should exist, the magnitude of the problem is small upon first examination since investments in computers form a relatively minor part of all capital input. For others, although the paradox is real, it represents but a transitory phase, not unlike the productivity lag produced in the past by the transition to technological systems such as the diffusion of electric power. And as is the case for other learning processes, it takes a protracted period of time before the economic benefits show up (David, 1990; Petit and Soete, 1997; Davenport, 1997). Still other observers see the productivity paradox not as a gap that reflects economic realities, but rather as an indicator of intellectual or theoretical deficits in economic discourse (Jorgenson, 1997).[8] Last but not least, though already contested, some economists have recently signaled that the danger has passed and that the productivity paradox had disappeared by 1991 (e.g. Brynjolfsson and Hitt, 1996; Sichel, 1999).[9]

Castells (1996: 74) does refer to the slowing down of *overall* productivity[10] rates in the 1973–1993 period. He notes that the timing of the kind of technological change of interest to him and the pace of productivity growth from the mid-1970s to the mid-1990s does not seem to covariate with the timing of the emergence of informational capitalism. The lack of productivity gains threatens his very distinction between industrial and informational capitalism.

Not surprisingly, perhaps, Castells takes a view that has been part of the debate among economists for some time, namely that the methods of measurement that are utilized to represent the output of the economy are subject to measurement error and that these errors conceal the productivity growth that is 'really taking place (cf. Diewert and Fox, 1997). Castells (1996: 78) sums up his own investigation with the suspicion that validity issues may be responsible for the observations of an overall slowdown in productivity gains. Perhaps the entire enigma is not even authentic, and productivity is not really vanishing at all but increasing: 'It may well be that a significant proportion of the mysterious productivity slowdown results from a growing inadequacy of economic statistics to capture movements of the new informational economy, *precisely because of the broad scope of its transformations under the impact of information technology and related organizational changes.*'[11]

Attewell (1994, 1992a, 1992b), in a series of studies at the levels of both the firm and economic sectors, has specifically examined possible mechanisms that could undercut or attenuate productivity changes following from investments in information and communication technologies. He argues that productivity payoffs or their lack may result from a series of trade-offs at both the individual and collective levels within firms. For example, the 'potential benefits of the technology may be channeled into alternative

HISTORY AND PERSPECTIVES

directions – either doing the original work more efficiently (productivity enhancing) or doing a different kind of activity or the same activity more often' (Attewell, 1994: 48). A further explanation offered by another group of authors suggests that the productivity paradox might encompass and manifest learning processes at all levels. Such a nexus points to the experiences observed in the transition from one technological regime to another in the past, for example in the case of the diffusion of the dynamo and electric power. The electric motor was introduced in the early 1880s but did not produce noticeable productivity gains until the 1920s. As Petit and Soete (1997: 1) indicate, the (negative) effects of major technological changes could be 'transitory or resulting from uncertainty and risk-adverse reactions that will disappear in time through experience and learning'. By the same token, and as the economist Paul Krugman (1994: 208) has argued, the 'highest rate of U.S. productivity growth before the 1950s was in the 1920s, driven by the automobile industry – even though automobiles had been in existence and even in fairly widespread use since the turn of the century'. Whether such analogies to past technological regimes have any relevance today is an open and contested question.

In my view, the specific paradox that pertains to information technology investments and productivity gains remains an open issue, as does the question: What mechanisms account for the productivity paradox?[12]

As Kenneth Arrow (1974: 47) observes with respect to the conditions for the possibility of innovation, 'innovation by firms is in many cases simply a question of putting an item on its agenda before other firms do it'. What counts and what increasingly drives the transformation of the modern economy is the quality of the *supply* of labor or the extent to which not only technological change but the transformation of work and the structure of the labor force is skill-based. Investments in communication and information technologies in the 1980s and 1990s have been accompanied, perhaps even precipitated, by a noticeable substitution of skilled labor. Initial empirical work appears to support such a contention. For in a broadly based cross-sectional empirical study at the level of individual manufacturing firms and using individual rather than aggregate data for the US economy, Doms *et al.* (1997), for example, have examined the relationship between technology use[13] and the education, occupation and wages of the employees in the manufacturing sector. On the basis of the data one is able to conclude that there is a growing covariance between the degree of technology use in firms, that is to say, the progress made in automating both the development and the production processes, and the educational level of the employees. The conclusion therefore is not only that 'skilled workers and advanced manufacturing technologies are complements' but also that the proportion of employees 'in skilled occupations rises significantly with the number of technologies employed' (Doms *et al.*, 1997: 261, 263; also Berman *et al.*, 1994) *as well as* the proportion of employees not directly active in the production process.[14] A variety of controls confirm these findings. In addition, the authors report that employees in firms with extensive technology deployment earn higher wages and salaries.

The cross-sectional data cannot, however, offer an answer to questions about the timing of the observed marked substitution in favor of skilled labor in the manufacturing firms that are technology intensive. As a result, Doms *et al.* attempt to extend their analysis by relating the utilization or adoption of different technologies over time in these firms to changes in the different variables such as the wage levels, the proportion of employees not directly involved in the production process, etc. Aside from methodological problems such a procedure may have as the result of the absence of valid longitudinal data, the overall result of their efforts to operationalize 'technology adoption' is that 'technology adoption is relatively uncorrelated with the changes in the nonproduction labor share, workers wages, or labor productivity' (Doms *et al.*, 1997: 277).

One possible 'explanation' for the 'negative' finding could be that the firms the authors included in their study had already employed or hired a large number of highly skilled employees *prior* to the adoption of new technological means. Thus, 'if plants that adopt technologies have more skilled workforces prior to adoption, then we would expect that the pre-adoption wages and labor productivity should be correlated with future technology use' (Doms *et al.*, 1997: 277). The results of their study are once more far from transparent. The authors sum up the relations they are able to document as follows: 'Plants that adopt a large number of new technologies have more skilled workers both pre- and postadoption' (p. 279). In other words, it is entirely possible that highly skilled or educated employees produce the 'scientification and technological modernization of their work places and therefore of the world of work. It is the growing supply of highly qualified workers, rather than the growing complexity or the pre-existing skill requirements of the world of work, that are the motor and the motivating force behind the transformation of work.[15]

In the modern economy, knowledge is the most important resource. As a result the production of knowledge and learning is the most significant process in the knowledge society. Public policy in turn must be attuned and attend to these features of modern society (cf. Alexander, 1997).[16] In response to the question of the reasons for the immense growth of the service sector in recent decades, Landauer (1995: 74–5) also offers an account that stresses factors induced by the demand for jobs. Thus, new jobs were needed, so new services were invented. Many new or expanded services depended on computers: a plethora of investment instruments – complex new mutual funds and trading schemes, a deluge of new insurance policies and options, a myriad of debit and credit cards, dozens of new kinds of bank accounts and novel banking services offered from widely dispersed branches and machines, multitudes of new medical techniques and therapies, fast food

HISTORY AND PERSPECTIVES

restaurants, fast copy stores, fully filled planes with frequent flyer plans, 'mom and pop' mail order firms, direct marketing, PC maintenance, and so forth (Landauer, 1995: 74–5).

Conclusions

Proponents of the 'new economy' argue, as does Manuel Castells, that modern society has experienced a far-reaching transformation. The economy has been fundamentally retailored by the spread of computers and digital technology. With the advent of information technology it has really become a *network* society. Castells's claims that this is a more adequate description than *information* society, because it highlights major organizational changes which accompany this technological transformation. It seems to me that the distance between the network society and the more established (although now declining) idea of modern society as an information society is not as large as Castells thinks. Both ideas rest on premises that resonate with technological determinism. Moreover, both perspectives are insufficient because they do not deal adequately with the productivity paradox. The productivity paradox can be better understood if one recognizes three empirical facts. First, highly skilled labor appears on the scene before information technology. Second, the increasing importance of highly skilled labor is not a reaction to demand for such labor, but rather there is an autonomous (i.e. societally driven) supply shift. And third, information technology actually helps entrepreneurs and managers to catch up with and reverse the rising labor costs implied by this supply shift. Therefore, the productivity paradox can help us to understand that we are not faced with a technology-driven transition from industrial to informational society or something of that kind, but rather with a societally driven transition from an industrial to a knowledge society (cf. Stehr, forthcoming). In this sense, then, we have entered a new modernity. The particular strength of Castells's analysis of modern society extends to observations about the nature of the new modernity rather than its antecedents.

Notes

I gratefully acknowledge the critical comments by Carlo Jaeger and Volker Meja.

1 In contrast to much of the discussion of the contentious idea that we are entering or already living in a postmodern era for example, Castells's reflections on modern societies as network societies have the distinctive merit to incorporate discussion of the (material) conditions for the possibility of the transformation of industrial society into a network society. On the material foundation of postmodernity and its neglect in theories of postmodernity see Stehr, 1997.

2 In a justification for assigning a core function to the new information of communication technologies in economic restructuring, Castells and Henderson (1987: 5),

DECIPHERING INFORMATION TECHNOLOGIES

using Colin Clark's (1940) probably obsolete three-economic sector hypothesis, stress the contribution to a *'qualitative* increase in productivity, across the board, in manufacturing, agriculture . . . and services. In fact, productivity growth is particularly crucial in the service sector of the economy' (emphasis added). The qualification of a 'qualitative' rise in productivity can of course be read to constitute a cautionary qualification of the universal thesis of a productivity growth in response to corporate and state investments in information technologies. I will return to this issue.

3 According to Castells (1996: 13), the state apparatus continues to play an active and significant role in the emerging network society because it mediates in definitive ways between technological developments and societal changes: 'The role of the state, by either stalling, unleashing, or leading technological innovation, is a decisive factor in the overall process, as it expresses and organizes the social and cultural forces that dominate a given space and time.' The application and use of the new technologies, as Castells and Henderson (1987: 5) emphasize elsewhere, 'are basically shaped' by capitalist policies and therefore a restricted economic logic that is dramatically enhanced in turn by the 'power of the new technological means' at its disposal.

4 Castells (1996: 17) emphasizes for example why he cannot detect any persuasive reasons for disagreeing with the reductionist definition of (theoretical) knowledge advocated by Daniel Bell (1973: 175) in his theory of post-industrial society. 'Information technology' is defined by Castells (1996: 30) in such a fashion that it is in important respects identical to scientific work ('I also include in the realm of information technologies genetic engineering'; perhaps one could add climate science, cognitive science, econometric modeling, and impact assessment as further examples) and therefore to scientific fields that resonate strongly with Bell's conception of theoretical knowledge.

5 Recent critiques of the technological determinism paradigm may be found in Heilbroner (1995), Grint and Woolgar (1997) and Leyshon and Thrift (1997).

6 As David Nye (1997: 180), in his enlightening examination of the deployment of narratives to understand technology in the twentieth-century, observes, 'the misleading sense of determinism so common to technological narratives is fostered in part by the Cartesian sense of space, which seems to predicate linear developments seen in log perspective. In this neutral space, the world is raw material, waiting to be worked up, and it offers only temporary resistance to what seems an inexorable sequences of events.'

7 But Touraine's alternative designation of modern society as a 'programmed society' appears to resonate with Castells's notion of a network society in as much as the concept of the programmed society also stresses decisive symbolic transformations that occur in contemporary society. According to Touraine ([1984] 1988: 104) the term 'programmed society' aptly captures changes underway in modern society, because the metaphor highlights the capacity of society to 'create models of management, production, organization, distribution, and consumption, so that such a society appears, at all its functional levels, as the product of an action exercised by the society itself.'

8 Jorgenson (1997: 4) sees the productivity paradox as arising from the prevailing identification of 'productivity growth with technological change'. Technological change and productivity gains are distinct. Productivity growth is but a minor component to growth. Technological change occurs, he argues, as a result of investments; economic growth, too, is due to capital investment. Capital investments can be categorized into investments in tangible assets, human and intellectual capital. The purchase of computers constitutes an investment in tangible assets.

But the key concept in this context, intellectual capital, remains but a vague (and perhaps even more irritating to economists) an unmeasured and unmeasurable concept.

9 The chairman of the US Federal Reserve Bank, Alan Greenspan, has reiterated the point: 'A perceptible quickening in the pace at which technological innovations are applied argues for the hypothesis that the recent acceleration in labor productivity is not just a cyclical phenomenon or a statistical aberration, but reflects, at least in part, a more deep-seated, still developing, shift in our economic landscape' (Speech at the Federal Reserve Bank of Chicago, 6 May 1999; see also note 11).

10 It is necessary to stress 'overall' productivity gains because the responsibility for productivity changes can of course be due to a host of factors.

11 Castells does not indicate how one might be able to specifically 'heal' the deficiencies of the current statistical regime (compare the appendix on 'tools for measuring and managing intellectual capital' in Stewart, 1997: 222–46 for a list of specific suggestions). Castells's skepticism when it comes to the conventional regime of measuring productivity performance is not without merit. For example, according to official US statistics, a bank today is only about 80 percent as productive as a bank in 1977 (*New York Times*, 14 April 1999, 'Computer age gains respect of economists').

12 Recent productivity statistics for the United States indicate that productivity growth has picked up from 1996. Moreover, initial disaggregations of factors that could be responsible for recent improvements in productivity suggest that information technologies could be among the factors that contribute to productivity performance. But the issues that have divided economists in their analysis of the productivity paradox in the past are far from being resolved. As one economist maintains, for example, the improved productivity performance could have much more to do with low interest rates than with the growing use of information and communication technologies (*New York Times*, 14 April 1999, 'Computer age gains respect of economists').

13 The degree of technology intensity in individual firms was measured by the authors of the study by counting the number of technical processes or devices such as computer-driven machines, robots and so on found in the plants (see Doms *et al.*, 1997: 287–8 for a detailed description of the different processes and devices).

14 More concretely, 'the positive relationship between technology use and the percent of skilled workers is primarily due to a dramatic increase in the percent of scientists and engineers in the most technologically advanced plants' (Doms *et al.*, 1997: 263).

15 A further but roundabout confirmation of the supply-side induced transformation of the world of work is aggregate data about the growing 'skill level' of the population in most OECD countries. According to Johnson (1997: 42), the relative skill supply measured as a ratio in the population of high school to college equivalency in the US has risen from .105 in 1940 to .496 in 1993. In five decades, the proportion of the population with a college-education has increased fivefold. The increase of college-educated labor is particularly strong in the 1970s, reflecting a growing proportion of college students in the latter half of the 1960s. It would be far too simple to suggest that the tremendous increase in the collective skill level of the work force is in direct response to market forces. Although individuals will respond to perceived market opportunities, the fit not only in terms of time between perceived market opportunities and education could hardly be expected to be exceptionally close. Too many other factors and forces impinge

upon those choices and after many years of education perhaps result in 'higher skill levels'.

16 Concerns that the quality of the available jobs might not be compatible with rising educational levels (Harman, 1978: 209) correspond to exactly the opposite perspective, namely that the quality of the world of work is primarily driven by the nature of the demand.

References

Alexander, T. J. (1997) '"Human" Capital Investment: Building the "Knowledge Economy"', *Policy Options* 18: 5–8.

Arrow, Kenneth (1974) *The Limits of Organization*. New York: W.W. Norton.

Attewell, Paul (1992a) 'Skill and Occupational Changes in U.S. Manufacturing', in Paul S. Adler (ed.) *Technology and the Future of Work*, pp. 46–88. Washington, DC: The Brookings Institution.

—— (1992b) 'Technology Diffusion and Organizational Learning: the Case of Business Computing', *Organization Science* 3: 1–19.

—— (1994) 'Information Technology and the Productivity Paradox', in Douglas H. Harris (ed.) *Organizational Linkages: Understanding the Productivity Paradox*, pp. 13–53. Washington, DC; National Academy Press.

Bell, Daniel (1973) *The Coming of Post-Industrial Society: A Venture in Social Forecasting*. New York: Basic Books.

Berman, Eli, Bound, John and Griliches, Zvi (1994) 'Changes in the Demand for Skilled Labor within U.S. Manufacturing Industries: Evidence from the Annual Survey of Manufacturing', *Quarterly Journal of Economics* 59: 367–98.

Brynjolfsson, E. and Hitt, L. (1996) 'Paradox Lost? Firm-level Evidence on the Returns to Information Systems Spending', *Management Science* 42: 541–58.

Castells, Manuel (1996) *The Information Age: Economy, Society and Culture*, Vol. I, *The Rise of the Network Society*. Oxford: Blackwell.

Castells, Manuel and Henderson, Jeffrey (1987) 'Introduction. Techno-economic Restructuring, Socio-political Processes and Spatial Transformation: a Global Perspective', in Jeffrey Henderson and Manuel Castells (eds) *Global Restructuring and Territorial Development*, pp. 1–17. London: Sage.

Clark, Colin (1940) *The Conditions of Economic Progress*. London: Macmillan.

Davenport, Paul (1997) 'The Productivity Paradox and the Management of Information Technology', paper presented to the Centre for the Study of Living Standards Confererence on Service Sector Productivity and the Productivity Paradox, Ottawa, 11–13 April.

David, Paul A. (1990) 'The Dynamo and the Computer: an Historical Perspective on the Modern Productivity Paradox', *American Economic Review Papers and Proceedings* 80: 355–61.

Diewert, Erwin and Fox, Kevin (1997) 'Can Measurement Error Explain the Productivity Paradox?', paper presented to the Centre for the Study of Living Standards Conference on Service Sector Productivity and the Productivity Paradox, Ottawa, 11–13 April.

Doms, Mark, Dunne, Timothy and Troske, Kenneth (1997) 'Workers, Wages and Technology', *The Quarterly Journal of Economics* (February): 253–90.

HISTORY AND PERSPECTIVES

Grint, Keith and Woolgar, Steve (1997) *The Machine at Work: Technology, Work and Organisation*. Oxford: Polity Press.

Harman, Wills W. (1978) 'Chronic Unemployment: an Emerging Problem of Post-industrial Society', *Futurist* 12: 209–14.

Heilbroner, Robert L. (1995) 'Do Machines Make History?', in Merritt Roe Smith and Leo Marx (eds) *Does Technology Drive History?* Cambridge, MA: MIT Press.

Johnson, George F. (1997) 'Changes in Earnings Inequality: the Role of Demand Shifts', *Journal of Economic Perspectives* 11: 41–54.

Jorgenson, Dale (1997) 'Computers and Productivity', paper presented to the Centre for the Study of Living Standards Conference on Service Sector Productivity and the Productivity Paradox, Ottawa, 11–13 April.

Krugman, Paul (1994) *The Age of Diminished Expectations: U.S. Economic Policy in the 1990s*, revised and updated edn. Cambridge, MA: MIT Press.

Landauer, Thomas K. (1995) *The Trouble with Computers: Usefulness, Usability, and Productivity*. Cambridge, MA: MIT Press.

Leyshon, Andrew and Thrift, Nigel (1997) *Money/Space: Geographies of Monetary Transformation*. London: Routledge.

Mokyr, Joel (1990) *The Levers of Riches: Technological Creativity and Economic Progress*. New York: Oxford University Press.

Nye, David E. (1997) *Narratives and Spaces: Technology and the Construction of American Culture*. New York: Columbia University Press.

Petit, Pascal and Soete, Luc (1997) 'Is a Biased Technological Change Fuelling Dualism?', paper presented to the Centre for the Study of Living Standards Conference on Service Sector Productivity and the Productivity Paradox, Ottawa, 11–13 April.

Quinn, J. B. (1996) 'The Producivity Paradox is False: Information Technology Improves Service Performance', *Advances in Services Marketing and Management* 5: 71–84.

Sichel, Daniel E. (1999) 'Computers and Aggregate Economic Growth: an Update', *Business Economics* 34: 18–24.

Stehr, Nico (forthcoming) *The Fragility of Modern Societies*. London: Sage.

Stehr, Nico (1994) *Knowledge Societies*. London: Sage.

Stewart, Thomas A. (1997) *Intellectual Capital: The New Wealth of Organizations*. New York: Doubleday.

Touraine, Alain ([1984] 1988) *Return of the Actor: Social Theory in Postindustrial Society*. Minneapolis: University of Minnesota Press.

US Department of Commerce (1991) *U.S. Industrial Outlook*. Washington, DC: US Department of Commerce.

19

AN ARCHAEOLOGY OF
THE GLOBAL ERA
Constructing a belief[1]

Armand Mattelart

Source: *Media, Culture & Society* 24(5) (2002): 591–612.

Into the Global Age . . .

(Giddens, 1999)

As in any serious discussion, words are sovereign.

(Braudel, 1979)

Few terms have been stretched as far or proved to be as infinitely extendable as the word 'globalization'. Few terms have come into widespread use at such a 'global speed', as Paul Virilio would say, taken over from English by every other language on earth. And few terms have been so widely disseminated in a context of such widespread social atopia, without any prior inventory of its possible significance or time for scrutiny by citizens, thus leaving an aura of doubt concerning the conditions and meaning of its source. It is a notion that refers not just to an actual process but also to a project, not just to fragments of reality but also to firmly established beliefs. Indeed, the terms governing interdependence have profoundly changed. National systems, whether technological, economic, cultural, socio-political, civilian or military, are all permeated by a logic that transcends and reconfigures them.

The project would have us believe that self-regulated trade is the necessary path, the Caudine Forks of 'prosperity for all' or 'happiness for everyone'. This is what gives the notion of globalization the configuration of a new totalizing ideology, lending support and legitimacy to the neo-liberal scheme. Incorporating all individual societies into the world is now reduced to incorporating them into a social and productive system, based on what is conventionally known as integrated, global capitalism. The ideology of corporate globalization is indissolubly linked to the ideology of worldwide communication. Together, they form the matrix both for the symbolic management of the worldwide scheme and for the further, unacknowledged reality of a world ruled by the logic of social and economic segregation.

This technoglobal newspeak operates like a latter-day *lingua franca*, making its pronouncements as if they were self-evident truths requiring no discussion. It stipulates how we must talk about the present and future. It endows the historical process of world unification with its own particular features. It transmutes a phenomenon with multiple dimensions both symbolic and real into a single body of beliefs. In the end, it blurs our grasp of what is at stake in the complex new forms of contemporary interaction and transaction between economies, societies and cultures. In this article, I propose to unearth the archaeology of some of the expressions of this *pensée unique* (one-sided thinking), in keeping with the intellectual project I have been pursuing since the second half of the 1980s (Mattelart, 1994, 1999, 2001). This archaeology appears all the more necessary to make the politics of the contemporary era intelligible as words convey beliefs which summon symbolic forces, a *mana* which forces action in one direction within the limits it imposes and prohibits our going in the opposite direction. Whether we like it or not, these beliefs conceal uncertainties that weigh on the process by which the world is being rearranged and, at the same time, they keep history on a path that far from represents our universal best interests.

Forgetting history

History is bunk. A glance through the panegyric discourse and meta-discourse concerning our entry into the global era seems to suggest that this observation, once uttered by Henry Ford on the threshold of his industrial triumph, is now making a conspicuous come-back. Global integration is being achieved through a multi-secular movement divested of any memory of conflict and, hence, of any grasp of what is now at stake. The historian Marc Ferro, a disciple of Fernand Braudel, is right to warn us against repressing the historical view:

> The end of this millennium is dominated by the idea that we have entered a new historical era, that of globalization. But isn't this simply an optical illusion? The movement in the direction of world unification appeared long ago, even though it has recently been extended and expanded at an accelerated pace.
>
> (Ferro, 1999: 28)

Historians are not the only ones to remind us of the need to take a long-term view of this process. Some economists have expressed a similar concern. Robert Boyer, the leading economist of the so-called 'regulatory' school,

AN ARCHAEOLOGY OF THE GLOBAL ERA

insists on the fact that history seldom repeats itself in an identical fashion and that the contemporary situation of the global economy represents an original configuration. He speaks of 'true' and 'false' novelty with regard to globalization, and argues that we must urgently transcend the 'retrospective analyses of economists and most researchers in social science which deal at best with a period of one or two decades' in order to 'take the long-term view of capitalism into account' (Boyer, 2000: 32). Pierre Bourdieu and Loïc Wacquant have expressed a similar need for caution:

> The globalization of material and symbolic exchange and the diversity of cultures are not products of the 20th century, they are co-extensive with human history, as Emile Durkheim and Marcel Mauss already pointed out in their *Note on the notion of civilisation*.
> (Bourdieu and Wacquant, 2000: 7)

We might add that the concept of interdependence, which sounds like a recent invention, was in fact forged at the end of the 19th century. It is actually a metaphor borrowed from biology, which used it to designate the close ties linking the cells of an organism to each other. The metaphor was developed at the time by the advocates of what was called 'worldism' or 'worldwide solidarism' to signify the 'new meaning of the world' which, in their view of the evolution of international life, was already emanating from the planet-wide network of underwater cables and communication routes. The notion of interdependence was at the root of the new project of creating an 'international community', first achieved in the League of Nations, and simultaneously lent legitimacy to the national plans for creating the welfare state.

One thing is certain: defective memory has encouraged the return of an eschatology with a religious connotation, drawn from the writings of the theologian and palaeontologist Pierre Teilhard de Chardin, the early inventor of the notion of 'planetization' (Teilhard de Chardin, 1955). Marshall McLuhan, who was a convert to Catholicism, was already steeped in Teilhard's writings when he launched the cliché of the 'global village', the modern version of the old Christian myth of the 'great human family' that keeps coming back in new garb (McLuhan, 1962). One can find repeated references to Teilhard de Chardin, the thinker of the noosphere and of 'cosmic totality', among the authors who originally constructed the notion of the 'global society', such as Zbigniew Brzezinski. Since the sudden arrival of the Internet, however, there has been a qualitative leap in the use of Teilhard's name through intensive appropriation by the techno-libertarian crusaders of cyberspace (Lévy, 2000). He has even been claimed as a kind of patron saint by American Net-war strategists, who introduced the concept of 'noopolitics' in a report prepared for the Pentagon under the aegis of the famous think-tank, the Rand Corporation (Arquilla and Ronfeldt, 1999).

Amnesia provides the foundation for a modernity without substance. Instead of a genuine social project, techno-mercantile determinism has instituted endless, unlimited communication, the heir to the notion of ongoing, limitless progress. In the process, the old scheme to westernize the world has been recycled along with the coming of the so-called knowledge-based society. 'The educated person of the future will have to expect to live in a globalized world, which will be a westernized world', proclaims the management theoretician Peter Drucker (1990) in his book on 'post-capitalist society', a society free from friction. The diffusion theory of linear progress, first formulated by 19th-century classical ethnology and updated a century later by the sociologies of modernization and westernization in the fight against 'underdevelopment' of the 1960s and the first half of the 1970s, has resurfaced with a new liberal Darwinist twist, on the pretext that today's technology has made 'universal knowledge' accessible to the whole world. The cultural models of modernity can only branch out from the centre towards the periphery. It is a modernity in line with a Euro-American centre, which anticipates the future of the rest of the world, provided it faithfully follows the canonical stages of the evolutionary process through which adult nations have already passed. The global age, which both *ingénues* and cynics view as the end of imperialism, has hardly put an end to the ethnocentrism of the age of empires. The obvious fiasco of development strategies in the 1970s had, or so one assumed, sealed the fate of the schematic steps of historical maturation: history – modernization – progress. Corporate thinking ignores the fact that, in the meantime, new critical ways of understanding the formation of modernity have been developed – starting in the 1980s – which compel us to question the processes whereby global flows are being appropriated by individual cultures and territories. In arguing that the information revolution has resulted in a new westernization of the world, Drucker makes a case for a broad alliance between managers and intellectuals, which he considers the main prerequisite to successfully achieving the plan for a planetary society guided by the knowledge industry:

> They [managers and intellectuals] are opposites; but they relate to each other as poles than as contradictions. They surely need each other. The intellectual's world, unless counterbalanced by the manager, becomes one in which everybody does his own thing but nobody achieves anything.
>
> (Drucker, 1990: 215)

Thus, the old demons of anti-intellectual populism surreptitiously rear their ugly heads.

The refusal to join historians in 'seeing the future in the mirror of the past' means deliberately overlooking the underlying moments of conflict that have built up the imaginary picture that we carry in our minds of planetary society and consciousness. Indeed, from the 15th century to the present, it is possible to track the dream of world unity as variously coming under the sign of a religion, an empire, an economic model or the struggle of the oppressed. There has been a profusion of plans and schemes for reorganizing and 'pacifying' the planet. In the early 18th century, Abbot Saint-Pierre imagined a world government, a conception that was to haunt every plan for world integration until the Treaty of Versailles and the founding of the League of Nations (1919). In 1776, Adam Smith spoke of a universal mercantile republic and a single worldwide factory. In 1794, in the midst of the French Revolution, Condorcet drew up plans for a universal republic of the sciences, taking his inspiration from the *New Atlantis* by Francis Bacon, the founder of the experimental method. In the first quarter of the 19th century, the followers of Claude Henri de Saint-Simon formulated the first doctrine of 'Universal Association' through technological networks. Throughout this long history, the generosity of exchange often fell back into the tyranny of *la pensée unique*, just as utopias were in danger of withering in prison. The 'discovery' of a New World, opened up the prospect of dialogue and, thanks to 16th-century Spanish scholastic theologians such as Francisco de Vitoria who justified the *jus communicationis* (the right to communicate), paved the way to modern international public law, but ended in massacres and the negation of Native Amerindian culture. Yet, four centuries later, the self-same international public law made it possible to indict General Pinochet for genocide. The philosophy of the Enlightenment sketched out a plan for the joint control of nature and provided a justification for the great colonial enterprises. The international thrust of true socialism was diluted as it gave way to nationalism. Free trade turned into an imperialist nightmare. To an unusual degree, the promise of redemption by building a universal community veered into damnation of the 'wretched of the earth', to borrow the expression of the Martinique-born writer Frantz Fanon.

Each of these historical moments has contributed successive notions of universality and of our relationship to others, which in turn were reflected in utopias that emphasized either technological networks or social networks in the service of building a 'supranational social bond' or both.

To exorcise the technoglobal representation of the world's destiny that forces us to adopt the short-term view and allow ourselves instead a clear picture of our *devoir de mémoire* (duty to remember), we might well go back and read through some of the essays by the Argentine writer Jorge Luís Borges on the Holy Grail of the 'universal library', 'Babel' or 'The Congress', on the impossible quest for a 'planet-wide organization'. Or yet again, 'The Analytical Language of John Wilkins' which recounts the equally quixotic quest for the 'principles of a world language', undertaken at the time of the great intellectual restoration, which translate into a 'thought chart' enabling all creatures to be ordered and classified, the same utopian scheme at work in all the ensuing projects to develop a 'universal language', including the new language of 'computerese'.

Let us shift our gaze from this brief look at the founding moments of the project for world integration and unification and take up a vantage point in the more recent past. This angle is just as essential, for it has resulted in the one-dimensional discourse announcing the entry of human societies into the global age and the development of the 'end-of' thesis, responsible for the insidious infiltration of an ideology that prefers to remain nameless.

The 'end-of' thesis

In the early 1970s, the manufacturing of an imaginary related to a new era in history was already well under way. By 1977, an IBM advertisement declared: 'Information age: there's growing agreement that it's the name of the age we live in.' As the processes of deregulation and privatization were stepped up, the image of the information age encountered that of the 'global age'. In March 1994 in Buenos Aires, Albert Gore, the then Vice-President of the United States, announced his plan for a Global Information Infra-structure, holding out to the 'great human family' the prospect of a new Athenian agora on a planetary scale. The notion of the New Economy appeared for the first time in official speeches that same year. In February 1995, the G7 countries met in Brussels where they ratified the notion of the Global Information Society, along with the decision to speed up the pace of telecom market deregulation. We had come full circle, ending the long conceptual flight forward during which – bearing the stamp of determinism – the field of ideas about technological change was formed.

The process had begun in the wake of the Second World War. The Cold War set the stage, overseeing the construction of concepts intended to announce, if not explain, that humanity had reached the threshold of a new information age and, hence, of a new universalism. There were three successive sources of this discourse: first, the social sciences, then forecasting techniques and, finally, geopolitics.

The first step involved decreeing the death of the previous age of 'ideology', which, according to its gravediggers, was consubstantial with the 19th century and the first half of the 20th century, and of 'mass society'. That was precisely the task assigned to the participants at a meeting in Milan in September 1955 on the topic of 'The Future of Freedom' sponsored by the Congress for Cultural Freedom. The latter organization was founded in Berlin in 1950 and, apparently unbeknownst to the meeting's organizers, financed by the CIA under the cover of a private foundation. The list of participants included the economist Friedrich A. von Hayek, Raymond Aron, who had just published *L'Opium des intellectuels*, and the American sociologists Daniel Bell, Seymour Martin Lipset and Edward Shils. The agenda referred to a series of endings, among them the end of ideology, the end of politics, the end of classes and of class struggle, as well as the end of protesting intellectuals and the end of political commitment. The idea was put forward that 'sociological analysis' was in the process of sweeping away the prejudices of 'ideology', testifying to the new legitimacy of the 'Western liberal intellectual' (Shils, 1955, 1960; Lipset, 1960). Another recurring thesis, first expressed in 1940 by the American philosopher James Burnham, who had broken from the Trotskyist Fourth International, played into the hands of the 'end-of' discourse: the managerial revolution and the irresistible rise of organization men, bearing with them the new society, the managerial society that prefigured the convergence of the capitalist and Communist systems (Burnham, 1941).

In 1960, Daniel Bell, director of the international seminar program of the Congress for Cultural Freedom, published *The End of Ideology*. Between 1965 and 1968, he chaired the Commission on the Year 2000, set up by the American Academy of Arts and Sciences, during which he worked on the concept of the 'post-industrial society'. In 1973, he brought out *The Coming of the Post-Industrial Society* in which he correlated his earlier thesis of the end of ideology with the concept of the 'post-industrial society'. The latter, also called the 'information society' or 'knowledge-based society', would be free from ideology. Bell was making a prediction; hence the subtitle of the book: *A Venture of Social Forecasting*. It is worth coming back briefly to this text, particularly in view of the fact that a new edition has just been brought out with a 30,000-word preface by the author, on the occasion of the publication of Manuel Castells's magnum opus on the 'network society'. Castells pays tribute to his American colleague, by the way, while taking him out of context. Even Bell himself, in his eagerness to demonstrate the validity of *The Coming* in the age of the Internet, presents his ideas out of context in the new preface, thereby offering further proof of how little regard is shown for history when the point is to celebrate the future (Bell, 1999).

Bell extrapolates from observable structural trends in the United States to construct an ideal model of society, a society featuring the rise of new elites whose power lies in the new 'intellectual technology' geared to decision-making and by the pre-eminence of the 'scientific community', a 'charismatic', universally oriented, disinterested community, 'without any ideology'; a hierarchical society, governed by a centralized welfare state in charge of planning change (hence his insistence on methods for monitoring and evaluating technological changes); a society allergic to network thinking and the topic of 'participatory democracy', an issue that cable television had, however, already put on the US agenda at the time. In such a society, where the economy is gradually shifting towards 'technical and professional services', growth will be linear and exponential. The prevailing 'history–modernity–progress' view is in keeping with mathematical information theory and the westernized-evolutionary model sketched out in 1960 by Walt W. Rostow in his 'Non-Communist Manifesto' concerning the 'stages of economic growth'.

HISTORY AND PERSPECTIVES

Uncertainty about growth and the 'crisis of governability of western democracies', diagnosed by the Trilateral Commission, the informal headquarters for representatives of the political and intellectual world of the triad (Japan, Western Europe and North America), soon made the hypotheses of the initial projected schema of the information society look shaky (Crozier *et al.*, 1975). Though this scientistic vision was flagrantly contradicted by subsequent events, it nevertheless succeeded in establishing the idea that organizational doctrines had supplanted politics. The new society was functional and would be run according to the principles of scientific management. Among his illustrious precursors, Bell mentions Claude-Henri de Saint-Simon, Frederic Winslow Taylor and Robert McNamara, former head of the Ford Motor Company, who oversaw the rationalization of Pentagon operations in the early 1960s, and later became president of the World Bank.

The professional forecasters

The idea that objective methods existed to explore the future gained legitimacy during the 1960s, and a market for the production of future-oriented scenarios developed. Professional forecasters offered their services to companies and governments, eager for advice and ready to pay for it. Through them, the general public became familiar with the new techno-information age.

One of them was Herman Kahn, director of the Hudson Institute, which made a number of forecasts under the aegis of the Commission on the Year 2000, headed by Bell. Kahn predicted, among other things, that Argentina and Spain would arrive side by side at the threshold of the post-industrial society and that, in the coming post-industrial (and therefore post-scarcity) society, people would work no more than 5–7 hours a day, four days a week, 39 weeks a year. The leading voice among forecasters was the independent consultant Alvin Toffler, author of the bestsellers *Future Shock* (1970) and *The Third Wave* (1979). A former Marxist, Toffler clearly indicated the role that anticipatory scenarios were designed to play: it was necessary to generate a desire for the future among the citizenry in order to avoid the 'trauma of future shock'. He publicized his expectations for the foreseeable future, including interactive democracy, the end of 'mass' media, customization, the return of the consumer, pluralism, full employment and flexibility. Above all, he predicted the end of that 'dangerous anachronism', the nation-state, which would be swept away by the 'matrix organization' of global companies. Instead of pitting the rich against the poor, or capitalism against communism, the new dichotomy would oppose the Archaic to the Modern. At the time, 'interactive democracy' meant the 'wired cities' still on the drawing boards that were taken over by think-tanks and transformed into laboratories for experiments in technocommunitarian ideology.

The precocious determination, revealed by the wave of forecasting, to give political legitimacy to the idea of a real 'information society', here and now, overcame any doubts one might have had about its epistemological soundness. By the 1970s, it was a *fait accompli*, with strategies for achieving economic recovery being formulated through information technologies in the major industrial countries. There was an increasing tendency to assimilate information in statistical terms (as data) and to recognize it as such only when a technology capable of processing it was available. As a result, a purely instrumental concept of the information society took hold. Along with the vagueness of the concept, which was supposed to indicate the new destiny of the world, came a gradual fading of the socio-political stakes involved.

Soft power networks

By the end of the 1960s, Zbigniew Brzezinski, a specialist in the problems of communism, in his analyses of the worldwide consequences of the convergence of data processing and telecommunications, was explicitly presenting a geopolitical grid that lent legitimacy to the notion of the information society as a global society. In fact, his book on the technotronic revolution published in 1969 can be read as the final outcome of 'end-of' discourse, expressed as a strategy for worldwide hegemony. His central thesis went like this: President J. F. Kennedy was the first president of the global era, because he viewed the entire world as a domestic policy problem; since the United States controlled world networks, it was the 'first global society in history', the one that 'communicates the most'; the 'global society' model represented by the US foreshadows the destiny of the other nations; the new universal values flowing from the US will inevitably captivate the imagination of humanity as a whole, which will then imitate them. The moral of the story: the time of gunboat diplomacy was over; the notions of imperialism, Americanization and a *Pax Americana* were obsolete; long live the new 'network diplomacy'. In 1974, two years before his appointment as national security advisor to James Carter, Brzezinski proposed setting up a special inter-ministerial body to manage the 'economic-political-international machinery' or 'global system', which would report to the Vice-President and be in charge of 'global matters'. The plan did not materialize, however, until the Clinton administration, which created an ad hoc Under-Secretary of State position.

With the expression 'network diplomacy', we find ourselves projected three decades into the future. In 1996, the political analyst Joseph S. Nye and Admiral William A. Owens, both of them advisers to the Clinton administration, said exactly the same thing when they introduced the notion of soft power as the basis of the new doctrine of 'global security':

HISTORY AND PERSPECTIVES

Knowledge, more than ever before, is power. The one country that can best lead the information revolution will be more powerful than any other. For the foreseeable future, that country is the United States.... The information edge is equally important as a force multiplier of American diplomacy, including soft power – the attraction of American democracy and free markets.

(Nye and Owens, 1996)

Conclusion: only modern communications, first and foremost the Web, can 'encourage the expansion of a peaceful community of democracies, which will be the best guarantee of a safe, free, prosperous world'. The notion of 'soft power' was launched by Nye in a book bearing the telling title *Bound to Lead: The Changing Nature of American Power*, published a year after the fall of the Berlin Wall. It was defined as:

> ... the ability to achieve desired outcomes in international affairs through attraction rather than coercion. It works by convincing others to follow, or getting them to agree to, norms and institutions that produce the desired behavior. Soft power can rest on the appeal of one's ideas or on the ability to set the agenda in ways that shape the preferences of others. If a state can make its power legitimate in the perception of others and establish international institutions that encourage them to channel or limit their activities, it may not need to expend as many of its costly traditional economic and military resources.

(Nye, 1990: 12)

In contrast to this definition, it is helpful to remember the warning issued as early as 1931 by Aldous Huxley: 'In an age of advanced technology, the greatest danger to ideas, culture and the mind may well come from an enemy with a smiling face rather than from an adversary who inspires terror and hatred' (Ramonet, 2000).

There is another leitmotif at the core of the doctrine of soft power, which tends to eliminate any sense of responsibility: the interdependence of nations, the increase in the number of players and stakes involved, and the weakening of hierarchies across the world makes the notion of power so 'complex, volatile and interactive' (Nye uses all of these terms) that it loses all consistency. The world system has no head, and therefore none of the players in the global scenario can be held accountable for their actions. In *Mythologies*, Roland Barthes described the bourgeoisie as a 'limited company'. The same name could well apply to today's 'global business class', as global leaders like to describe themselves.

As everyone knows, the year that the Berlin Wall came down also gave fresh impetus to the 'end of history' discourse, in a new version devised by Francis Fukuyama, in the light of the victory of free-market democracy.

Global security or the 'revolution in military affairs'

The concept of soft power reflects the hidden side of globalization doctrines, namely the thinking of the military establishment. A new doctrine arose in connection with the Gulf War, and was later consolidated with regard to the war in Bosnia and the implosion of Africa. The new strategic idea that enshrined the position of the United States as the 'lonely superpower' to use Samuel Huntington's expression, or head of the 'system of systems', was an updated notion of 'American national interests' at a time when US information dominance was becoming obvious. Pentagon experts, inspired in part by Admiral Owens, immediately dubbed this new geo-strategic outlook resulting from the disappearance of the 'global enemy', i.e. the communist bloc, a 'revolution in military affairs'.

The doctrinal revision aimed at redefining 'military control in an uncontrollable world' where the players in the 'global system' have increased in number, along with their modes of action. According to its proponents, wars of agrarian and industrial civilization in the era of information war were a relic of the past, requiring careful doses of intervention and abstention. War, which acquired legitimacy in the name of humanitarian universalism, thus had a number of targets, from which America's overriding national interests would choose. The US should avoid intervening in local wars, in which belligerents solved their problems by hacking each other to death. In any case, when intervention did occur, it should be limited to the commitment to bringing into play the resources of cyberwar, namely, control of the skies. Ideally, the US alone should decide on the military operations, including those outside the European-Atlantic zone, within the scope of NATO, which they tried to turn into a virtually autonomous security organization. At the bottom of the ladder were the countries destined to remain fatally 'unconnected', the irretrievable 'failed states', still mired in agrarian or industrial conflicts. State organization in these countries was decomposing and was obviously incapable of fulfilling the geo-economic tasks assigned to it by the new world order (Joxe, 1996). What was new was the fact that the military was starting to use geoeconomic criteria for decision-making. It was promoting an offensive strategy of peaceful enlargement of the world market as a paradigm, in place of the defensive strategy of containment adopted during the polar opposition of the Cold War years. Hence, the revolution in military affairs assigned prime importance to extending the realm of free trade, revealing the close links it was developing among the control of information networks, the universalist model of market democracy and the so-called 'global security' strategy intended to ensure the stability of the planet viewed strictly through the prism of the new liberalism. The concentration of geopolitical power in the hands of the lonely superpower was the logical counterpart to economic globalization, defined as nothing less than decentralization at the planetary level.

Since the fall of the Berlin wall, experts in the military establishment have delighted in celebrating the 'revolution in military affairs'. The antiseptic wars in the Gulf and Kosovo seemed to confirm this vision, with its traces of technological determinism, until the attacks on 11 September 2001, when they were forced to observe that the macro system of remote surveillance via spy satellites and planetary eavesdropping had not been able to anticipate the terrorist actions, since old-fashioned human information gathering methods ('humint', as they call it in intelligence circles) had been relegated to the dustbin. Similarly, the doctrine of zero casualties from among their own ranks appeared totally outdated when formulating a counterattack on a faceless enemy.

The rise of management metaphors

In a tribute to the new legitimacy of geo-economic reasoning, a number of metaphors bloomed to designate the global company, such as 'hologram-firm' or 'amoeba-firm'. A global company was composed of relationships and information, a paradigm of the fluid, 'circulating' society. It was free of the complex modes of Fordist compartmentalized, hierarchical organization and could adopt the credo of company flexibility, employee autonomy and the 'good-citizen firm'. The watchword of this new form of organization was 'integration'. First of all, this meant the integration of geographical levels: the local, national and international levels would no longer be compartmentalized, but would instead interact with each other and be thought about simultaneously. Integration also meant combining design, production and marketing. It meant joining together activities that were once separate (the giant mergers of software and hardware firms, of contents and containers, come to mind). This cluster of convergences generated its own neologisms, such as 'glocalize', a term invented by Japanese management theorists to describe local–global circularity, and 'co-producer' or 'prosumer', which designated the consumer's new interactive function. The word 'integration' naturally refers explicitly to a 'holistic' or better still, 'cybernetic' philosophy, whereby the world is organized into large economic units. This new 'management-speak' had only one obsession: the death of the infamous nation-state (Ohmae, 1985, 1995).

This system-oriented view distilled its own imaginary. The 'network-based company' was another name for the 'postmodern company', an immaterial, abstract unity, a world of forms, symbols and information flows. The more aesthetically inclined management gurus unabashedly quoted the most scholarly references from Derrida, Lyotard and Foucault to lend legitimacy to the new fluid order of so-called 'dissipative' structures (Cooper, 1989).

What stands out clearly in this hazy picture of the entrepreneurial world is the dissipation of the stakes involved in restructuring the world economy, the failure to mention the appearance of neo-Tayloristic methods applied in the face of stiff competition and the quiet acceptance of the shameful exploitation of workers making electronic devices on assembly lines in tax-free zones. It confused words with realities, since only a few companies could be properly called 'global firms'. 'The global firm is more of a project than a reality'. It also ignored the fact that 'globalization deepens the specific features of each economy and greater globalization need not be an impediment to diverse production models which take the particular social and economic aspects of the various countries into account' – in short, that 'complex hybrids' exist (Boyer, 2000: 21).

The weightlessness of the postmodern corporation and the Net economy do not offer any protection against reality. With the attacks on the World Trade Center and the Pentagon, the techno-libertarian myth of the end of the nation-state has suddenly been cracked at the seams by the force of renewed patriotism and state intervention.

The global democratic marketplace and freedom of commercial speech

Globalization walks hand in hand with deregulation. The debate on culture, information and communication has gone beyond UNESCO and shifted to technical organizations, the first and foremost of which is the GATT or General Agreement on Tariffs and Trade, renamed the World Trade Organization in 1995. In administrative terminology, these areas now come under the heading of 'services'.

A new version of free speech and choice appeared in response to initial controversies surrounding deregulated advertising and television. The very definition of the citizen's right of free speech was now competing against 'freedom of commercial speech', which was claimed to be a new 'human right'. This has generated a recurring tension between the empirical law of the marketplace and the rule of law, between the absolute sovereignty of consumers and that of citizens, guaranteed by their parliaments. It was in this context that the neo-populist notion of a global democratic marketplace, the cornerstone of free trade legitimacy, arose.

The management language (not to say the language of states that are accomplices to their own dispossession) used to describe the information society is the outcome of this ideological project: the definition of cultural diversity is transmuted into offering a plurality of services to sovereign consumers; the cultural term 'work' has been supplanted by the market notions of 'service' and 'product'. In 1998, a European Directive was issued concerning the protection of personal data, to the indignation of global marketeers who consider building databanks to be one of the main driving forces of targeted e-commerce. The objections to the Directive raised by information industry pressure groups were based on the same 'philosophy' of the freedom of commercial speech: 'Restrictions laid down in the name of protecting privacy should not be allowed to prevent legitimate business from being carried on electronically both inside and outside our borders' (Eurobit *et al.*, 1995). Here Pierre Legendre's analysis takes on its full significance: management doctrine is indeed the 'technical version of politics' (Legendre, 1992: 26).

Lobbies immediately denounced legitimate objections to the market concept of freedom as an attempt to restore censorship: there should be no restrictions on the freedom to communicate. The movement of cultural and information flows should be regulated only by the consumer's free will in a free marketplace of products. With this axiom, any attempt at formulating national and regional public policies in this domain lost its legitimacy. There was no point in debating whether or not the state should play a role in organizing information and communication systems with a view to protecting citizens' free speech from the logic of market and technological segregation, nor was there any reason to examine how organizations in civil society might act as decisive pressure groups to demand arbitration from public authorities on this issue.

Clearly, the claim of full rights to freedom of commercial speech was an attempt to push back the limits imposed by society to 'using the public sphere for public relations purposes', as Habermas would say. The notion of the freedom of commercial speech, as a principle of world organization, is indissolubly linked to the old principle of the free flow of information, which American diplomats began using at the start of the Cold War, but which was actually developed during the middle of the Second World War (Mattelart, 1995). The business management doctrine of globalization is a recycled version of this principle, which equates freedom itself with freedom to trade. Hence, any position that holds that the principle of the free flow of information is not synonymous with justice and equality among people is considered obsolete, if not altogether antediluvian.

In the GATS (General Agreement on Trade in Services) negotiations which were slated to begin at the third WTO conference, known as the Millennium Round, organized in Seattle, Washington from 30 November to 3 December 1999, one of the issues was to make sure the doctrine of free trade was not applied to all types of goods and services. The aim was to have not only culture but also health, education and the environment recognized as universal public goods.

The search for the global standard

The search for a 'global standard' has stepped up the production of possible scenarios for future society. By 'publicizing' a future free from the weight of

AN ARCHAEOLOGY OF THE GLOBAL ERA

'centralization', 'territoriality' and 'materiality', these scenarios plainly seek to hasten its arrival. The bestsellers by Nicholas Negroponte (1995) or Bill Gates (1995) are typical of this logistical system, which has been given the task of supporting the promise of *le grand soir* of 'frictionfree capitalism'. 'The digital' turns into a 'natural force'; there is no way of 'stopping' it or 'holding it back'. Its power lies in 'decentralizing', 'globalizing', 'harmonizing' and 'empowering' (Negroponte, 1995). The verb 'globalize', like its ally 'communicate', has become intransitive, testifying to the implosion of thought.

As for think-tanks, they have become the purveyors of 'organic' system-bound intellectuals and salesmen of deregulation. In a January 2000 interview in *Le Monde de l'économie,* one of the heads of the Cato Institute summed up his 'liberal philosophy' this way:

> The 20th century has been nothing but one long state-oriented parenthesis. We are responding to the issue of poverty by saying that, the freer the economy, the more jobs it creates, the better it pays its employees, the fewer poor people it creates. State intervention is only necessary for the army, the police and the law. Everything else can be managed by the private sector. As far as I'm concerned, the new economy is clearly in tune with this project for freedom.
>
> (Boaz, 2000: III)

This think-tank, specializing in monitoring public policy, belongs to the most radical libertarian current in the neo-liberal family, precisely because of its anti-government stance. It has only one doctrine regarding network regulation: the application of common business law. The role of the state should be restricted to creating an environment conducive to free trade.

Free-market fundamentalists are by no means the sole proponents of this vision, as the discussion on digital convergence has shown. At the present time, an attempt is being made to merge the regulatory systems applied to audiovisual communication and telecommunications and make both of them subject to a 'simplified' standard dictated by 'market forces'. This is tantamount to putting telephonic communication on an equal footing with cultural products, and the latter would thereby cease to be given special treatment.

The new messianism

Globalization also goes hand in hand with megalomania. Discourse on the values of the global firm and the market totality exudes overweening self-confidence: 'Where conquest has failed, business can succeed.' The global business community has continually claimed for itself the messianic role of midwife of world peace. In fact, the organizers of the economic forum in Davos (transferred from this Swiss city to New York after 11 September

2001), where the business elite comes together every year, have defined their undertaking as a 'sort of global social conscience', but only after first recalling its 'apolitical' nature. In an astonishing interview broadcast by the TV channel Arte in November 1997 as part of a documentary film, Ted Turner, the founder of CNN, pushed this new-millennium position to an extreme:

> We have played a positive role. Since CNN was set up, the Cold War has ended, the conflicts in Central America are over, there is peace in South Africa, etc. People can see how stupid war is. But nobody wants to look stupid. With CNN, information circulates throughout the world and nobody wants to look like a jerk. So, they make peace, because it's smart.
>
> (Laffont, 1997)

Two years later, this determinism with its crusader-like tone was especially piquant in light of the *realpolitik* of the Allied Forces in ex-Yugoslavia.

The rudimentary discourse used to give legitimacy to the ideology of corporate globalization is an affront to the real complexity of our interconnected world. Its increasing social legitimacy has been indissolubly linked to conceptual destabilization resulting from the deregulation of the information and communication systems. That is exactly the point Gilles Deleuze and Félix Guattari were making when they denounced the use of 'communication universals', the most basic of which is the notion of globalization. As they wrote:

> The absolute low-point of shamefulness was reached when data processing, marketing, design and advertising, all the communication disciplines, took over the word 'concept' itself and said: this is our business. . . . It is profoundly depressing to learn that 'concept' now designates a service and computer engineering society.
>
> (Deleuze and Guattari, 1991: 15)

Deleuze saw this semantic expropriation as a further sign supporting his definition of the new society as a 'control society': a society in which the company serves as a paradigm and control is exercised in the short term, in rapid yet ongoing, unlimited turnover, replacing the mechanisms of the disciplinary societies revealed by Michel Foucault.

The asymmetrical planet

By announcing the arrival of the Global Information Infrastructure to the 'great human family', the then Vice-President of the United States, Albert Gore, was holding out the dazzling prospect to underdeveloped countries of escaping from their problems, along with a 'new Athenian age of democracy forged in the forums that this network is going to create' (Gore, 1994). Experience has shown, however, that communication networks not only link people together, but often widen the gap between economies, societies and cultures along the lines taken by 'development' (Braudel, 1979; Wallerstein, 1983).

In 1999, the United Nations Development Programme (UNDP) made a critical assessment of globalization, confirming the growing marginalization of most of the world's countries from the standpoint of information technology. Ninety-one percent of Internet users were found in the OECD countries, which comprise the 29 richest countries in the world and represent 19 per cent of the world's population. More than half of them were in the United States, which accounts for only 5 per cent of the world's population. To finance computer connections for the planet's cyberspace misfits, the UN proposed the shock therapy of a 'byte tax', a sort of network tax, equivalent to the 'Tobin tax' on financial transactions worldwide proposed by French anti-globalization social movements (UNDP, 1999).

The World Report on Culture published by UNESCO for the year 2000 presents a telling picture of enormous disparities in new technology equipment. In the industrialized world, for every 10,000 inhabitants, the study documented the existence of 1,822 cellular phones (compared to 163 among the other [majority] portion of the planet), 444 faxes (compared to 13), 1,989 personal computers (compared to 113) and 2000 Internet addresses (compared to 4.7). More than 50 percent of the earth's inhabitants do not have a telephone line, or even electricity. In order to access basic telecommunication services, there must be one telephone for every hundred people, whereas a quarter of the world's population has yet to reach that point. As if that were not enough, the cost of Internet access is directly proportionate to the density of the country's Net-user population. Whereas the average cost of 20 hours of Internet connection in the United States is $30, it jumps to well over $100 in countries with few Net users.

The world economy can best be described as an 'archipelago' or 'techno-apartheid' global economy, due to the growing dichotomies within it, which are also found, in their own way, inside the rich countries themselves. The gap becomes a gulf when the potential for information technology development is used as a veneer for an economic model that many countries and social groups today correctly perceive as unbridled. In a similar context, the way the digital era is reconfiguring the physiognomy of cities offers further testimony. Increasingly, we find fortified centres, veritable enclaves along the lines of private towns in the United States, and companies where the employees live closed in upon themselves on planned sites linked by new information technologies, in opposition to the vast no-man's land of the information-poor and excluded. The neo-liberal fundamentalists readily admit that this is the world's unavoidable new deal, invoking a magical figure of 20/80, which means that the global economy model can benefit only 20 per cent of the world's population, whereas the fate of everyone else will remain precarious. People are being openly encouraged to believe that the former plan for a modern world based on the desire to end inequality and injustice is a thing of the past. It is a 'stupefying period of mass mystification', says Alain Joxe; the 'ideologists of global laissez-faire' are concealing the de facto 'exclusion of those condemned to death by economic war'. Joxe, an expert on war and peace studies, concludes: 'The war against the poor, and even the genocide of the poor, is the agenda of modernity' (Joxe, 1997: 24).

Contrary to the geo-techno-economic vision of a world supposedly held together by free trade, there are signs everywhere that given socio-cultural systems are being unhitched from the drive towards a unified economic field. The dissociation between the two is an ongoing source of conflict and tension that feeds the various networks of planetary disorder which take on their own form of globalization. In contrast to new hybrid landscapes, some assertions of cultural difference respond to the threat of creeping homogeneity by refusing otherness, even though they are inextricably linked to the common reconstruction of identity-affirming processes in the age of global flows.

A global system with new global actors

By taking to the streets in the 1990s to protest against the rule of the market, new social movements on a worldwide scale revealed the harshness of the notion of globalization that was coming dangerously close to achieving a consensus. The protest movement was a salutary awakening of citizens who brought to the fore terms such as domination, power struggle and inequality, which had been called into question by the project for neo-liberal flexibility.

As the stakes became planetary in scope, they ignited equally far-reaching protests. The new political deal came into focus most clearly in Seattle, at the time of the mobilization (a genuinely global event) of nongovernmental organizations, trade unions and associations against the drive towards, and danger of, a wholly market-oriented world. While less spectacular, in 1998 the concerted action of 600 organizations in some 70 countries, linked together by the Internet, had already succeeded in interrupting the MAI (Multilateral Agreement on Investment) negotiations on the deregulation of unbridled investment. For three years, one example of using the Internet to lodge protests was in the back of everyone's mind: the 'information guerrilla' action in Mexico's Chiapas region by the neo-Zapatistas and Sub-Commander Marcos. Downstream, this emblematic experiment gave food for thought about social movements to theorists of the global network society (Castells, 1996). Upstream, it called forth a Net-war strategy at the Pentagon, where new forms of political activism were eagerly monitored (Swett, 1995; Arquilla and Ronfeldt, 1998).

The unification of the economic sphere presents a major challenge when it comes to choosing the form of protest. It requires that social organizations, anchored in a historically situated territory but capable of broadening their scope beyond national boundaries, discover what binds them to other realities and struggles. Searching for multilevel articulations was one of the main tasks of the global movements gathered in the two first World Social Fora of Porto Alegre, Brazil, in 2001 and 2002. They testify to the different forms of social interaction emanating from the grassroots, pervading national societies and ultimately achieving true global reach.

Buoyed by the high visibility and efficient communication of the cyber-mobilization of the new social networks on a worldwide scale, groups from one end of the political spectrum to the other soon began proclaiming the arrival of a 'global civil society'. In examining how that notion was manipulated, however, one must be more circumspect, especially as the notion of 'civil society' itself carries with it a long history of ambiguities. Such extrapolation generally ignores the complex ways in which the nation-state has been reconfigured in its articulation with national civil society, both of them being faced with the logic of global system integration. It masks a refusal to think about the state outside of the ready-made idea of the 'end of the nation-state'.

Like it or not, the territory of the nation-state remains the place where the social contract is defined. It has by no means reached the degree of obsolescence suggested by the crusade in favour of deterritorialization through networks. It takes the nearsightedness of techno-libertarians to support this kind of globalizing populism, which avails itself of the simplistic idea of a somewhat abstract and evil state in opposition to that of an idealized civil society – an area of free exchange between fully sovereign individuals. Despite all the talk that relativizes the position of the nation-state, negotiations between states continue to be necessary as a counterforce to the deviations of ultra-liberalism. One of the tasks of organized civil society is indeed to ensure that the state is not robbed of its regulatory function. That is precisely what the sociologist Anthony Giddens, promoted to advisory status by Tony Blair, has rejected in his search for a 'third way', tinged with a Christian communitarian spirit, to rebuild worldwide social democracy (Giddens, 1999). What he calls the 'global age' functions as a kind of determinism. The corollary to his univocal celebration of the mythical power of a global civil society shaped by new social movements is the disempowerment of public authorities. This type of meta-discourse can only be formulated within a national situation in which ultra-liberalism has already swept away social achievements and reduced state intervention to a minimum. Once again, the 'global' keeps showing its 'local' face.

To conclude, I would say that the current confusion surrounding words, concepts and notions relating to the global age, which appear to make sense and generate consensus in the most varied cultural and political contexts, forces us to remain on our epistemological guard. Long study trips to China, the Indian Ocean islands and the Middle East during the past year have prompted me to emphasize the visible wish of citizens throughout the world to reappropriate the process of worldwide integration by starting with the idea of a 'regional cultural community'. In spite of numerous political tensions, such attempts to build large geo-cultural entities (with their own specific features) are an essential response to the plan for a globalization that can grasp culture only in instrumental terms. Of these attempts, which I have observed in every cultural area, what pleased me the most was the fact that they not only reached across physical borders but also across academic disciplines. Geographers, anthropologists, historians, economists as well as life scientists and many others have all been invited to think and rethink the new world of networks. On the fringe of global events, on the fringe of the new totalizing theories about the future of the world led by a techno-globalizing ideology, an alternative way is being paved to build a viable planet for everyone.

It is significant that the United Nations placed the year 2001 under the auspices of the 'Dialogue between Civilizations' proposed by President Khatami of Iran, who was seeking thereby to counter Samuel Huntington's thesis on the inevitable 'clash of civilizations'. The call for dialogue seems increasingly like a premonition, in the light of the spectre of the crusade and holy war following the 11 September terrorist attacks.

To date, the most important narrative accounts of a social utopia have talked about 'nowhere'. The slow rebuilding of a utopian vision on the threshold of the 21st century needs its *genius loci,* the spirit of each place, the singularity of places. No doubt, this is the only way to accomplish a new vision of the universe and of the universal.

Note

1 Translated from the French by Susan Taponier with Philip Schlesinger.

References

Arquilla, J. and D. Ronfeldt (1998) *The Zapatista Social Netwar in Mexico.* Santa Monica, CA: Rand Corporation.
Arquilla, J. and D. Ronfeldt (1999) *The Emergence of Noopolitik: Toward an American Information Strategy.* Santa Monica, CA: Rand Corporation.
Bell, D. (1960) *The End of Ideology.* Glencoe, IL: Free Press.
Bell, D. (1973) *The Coming of Post-Industrial Society: A Venture in Social Forecasting.* New York: Basic Books.
Bell, D. (1999) 'Foreword', in *The Coming of Post-Industrial Society*, 3rd edn. New York: Basic Books.
Boaz, D. (2000) 'Entretien', *Le Monde de l'économie* (Paris) 25 Jan.

AN ARCHAEOLOGY OF THE GLOBAL ERA

Bourdieu, P. and L. Wacquant (2000) 'La Nouvelle Vulgate planétaire', *Le Monde diplomatique* March.

Boyer, R. (2000) 'Les Mots et la réalité', in S. Cordellier (ed.) *Mondialisation audelà des mythes.* Paris: La Découverte.

Braudel, F. (1979) *Le Temps du monde, vol. III, Civilisation matérielle, économie et capitalisme XVe–XVIIIe siècle.* Paris: Armand Colin. (English trans., *Civilisation and Capitalism: 15th–18th Century, vol. III.* London: Collins, 1984).

Brzezinski, Z. (1969) *Between Two Ages: America's Role in the Technetronic Era.* New York: Viking Press.

Burnham, J. (1941) *The Managerial Revolution.* Bloomington: Indiana University Press.

Castells, M. (1996) *The Rise of Network Society.* Oxford: Blackwell.

Cooper, R. (1989) 'Modernism, Post-Modernism and Organizational Analysis: The Contribution of Jacques Derrida', *Organizational Studies* 10(4).

Crozier, M., S. Huntington and J. Watanuki (1975) *The Crisis of Democracy: Report on the Governability of Democracies to the Trilateral Commission*, Preface by Z. Brzezinski. New York: New York University.

Deleuze, G. and F. Guattari (1991) *Qu'est-ce que la philosophie?* Paris: Minuit.

Drucker, P. (1990) *Post-Capitalist Society.* New York: Harper Business.

Ferro, M. (1999) 'Le Futur au miroir du passé', *Le Monde diplomatique* September.

Gates, B. (1995) *The Road Ahead.* New York: Viking Penguin.

Giddens, A. (1999) *The Third Way: The Renewal of Social Democracy.* Cambridge: Polity Press.

Gore, A. (1994) 'Remarks Prepared for Delivery by Vice-President Al Gore to the International Telecommunications Union', Buenos Aires, 21 March. Washington, DC: Department of State.

Joxe, A. (1996) *Le Débat stratégique américain 1995–1996: révolution dans les affaires militaires.* Paris: Cirpes.

Joxe, A. (1997) 'La Science de la guerre et la paix', Lecture at the Autonomous University of Mexico, Centre for Interdisciplinary Studies, mimeo, January.

Laffont, F. (1997) *'La Planète CNN'*, documentary film, *Arte* channel, Paris, 14 November.

Legendre, P. (1997) *La Fabrique de l'homme occidental.* Paris: Editions Arte.

Lévy, P. (2000) *World Philosophie.* Paris: Odile Jacob.

Lipset, M. S. (1960) *Political Man: The Social Basis of Politics.* New York: Doubleday.

McLuhan, M. (1962) *The Gutenberg Galaxy.* Toronto: Toronto University Press.

Mattelart, A. (1994) *L'Invention de la communication.* Paris: La Découverte (English trans., *The Invention of Communication.* Minneapolis and London: University of Minnesota Press, 1996).

Mattelart, A. (1999) *Histoire de l'utopie planétaire: de la cité prophétique à la société globale.* Paris: La Découverte.

Mattelart, A. (2000) *Networking the World: 1794–2000.* Minneapolis: University of Minnesota Press.

Mattelart, A. (2002) *Histoire de la société de l'information* [The Information Society]. Paris: La Découverte. London: Sage.

Mattelart, T. (1995) *Le Cheval de Troie audiovisuel: le rideau de fer à l'épreuve des radios et télévisions transfrontières.* Grenoble: PUG.

Negroponte, N. (1995) *Being Digital.* New York: Vintage.

Nye, J. S. (1990) *Bound to Lead: The Changing Nature of American Power*. New York: Basic Books.

Nye, J. S. and W. A. Owens (1996) 'America's Information Edge', *Foreign Affairs* 75(2).

Ohmae, K. (1985) *The Triad Power*. New York: Free Press.

Ohmae, K. (1995) *The End of the Nation State: The Rise of Regional Economies*. London: Harper-Collins.

Ramonet, I. (2000) 'Un délicieux despotisme', *Le Monde diplomatique* March.

Rostow, W. W. (1960) *The Stages of Economic Growth: A Non-Communist Manifesto*. Cambridge: Cambridge University Press.

Shils, E. (1955) 'The End of Ideology?', *Encounter* 5(5).

Shils, E. (1960) 'Mass Society and Its Culture', *Daedalus* spring.

Swett, C. (1995) *Strategic Assessment: The Internet*. Washington, DC: Department of Defense.

Teilhard de Chardin, P. (1955) *Le Phénomène humain*. Paris: Seuil.

UNDP (1999) *Rapport mondial sur le développement humain*. Geneva: UNDP.

Wallerstein, I. (1983) *Historical Capitalism*. London: Verso.

20

CLASS ANALYSIS AND THE INFORMATION SOCIETY AS MODE OF PRODUCTION

Nicholas Garnham

Source: *Javnost–The Public* 11(3) (2004): 93–103.

Abstract

In analysing the current usefulness of a class analysis of the media this article places the political economy of the media in the context of a political economy of the Information Society. It argues that the Information Society does not refer to one thing or trend, but is made up of a number of competing, and often contradictory analyses of the development of the mode of production, each with different concepts of the role of information in economic development and different definitions of information workers. Media centric versions of the Information Society are then critiqued in the light of empirical evidence. Finally an assessment is made of what Information Society theory can contribute to our understanding of changes in the structure of the labour market associated with the growth of information work in relation to class and of globalisation through the concept of the death of distance.

This paper is focused on the question of the continuing usefulness of a class analysis of communication as a defining characteristic of a critical, left or progressive approach. In response to this question I should say first that it seems to me that it is the primary function of critical scholars to analyse the world as it is. The purpose is to show what is going on and with what consequences and for whom without worrying as to whether it is left or progressive.

363

However it is undoubtedly the case that much critical scholarship has seen itself and been seen by others as based upon a class analysis. It is also the case that classes – in the classic sense of social groups whose broad life chances, relative social power, and possibly also views of the world, are determined by their sources and levels of income – exist and remain one important basis for the analysis of social structure and dynamics.

The left's use of class analysis is, however, more specific than this. It has been characterised by two basic arguments. First that the basic social cleavage is between owners of capital and labour and that this cleavage is conflictual because it is exploitative. Second that from this basic cleavage can be derived distinct ideologies, political programmes and perhaps cultural tastes. Within this broad framework critical communication scholars have either analysed the media as exemplars of class division at the point of production within a broader political economy or they have analysed them as vehicles for ideological domination.

It is my view, for what it is worth, that the class based dominant ideology approach has for long been a busted flush. We do not require it in order to explain the relatively smooth reproduction of capitalism and it has proved an unreliable vehicle for explaining the nature of the social, political and cultural beliefs and practices of individuals and groups. In fact most current critiques of this type are broadly liberal in origin (they are none the worse for that).

This then leaves us with the production based concept of class and its relationship to an analysis of the political economy of the communication sector. In this paper I will illustrate my views of its relevance and usefulness through an outline analysis of information society policy rhetoric and of current developments in the media sector within that framework. Above all, the classic Marxist version of class, derived from Smith and Ricardo, saw the basic class structure as derived from the relations of production of a given mode of production and future changes in class structure and relations as stemming from major shifts in the mode of production. From a class analysis perspective therefore, the key question posed by Information Society thinking is whether it is, as some claim, a new mode of production.

My argument in this paper starts from the assumption that, in the present period, we need to tackle the political economy of media within the wider political economy of the information society. There are at least two indications that this is the case. During the period of "irrational exuberance" that marked the so-called dot-com boom of the late 1990s the financial markets created a new sector, TMT (Technology, Media and Telecommunications), under the assumption, erroneous as we shall see, that their economic dynamics and thus financial futures were as though one. Regulatory policy both in the US, Europe and the WTO is driven by a rhetoric that legitimates changes in intellectual property law, the deregulation of media and telecommunication markets and liberalisation of world trade in cultural services as the removal of barriers to innovation and competition required for the development of the information society.

The political economy of the media is in particular linked to information society thinking in two specific ways. On the one hand it is argued that the media are a key growth sector, creating jobs and export earnings, and that therefore economic and regulatory policy in each country must be designed to ensure that supposed barriers to this growth and to national competitive success on global markets for media products and services are removed. It is this view that is captured in designating the creative or copyright industries as the focus of attention and in seeing the World Wide Web and multi-media as the revolutionary driving forces. On the other hand it is argued that the media sector's economic history, structure and dynamics are precursors for the whole economy as it becomes an information economy, producing, distributing and consuming symbolic goods and services. It is this view that is captured in the terms knowledge, weightless and digital economies.

The central argument of this paper is that in order to test these claims and the efficacy, or otherwise, of the policies which derive from them it is necessary to deconstruct the information society discourse. In so doing we will see that there are a range of different economic theories/analyses, each with its own history, intertwined in the concept of the information society. These theories are each a response to specific economic/social problems with different policy goals. They require specific empirical testing and benchmarking. For instance, the notion that broadband penetration per se tells us anything useful or meaningful as a benchmark about wider economic and social dynamics is a bizarre fetishism. What is more both the analysis and the goals are in part contradictory. For instance, and I will return to this, a theory of price based market competition drives deregulation and competition law, while a Schumpeterian theory of growth based upon market entering innovations and driven by the excess rents that the resulting technical monopoly produces drives innovation policy. Each has something to recommend it, both as analysis and prescription, but from a policy perspective you have to choose between one or the other.

The range of theoretical/empirical analyses and the related policies and policy discourses jostle beneath a number of names – information, knowledge, creative, copyright, digital, e-economy or society. Often the names appear to be used randomly. But their choice may reflect the nature of the explanatory theory being deployed or the interest being promoted. For instant digital nuances the discourse towards the ICT (Information and Communication Technologies) industries; e-economy towards Net based business processes; information and knowledge towards science, innovation, and research and development; creative and copyright towards the media and cultural industries. One of the great ideological advantages of the information society discourse is that in its vagueness of concept and nomenclature it enables many to jump on the bandwagon and find a seemingly comfortable home in its promiscuous warmth. Witness the ways in which education, and especially higher education, has uncritically adopted it as it fights at the fiscal trough.

Let me then turn to deconstructing Information Society discourse as a range of theories which try to explain what is happening to the capitalist economy and as a range of policy responses to problems thrown up by those developments. Sometimes these problems and responses will be found at a very general level among economists, corporate strategists and managers and national and international policy makers. For instance how to explain and then what to do about stagnation, evidenced by falling rates of productivity growth and rates of profit in the leading industrial economies in the 1970s and 1980s. Or, and these are related, how to understand and respond to the implications of the shift from manufacturing to services. Sometimes they will stem from the interests of an industry and its lobbyists – for instance the marketing needs of ICT hardware and software industries or the investment needs, and intrasectoral competition of telecom operators.

1. Knowledge as the core of value added

This is Daniel Bell's "Post-Industrial Society" thesis. It stresses the centrality of organised technical innovation through harnessing science to capitalist growth. In this model ICTs are both a key exemplary product of this innovation process and also a tool within it. It places a stress on industrial research and development (R & D) and on relative rates of R and D spending as a test of national competitiveness – see for instance current EU policies. It is this model that now drives UK research policy and its search for elite, "world class research" centres. It is associated with theories of systems of innovation and endogenous growth theory – for instance stress on university/ industry collaboration, industrial clusters, the intrafirm learning curve and the knowledge organisation (see Castells 1996 and the concept of the network firm). It has become associated with –

2. Schumpeterian growth theory

Much Information Society analysis and policy is, often without knowing it, Schumpeterian. Indeed one could argue that he is at present the most influential of the great economists, that we have passed through Keynesianism and Monetarism and are now passing through Schumpeterianism. So it is important to be clear what Schumpeter was arguing and to what problem in capitalist development and its theorisation he was responding. It was widely recognised at the time Schumpeter (Schumpeter 1934; 1939) wrote that the classic explanation of capitalist dynamics, and at the same time its legitimation, namely interfirm price competition, was leading to stagnation, static sectoral oligopoly and normal profits and thus an investment slump. It was in this context that state planning and direction of investment looked attractive. Schumpeter's response was to argue that interfirm price competition was not the secret of capitalist growth – that it did indeed, as Walrasians argued, lead to equilibrium but a static equilibrium. The secret of capitalist growth was not competition through price between homogeneous commodities but the innovation of new heterogeneous products or processes which created new markets. However there was a high risk associated with innovation and thus the innovating entrepreneur (the *deus ex machina* in Schumpeter's system) required the promise of a monopoly in the new product and thus superprofits or rents. It is essentially this theory that was used to defend Microsoft against antitrust action.

This theory of the centrality of innovation and the entrepreneur to capitalist growth, and the innovation encouraging policies associated with it (everyone's search for the next Silicon Valley), has to face two problems. First, as I have noted above, and as the Microsoft case illustrates, it is quite incompatible with the neoclassical equilibrium model of market competition, and especially price competition, which underpins deregulation and competition policy. Secondly it raises the question of how long the monopoly should last if it is not in its turn to lead to stagnation. In Schumpeter it is assumed that innovation is external to the market and will always lead to a renewed process of market entry which will break the monopoly of the previous generation of successful innovators. However, much recent work has focused on barriers to market entry; on first mover advantage, intrafirm learning curves, constant returns to scale, path dependency and lock- in, all of which cast doubts on the Schumpeterian model and point more to a renewal of Chandler's model (Chandler 1977) of the dominance of economies of scale and scope and thus constant consolidation. I want to stress that this is a real and important argument about economic growth but it is about general processes of innovation, risk and reward which have not been changed as some would argue by ICTs. They connect with debates about the media in only one respect to which I will return – one of the arguments used to justify copyright extension, as also the widening of patent protection, is that it is to ensure the returns which motivate the creative entrepreneur.

3. Digitalisation and the frictionless economy

One version of the new information economy argument is a version of interfirm price competition as the key determinant of economic growth and consumer welfare. Its variant as applied to the media sector and the impact of the Internet is disintermediation. This approach focuses on transaction costs and in particular on the costs of information as key structural determinants of markets and argues that ICTs are creating both more transparent markets and thus both greater consumer choice and lower prices, and are at the same time making firms both more efficient and more flexible by drastically lowering transaction costs. From this perspective e-business is the core of the information society. So far as the media sector is concerned the issue is whether web based distribution and transaction systems have or have not radically shifted the relationship between symbol production and consumption and thus the basic economics of the industry – in particular has it broken the power of the distribution based conglomerates. The music industry is clearly at present the focus of this debate.

4. The information/copyright/creative industries as the new growth sector

This version of Information Society theory has been particularly attractive, both to those who study the media and those who work in it, for obvious reasons. Here much theorising is part of a long tradition which first focused on the shift from manufacturing to services and was then developed in Post-Fordist theory. This analytical tradition stressed the problems associated with the market exchange of intangibles (associated with a general growth of interest in information economics), with the increased importance of human capital, and with necessarily low productivity in the service sector. For the purposes of our discussion on the relevance of class it is important to stress that this approach, linked to the focus on innovation, was closely linked to theories of labour market restructuring, the rise of the so-called service class and, for instance in Bell and his followers such as Castells, a shift in the axial principle and thus in the basis of class power from industrial capital invested in tangible machines, plants and homogeneous labour power and to human capital invested through education and training in heterogeneous knowledge workers themselves. On the consumption side this approach also stressed the increased freedom of more knowledgeable consumers and links to the frictionless market approach. So far as the media are concerned the view of the information industries as key growth sectors has underlaid much of the drive to deregulation and the reform of intellectual property.

In my view this approach has tended a) to take the propaganda (or wish fulfilment) of the media sector itself at face value, and b) failed to distinguish the economics of content production from the economics of distribution. Critical scholars have been as guilty, perhaps more guilty of these failings, as anyone else. In my opinion this leads, for instance, to an absurd exaggeration of the power, reach and importance of media conglomerates and moguls.

When all is said and done it would be my contention that most of what is now called the information economy/society is in fact the service economy/ society revisited.

5. The mediacentric view of the Information Society

As I have said there is one version of the development of the information society which sees it as a shift from an economy dominated by material goods production to one dominated by the production, distribution and consumption of information or symbolic goods and services. This view was encapsulated in Negroponte's slogan "from atoms to bites" and is sometimes expressed as the information economy's weightlessness. This general position was also a central aspect of Post-Fordist theory and of Alvin Tofler's *Third Wave* (Tofler 1981). It has been central to the ideology of the Internet and dot.com boosters. It has been too readily accepted in my view by soi-disant post-modern radicals such as Scott Lash.

There has been a seamless move from this general argument to see the media sector, now retitled the information industries, as the major economic beneficiaries of this development. The policy imperative is well captured in the title of a recent OECD report "Content: the new growth industry." In examining the reality of this argument we need first to be extremely wary of the slippery term "creative" and thus the slide in the policy discourse from media or information industries to creative industries. No one of course can be against creativity. Its recent high valuation within information society discourse stems from a) the high value placed upon innovation, b) the stress in developed economies on the returns to human capital and its relation to a high skill/high value added strategy in the face of competition from cheap labour economies, and c) the centrality in production in service dominated economies of human to human relations rather than human to machine. It has little to do with creativity in the artistic or cultural sense, although the cultural industries and some sectors of education have adopted the creative industries nomenclature in an attempt to capture the concept of creativity exclusively for themselves. In fact the claimed economic weight and growth prospects of the "creative industries," certainly within the UK policy realm, rested largely on the inclusion of computer software and industrial design. Within the media sector itself it was traditional print publishing that loomed largest rather than the high tech electronic sectors.

So what is happening in the media sector? In order to understand the structure and dynamics of the media sector in relation to the larger economic context, whether of an information economy or not, we need to make a crucial distinction that is too often ignored. The media industries serve two distinct markets – that for intermediate goods and services as well as that for final consumer demand or, as Marxists used to say, Dept. 1 and Dept. 2. This is important because central to classic political economy has always been the problem, in relation to the analysis of reproduction, of the business cycle and crisis of the co-ordination between Dept. 1 and Dept. 2. It is also important because information industry growth in recent years, as Charles Jonscher (Jonscher 1983) pointed out long ago, has been largely in business services NOT in final consumer demand. But it is the media as suppliers of goods and services to consumers in their leisure time that has dominated attention and analysis. The problem is further complicated in the media sector by advertising. Advertising is a business service. Its cyclical growth dynamic is determined by corporate profitability and the intensity of competition between firms. But it is an essential ingredient in the financing of consumer media. Thus the media sector marches to two tunes which, as the most recent cycle shows, are often out of sync. It is important to stress that there is a deep contradiction between the growth of business information services and of advertising on the one hand and the claims of the information society (read new economy) advocates that ICTs in general and the Internet in particular make the economy more productive and efficient thus increasing consumer welfare by making markets more transparent and in Bill Gates words "frictionless." In fact this claim does not stand up to any serious analysis, but if it were true the prospects for the media broadly understood would not be good.

So far as consumer media are concerned we can observe a modest growth above the growth rate of GDP a large component of which has been a cyclical boom in advertising (now followed by an equally severe slump) a large fraction of which was internal to the information sector itself (dot.com advertising, etc.). But this has been largely a relative price effect since consumption itself has not risen proportionally. Indeed it is better to understand recent media developments as intensified competition for stagnant demand than as driven by explosive demand growth. The result of this has been the rise in the price to consumers of each unit of media consumption time, in economic theory not a good recipe for dynamic sectoral growth. Of course the information society theorists were arguing that prices would fall because of the cost of distribution was falling. This was central to the whole Third Wave, deregulation argument that saw the Internet as the provider of nil cost information abundance. Unfortunately they overlooked both the rising relative costs of production (including importantly rising marketing costs) and the demand side. In fact rising disposable income has not been mainly channelled towards media demand growth. Rather it has gone to higher cost, but now affordable, ways of enhancing leisure, tourism, restaurants, interior decoration, fitness, and health and beauty (It should not be forgotten that the largest service sector growth has been financial services, themselves a major driver of both ICT investment and information society boosterism).

The big story of the last decade in the media sector has not been growth in demand but a struggle for market share, which has taken the form of a struggle over distribution. If we look at US figures we see that the result has been declining margins, declining rates of return on capital and declining rates of profit, especially in the high growth sectors of cable and satellite. Beneath the froth we see a classic over investment boom driven by a search for market share during a period of technological uncertainty in distribution. To this extent the media are part of TMT since it was this sector that fuelled the general over investment boom that characterised the new economy period of irrational exuberance.

In part this was a side effect of developments in the telecom sector. Driven by regulatory induced competition and technological uncertainty telecom operators, both incumbents and new entrants, overbuilt networks and at the same time went in search of the increased traffic that would provide the economies of scale essential to make those network investments pay back. The economics of the sector are such that it was a "last person standing takes all" game. As part of this strategy the telecom operators bought into the argument, at least temporarily, that it was media consumption that would eat up the bandwidth they were so profligately providing. Hence the Content is King/Content; the new growth industry arguments and the search for so-called killer applications. On the other side the media industry bought into the convergence argument – that digitalisation enabled the exploitation of a range of content across delivery platforms and that to ensure economies of scale and scope it was necessary to be present on all platforms. Vivendi/Universal and AOL/Time Warner stand as decaying monuments to the fallacies of this strategy.

Here I would like to consider what implications my analysis has for a class analysis of the media sector. The critical approach has focused overwhelmingly on concentration of ownership. The underlying argument is that the media, because privately owned and controlled, are vehicles for the propagation of ruling class ideology and that therefore concentration strengthens this power. The proposed alternatives are either public service or working class owned and controlled media. It is important to stress that the critique of concentration per se is more of a liberal than a left critique. It is also important to stress that the critique of commercialisation that often accompanies it is often closer to the elitist mass culture critique than to a class analysis.

One version of the information society argument (Third Wave, Internet, etc.) is that it will/has produced a multiplicity of content (e.g., de Sola Pool's *Technologies of Freedom*, 1984). The alternative left argument has focused on concentration and commercialisation. In my view both positions largely miss the point.

While the plurality boosters are largely simply wrong the left has both exaggerated the extent of concentration and the power of conglomerates. On the one hand both parties fail to recognise that the mass media are, by their very nature, for better or worse the products of economies of scale and scope and thus are by their very nature concentrated. Diversity and mass media are simply contradictions in terms.

It is also the case, at least for the US market, that concentration has not increased either within sectors or cross sectorally. What has taken place is a shift from private to public company control and thus an increased financialisation. This has important consequences but they are not those of concentration. It is not ideological control that drives the managers of these companies but the drum beat of Wall Street, quarterly returns and the stock price. To improve these they would happily advocate a Bolshevik revolution if necessary. The bottom line in my view is that you simply do not need a dominant ideology explanation for the relative stability and reproduction of the capitalist system.

6. Digitalisation and the death of distance

This approach links a shift to an economy of intangibles to an analysis that sees the rapidly reducing costs through digitalisation of communication transport and switching as the key economic determinants where globalisation is a key aspect of the information society. According to this view a key historical determinant of achievable market size and thus of the general efficiencies derived from economies of scale and scope at the level of both firm and economy have been transport and communication costs and barriers. Their removal or reduction therefore leads to the realisation of capitalism's promise of a global market both in the production and sale of tangible commodities and increasingly in services. This in its turn leads, it is argued, to the declining regulatory power of nation states and the need to remove regulatory barriers to global flows and exchanges of all sorts. That there is some truth to this argument is certain. The issue is the extent of the effect and whether the process is on balance beneficial or negative and in each case for whom. In my view the extent and speed of globalisation has been much exaggerated and its effects insufficiently disaggregated. But it must also be stressed that there is a perfectly good critical/progressive case to be made for globalisation in the media sector as elsewhere.

7. Finally, information workers

It is clear that much thinking about the information society derives from the post-industrial tradition. Central to Daniel Bell's original thesis, and explicitly derived from Marx's own approach, was an argument about class power and its relationship to what Bell saw as a new mode of production within a stage theory that went feudalism, industrial capitalism, post-industrialism (Bell 1980). According to Bell, following Marx, industrial capitalism and its associated class structure was based upon capital's control of the physical means of production enabling them to control and exploit propertyless labour – so far so familiar. Bell then argued that the growth and value added of the nascent post-industrial economy was based upon the mobilisation/exploitation of knowledge (in particular scientific knowledge) which was not owned by capitalists but embedded as human capital in workers. Bell's thinking, derived in part from his Trotskyist past, was clearly part of a wider current of thought about the changing nature of capitalism and its implications both for capitalist development and for class politics. I mention Burnham and Galbraith as examples. Indeed it was precisely against this current of thought and its counterposing of a planned, bureaucratised industrialism and the social-democratic politics that went with it, as against an anarchic, competitive capitalism that Schumpeter developed his analysis.

The Bell approach then went on, first in the US in the work particularly of Porat, and then more widely through the OECD, to count information workers. In the early 1980s the percentage of information workers was seen as the key indicator of national economic development, holding much the same talismanic status then as broadband penetration has now.

The continuing power of this paradigm can be seen in the centrality given to "networkers" in Castells' trilogy (Castells 1996).

Indeed it would be hard to exaggerate the influence on both thinking generally and on policy of this approach. We can see it in particular in the policy stress now given everywhere, associated with the work of such gurus as Michael Porter and with endogenous growth theory, to the contribution to relative national competitiveness of education and training. It is, I think, a particularly well entrenched position precisely because it is designed to appeal to intellectual elites everywhere and to those potential centres of critical thinking we call universities.

For our purposes there are here both theoretical and empirical questions at issue. Empirically we need to place the claims made for a shift in labour composition against actual figures. In doing so we need firmly to distinguish between high level scientific research and development, the varied skill levels needed for different applications of technology and the embedded "touchy/feely" skills involved in much managerial and service work. Pace Bell claims (reference) it is largely the demand for the later that has increased. So far as levels of remuneration are concerned while in some specialised sectors a star economy and wider wage differentials have developed this has not and cannot be generally replicated. Indeed US data seems to show that, as one would expect, an increase in the supply of graduates lowers their market price. Nor as certain management gurus and politicians have argued has the increased importance of embedded human capital led to a shift in power between employer and employee or to the claimed resulting development of a generalised freelance, portfolio worker culture. Indeed all current evidence points to a remarkable stability over time in the average length of employment with one firm. Contrary to the hype on both right and left the OECD economies are not becoming significantly more part-time or freelance, even in the US. What does appear to be true, and this chimes ill with claims to higher productivity associated with high skill information work, and in passing has serious implications for a media growth scenario, is that the long term trend within industrial capitalism of reduced working hours appears to have stopped or possibly reversed and this is particularly true for the high tech-high skill workers and service workers. This may of course be a temporary response to skill shortages but this seems unlikely.

At a theoretical level what is at issue is how useful a general class approach that simply opposes capital to labour is in analysing changes in the labour market and their possible wider sociological and political effects as opposed to a more Weberian status group analysis which takes the division between capital and labour as given and then analyses shifts in the internal composition of labour. This is, in my view, of particular relevance in a situation in which capital has become more socialised and labour less homogenous. The problem for a general class analysis is the Marxist concept of exploitation. There are two versions of this: One stresses the labour theory of value and thus sees any returns to capital as theft from workers; the other stresses alienation and thus sees the labour process as the villain rather than the wage bargain. In practice these two may of course be combined. I have to confess that while I fully understand the Hegelian roots of alienation it in general remains a romantic load of hogwash and no basis for a sensible analysis of the social relations of capitalism. This does not of course mean that there are not unpleasant, stressful and unhealthy forms of work into which people are forced by economic necessity and too often for levels of pay, which are a disgrace and that this is not a proper matter of social and political concern. But I see little evidence either theoretical or practical that some generalised concept of class struggle will do anything to address the problem.

So, at a general level we are left with the division between wages as a return to labour and profits as a return to capital. While there is indeed a fluctuation in their relative shares, what is striking is the long-term stability of the shares in all developed industrial capitalist economies at around 65% to wages and 35% to profits. Any economy that at least reproduces itself, let alone grows, needs a mechanism for dividing output between current consumption and investment. The issue therefore is not the consumption levels of a few egregiously wealthy capitalists, as the populist media coverage of fat cats might lead one to believe, but whether current mechanisms are either economically or socially the most efficient and/or whether there is a viable and superior alternative. This, in practice, is what most economic policy debates are about. The second issue is then not the division between capital and labour but the distribution among labour and a general class analysis is just not useful, in my judgement, in either explaining the current mechanism and structure of distribution or in developing any alternative. To take one relevant example, the recent history of the US corporate sector, of which the revealed financial scandals were only the most flagrant form, involved through the exploitation of stock options and the manipulation of employment contracts a massive transfer of resources (in effect a theft) from shareholders by senior managerial employees, NOT some exploitative

374

behaviour by a capitalist class vis-à-vis workers. Similarly the AOL/Time Warner merger involved AOL shareholder managers stealing from Time Warner shareholders. One can take what view of such shenanigans one likes but they are not a question of class and class exploitation except in cases where pension funds were raided to the benefit of shareholders. Similarly much economic policy, including information society policy, is the outcome of intracapitalist struggle, for instance between finance and industrial capital, with no necessary impact on broader class relations.

References

Bell, Daniel. 1980. The Social Framework of the Information Society. In T. Forester (ed.), *The Microelectronics Revolution*, 500–549. Oxford: Blackwell.

Castells, Manuel. 1996. *The Rise of Network Society*. Oxford: Blackwell.

Chandler, Alfred. 1977. *The Visible Hand: The Managerial Revolution in American Business*. Cambridge, Mass.

De Sola Pool, Ithiel. 1984. *Technologies of Freedom*. Cambridge, MA: MIT Press.

Jonscher, Charles. 1983. Information Resources and Economic Productivity. *Information Economics and Policy* 1, 1, 13–35.

Schumpeter, Joseph. 1934. *The Theory of Economic Development*. Cambridge, MA:

Schumpeter, Joseph. 1939. *Business Cycles: A Theoretical, Historical and Statistical Analysis of the Capitalist Process*. New York: McGraw-Hill.

Tofler, Alvin. 1981. *The Third Vawe*. New York: Bantam Books.

21

MAKING SENSE OF THE INFORMATION AGE

Sociology and Cultural Studies

Frank Webster

Source: *Information, Communication & Society* 8(4) (2005): 439–58.

This article traces the development in Britain of research on information and communications in relation to trends in Sociology and this discipline's relations with Cultural Studies. It observes at the outset the seminal contribution of Daniel Bell's conception of Post-Industrial Society, characterizing it as blending theory with empirical observation while providing an account of the most consequential features of change. Sociology in the UK during the 1980s largely ignored macro-level analysis and focused on work and employment, took its starting point as opposition to the technological determinism associated with this first wave enthusiasm for the 'microelectronics revolution', and produced localized and textured studies. Manuel Castells' conception of the Network Society, while distinctive, signalled a return to the scale and scope offered by Bell, notably in being a macro analysis that combined theory and empirical evidence. Castells' contribution coincided with a second wave of technological enthusiasm associated especially with the Internet. Alongside this Sociology in Britain has experienced the rise of Cultural Studies, a field that has competed for important parts of what might have been considered Sociology's terrain. Indeed, Cultural Studies has outpaced Sociology in response to recent changes in the information domain. Its emergence expressed little concern with technological determinism, embracing 'virtuality' and being more open to the exploration of expanding culture. Nonetheless, Cultural Studies remains methodologically flawed while, like so much sociological research on ICTs and information, seemingly incapable of combining theory and empirical evidence that identify and explain the major contours of change.

Introduction

I have been thinking and writing about information trends and information and communications technologies (ICTs) for over 25 years. I have done so as a Sociologist, located chiefly in universities in the United Kingdom, with almost a decade as an academic visitor in a Scandinavian university plus regular periods spent in the United States. During this quarter century the discipline has developed in many ways, for instance coming to terms with Feminism, embracing and then spurning multiple shades of Marxism, and warming and cooling with regard to the relative importance of quantitative and qualitative approaches to research. Along the way, postmodernism – as both substantive development and epistemological assault – has been encountered. Of the challenges for Sociology over these years few have been more consequential than having to come to terms with the emergence of Cultural Studies (and its close cousin Media Studies). Indeed, if bookshops are any guide, one may even suggest there has been a takeover of much Sociology by Cultural Studies, or at least the occupancy by Cultural Studies of territory towards which one might have supposed Sociology had a prior claim. If one is suspicious of bookstore stocks as indicative of the health of a discipline, then witness the explosive growth of university courses in communications, media and Cultural Studies itself while Sociology numbers have grown at a much slower rate. In this article I should like to reflect on approaches to, and issues concerning, information and ICTs particularly in light of the sometimes troubled relations between Sociology and Cultural Studies during this period. I shall argue that there has been a shift, amongst students of change, away from interest in the Information Society (a term coined by Sociology) towards concern with the character of Cyberspace and Virtuality that reflects the emergence of Cultural Studies and its impatience with Sociology's inability to keep pace with the dynamism of change. I shall continue to argue, however, that sociological research on ICTs and information consistently proved incapable of developing work with the ambition and scope to match that offered by the leading thinkers Daniel Bell and Manuel Castells. Cultural Studies, while it has kept pace with change and responded more imaginatively than Sociology in its analyses, is methodologically weak and, like much Sociology, has been unable to match the vision and combination of empirical and theoretical work of analysts such as Daniel Bell and Manuel Castells.

The Information Society

The notion of the Information Society has wide currency within Sociology and, indeed, far beyond the discipline's borders. For most of my career the concept, Information Society (and its earlier synonym Post-Industrial Society), has been a major reference point for thinking about the information domain and associated technological innovation. It is far and away the most thorough and systematic attempt to delineate the new society, how it came about and where it is likely to take us. Necessarily, then, it is something with which analysts must come to terms. This has been the case even when scholars have been disposed to reject the term (Webster 2002).

The concept of the Information Society was conceived by Daniel Bell (born May 1919), arguably the most influential sociologist of the late twentieth century. Bell is an American, and critics have been quick to observe that his model of the Information Society is US-centric (Ross 1974; Steinfels 1979). This is so, though in return one might note that Bell's work has distinctively European reference points – evident in the literary style, the scope of his imagining, as well as his deep knowledge of and recourse to European thinkers (from as far apart – and as close – as Max Weber and Georg Lukacs [cf. Bell 1981, 1991]). That Bell is a first-generation American, born in the Lower East Side of New York City to Polish immigrants Benjamin and Anna Bolotsky who were fleeing anti-Semitism and poverty, is not inconsequential to his mode and substance of thinking.

Bell originated the concept as early as the 1960s, but it was launched definitively with the publication of his book, *The Coming of Post-Industrial Society* in 1973. This seems to me to be a remarkable text and not only because of the extraordinary intellectual influence it has had. It is noteworthy also because it stood apart from the then penchant in Sociology for what one might term *high theory*. By this I mean the enthusiasm in Sociology, during the late 1960s and 1970s, for theory that merged with (perhaps more accurately aped) Philosophy, stuck to an intensely abstract level of analysis, and determinedly resisted coming to terms with empirical matters. The hold of Talcott Parsons's Structural Functionalism was weakening by this time, but the heavyweight alternative in Sociology came in the shape of the equally reified theorizations of Althusserian Marxism, while for the less ideologically enthusiastic, aspects of Wittgenstein – leavened by Peter Winch and conjoined with Garfinkel's ethnomethodology and some phenomenology – had considerable appeal. Across Sociology there was a widespread contempt for mere 'empiricism', something dismissed as a naive and outdated 'positivism'.

Against this, Bell's project stood apart in that, while theoretically adept and ambitious, it insisted that theory should be developed in close accord with evidence. This was not a call for abandonment of theory, defined as a search for abstract and codified generalization. Indeed, it held to the ambition to produce what later came to be called, disparagingly, 'grand narratives' – i.e. attempts to identify the most consequential features of social life and to trace their trajectory. But it was an insistence that generalizations should be informed by evidence rather than philosophical speculation (Mouzelis 1995) and it had a good deal in common with Robert Merton's (1968) advocacy of 'theories of the middle range'. This approach to theory, one that stressed the indivisible connections of theory and real-world observation, was unfashionable when Bell developed his notion of Post-Industrial Society, but he was not alone. The approach was one pursued by sociologists as diverse as Ralph Dahrendorf, Alain Touraine, A. H. Halsey, C. Wright Mills, and Ralph Miliband. It is, in my view, an admirable tradition, one aiming to produce generalized statements of significance regarding the character of societies while committed to ensuring that theories are substantively grounded and subject to reconceptualization in light of empirical evidence.

The main elements of Post-Industrial Society have been well rehearsed: Daniel Bell presented it in terms of what has been called a 'march through the employment sectors' (Kumar 1995, p. 26). That is, he argued that over time one could see a transfer from a time when most people gained their livelihoods in agriculture (Pre-Industrial Society), later moving into manufacturing (Industrial Society), and most recently transferring into service employment (Post-Industrial Society). The vast majority of people in advanced societies such as North America, Japan and Europe are employed in service jobs such as teaching, counselling, finance and management, something which, *prima facie*, endorses Bell's account of change. The emergence of a 'service economy' means also that we have entered an Information Society since the major feature of service work is information. In the past work was a matter of engaging with the elements and/or working with machinery of one sort or another, but today it is a matter of relating to other people in terms of information. As Bell (1973) says, 'what counts (now) is not raw muscle power, or energy, but information' (p. 127). For this reason, says Bell, a Post-Industrial Society is also an Information Society.

On the matter of causation Bell is clear: the driving force of change is increased productivity, or what he terms, consciously echoing Max Weber and Henri St Simon, 'more for less'. So long as subsistence agriculture is the norm, then everyone must work the land to eke a bare living. However, once a society manages to feed itself without everyone being so engaged (this process began with the Agricultural Revolution in the eighteenth century), then surplus labour can be transferred to industrial occupations while being assured of having sufficient to eat. Through time, continuous increases in agricultural productivity have meant there are now tiny proportions of workers employed in farming, yet we have benefited from enormously increased output from the land, so much so that nowadays almost all people in the North have access to plentiful, varied and cheap food. Such productivity increases mean today that we have more food than ever, yet only 2–3 per cent of the workforce in the UK and USA are involved with farming. Much the same process of increased productivity and transfer out of excess workers goes on in industry, starting from the early days of industrialism when there was intensive labour in workshops, to the modern highly automated assembly line. Bell argues that the huge productivity increases in industry resulted in surplus wealth being generated, a consequence of which was the creation of ideas to spend this. These found expression in calls for services (leisure activities, smaller classrooms, extension of education, medical facilities, . . .) that create jobs for people no longer required by industry (though productivity from that quarter continues to increase). The wonderful thing is that, so long as productivity keeps on growing, thereby generating additional wealth even while requiring fewer workers in farming or industry, service jobs will always be created to use this wealth since service needs are insatiable and service occupations are especially difficult to automate (for instance, witness the expansion of counsellors, therapists and 'personal trainers' over the last decade or so). Indeed, attests Bell (and this several years before the ecological movement took hold of imaginations) a Post-Industrial Society may become so wealthy as to turn its back on an inflexible principle of 'more for less', for instance refusing a new factory location in favour of environmental protection.

There can be no doubt that the driver of this route towards the Information Society is technology and technique, since this is what enables the increased productivity on which services depend. It is also an evolutionary conception, being presented as desirable and more or less smoothly achieved, the development model being North America. Francis Fukuyama published his controversial essay in 1989 and the book-length *The End of History and the Last Man* (1992) shortly afterwards. The message here – capitalism has triumphed over communism – appears on the surface to be very different from that of Daniel Bell. Yet at root Fukuyama presents much the same thesis: it is productivity that changes the world, capitalism has won out because it out-produced communism, and thus the direction of history is firmly set. While Bell adopted the language of rationalization, Fukuyama prefers the terms of the market economy, yet in all essentials his analysis follows the same logic and trajectory as does Bell's.

On any measure Bell's account of Post-Industrial Society was an impressive achievement. Well before there was public interest in informational developments beyond the recondite realms of Library Science, he was presenting a serious and sustained analysis and explanation of the Information Society. It scarcely matters that, professionally, *The Coming of Post-Industrial Society* was savaged, theoretically and empirically (e.g. Gershuny 1978; Kumar 1978; Gershuny & Miles 1983). Bell had set the agenda to which critics had to respond. Moreover, in the late 1970s and early 1980s, events were happening outside academe that both made Bell seem especially perspicacious and impelled a response from Sociology.

The microelectronics revolution

Late in 1978, the then UK Prime Minister James Callaghan announced that the British people must 'wake up' to the microelectronics revolution.

Accompanying this was a spate of television documentaries and paperback books with titles such as 'The Chips are Down', 'Silicon Civilization' and 'The Mighty Micro'. The message was that an enormously significant technological breakthrough had been made (in a place gnomically evoked as 'Silicon Valley') and it was set to sweep away all in its path. In the metaphor of the popular futurist, Alvin Toffler (1980), this was comparable to a tidal wave that engulfs everything before it. Technology, we were told, was set to have impacts on society on a scale unknown since the Industrial Revolution (and there was indeed interminable talk of this being a 'second industrial revolution'). The main concern – significantly so in view of more recent commentary – was with work and employment. Not surprisingly perhaps there was a rush of major impact predictions, and many of these were dire. Anticipated increases in productivity created apprehension for many. For instance, Clive Jenkins and Barrie Sherman (1979) predicted a 'collapse of work' before the 1990s (a theme refrained by Jeremy Rifkin [1995]). Even the optimists here foresaw a massive reduction in jobs, only then to remain cheerful by suggesting this might translate into a 'leisure society' provided that enlightened government increased wages, shortened working hours and increased holiday entitlements (Gorz 1982).

When the analyses were not doleful or apocalyptic (and for obvious reasons government and industry tended to embrace the 'microelectronics revolution'), there was consensus that old-style jobs would go but an assurance that, in place of positions in coal-mining, steel works and manufacture, services would expand to take up the slack. Margaret Thatcher (1983), then politically pre-eminent in the UK, insisted that there would be 'many, many jobs . . . in the service industries'. Such interpretations were straightforwardly with Daniel Bell's 'march through the sectors', even where his writing had not been consulted (Webster & Robins 1986).

My main point here is chiefly directed at commentary on what might be termed the societal, or macro, level. Whatever its particular takes, this operated within a technological determinist framework. The underlying premise was that technology caused social change, that microelectronics was an especially powerful technology and thus would have prodigious consequences (one popular metaphor was to describe microelectronics as a 'heartland' technology [Barron & Curnow 1979]), and that this technology, while itself asocial, more or less directly impacted on society. In this frame, some imagined the 'collapse of work' while others were convinced that services would come to the rescue.

Where did sociological research fit into this picture? Surprisingly little in the UK ventured onto the macro terrain. The major support agency, the Economic and Social Research Council (ESRC), made funds available for research on the 'microelectronics revolution'. It even established a programme called PICT (Programme in Information and Communications Technologies) that ran from 1985 for a decade. Perhaps it was the ESRC's insistence that projects should offer policy guidance that contributed to increased competition by the nation that led to the sociological studies turning away from the big picture. Whatever the reason, what we got were focused and grounded projects concerned with matters such as innovations in banking, medical uses of technologies, regulatory regimes, women's employment in offices and the introduction of technologies on the shop floor (Dutton 1996).

More interestingly, there was a marked reluctance amongst sociologists to accept the starting premise of the ESRC – that the microelectronics revolution was set to change the world, and that social science must study and advise upon adaptation to this innovation – which found expression in resistance to the technological determinist presumption of the funders (and so many others). Indeed, it became orthodoxy for sociologists, paid to study technology's impacts, to reject the notion that technology caused social change (Dutton 1999). This sat with highly context-specific studies which demonstrated that technologies always incorporated values, that innovation was a highly negotiated affair, and that the presupposition of technology's privileged role in bringing about social change was misplaced. Steve Woolgar (1996), one of the major and most insightful players in this game, noted the irony of there being a fierce rejection of technological determinism by researchers whose funding arrangements meant that we had 'technological determinism in practice' (p. 89). Nonetheless, while there were differences in approach between the 'social shapers' and the 'social constructivists', over this period social studies of technology boomed and, alongside, there was a consensus as regards technology being indivisible from the social. Bruno Latour's (1993, 1996) 'actor-network' theory grew in popularity until it became the dominant theoretical perspective amongst researchers.[1]

It is my view that this period saw, from the research community in Britain, the production of interesting, textured and localized studies. These demonstrated, time and again, that the technological determinism which underscored government debate and most other discussion of the 'microelectronics revolution' was intellectually weak. Nonetheless, what seems evident to me is that the research community at this time was unable to come up with any 'big' thinking as regards the character of change at the time. In sum, there was nothing to begin to match the scale and scope of Daniel Bell's theory of Post-Industrial Society. Bell was certainly criticized by fine scholars (Kumar 1978), but Sociology was incapable of matching him with a positive and general analysis of contemporary social change.

The Network Society

This situation continued until the 1990s. Daniel Bell's conception of a Post-Industrial Society was routinely criticized in the professional literature (Webster 1995, ch.3) for numerous inadequacies, but none offered an alternative. Meanwhile the research community most closely involved with researching informational matters by and large concerned itself with unambitious studies of particular localities while subscribing to social constructivism. Outside academe, even beyond the border of Sociology, others appeared content to embrace Bell's conceptualization as the most appropriate for the current epoch.

Things changed with the publication of the remarkable trilogy of Manuel Castells (born February 1942), *The Information Age*, between 1996 and 1998. What Castells offered was worthy of succeeding and superseding Daniel Bell. *The Information Age* was distinctively ambitious in its endeavour to account for the major patterns of contemporary civilization, but it was also the work of a self-described and determinedly 'empirical sociologist' who wore his theoretical clothes lightly (Castells [2000] advocates 'disposable theory', theory being an essential tool, but something to be discarded when it becomes incapable of illuminating the substantive world). Castells' achievement has received widespread praise as well as close criticism (Webster and Dimitriou 2004). In my view it is right that he is perceived to be standing in the tradition of Karl Marx and Max Weber, though I welcome *The Information Age* too as a worthy successor to Daniel Bell's attempt to produce ambitious theoretical insights – abstract generalizations – based on detailed empirical evidence that capture the most consequential characteristics of out times. In this endeavour to paint the big picture of the world today, capturing its primary colours and its detail, it is noteworthy that Castells runs counter to the postmodern enthusiasm for specification, particularity and difference that expresses scepticism towards 'grand narratives'.

Castells' contribution coincided with the arrival of what I would call the second wave of technological enthusiasm – by which I mean to identify a torrent of comment that accompanied the development of information and communications technologies, the Internet especially, in the 1990s (Negroponte 1995). This evoked memories of the first wave that had been manifested in the 'mighty micro' language of the late 1970s and early 1980s. I shall return to this, but for now would emphasize ways in which Castells' work helped us reconceive the current era. His metaphor of the 'network society' and his detailing of 'flows of information' have helped us think more clearly of the *mobilities* of peoples, products and information in a globalizing world and it has been developed in the writings notably of John Urry (2000, 2003) and Scott Lash (2002). It is consonant with current interest in matters such as 'electronic communities', 'e-democracy', 'diasporas', 'transnationalism', 'urban cultures', and the emergence of 'symbolic politics'.

Castells' work also sits comfortably with a good deal of popular comment on information and communications technologies. His stress on the movement of information, such that nowadays we are reaching a situation of real-time action on a planetary scale, is well in line with technology-led images of an 'information superhighway', with excited talk about 'connectivity', and with all things digital (e.g. Mulgan 1997). But it is worth noting that Castells distances himself from technological determinism in important ways. For a start, he refuses Bell's conception of Post-Industrialism as a novel society built on technological excess, referring instead to 'informational capitalism', thereby emphasizing the continuities of the present with the past. More interestingly, though Castells has a somewhat eclectic notion of information (and it is one that frequently does prioritize technology), in his trilogy he helps shift attention away from the hardware to the softer side (i.e. from technologies towards human capital). This is especially so in his conception of 'informational labour' being the key category for the new age. This is the group in the 'information age' that manages, initiates and shapes affairs, by being well-educated, having initiative, welcoming the frenetic pace of change which typifies the current epoch, and having, perhaps above all, the capacity to 'self-programme' itself. Informational Labour jobs 'embody knowledge and information' (Castells 1997, ch. 6), and inevitably this group leads in research and development, in entrepreneurial activity, in finance, in media, even in alternative politics: everywhere it is on top, with its ease in initiating campaigns, in developing strategy, in connecting with other actors across the globe. It highlights ways in which work and living appear to be shifting towards flatter organizations, portfolio careers and living with continuous uncertainty. More than this, Informational Labour identifies what Lash and Urry (1994) termed 'reflexive accumulation', something that may be understood as information-intensive labour where the process and product are constantly scrutinized to be changed and revalued. This echoes Zuboff's (1988) concern for the feedback loops established in modern production, the design intensity of so many products (the whole fashion industry, the branding of goods, companies and even people), the centrality of modern marketing, and the increased importance of cognitive employment (finance, business, consultancy etc.) as well as of creative work (few people seem to buy a kettle now, they want it to enhance their designer kitchen).

There are few measures of this transformation, though Castells does estimate that some 30 per cent of positions in OECD nations are concerned with informational labour. But it does gel with perceptions that, in the present era, imaginative and innovative people who are at ease with change are at a premium, and that those who are not – what Castells terms 'routine labour' – are fatally disadvantaged and continuously threatened since their assumptions of and aspirations for stability ('I want a steady job; I trained for this as a young man and expect to do it for the rest of my life') are mistaken since 'informational labour' can and will redesign pretty well any form of repetitive work, either by automation or by reorganizing affairs on a world scale.

It bears repeating that this is not a technology-dominated approach to the Information Age. The ICTs (Information and Communications Technologies) are part and parcel of 'informational labour's' day-to-day functioning, but the key qualities are education, imagination, and capability to innovate (cf. Reich 1991). In terms of research agendas, Castells' work helps shift attention away from technology impact studies towards new forms of stratification, changes in education systems (Robins & Webster 2002), new forms of political engagement (e.g. the organization and mobilization of campaigners such as anti-globalizers, environmentalists and human rights activists), changes in political parties and the conduct of politics (Bimber 2003), and contemporary forms of conflict such as information war (Webster 2003).

Culture and Cultural Studies

I have thus far argued that Daniel Bell's conception of the Information Society was singular both in its intellectual sophistication and in its ambition to paint the big picture in sociological thinking during the 1970s. The first wave of technological enthusiasm did much to highlight the pre-science of his work. In the UK the research on new technology was of much less ambition than that presented by Bell, being focused in approach, while routinely rejecting technological determinism. In the 1990s Manuel Castells' notion of a 'network society' recalled the scale and scope of Daniel Bell. Castells' offering coincided with the second wave of technological enthusiasm that was associated with ICTs and the Internet. Beside, and often beneath, these developments were two connected phenomena of major importance to Sociology itself and to analysis of how we live today. I refer to the exponential growth of culture and to the related spread of Cultural Studies to social analysis. Culture is of course a famously difficult term, but here I refer to the realm of the *symbolic*, the places where we discuss and decide about what and who we are, how we feel about ourselves and others, how we display ourselves to one another. . . .

I do not think anyone would deny that there has been an enormous expansion of the symbolic over recent decades, something which involves technologies but which reaches far beyond. Think for instance of the expansion and digitalization of media such as satellite, television, radio, telecommunications, DVD, and latterly the Internet, such that nowadays symbols are transmitted, sent and received pretty well anywhere, anytime and by anyone. One must add to this the huge growth of fashion and style (of the body, hair, face, clothing, . . .), the spread of youth cultures, of different lifestyles, of advertising, of varied cultures that have accompanied migration, travel and tourism as well as the globalization process, and the plethora of brands which means that images of the Nike swoosh, David Beckham and Naomi Campbell are recognized round the globe. Much might be written on this subject, but here I simply announce the enormous growth of the cultural environment of people over the past few decades. This is evident in just about anything from the Walkman to the dress of multi-ethnic communities, from styling of the body to architectural design, from cityscapes to the variety of cuisine in any English town, from the composition of Premier League soccer to the decoration of living rooms. It is an inescapable feature of living in the twenty-first century – it is now inconceivable that one might live, as many once did, solely within one's own culture, try as one might. Contemporary media, urban experiences and everyday matters of style demand that one immerses oneself, to a greater or lesser degree, in the diverse and hybrid cultural ambiances that surround us today. Unsurprisingly, identity – and identity politics – is of major concern in this milieu.

Cultural Studies has developed in response to these trends. Faced by so much more culture, and so much more varied cultures, there has been a pressing need for academe to engage. However, a reasonable question is: why did Sociology not develop to incorporate these matters from an early date? I would suggest several reasons (cf. Webster 2001). One is that Sociology seemed rather 'slow' when faced by the energy, dynamism and often-ephemeral character of cultural growth. Perhaps academic respectability, and professional institutionalization, played a part here. After all, in the 1960s Sociology was to the fore in accounting for things such as 'moral panics' and the 'new criminology'. But the discipline had experienced hard times in the 1980s when government disparaged and starved it of funds, leaving Sociologists to hang on to whatever posts they had in universities. There were scarcely any new appointments in Sociology over that decade, and many talented postgraduates had to find employment in expanding areas such as Business Studies, Communications and – ironically – Cultural Studies that were open to new ideas and were vitalizing areas (Webster 2004). Such circumstances perhaps induced conservatism in the discipline, an urge to seek respectability that found expression in doing 'solid' work and insisting that the discipline adopted rigorous 'scientific' methods.

A second reason lies in the particular concern of British Sociology with the connected areas of *work/occupation* and *production* that were key elements of the prioritization of *class analysis*. Class analysis predominated in British Sociology in the postwar years right through to the late 1980s. This extended across the major paradigmatic divide – Marxism versus Weberianism – so much that, looking back, we may see that a good many of those disputes ('was class a matter of relations of production, or was it more to do with authority, or was it expressive of market situation?') were largely internecine. The shared supposition was that class (and this was taken to be represented by the male head of household) was the primary source of a whole host of other phenomena. Hence from someone's class (and most analysts in British Sociology worked on the assumption that class was a matter of occupational position, and that it was divisible into two categories, working and middle class) could be 'read off' a host of other factors – likelihood of educational success or failure, leisure habits, voting preferences, domestic relationships, choice of marriage partners and so on. Increasingly, this position came to be regarded as adopting a determinist approach to sociological subjects, even an essentialist account of the social world ('at root class is what really matters'). Those who did not share its worldview became increasingly unhappy with Sociology. What attention was it paying, and what might it offer, say, to understanding of 'race' and ethnicity, gender relationships, media analysis (outside of news), shopping, sport, tourism or the manifest expansion of consumption that accompanied sustained increases in living standards (Obelkevitch 1994)?

In brief, culture had emerged, and continued to expand at breakneck speed, as a huge feature of contemporary life, but Sociology, perhaps excessively committed to class analysis, appeared to ignore it and, where the discipline did approach, tended to reduce culture to an expression of class circumstances that were themselves increasingly being subverted by the decline of manufacturing occupations, the growth of services, the participation of women in the labour force, and evidence that work was declining in significance as regards the experiences and identities of many people. In this light it was not altogether surprising that Ray Pahl (1989), one of the most eminent British sociologists in postwar Britain, exasperatedly declared that 'class as a concept is ceasing to do any useful work for sociology' (p. 709) and that perhaps market researchers, with their categories such as DINKIES (dual income, no kids), GUPPIES (Greenpeace Yuppies), and WOOFs (well off older folk), were more insightful than the class concept beloved of the discipline.

Cultural Studies thrived on this expansion of culture and the inadequacies of Sociology. For instance, it was Cultural Studies that led the way in studying soap operas, in taking seriously fashion and clothing, in paying attention to race and the media, and in exploring hydrities. More than that, Cultural Studies characteristically paid attention not to the determinants of class to behaviour but to the active choices of actors, to the capacities of people, young and old, of varied ethnicities, to find pleasure and creativity in surprising areas. . . . In short, Cultural Studies highlighted the resistance of people to impositions of constricting circumstances.

Virtuality

This took place alongside the spread of what I termed earlier the second wave of technological enthusiasm, something associated especially with the coming of the Internet, but also in an especially rapid development of digital media, mobile telephony, and widespread awareness of the potential of genetics to transform the most intimate areas of life. It is clear that the spread of new media and ICTs was integral to the explosive growth of cultures. Cultural Studies did not, like its Sociologist counterparts, seek to assess the impacts of these new technologies. Such an approach was antipathetic to Cultural Studies' concern to appreciate the creativity of people. Neither was Cultural Studies much drawn to social constructivism: such a proposition – that technologies were constitutive of human values – was so axiomatic to Cultural Studies that it scarcely seemed worthwhile labouring the point or applying it to particular situations. When it comes to issues such as cyborgs (cybernetic organisms), what is the point of arguing that humans and technology are melded? What is more exciting is what and how people are constituted and how they might reconstitute themselves in an era of spare-part surgery, cosmetic surgery, exercise regimes, body design and extensive use of drugs such as Viagra and Prozac.

Cultural Studies embraced this new technological ambiance as the milieu of *virtuality*, one in which emphasis is on the mediation of relations, their malleability, their artifice, and the constant possibilities of arrangements and imminent rearrangements. Not surprisingly, Cultural Studies paid a lot of attention to media in this situation, looking at media as a field of creativity and artifice, but foregrounding ways in which actors also could negotiate and find meaning in this rich symbolic seam. Elsewhere, we find with Cultural Studies strong resistance to notions of authenticity, indeed to any essentialist claims. Thereby it would examine realms of culture as necessarily manufactured, hence inauthentic, phenomena. For instance, tourism would be paid serious attention, the tourist experience being regarded not as the search for the 'true' history or peoples of a region, but rather as an artifice that all might appreciate, but still enjoy. Thus we have the 'true' Grecian taverna with its ice-cold beer, the carefully staged traditional dancing (complete with breaking of plates, costed and pre-purchased), the authentic Greek music played through the CD system and composed not a decade ago. . . . Everyone knows this is ersatz culture, but still it is enjoyable for the postmodern tourist (Urry 2002). What is characteristic of this, the 'cultural turn' that British social thinking has encountered in this last decade or so, is that it is acknowledged that everything is 'virtual' in the sense that it is socially manufactured, and this takes material forms, though no necessary constraint follows from this. Thus the tourist experience will vary enormously depending on the 'knowingness' of the tourist. Again, urban reinvention is a material process – it involves new streets, new architecture and new ambiances – which are all about diverse and coexisting cultural expressions (cuisine, shops, entertainment, . . .). But still people have enormous capacity to make sense of, and indeed shape, these in imaginative and unexpected ways.

Mark Slouka (1995) rebels against the excessive voluntarism of Cultural Studies, a subject that, in often converging postmodern sensibilities with new technology enthusiasm, represents 'a mating of monsters'. I share unease at Cultural Studies' willingness to ignore the real limits imposed on so many people today (Webster 2000). What might 'virtuality' offer the 1.3 billion people of the world existing on less than a dollar a day? Or the one in six who are illiterate? (United Nations 2002). And yet I cannot but recognize Cultural Studies' capacity to open up social science to new areas of research that are demonstrably important in today's world. Without it, I fear that Sociology would have continued to sideline interest in consumption, in media, in identity issues, in sexualities. . . . To be sure, Sociology has not been uninfluenced by Cultural Studies itself. The journal *Theory, Culture and Society* has been an important bridge linking Cultural Studies work and Sociology. In England the leading Cultural Studies figure, Stuart Hall (born 1933), came to occupy a chair in Sociology at the Open University and served two years as the British Sociological Association's President in the 1990s, though his academic background is English Literature and he possesses no training in Sociology. Moreover, he has neither received awards from the ESRC nor does he publish his work in Sociology journals. There have been a few departments of Sociology, notably Lancaster, which have welcomed the 'cultural turn' and have seriously studied issues such as 'heritage' invention and environmental design in ways decidedly influenced by Cultural Studies. These are signs that Sociology is more willing to take on the insights of Cultural Studies, though it should be said that much suspicion and even antipathy remains, with Cultural Studies' undoubted weaknesses in method (inadequate research design, proneness to solipsism . . .) readily allowing wholesale rejection of the field.

Conclusion

I began this article with a tribute to Daniel Bell, to his conception of Post-Industrial Society, his attempt to present a 'grand narrative' that was sensitive to both theory and empirical observation. In the United Kingdom Sociology was pretty hostile to Bell, but when it came to respond to the 'microelectronics revolution' researchers could come up with nothing to match his work. To be sure, they rejected technological determinism *tout court*, and embraced social constructivism wholeheartedly (the 'conservatives' stuck with 'social shaping' approaches to technology), but none could present a persuasive alternative account of 'how we are now'. On the contrary, sociological research that was undertaken in this arena was, by and large, determinedly local, small-scale and particular.

In the 1990s Manuel Castells revitalized the mode of analysis first offered by Daniel Bell. *The Information Age*, with its metaphors of 'networks' and 'flows', is a major achievement. Its stress on the category 'informational labour' does much to shift away from technological determinism without abandoning the big picture. The trilogy has already had an important influence on researchers, for instance in analysis of 'electronic communities' and 'information warfare'. Of course, the critical mice have been quick to gnaw at various aspects of *The Information Age*, but few have been able to inflict serious damage.

It should be emphasized that macro analysis per se is not superior (and the term 'macro' itself misses the intimate connectedness with the substantive that I would want to insist upon). One needs look no further than the ridiculously assured statements that came, and continue to come, from futurists to recognize that 'big picture' accounts are not inherently better. It is the combination of rich empirical analysis and its complex relations with wider contexts and conceptualizations (themselves subject to rigorous empirical scrutiny) that does seem to me superior to studies which remain, as it were, with their intellectual blinkers fixing them on the merely particular. Such studies can be fascinating, and they may demonstrate the intricacy of human/technology relations, but they do little more than this, confirming only the truistic 'life is complicated, contingent and constantly created'.

But Sociology has been somewhat outpaced by Cultural Studies when it comes to examination of the culture and cultural changes that have been such a key feature of our time. Cultural Studies has seized on *virtuality* to address some of the most arresting issues of the contemporary epoch – sexualities, the body, pervasive media experiences, identities. . . . In this it has been ahead of Sociology. Though some of the discipline has welcomed the 'cultural turn' there has also been fierce resistance from other parts (cf. Goldthorpe 2000). Significantly, Steve Woolgar's (2002) edited collection, *Virtual Society?*, evidenced sympathy and sensitivity towards Cultural Studies concerns, highlighting some of the discipline's openness in recent years.

Nonetheless, it should not be entirely surprising to come across agreement between social constructivist analyses of technology and Cultural Studies, since both stress the malleability of relationships and the importance of particularities. Moreover, there are commonalities of epistemology and method that further encourage agreement. In spite of this convergence, still I remain disappointed with the common failure of much sociological research on ICTs and Cultural Studies to address wider questions of change. One does understand wariness of facile generalization, still more of forms of functionalism that have bedevilled a good deal of macro-analysis in the past, especially that which limits itself to armchair theorizing and/or abstracts technology from the substantive realm while asserting that this technology is the *primum mobile* of change. So one is not calling here for a social analysis capable of grandly explaining everything. Rather the plea is for accounts that, empirically testable and conceptually sensitive, strive to identify the most consequential characteristics of how we live. This is necessarily a contested affair, involving debate between arguments and evidence, but it is not a hopelessly subjective task. It also requires some notion of the interconnectedness of phenomena, not to subsume them into a presupposed whole but that we may struggle towards studies that make the most consequential features of the world we inhabit evident and comprehensible (cf. Preston 2001; Schuler & Day 2004). No amount of localized ethnographies, however rewarding in themselves, can replace the need for social science to aspire and attempt to reach the levels of Daniel Bell and Manuel Castells.

Acknowledgement

A first draft of this paper was presented as a plenary address at the Hungarian Sociological Society Annual Conference, 27–28 November 2003, Budapest and an earlier version appeared in *Concentric: Literary and Cultural Studies* 31(1) 2005.

Notes

1 An intriguing division amongst scholars who rejected technological determinism at this time was discernible. On the one side were critics, often outside higher education, who aligned typically with Marxian traditions to stress ways in which technological innovation advantaged sectional interests by presenting change as a merely technical (hence untouched by social values) matter, while incorporating their own values into new technologies that disadvantaged workers especially. David Noble (1977, 1984), David Dickson (1974, 1984), Steven Rose, and Robert Young and Les Levidow (with the journal they pioneered, *Science as Culture*), were key players in this school that situated technology in the wider milieu of capitalist endeavour. On the other side were the social constructivists, overwhelmingly employed in universities, who, while sharing the premise that technology (and science) is inherently social, were committed to localized and textured studies of innovation such as laboratory relationships and the nuances of producing software. These were influenced by ethnomethodology and associated forms of micro and interpretivist philosophy. Prominent amongst them were Steve Woolgar (1988), John Law (1991), and Wiebe Bijker (Bijker *et al.*, 1989), while pre-eminent was Bruno Latour.
2 It seems that the two sides, while agreeing on the limits of orthodox approaches to technology, scarcely spoke to one another; they rarely cited writings from respective schools. Social constructivists focused on producing ethnographic micro studies and became the dominant force in ESRC-funded research in the UK. Perhaps they found the 'politicos' too crude and reductionist for their tastes, likely to manifest what Woolgar (2002) calls 'clumping tendencies' (p. 6) that did a disservice to the complexities of change. With a few noteworthy exceptions (cf. MacKenzie 1998), researchers in the UK ignored the likes of Noble and Young and favoured social constructivism, eclipsing their followers when it came to research funding.

References

Barron, I. & Curnow, R. (1979) *The Future with Microelectronics: Forecasting the Effects of Information Technology*, Pinter, London.
Bell, D. (1973 [1976]) *The Coming of Post-Industrial Society: A Venture in Social Forecasting*, Penguin, Peregrine Books, Harmondsworth.
Bell, D. (1981) 'First love and early sorrows', *Partisan Review*, vol. 48, no. 4, pp. 532–551.

HISTORY AND PERSPECTIVES

Bell, D. (1991) 'After the age of sinfulness', *Times Literary Supplement*, 26 July, pp. 5–8.

Bijker, W., Hughes, T. & Pinch, T. (eds) (1989) *The Social Construction of Technological Systems*, MIT Press, Cambridge, MA.

Bimber, B. (2003) *Information and American Democracy*, Cambridge University Press, New York.

Castells, M. (1996–98) *The Information Age: Economy, Society, and Culture*, Blackwell, Oxford [1998]. Volume I: *The Rise of the Network Society* (1996). Volume II: *The Power of Identity* (1997). Volume III: *End of Millennium* (1998). Revised edition for volumes I and III (2000).

Castells, M. (2000) 'Materials for an exploratory theory of the network society', *British Journal of Sociology*, vol. 51, no. 1, pp. 5–24.

Dickson, D. (1974) *Alternative Technology and the Politics of Technical Change*, Fontana, London.

Dickson, D. (1984) *The New Politics of Science*, Pantheon, New York.

Dutton, W. (ed.) (1996) *Information and Communications Technologies: Visions and Realities*, Oxford University Press, Oxford.

Dutton, W. (ed.) (1999) *Society on the Line: Information Politics in the Information Age*, Oxford University Press, Oxford.

Fukuyama, F. (1989) 'The end of history?', *The National Interest*, vol. 16, Summer, pp. 3–18.

Fukuyama, F. (1992) *The End of History and the Last Man*, Hamish Hamilton, London.

Gershuny, J. I. (1978) *After Industrial Society? The Emerging Self-Service Society*, Macmillan, London.

Gershuny, J. I. & Miles, I. (1983) *The New Service Economy: The Transformation of Employment in Industrial Societies*, Pinter, London.

Goldthorpe, J. H. (2000) *On Sociology: Numbers, Narratives, and the Integration of Research and Theory*, Oxford University Press, Oxford.

Gorz, A. (1982) *Farewell to the Working Class: An Essay on Post-Industrial Socialism*, Pluto Press, London.

Jenkins, C. & Sherman, B. (1979) *The Collapse of Work*, Eyre Methuen, London.

Kumar, K. (1978) *Prophecy and Progress: The Sociology of Industrial and Post-Industrial Society*, Allen Lane, London.

Kumar, K. (1995 [2005]) *From Post-Industrial to Post-Modern Society: New Theories of the Contemporary World*, 2nd edn, Blackwell, Oxford.

Lash, S. (2002) *Critique of Information*, Sage, London.

Lash, S. & Urry, J. (1994) *Economies of Signs and Space*, Sage, London.

Latour, B. (1993) *We Have Never Been Modern*, Harvard University Press, Cambridge, MA.

Latour, B. (1996) *Aramis, or the Love of Technology*, Harvard University Press, Cambridge, MA.

Law, J. (ed.) (1991) *A Sociology of Monsters: Essays on Power, Technology and Domination*, Routledge, London.

MacKenzie, D. (1998) *Knowing Machines: Essays on Technical Change*, MIT Press, Cambridge, MA.

Merton, R. K. (1968) 'On sociological theories of the middle range', in *Social Theory and Social Structure*, Free Press, New York, pp. 39–72

Mouzelis, N. (1995) *Sociology Theory, What Went Wrong? Diagnosis and Remedies*, Routledge, London.

Mulgan, G. (1997) *Connexity: Responsibility, Freedom, Business and Power in the New Century*, Chatto & Windus, London.

Negroponte, N. (1995) *Being Digital*, Hodder & Stoughton, London.

Noble, D. (1977) *America by Design: Science, Technology and the Rise of Corporate Capitalism*, Knopf, New York.

Noble, D. (1984) *Forces of Production: A Social History of Industrial Automation*, Knopf, New York.

Obelkevitch, J. (1994) 'Consumption', in *Understanding Post-War British Society*, eds J. Obelkevitch & P. Catterall, Routledge, London, pp. 141–154.

Pahl, R. (1989) 'Is the Emperor naked? Some questions on the adequacy of sociological theory in urban and regional research', *International Journal of Urban and Regional Research*, vol. 13, no. 4, pp. 709–720.

Preston, P. (2001) *Reshaping Communications: Technology, Information and Social Change*, Sage, London.

Reich, R. (1991) *The Work of Nations: Preparing Ourselves for Twenty-First Century Capitalism*, Vintage, New York.

Rifkin, J. (1995) *The End of Work: The Decline of the Global Labor Force and the Dawn of the Post-Market Era*, Putnam, New York.

Robins, K. & Webster, F. (eds) (2002) *The Virtual University? Knowledge, Markets and Management*, Oxford University Press, Oxford.

Ross, G. (1974) 'The second coming of Daniel Bell', in *Socialist Register, 1974*, eds R. Miliband & J. Saville, Merlin, London, pp. 331–148.

Schuler, D. & Day, P. (eds) (2004) *Shaping the Network Society: the New Role of Civil Society in Cyberspace*, MIT Press, Cambridge, MA.

Slouka, M. (1995) *War of the Worlds: Cyberspace and the High-Tech Assault on Reality*, Abacus, London.

Steinfels, P. (1979) 'Daniel Bell, theoretician and moralist', in *The Neoconservatives*, Simon & Schuster, New York. pp. 161–187.

Thatcher, M. (1983) 'Speech at Conservative Party conference', Blackpool, 14 October, reported in *The Times*, 15 October, p. 2.

Toffler, A. (1980) *The Third Wave*, Collins, London.

United Nations (2002) *Human Development Report*, UN, New York.

Urry, J. (2000) *Sociology Beyond Societies: Mobilities for the Twenty-first Century*, Routledge, London.

Urry, J. (2002) *The Tourist Gaze*, 2nd edn, Sage, London.

Urry, J. (2003) *Global Complexity*, Polity, Cambridge.

Webster, F. (1995) *Theories of the Information Society*, Routledge, London.

Webster, F. (2000) 'Virtual culture: knowledge, identity and choice', in *Knowledge, Space, Economy*, eds J. R. Bryson, P. W. Daniels, N. Henry & J. Pollard, Routledge, London, pp. 226–241.

Webster, F. (2001) 'Sociology, Cultural Studies, and disciplinary boundaries', in *A Companion to Cultural Studies*, ed. Toby Miller, Blackwell, New York, pp. 79–100.

Webster, F. (2002) *Theories of the Information Society*, 2nd edn, Routledge, London.

Webster, F. (2003) 'Information warfare, surveillance and human rights', in *The Intensification of Surveillance: Crime, Terrorism and Warfare in the Information Age*, eds K. Ball & F. Webster, Pluto, London, pp. 90–111.

HISTORY AND PERSPECTIVES

Webster, F. (2004) 'Cultural Studies and Sociology at, and after, the closure of the Birmingham School', *Cultural Studies*, vol. 18, no. 6, pp. 847–862.

Webster, F. & Dimitriou, B. (eds) (2004) *Manuel Castells: Masters of Modern Social Thought*, 3 vols, Sage, London.

Webster, F. & Robins, K. (1986) *Information Technology: A Luddite Analysis*, Ablex, Norwood, NJ.

Woolgar, S. (1988) *Science: The Very Idea*, Ellis Horwood, Chichester.

Woolgar, S. (1996) 'Technologies as cultural artefacts', in *Information and Communications Technologies: Visions and Realities*, ed. W. Dutton, Oxford University Press, Oxford, pp. 87–102

Woolgar, S. (ed.) (2002) *Virtual Society? Technology, Cyberbole, Reality*, Oxford University Press, Oxford.

Zuboff, S. (1988) *In the Age of the Smart Machine: The Future of Work and Power*, Heinemann, Oxford.

22

PUTTING THE CRITIQUE BACK INTO A *CRITIQUE OF INFORMATION*

Refusing to follow the order

Paul A. Taylor

Source: *Information, Communication & Society* 9(5) (2006): 553–71.

This paper argues that Scott Lash's *Critique of Information* is one of the most important works of the new informational order: the *Order*. However, despite its comprehensive and insightful analysis, it illustrates a common trend amongst theorists whereby the inherent pessimism of their arguments' logic tends to be replaced by an unwarranted optimism regarding their conclusions. This criticism is applied to Lash's critique, which is further supplemented by a rejection of Lash's argument that the transcendent perspective necessary for critical theory has been supplanted in the information age by an immanent all-at-onceness. The much more negative perceptions of the social and cultural effects of the Order to be found within literature and cultural history are defended as valuable sources of critical perspectives that may still help to aid theory as it struggles to keep up with the Order's discombobulating flows.

Introduction

Historical materialism wishes to hold fast that image of the past which unexpectedly appears to the historical subject in a moment of danger. The danger threatens both the content of the tradition and those who inherit it. For both, it is one and the same thing: the danger of becoming a tool of the ruling classes. Every age must strive anew to wrest tradition away from the conformism that is working to overpower it.

(Benjamin 2003/1940, p. 391)

This paper proposes that Scott Lash's *Critique of Information* (2002) represents one of the most significant contributions of recent years to our

HISTORY AND PERSPECTIVES

understanding of contemporary informational society and it sits worthily alongside other defining works of a new informational order (henceforth referred to as the *Order*) such as Mark Poster's *The Mode of Information* (1990). It also argues, however, that, despite its title, Lash's work suffers from an essential lack of critique and risks becoming, as in Benjamin's above admonitory quotation, part of a conformist problem of uncritical acceptance of media-driven exigencies. From the perspective of Critical Theory, this is a strong trend amongst academics who, in various works sympathetic to cultural populism, tend to confuse any interpretive activity within the masses as critical activity per se. We shall see in the following sections how Lash arguably partakes of this trend as it applies to the mass information society. This is despite the fact that there is plenty of material from his own analysis that should cause deep concern about the serious political and social consequences of our rapid informationalization. This omission of a critical perspective is consistent with a central premise of his argument, namely that the traditional ground for Critical Theorists has been cut from under their feet by the advent of the Order: the position from which a transcendent, critical perspective can be taken simply does not exist any more. Having dismissed traditional modes of critical thought, however, Lash fails to replace them. This would not be such a problem were it not for the fact that the book and its title are devoted to presenting alternative grounds for proactive engagement/critique with the Order's flows. The *informationcritique* he does offer up acts more as a vehicle for an implicit (albeit denied) media determinism than as the basis of substantive social critique. Lash's account nevertheless remains important because his failure to produce an adequate alternative is not itself evidence that his analysis is wrong; it merely suggests that the acuity of his diagnosis is stronger than the feasibility/political desirability of his somewhat Panglossian prescriptions. I write from the perspective of a researcher who has spent the majority of his career sympathetically analysing the strategies of those groups that have embraced the informational immanence Lash describes. But, contra Lash, I argue that the enthusiasm of a call to accommodate to the requirements of the Order should not displace a more realistic and unabashedly critical assessment of the ultimate political potency of such accommodations.

This paper engages with Lash's critique in two main ways. Firstly, and most conventionally, it seeks to defend the continued importance of a critical theory Lash claims has (ironically) become transcended due to its anachronistic reliance upon transcendence. Secondly, and more in keeping with Lash's argument that such causally based theory needs to be replaced by non-linear concepts more sensitive to the new, more mosaic, technological life-world represented by the Order, the paper uses material from literature and cultural analysis to question the ultimate wisdom of following Lash's precepts. This paper's borrowing of insights from literature to supplement the alleged inadequacies of Critical Theory is in further keeping with Lash's own

396

assessment that 'The supplement, not the representation is at issue as we move from mechanical-age linearity to information-age discontinuity' (ibid, p. 180). Elsewhere (Taylor 2001) I have argued at length for the importance of the artistic imagination as a resource with which to understand better the informational zeitgeist. It is a view shared by several key theorists of the Order including Kittler (1997, 1999) and McLuhan (1995/1964). Whilst Lash highlights McLuhan and the like-minded Baudrillard as important, he does not consider Kittler. It is nevertheless worth drawing attention in this context to Kittler's belief that within a technological episteme such as the Order, understanding media (which provided the title of McLuhan's seminal work) is an oxymoron. It is only when one has left a technological life-world for the next that one can fully appreciate its nature (see Taylor & Harris 2005, p. 70). McLuhan (1995/1964) made a similar point when he compared analysing technology to driving a car whilst only being able to look through the rear view mirror and made his observation that the sound barrier is only visible on the end of a plane's wings when it is being broken and left behind. So for all those who would wish to theorize the Order, there are intrinsic difficulties. Theory would seem to take one only so far.

Rather than theory, as a result of its difficulties, needing to meekly capitulate to an Order (paradoxically constituted from the disorder of an environment dominated by emergent processes) this paper suggests that it simply needs to be more sensitive to, and realistic about, its natural limits and capabilities. Acceptance of theory's limitations does not, however, equate with Lash's stronger claim that 'theory itself is swept up in this logic of communication' (Lash 2002, p. viii). Apart from the risk that the claim, by Lash the theorist, that theory is inadequate smacks of the similar contradictory canard of the postmodern theorist authoritatively declaring as a meta-narrative the death of meta-narratives, there is an additional, significant contradiction in Lash's project. Thus, he states that: 'A major aim of this book is to explore the contours of an emergent informational regime of power (Lash 2002, p. vii) yet simultaneously he denies theory the transcendent, elevated perspective needed for the act of mapping that contours, by their very nature, intrinsically require. Deepening the contradiction later in the book, Lash distances himself from his own major aim by arguing 'Networks unlike roads are discontinuous. They are "topological", as Latour (1993) stresses, not "topographical"' (Lash 2002, p. 180). In opposition to Lash and Latour, this paper defends theory's right to maintain the elevated perspective, but it also takes them at their word. It pursues the topological, in keeping with Benjamin's description of how the *flâneur* goes 'botanizing on the asphalt' (Benjamin 1983/1938, p. 36), by exploring literary representations of the social nature (flora) of the Order and tracing the continuities that exist with its precursor – the nascent urbanity of early modernity.

The original precedent for this literary approach resides in Baudelaire's focus upon the French realist illustrator Constantin Guys. This *Painter of*

Modern Day Life (Baudelaire 2003/1859) attempted to give comprehensible form to modernity's earliest manifestations: 'Observer, philosopher, *flâneur* – call him what you will; . . . Sometimes he is a poet; more often than not he comes closer to the novelist or the moralist; he is the painter of the passing moment and of all the suggestions of eternity that it contains' (cited in Gilloch 2002, p. 213). Lash shares with other academics a reluctance to confront the pessimism of outlook that can result from the combined application of theoretical and literary analysis. For example, there is precious little optimism to be found in Baudelaire's perception of modernity's early flows: 'Lost in this base world, jostled by the crowd, I am like a weary man whose eye, looking backward into the depths of years, sees only disillusion and bitterness, and looking ahead sees only a tempest which contains nothing new, neither instruction nor pain' (cited in Benjamin 2003/1939, p. 343). Theory may not have any practical solutions to offer the various profound social problems to be associated with the Order that has speeded up Baudelaire's world still further, but like Adorno's concept of resignation (Adorno 2001/1978), it is sometimes necessary to defend pessimism's analytical credentials in the face of unwarranted optimism.

The new sociality: play and spatial materialism

Too many analysts limit themselves to enthusing over expanding postindustrial horizons of innovation and choice.

(Lash 2002, p. vii)

What is needed instead is a more *situated* semiotics, *grounded* especially in forms of sociality.

(ibid., p. ix, emphasis added)

I will propose sociality as an alternative mode of critique.

(ibid., p. 80)

The fact that Lash's *informationcritique* does not over-emphasize innovation and choice as great social benefits of the Order is a double-edged sword. This is because, in the absence of such a strong emphasis, and despite Lash's enthusiasm for a practical phenomenology with which to make sense of the technological life-world, the Order's contours remain just that: rather vague contours that lack a fuller sense of their actual lived-in nature. Lash does mention the opportunities opened up for new social forms based on innovation such as design studios and science laboratories (and their increasingly similar processes) but beyond these commerce-based social forms the improved opportunities for critical consciousness seem limited. For Lash this is because prior forms of Critical Theory consisted of either 'aporetics' or 'dialectics'. Both involved a transcendental perspective to the empirical that is no longer viable since the defining feature of the Order is its conflation of the transcendental and the empirical within the immanent. To engage properly in the Order: Lash seeks to ground such 'situated semiotics' and the new forms of sociality that result in a technological phenomenology and a new theory of power that draws on an array of thinkers including Lefebvre, McLuhan, Haraway and Garfinkel. These and other theorists are chosen to the extent that Lash can use them to deal with the new-found dominance of the interface as a social mode. This dominance is such that previous modes of discourse and narrative have been supplanted by the new 'axial principle of culture': the communication. Reliant as they are on a transcendent perspective, previous forms of critical theory are swept away by this pervasive new logic of communication. Critical theory is not the only thing that is swept away: 'society – or the social – is being displaced by the rise of the cultural' (ibid., p. 79). Whilst recognizing that the logic of commodification is contained within the rise of this networked culture, the rise of the interface means that representational modes of discourse have collapsed, *à la* McLuhan and Baudrillard's media-induced implosion of 'reversibility', to be replaced for Lash by potentially two new modes of proactive engagement with informational flows: the *spatial materialism* of Lefebvre and the mode of *play*. It is worth assessing the possibilities that both these concepts offer to the generation of Lash's new sociality.

In terms of Lefebvrian spatial materialism, various writers have explored the potential for radical engagement with, and re-engineering of, informational flows. For example, in a similar fashion to Lash's citation of Lefebvre's proposal for a spider-like utilization of space that combines the technicity of the network with the organicity of social webs, Klein approvingly cites the case of American students who identify themselves as 'Spiders' and he suggests that: 'Activists are now free to swing off this web of logos like spy/ spiders (Klein 2001, p. xx), a theme that I have also dealt with in depth (see Jordan & Taylor 2004, Taylor 2005). The problem for critique based on such spatially materialist practices is the limited nature of the empowerment they promise. Detailed studies of hacktivist initiatives and the underlying political philosophy of engagement in a technological environment (e.g. Latour 1988, Hardt & Negri 2000, 2005) would seem to suggest that a difficult task faces those seeking to get ahead of power's curve whether that power be perceived in terms of *Empire* (Hardt & Negri) or *The Prince* (Latour). Hardt and Negri's analysis of the potential that resides in what they term *the multitude* illustrates well the tension involved in Lash's desire to set up a 'situated semiotics' that can be used in the lifted out, disembedded space of the Order, yet which is still somehow 'grounded':

> We should recognize from the outset the extent of capital's domain. Capital no longer rules merely over limited sites in society. As the impersonal rule of capital extends throughout society well beyond the factory walls and geographically throughout the globe,

capitalist command tends to become a 'non-place' or, really, an 'every place'. There is no longer an outside to capital, nor is there an outside to the logics of biopower . . . capital and biopower function intimately together.

(Hardt & Negri 2005, pp. 101–102)

Hardt and Negri's assertion that 'there is no longer an outside to capital' mirrors Lash's claims for the lack of an outside from which theory can critique the Order. This shared belief in the loss of the outside/inside distinction is what lies behind both the notion of biopower and Lash's similar argument that the social has been superseded by the cultural. The subsequent challenge for such an argument is to resolve the imbalance between capital's reliance upon lifted-out non-space and the fact that, as Hardt and Negri themselves admit, 'The places of exploitation, by contrast, are always determinate and concrete' (ibid., 102).

Lash presents play as a cultural mode in which this exploitation can be resisted in equally concrete ways. The agonistic replaces the utilitarian, unlike outmoded critical theory: 'play gives us the empirical without the transcendent' (Lash 2002, p. 161). The weakness of such an argument is evident from a closer look at this empirical nature of play within the Order. People's experience of the agon in North America, for example, is dominated by professional sports coverage, which in turn is dominated by its saturation with statistical frameworks, a situation that does little to move us on successfully from Adorno's claim that the culture of the culture industry is merely to keep the workers in a receptive frame of mind to the needs of industry proper. Elsewhere, subversive strategies of play may well occur with GameBoys but it is difficult to see how capital is significantly undermined by consumption of more consoles and DVDs. Unperturbed, Lash claims, 'The player is in the global information order with Nike' (ibid., p. 161) but this sounds disturbingly like the bio-political merging of the theorist himself with the advertising slogan 'Just do it'. Similarly, the playful elements of hacking (see Taylor 1998, 1999) were easily recuperated by either the games industry or Microsoft. Such real-world recuperation was consistently prefigured in the plots of numerous cyberpunk novels where, instead of offering potential sites of critique, technological innovation is tolerated as a necessary sandpit for the mavericks capitalism depends upon, as Gibson puts it: 'Night City wasn't there for its inhabitants, but as a deliberately unsupervised playground' (Gibson 1984, p. 18). I recognize the biopolitical potential of initiatives such as Open Source programming (see Taylor & Harris 2005, Harris & Taylor 2005) but I also recognize that its influence in the Order's broader scheme of things may be disappointingly slight.

Notwithstanding his assertion that commodification is also subordinate to the interface, the contours of the Order's new regime of power that Lash

PUTTING CRITIQUE INTO A *CRITIQUE OF INFORMATION*

proceeds to explore are disproportionately based on commodified cultural products: 'this all-at-once mosaic is iterated again and again and again and again. Always new. Yet always repeated. As ephemeral, as useless, as yesterday's papers. But then there are today's papers. There is today's big match. The next number one hit. There is this summer's blockbuster movie' (Lash 2002, p. 185). Again, the critique here seems suspiciously akin to the enthusiastically uncritical acceptance of the culture industry's output. The political problem of insubstantial products, exclusively driven by the needs of marketing, is celebrated as a solution. Lash's repeated attempts to provide more authentic examples of non-commodified cultural empowerment invariably fail. For example, there seems little distinction between his expression of the sporting imagination at its freest and soccer at its most commodified: 'We play in disguise, in for example the replica kit of Arsenal or Real Madrid' (Lash 2002, p. 157). Even imagination has to pay its dues at the souvenir shop – a fact that entrepreneurs of the Order such as Malcom Glazer have been quick to realize (in both senses of the word) in their rejection of Lash's precept that in playing 'you are immediately in the world with things and people: you use neither as instrument, neither for benefit maximising' (ibid., p. 156). In a similar vein, it would not appear unduly cynical to question whether the Olympic ideal illustrates the vulnerability of the cultural to the branded non-space. The success of the London bid for the Games of 2012 is at the under-reported social and environmental cost of such vibrant local arenas of play as Hackney marshes. True inter-racial and inter-generational agon is forced to make way for play defined as the Olympic brand (see Beard 2005; Kelso 2005).

Pattern recognition in *The Man without Qualities*

> There is no escaping from the information order, thus the critique of information will have to come from inside the information itself.
>
> (Lash 2002: vii)

> The point that this book has tried to make is that we can no longer step outside of the global communications flows to find a solid fulcrum for critique. There is no more outside. The critique of information is in the information itself.
>
> (ibid., 220)

Critique of Information is bookended by the above two quotations. The first sentence ends the very first paragraph whilst the second constitutes the book's final sentence and the point is re-emphasized in various other sections throughout the rest of the book. It is therefore clear from both the prominence of their positions and, separated by the length of the book, their consistency of theme, that they represent a succinct summary

HISTORY AND PERSPECTIVES

of Lash's key concern that the information Order is both inescapably enframing and irredeemably unsolid. The fluid instability Lash describes predates the Order. Baudelaire defines modernity as 'the ephemeral, the fugitive, the contingent' (Baudelaire 2003/1859, p.12). He approving cites Edgar Allan Poe's *Man of the Crowd* (1845) who 'hurls himself headlong into the midst of the throng' (ibid., p. 7). For the *flâneur*, 'The crowd is his element, as the air is that of birds and water of fishes. His passion and his profession are to become one flesh with the crowd . . . it is an immense joy to set up house in the heart of the multitude, amid the ebb and flow of movement, in the midst of the fugitive and the infinite' (ibid., p. 9) and, using imagery extremely prescient of the later cyberpunk's urge to dive into the Matrix, 'the lover of universal life enters into the crowd as though it were an immense reservoir of electrical energy' (ibid., pp. 9–10). Like Baudelaire, Lash consistently highlights the manner in which the information age creates an immanent plane of flows and communicational pulsions. Similarly, also following McLuhan, he argues that this creates a cultural environment pervaded by a sense of 'instant all-at-onceness' (Lash 2002, p. 185) and 'deep participation' (ibid., p. 184). In this context of immersive speed, reading and traditional lineal forms of discourse are replaced by an accommodative ability to sense patterns: *pattern recognition*. Whilst Gibson's fictional *Neuromancer* trilogy is famous for popularizing the notion of cyberspace as a working concept within the Order, such influence works in both directions so that Gibson's later work fleshes out the cultural implications of this theoretical concept:

> Fully imagined cultural futures were the luxury of another day, one in which 'now' was of some greater duration. For us, things can change so abruptly, so violently, so profoundly, that futures like our grandparents' have insufficient 'now' to stand on. We have no future because our present is too volatile. . . . We have only risk management. The spinning of the given moment's scenarios. *Pattern recognition.*
>
> (Gibson 2003, p. 57, emphasis added)

The roots of pattern recognition and a succinct summary of Lash's argument can be seen in McLuhan where, 'community is based in pattern recognition. . . . Central here is not the citizen, but the communicant. McLuhan's nomads are bad citizens' (Lash 2002, p. 185). In this context, McLuhan cites Margaret Mead to argue: 'There are too many complaints about society having to move too fast to keep up with the machine. There is great advantage in moving fast if you move completely, if social, educational, and recreational changes keep pace. *You must change the whole pattern at once* and the whole group together and the people themselves must decide to move' (cited in McLuhan 1995/1964, emphasis added). In addition to the sense of reactive media determinism implied by this keeping pace with the machine, cultural analysis of the social consequences of an Order with 'bad citizens' is not inspiring.

From the imaginative extreme of Bret Easton Ellis's *American Psycho* (1991) to Mark Seltzer's panoptic account, *Serial Killers* (1998), immersion within the Order's 'field of impulses' would seem to suggest pathological forms of sociality. Less threatening, but still similarly indicative of the anomic disposition of those best adapted to the Order's life-world, is Hari Kunzru's *Transmission* (2004). Resonant of the earlier recorder of flows, Guys Constantin, Kunzru gives us the aptly named protagonist Guy Swift: 'On the far side, legs ostentatiously crossed, lounged a man who appeared to be less of a human being than a communications medium, a channel for the trans-mission of consumer lifestyle messages' (Kunzru 2004, p. 8). Where Gibson depicts the near-future urban settings of Chiba and Night City, Kunzru gives us Noida and, for another of his protagonists, aspiring to become part of the global Order, 'lost in his inner retail space' (ibid., p. 11); there is little room for a critical response to the pervasive *Chokerlebnis* (shock effect) of its speeded up atmosphere: 'All the action of Noida fizzed through Arjun's sensorium without leaving a trace' (ibid., p. 13). Swift would seem to fit well with Lash's call to learn to deal with the deep immersive flows of the Order: 'he had experienced a personal epiphany, the realization . . . that his future lay in the science of "deep branding", the great quest to harness what . . . he termed the "emotional magma" that wells from the core of planet brand' (ibid, p. 20). But, from the literary perspective, the new forms of sociality Lash seeks from the Order promise slim pickings. In both *Pattern Recognition* and *Transmission*, a competitive advantage to others is created by a hypersensitivity to the informational zeitgeist that is rich in the buzz from the 'biz' for the individual, but much less amenable for the cultivation of wider social interactions. This explains the continued tension between the physical and the abstract that exists in analyses of both early modernity and the Order.

We can see in the previously cited excerpts from Baudelaire that the 'flesh of the crowd' is juxtaposed with the same crowd seen as an 'immense reservoir of electrical energy'. In cyberpunk, the portrayal of crowds and urban environments also reflect this im/material ambivalence so that such urban physicality (in this case Ninsei) merges with the individual's irrational enjoyment of accessing abstract flows of data:

> He felt a stab of elation, the octagons and adrenaline mixing with something else. You're enjoying this, he thought; you're crazy. Because in some weird and very approximate way it was like a run in the matrix . . . it was possible to see Ninsei as a field of data. . . . Then you could throw yourself into a highspeed drift and skid, totally engaged but set apart from it all, and all around you the

HISTORY AND PERSPECTIVES

dance of biz, information interacting, *data made flesh* in the mazes of the black market.

(Gibson 1984, p. 26, emphasis added)

This juxtaposition of data and flesh is often described in terms that never-theless reflect a certain distaste with the corporal. Two particularly vivid examples in Neil Stephenson's *Snowcrash* (1992) are where moving through a crowd at a rock concert is compared to walking across a room full of puppies wearing crampons and the sound of a bullet hitting a bulletproof vest is described as like that of a wren hitting a patio door. In cyberpunk, the social environment is downgraded to the husk left over from the cumu-lative effects of individuals enjoying the Order's flux, so that amidst the hi-tech surroundings social dystopia reigns to the extent that tramps can be found roasting a dog over an open spit and neighbourhoods have been replaced by private franchised 'communities' of 'burbclaves'.

Lash talks in terms of areas within global capitalism that due to the lightness or heaviness of their communicational flows and stability of their identity qualify as 'live' or 'dead' zones, 'tame' or 'wild' zones, and com-binations thereof (see Lash 2002, pp. 28–30). Again, language rich with physicality is used within fiction to describe the social alienation that accom-panies such a society disproportionately built upon informational flows. Randal, the lead character of *Spares*, describes, using a much more negative perception of a spider's web than either Klein or Lefebvre, the consequences for communities of membership of a live or dead zone:

I saw America itself as one big matrix: bright, dangerous cities crammed with sharp and needy people, interconnected by a spider's web of highways and toll roads and bordered at the edges by the slow coasts peppered with perambulating old people. And in between, in the gaps, a sagging mass of flatline towns which hadn't made it into the twenty second century – alive and technically equal to everyone else, but actually breaking up, losing their cohesion like skin on the face of someone very ill for a long time. The nose might still look sharp, the eyes bright, the cheekbones in place; but the flesh in between falls loosely between the peaks.

(Smith 1996, p. 184)

These examples from cyberpunk provide a more up-to-date, relevant to the Order, version of what Benjamin termed, 'the gaze of the alienated person. It is the gaze of the flâneur, whose way of living still bestowed a conciliatory gleam over the growing destitution of human beings in the metropolis' (cited in Frisby 1986, p. 228). They describe the price paid in terms of lost sociality for the solipsistic, individually internalized enjoyment of flows for their own sake. Kunzru describes this paradoxical over-identification with impersonal forces felt at a very personal level. He describes, 'Guy Swift's personal relationship to the future . . . he felt it was physically connected to him, as if through some unexplained mechanism futurity was feeding back into his body: an alien fibrillation, a flutter of potential' (Kunzru 2004, p. 20). As with the *flâneur* who liked to feel *in* the crowd but not *of* the crowd, being part of the Order tends to make others merely backdrop-filling extras for the lifted-out generic non-space Lash describes as the Order's milieu: 'Surrounded by people on their way to other places, he would feel cocooned in the even light and neutral colours of a present that seemed to be declaring its own provisionality, its status as non-destination space' (ibid., p. 20). Living in the future like Guy Swift means that 'Unlike the package tourists, the high-street shoppers and all the other yearners and strivers, your existence is extreme' (ibid., p. 21). For Swift, 'The thrills are tremendous, but they come at a price' (ibid., p. 21). This 'price' is twofold. First, it takes the form of a different form of immersion from that envisaged by Lash, Swift (the arch-communicant), 'knew that the tiniest lapse of concentration, the smallest failure of response would send him tumbling down towards the place of discount clothing outlets, woodchip wallpaper and economy chicken pieces' (ibid., p. 21). Despite Lash's claim that there are no longer transcendent perspectives, Swift fears the failure of being re-immersed in the masses below. Second, since, 'Sometimes at night his twitching took on a regular myoclonic rhythm, a constant cycle of fall and recovery. Boom and bust' (ibid., p. 21), this 'natural attitude' of the technological phenomenology sought by Lash seems anything but natural.

The vestigial manifestations of modern processes of urban spatialization initially provided the *flâneur* with fodder for his curiosity and entertainment (see Tester, 1994) but the onward march of capitalist modernity proved too rapid for the survival of the idly strolling dandy. As the nineteenth century progressed, the *flâneur* increasingly lost his aura of detached superiority and carefree flippancy. In Balzac's portrayal, for example, the *flâneur* is said to become: 'a truly hapless soul, whom the city overwhelms rather than fascinates. Far from empowering the walker in the street, the altered urban context disables the individual. Distance and inactivity no longer connote superiority to the milieu, but suggest quite the opposite – estrangement, alienation, anomie' (Ferguson in Tester 1994, p. 33). Guy Swift is merely the latest in a long line of literary figures who symbolize the essential emptiness at the heart of the Order. Perhaps the most symbolic of these figures is contained in Robert Von Musil's novel *Der Mann ohne Eigenschaften* (The Man without Qualities). The following is part of his description of the apparent death of a pedestrian (his ultimate fate is never revealed), knocked down by a lorry in the rapidly urbanizing city of Vienna:

> Motor-cars came shooting out of deep, narrow streets into the shallows of bright squares. Dark patches of pedestrian bustle formed

HISTORY AND PERSPECTIVES

into cloudy streams. Where stronger lines of speed transected their loose-woven hurrying, they clotted up – only to trickle on all the faster then and after a few ripples regain their regular pulse-beat ... the general movement pulsed through the streets.... Like all big cities, it consisted of irregularity, change, sliding forward, not keeping in step, collision of things and affairs, and fathomless points of silence in between, of paved ways and wilderness, of one great rhythmic throb and the perpetual discord and dislocation of all opposing rhythms, and as a whole resembled a seething, bubbling fluid in a vessel consisting of the solid material of buildings, laws, regulations, and historical traditions.

(Musil 1979/1930, pp. 3, 4)

Musil's scene neatly represents the point at which the *flâneur* becomes over-whelmed rather than fascinated. He counterposes the human and biological (like blood the crowd 'clotted up' and has a 'regular pulse-beat') with the technological and its inhuman movement of increasing abstraction. Like the geometric lattices of light used by Gibson to portray the Matrix, 'stronger lines of speed' transect the more organic movements of the crowd to create a bubbling vessel that resonates with Marx's description of capitalism's effects as 'all that is solid melts into air' (Marx & Engels 1977/1848, p. 38). Musil's description thus represents more than just the literary death of the *flâneur*. It is a vivid portrayal of the fatal implications the 'lines of speed' have for non-capitalist life-worlds, whether they come in the form of a lorry or a fibreoptic cable.

Memory & mourning

... the empirical world of technology and shock experience and speed has levelled Being and Reason into a wasteland, but in which *the transcendental moment is preserved as memory and mourning.*

(Lash 2002, p. ix, emphasis added)

This stuff is simulacra of simulacra. A diluted tincture of Ralph Lauren, who had himself diluted the glory days of Brooks Brothers, who themselves had stepped on the product of Jermyn Street and Savile Row.... But Tommy surely is the null point, the black hole. There must be some Tommy Hilfiger event horizon, beyond which it is impossible to be more derivative, more removed from the source, more devoid of soul.

(Gibson 2003, p. 18)

In contrast to his generally go-to attitude, his Benjamin-inspired notion that memory and mourning provide Being and Reason's best hopes of dealing with

PUTTING CRITIQUE INTO A *CRITIQUE OF INFORMATION*

Chokerlebnis actually fits better with the logic of his general argument. Thus, Lash fails to make clear how sociality can be built within a cultural environment that appears to have most of the characteristics of a speeded-up version of Lukács's theory of social reification (Lukács 1968/1922). Lash sees Lefebvre's work as a valuable theoretical framework with which to create the situated semiotics needed to make social sense of this situation. It provides a radical materialist critique with which to deal effectively with the complex admixture of the abstract and material in the spaces produced (not reproduced – because reproduction based on the previous mechanical, manufacturing order collapses) in the new global Order: 'It is the imminent impossibility of reproduction, in whose stead all we have is production: incessant production; the production of flux. Of flow. At stake are both psychic and social systems' (ibid., p. 214). This recognition in the last few pages of *Critique of Information* is resonant of McLuhan and his claim that electronic technologies represent the 'outering' of the human sensorium into the world at large. Lash devotes a significant amount of space to McLuhan's mediology but underestimates the extent to which McLuhan was wary of the potentially catastrophic nature of this psychic and social stake. A closer reading of McLuhan's work suggests he had more ambivalent feelings about media effects than he is normally allowed. Because of McLuhan's posthumous re-adoption by the techno-evangelists, who have brought him out 'from behind a potted palm again' (Moos 1997, p. xvi), we tend to forget that whilst 'McLuhan predicted packages would be obsolete, he himself was being packaged in a manner which ensured that the implications of what he was saying would be deflected, diffused, and deferred, filed with playful bewilderment' (Moos 1997, p. 140). In *Understanding Media*, McLuhan hints at the possible scale of the psychic stake by suggesting that belief in the essential neutrality of the media we use 'is the numb stance of the technological idiot. For the "content" of a medium is like the juicy piece of meat carried by the burglar to distract the watchdog of the mind' (McLuhan 1995/1964, p. 18), and similarly suggestive of dark consequences: 'The threat of Stalin or Hitler was external. The electric technology is within the gates, and we are numb, deaf, blind, and mute about its encounter with the Gutenberg technology, on and through which the American way of life was formed' (ibid., p. 18).

Memory and mourning are all that is left in the face of *Chokerlebnis* because, along with the conditions from which one can create a transcendental critique, Lash seems to have removed the basis upon which he could be critical of the technological life forms' tendency to remove particularity from the grounded. He therefore uncritically describes technological forms of life as 'disembedded', and asserts that this 'lifted out space of placelessness is a generic space'(Lash 2002, p. 21). Notwithstanding his assertion that commodification is subordinate to the mode of the interface, the contours of the Order's new regime of power, the cultural space that has supplanted the social, becomes disproportionately commodified because, as Lash himself points out, commerce has a pre-existing suitability for these new modes of space since 'Brand environments are lifted out, generic spaces' (ibid., p. 23). The resulting wasteland for Being and Reason is manifested in such extreme forms as Disney, although Baudrillard (1983) would have us believe that Disney's excesses merely prevent us from realizing how much the Western world is already fundamentally Disney-like. The hyperreality of 'Mousewitz' and 'Duckau' threatens to become the template for already increasingly thematized urban centres where past manufacturing activities are repackaged for tourist consumption:

> Disney invokes an urbanism without producing a city. Rather, it produces a kind of aura-stripped hypercity, a city with billions of citizens (all who would consume) but no residents. Physicalized yet conceptual, it's the utopia of transience, a place where everyone is just passing through. This is its message for the city to be, a place everywhere and nowhere, assembled only through constant motion.
>
> (Sorkin 1992, p. 231)

There is indeed literary evidence of the role played by memory and mourning but it is not inspiring. Despite attempts to escape them – 'Memories are nothing more than a book you've read and lost, not a bible for the rest of your life' (Smith 1996, p. 301) – there remains, amidst the flux and flows of the Order, a wistful presence of anachronistically simple objects valued for their ability to halt, even if only momentarily, the inexorable flows of the Order: 'I passed a couple of Children's trikes laid casually on the path, but a nudge with my foot proved what I already knew. They were welded to the path. Show trikes, for atmosphere. Nobody here was letting their kids just ride around the neighbourhood' (ibid., p. 100). Such nostalgia is dealt with in a more thematically substantial manner in Gibson's *Count Zero* (1986) where the character Marly discovers a rather old-fashioned robot akin to those presently used in car-assembly work. It is called the 'box-maker' and its purpose is to produce antiquated pieces of art that consist of an odd collection of family objects.

Gibson neatly summarizes the significance of these apparently anachronistic objects produced by the box-maker in terms of a 'slow-motion hurricane of lost things' (Gibson cited in Cavallaro 2000, p. 62). The oxymoronic choice of words is instructive. Set against the overwhelming pace of change around them, such objects achieve a compensatory power through their very stillness. In *Pattern Recognition* (Gibson 2003) this power is something that Cayce clings on to in an attempt to make sense of another form of unreal slow-motion hurricane: the 9/11 tragedy. At the time of the crash, Cayce was in a street nearby and when the first plane to hit the Twin Towers passes over her very low, with a hint of the internal/external blurring of reality, she assumes that 'They must be making a film'. In a novel whose key

PUTTING CRITIQUE INTO A *CRITIQUE OF INFORMATION*

focus is the surface-level and essential insubstantiality of commodities in the Order, it is once again significant that an emphasis is placed upon antiques so that we read how:

> She had watched a single petal fall, from a dead rose, in the tiny display window of an eccentric Spring Street dealer in antiques. . . . The dead roses, arranged in an off-white Fiestaware vase, appeared to have been there for several months. They would have been white, when fresh, but now looked like parchment . . . the objects in the window seemed to change in accordance with some peculiar poetry of their own, and she was in the habit, usually, of pausing to look when she passed this way. The fall of the petal, and somewhere a crash, taken perhaps as some impact of large trucks, one of those unexplained events in the sonic backdrop of lower Manhattan. Leaving her sole witness to this minute fall. Perhaps there is a siren then or sirens, but there are always sirens, in New York.
>
> (Gibson 2003, pp. 135–136)

Later, on her way up to a friend's apartment and before they both witness the impact of the second plane: 'As the elevator doors close behind her, she closes her eyes and sees the dry petal falling. The loneliness of objects. Their secret lives' (ibid., p. 136). When Roquentin, Sartre's protagonist in *Nausea* (1983/1938), is overcome by the sheer facticity of a chestnut tree, the experience takes place in the domesticated nature of a city park. By contrast, Gibson gives Cayce an exclusively urban existential moment. Encased in glass, nature's entombed particularity is presented as a minute particle of the surrounding urban maelstrom, a point adumbrated further by the backdrop of the disembodied, haunting wail of sirens. The apparent autonomy of the window objects, which 'seemed to change in accordance with some peculiar poetry of their own', seems to appear as a nostalgically manageable counterpoint to the rest of the novel's (and by extension Gibson's extended oeuvre) focus upon Marx's description of the topsy-turvy nature of a society built upon flows in which people begin to circulate in the world of objects/ technologies rather than vice versa. Despite Lash's claims for the novel implications of the Order, at least the novel itself has not departed far from Benjamin's mournful understanding of a modernity as 'a world of dead objects' (Lash 2002, p. 61) surrounded by the crashes of lorries in Vienna and New York at the turn of different centuries.

Conclusion: Adorno in the living room

> In an age of generalized informational indifference, the critic can make a difference.
>
> (Lash 2002, p. xii)

HISTORY AND PERSPECTIVES

for the last ten minutes, watch in hand, he had been counting the cars, carriages, and trams, and the pedestrians' faces, blurred by distance, all of which filled the network of his gaze with a whirl of hurrying forms. He was estimating the speed, the angle, the dynamic force of masses being propelled past, which drew the eye after them swift as lightning, holding it, letting it go, forcing the attention – for an infinitesimal instant of time – to resist them, to snap off, and then to jump to the next and rush after that. . . . "It doesn't matter what one does," the Man Without Qualities said to himself, shrugging his shoulders. "In a tangle of forces like this it doesn't make a scrap of difference."

(Musil 1979/1930, pp. 7–8)

This paper has argued that the problem with the Order is not so much the death of critical theory as the death of the grounded life-world represented in the fate of the Viennese pedestrian and the desiccated rose petal. This is what makes the new sociality desired by Lash part of the problem and not the solution. The desire to live in a truly immanent Order perhaps requires greater sensitivity to the continuities this Order has with the 'dead zones' of a world where *Living on Thin Air* (Leadbetter 2000) is a death-dealing reality rather than merely a title for New Age corporate techno-porn. Lash's above claim that the critic can still make a difference is a view diametrically opposed in Musil's narrative from the transcendent perspective of a man in the upper-storey living room of a miniature chateau that overlooks the death of the pedestrian. The man pointedly described as *The Man Without Qualities* is presented to us in terms of a time-and-motion Taylorist functionary measuring with a stopwatch the impersonal vectors and implicit matrices lying behind the frenetic social pace of modernity he looks down upon. Like Lash he recognizes the social primacy circulation has assumed in which people are reduced to constituting 'a whirl of hurrying forms' and its enframing quality in the way that flow 'filled the network of his gaze'. Unlike Lash, and perhaps more like Adorno the oft-charged elitist, Musil's critic reserves his right to an elevated perspective and refuses to fall into the trap of immersing himself in the deterministic 'tangle of forces', impervious as they are to interference and redirection.

Lash approvingly cites, with regard to the Order, Nietzsche's idea of *amor fati* (the embracement of fate). Nietzsche, echoing the previously cited notion of activists as spiders, also called for:

The madly thoughtless shattering and dismantling of all foundations, their dissolution into a continual evolving that flows ceaselessly away, the tireless unspinning and historicising of all there has ever been by modern man, the great cross-spider at the node of the

410

PUTTING CRITIQUE INTO A *CRITIQUE OF INFORMATION*

cosmic web – all this may concern and dismay moralists, artists, the pious, even statesmen; *we* shall for once let it cheer us. . . .
(Nietzsche, cited in Frisby 1986, p. 28 emphasis in the original)

Such *amor fati* is problematic for two reasons. Past experience of the corporate recuperation of hackers who had previously voiced similar sentiments (e.g. Chip Tango in Taylor 1999, p. 170) would seem to militate against the concept on a pragmatic level, whilst, more symbolically, in Musil one can see an early warning of the danger to be found in the Order's fathomless points of silence. Lash's analysis is strongest when it dares to pose more questions about the Order than answers: 'What happens when meaning is not successfully transmitted over generations, when signifiers refuse to signify? What happens when death, previously on the outside and constituting the existential meaning of life, is now on the inside and all amongst us?' (Lash 2002, p. 215). Despite Lash's best efforts, the essential political question remains. Whither critique when, like a Viennese pedestrian, it has been hit by an informational juggernaut? Then again, perhaps Lash and other theorists of the Order, distracted by the beeps of its global positioning system, are driving the lorry?

References

Adorno, T. (2001/1978) *The Culture Industry*, Routledge, London.
Baudelaire, C. (2003/1859) *The Painter of Modern Life and Other Essays*, Phaidon Press, London.
Baudrillard, J. (1983) *Simulations*, trans. P. Foss, P. Batton & P. Beitchman, Semiotext(e), New York.
Beard, M. (2005) 'Hackney Marshes, home of Sunday football, to be bulldozed for Olympics coach park', *Guardian*, 1 January.
Benjamin, W. (1983/1938) *Charles Baudelaire: A Lyric Poet in the Era of High Capitalism*, Verso, London.
Benjamin, W. (2003/1939–40) *Selected Writings, Volume 4: 1938–40*, Harvard University Press, Cambridge, MA.
Cavallaro, D. (2000) Cyberpunk and Cyberculture: science fiction and the work of William Gibson, Athlone Press, London.
Ellis, B. E. (1991) *American Psycho*, Picador, London.
Ferguson, P. P. (1994) 'The flâneur on and off the streets of Paris', in *The Flâneur*, ed. K. Tester, Routledge, London, pp. 22–42.
Frisby, D. (1986) Fragments of Modernity: Theories of Modernity in the Work of Simmel, Kracauer and Benjamin, MIT Press, Cambridge, MA.
Gibson, W. (1984) *Neuromancer*, Grafton, London.
Gibson, W. (1986) *Count Zero*, Grafton, London.
Gibson, W. (2003) *Pattern Recognition*, Penguin, London.
Gilloch, G. (2002) *Walter Benjamin: critical constellations*, Polity Press, Cambridge.
Hardt, M. & Negri, A. (2000) *Empire*, Harvard University Press, Cambridge, MA.

HISTORY AND PERSPECTIVES

Hardt, M. & Negri, A. (2005) *Multitude*, Hamish Hamilton, London.

Harris, J. & Taylor, P. A. (2005) 'Hacktivism', in *The Handbook of Information Security*, ed. H. Bidgoli, Wiley, Hoboken, NJ.

Jordan, T. & Taylor, P. A. (2004) *Hacktivism: Rebels with a Cause*, Routledge, London.

Kelso, P. (2005) 'Protest stirs in troubled east', *Guardian*, 15 February.

Kittler, F. A. (1997) *Literature Media, Information Systems*, ed. J. Johnston, Overseas Publishers Association, Amsterdam.

Kittler, F. A. (1999) *Gramophone, Film, Typewriter*, trans. G. Winthrop-Young & M. Wutz, Stanford University Press, Stanford, CA.

Kunzru, H. (2004) *Transmission*, Hamish Hamilton, London.

Klein, N. (2001) *No Logo*, Flamingo, London.

Lash, S. (2002) *Critique of Information*, Sage Publications, London.

Latour, B. (1988) 'The prince for machines as well as for machinations', in *Technology and Social Processes*, ed. B. Elliot, Edinburgh, Edinburgh University Press, pp. 20–43.

Latour, B. (1993) *We Have Never Been Modern*, trans. C. Porter, Harvard University Press, Cambridge, MA.

Leadbetter, C. (2000) *Living on Thin Air: The New Economy*, Penguin, London.

Lukács, G. (1968/1922) 'Reification and the consciousness of the proletariat', in *History and Class Consciousness*, Merlin Press, London.

Marx, K. & Engels, F. (1977/1848) *Manifesto of the Communist Party*, Progress Publishers, Moscow.

McLuhan, M. (1995/1964) *Understanding Media*, Routledge, London.

Moos, M. (ed.) (1997) *Media Research: Technology, Art, Communication*, Overseas Publishers Association, Amsterdam.

Musil, R. (1979/1930) *The Man without Qualities*, vol. 1, Picador, London.

Poster, M. (1990) *The Mode of Information*, Polity Press, Cambridge.

Sartre, J. P. (1983/1938) *Nausea*, Penguin, London.

Seltzer, M. (1998) *Serial Killers: Death and Life in America's Wound Culture*, Routledge, London.

Smith, M. M. (1996) *Spares*, London, HarperCollins.

Sorkin, M. (1992) *Variations on a Theme Park*, Hill & Wang, New York.

Stephenson, N. (1992) Snow Crash, RoC, New York.

Taylor, P.A. (1998) 'Hackers: cyberpunks or microserfs?', *Information, Communication and Society*, vol. 1, no. 4, pp. 401–419.

Taylor, P. A. (1999) *Hackers: Crime in the Digital Sublime*, Routledge, London.

Taylor, P. A. (2001) 'Informational intimacy and futuristic flu: love and confusion in the matrix', *Information, Communication & Society*, vol. 4, no.1, pp. 74–94.

Taylor, P. A. (2005) 'From hackers to hacktivists: speed bumps on the global superhighway?', *New Media & Society*, vol. 7, no. 5, pp. 625–646.

Taylor, P. A. & Harris, J. L. (2005) *Digital Matters: Theory and Culture of the Matrix*, Routledge, London.

Tester, K. (ed.) (1994) *The Flâneur*, Routledge, London.

23

COMMUNICATION, POWER AND COUNTER-POWER IN THE NETWORK SOCIETY[1]

Manuel Castells

Source: *International Journal of Communication* 1(1) (2007): 238–66.

This article presents a set of grounded hypotheses on the interplay between communication and power relationships in the technological context that characterizes the network society. Based on a selected body of communication literature, and of a number of case studies and examples, it argues that the media have become the social space where power is decided. It shows the direct link between politics, media politics, the politics of scandal, and the crisis of political legitimacy in a global perspective. It also puts forward the notion that the development of interactive, horizontal networks of communication has induced the rise of a new form of communication, mass self-communication, over the Internet and wireless communication networks. Under these conditions, insurgent politics and social movements are able to intervene more decisively in the new communication space. However, corporate media and mainstream politics have also invested in this new communication space. As a result of these processes, mass media and horizontal communication networks are converging. The net outcome of this evolution is a historical shift of the public sphere from the institutional realm to the new communication space.

Introduction: power making by mind framing

Throughout history communication and information have been fundamental sources of power and counter-power, of domination and social change. This is because the fundamental battle being fought in society is the battle over the minds of the people. The way people think determines the fate of norms and values on which societies are constructed. While coercion and fear are critical sources for imposing the will of the dominants over the dominated, few institutional systems can last long if they are predominantly based on sheer repression. Torturing bodies is less effective than shaping minds. If a majority of people think in ways that are contradictory to the values and norms institutionalized in the state and enshrined in the law and regulations, ultimately the system will change, although not necessarily to fulfill the hopes of the agents of social change. But change will happen. It will just take time, and suffering, much suffering. Because communication, and particularly socialized communication, the one that exists in the public realm, provides the support for the social production of meaning, the battle of the human mind is largely played out in the processes of communication. And this is more so in the network society, characterized by the pervasiveness of communication networks in a multimodal hypertext. Indeed, the ongoing transformation of communication technology in the digital age extends the reach of communication media to all domains of social life in a network that is at the same time global and local, generic and customized in an ever-changing pattern. As a result, power relations, that is the relations that constitute the foundation of all societies, as well as the processes challenging institutionalized power relations are increasingly shaped and decided in the communication field.

I understand power to be the structural capacity of a social actor to impose its will over other social actor(s). All institutional systems reflect power relations, as well as the limits to these power relations as negotiated by a historical process of domination and counter-domination. Thus, I will also analyze the process of formation of counter-power, which I understand to be the capacity of a social actor to resist and challenge power relations that are institutionalized. Indeed, power relations are by nature conflictive, as societies are diverse and contradictory. Therefore, the relationship between technology, communication, and power reflects opposing values and interests, and engages a plurality of social actors in conflict.

Both the powers that be and the subjects of counter-power projects operate nowadays in a new technological framework; and this has consequences for the ways, means, and goals of their conflictive practice. In this article I will present some hypotheses on the transformation of this relationship, as a result of several trends that are connected but independent:

- the predominant role of media politics and its interaction with the crisis of political legitimacy in most countries around the world;
- the key role of segmented, customized mass media in the production of culture;
- the emergence of a new form of communication related to the culture and technology of the network society, and based on horizontal networks of communication: what I call mass self-communication;
- and the uses of both one-directional mass communication and mass self-communication in the relationship between power and counter-power, in formal politics, in insurgent politics, and in the new manifestations of social movements.

The understanding of this transformation between communication and power must be placed in a social context characterized by several major trends:

a) The state, traditionally the main site of power, is being challenged all over the world by:

- globalization that limits its sovereign decision making
- market pressures toward deregulation that diminish its capacity to intervene
- a crisis of political legitimacy that weakens its influence over its citizens[2]

b) Cultural industries and business media are characterized at the same time by business concentration and market segmentation, leading toward heightened oligopolistic competition, customized delivery of messages, and vertical networking of the multimedia industry[3]

c) Around the world, the opposition between communalism and individualism defines the culture of societies as identity construction works at the same time with materials inherited from history and geography and from the projects of human subjects. The culture of communalism roots itself in religion, nation, territoriality, ethnicity, gender, and environment.[4] The culture of individualism spreads in different forms[5]:

- as market-driven consumerism,
- as a new pattern of sociability based on networked individualism, and
- as the desire for individual autonomy based on self-defined projects of life.

In spite of this complex, multidimensional social evolution, the decisive process shaping society, both individually and collectively, is the dynamics of power relations. And power relations, in our social and technological context, are largely dependent on the process of socialized communication in ways that I will now analyze sequentially.

Mass communication and media politics

Politics is based on socialized communication, on the capacity to influence people's minds. The main channel of communication between the political system and citizens is the mass media system, first of all television. Until recently, and even nowadays to a large extent, the media constitute an articulated system, in which, usually, the print press produces original information, TV diffuses to a mass audience, and radio customizes the interaction.[6] In our society, politics is primarily media politics. The workings of the political system are staged for the media so as to obtain the support, or at least the lesser hostility, of citizens who become the consumers in the political market.[7]

Of course, this does not mean that power is in the hands of the media. Political actors exercise considerable influence over the media.[8] In fact, the current 24-hours news cycle increases the importance of politicians for the media, as media have to feed content relentlessly.

Neither that the audience simply follows what the media say. The concept of the active audience is now well established in communication research. And media have their own internal controls in terms of their capacity to influence the audience, because they are primarily a business, and they must win the audience; they are usually plural and competitive; they must keep their credibility in front of their competitors; and they have some internal limits to the management of information coming from the professionalism of journalists.[9] On the other hand, we should remember the current rise of ideological, militant journalism in all countries (actually a good business model in the U.S., e.g. Fox news or in Spain, e.g. El Mundo), as well as the diminishing autonomy of journalists vis-à-vis their companies, and the intertwining between media corporations and governments.[10]

The practice of what Bennett (1990) has named "indexing," in which journalists and editors limit the range of political viewpoints and issues that they report upon to those expressed within the mainstream political establishment, weighs heavily on the process of events-driven reporting.

Yet, the main issue is not the shaping of the minds by explicit messages in the media, but the absence of a given content in the media. What does not exist in the media does not exist in the public mind, even if it could have a fragmented presence in individual minds.[11] Therefore, a political message is necessarily a media message. And whenever a politically related message is conveyed through the media, it must be couched in the specific language of the media. This means television language in many cases.[12] The need to format the message in its media form has considerable implications, as it has been established by a long tradition in communication research.[13] It is not entirely true that the medium is the message, empirically speaking, but it certainly has substantial influence on the form and effect of the message.

So, in sum: the media are not the holders of power, but they constitute by and large the space where power is decided. In our society, politics is dependent on media politics. The language of media has its rules. It is largely built around images, not necessarily visual, but images. The most powerful message is a simple message attached to an image. The simplest message in politics is a human face. Media politics leads to the personalization of politics around leaders that can be adequately sold in the political market. This should not be trivialized as the color of the tie or the looks of a face. It is the symbolic embodiment of a message of trust around a person, around the character of the person, and then in terms of the image projection of this character.[14]

The importance of personality politics is related to the evolution of electoral politics, usually determined by independent or undecided voters that switch the balance, in every country, between the right or center-right and the center-left. Thus, although there are substantial differences between parties and candidates in most countries, programs and promises are tailored toward the center and the undecided, often by the same political advertising companies and political marketing consultants working across party lines in alternating years.[15] However, more critical than political marketing techniques and the tailoring of political platforms, is the values associated with and drawn upon by different candidates. As George Lakoff writes, "issues are real, as are the facts of the matter. But issues are also symbolic of values and of trustworthiness. Effective campaigns must communicate the candidates values and use issues symbolically, as indicative of their moral values and their trustworthiness."[16] Citizens do not read candidate platforms. They rely on media reports of the candidates' positions; and ultimately their voting decision is a function of the trust they deposit in a given candidate. Therefore, character, as portrayed in the media, becomes essential; because values—what matters the most for the majority of people—are embodied in the persons of the candidates. Politicians are the faces of politics.

If credibility, trust, and character become critical issues in deciding the political outcome, the destruction of credibility and character assassination become the most potent political weapons. Because all parties resort to it, all parties need to stockpile ammunition in this battle. As a consequence a market of intermediaries proliferates, finding damaging information about the opponent, manipulating information, or simply fabricating information for that purpose. Furthermore, media politics is expensive, and legal means of party financing are insufficient to pay for all advertising, pollsters, phone banks, consultants, and the like. Thus, regardless of the morality of individual politicians, political agents are on sale for lobbyists with different degrees of morality. This is so even in European countries in which the finance of politics is public and regulated, because parties find ways to circumvent the controls by receiving donations from undisclosed donors. These funds are used for discrete forms of political campaigning, such as paying informants and producers of information. So, more often than not, it is not difficult to find wrongdoing and damaging material for most parties and candidates. Since it is rare that personal lives are without shadows, and given the tendency of many people, particularly men, to brag and be indiscrete, personal sins and political corruption brew a powerful cocktail of intrigues and gossip that become the daily staple of media politics. Thus, media politics, and personality politics lead to scandal politics, as analyzed by scholars and researchers, such as Thompson (2000), Tumber and Waisboard (2004), Esser and Hartung (2004), Liebes and Blum-Kulka (2004), Lawrence and Bennett (2001), and Williams and Delli Carpini (2004) to mention a few. Scandal politics is credited with bringing down a large number of politicians, governments, and even regimes around the world, as shown in the global account of scandal politics and political crises compiled by Amelia Arsenault (forthcoming).

Media politics, scandal politics, and the crisis of political legitimacy

Scandal politics has two kinds of effects on the political system. First, it may affect the process of election and decision-making by weakening the credibility of those subjected to scandal. However, this kind of effect varies in its impact. Some times, it is the saturation of dirty politics in the public mind that provokes reaction or indifference among the public. In other instances, the public becomes so cynical that it includes all politicians in their low level of appreciation, thus they choose among all the immorals the kind of immoral that they find more akin or closer to their interests. Furthermore people some times consider the exposure of inappropriate behavior as good entertainment, while not drawing political implications from it. This seems to be the process that explains the high level of popularity of Clinton at the end of his presidency, based on his policy record, in spite of his televised lying act to the country.[17] However, some interesting research by Renshon (2002) seems to indicate that the second order effect of this low morality had the consequence of bringing additional votes in the 2000 election to George W. Bush, the candidate that appeared to be, at that time, more principled than the incumbent administration.

There is a second kind of effect of scandal politics, one that may have lasting consequences on the practice of democracy. Because everybody does something wrong, and there is generalized mudslinging, citizens end up putting all politicians in the same bag, as they distrust electoral promises, parties, and political leaders.[18] The crisis of political legitimacy in most of the world cannot be attributed exclusively, by any means, to scandal politics and to media politics. Yet, scandals are most likely at the very least a precipitating factor in triggering political change in the short term and in rooting skepticism vis-à-vis formal politics in the long term.[19] It would seem that the pace and shape of media politics stimulate the disbelief in the democratic process.[20] This is not to blame the media, since in fact political actors and their consultants are more often than not the source of the leaks and damaging information. Again, media are the space of power making, not the source of power holding.

At any rate, we do observe a widespread crisis of political legitimacy in practically all countries with the partial exception of Scandinavia. Two thirds of citizens in the world, according to the polls commissioned in 2000 and 2002 by the U.N. secretariat and by the World Economic Forum, believed that their country was not governed by the will of the people, the percentage for the U.S. being 59% and for the EU 61%. In recent years,

COMMUNICATION, POWER AND COUNTER-POWER

the Eurobarometer, the UNDP Study on Democracy in Latin America, the World Values Survey, and various polls from Gallup, the Field Institute, and the Pew Institute in the United States, all point toward a significant level of distrust of citizens vis-à-vis politicians, political parties, parliaments, and to a lesser extent, governments.[21] This partially explains why everywhere a majority of the people tend to vote against rather than for, electing the lesser of two evils, or switch to third party or protest candidates who are often propelled by a colorful presence in the media that makes for good footage or noteworthy news, opening the way to demagogic politics.[22] At the same time, distrust of the system does not equate depoliticization.[23] A number of studies, including the World Values Survey, indicate that many citizens believe they can influence the world with their mobilization.[24] They just do not think that they can do it through politics as usual. Thus, at this point in the analysis, I will consider turn to the emergence of processes of counter-power linked to social movements and social mobilization.

However, any political intervention in the public space requires presence in the media space. And since the media space is largely shaped by business and governments that set the political parameters in terms of the formal political system, albeit in its plurality, the rise of insurgent politics cannot be separated from the emergence of a new kind of media space: the space created around the process of mass self-communication.

The rise of mass self-communication

The diffusion of Internet, mobile communication, digital media, and a variety of tools of social software have prompted the development of horizontal networks of interactive communication that connect local and global in chosen time. The communication system of the industrial society was centered around the mass media, characterized by the mass distribution of a one-way message from one to many. The communication foundation of the network society is the global web of horizontal communication networks that include the multimodal exchange of interactive messages from many to many both synchronous and asynchronous. Of course, the Internet is an old technology, first deployed in 1969. But it is only in the last decade that reached out throughout the world to exceed now 1 billion users.[25] Mobile communication has exploded reaching over 2 billion mobile phone subscribers in 2006 in contrast to 16 million in 1991.[26] So, even accounting for the differential diffusion in developing countries and poor regions, a very high proportion of the population of the planet has access to mobile communication, some times in areas where there is no electricity but there is some form of coverage and mobile chargers of mobile batteries in the form of merchant bicycles. Wifi and wimax networks are helping to set up networked communities. With the convergence between Internet and mobile communication and the gradual diffusion of broadband capacity,

419

HISTORY AND PERSPECTIVES

the communicating power of the Internet is being distributed in all realms of social life, as the electrical grid and the electrical engine distributed energy in the industrial society.[27] Appropriating the new forms of communication, people have built their own system of mass communication, via SMS, blogs, vlogs, podcasts, wikis, and the like.[28] File sharing and p2p (i.e. peer-to-peer) networks make possible the circulation and reformatting of any digitally formatted content. As of October 2006, Technorati was tracking 57.3 million blogs, up from 26 million in January. On average 75,000 new blogs are created every day. There are about 1.2 million posts daily, or about 50,000 blog updates an hour. Many bloggers update their blogs regularly: against a usual belief, 55% of bloggers are still posting 3 months after their blogs are created.[29] Again, according to Technorati, the blogosphere in 2006 was 60 times bigger than in 2003, and doubles every six months. It is a multilingual and international communication space, where English, dominant in the early stages of blog development, accounted in March 2006 for less than a third of blog posts, with Japanese representing 37% of blogs, followed by English (31%) and Chinese (15%). Spanish, Italian, Russian, French, Portuguese, Dutch, German, and most likely Korean are the languages that follow in numbers of posts.[30]

Most blogs are of personal character. According to the Pew Internet & American Life Project, 52% of bloggers say that they blog mostly for themselves, while 32% blog for their audience.[31] Thus, to some extent, a good share of this form of mass self-communication is closer to "electronic autism" than to actual communication. Yet, any post in the Internet, regardless of the intention of its author, becomes a bottle drifting in the ocean of global communication, a message susceptible of being received and reprocessed in unexpected ways. Furthermore, RSS feeds allow the integration and linking of content everywhere. Some version of the Nelsonian Xanadu has now been constituted in the form of a global multimodal hypertext. This includes: low power FM radio stations; TV street networks; an explosion of mobile phones; the low cost, production and distribution capacity of digital video and audio; and nonlinear computer based video editing systems that take advantage of the declining cost of memory space. Key developments are: the growing diffusion of IPTV, p2p video streaming, vlogs (i.e. a blog that includes video), and a flurry of social software programs that have made possible the blossoming of online communities and Massively Multiplayer Online Games (MMOGs). There is a growing use of these horizontal networks of communication in the field of mass communication. Certainly, mainstream media are using blogs and interactive networks to distribute their content and interact with their audience, mixing vertical and horizontal communication modes. But there are also a wealth of examples in which the traditional media, such as cable TV, are fed by autonomous production of content using the digital capacity to produce and distribute. In the U.S., one of the best-known examples of this kind is Al Gore's

Current TV, in which content originated by the users, and professionally edited, already accounts for about one-third of the content of the station.[32] Internet-based news media, such as Jinbonet and Ohmy News in Korea or Vilaweb in Barcelona, are becoming reliable and innovative sources of information on a mass scale.[33] Thus, the growing interaction between horizontal and vertical networks of communication does not mean that the mainstream media are taking over the new, autonomous forms of content generation and distribution. It means that there is a contradictory process that gives birth to a new media reality whose contours and effects will ultimately be decided through a series of political and business power struggles, as the owners of the telecommunication networks are already positioning themselves to control access and traffic in favor of their business partners, and preferred customers.

The growing interest of corporate media for Internet-based forms of communication is in fact the reflection of **the rise of a new form of socialized communication: mass self-communication**. It is mass communication because it reaches potentially a global audience through the p2p networks and Internet connection. It is multimodal, as the digitization of content and advanced social software, often based on open source that can be downloaded free, allows the reformatting of almost any content in almost any form, increasingly distributed via wireless networks. **And it is self-generated in content, self-directed in emission, and self-selected in reception by many that communicate with many**. We are indeed in a new communication realm, and ultimately in a new medium, whose backbone is made of computer networks, whose language is digital, and whose senders are globally distributed and globally interactive. True, the medium, even a medium as revolutionary as this one, does not determine the content and effect of its messages. But it makes possible the unlimited diversity and the largely autonomous origin of most of the communication flows that construct, and reconstruct every second the global and local production of meaning in the public mind.

Mass self-communication and counter-power

By counter-power I understand the capacity by social actors to challenge and eventually change the power relations institutionalized in society. In all known societies, counter-power exists under different forms and with variable intensity, as one of the few natural laws of society, verified throughout history, asserts that wherever is domination, there is resistance to domination, be it political, cultural, economic, psychological, or otherwise. In recent years, in parallel with the growing crisis of political legitimacy, we have witnessed in most of the world the growth of social movements, coming in very different forms and with sharply contrasted systems of values and beliefs, yet opposed to what they often define as global capitalism.[34]

Many also challenge patriarchalism on behalf of the rights of women, children and sexual minorities, and oppose to productivism in defense of a holistic vision of the natural environment and an alternative way of life. In much of the world, identity, be it religious, ethnic, territorial, or national, has become source of meaning and inspiration for alternative projects of social organization and institution building. Very often, social movements and insurgent politics reaffirm traditional values and forms, e.g. religion, the patriarchal family or the nation, that they feel betrayed in practice in spite of being inscripted in the forefront of the institutions. In other words, social movements may be progressive or reactionary or just alternative without adjectives. But in all cases they are purposive collective actions aimed at changing the values and interests institutionalized in society, what is tantamount to modify the power relations.[35]

Social movements are a permanent feature of society. But they adopt values and take up organizational forms that are specific to the kind of society where they take place. So, there is a great deal of cultural and political diversity around the world. At the same time, because power relations are structured nowadays in a global network and played out in the realm of socialized communication, social movements also act on this global network structure and enter the battle over the minds by intervening in the global communication process. They think local, rooted in their society, and act global, confronting the power where the power holders are, in the global networks of power and in the communication sphere.[36]

The emergence of mass self-communication offers an extraordinary medium for social movements and rebellious individuals to build their autonomy and confront the institutions of society in their own terms and around their own projects. Naturally, social movements are not originated by technology, they use technology. But technology is not simply a tool, it is a medium, it is a social construction, with its own implications. Furthermore, the development of the technology of self-communication is also the product of our culture, a culture that emphasizes individual autonomy, and the self-construction of the project of the social actor. In fact, my own empirical studies on the uses of the Internet in the Catalan society show that the more an individual has a project of autonomy (personal, professional, socio-political, communicative), the more she uses the Internet. And in a time sequence, the more he/she uses the Internet, the more autonomous she becomes vis-à-vis societal rules and institutions.[37]

Under this cultural and technological paradigm, the social movements of the information age, and the new forms of political mobilization are widely using the means of mass self-communication, although they also intervene in the mainstream mass media as they try to influence public opinion at large. From the survey of communication practices of social movements around the world that we have carried out with Sasha Costanza-Chock, it appears that without the means and ways of mass self-communication, the new movements and new forms of insurgent politics could not be conceived. Of course, there is a long history of communication activism, and social movements have not waited for Internet connection in order to struggle for their goals using every available communication medium.[38] Yet, currently the new means of digital communication constitute their most decisive organizational form, in a clear break with the traditional forms of organization of parties, unions and associations of the industrial society, albeit these social actors are now evolving toward the new organizational model built around networked communication. For new social movements, the Internet provides the essential platform for debate, their means of acting on people's mind, and ultimately serves as their most potent political weapon. But social movements do not exist only in the Internet. Local radio and TV stations, autonomous groups of video production and distribution, p2p networks, blogs, and podcasts constitute a variegated interactive network that connects the movement with itself, connects social actors with society at large, and acts on the entire realm of cultural manifestations. Furthermore, movements, in their wide diversity, also root themselves in their local lives, and in face-to-face interaction. And when they act, they mobilize in specific places, often mirroring the places of the power institutions, as when they challenge meetings of WTO, the IMF or the G8 group in the localities of the meetings.[39] Thus, the space of the new social movements of the digital age is not a virtual space, it is a composite of the space of flows and of the space of places, as I tried to argue time ago in my general analysis of the network society.[40] Social movements escaped their confinement in the fragmented space of places and seized the global space of flows, while not virtualizing themselves to death, keeping their local experience and the landing sites of their struggle as the material foundation of their ultimate goal: the restoration of meaning in the new space/time of our existence, made of both flows, places and their interaction. That is building networks of meaning in opposition to networks of instrumentality.

This analysis is supported by a number of recent social trends such as:

- The existence of the global movement against corporate globalization in the Internet, in the network of communication built around Indymedia and its affiliated networks, as forms of information, organization, debate, and action planning.[41] But also the use of symbolic, direct action against the sites of power to impact the mainstream media and through them the mainstream public opinion.
- The building of autonomous communication networks to challenge the power of the globalized media industry and of government and business controlled media. As it has been the case in Italy with pirate radio stations and street television (e.g. Tele Orfeo), fed by audiovisual material via

HISTORY AND PERSPECTIVES

p2p networks and RSS feeds, to counter the monopoly of Berlusconi over both private and public television networks. Or the spread of activist neighborhood TVs such as Zalea TV in Paris, Okupem les Ones in Barcelona, TV Piquetera in Buenos Aires, and numerous similar experiences around the world.[42]

- The development of autonomous forms of political organizing in political campaigns, including fund raising and mobilization of volunteers to get out the vote, as exemplified in the U.S. presidential primaries by the Howard Dean Campaign in 2003–2004 following the analysis we conducted with Araba Sey.[43] Initiatives such as Dean supporters' use of MeetUp exemplified the ability of networks of affinity to leverage the Internet and to translate virtual affinity into physical vicinity, and community action.[44] True, the defeat of Howard Dean in the primaries showed the strength of traditional media politics vis-à-vis the fragile forms of Internet-based mobilization. But we should not extrapolate too much from a limited experience in which other variables, such as the limitations of the candidate himself, as well as the concern about terrorism in a country at war, also weigh heavily in the voters decision.

- The spread of instant political mobilizations by using mobile phones, supported by the Internet, is changing the landscape of politics. It becomes increasingly difficult for governments to hide or manipulate information. The manipulation plots are immediately picked up and challenged by a myriad of "eye balls," as debate and mobilization are called upon by thousands of people, without central coordination, but with a shared purpose, often focusing on asking or forcing the resignation of governments or government officials. With Mireia Fernandez, Jack Qiu, and Araba Sey, we have analyzed recent experiences of mobilization around the world, from Korea, the Philippines, Thailand, and Nepal to Ecuador, Ukraine, or France, with results as dramatic as the prompting of the electoral defeat of Prime Minister Aznar in Spain on March 14th, 2004, after his attempt to manipulate the public opinion lying about the authors of something as tragic as the Madrid massacre on March 11th backfired at the last minute, thanks to the spontaneous mobilization of Spanish youth armed with their cell phones. But this is not a technological effect, but the ability of network technology to distribute horizontally messages that resonate with the public consciousness in ways that are trustworthy.[45] In December 2005 the first Mobile Active conference met in Canada, bringing activist from around the world to share experience, skills, tools, and tactics on the new landscape of socio-political activism.[46] Action research networks are being formed, such as Our Media/Nuestr@s Medios, to diffuse tools, research, and ideas being produced by the new social movements of the information age.[47]

The grand convergence: power relations in the new communication space

The distinction between mass media and mass self-communication has analytical value, but only on the condition to add that the two modes of communication are interacting in the practice of communication, as communication technologies converge. Media businesses aim at positioning themselves in the Internet-mediated communication realm; mainstream media set up direct links to the horizontal network of communication and to their users, so becoming less one-directional in their communication flows, as they relentlessly scan the blogosphere to select themes and issues of potential interest for their audience; actors striving for social change often use the Internet platform as a way to influence the information agenda of mainstream media; and political elites, across the entire political spectrum, increasingly use the ways and means of mass self-communication, because their flexibility, instantaneity, and unfettered capacity to diffuse any kind of material are particularly relevant for the practice of media politics in real time. Therefore, the study of the transformation of power relations in the new communication space must consider the interaction between political actors, social actors, and media business in both the mass media and networked media, as well as in the interconnection between different media that are quickly becoming articulated in a reconfigured media system. I will illustrate these new developments with some examples, while trying to make analytical sense of observed trends with the support of contributions from communication scholars.

Business media strategies

The clearest evidence that corporate media are redirecting their strategies toward the Internet is via their investments. For instance, in 2006 NewsCorp (the media conglomerate headed by Rupert Murdoch) acquired MySpace, a network of virtual communities and personal pages that by mid-2006 counted with over 100 million pages and 77 million subscribers. At a NewsCorp shareholders meeting on Oct. 20, 2006, Murdoch heralded the company's move into the Internet: "to some in the traditional media business, these are the most stressful of times. But to us, these are great times. Technology is liberating us from old constraints, lowering key costs, easing access to new customers and markets, and multiplying the choices we can offer."[48] However, NewsCorp's strategy includes an understanding of the new rules of the game. The key to successfully integrating MySpace into the overall NewsCorp strategy, is to allow MySpace communities to remain free, and set up their own rules, indeed inventing new forms of expression and communication. By attracting millions of people to MySpace, NewsCorp amasses a huge potential advertising market. But this potential has to be used with

HISTORY AND PERSPECTIVES

prudence so that users feel as at home as their parents feel while consuming advertising from television networks in the privacy of their living room. As long as NewsCorp does not inhibit the already established pattern of customizability that made MySpace popular in the first place, users may accept the commercialization of their online space.[49]

Other instances of major business deals that merge old and new media for either purchasing or content provision include Google's acquisition of YouTube in October 2006 for 1.6 billion dollars. While at the time of purchase, YouTube, generated little if any revenue, its potential as an advertising venue provided a key source of attraction for Google. In the weeks following the purchase corporations have flocked to YouTube. For example, Burger King launched its own channel on YouTube; Warner Music recently signed a deal to provide music videos via YouTube with embedded advertising; and NBC, who formerly led the charge in forcing YouTube to remove copyrighted content, recently signed a major cross-promotional deal with YouTube. Other media giants are planning to launch similar sites to YouTube. Microsoft is developing its own version; and Kazaa and EBay are developing the Venice Project, a video sharing service built upon p2p technology rather than streaming video.[50]

Corporate investment into YouTube and attempts to control these networks financially also help to ensure the continued success of mainstream media. Now that YouTube has the financial backing of Google, media conglomerates can pressure it to remove copyrighted content (previously YouTube had very little assets so there was nothing to sue). Similarly, MySpace is now a place where NewsCorp can provide and market its movies, television programs, and other content. Moreover, ABC and other mainstream stations are now adapting to the trend toward convergence by providing streaming their televised content free online with embedded advertising.

However, this process of consolidation of networking sites around a few major corporations is not inevitable. There is evidence that smaller less commercial networking sites are becoming increasingly popular and that young people are migrating from larger networks like MySpace (where amassing the largest number of friends/acquaintances was previously the trend) to smaller more elitist networks not readily accessible or locatable by all, (most importantly the parents trying to monitor them).[51]

What we are observing is the coexistence and interconnection of mainstream media, corporately owned new media, and autonomous Internet sites. Here again, the autonomy of networking sites does not imply competition against mainstream media. In fact, networking services can boost the power of traditional media outlets. For example, Digg (now the 24th most popular site on the web) can help articles posted on FoxNews.com or the New York Times website move up in the search engine rankings. Because the Digg's demographic is almost entirely upwardly mobile and male (a key advertising target) several major companies were trying to buy it at the time of this writing.[52] Similarly, Facebook just brokered a deal with mainstream news providers like the *New York Times* and the *Washington Post* to provide a new service for users that allows them to easily link and feature articles and photos from these sites on their personal pages.

A major reason for the persistence of relatively autonomous social networking sites, regardless of their connections for new media corporate strategies is that the *authentic* nature of these social networking services seems to be critical. For example, AOL tried to launch a rival to Digg by offering the 50 top contributors $1,000 to start participating in their version. It failed. Users want to trust their spaces of sociability, and feel a personal connection to their sites. Furthermore, the "cool factor," that is the cultural construction of the social space to the taste of its users, is of essence. Companies trying to position themselves into this new media market brand the websites they acquire very discretely, or not at all, so that users while exposed to new ads will not be fully aware they are using a corporate product and are less likely to migrate elsewhere. Therefore, it seems to be a better business strategy for old media companies to buy innovative networking services than to initiate them. The result is that rather than separation between old and new media, or absorption of the latter by the former, we observe their networking.

Electoral politics in the age of the multimodal Internet

In the traditional theory of political communication political influence through the media is largely determined by the interaction between the political elites (in their plurality) and professional journalists. Media act as gatekeepers of the information flows that shape public opinion.[53] Elihu Katz (1997) emphasized the transformation of the media environment through the fragmentation of the audience, and the increasing control that new communication technologies give to the consumers of the media. The growing role of on-line, multimodal social networking accelerates this transformation. According to Williams and Delli Carpini (2004), the new media environment disrupts the traditional "single axis system" of political influence and creates a fluid "multiaxity" of power in three ways: (1) The expansion of politically relevant media and the blurring of news and entertainment has led to a struggle within the media itself for the role of authoritative gatekeeper of scandals. (2) The expansion of media outlets and the move to a 24-hour news cycle have created new opportunities for nonmainstream political actors to influence the setting and framing of the political agenda (as in the case of Matt Drudge bypassing the mainstream media via his Drudge Report on-line, to start the Monica Lewinsky scandal that CBS and other media suppressed for about two weeks). Twenty-four hour cable news outlets now not only gather news as fast as possible but also broadcast

HISTORY AND PERSPECTIVES

it rapidly as well, effectively eliminating the role of editors in the news production process. And (3) this changed media environment has created new opportunities and pitfalls for the public to enter and interpret the political world. According to Williams and Delli Carpini, the rise of cell phones, videogames, ipods, and other new technologies has broken down the binary between media and the rest of everyday life on which most of political communication used to rest.

In line with this analysis, observation of recent trends shows that the political uses of the Internet have substantially increased with the diffusion of broadband, and the increasing pervasiveness of social networking in the Internet.[54] Some times the aim of political actors in using the Internet is to bypass the media and quickly distribute a message. In the majority of cases the purpose is to provoke media exposure by posting a message or an image in the hope that the media will pick it up. The 2006 U.S. Congressional election was marked by a sudden explosion of new media uses by candidates, parties, and pressure groups across the entire political spectrum. The sharp polarization of the country around the Iraq war and around issues of social values coincided with the generalization of mass self-communication networks. Thus, the campaign marked a turning point in the forms of media politics in the United States and probably in the world at large. Countless politicians (most notably, Congressman Nancy Pelosi) posted videos on Youtube and set up pages on Myspace.[55] Moreover, there is increasing use by the political agency of these networks—using them as a tool—particularly for scandal politics. A common practice consists in sending trackers to shadow the opponents' public appearances, recording his words and gestures, in the hope to produce a damaging video that is immediately posted on a popular website. It has become customary to post either on Youtube or similar sites embarrassing clips of opponent, some times recording a direct hit on the targeted candidate.[56]

The new media politics shows remarkable capacity to innovate, following the steps of the culture of social networking reinvented every day by web users. For instance, in October 2006, political strategists in the U.S. launched HotSoup.com an online community that allows users to create profiles, publish messages, and post images. Its first homepage featured five panelists sharing their viewpoints on a single issue. HotSoup.com's founders include former Clinton press secretary Joe Lockhart, and Matthew Dowd, chief strategist for the 2004 Bush presidential campaign, in a significant attempt by political professionals to ride the tiger of "youtube politics." MSNBC recently signed a partnership deal with HotSoup involving the creation of a cross-linked political forum where users can debate issues and the regular appearance of HotSoup panelists on MSNBC programs. In another expression of the migration of media politics into the Internet' social space, MySpace.com set up a voter registration drive in the weeks preceding the 2006 election.[57]

Overall, electoral campaigns have become, using Philip Howard's (2006) term, "hypermedia campaigns", thus changing the dynamics, forms, and content of media politics.

Grassroots politics and the new media

Bennett (2003) has identified the changes facilitated by new media technologies in the realm of political communication. As he wrote, "mass media news outlets are struggling mightily with changing gatekeeping standards due to demands for interactive content produced by audiences themselves. As consumer-driven content progresses beyond chats and click polls, new possibilities arise for high-quality political information governed by more democratic and less elite standards. Technologically savvy activists are writing software that enables automated and democratic publishing and editing. Ordinary people are empowered to report on their political experiences while being held to high standards of information quality and community values. In the long run, these trends maybe the most revolutionary aspects of the new media environment."[58]

However, if there is such a revolution it may come in unexpected formats, not necessarily abiding to high standards of information quality. New media politics creates new political tricks. Thus, according to the Pew Internet and American Life project, the most frequent political use of the Internet by citizens is to search for information about candidates they have little knowledge. Bloggers and campaign staffers have responded to this trend by using Google Bombing—meaning that bloggers have launched frequent attempts to alter search term results by linking political issues to damning key words. For example, in 2002, bloggers posted numerous links between George W. Bush's biography and the search term "miserable failure" and Tony Blair is now indexed to the word "liar." In the U.S., in 2006, a sex columnist also launched a Google bomb against the publicly homophobic Senator Rick Santorum by urging other bloggers to use a new definition for the word Santorum that related to homosexual sex. A search for santorum will now result in the appearance of several highly ranked websites about homosexuality and sexual deviance. In France, groups opposed to the DADVSI copyright bill, proposed by minister Renaud Donnedieu de Vabres, mounted a Google bombing campaign linking the bill to *ministre blanchisseur* ("laundering minister") and an article chronicling Donnedieu de Vabres' conviction for money laundering. While survey data shows that mainstream and corporate websites tend to be the most visited—this "Google bombing" in effect combats this trend by altering the perception, if not the reality of the most important news and views available to web users. Other expressions of this new form of alternative info-politics is the use of spoof websites: for example whitehouse.org is a anti-Bush humor website. Whitehouse.com was a pornography site until the Clinton's White House brought legal challenges.[59]

In broader terms, a number of studies, including Shah *et. al* (2005) find strong evidence that Internet usage facilitates civic engagement.

The interplay between political actors in the new communication realm

The observations presented above illustrate the interplay of business, political actors, and grassroots activists in the new forms of communication, increasingly articulated to the traditional mass media. Thus, there is double process of convergence: technological and political. All political actors are present in both the mass media and in the networks of mass self-communication, and all aim at finding bridges between the two media systems to maximize their influence on the public opinion. In this new context, Williams and Delli Carpini sum up the ongoing debate in the field of political communication when they write, "optimistically we believe that the erosion of gatekeeping and the emergence of multiple axes of information provide new opportunities for citizens to challenge elite control of political issues. Pessimistically we are skeptical of the ability of ordinary citizens to make use of these opportunities and suspicious of the degree to which even multiple axes of power are still shaped by more fundamental structures of economic and political power."[60]

Indeed, in this article I have shown that corporate media are fully present in the horizontal networks of communication, and that grassroots activists and social movements are not alone in the effective use of these networks to communicate among themselves and with society. Furthermore, the structures of power are rooted in the structure of society. However, these power structures are reproduced and challenged by cultural battles that are fought to a large extent in the communication realm. And it is plausible to think that the capacity of social actors to set up autonomously their political agenda is greater in the networks of mass self-communication than in the corporate world of the mass media. While the old struggle for social domination and counter-domination continues in the new media space, the structural bias of this space toward the powers that be is being diminished every day by the new social practices of communication.

Conclusion: communication as the public space of the network society

Societies evolve and change by deconstructing their institutions under the pressure of new power relationships and constructing new sets of institutions that allow people to live side by side without self-destroying, in spite of their contradictory interests and values. Societies exist as societies by constructing a public space in which private interests and projects can be negotiated to reach an always unstable point of shared decision making toward a common good, within a historically given social boundary. In the industrial society, this public space was built around the institutions of the nation-state that, under the pressure of democratic movements and class struggle, constructed an institutional public space based on the articulation between a democratic political system, an independent judiciary, and a civil society connected to the state.[61] The twin processes of globalization and the rise of communal identities have challenged the boundaries of the nation state as the relevant unit to define a public space. Not that the nation-state disappears (quite the opposite), but its legitimacy has dwindled as governance is global and governments remain national. And the principle of citizenship conflicts with the principle of self-identification. The result is the observed crisis of political legitimacy. The crisis of legitimacy of the nation-state involves the crisis of the traditional forms of civil society, in the Gramscian sense, largely dependent upon the institutions of the state. But there is no social and political vacuum. Our societies continue to perform socially and politically by shifting the process of formation of the public mind from political institutions to the realm of communication, largely organized around the mass media. Ingrid Volkmer (2003) has theorized the emergence of communication as the public sphere in our kind of society and has investigated the emergence of global communication networks, built around mass media, as the incipient global public sphere. To a large extent, political legitimacy has been replaced by communication framing of the public mind in the network society, as Amelia Arsenault and myself have tried to argue empirically in an article on the communication strategy of the Bush Administration concerning the Iraq war.[62]

I am extending this analytical perspective to the historical dynamics of counter-power, as new forms of social change and alternative politics emerge, by using the opportunity offered by new horizontal communication networks of the digital age that is the technical and organizational infrastructure that is specific of the network society. Therefore, not only public space becomes largely defined in the space of communication, but this space is an increasingly contested terrain, as it expresses the new historical stage in which a new form of society is being given birth, as all previous societies, through conflict, struggle, pain, and often violence. New institutions will eventually develop, creating a new form of public space, still unknown to us, but they are not there yet. What scholarly research can observe is the attempt by the holders of power to reassert their domination into the communication realm, once they acknowledged the decreasing capacity of institutions to channel the projects and demands from people around the world. This attempt at new forms of control uses primarily the mass media. On the other hand, dominant elites are confronted by the social movements, individual autonomy projects, and insurgent politics that find a more favorable terrain in the emerging realm of mass self-communication. Under such circumstances, a new round of power making in the communication

HISTORY AND PERSPECTIVES

space is taking place, as power holders have understood the need to enter the battle in the horizontal communication networks. This means surveilling the Internet as in the U.S., using manual control of email messages when robots cannot do the job, as in the latest developments in China, treating Internet users as pirates and cheaters, as in much of the legislation of the European Union, buying social networking web sites to tame their communities, owning the network infrastructure to differentiate access rights, and endless other means of policing and framing the newest form of communication space.

Thus, as in previous historical periods, the emerging public space, rooted in communication, is not predetermined in its form by any kind of historical fate or technological necessity. It will be the result of the new stage of the oldest struggle in humankind: the struggle to free our minds.

Notes

1 The author acknowledges and thanks the substantial contribution made to the research and elaboration presented in this article by Amelia Arsenault and Sasha Costanza-Chock, doctoral students at the Annenberg School of Communication, University of Southern California. An earlier version of the hypotheses proposed in this text was presented as the Opening Lecture of the Annual Meeting of the International Communication Association, Dresden, 18 June 2006. The author wishes to express his recognition to the Board of the ICA, and particularly to Professors Ronald Rice and Ingrid Volkmer for their kind invitation to deliver the lecture.

2 (Beck, 2006; Castells, 2005, and Held & McGrew, 2007).

3 (Crouteau & Hoynes, 2006; Hesmondhalgh, 2007; and Klinenberg, 2007).

4 (Castells, 2004; and Ong, 2006).

5 (Barber, forthcoming; Touraine, 2006; and Wellman & Haythornwaite, 2002).

6 (Bennett, 1990).

7 Mazzoleni refers to the increased centrality of the media in Italian politics as a "Copernican revolution" in political communication: "yesterday everything circled around the parties, today everything circles around and in the space of, the media (1995, p. 308)." See also Curran (2002) and Graber (2007).

8 Thus, Hallin (1986), in his classical study of public opinion concerning the Vietnam War, argued that the vast majority of American media were largely uncritical of the war effort until after the 1968 Tet Offensive, and that this turn was "intimately related to the unity and clarity of the government itself, as well as to the degree of consensus in the society at large (p. 213)." In the same vein, Mermin (1997) demystifies the notion that the media induced the decision by the U.S. to intervene in Somalia by showing that while journalists ultimately made the decision to cover the crisis, that key media coverage on network television followed rather than preceded attention to the issue by key Washington officials (p. 392). See also: Entman (2003) in which he provides evidence for a theory of "cascading activation," in which media frames activate elite policy decisions and vice versa.

9 Hallin and Mancini (2004) include a model of media systems based on a survey of 18 countries.

10 Tumber and Webster (2006) explore the tensions between nationalism, journalism, globalization, warfare, and outline how nation states can and cannot navigate the altered power dynamics.

11 This is in line with Thompson's (2005) analysis of mediated visibility.

12 The Pew Research Center (2006a) documents the fact that television continues to be the dominant source of news in America. In fact the increase in the number of people going online for news has slowed considerably since 2000. The 2006 survey found that 57% accessed Television "yesterday" (compared to 56% in 2000 and 60% in 2004) for their news as compared to 23% accessing the Internet (compared to 24% in 2004). Moreover, people not only tend to access television more often for their news and information, they spend more time consuming it. Only 9% of those who access news on the Internet spent a half-hour or more online looking at news (Pew Research Center, 2006a, p. 2). News consumption patterns of course varies by age and this difference in behavior has important connotations for the role of the Internet vis-à-vis television in the future: 30% of 18–24 year olds regularly get their news online (up 1% from 2000) compared to 42% of 25–29 year olds (up 11% from 2000), 47% of 30–34 year olds (up 17% from 2000), 37% of 35–49 year olds (up 12% from 2000), and 31% of 50–64 year-olds (up 12% from 2000) (Ibid.). However, there do appear to be greater increases in people accessing the Internet for campaign news during election times (still around 20%). A post-election, nationwide survey by the Pew Internet & American Life Project shows that the online political news consumer population grew dramatically from 18% of the U.S. population in 2000 to 29% in 2004. There was also a striking increase in the number who cited the Internet as one of their primary sources of news about the presidential campaign: 11% of registered voters said that the Internet was a primary source of political news in 2000 and 18% said that in 2004 (Raine, Horrigan & Cornfield, 2005). Yet, television continues to be the primary source.

13 See for example: Norris and Sanders (2003).

14 For more analysis on parasocial interaction, see Giles (2002).

15 (Farrell, Kolodny & Medvic, 2001; Jamieson, 1996; and Thurber & Nelson, 2000).

16 (Lakoff, 2006, p. 7).

17 (Williams & Delli Carpini, 2004).

18 Treisman (1997) using data from the World Values Survey finds a relationship between levels of perceived corruption and low levels of trust in the political system. Newer studies find similar trends. For example, Chang and Chu (2006) discovered similar results in the Asian case (Japan, Thailand, Philippines, Taiwan, & South Korea). Using data from 16 Western and Eastern European countries, Anderson and Tverdova (2003) found that citizens in corrupt countries express lower levels of political trust. Similarly, using cross-national survey data from four Latin American countries, Seligson (2002) found that exposure to corruption correlates with erosion in belief in the political system and interpersonal trust. To be sure, perceived corruption is not the same as scandal, but it is the raw material from where scandals are fabricated.

19 There is some question of causality here: whether there is greater corruption or perceived corruption in societies that are distrustful or whether people tend to trust less when they perceive that corruption is high. However, Treisman (2000) and Uslaner (2004) are just a few scholars that find greater evidence for the latter.

20 There is disagreement about whether scandal politics directly influence voting behavior. However, in the United States, a Pew Research Center for the People and the Press survey conducted in March 2006 documented the fact that news of corruption influences voting behaviors, although not necessarily political orientation. Sixty-nine percent of those who reported that they followed media coverage of corruption and scandal in Congress closely believed that most sitting members

HISTORY AND PERSPECTIVES

of Congress should be voted in the elections of Fall 2006, compared to 36% of those who reported following the media very little or not closely at all. This trend was even more pronounced in Independent voters (a critical force in American politics): 77% of Independents who followed media scandals closely thought that most of Congress should be voted out in 2006 (Pew Center for the People and the Press, 2006b). Other studies have illustrated that scandal politics may be linked to trust in the system overall but not to how individuals vote for their particular representative. However, it is clear that scandal politics have altered both the form and the method of political and journalistic practices (Tumber & Waisboard, 2004; Thompson, 2002; and Williams & Delli Carpini, 2004).

21 A GlobeScan poll commissioned by the World Economic Forum (WEF) in 2005 finds declining levels of trust in every country measured except for Russia across a variety of institutions (NGOs, the United Nations, National Governments, Global Corporations, and National Corporations). In only six of the sixteen countries for which data was available did more citizens trust their national governments than distrust them (GlobeScan/WEF, 2006); According to the 2005 Gallup International Voice of the People survey also commissioned by the WEF, 61% of people surveyed viewed politicians as dishonest (Gallup/WEF, 2006); According to the latest Eurobarometer survey only 33% of Europeans surveyed trust their national government and 39% trust parliament (2006, p. 25). And trust in the European Union institutions continues to decline across the board (Eurobarometer, 2006, p. 72); According to the Pew Research Center for the People and the Press, 65% of Americans say they trust the government only sometimes or never (2006b, p. 11); The latest Latinobarometro does show slight declines in trust between 2002–2005. However, there is a clear break between trust in governmental institutions and trust in elites. Trust in government is generally higher overall, but trust in elites has risen slightly while trust in government has dropped slightly. For example, in the wake of the Lula scandal, trust in government institutions dropped 20% to 47%, but he retained the support of over half the population (Latinobarometro, 2005, p. 10). See also: Dalton (2004), Dalton (2005), and Inglehart and Catterberg (2002) for analyses of the World Values Survey data on levels of government trust.

22 Using various election survey data from around the world, Dalton (2004) documents serious declines in party bonds in countries around the world. New Zealand has exhibited the highest decline in partisanship (33%), followed by Ireland (32%). Other countries with evidence of declining partisanship include: the United States (17%), Japan (22%), France (19%), and Germany (10%). The Eurobarometer data released in June 2006 showed that only 19% of the sample population trust their political parties; Transparency International's Global Corruption Barometer finds that in a survey of 62 countries, political parties are perceived by far to be the most corrupt institutions in society (Transparency International, 2006, p. 3).

23 Dalton (2005) using data from the Comparative Study of Electoral Systems presents an argument that Americans and indeed citizens around the World remain engaged in politics: "Why have past analyses—excluding Tocqueville's —missed the continuing participatory nature of Americans? We suspect that part of the reason is the changing nature of participation in the United States. Those factors that are easiest to count—turnout in national elections and formal membership in large national associations—are showing decreased activity levels." In other words, social and political mobilization remain significant, both in the U.S. and in the world at large, in contrast to participation in civic associations and electoral turnout.

COMMUNICATION, POWER AND COUNTER-POWER

24 According to the 2005 Center for the Digital Future Report: in 2005, 39.8% (up from 27.3% in the previous study) of Internet users believe "that going online can give people more political power." And, 61.7% of all respondents (both Internet users and nonusers) believe that going online "has become important to political campaigns (2005, p. 102)." Castells, Tubella, Sancho, Diaz de Isla, and Wellman (2003), in a survey of 3,000 persons, representative of the population of Catalonia, found that while only 1% were involved in activities of political parties, and the majority did not trust parties or governments, one third were engaged in associations and movements of various kinds, and over 70% thought that they could "influence the world" by their own social mobilizations.

25 The Pew Global Attitudes Project (2006a) documents significant increases in Internet usage in all countries (Western and non-Western) in which historical comparisons are available; The Center for the Digital Future (2005) reports similar trends for the United States.

26 Current statistics are available from the International Telecommunications Union (ITU), http://www.itu.int.

27 See for example: Castells, Qui, Fernandez-Ardevol, and Sey (2006) and Castells (Ed, 2004). However, while some level of connectivity is increasingly available everywhere, the diffusion of broadband connectivity remains highly uneven along traditional lines of inequality, with income, geography (urban/rural location), race/ethnicity, gender, level of education, and age remaining significant predictors of broadband Internet access and skill levels. See for example: Tolbert and Mossberger (2006).

28 (De Rosnay & Failly, 2006; Gillmor, 2004; Drezner & Farrell, 2004; and Cerezo, 2006).

29 This data was retrieved on Oct. 22, 2006 from www.technorati.com/about.

30 (Sifry, 2006).

31 Moreover, also according to the same Pew survey only 11% of new blogs are for politics (Lenhart & Fox, 2006, pp. ii–iii).

32 Current TV is available on DirectTV, TimeWarner, and Comcast in the United States (in top tier cable packages) and a British version has launched on BSkyB in the United Kingdom. Current also has deals with Google to update its searches hourly and a content provision contract for four broadband channels with Yahoo video (see: http://video.yahoo.com/currenttv).

33 Jinbonet is South Korea's progressive media network, and is the primary tool for South Korean civil society and social movement communication. However, OhMy News has moved steadily toward centrist politics and a traditional vertical news organization structure. Kim and Hamilton (2006) present an analysis of OhMy news illustrating how it replicates many of the consumerist-based practices of mainstream news publications even as it markets itself as an alternative voice of social activism.

34 (Keck & Sikkink, 1998; O'Brien, Goetz, Scholte, & Williams, 2000; Kaldor, 2003; Juris, 2004; and Amoore, ed., 2005).

35 (Castells, 2004).

36 (Juris, 2004; Couldry and Curran, eds., 2003).

37 (Castells, Tubella *et al*, 2003; Castells, Tubella *et al*, 2004).

38 For a theoretical and historical overview of social movements in communication, see for example: Downing (2001). I also refer here to the proceedings of the International Workshop on Horizontal Networks of Communication, convened by the Annenberg Research Network on International Communication, at the Annenberg Center for Communication, University of Southern California, Los Angeles, Oct. 6–7, 2006.

HISTORY AND PERSPECTIVES

39 All of this takes place even though different movement actors have different levels of access to the advanced communication networks. For example, Burch, León, and Tamayo (2004) document how campesino and indigenous organizations in Latin America are connected, but primarily only through email. Furthermore, their email use is often limited to movement leaders at the national or regional level

40 (Castells, 2000).

41 Academic study of online news has so far mostly ignored Indymedia, which is odd given that traffic to the Indymedia network of sites in 2006 is similar to that of the U.S. top-ranked political blog DailyKos. Existing publications on Indymedia include, work by Kidd (2003); Downing (2003); and Juris (2004). Indymedia relies on a global network of committed reporters, that some times pay their service with their lives, as it was the case of Brad Will, an American Indymedia reporter shot and killed by the Mexican gunmen at the service of the governor Ulises Ruiz, while capturing in video the violent repression of grassroots activists in the city of Oaxaca on Oct. 28, 2006.

42 O'Connor (2004), Opel (2004), Soley (1999), Tyson (1999), and Ward (2004) among others have documented the long history of the role of pirate or free radios in social movements. There is non-academic work on free TV stations, see the article "Telestreet Movement" by Web of Struggles (2006).

43 (Sey & Castells, 2004).

44 For a detailed insider description of this process see: Trippi (2004).

45 (Castells, Fernandez-Ardevol, Qui, & Sey, 2004).

46 See http://www.mobileactive.org. More recent developments in the use of mobile phones by social movements involve the enhanced ability of phones to create and transmit content other than SMS. Higher quality photo and video capability in the newest generation of mobile phones has led to several software tools that allow people to publish photos, audio, and videos from mobilizations directly to social movement websites.

47 See http://www.ourmedianet.org.

48 (Murdoch, 2006).

49 (Boyd, 2006a; and Newman, 2006); Rupert Murdoch discusses his Internet strategy in a recent interview with *Wired Magazine* (Reiss, 2006).

50 There are numerous other examples in which mainstream media and Internet companies are seeking to capitalize on the success of start-up Internet-based social communication networks. Yahoo! recently purchased Flickr.com (a photo sharing site), Del.icio.us.com (a social bookmarking website), and is reported to be interested in Digg.com (the hybridized social bookmarking/ news aggregation service).

51 (Boyd, 2006a; and Boyd, 2006b).

52 Digg is a user-powered news content site—users post news stories and links. Other users vote on them—pushing some up on the site and others deemed less interesting irrelevant (Lacy & Hempel, 2006).

53 (Peterson, 1956; Iyengar, 1994).

54 (Sey & Castells, 2004).

55 (Cassidy, July 11, 2006). There are multiple examples of politicians using YouTube either as a position platform or an weapon against their opponent with varying levels of success. For example, in the United Kingdom, Conservative leader David Cameron has launched his own vlog called WebCameron (www.webcameron. org.uk) networked via YouTube in which he talks about the new Conservative platform while conducting mundane tasks like washing the dishes or tending to his baby. In early October 2006, a Labor party backbencher Sion Simon posted

COMMUNICATION, POWER AND COUNTER-POWER

a spoof of WebCameron on YouTube. After the Guardian picked up the story the number of views of the spoof video skyrocketed from 250 to 50,000 in under 24 hours time (Sweney, Oct. 13, 2006). In late October another anonymous spoof site www.webcameron.org appeared. The site provides links to YouTube spoofs and sites its mission as "seeking to expose the shallow, insincere image-politics of David Cameron." In another example of the political uses of YouTube, in Minnesota, E-Democracy hosted the first-ever exclusively online Gubernatorial debate on YouTube between Oct. 9–19, 2006. All candidates participated via video streaming and were asked to debate four major themes and then to answer 10 questions provided by citizens. Citizens were then invited to comment on their statements either via text message, video response, or comment posting (see http://www.e-democracy.org/edebatemn06/).

56 The most high profile case of "YouTube politics" involved the posting of a video in which Virginia Senator George Allen says to a man of Indian descent "Let's give a welcome to Macaca [a racially charged term for Monkey] here. Welcome to America." The video unleashed a full-fledged mainstream media scandal and facilitated investigations into Allen's racist past. In another example, Florida Congressional Republican candidate Tramm Hudson lost his primary after a video of him was posted on redstate.com (a networking and blog site for republicans). In the video he said: "I know this from my own experience that blacks are not the greatest swimmers or may not even know how to swim." The video was posted on a Thursday, made headlines in the local media by Friday, and on Tuesday, the once-unknown Tramm Hudson was already a punch line on "The Daily Show." in TV (CBS.com, September 26, 2006); YouTube politics may also have implications for transnational politics. For example, a short clip of George W. Bush rubbing the German Chancellor Angela Merkel's shoulders originally screened on Russian television would most likely have remained out of the media sphere. However, after the clip was posted on YouTube it became an international news story. As of October 2006, if you put in the search terms Bush and Merkel, the YouTube video is the first thing to appear. Indeed, YouTube is not only a U.S. phenomenon. According to the Internet analysts ComScore, in July 2006, YouTube provided nearly 3 billion video streams worldwide, less than $1/4$ of which streamed to U.S. locations. On an average daily basis for the month, 96 million streams were served worldwide, and 21 million in the U.S.

57 See http://www.myspace.com/declareyourself.

58 (Bennett, 2003, p. 35).

59 See Greenfield (2006) for a description of plans by political bloggers to use Google bombs during the November 2006 election and Lizza (August 20, 2006) for journalistic analysis on YouTube politics.

60 (Williams & Delli Carpini, 2004, p. 1209).

61 (Habermas, 1976).

62 (Arsenault & Castells, 2006).

References

Amoore, L. (Ed.). (2005). *The global resistance reader.* London: Routledge.

Anderson, C. J. & Tverdova, Y. V. (2003). Corruption, political allegiances, and attitudes toward government in contemporary democracies. *American Journal of Political Science, 47(1)*, 91–109.

Annenberg Research Network on International Communication (2006). *International Workshop on Horizontal Networks of Communication.* Los Angeles, CA, Oct. 5–7.

HISTORY AND PERSPECTIVES

Arsenault, A. (forthcoming). Scandal politics and the media: a global accounting. Working paper. Los Angeles: Annenberg Center for Communication.

Arsenault, A. & Castells, M. (2006). Conquering the minds, conquering Iraq: The social production of misinformation in the United States—a case study. *Information, Communication, & Society*, *9(3)*, 284–307.

Barber, B. R. (forthcoming). *Consumed. The decline of capitalism and the infantilist ethos.* New York: Norton.

Beck, U. (2006). *Power in the global age.* Cambridge: Polity.

Bennett, W. L. (2003). New Media Power: The Internet and Global Activism. In N. Couldry & J. Curran (Eds.), *Contesting Media Power: Alternative Media in a Networked World.* Oxford: Rowman & Littlefield.

Bennett, W. L. (1990). Toward a theory of press-state relations in the United States. *Journal of Communication*, *40(2)*, 103–127.

Boyd, D. (2006a). Identity production in a networked culture: Why youth heart MySpace." Conference paper talk at AAAS 2006 (part of panel: "It's 10PM: Do You Know Where Your Children Are . . . Online!"). St. Louis, Missouri: February 19, 2006.

Boyd, D. (2006b). Presentation. Horizontal communication and the media industries panel. Annenberg Research Network on International Communication (ARNIC) Conference. Annenberg Research Center. Los Angeles, CA, Oct. 6–7, 2006.

Burch, S., León, O., & Tamayo, E. (2004). *Se cayó el sistema: Enredos de la sociedad de la información.* Quito: Agencia Latino Americana de Información.

Cassidy, M. (July 11, 2006). YouTube hits the big time in a short time. *The Mercury News.*

Castells, M. (2000). *The rise of the network society* (2nd ed.). Oxford; Malden, Mass: Blackwell Publishers.

Castells, M. (2004). *The power of identity.* Malden, Mass: Blackwell Pub.

Castells, M. (Ed.). (2004b). *The network society: A cross-cultural perspective.* North Hampton, MA: Edgar Elgar.

Castells, M. (2005). Global governance and global politics. *PS: Political Science & Politics*, *38(1)*, 9–16.

Castells, M., Fernandez-Ardevol, M., Qiu, J., & Sey, A. (2004). The mobile communication society: A cross-cultural analysis of available evidence on the uses of wireless communication technology. Presentation to the International Workshop on Wireless Communication. Annenberg School for Communication, University of Southern California, Los Angeles.

Castells, M., Qui, J., Fernandez-Ardevol, M., & Sey, A. (2006). Mobile communication and society. A global perspective. Cambridge, MA: MIT.

Castells, M. & Tubella, I, Sancho, T., Diaz de Isla, I, & Wellman, B. (2003). La Societat Xarxa a Catalunya. Barcelona: La Rosa del Vents Mondadori.

Castells, M., Tubella, I, et alter (2004). Social Structure, Cultural Identity, and Personal Autonomy in the Practice of the Internet: The Network Society in Catalonia. In M. Castells (Ed.), *The Network Society: A Cross-cultural Perspective.* Cheltenham, UK: Edward Elgar.

Castells, M., Tubella, I., Sancho, T., & Wellman, B. (2003). The network society in Catalonia: An empirical analysis. Barcelona: Universitat Oberta Catalunya. http://www.uoc.edu/in3/pic/eng/pdf/pic1.pdf

CBSNews.com (September 27, 2006). Politics in the age of Youtube. CBSNews. com. Retrieved on Oct. 1, 2006 from http://www.cbsnews.com/stories/2006/09/27/eveningnews/main2046159.shtml.

Center for the Digital Future (2005). The digital future report 2005: Surveying the digital future, year five. Los Angeles, CA: Center for the Digital Future, Annenberg School for Communication.

Cerezo, J. M. (2006). "La blogosfera hispana: pioneros de la cultura digital", Madrid: Fundacion France Telecom-Espana.

Chang, E. C. & Chu, Y. H. (2006). Corruption and trust: exceptionalism in Asian democracies? *The Journal of Politics*, *68*, 259–271.

Costanza-Chock, S. (2006). Analytical note: Horizontal communication and social movements. Annenberg School of Communication, 2006.

Couldry, N. & Curran, J. (2003). *Contesting media power: Alternative media in a networked world (critical media studies)*. Lanham, Maryland: Rowman & Littlefield.

Croteau, D. & Hoynes, W. (2006). *The business of media: Corporate media and the public interest* (2nd edition). Thousand Oaks, CA: Pine Forge Press.

Curran, J. (2002). *Media and power*. London: Routledge.

Dalton, R. J. (2004). *Democratic challenges, democratic choices: The erosion of political support in advanced industrial democracies*. Oxford: New York: Oxford University Press.

Dalton, R. (2005). The myth of the disengaged American. *Public Opinion Pros*. Retrieved Oct. 1, 2006 from http://www.umich.edu/~cses/resources/results/POP_Oct2005_1.htm.

De Rosnay, J. & Failly, D. (2006). *La révolte du pronétariat: Des mass média aux média des masses*. Paris: Fayard. Retrieved on Oct. 1, 2006 from http//www.pronetariat.com.

Downing, J. (2001). Radical media: Rebellious communication and social movements. London: Sage.

Downing, J. (2003). The independent media center movement and the anarchist socialist tradition. In N. Couldry & J. Curran (Eds.), *Contesting media power: Alternative media in a networked world*. (pp. 243–257). Lanham, MD: Rowman & Littlefield.

Drezner, D. & Farrell, H. (2004). *The power and politics of blogs*. Paper presented at the American Political Science Association, Chicago, Illinois, September 2–5, 2004.

Entman, R. M. (2003). *Projections of power: Framing news, public opinion, and U.S. foreign policy*. Chicago: University of Chicago Press.

Esser, F. & Hartung, U. (2004). "Nazis, pollution, and no sex: Political scandal as a reflection of political culture in Germany." *American Behavioral Scientist*. 47(8), 1040–1078.

Eurobarometer (2006). Eurobarometer 65: Public opinion in the European union, First results. Standard Eurobarometer.

Farrell, D. M., Kolodny, R., & Medvic, S. (2001). Parties and campaign professionals in a digital age: Political consultants in the United States and their counterparts overseas. *The Harvard International Journal of Press/Politics*, *6(4)*, 11–30.

Gallup International/World Economic Forum (2006). Voice of the People Survey. Geneva: World Economic Forum. Accessed Oct. 2, 2006 from http://www.voice-of-the-people.net/.

HISTORY AND PERSPECTIVES

Giles, D. C. (2002). Parasocial interaction: A review of the literature and a model for future research. *Media Psychology*, *4(3)*, 279–305.

Gillmor, D. (2004). *We the media: Grassroots journalism by the people, for the people.* Sebastopol, CA: O'Reilly.

GlobeScan/World Economic Forum (2006) "Trust in governments, corporations, and global institutions continues to decline." Global Public Opinion Survey. Retrieved September 1, 2006 from http://www2.weforum.org/site/homepublic.nsf/Content/Full+Survey_+Trust+in+Governments,+Corporations+and+Global+Institutions+Continues+to+Decline.html.

Graber, D. A. (Ed.). (2007). *Media power in politics*. (5th ed.). Washington, D.C: CQ Press.

Greenfield, H. (Oct. 25, 2006). Political bloggers coordinate Google bombs. *National Journal.*

Habermas, J. (1976). *Legitimation crisis* (T. McCarthy, Trans.). London: Heinemann Educational Books.

Hallin, D. C. (1986). *The "uncensored war": The media and Vietnam.* New York: Oxford.

Hallin, D. C. & Mancini, P. (2004). *Comparing media systems: Three models of media and politics.* Cambridge: Cambridge University Press.

Held, D. & McGrew, A. G. (Eds.). (forthcoming 2007). *Globalization theory: Approaches and controversies.* London: Polity.

Hesmondhalgh, D. (forthcoming 2007). *The cultural industries* (2nd edition). Thousand Oaks, CA: Sage.

Howard, P. N. (2006). *New media campaigns and the managed citizen.* New York: Cambridge University Press.

Inglehart, R. & Catterberg, G. (2002). Trends in political action: The developmental trend and the post-honeymoon decline. *International Journal of Comparative Sociology*, *43*(3–5), 300–316.

Iyengar, S. (1994). *Is anyone responsible?: How television frames political issues.* Chicago: University of Chicago Press.

Jamieson, K. H. (1996). *Packaging the presidency: A history and criticism of presidential campaign advertising* (3rd ed.). New York: Oxford University Press.

Juris, J. (2004). Networked Social Movements: the Movement Against Corporate Globalization. In M. Castells (Ed.), *The network society: A cross-cultural perspective.* Cheltenham, UK; Northampton, MA: Edward Elgar Pub.

Kaldor, M. (2003). *Global civil society: An answer to war.* Malden, MA: Blackwell Pub.

Katz, E. (1996). And deliver us from segmentation. *Annals of the American Academy of Political and Social Science*, 546, 22–33.

Keck, M. E. & Sikkink, K. (1998). *Activists beyond borders: Advocacy networks in international politics.* Ithaca, N.Y: Cornell University Press.

Kidd, D. (2003). Indymedia.org: A New Communications Commons. In M. McCaughey & M. D. Ayers (Eds.), *Cyberactivism: online activism in theory and practice.* (pp. 47–69). New York: Routledge.

Kim, Eun-Gyoo & Hamilton, J. W. (2006). Capitulation to capital? Ohmynews as alternative media. *Media Culture Society*, *28(4)*, 541–560.

Klinenberg, E. (2007). *Fighting for air: Conglomerates, citizens, and the battle to control America's media.* New York: Henry Holt & Co.

Lacy, S. & Hempel, J. (August 16, 2006). Valley Boys: Digg.com's Kevin Rose leads a new brat pack of young entrepreneurs. *BusinessWeek*. Retrieved Oct. 20, 2006 from http://www.businessweek.com/magazine/content/06_33/b3997001.htm.

Lakoff, G. (2006). *Thinking points. Communicating our American values and vision.* New York: Farrar, Strauss and Giroux.

Latinobarometro (2005). Latinobarometro: Report 2005. Santiago: Corporation Latinobarometro.

Lawrence, R. G. & Bennett, W. L. (2001). Rethinking media and public opinion: Reactions to the Clinton-Lewinsky scandal." *Political Science Quarterly*, 116(3), 425–446.

Lenhart, A. & Fox, S. (2006). Bloggers: A portrait of the Internet's new story tellers. Washington, DC: Pew Internet & American Life Project.

Liebes, T. & Blum-Kulka, S. (2004). It takes two to blow the whistle: Do journalists control the outbreak of scandal? *American Behavioral Scientist*, 47(9), 1153–1170.

Lizza, R. (August 20, 2006). The Youtube election. *New York Times*, Week in Review.

Mazzoleni, G. (1995). Towards a 'videocracy'?: Italian political communication at a turning point. *European Journal of Communication*, *10*(3), 291–319.

McCaughey, M. & Ayers, M. D. (2003). *Cyberactivism: Online activism in theory and practice.* New York: Routledge.

Mermin, J. (1997). Television news and American intervention in Somalia: The myth of a media-driven foreign policy. *Political Science Quarterly*, *112(3)*, 385–403.

Newman, J. (2006). Director of Digital Media for Fox Interactive. Presentation. Horizontal communication and the media industries panel. Annenberg Research Network on International Communication (ARNIC) Conference. Annenberg Research Center. Los Angeles, CA, Oct. 6–7, 2006.

Norris, P. & Sanders, D. (2003). Message or medium? Campaign learning during the 2001 British general election. *Political Communication*, *20*(3), 233–262.

O'Connor, A. (2004). *Community radio in Bolivia: The miners' radio stations.* Lewiston, NY: Edwin Mellen Press.

O'Brien, R., Goetz, A. M., Scholte, J. A., & Williams, M. (2000). *Contesting global governance: Multilateral economic institutions and global social movements.* Cambridge: Cambridge University Press.

Ong, A. (2006). *Neoliberalism as exception: Mutations in citizenship and sovereignty.* Durham, NC: Duke University Press.

Opel, A. (2004). *Micro radio and the FCC: Media activism and the struggle over broadcast policy.* Westport, CN: Praeger.

Pew Global Attitudes Project (2006). Truly a world wide web: Globe going digital. *2005 Pew Global Attitudes Survey.* Washington, DC: Pew Research Center. Retrieved June 1, 2006, from www.pewglobal.org.

Peterson, T. (1956). The social responsibility theory of the press. In F. S. Siebert, T. Peterson, & W. Schramm (Eds.), *Four Theories of the Press:*. (pp. 73–103). Urbana, IL: University of Illinois Press.

Pew Research Center for the People and the Press (2006a). Maturing Internet news audience—broader than deeper: Online papers modestly boost newspaper readership. *Pew Research Center Biennial News Consumption Survey.* Washington DC: Pew Research Center. Retrieved Oct. 22, 2006, from http://people-press.org/reports/display.php3?ReportID=282.

Pew Research Center for the People and the Press (2006b). Hillary Clinton seen as leader of Democratic Party. Pew Research Center: Washington, DC. Retrieved on Oct. 1, 2006 from http://peoplepress.org/reports/pdf/270.pdf.

Raine, L., Horrigan, J., & Cornfield, M. (2005). The Internet and campaign 2004. Pew Internet and American Life Project Report. Washington, DC: Pew Research Center. Retrieved Oct. 26, 2006, http://www.pewinternet.org/PPF/r/150/report_display.asp.

Reiss, S. (2006). His space. *Wired Magazine*, 14(06). Retrieved Oct. 1, 2006 from http://www.wired.com/wired/archive/14.07/murdoch.html.

Renshon, S. A. (2002). The polls: The public's response to the Clinton scandals, part 2: Diverse explanations, clearer consequences. *Presidential Studies Quarterly*. 32(2), 412–427.

Seligson, M. A. (2002). The impact of corruption on regime legitimacy: A comparative study of four Latin American countries. *The Journal of Politics, 64(2)*, 408–433.

Sey, A. & Castells, M. (2004). From Media Politics to Networked Politics: The Internet and the Political Process. In M. Castells (Ed.), *The network society: A cross-cultural perspective*. Cheltenham, UK; Northampton, MA: Edward Elgar Pub.

Shah, D. V., Cho, J., Eveland, W. P., & Kwak, N. (2005). Information and expression in a digital age: modeling Internet effects on civic participation. *Communication Research, 32(5)*, 531–565.

Sifry, D. (2006). *State of the blogosphere August 2006*. Blog post by founder and CEO of Technorati. Retrieved on Oct. 22, 2006 from http://www.sifry.com/alerts/archives/000433.html.

Soley, L. C. (1998). *Free radio: Electronic civil disobedience*. Boulder, CO: Westview Press.

Sweney, M. (Oct. 13, 2006). "Cameron spoof removed from YouTube." *The Guardian*.

Thompson, J. B. (2000). *Political scandal: Power and visibility in the media age*. Cambridge: Polity Press.

Thompson, J. B. (2005). The new visibility. *Theory, Culture & Society, 22(6)*, 31–51.

Thurber, J. A. & Nelson, C. J. (Eds.). (2000). *Campaign warriors: The role of political consultants in elections*. Washington, D.C: Brookings Institution Press.

Tolbert, C. J. & Mossberger, K. (2006). New inequality frontier: Broadband Internet access. *Working Paper No. 275*, Economic Policy Institute. Retrieved on Oct. 22, 2006 from http://www.epinet.org/workingpapers/wp275.pdf.

Touraine, A. (2006). *Le monde des femmes*. Paris: Fayard.

Transparency International (2006). Report: Global corruption barometer 2005. Berlin: Transparency International.

Treisman, D. (1997). The causes of corruption: A cross-national study. UCLA Mimeo.

Treisman, D. (2000). The causes of corruption: A cross-national study, *Journal of Public Economics*, 76, 399–457.

Trippi, J. (2004). *The revolution will not be televised: Democracy, The Internet, and the overthrow of everything*. New York: Regan Books.

Tumber, H. & Webster, F. (2006). *Journalists under fire: Information war and journalistic practices*. London: Sage.

Tumber, H. & Waisbord, S. R. (2004). Political scandals and media across democracies volume II. *The American Behavioral Scientist, 47(9)*, 1143–1152.

Tyson, T. B. (1999). *Radio free Dixie: Robert f. Williams and the roots of black power.* Chapel Hill: University of North Carolina Press.

Uslaner, E. M. (2004). Trust and Corruption. In J. G. Lambsdorf, M. Taube, & M. Schramm (Eds.), *Corruption and the New Institutional Economics.* London: Routledge.

Volkmer, I. (2003). The global network society and the global public sphere. *Development,* 9–16.

Ward, B. (2004). *Radio and the struggle for civil rights in the south.* Gainesville: University Press of Florida.

Web of Struggles (2006). "Telestreet movement." Retrieved Oct. 28, 2006 from http://www.affinityproject.org/practices/telestreet.html.

Wellman, B. & Haythornthwaite, C. A. (2002). *The Internet in everyday life.* Malden, MA: Blackwell.

Williams, B. A. & Delli Carpini, M. (2004). Monica and Bill all the time and everywhere: The collapse of gatekeeping and agenda setting in the new media environment." *American Behavioral Scientist.* 47(9), 1208–1230.